WASHINGTON

VOLUME II

CAPITAL CITY

1879-1950

WASHINGTON

CAPITAL CITY

1879-1950

BY CONSTANCE MC LAUGHLIN GREEN

PRINCETON, NEW JERSEY
PRINCETON UNIVERSITY PRESS
1963

IN MEMORY OF MY MOTHER AND FATHER

Lois Angell

AND

Andrew Cunningham McLaughlin

FOREWORD

STUDENTS of the American capital usually call Washington unique. Certainly nowhere else do national politics and execution of national policies loom so large day in and day out. Although the men directing those affairs have not always survived in history as major figures, there is probably no time when they did not command wider public attention than did Americans in other places. Accompanying that political prestige are the physical attributes of the capital of a wealthy and powerful nation: monumental government buildings, stretches of parks, foreign embassies, headquarters of national scientific institutions, learned societies, international labor unions, and a host of other non-profit or eleemosynary associations. As these institutions occupy great expanses of land, Washington is the only city in the United States in which more than half the real estate is tax-exempt. Other unique features, while clearly in evidence, are not an inevitable consequence of her national status.

In none of the old European capitals or newer twentieth-century creations such as Canberra and Brazilia is suffrage denied to local citizens. The twenty-third amendment to the Constitution, ratified in 1961, gives Washingtonians votes for President and Vice President but leaves them without representation in Congress, without a popularly elected city government, and, alone among American citizens, without any voice in the management of their own municipal affairs. A non-industrial, essentially non-commercial city, Washington is also set apart by the phenomenon of the indirect power exercised by a small group of businessmen, the Board of Trade. And the city expands less in years of country-wide economic prosperity than in periods of war and national crisis. Another characteristic has been the extraordinary cultivation and intellectual distinction of the upper-class colored community, which, though seldom fully recognized by white citizens, long made the city the undisputed center of American Negro civilization. Still another factor peculiar to Washington has been the number and social influence of high-ranking military men who chose upon retirement to live out their days here; the post-World War II era, in which big industrial corporations took to engaging the services of newly retired generals, admirals, and Navy captains, has diminished the role of elderly officers in the city's life, but until about 1948 that rootless, politically conservative group constituted an important element.

One of the most decisive features of Washington's history is the psychological impermanence of much of the upper strata of her population—"psychological" rather than "physical," because uncounted thousands of people who have lived here pleasurably for years have never labelled themselves Washingtonians, or they delayed so long in acknowledging their allegiance that the community lost much of the benefit of their participating presence. Thus vigorous young men who came in the 1930's to take jobs under the New Deal paid scant attention to the local community; they expected to leave within a year or two. Ten, twenty, or thirty years later, still in Washington, they would realize that their detachment had been costly to the city if not directly to themselves; at critical moments they had failed to support or oppose local projects about which they would later feel strongly. If most noticeable from World War I onward, the long-enduring unconcern of permanent temporary residents has handicapped the city for the past eighty-odd years.

In important respects, on the other hand, Washington is like other big American cities. Her aspirations and troubles duplicate theirs—the struggle to develop a sound public school system, to eliminate juvenile delinquency and reduce crime to a minimum, to provide humane, intelligently run welfare services, maintain an adequate water supply and sewage facilities, build highways capable of handling the evergrowing volume of traffic, and create and preserve beauty amidst the turmoil. Nor are the newer problems of mid-twentieth-century metropolitan areas pronouncedly different in the District-of-Columbia-Maryland-Virginia complex from those of other American metropolitan regions that cross state lines. The details vary, but the broad outline is the same.

One or two significant features of Washington's life, however, fall between the categories of the unique and the recognizable urban "norm." From 1880 down to World War I, the years of heaviest European immigration to the United States, the city attracted far fewer foreigners than did rapidly growing northern industrial centers. Like a number of southern cities, she escaped the social problems brought in the wake of the waves of non-English-speaking aliens, but at the same time she lost the enrichment of their varied cultural backgrounds. A large part of her in-migrants were Negroes from the agrarian South, an element that moved also into northern manufacturing cities during World War I and after. In the voteless District of Columbia one result early in the twentieth century was a curious local arrangement: colored people excluded from white neighborhood groups formed civic associations in endeavor to counterbalance the influence of white citizens' associations.

These strands of the unique, the distinctive, and the universal interweave to form the fabric of Washington's history. From it emerges a double pattern. Indeed this book might well borrow the title of a recent pamphlet published by the District League of Women Voters: *Washington D.C.: A Tale of Two Cities.* For the historian quickly discovers that alongside a pride-inspiring capital, a place captivating to residents and visitors, stands a city ridden by frustration and impotence. That duality, only faintly perceptible in the 1880's and not pronounced until World War I, sharpens with the sloughing off of federal responsibility for District finances in the 1920's and becomes thereafter the single most compelling factor in Washington's civic development.

Men and women, not abstract forces, brought about this and less dramatic elements of change over the years, but the further the story progresses in time and the larger the city grows, the less clear-cut the role of particular individuals. Hence my text takes on an impersonal quality, particularly after 1930, in spite of the colorful people who trod the stage of New Deal and wartime Washington. The submergence of the city as a community between 1940 and 1945 has led me merely to outline events that constitute part of world history and only to touch upon episodes that had special local impact. The postwar years opened up new vistas, but whither they would lead, or which of the series of alternatives would seem most desirable was uncertain at midcentury. My last chapter, therefore, attempts only to set the scene for acts that would be played out after 1950. As city becomes part of megalopolis and regional problems overreach political boundaries, city planners, sociologists, political scientists, and urban historians confront new themes that call for exhaustive study.

Not all readers will agree with my choice of emphasis. The course of race relations, for example, from the heartbreaking deterioration after the 1870's to about 1906, and the upward turns and the reversals thereafter, might be summarized at intervals merely by the phrase "more of same." And yet manifestly it was never exactly "same." Careful exploration of the painfully slow evolution has seemed to me essential. Why I pursue the half-century of conflict between the Board of Trade and other elements in the city may be less obvious. In Washington, the "power structure," a term beloved of sociologists and political scientists, rests on the Hill, in Congress; the President himself functions chiefly as interior decorator, and the community has been confined to strengthening or attacking the "influence structure." Hence the necessity, as I see it, of tracing the steps in that struggle. In examining the seamy side of the city's life, perhaps here and there I tend unwarrantably to exculpate Washingtonians themselves for their plight; if so, I can only defend that uncritical excess by pointing to the provocation: the sympathy evoked by observing the narrowness of the cleft stick in which they are caught. And if I spend more time in describing ineptness in city management than in discussing the growing dedication to music and painting and the pursuit of ideas, perhaps it is reasonable to point out that the emotion inspired by a Bach Invention, the appeal of a Rembrandt portrait, or growing awareness of the relationship of the fourth dimension to everyday life do not lend themselves to exact analysis, particularly as the responses of a half-million individuals are involved.

While the interpretations I have put upon my findings are my own, I am indebted to many people for assistance in locating data and for giving me the benefit of their experience in using them. Unlike my first volume on Washington, the second draws heavily upon interviews with participants in or observers of past events. In arriving at generalizations I cannot pretend to having employed a sampling technique on a large enough scale to rate as sociologically scientific. The last seven chapters, on the research and writing of which I worked single-handed, would especially have benefited from deploying a team of skilled interrogators to assemble an adequate cross-section of local opinion. As it is, a number of people with special information that nowhere else appears in print have discussed with me the questions under consideration, and several have read critically the chapters which deal with the problems they are peculiarly qualified to pass upon. Besides the staff of the Library of Congress and the Washingtoniana Room of the Public Library, the men and women of the recently organized Washington Center for Metropolitan Studies have given me invaluable help, most particularly my former assistant, Atlee Shidler.

Until the expiration in 1960 of the grant from the Rockefeller Foundation that inspired this study, an advisory committee of eminent scholars read every chapter as it appeared in draft. Dr. Waldo Leland, director-emeritus of the American Council of Learned Societies, Doctors Ernest Posner, Ralph Gabriel, and Arthur Ekirch of American University, Dr. Caroline Ware, recognized expert on community organization, and Dr. Oliver Wendell Holmes of the National Archives composed the active members of the committee; the ill-health of Dr. Solon J. Buck and the death of John Ihlder, authority on Washington housing problems, early denied me their invaluable help. Louis Brownlow has contributed more to this volume than any other one person with no official responsibility for it. A newspaperman when he first came to Washington in 1904, a District commissioner for five and a half critical years, and later the head of the Public Administration Clearing House, "Brownie" has supplied me with facts and insights I could have obtained in no other way, and, by his reading of most of the chapters covering the period of his years here, he has saved me more than once from drawing faulty conclusions. Dr. Rayford Logan of Howard University, Dr. John Hope Franklin of Brooklyn College, and Eugene Davidson, a leader in the fight for Negro civil rights, have between them scrutinized most of the text on colored Washington. Doctors Charles Wiltse and Louis Hunter have similarly gone over carefully the story I present from 1933 to 1950. In addition to many others on whose encouragement and help I depended, I wish to thank the trustees of the Chapelbrook Foundation for the two-year grant that enabled me to complete this study.

CONSTANCE MC LAUGHLIN GREEN

Washington, D.C.
November 1962

CONTENTS

ILLUSTRATIONS

16. Sailing on the Washington Channel. Beyond stands the line of officers' houses built by Stanford White on the grounds of the Army War College. Courtesy Library of Congress

Illustrations 17 through 30 following page 334

17. President Wilson addressing Congress, April 2, 1917, to ask for a declaration of war. Courtesy Library of Congress
18. War workers' dormitories under construction in the Union Station Plaza, October 1918. Courtesy National Archives
19. Eminent Washingtonians; top, left to right, Gardiner Hubbard, ca. 1897, a founder of the Washington Academy of Sciences and of the National Geographic Society, John Joy Edson, ca. 1920, civic leader and one-time president of the Board of Trade, Herbert Putnam, ca. 1901, Librarian of Congress; center, Commissioner Louis Brownlow, ca. 1915; bottom, left to right, Archibald Grimke, ca. 1920, president of the Washington branch of the NAACP and of the American Negro Academy, Mary Church Terrell, ca. 1930, one of the first two women to serve on the School Board and first president of the National Association of Colored Women, Kelly Miller, ca. 1929, professor of sociology at Howard University
20. Bonus Army on the Capitol grounds, 1932. Photograph by Underwood & Underwood
21. General Glassford inspecting Camp Marks. Photograph by Underwood & Underwood
22. "Tiny Veterans" and posters at Camp Marks. Photograph by Underwood & Underwood
23. Ku Klux Klan Parade, 1925. Courtesy National Archives
24. The Elder Lightfoot Michaux baptizing his sheep in water from the River Jordan, 1938.
25. Alley dwellings near the Capitol in Dingman Place, where four-room tenements with outdoor water taps and privies rented at about $15 a month each. Courtesy Library of Congress
26. Schott's Alley with the Senate Office Building in the background. Courtesy Library of Congress
27. Federal Triangle, looking west along Constitution Avenue from 10th Street. Courtesy Library of Congress
28. At the zoo. Courtesy Library of Congress

WASHINGTON

VOLUME II
CAPITAL CITY
1879-1950

CHAPTER I

THE INHERITANCE OF THE PAST

TO A LONG-LIVED MEMBER of the Oldest Inhabitants' Association, the Washington of 1879 undoubtedly looked very different from the village of the early years of the century. By the end of the 1870's the capital had acquired 140,000 permanent residents; another 9,000 lived beyond Rock Creek in Georgetown. The orchard that had covered the upper half of the President's Square in 1800 had become a park edged by the harmoniously proportioned St. John's Church and handsome houses looking out through elm and sycamore branches toward the equestrian statue of General Andrew Jackson. The Treasury erected in President Jackson's day and the new, ornate State Department building interrupted the sweep of Pennsylvania and New York Avenues to the east and the west of the White House; the tracks of the Baltimore and Potomac Railroad laid across the Mall between the foot of Capitol Hill and the red sandstone castle housing the Smithsonian Institution broke the stretch that L'Enfant had intended for a magnificent promenade reaching to the river; and the heavy Gothic stone railroad depot jutting out upon the Mall and North 6th Street underscored the recent changes in architectural taste more emphatically than did the red-brick mansard-roofed Department of Agriculture building placed to the west of the Smithsonian. Like a stubby thumb the unfinished Washington Monument cut the skyline above the tidal marshes along the Potomac and the ponds formed by draining and filling the old Washington Canal. Otherwise the main outlines of L'Enfant's original plan were still visible.

An unprepossessing huddle of sheds and small houses clustered along lower Pennsylvania Avenue above and below the new Centre Market, and, nearby, the National Hotel, once Washington's most famous hostelry, still offered competition to the more elegantly equipped Willard and the Ebbitt House. Office buildings interspersed with livery stables now flanked most of F Street from the Treasury to Judiciary Square, where the beautiful simple lines of the old City Hall caught the eye. Fashionable early and mid-Victorian dwellings along 6th Street still formed a select residential area as desirable as the newer section in the neighborhood of the British Legation on Connecticut Avenue below Dupont Circle. Tracks for the horse-drawn street-railway cars threaded a half-dozen thoroughfares out as far as Boundary Street and down to the Eastern Branch at the Navy Yard and the wharves below. At night yellow gas lights winked through the branches of the saplings planted in Boss Shepherd's heyday.

Yet, compared to the transformations in other cities, the physical changes in Washington were minor. New York, with more than a million inhabitants spread from the Battery nearly to 60th Street, had become one of the great commercial cities of the world—a city displaying all the elegance of wealth and all the squalor of poverty. Baltimore now contained solid lines of shops, warehouses, and dwellings for 332,000 people. Cincinnati had grown from a frontier settlement of 800 souls and a hundred-odd log houses to a river port and manufacturing center supporting a population of 255,000; Chicago, from an empty stretch of prairie on Lake Michigan's shore, had turned into a huge sprawling polyglot city fed by a network of railroads.

Washington's leading citizens nevertheless were gratified by what they saw about them. Largely because of that satisfaction they had acquiesced cheerfully in the new political order introduced in 1874, when bankruptcy had undermined the three-year-old territorial government. Congress, in enacting first a temporary law and then the Organic Act of June 1878, had stripped them of all local self-government but at the same time had guaranteed the solvency of the District of Columbia by underwriting its public debt and by pledging the United States to share equally with local taxpayers the annual expense of

4

running the capital. To arch-southerners in Washington dis-enfranchisement represented a safeguard against a city govern-ment partly manned by Negroes, and many a big taxpayer, whatever his origins, had seen advantages in a regime free of pressures from non-propertied "riff-raff." Men who perceived dangers in rule by a three-man presidentially appointed com-mission with Congress in control of the purse-strings had the consolation of believing that this was only a temporary arrange-ment that they could bring to an end when the time was propi-tious. In the interim the seventy-year-old struggle to obtain federal funds for the public schools appeared to be a problem of the past. What optimists lost sight of was the depth of the conviction that had permeated Congress and would linger on for the next eighty years that Washingtonians were financially irresponsible, that if given another chance they would again plunge the District into heavy debt and again force the federal government to bail them out as it had twice since 1835. That distrust on the Hill would balk every effort of the next three generations to return to local citizens control of their own taxes and municipal expenditures seemed inconceivable to Washing-tonians in 1879.

Intelligent colored men, however reluctant to lose the local voting rights they had enjoyed since 1867 as the political equals of whites, had not protested publicly against the new scheme of local government. Presumably the President, Congress, and the federal courts would protect Negroes' recently won civil rights; less than a decade earlier two municipal ordinances and sub-sequently an act of the territorial legislature had fortified those rights by prohibiting racial discrimination in public places. The tax-supported colored schools, opened in 1864, had so expanded that Negro illiteracy in Washington might well disappear with-in another generation. Howard University provided higher edu-cation and professional training for exceptionally able Negroes. Meanwhile, although white people tended to think of the colored community as one, it had become two—one group made

5

up largely of black field hands who had migrated to the District of Columbia during and after the Civil War, and a second relatively small group of aristocratic old Washington families and newcomers with as much white as Negro blood who had been drawn to the capital by the exceptional opportunities open to them. While the black masses greatly predominated and at least half of them lived at a bare subsistence level, colored Washington included more upper-class Negroes than any other one place in the country. Perceptive and ambitious, these men expected to lead their people out of the wilderness. Hopes of rapidly reducing race prejudice had, to be sure, dwindled during the mid-seventies, but faith remained that its overt expression in discriminatory practices could be kept in check until experience taught white men that dark-skinned Americans were capable of responsible citizenship.

The social structure of the white community, in turn, had undergone changes since 1860. The very term "Federal City" had dropped out of use, as the enlargement of national power at the expense of the states enhanced Washington's political and social importance. What transpired in Richmond, Columbia, or Baton Rouge, or indeed in Albany, Topeka, or Sacramento, now mattered far less than what politicians decided on Capitol Hill; Americans must go to Washington to be in the swim. While the vulgarity of a new plutocracy had permeated much of official society during most of the postwar decade, after the panic of 1873 the social carpetbaggers had gradually ceased to exercise much influence. Old residents imbued with a strong sense of tradition, newcomers ready to share in community responsibilities, and a number of cultivated, highly trained men willing to risk the precariousness of government employment had succeeded in restoring dignity to social intercourse. Thus the upper brackets of Washington society felt able thenceforward to handle any new invasions of frivolous, wealthy, temporary residents. Four universities and the Library of Congress endowed the city with some scholarly standing.

The increasingly significant role of government scientists in itself enriched community life. Joseph Henry, eminent secretary of the Smithsonian Institution, had remarked in 1871 that no other city in the United States had "in proportion to the number of its inhabitants, so many men actively engaged in pursuits connected with science as in Washington."[1] Before the end of that decade residents knew that a city claiming a John Wesley Powell, a Simon Newcomb, a Cleveland Abbe, and a Lester Ward, let alone a Henry Adams, need no longer fear being branded a provincial village, a stage for tawdry display, or a nursery of bad taste.

At the end of the 1870's knowledgeable Washingtonians had come to see the city's future as forever tied to her status as national capital. Ambitions to use the Potomac waterway as a means of making her the chief "emporium" of the continent had evaporated in the 1850's; and determination to develop a commercial empire sustained by a complex of railroads had faded during the next two decades. The long lines of the unemployed drawn up at soup kitchens in America's big industrial centers and the violent railroad strike of 1877 that crippled and terrified commercial cities had deepened Washingtonians' gratitude for escaping the worst consequences of the country-wide panic and depression. Service to the United States government, to sight-seers in the capital, or to citizens who wanted to enjoy its pleasures during the "season" promised a more stable and satisfactory source of livelihood than could further costly attempts to develop manufactures and shipping. The community had emerged from the social revolution which the Civil War had launched and from the economic and political troubles of the 1870's into a stronger position than she had ever known before. Talk of moving the capital to the Middle West had ceased.

[1] Garrick Mallery, "Relations between Professor Baird and Participating Societies," *Annual Report of the Smithsonian Institution*, 1888, p. 719.

7

Washington still had nothing except national political news to sell in the markets of the rest of the country, but the seasonal crop of congressmen, lobbyists, and visitors ready to spend freely kept considerable money in circulation. The extravagances of senators who, if not commanding the $500,000 monthly income ascribed in 1878 to Senator Fair of Nevada, nevertheless had fabulous fortunes, inevitably benefited local business. The recently regained sense of permanence, coupled with the physical attractions of the modernized city, had brought her new residents and a certain amount of investment capital. Poverty was no less extreme in some parts of Washington than in big industrial cities, but here it was probably less widespread and certainly less evident to the casual observer. Although the gain in per capita wealth did not eradicate the miseries of the city's destitute, other residents could look upon it as proof of material progress and a hopeful portent. Rich or poor, white or black, people who had lived through the heartbreak of the Civil War and the harassing years that followed were not likely to believe in an untroubled future. Nevertheless, as 1878 drew to a close, an atmosphere of cautious confidence had begun to envelop Washington.

CHAPTER II

REAL ESTATE AND CIVIC ENTERPRISE, 1879-1901

THE economic history of Washington during the last years of the nineteenth century becomes a story of real estate. Convinced by the long depression of the folly of seeking to develop heavy industry and the far-flung commercial empire that had once seemed so desirable, after 1878 business leaders acquiesced in keeping Washington outside America's commercial and industrial orbit. Even the dismantling of the government's ordnance workshops at Arsenal Point occasioned little protest, and the halfhearted attempt to whip up fresh interest in exploiting the water power of the Great Falls quickly subsided before the greater attractions of investment in local residential property. The consensus ran that service to the federal government and to the host of yearly visitors offered the national city a sound basis for her economy; rooted in so fertile a soil, it needed nothing more to secure a sturdy growth. When the panic of 1893 checked real estate and building activities, a committee of businessmen spoke of the District's eligible factory sites and the unemployed workmen available as mill hands, but the committee insisted that the city must remain primarily a center of "learning and culture." Certainly only light industry of an "inoffensive" kind would be welcome; at most citizens should persuade the federal government to manufacture its supplies here.

Manufacturing, to be sure, expanded within a narrow range, but small shops without power-driven machinery still accounted for most of the local output except building materials, illuminating gas, flour, beer, and printing. (See Table I.) Two years after the Potomac Electric Power Company acquired land and water rights at the Great Falls in 1898, all manufacturing concerns together used less than 9,600 horse power, the equivalent potential of about seventy family automobiles of mid-twentieth

9

century.[1] The production of consumer goods for a local public suited community leaders fearful of "the possible unrest . . . in the population whenever an unsatisfactory relation between labor and capital might arise." Although growth was more pronounced between 1880 and 1890 than in the next decade, the depression-ridden 1890's brought the District more establishments with more money invested, bigger payrolls, and a larger dollar value of product. Flour milling, on the decline since 1870, dropped off sharply after 1889 when a devastating flood so damaged the C & O Canal that for seven or eight years canal traffic ceased altogether. Brewing, on the other hand, grew in twenty years from a $275,000 to a $1,340,000 business, and the beer produced in Christian Heurich's imposing brick brewery near the mouth of Rock Creek commanded a wide market. Private book publishing and job printing gradually yielded in importance to newspaper and magazine publishing, but the tonnage of books and reports issuing from the Government Printing Office kept the balance about as before.

For stockholders probably the most profitable enterprise was the Washington Gas Light Company; its monopoly, unchallenged until electricity offered a glimmer of competition in the 1890's, permitted minimum dividend payments of 10 percent annually, although, compared to the 65 percent of the depression year of 1876, the return was small. A swelling population which included 350 bankers, about 9,000 well-to-do professional people, and a number of men listed in the city *Directory* merely as "capitalist" meant, as the Washington Board of Trade observed in 1899, an "unprecedented growth of demand on the part of consumers of every kind [which] has

[1] *Evening Star*, 22, 29 Mar, 19 Apr, 17 May 1879, 24 May 1884 (hereafter cited as *Star*); Andrew J. Rogers to Sayles J. Bowen, 8, 16 Jan 1878, and Memorial of Great Falls Manufacturing Co., 1882, Sayles J. Bowen Mss (in possession of Charles A. Barker of the Johns Hopkins University); *Annual Reports of the Washington Board of Trade*, 1894, pp. 6-7, 1896, pp. 6-7, 34-35, 1898, pp. 44-47, 1899, p. 52 (hereafter cited as *Rpt B/Tr*); *Twelfth U.S. Census*, 1900, *Manufactures*, Pt. ii, p. 115.

taxed the facilities and ingenuity of merchants and manufacturers, absorbing their attention so completely as to leave little time or room for thoughts or theories of further expansion of industries."[2]

Shoppers were delighted when Isadore Saks opened his fine clothing store and S. Walter Woodward and Alvin Lothrop a department store modelled upon Wanamaker's of Philadelphia and Marshall Field's of Chicago. But despite advertisements of the latest Parisian pelisse, Washington, as one disappointed young woman noted, was not "a brag shopping place." Wholesaling firms were few. Well before the final collapse of the C & O Canal, the city focused her commercial aims upon becoming the convention center and show place of the country. As early as 1878 some three hundred businessmen obtained from Congress a charter for a National Fair Association. Although the thirty-year-old campaign again failed to win federal money for a large public auditorium, two or three exhibitions held at Ivy City near the Kendall Green school for the deaf were modest successes. In the late eighties Washingtonians proposed to stage a world's fair to celebrate Columbus' discovery of America, but, when Chicagoans outmaneuvered them, they found comfort in the steady rise of the tourist and convention trade,[3] and took pride in seeing the city turn into "a favorite place of residence for people of talent, culture and fortune."[4]

The ideal of making and keeping Washington "a favorite place of residence" was at once the cause and the result of widespread interest in local real estate. The purchase of city lots or suburban tracts became a fetish among people of small

[2] *Star*, 1 Jan 1890; Senate Miscellaneous Document 91, 53C, 2S, Ser 3167 (hereafter cited as S Mis Doc); Cleveland *Leader*, 19 Apr 1883; *Directory*, 1878 and 1900; *Rpt B/Tr*, 1899, p. 51.

[3] Virginia Grigsby to Hart Grigsby, Jul 1883, Gibson-Humphreys Mss (Southern Historical Collection, hereafter cited as SHC); *Star*, 22 Aug, 21, 23 Oct 1879, 8, 16 Oct 1880, 20 May, 18, 23 Nov 1882, 17 May 1883, 14 Jan 1885, 13 Sep 1887; *Sunday Chronicle*, 21 Aug 1881, 4 Jun 1882 (hereafter cited as *Sun Chronicle*); *Sentinel*, 12 Oct, 30 Nov 1889; Washington *Post*, 2, 4, 11 Oct 1889; *Rpt B/Tr*, 1891, p. 18.

[4] S Mis Doc 222, 52C, 1S, pp. 25-26, Ser 2907.

means as well as large: Washington real estate looked fool-proof. Thus in 1883 Mrs. Susan Grigsby, an impoverished southern gentlewoman newly appointed to a $900-a-year clerk-ship in the government Land Office, wrote to her sister: "There are still big fortunes to be made in this city on very small real estate investments and I hope you and I will be amongst the fortunate ones." That Mrs. Grigsby's venture did not pay off in no way discouraged others. A building boom accompanied the snowballing speculation in land. While new office buildings and stores rose along F Street, houses multiplied in the rest of the city, some of them designed by expensive architects for individual clients, more of them contractor-built pseudo-Queen-Anne red brick rows.[5] Impressed by these signs of prosperity a young newspaper correspondent questioned a leading citizen about its source. "Washington," came the answer, "is more of a business town than most people think. Washingtonians have some wholesale groceries here which do a business up into millions." And, he added, "real estate values have been making regular jumps upward for the past two years . . . the day will come—I ought to say it has already come—when it will be as fashionable to have a winter house at Washington as it is to have a summer one at Newport or at Saratoga . . . Washington in the winter is the gayest of the gay."[6]

Washington, known since the 1840's for the gaiety of her season, had never enjoyed a comparable boom. Formerly most public officials and people who came for the winter's social whirl had rented houses or lived in hotels and boarding houses; now men holding important public office generally made a point of owning their houses, and scores of other temporary residents hastened to build or buy. For as industrial fortunes began to create a new American elite, men long preoccupied with en-trenching themselves behind the power of money increasingly

[5] Susan Grigsby to Sarah G. Humphreys, 5 Aug 1883, 3 Aug, 5 Oct 1884, Gibson-Humphreys Mss; *Star*, 18 Jun 1881, 30 Sep 1882, 28 Apr 1883, 27 Mar 1884; *Sun Chronicle*, 21 Nov 1880, 24 Sep 1882.
[6] Cleveland *Leader*, 30 Sep 1883.

aspired to national political power and the more subtle power of social prestige. To achieve those aims a recognized position fortified by a fixed establishment in the national capital might be important, if only because it permitted frequent association with members of the *Corps Diplomatique*. For people already socially secure, a *pied à terre* in Washington also held the attraction of a place in which to entertain internationally known figures in agreeable surroundings. There was little to lose, since the federal government's commitment of 1878 to share District expenses kept taxes low. Assessments upon the rich were moderate: in 1893 the property of only 4,119 of the 31,700 District taxpayers was valued at over $10,000 and, despite frequent allusions to the city's large array of costly "mansions," only 1,300 holdings were assessed at more than $25,000.[7] The "opulent New Yorker," a merchant prince such as Levi Leiter of Chicago, or a Pittsburgher such as George Westinghouse, grown rich on his inventions, could build or buy his own residence in Washington, occupy it a few months of the year, and, when he wanted to dispose of it, count on making money on the transaction. What the very wealthy chose to do seemed desirable to people not so wealthy.

Permanent residents consequently began to build houses to sell or to furnish and rent. It was a very ill-equipped or badly located house that would not lease for the winter at a price high enough to bring the owner a handsome annual return. Rentals of furnished houses ranged in the mid-eighties from $75 to $3,733 a month; the average was $200. As land values rose, high-priced flats began to appear, a sign of urban growth both gratifying and slightly alarming to old residents. One businessman, marvelling at the changes he had witnessed since the war, noted that in 1865 Washington brokers never dealt exclusively in real estate but handled it along with claims, insurance, and stocks; fifteen years later the realtor

---

[7] *Rpt B/Tr*, 1893, p. 33; *Annual Report of the Commissioners of the District of Columbia*, 1893, p. 17 (hereafter cited as Comrs Rpt).

had come into being. Dozens of newcomers who had begun as government clerks turned into real estate dealers. So in 1863 fifteen-year-old Brainard Warner arrived from a small town in Pennsylvania, took a clerical job in the Judiciary Square Hospital and other clerkships in the next several years, and, after reading law with the famous Thaddeus Stevens and graduating from the Columbian Law School in 1869, founded a highly successful real estate business. George Truesdell, a New Yorker trained as a civil engineer, began his Washington career in 1872 as a clerk in the Treasury, only to open his own real estate office within a few years. And other ambitious young men followed the same path from government clerkships to heads of real estate companies. By 1885 there were a hundred-odd firms.[8] "The real estate men occupy the best offices, and along F street where they are mostly found, their carriages line the street curbs during business hours." More than 2,450 buildings went up in Washington in 1887 alone, and ground that had sold for 8¢ a square foot five years before sold for 48¢.[9]

Abetted by a new generation of astute young bankers, real estate syndicates embarked in the mid-1880's upon large-scale operations in the suburbs. One group bought Kalorama Heights, once part of Joel Barlow's estate lying between Boundary Street and Rock Creek; another acquired 240 acres along Massachusetts Avenue extended from the creek to the Tenley-town road, the Wisconsin Avenue of today; and in 1887 still a third purchased Chevy Chase, the old Joseph Bradley farm on the District's northwestern line, soon to be the site of Washington's first country club. The profits on these transactions were frequently quick and reportedly enormous. A house in one of these new sections virtually guaranteed the occupant

[8] Cleveland *Leader*, 5 Jan 1883, 17 Jun 1885; S. J. Bowen to Phebe Barker, 8 Nov 1881, Bowen Mss; *Star*, 10 Feb, 10 Mar 1883, 27 Oct 1888, 1 Jan 1890; John Hitz, "Homes for the People in the City of Washington," *Journal of Social Science*, xv, 145.

[9] Cleveland *Leader*, 1 Nov 1884; *Star*, 8 Oct 1887.

a place on the *Elite List*, a compilation of the names of socially acceptable Washingtonians. Less sophisticated residential areas beyond the city limits also rose sharply in value, although the appreciation was slower. Washington Heights, a section above Boundary Street near Columbia Road, increased in seventeen years from an assessed value of $112,000 to $1,137,400. Cleveland Heights, so named because the President's fifteen-room summer "cottage" was located on Woodley Road near the Tenleytown street railway, boomed in the late eighties; and a few years later, when the Naval Observatory rose on a hilltop in the vicinity, Cleveland Park came into existence.

As Washington became "a city for the rich," people of modest means found housing costs an acute problem. "It is strange," remarked John Forney's *Sunday Chronicle*, "that the capitalists and moneyed men of Washington seeking good opportunities for investment never think of building blocks of small houses within the reach of poor men and government clerks." Le Droit Park, a model cooperative apartment building venture of the 1870's, quickly became too expensive for many householders. Multiplying home loan and building associations helped the impecunious finance new homes, and some owners met the monthly payments on buying a house by occupying only a part and renting out the rest. Other families had to find quarters in localities beyond the reach of the street railways or in suburbs lacking piped water, such as Uniontown across the Anacostia or Mt. Pleasant to the north. Government clerks without children generally lived in Washington boarding houses; single women in fact had little choice.[10] Timid ladies whom the Civil War had impoverished and who were struggling to earn a living as federal employees were fearful of the remoteness of the suburbs and the expense of daily

[10] *Directory*, 1890; *Star*, 8 Nov 1879, 15 Mar 1882, 28 Jul 1883, 24 May 1884, 14 Feb, 27 May 1885, 7 May, 18 Jun, 9 Jul, 26 Nov, 3 Dec 1887, 7 Jan, 16 Jun 1888; *Post*, 27 Oct 1889; *Sentinel*, 16 Jul 1892; *Sun Chronicle*, 21 Aug 1881; Comrs Rpts, 1899, ii, 131, 1900, i, 28-29; Joseph W. Moore, *Picturesque Washington*, pp. 244-45; Hitz, "Homes," pp. 135-45.

carfare.[11] The real estate boom, if sauce for the gander, was certainly not sauce for the goose.

What twentieth-century planners would call "suburban sprawl" had a twenty-year start before Congress took steps to ensure some order in the future outward thrust of the city. By 1888 a belt of "inharmonious subdivisions" where streets had no relation to those of the city ringed Washington's northern bounds. Recognizing for the first time a "metropolitan area" problem, Congress enacted a law requiring suburban developers to lay out their subdivisions in conformity with the street plan of the city. The act for a time checked the mushrooming of relatively inexpensive settlements on Washington's periphery but later simplified the extension of sewers, water mains, and street lights into the county. Even without those urban conveniences, real estate values in parts of the county increased nearly 500 per cent during the eighties. Until street railway lines ran over the Aqueduct Bridge into Virginia in the late nineties, Washington's suburbia included none of the area beyond the Potomac. But within the District the spectacular growth elicited rhapsodic comment: "In time the District will be one vast city, the most beautiful, uniform and attractive of any to be found, the centre of learning, thought, wealth and station, the pride of our Republican empire and the envy of the world."

The slowing of all business after 1893 retarded building operations in both city and suburbs, but recovery, beginning in 1898, was so rapid that the District building inspectors were swamped with work. While a group of civic-minded men intent on ending alley-dwelling in Washington organized the Sanitary Improvement Company and built a number of row houses suited to the purses of workingmen, extension of the trolley lines into the county beyond the Anacostia River hastened the peopling of that area "to the proportion of a

[11] Virginia to Hart Grigsby, Jul 1883, Gibson-Humphreys Mss.

city."[12] Carroll D. Wright, federal Commissioner of Labor, wrote in 1899: "These movements for the improvement of the city have given some wag the opportunity to say that the population of Washington is divided into two classes—real estate agents and those who are not—but the usual facetious remark about real estate agents is offset . . . by the fact that they have been instrumental in a very large degree in carrying on the improvements that make the present city."[13]

In 1882 a newspaper man estimated the personal fortunes of seventeen senators at over $600,000,000. Although rumors later circulated that a good many members of Congress acquired their wealth in shady local real estate deals and manipulation of public utility stocks, the money these men spilled about the city was a boon to business. The salaries paid by railroad magnates and powerful industrialists to lobbyists in the capital further swelled the sums spent on high living. Lengthening rosters of government clerks also increased the demand for commodities, services, and housing. Salaries, though very small, meant a regular monthly income worth fighting for. After as well as before the inauguration of competitive civil service examinations in 1883, every month about twenty newspaper advertisements read typically: "Will give $100 for a place as clerk or messenger in any of the departments: first class references." The 7,800 government employees of 1880 rose in number to 23,000 in 1890—more than Washington's entire population in 1840—and by 1901 the total ran to over 26,000. Moreover, as one promoter bragged, "We have at Washington, in all departments of

[12] Comrs Rpts, 1886, pp. 40-43, 1890, p. 43, 1896, p. 17, 1899, I, 12-14, 1900, I, 28; 25 *United States Statutes at Large*, 451; S Rpt 623, 53C, 2S, Ser 3192; petitions, Senate 51A-J1S, 22 Jul 1890, Record Group 46, National Archives, and House 53A-H6.1, 21 Feb 1895, Record Group 233 (hereafter cited as ptns, S or H); S Doc 234, 54C, 1S, Ser 3354; Washington *Bee*, 7 Jan 1893; *Chronicle*, 14 Sep 1890; *Rpts B/Tr*, 1896-1900; *Star*, 1 Jan 1898, 1 Jan 1900, and 1 Jan 1901. Beginning in 1890 the New Year's day issues of the *Star* carried summaries of developments of the year past; these are hereafter cited as *Star* summaries.

[13] Carroll D. Wright, "The Economic Development of the District of Columbia," *Proceedings of the Washington Academy of Sciences*, I, 180.

the Government, nearly a thousand experts . . . the whole body of them constituting the most important cluster of men of genius and rare attainments in the world."[14]

Federal public works, although less vitally important to the city than those of the 1850's, provided jobs for common laborers and skilled artisans—work digging the foundations, laying the brick, and emplacing the frieze of red and blue tile medallions of the National Museum on the Mall, completing the stone work of the Washington Monument, putting the finishing touches on the State, War, and Navy Building west of the White House, erecting on Pennsylvania Avenue the new granite city Post Office with its heavy Gothic clock tower, and building the Italian Renaissance Library of Congress on Capitol Hill. Redemption of the "Potomac Flats" gave day laborers several years' work when Congress in 1882 at long last appropriated funds for filling the tidal marsh that had stretched since the 1830's from 17th Street below the White House to the Long Bridge. Under the direction of the District engineer commissioner, the laying of water mains and sewers further increased employment during the 1880's. Although a few Washington contractors had earned the title of "eight-hour bosses," strikes aimed at an eight-hour day occurred in 1886, but the local unions, alarmed by the public hysteria over Chicago's Haymarket Riot on May Day, condemned any recourse to violence. When the building trades unions risked a fresh round of strikes four years later, they again failed to win any major concession. As wages were slightly higher here than elsewhere and working conditions no worse, labor organizations thereafter limited their activities to talk.

To Washington, secure in her own prosperity and seemingly walled off from the industrial strife that had shaken much of the country during the 1880's, the consequences of the world-wide depression of the early 1890's came as a shock. Private

[14] Cleveland *Leader*, 21 Dec 1882, 2 Jul 1883, 24 Mar 1884; *Official Register of the United States*, 1881 and 1901; *Bee*, 28 Aug 1886; S Rpt 825, 52C, 1S, Ser 2914.

building enterprise in the city declined before the end of 1893, and, except for brewers and bakers, wages dropped, but full realization of what had been happening in the rest of the country first struck the capital in the spring of 1894, when the "Army of the Unemployed," its initial contingent led by "General" Coxey of Ohio, began to roll in to ask the federal government for help. Washingtonians became increasingly apprehensive as the rag-tag bob-tail throng, arriving by tens and twenties, gradually swelled to several thousand men. There were no jobs for them in the District or nearby Maryland and Virginia, and the prospect of their settling down for an indefinite period in their makeshift camps was as alarming to the local labor unions as to other citizens. Few people, however great their sympathy for the unemployed, expected Congress to enact any measure of relief for men who appeared to be challenging the rights of capital to control labor. Yet the community was not prepared for the action taken in early May to halt a fifteen-minute "riot" on the Capitol grounds; billy clubs wielded by the Capitol guards drove back the men attempting to make their way to the building, mounted police trampled into the crowd, and General Coxey and his two principal lieutenants were arrested for walking on the grass. By June some of the "army" had drifted away, but several hundred men stayed on, hoping for something to turn up. For weeks the generous Frank Hume, Washington's biggest wholesale grocer, supplied them with food, and it was he who finally arranged with the District commissioners to pay for railroad tickets to take them home in mid-August.

American workingmen nevertheless concluded that Washington might well be a useful location for the headquarters of organized labor, such as it was. In 1895 the emasculated Knights of Labor, still headed by its founder, Terence Powderly, moved its central office from Philadelphia to a building "within the very shadow of the Capitol," while the American Federation of Labor, with some 2,000 new members and a newly organized labor bureau, found jobs for about 150 men. And as private building picked up at the end of the century, the building trades, always the mainstay of labor in Washington, regained some confidence.[15]

Congress, if unwilling to interfere with the workings of the American industrial order, displayed meanwhile a welcome interest in improving the capital. Reclamation of the Potomac Flats, a vital sanitary measure, was the most needed public project, but scarcely less important to the city were the founding of the zoo, the opening of Rock Creek Park, and the creation of Potomac Park, after the courts had vested in the United States title to the made land on the water front. Far-sighted citizens perceived that the skillful use of open space might ultimately contribute more to Washington's appearance and hence to her attractions for tourists than could a formless proliferation of individually handsome buildings. Prodded by the petitions of District residents and the occasional urgings of federal officials, Congress had talked since 1867 of acquiring the Rock Creek valley for a park, but not until 1889, when fears rose lest sewage from nearby dwellings irretrievably contaminate the creek, was money forthcoming. The District appropriation act for 1890 included $200,000 for the purchase of land for a National Zoological Park a mile north of the city limits. Eighteen months later additional funds permitted negotiation for a much larger stretch of the upper valley for Rock Creek Park, "a pleasuring ground for the benefit and enjoyment of the people of the United States."

The appropriation for the zoo came first because Samuel Langley, secretary of the Smithsonian Institution, convinced Congress of the need of a proper home for the live animals then kept on the Smithsonian grounds as models for the insti-

[15] Donald L. McMurry, *Coxey's Army, A Study of the Industrial Army Movement of 1894*, pp. 113-26, 256-58; *Star*, 4 Oct 1884, 14 Feb 1885, 24 Jun 1886, 3 Nov 1887, Summaries, 1890-1896; *Chronicle*, 12 Aug 1894; *Sentinel*, 24 Apr 1894, 29 Apr 1899.

tution's taxidermists. Besides "Dunk" and "Gracie," two magnificent elephants, the first denizens of the zoo included herds of deer and peccary, some rather moth-eaten buffalo, several cages of monkeys, and about two hundred other specimens of wild creatures. A former Barnum and Bailey man took charge as head keeper. Inasmuch as the law gave the regents of the Smithsonian direction of the zoo but put the entire cost of maintaining it upon local taxpayers, some angry complaints sounded at Congress for forcing the District to pay for national "monkey parks." Since, ran the argument, the zoo and Rock Creek Park were inaccessible for people without bicycles or horses and carriages, only speculators in the real estate adjoining the creek would benefit; the money might have been better spent on improving the Mall.

In actuality "the extremely economical ideas" of the House Committee on Appropriations dictated leaving the stretch of Rock Creek Park above the "Zoological Gardens" in its natural state; even at the end of the century only a few dirt roads wound through the woodlands. The new parks, however, formed a point of departure upon a course that would eventually restore salient features of L'Enfant's plan of the city. In response to pleas of Washington's Board of Trade and a committee in charge of the city's centennial celebration, in March 1901 Senator James McMillan proposed that the Senate appoint a commission to plan a complete park system linking the Capitol grounds, which had been landscaped by Frederick Law Olmsted in the seventies, the Mall, and Potomac Park with the zoo and Rock Creek Park. From that beginning would spring an elaborate plan for beautifying the city.[16]

The relations of Congress with the local community, while

[16] Comrs Rpts, 1886, p. 44; House Report 3820, 49C, 2S, Ser 2501 (hereafter cited as H Rpt); H Rpt 3866, 50C, 2S, Ser 2673; ptns, H50A-D1, 19 Feb 1889, H51A-D1, n.d.; H Mis Doc 72, 51C, 1S, Ser 2760; S Ex Doc 127, 51C, 1S, Ser 2688; S Rpt 1919, 56C, 2S, Ser 4064; *Star*, 2 Jan 1893; "The Parks and Proposed Parks of Washington City," *American Architect and Building News*, XLVII, 72; *Rpts B/Tr*, 1894, pp. 27-28, 1898, p. 55, 1899, pp. 65-66, 1901, pp. 20, 64-66.

now and again touched by controversy, eventually achieved a surface serenity that contrasted noticeably with the anger and frustration of the 1860's and 1870's. Not all congresses, it is true, gave the District much attention, and even those most inclined to constructive legislation shelved some bills important to Washingtonians. Congressmen frequently begrudged the time spent on District affairs. Whenever questions of property rights arose, one senator grumbled, "the Senate of the United States is converted . . . into a mere town council, and the wrangles that go on here resemble very much the interesting debates that occur in such bodies." Yet congressional impatience tended to yield to pride in the capital or, as some critics implied, to zeal for protecting congressmen's investments in local property. Whatever the reason, in the 1890's men on the Hill devoted a good deal of thought to the District and, in investigating problems such as the organization of charities, the public school system, or the tax structure, the District committees often revealed genuine interest in bettering matters. Despite some short-sighted obstructionism, frequently born of newcomers' objections to forcing their constituents to contribute to District expenses, congressional debates on local bills generally ended in accepting committee recommendations. Until 1893 appropriations went through yearly with at most minor deviations from the principle of equal sharing set forth in the Organic Act, and thereafter the chief exception was in meeting the costs of extending streets into the county. A bill to cancel the half-and-half arrangement in 1896 got very short shrift indeed after figures showed that the value of taxable property in the District came to about $191,418,000, whereas federal property, exclusive of the streets and alleys, was worth over $198,000,000.[17]

[17] Frederick L. Siddons, "Municipal Conditions of Washington," *Proceedings of the Second . . . and Third National Conference for Good City Government*, pp. 362-63; *Congressional Record*, 46C, 2S, p. 3063, 47C, 2S, pp. 890-93, 52C, 1S, pp. 1636-58, 54C, 1S, pp. 1178, 5599 (hereafter cited as *Rec*); H Rpt 1978, 54C, 1S, Ser 3464.

District taxpayers, for their part, understood the importance of the annual federal contribution. Although they resented having to carry the costs of the zoo, an explicitly national park under the direction of a federal agency, they knew that without federal money the park could not have come into being. Their anger rose at congressional refusal to apply the half-and-half principle to the county as well as the city when the time came to extend streets beyond Washington's and Georgetown's original limits; the law of 1878 had pledged the federal government to sharing the expenses of the entire District, not merely the part formerly under municipal jurisdiction. If charging half the cost of laying out suburban streets to abutting private property could be justified, only bad faith, local citizens believed, could account for putting the rest of the cost upon the District without any federal contribution at all. Still worse, after exercise of the right of eminent domain and assessment of half the expense upon abuttors' property, Congress again and again failed to vote the appropriation of District funds necessary to open up a street, thereby leaving adjacent land without the improvements for which its owners had already paid. In the House defenders of the scheme called it the means of saving their constituents and small local taxpayers from having to foot the bills of real estate speculators.

Summary dismissals of grievances periodically sharpened citizens' sense of helplessness. Disagreements among themselves admittedly often hampered congressional response to community appeals, but even when public opinion was virtually unanimous a mere whim on the Hill could block a measure. For example, in the face of city-wide uneasiness about the paucity of charitable institutions for colored children, House and Senate haggled over the terms on which they would accept the gift of a civic-minded Negro who offered his farm as a home for "the poor colored waifs of the city." Congressional inaction on codification of District law became so intolerable that private organizations finally paid a lawyer to draft a code;

Congress then adopted the first part of the two-part draft. Every new Congress presented a fresh hazard, since the men assigned to the District committees could impede badly wanted legislation or recast bills to suit their personal interests. Those assignments once thought undesirable were sought after in the 1890's because of "the chances open to that committee for promising speculation" in property in the politically impotent city.[18]

Rebellion against that impotence alternately waxed and waned during the 1880's. Ambivalence marked the thinking of most well-to-do people. While District representation in Congress looked desirable, could a non-voting delegate in the House be of any use and could the community obtain a voting voice in Congress without accepting a popularly elected local government? Reopening the questions settled by the Organic Act might result merely in scrapping the provision for federal appropriations without altering the District's non-voting status, or, more alarming to some Washingtonians, end federal financing but revive a city regime dominated by Negro and propertyless voters. Fear of prying the lid off a Pandora's box kept influential men silent except when provoked into speech by some flagrant congressional sin of omission or commission. Unlike wealthier citizens, the working classes were only incidentally concerned with perpetuation of the financial provisions of the Organic Act. Inasmuch as white workingmen obviously believed two whites could always outvote one Negro,

[18] Memorial, . . . Joint Executive Committees of the Citizens' Associations of the District of Columbia Against the Repeal of the Fifty Percent Annual Congressional Appropriation Law, Jan 1894; 27 Stat. 532; Rec, 52C, 1S, pp. 4570-82, 5665-74, 52C, 2S, pp. 1157, 2249; Comrs Rpts, 1899, II, i-v, 1900, I, 31, 1901, I, 84; Rpts B/Tr, 1897, p. 65, 1901, p. 29; Star, 5 Apr 1879, 1 Sep 1881, 5 Mar 1887, 18, 25 Feb, 3, 10 Mar 1888, 2 Jan 1899; Capital, 1 Jan 1888; Sun Chronicle, 23 Jan, 6 Feb 1881, 5 Mar 1882; Chronicle, 14 Sep 1890; ptns, H46A-D1, 8 Mar 1880, S50A-J12, 9 Jan 1888, H52A-D1, 30 Mar 1892; S Mis Doc 161, 53C, 2S, Ser 3171; S Rpt 1150, 55C, 2S, Ser 3625; Siddons, "Municipal Conditions," p. 365; Mary Noble Lee, "City Government of Washington," Chautauquan, XXII, 170.

labor groups from time to time repeated their earlier appeals for suffrage.

The local press generally opposed restoration of a popularly elected District government. Until 1888 the *Star* insisted that all the faults of the existing regime lay in the men appointed, not in the system. The *Post* and the *Sentinel*, a paper directed mainly to Washington's German population, at first held votes for municipal officials better than nothing but later veered away from that position. The *People's Advocate*, a short-lived Negro newspaper, declared: "Universal suffrage is wrong in policy of [sic] not in principle when applied to cities," and the *Bee*, a second Negro paper, switched back and forth but generally argued that colored people were better off under the protection of Congress than they would be under city officials elected by Negro riff-raff. Only the *Chronicle* and John Forney's *Sunday Chronicle* consistently took the line that a local electorate including colored men could do no worse for itself than did federal appointees.[19]

In 1888 Theodore Noyes, son of the editor of the *Star*, published a series of articles reviewing the eigthy-eight years of what he termed congressional neglect of Washington. Coming on the heels of a congressional session that had seen no action on important local bills, the analysis struck home with peculiar force. He rejected popularly elected municipal officers as useless. "Without representation," he argued, "suffrage is of no value; and, shut out from the bodies which make its laws and imposes taxes upon it," the District would gain nothing from seating a delegate in the House. The one measure that could give District citizens any power over their own destiny was a constitutional amendment enabling qualified voters to elect representatives to Congress and a corresponding

[19] Siddons, "Municipal Conditions," pp. 370-71; "A Study in City Government," *The Nation*, xxxviii, 335; ptns, H51A-D1, 5 Dec 1890, H52A-D1, 30 Mar 1892, S55A-J18, 8 Dec 1897; frequent pieces in *Star*, 1879-1888, *Sentinel*, 1886-1894, *Post*, 1879, *Sun Chronicle*, 1881-1882, *Chronicle*, 1884-1895, *People's Advocate*, 1882, and *Bee*, 1883-1898.

number of members to the presidential electoral college. Later that year a Citizens' Committee of One Hundred examined Noyes' proposal. When a Washington notary had assembled letters expressing the ideas of well-known residents and had collected figures comparing the District's population, wealth, and contributions to the nation with those of a half-dozen states, the committee dispatched a memorial to the Hill. "They are unable to see," read the statement, "why they should be excluded from participation in the General Government any more than the people of State capitals should be excluded from participation in State governments." Several of the accompanying letters asked for an elected local government as well as national representation.[20]

Senator Henry W. Blair of New Hampshire presented the plea in the form of a resolution. In May 1890 the Senate committee to whom the matter was referred reported it back adversely. Incensed at the committee for holding no hearings on the measure, Blair spoke of the evil effects of civic irresponsibility upon young men growing up in Washington, where business monopolies exercised control through "combinations and rings and syndicates which derive their strength from unholy or indifferent relations to and with the representatives of national power." Because a constitutional amendment would take time to ratify, Congress must start the process at once in order to free the community from the prevailing "absolute political despotism, all the more alarming because so many are in love with it." Curiously enough, the newspapers did not pick up Blair's allusion to an unholy alliance between Congress and special interests in Washington, and substantiating comment was slow in coming into the open. Blair's speech began and ended the Senate discussion. Republicans ignored the issue.

[20] *Star*, 5 Mar, 15 Jun 1887, 18, 25 Feb, 3, 10 Mar 1888; *Rec*, 49C, 2S, p. 1172; S Mis Doc 126, 50C, 1S, Ser 2517; District of Columbia Citizens' Representative Committee of One Hundred, *Proposal to Improve the Present Form of Government of the District of Columbia*, 14 Feb 1888; S Mis Doc 237, 51C, 1S, Ser 2700; ptns, S51A-J15, 17 May 1890, H51A-D1, 19 Aug 1890.

TABLE I

MANUFACTURING AND ALLIED ENTERPRISES IN THE DISTRICT OF
COLUMBIA, 1880-1900[a]

	1880	1890	1900
BUILDING MATERIALS AND CONSTRUCTION ENTERPRISES			
No. of Establishments	251	565	744
Persons Employed	1,718	7,321	7,322
Wages and Salaries	$ 596,042	$ 4,734,360	$ 4,186,013
Capital Investment	755,505	4,602,692	7,425,342
Value of Product	1,904,206	12,543,013	13,928,690
FOODS AND BEVERAGES			
No. of Establishments	82	99	119
Persons Employed	283	858	1,092
Wages and Salaries	$ 124,842	$ 518,995	$ 666,683
Capital Investment	559,040	2,192,020	3,510,117
Value of Product	2,053,843	3,827,437	4,010,971
CLOTHING			
No. of Establishments	37	140	208
Persons Employed	237	967	904
Wages and Salaries	$ 102,850	$ 512,318	$ 475,989
Capital Investment	115,550	601,173	648,813
Value of Product	386,415	1,170,353	1,526,326
PRINTING AND ENGRAVING[b]			
No. of Prvt Plants	{ 30	{ 69	137
Govt "	{	{	9
Persons Employed in Pvt Plants	{ 2,654	{ 4,593	1,648
" Gvt "	{	{	5,771
Wages & salaries in Ptv Plants	{ $ 2,175,578	{ $ 3,733,469	$ 1,066,713
" Gvt "	{	{	4,927,875
Capital Investment, Pvt	{ $ 2,118,800	{ $ 3,270,306	3,036,297
, Gvt	{	{	3,916,746
Value of Product, Pvt	{ $ 3,775,478	{ $ 6,121,703	2,687,369
, Gvt	{	{	6,566,663
OTHER[c]			
No. of Establishments	571	1,422	1,507
Persons Employed	2,254	9,665	10,039
Wages and Salaries	$ 935,300	$ 5,123,122	$ 5,123,878
Capital Investment	1,933,631	18,198,898	23,443,930
Value of Product	3,762,374	15,668,931	18,947,603
GRAND TOTALS			
No. of Establishments	971	2,295	2,754
Persons Employed	7,146	23,404	26,776
Wages and Salaries	$ 3,924,612	$14,622,264	$16,477,151
Capital Investment	5,552,526	28,865,089	41,981,245
Value of Product	11,882,316	39,331,437	47,667,622

a 10th U.S. Census, 1800, Vol. II, *Manufactures*, Pt. I, pp. 101-02; 11th U.S. Census, 1890, Vol. VI, *Manufactures*, Pt. II, pp. 598-605; 12th U.S. Census, 1900, Vol. VIII, *Manufactures*, Pt. II, pp. 118-21.

b Until 1900 the census made no differentiation between private and government printing and engraving.

c Mostly handicrafts.

The Democratic national party platform of 1892 included a District home rule plank; flimsy at best, it remained purely decorative until discarded.[21]

Thin hopes for success apparently lessened the petitioners' disappointment. If they were still, in Theodore Noyes' phrase, "political slaves," at least they had not become "bankrupt freemen" by loss of the federal sharing of District expenses. During the 1890's the suffrage question in one form or another cropped up occasionally but without arousing citizens to new efforts. In 1895 Frederick Siddons, a Washington lawyer whom Woodrow Wilson would make a District commissioner eighteen years later, prophesied at a national conference on good city government that growing dissatisfaction among the rank and file of Washingtonians would shortly invigorate the campaign for self-government, inasmuch as the existing system put them at the mercy of men uninformed about the needs of ordinary, socially obscure citizens. Siddons miscalculated. The suffering to be seen in other cities after the panic weakened the community's interest in political reorganization, since poverty and unemployment, bad enough in the District, could easily become worse. Furthermore, toward the end of the decade exceptionally generous appropriations made congressional rule relatively painless, and growing faith in citizens' associations and the new Washington Board of Trade persuaded taxpayers that, voteless though they were, they could make their wants known on the Hill and expect an eventual response.[22]

The citizens' associations were initially neighborhood groups each concerned with its own section of city or county. The East Washington Citizens' Association launched by property-owners on Capitol Hill in 1871 was the first, but others appeared

[21] *Rec*, 51C, 1S, pp. 10119-23; Lee, "City Government of Washington," 169; Robert Wickliffe Woolley, "The Plunderers of Washington," *Pearson's Magazine*, XXII, 623-36; Kirk Porter and Donald Bruce Johnson, *National Party Platforms, 1840-1956*, pp. 94-125.

[22] *Chronicle*, 7 Apr 1895; ptn, H52A-D1, 30 Mar 1892; Siddons, "Municipal Conditions," pp. 370-71; *Star*, 1 Jan 1900; *Sentinel*, 8 Jan 1901; Mary S. Logan, ed., *Thirty Years in Washington*, p. 524.

after 1874, and the number multiplied rapidly in the mid-eighties. Inasmuch as law forbade District borrowing and appropriations for public works were expressly tabbed for particular projects, each area had to compete with its neighbors to get the largest possible sum for itself. Every association ordinarily discussed only its own special needs. But now and again topics such as changes in the school system or methods of assessing property evoked city-wide interest, and the wish of all associations to have a voice in determining how taxes should be spent spurred efforts to set up a central body. In 1886 eight associations in Washington and the Mt. Pleasant association in the county proposed a presidentially appointed citizens' council empowered to prepare the District's annual budget for submission to Congress, but the failure of that petition, the dismissal of Noyes' plan for a constitutional amendment, and the frequently conflicting aims of the separate associations gradually undermined attempts at union.

The associations nevertheless were useful. While they had no purely social function, they bore some resemblance to the farmers' Grange and served the same purpose of clarifying and giving form to members' ideas. In the 1870's Colonel Henry Robert, later a District engineer commissioner, had drafted *Robert's Rules of Order* to help new associations conduct their meetings efficiently. "Difficult questions," remarked a detached observer, "are expounded with a fullness of detail and of technical precision that would never be dared before the usual political audience." The effort of Negroes excluded from White associations to form their own testified to the importance the community attached to these neighborhood pressure groups.[23]

Because it was more homogeneous, better organized, and possessed of wider vision of community needs, the Washington

[23] *Bee*, 14 May, 2 Jul, 12 Nov 1887, 28 Oct 1899; ptns, 51A-H4.2, 18 Apr 1890, H54A-H7.6, 30 Mar 1896; *Post*, 6, 12 Nov 1889; Louis Brownlow, *A Passion for Politics*, p. 63; C. Meriwether, "Washington City Government," *Political Science Quarterly*, XII, 418. From 1883 through 1888 the *Star* carried articles on citizens' associations at least once a month.

Board of Trade, founded in November 1889, immediately proved of greater value to the city as a whole than the avowedly parochial citizens' associations. Many a twentieth-century Washingtonian would come to look upon the Board of Trade as a body ruled by a handful of men for the sole benefit of real estate speculators and the bankers who financed them. Yet if, as the *Sentinel* contended, from its very beginning the board was a front for the street railway executives, bankers, insurance agents, and "sprinkling of real estate brokers, politicians and the like" who really governed the city, for some years they were of service to others than themselves. Although they showed little comprehension of workingmen's problems, in the main ignored the Negro third of the population, and took a complacent attitude toward the public schools, the committee reports from 1890 to 1901 in a dozen realms revealed painstaking investigation of civic wants and produced intelligent recommendations for meeting them.

Beriah Wilkins sent out the two hundred four-line letters of invitation to the meeting that gave birth to the Board of Trade. Having completed a third term in the House of Representatives as a member from Ohio, Wilkins had bought a controlling interest in the Washington *Post* and had chosen to settle permanently in a city he found at once congenial and challenging. He paved the way for the proposed Board of Trade in an editorial explaining that an organization of responsible businessmen could represent public opinion in the District more fully and would carry more weight with Congress and the commissioners than citizens' associations and individual petitions ever could.[24] The men who attended the meeting agreed.

Organization proceeded quickly. The charter members elected thirty-one directors; the next year the number was cut to thirty. The directors chose the president from their own

[24] *Sentinel*, 16 Jul 1892; *Rpts B/Tr*, 1890-1901; H. W. Crew, *Centennial History of the City of Washington*, pp. 460-61; *Post*, 12 Nov 1889. A copy of Wilkins' letter still hangs in the Board of Trade directors' room.

ranks, engaged the paid secretary, selected the treasurer, fixed
the annual dues—$5 for an individual, $10 for a partnership or
corporation—appointed the standing committees, and recommended or, as things worked out in practice, set policies. The
entire board might vote upon the admission of new members
and it annually reelected or replaced ten directors, but the
bylaws enabled thirty men to run the organization. It soon
came to exercise greater power in Washington than any body
except Congress and the presidentially appointed District commissioners. Within two years the District committees of Congress and the commissioners were turning to the Board of Trade
for advice, and by the end of the century it was an open secret
that the commissioners themselves owed their office to the
board's directors. Membership in the organization was much
more inclusive in the 1890's than later. Neither religion nor
color was a bar. Isadore Saks was a director during most of the
nineties and Simon Wolf, a leader in Jewish welfare work,
served on several committees. Interestingly enough in view of
twentieth-century attitudes, James T. Wormley, son of the
founder of the famous Wormley House, was a charter member,
and three other Negroes were elected in the course of the next
few years.[25]

While the board of directors never included all Washington's
wealthiest men, the fifty-seven individuals who served before
1902 represented the city's economic dominants. Alongside
such powerful persons as Charles Glover, president of the Riggs
National Bank, S. W. Woodward, department store owner,
and Brainard Warner, the city's foremost real estate broker,
were nationally known lawyers, journalists and editors, doctors
and engineers. The professional men were generally also directors of banks and other business enterprises, just as several
of the bankers and real estate brokers held law degrees. Con-

[25] *Rpts B/Tr*, 1890, 1891, and *By Laws*, 1893, pp. 54-57; *Bee*, 2 Feb
1901; memo, 23 Apr 1900, McKinley Mss (L. C.); Siddons, "Municipal
Conditions," pp. 366, 371.

trary to later popular belief, realtors as such were fewer than merchants and bankers, although the distinction between a real estate dealer and any other businessman was shadowy. Indeed a striking feature of the make-up of the Board of Trade directorate was the interlocking interests of its members.

Most of these men had come to Washington after the Civil War and in 1889 were still in their early forties. Several were completely self-made. Brainard Warner, an unknown country boy upon his arrival in Washington, had become head of the city's biggest real estate firm before he was thirty, the founder and first president of the Washington Loan and Trust Company at the age of forty-two in 1889, president of the Board of Trade in the nineties, and in the interim, while organizing a half-dozen other successful business enterprises, had built and moved into a red brick mansion in the millionaire section of Massachusetts Avenue beyond Dupont Circle. The dour-looking, witty Crosby Noyes, born in Maine, had walked into Washington on foot in 1848 and, by his literary skill, his insights, and his Yankee shrewdness, made his way up to a position of singular power not only as editor of the *Evening Star* but as a citizen passionately devoted to Washington's interests as he saw them. The suave Theodore Noyes, a native Washingtonian, inherited that devotion as well as the editorship of the *Star*.

Whether to the manor born or representing the rags to riches saga, the leaders of the Board of Trade all had some social finesse; over forty percent of them were listed in Washington's first *Social Register*. All played some part in guiding local charities and reform institutions. Beriah Wilkins acted for years as treasurer of the citizens' relief committee. The heavily built, round-faced, mustachioed Brainard Warner, outwardly the entrepreneur *par excellence*, repeatedly served on the school board and on the boards of the Industrial Home School and of the Central Free Dispensary and Emergency Hospital; he was president of the National Philharmonic Society, a vice president of the American National Red Cross, and a sponsor of the Washington Choral Society and Georgetown Orchestra. Another Board of Trade president, S. W. Woodward, identified himself closely with the YMCA; prim-looking behind his rimless eye-glasses and carefully pointed Vandyke beard, he held such firm religious convictions that he forbade the sale of playing cards in Woodward and Lothrop's department store, but he gave away thousands of dollars yearly and by his rectitude and gentleness won universal respect. That violent-tempered, blond giant, Charles Glover, threw his influence into getting public parks for the city and into launching the National Cathedral Foundation. Self interest, to be sure, usually went hand in hand with altruism but, according to their lights, the business leaders of this period were dedicated men. And Washingtonians by adoption were as eager as native sons to work for the city's well-being.

As the name "Board of Trade" implies, its first concern was to strengthen the city's economic position. The directors opposed local suffrage, but they saw that efficiently run charities, a sound public health program, and urban aesthetics were important assets to a residential city. Their aims, therefore, extended to reducing pauperism while providing for the helpless, to improving sanitation, and to realizing a plan for the "City Beautiful" which Congress through the Park and Fine Arts Commissions later largely adopted. Thus the board joined with the Associated Charities and the backers of a new Civic Center in organizing a company to build inexpensive model houses for workingmen. It was the board in collaboration with the District Bar Association that engaged Associate Justice Walter Cox of the District Supreme Court to codify District law, the board that campaigned successfully for a public library and led the fight to get the Pennsylvania Railroad tracks and the depot off the Mall. The organization was intrinsically undemocratic. When the membership committee in 1897 acknowledged that a tiny minority made all decisions, the remedies introduced still left an autocracy. Yet in light of the abuses of municipal governments elsewhere in America, Washingtonians who shrank from the mere idea of popularly elected city officials had reason to place faith in the Board of Trade. A political scientist writing for a learned journal indeed argued that this unofficial, self-appointed "city council" provided an ideal form of local government through a "representative aristocracy."[26]

[26] *Rpts B/Tr*, lists of officers and members, 1890-1901, and 1894, p. 50, 1895, pp. 47-48, 1896, p. 47, 1897, pp. 5, 39-40, 1898, pp. 22-24, 1899, pp. 21-22, 1900, pp. 37-43, 108-09; *Chronicle*, 12 Dec 1896; *Post*, 8, 9 Oct 1889; *Washington Social Register*, 1900; *A History of the City of Washington, Its Men and Institutions*, by the Washington *Post*, ed. Allen Slauson, pp. 69-70, 191-259, 341, 401-33 (hereafter cited as *Post History*); *Sentinel*, 18 Nov 1899; Meriwether, "Washington City Government," pp. 407-19.

CHAPTER III

MUNICIPAL HOUSEKEEPING, 1879-1901

THE long congressional debates which preceded the passage of the Organic Act of 1878 had convinced President and senators that they must put competent men, not party hacks, in charge of running a city which for seventy-one years had governed herself. With Congress enacting all local legislation and controlling all local public expenditures, the three commissioners must be men who commanded respect in the community, even though they were responsible to Congress and the President rather than to citizens of the District of Columbia.

Certainly the civilian commissioners between 1879 and 1901 were more conscientious than the politicians who had preceded them. *Bona fide* residents of Washington, they were familiar with the local scene, and the tacit understanding that one of the two appointees was to be a Republican and the other a Democrat minimized political partisanship in local administration. Except for John Ross, a former Georgetown University law professor who served from 1890 till his death in 1902, and the journalist Henry Macfarland, none of the commissioners possessed personal distinction. Lawyers, real estate dealers, and merchants with wide-ranging interests in the community, they represented Washington's top business stratum; all of them were members of the Board of Trade after its organization. Blind as they generally were to the problem of the little fellow, in their official acts they followed the line they thought Congress expected of them. A story published fifteen years after the rumored event told of a Grover Cleveland nominee who failed to win Senate confirmation because he had refused to promise to keep hands off certain powerful interests. But the charges of self-seeking or negligence which citizens occasionally levelled at one or another of the District commissioners rarely stuck. As public servants they ranked high in an era when municipal officials in America were by and large an unsavory lot.

By law, one of the three commissioners was always to be an officer of the Army Engineer Corps. Unlike his two civilian associates, he was usually a newcomer to Washington and consequently was ill-versed in the District's problems. Because his tour of duty was brief, he had little time to learn the job; in twenty years ten different officers held it. Washingtonians disliked what often seemed to be military highhandedness in the engineer's office. Since he had charge of all contracts for public works, he commanded considerable patronage and could exercise an arbitrary authority. Yet ordinarily the engineering work was efficiently executed, and much of it was planned with a vision that enabled two succeeding generations of Washingtonians to dismiss from mind a host of earlier problems.[1]

Past disasters had bred wariness in District residents. Although the Organic Act provided safeguards against irresponsible spending, taxpayers during most of the 1880's watched the commissioners' every move. In 1879 the financial tangle left by the territorial Board of Public Works was still a legacy of trouble. The new commissioners balked at imposing tax liens on property for assessments improperly levied or not paid because the improvements had never been made; adjustments cost the District about $2,000,000. But delinquency on all taxes continued. Citizens objected to the personal property tax and even more strongly to the haphazard methods of assessing real estate and handling appeals. Three-year intervals between appraisals piled up inequities of valuation in the rapidly growing community and fostered the rise of a single tax movement. The

[1] E.g., *Sentinel*, 20 Jul 1883, 27 Nov 1886, 2 Mar 1889, 16 Aug, 22 Nov 1890; *Bee*, 19, 26 Jul 1884; *Star*, 22 Sep 1887, 18 Feb, 28 Sep 1888, 9 Jan 1889; ptn, S50A-J12, 8 Oct 1888; S Rpt 2686, 50C, 2S, Ser 2620; *Chronicle*, 7 Sep 1890, 13, 20 Mar 1897; Henry Himber to S. J. Bowen, 14 Jun 1880, and Zalmon Richards to Bowen, 2 Jul 1881, Bowen Mss; Siddons, "Municipal Condition," *Third Ntl Conference for Good City Govt.*, pp. 365, 369; R. W. Woolley, "The Plunderers of Washington," *Pearson's Magazine*, XXII, 626; Louis Brownlow, *A Passion for Anonymity*, pp. 8-10.

commissioners themselves thought that taxes on improvements encouraged speculation in real estate and believed the personal property tax too easily evaded to be useful. In 1892, after scrutinizing the local tax laws, a congressional committee reported:

"[Since] land values are increasing at an enormous rate—on a conservative estimate to the amount of $40,000,000 annually . . . —the assessment of buildings and the under-assessment of land is operating to discourage greatly the growth and improvement of the capital . . . [On] a fair assessment of land alone it would be easy to obtain by a tax rate less than one-half of the present all the revenue required for the needs of the District."

The findings showed business property assessed frequently at less than 14 percent its true value and land held for speculation at less than 10 percent, while residential property "especially where the small homes are situated, is assessed at from 70 to 80 percent of its true value." Although reputable real estate dealers reluctantly admitted the validity of these data, at the last minute the committee shied away from any radical innovation. In 1894 a new law drafted largely by members of the Board of Trade merely required the assessors to conduct open hearings on complaints, to revise and equalize existing real estate valuations, and to systematize future assessments. The most glaring inequities disappeared thereafter. "Yet, as nearly every resident of the city of Washington is a single taxer," a congressman remarked at the end of the century, a tax on land alone would have better satisfied most of the local public.[2]

The $1,214,000 paid annually into the sinking fund, however, steadily pared down the District's long-term debt. As interest payments shrank and monies for reduction of the principal and for building up the fire and police department

[2] S Mis Doc 39, 46C, 2S, pp. 13, 90-97, Ser 1931; H Mis Doc 11, 46C, 3S, Ser 1981; Comrs Rpts, 1881, pp. 4-6, 1882, pp. 5, 176, 1887, p. 9; *Rec*, 47C, 1S, pp. 1317-24, 5352-54, 47C, 2S, pp. 3682, 3698; *Star*, 11 Dec 1879, 22 May 1880, 4 Aug 1888; *Sentinel*, 18 Dec 1886, 25 May 1889; ptns, H46A-D1, 8 Mar 1880 and dozens of similar petitions to every Congress during the 1880's.

pension funds dropped from 35.26 to 15.26 percent of the over-all budget, taxpayers felt easier. (See Table II.) They were dismayed at several congressional departures from the half-and-half principle, first in 1891 when the appropriation act charged the District with the full $3,000 cost of opening a public bathing beach, and then over the next six years by refusals to share some $357,000 of costs for street extension and minor items. But these exceptions were disturbing chiefly as warnings of restiveness in Congress over the 1878 commitment.[3]

Determined to forestall full repudiation of the financial arrangement, citizens generally swallowed their wrath. Although the murderous shooting of President Garfield in the summer of 1881 had called congressional attention to the need of a larger police force, for years the appropriation precluded engaging more patrolmen. (See Table II.) Two hundred men, only half of them on duty at any one time, were too few; ten years later, 365 were still too few for a city so geographically spread out. In actuality, in relation to population, neither violent crime nor less serious law-breaking was as frequent in the 1880's and 1890's as it had been in the 1850's and the Civil War era, but charges of police corruption, laxity, or brutality filled the newspapers until the replacement of venal officers and appointment of a new chief in 1886 restored some measure of public confidence. Gambling, vagrancy, and drunkenness were still the chief sources of trouble. In Washington, the *Star* suggested, "the general climate, the charitable disposition of the people who have means, the easy hours of work and the uncertain tenure of government employ, all contribute to help men downward." Every winter tramps and migrant seasonal laborers rolled in, and, as the commissioners reported gloomily, a national emergency like the war with Spain "brought many criminals and

[3] H Rpt 1469, 52C, 1S, pp. 1-4, 10, Ser 3046; S Bill 2046, 53C, 2S (mf, L.C.); *Star*, 1 Jan 1895; *Rec*, 56C, 2S, App, p. 181; S Doc 351, 57C, 1S, Ser 4245; *Rpt B/Tr*, 1897, pp. 62-63.

cranks to the city." New anti-gambling and anti-vagrancy laws failed to have much effect. The enlargement of the police force to 585 men and the addition of a bicycle squad at the end of the century helped far more.

As for years past, juvenile delinquency was a greater source of public anxiety than adult crime. Warfare between rival fire house gangs had ended when members of a paid fire department took up living quarters in the engine houses, but juvenile delinquents still roamed the streets. The Reform School for Boys and the school for incorrigible girls which opened in 1893 offered no cure, and the suggestion that lack of playgrounds encouraged mischief-making in a city where law forbade children's using the public reservations for ball grounds brought no response from Congress. As prohibition sentiment gained strength in the community, the newly organized Guardian League attempted to prove statistically the link between the growth of the liquor traffic and juvenile delinquency: between 1882 and 1887 there had been a 15-percent increase in population but a 40-percent rise in the number of licensed saloons and liquor wholesalers, a 90-percent increase in licensed billiard and pool halls, and countless places operating illegally. "Youths in consequence of these diabolical snares . . . abandon school and workshop and become tipplers, gamblers, harlots, vagabonds and paupers." Here juvenile arrests averaged 20 percent of all arrests, whereas in New York City the average was under 11, in Boston under 14, and in Chicago 15.5 percent. The *Star* disputed those findings; well-informed travellers were "ready to pronounce Washington the most orderly city of its size extant."[4]

Nevertheless, people throughout the United States petitioned Congress to institute in the capital reforms they frequently did not enjoy at home—freedom "from the curse of rum,"

[4] *Rec*, 47C, 1S, pp. 3801, 5232, 47C, 2S, pp. 188-89, 1452, 1526; Comrs Rpt, 1881, p. 101, 1887, pp. 14-16, 1890, pp. 66-67, 1898, pp. viii, xi, 1899, I, 12-15; *Star*, 17 Mar 1880; *Sentinel*, 3 Nov 1883, 20, 27 Nov, 4 Dec 1886; *Capitol*, 27 May 1883; S Mis Doc 24, 49C, 2S, Ser 2450.

TABLE II

DISTRICT OF COLUMBIA EXPENDITURES[a]

	1881	%	1891	%	1901	%	1911	%	1915	%	1917	%
TOTAL[b]	$3,737,049		$5,814,237		$9,437,829		$13,402,135		$14,845,469		$14,915,244	
GENERAL ADMINISTRATION & MISCELLANEOUS	203,690	5.45	325,770	5.60	503,562	5.33	915,382	6.9	1,481,237	10.0	1,839,689	12.3
DEBT RETIREMENT[c] & SPECIAL FUNDS	1,346,915	35.3	1,294,855	22.3	1,459,776	15.5	1,650,091	12.3	1,843,963	12.4	973,205	6.5
FIRE PROTECTION	106,262	2.9	147,726	2.5	339,025	3.6	756,051	5.6	731,015	4.9	768,705	5.2
LAW ENFORCEMENT Courts, Police & Reformatories	405,529	10.9	670,573	11.5	1,004,746	10.6	1,835,592	13.7	1,897,980	12.8	2,107,698	14.1
HEALTH SERVICES General; care of indigent D.C. patients at St. Elizabeths; other public hospitals[d]; subsidies to private hospitals; garbage removal	102,036	2.46	200,283	3.44	581,178	6.18	886,481	6.6	1,208,508	8.1	1,046,869	7.0
WELFARE Washington Asylum[e]; poor relief; after 1900, Board of Charities, Board of Children's Guardians, other public charities[f]; subsidies to private charities[f]; playgrounds and bathing beaches	106,281	2.84	143,158	2.46	195,852	2.98	378,137	2.8	460,943	3.2	515,094	3.5

PUBLIC EDUCATION	527,311	14.3	940,495	16.2	1,524,373	16.2	3,193,513	23.8	3,164,464	21.3	3,420,107	22.9
Salaries	330,343		600,919		939,260		1,831,353		2,071,785		2,261,796	
New buildings	117,981		230,205		341,457		815,639		621,255		609,670	
PUBLIC WORKS (exclusive of school buildings)	919,426	24.8	2,090,371	36.0	3,957,596	40.6	3,787,039	28.3	4,047,260	27.3	4,236,580	28.4
Streets	623,513		1,584,865		2,389,849		1,693,305		1,888,000		2,036,315	
Sewers	121,648		221,965		1,411,051		469,039		584,247		567,375	

a Computed from figures in Comrs Rpts, 1881-1917.

b Including cash balances, water fund, police and firemens' funds, and, in 1917, repayment to the U.S. of $518,505 for a deficiency in District accounts pertaining to St. Elizabeths and court fines of the late 1870's.

c Including, in 1915, $586,000 for interest on the 3.65% bonds for the fiscal years 1877 and 1878.

d Freedmen's only till 1901, when $73,639 went for a site for a new municipal hospital. Till 1894 Congress appropriated for Freedmen's hospital in the Sundry Civil bill and the U.S. Treasury bore the entire expense. Expenditures for the Asylum Hospital were lumped with those for the almshouse and workhouse. Before 1902 St. Elizabeths was included in Welfare in the reports but in this table is added to Health. In 1915 $394,000 went for a new Columbia Hospital.

e Including workhouse, almshouse and hospital before 1911, and jails in 1911, 1915, and 1917.

f Approximately three-fifths for child care.

"Sunday Rest," anti-vivisection, juster divorce laws, or the forbidding of kinetoscope reproduction of prize fights. The countrywide concern to have the capital an ideal municipality at once gratified and irritated the local public. The WCTU campaign particularly irked German-born citizens who wished to drink their Sunday beer in peace. The commissioners, after exploring a plan for raising the liquor license fee from $100 to $500, chose instead to enforce Sunday closing, to increase fines for illegal selling, and to reduce the number of licenses granted, especially in the notorious "Division," the former Murder Bay area in the triangle southeast of the Treasury between Pennsylvania Avenue and the old Washington Canal bed.[5]

More important to most residents was the meagerness of the water supply. A Senate investigation showed that since 1863, when the receiving reservoir of the aqueduct opened, daily per capita consumption of water had risen to over 155 gallons, whereas the Chicagoan used only 119 gallons daily, the Bostonian 75, and the Philadelphian 58. Increases in water rental rates and house-to-house inspections to check on dripping faucets improved service but failed to resolve the basic problem: the insufficient head of water at the reservoir above Georgetown, leakages in the distributing system, and the inadequacy of a single three-foot distributing main to meet the needs of the rapidly growing population. Georgetown, being nearer the reservoir, was better off than most of Washington. Gravity feed ensured proper pressure in only part of the downtown capital; the eastern half of the city and sections supplied by pumping stations suffered from a water famine, while many of the suburbs had no piped water at all; St. Elizabeths Hospital pumped its supply from the turgid Eastern Branch.[6]

[5] S Mis Doc 114, 51C, 1S, Ser 2698; ptns, H46A-H7, n.d., H50A-H31.3, H51A-H7, n.d., S54A-J20, n.d., and hundreds more; *Sentinel*, 11 Dec 1886, 18 Oct 1890, 28 Mar 1891, 18 Jun 1892, 9 Jun 1894; *Star*, 12 Feb 1887; Comrs Rpts, 1890, p. 12, 1899, p. 18, 1901, p. 24.
[6] S Rpt 39, 46C, 2S, Ser 1893; *Star*, 10, 11, 17, 25 Jul, 4 Aug 1879, 15 Jan 1880, 1 Aug 1885; *Capitol*, 26 Jan 1879; *Sun Chronicle*, 9 Jan

The most economical answer, Congress finally concluded, was to increase the capacity of the Georgetown reservoir by raising the height of the Great Falls dam and running it to the Virginia shore and then to extend the aqueduct to a second reservoir to be located between the Soldiers' Home and Howard University. The dam was finished in 1886, but cave-ins due to faulty masonry halted work on the new "Lydecker tunnel," named for the Army engineer commissioner in charge of extending the aqueduct; only complete rebuilding at an ultimate cost of over $1,500,000 would make the tunnel usable. As lack of funds caused a thirteen-year delay in starting the job, the new reservoir would not be in use until 1907. In the interim a new main from the Georgetown reservoir relieved the worst of the water shortage on the Hill and somewhat bettered service in the rest of the city and the suburbs. But at the end of the century forty out of eighty-two schoolhouses still had no water closets, and in the big Wallach School east of the Capitol no water flowed through the urinals during the day time.[7]

An equally urgent need was an adequate sewage and drainage system. In 1879 the sewers in Georgetown and northwesternmost Washington emptied into Rock Creek, a thin trickle of a brook in summer; those in east and south Washington fed into the James Creek, which flowed through a crowded slum area into the Eastern Branch near the Arsenal grounds; the pipes from the central part of the city drained into the "B Street main," the old Washington Canal turned into a covered culvert debouching into the tidal marshes beyond the White House. During heavy rainstorms surface water pouring down from the hills into a single storm sewer threatened to flood the heart

---

1881; *Rec*, 47C, 1S, p. 4665, 49C, 1S, pp. 5844, 7519-22; *Sentinel*, 11 Dec 1886, 20 Aug 1887, 16 Nov 1889, 22 Feb 1890.
   [7] 22 *Stat.* 168; 23 *Stat.* 132-33; 25 *Stat.* 573; "The Water Supply Problem in Washington," *Engineering Record*, xxxvii, 313; Capt. D. D. Gaillard, "Water Waste and Use in Washington," *Engineering Record*, xlii, 277-78; Comrs Rpts, 1883, p. 272, 1886, p. 25, 1887, pp. 18-19, 1889, pp. 292-93, 1890, pp. 11, 415-17, 1894, pp. 435-49.

of the city. During a freshet in 1877 the river had risen ten feet at 17th Street beyond the White House, and the next summer, when the Tiber arch broke, the lower part of the city had narrowly escaped "a horrible inundation." But the commissioners' proposed remedy required a $2,500,000 appropriation, and Senate objections to including a District sanitary measure in a general rivers and harbors bill delayed action until 1882. The undertaking then approved involved filling the marshes beyond the Monument grounds, building a tidal basin slightly downstream in order to control the flow of the tide, and dredging a deep channel that would skirt the shore from the Long Bridge to Arsenal Point.

As fill slowly reclaimed the swamps along the Potomac River front, Washingtonians began an ultimately successful campaign to have the new land turned into a permanent park. But hopes that elimination of the Potomac Flats would take care of sewage disposal were disappointed. In 1890 a special board of sanitary engineers reported the swamps at the source of the Anacostia and the tidal backwash into the James Creek canal still affecting the eastern part of the District, the flow of Rock Creek too sluggish to carry off the sewage of northwest Washington and Georgetown, and the pollution of the Potomac near the Monument grounds still a danger to the public. Thanks to correct estimates of Washington's future growth, Rudolph Henning, the foremost American sanitary engineer of the nineteenth century, helped the sanitary board draft a plan of such dimensions that it would serve the city adequately for the next sixty years; by extensions in the 1920's it would enable nearby Maryland communities also to feed sewage into the District's trunk lines; not until the late 1950's would sanitary experts find fault with a system that used the same mains for sewage and for the drainage of surface water.

The engineers of 1890 recommended construction of huge trunk sewers into which intercepting lines covering every thickly settled section of the District should flow; a pumping station at the foot of New Jersey Avenue would then force the sewage from the trunk lines into conduits laid under the Eastern Branch and extended three miles downstream to empty into deep water where the tides would not wash pollution back into Washington. Congress accepted the plan but refused to sanction a bond issue to pay for the work. A depleted federal Treasury during the mid-nineties shut off the other possible source of funds until the revival of the country's business in 1898 enabled the commissioners and the Board of Trade to prevail upon Congress to make yearly appropriations to meet the costs. By 1901, although sewage disposal was still "the most vital question" facing the city, an expenditure of over $2,000,000 saw the new system nearly half-finished.[8]

More than new sewer mains were needed to safeguard public health. In 1881 fewer than a third of the 30,474 houses in Washington and Georgetown had sewer connections. Hotels and boardinghouses rarely had more than one water closet to a floor. Many families pumped all their water from cisterns or carried it pailful by pailful from the wells in the public squares; where sanitation was primitive, seepage from the contaminated soil into wells spread typhoid and diarrheal diseases. Every year, to be sure, added to the number of dwellings equipped with plumbing, but in 1890 some 30,000 people, most of them Negroes, lived in squalid alley tenements which congressional views on the sanctity of private property prevented the District health officer from demolishing. Here tuberculosis flourished, annually the cause of one out of every four deaths. A forward step taken in 1892 was the enactment of a law prohibiting building of additional dwellings in alleys less than twenty

[8] S Mis Docs 13, 17, 19, and 25, 45C, 3S, Ser 1833; H Ex Doc 445, 51C, 1S, Ser 2752; ptns, H54A-H7.6, 14 Jan and 24 Feb 1897; Comrs Rpts, 1879, pp. 7-11, 1885, p. 184, 1887, pp. 20-21, 1889, p. 300, 1890, p. 535, 1900, i, 27, 1901, i, 30; *Star*, 16, 29 Jan, 4 Aug 1879, 1 Jan 1895; *Rec*, 47C, 1S, pp. 986, 2738-49, 3801, 5792, 5828-33; *Rpts B/Tr*, 1898, pp. 94-99, 1900, pp. 114-16; Staff Rpt, Joint Committee on Washington Metropolitan Problems, 86C, 2S, Dec 1958, *Water Supply and Sewage Disposal*, p. 13.

feet wide and not equipped with sewage and water mains and lights. Meanwhile periodic inspections of the public markets failed to stop the sale of spoiled foodstuffs. No dairy sold un-adulterated milk.

The appearance of cholera in the United States in 1893 brought things to a head. A Sanitary League divided the city into districts and set up committees in each to report upon its sanitary condition. The health officer was then able to carry out his long-cherished plan of conducting a house-to-house sanitary inspection, and public opinion forced landlords and householders to renovate run-down property, replace defective drains, clean out yards and area-ways, and burn tons of rubbish and offal. The result was 350 fewer deaths than in the previous year. Infant mortality still accounted for one death in three, but by 1898 the over-all death rate in the city had declined to 19.32 per thousand; in the county a rate of 35.82 was partly due to the high incidence of malaria at St. Elizabeths Hospital. In the meantime a stricter building code prevented speculators from putting up more ramshackle houses without installing plumbing, and a law of 1897 decreed that all premises must be connected with sewers. Although the law was not wholly en-forceable, the owners of 1,500 buildings promptly put in sewer connections.

At the same time the District health department closed a number of surface wells, placed dairies under surveillance, and with some success experimented with anti-toxin for diphtheria cases. When threatened smallpox epidemics emphasized the city's need of a contagious hospital, Congress voted to erect a suitable building on the site of the old jail and for the time being forced three existing hospitals to open isolation wards. Every new proposal, every innovating regulation, met with some opposition, and, as the health officer complained, small budgets constantly hampered the execution of useful laws. Nevertheless, the community became increasingly aware of the importance of his function, and, as interest in the "city beautiful" movement grew at the turn of the century, decent housing and clean well-kept streets began to command wider public support.[9]

Street paving, that never-ending chore in an expanding community, meanwhile continued to breed feuds. Rival citizens' associations resentfully saw the bulk of the funds spent in fashionable "Northwest" and in the suburbs beyond, where quick profits for speculators depended upon the early extension of paved streets and other urban conveniences. Taxpayers on Capitol Hill and in the Navy Yard section fumed over the sums poured into improvements along "Massachusetts Avenue extended" and Connecticut Avenue above Boundary Street until Northwest and its suburbs had twice as many miles of hard-surfaced streets as all the rest of the District. But when so powerful a politician as Senator John Sherman of Ohio insisted, for example, on giving priority to widening and grading 16th Street north of the city limits where he and some of his protégés owned land, property-owners elsewhere could only grumble futilely. That measure, followed by the extension of Massachusetts Avenue from Dupont Circle to Rock Creek, marked the first official recognition that Washington was outgrowing her old bounds. During 1888 the commissioners strove to evolve a rational scheme of naming a second and third tier of streets beyond the old "alphabet" streets, but not until 1905 was the present-day system adopted—two-syllable names of eminent Americans arranged in alphabetical order, followed by three-syllable names for the streets of "the third alphabet." In 1890 Boundary Street became Florida Avenue, in 1895 the name *Georgetown* officially disappeared by congressional mandate,

[9] Comrs Rpts, 1878, p. 48, 1880, pp. 294-303, 1881, pp. 365-66, 391-409, 1889, pp. 104, 394, 1890, p. 659, 1895, p. 13, 1897, p. 75, 1898, pp. xix-xx, 1899, I, 19-22; *Rec*, 46C, 2S, pp. 518, 2344-46, 2931; ptn, S51A-D1, n.d.; *Sentinel*, 20 Feb 1892; *Star*, 15 Mar 1882, 18 Dec 1888, and summaries, 1894-1896; H Mis Doc 188, 53C, 2S, Ser 3229; S Doc 385, 56C, 1S, Ser 3875; 25 *Stat.* 451; *Rpts B/Tr*, 1899, pp. 8, 11, 1900, pp. 10, 80, 1901, pp. 22-23; George M. Kober, *The History and Development of the Housing Movement in the City of Washington, D.C.*, pp. 6-9 (hereafter cited as Kober, *Housing Movement*); Lillian W. Betts, "The Every-day Washington," *The Outlook*, LXV, 868-73.

and in 1900 plans for bridging Rock Creek at both Massachusetts and Connecticut Avenues looked to the moment when Washington's streets would thread the entire area from the heights of the Potomac beyond Georgetown University to the upper reaches of the Anacostia.[10]

While the special interests of influential real estate owners undoubtedly affected the choice of areas to get first attention, the spread of the city into the county did not proceed in purely hit-or-miss fashion. On the contrary, a plan of orderly metropolitan expansion begun in 1888 acquired more precise form upon passage of a highway act in 1893 and the creation of the Park Commission in 1901. Those measures constitute the first conscious attempt to guide the suburban growth of an American community along lines that would ensure harmony between new developments and the parent city.

The act of 1888 merely required the platting of subdivisions of land in the county to conform to Washington's street plan; what represented acceptable conformity was uncertain. The highway act of 1893 carried planning very much further and provided the machinery to execute it. Instructed to engage a landscape architect to prepare a tentative layout of new streets and a system of parkways to ring Washington from Rock Creek to the Anacostia, the District commissioners were then to submit to a highway commission detailed maps of each suburban section; when the highway commission, consisting of the Secretary of War, the Secretary of the Interior, and the Chief of Engineers, had approved, the maps would represent the authorized plan of city enlargement. These "initiatory steps," taken before the opening of the Columbian World's Fair, indicate early stirrings of the "city beautiful" movement in America which the White City on Chicago's lake front brought to

10 S Mis Doc 37, 45C, 3S, Ser 1833; *Star*, 8, 25, 28 Jan, 4 Feb 1879, 13 Aug 1883, 22, 23 Oct, 19 Nov 1886, 8 Oct 1887; *Sentinel*, 4 Jul 1885, 5 Mar 1887; *Sun Chronicle*, 1 Oct 1882; Comrs Rpts, 1882, pp. 135-36, 1885, p. 169, map p. 184, 1886, pp. 28-32, 1887, p. 21, 1889, pp. 260-62, 1900, ii, 81; *Rec*, 47C, 1S, pp. 4619-32, 4663, 47C, 2S, p. 3159.

life. Frederick Olmstead, Jr., drafted the first layout of Washington's northwestern suburbs and, although the District commissioners had to modify it to meet the objections of propertyowners in long established areas, by 1900 maps of the future "greater Washington," complete with reservations for parks and open spaces at avenue intersections, had been officially adopted. This headstart would enormously ease the problem of the advisory commission established in 1901.

A height of buildings act passed in 1899 further testified to a new readiness to put the orderly development of a beautiful city ahead of private property interests, an act inspired by public dismay at the conspicuousness of the recently built "Cairo," a fourteen-story yellow brick apartment house above Scott Circle. Unlike the short-lived decree of Thomas Jefferson and the federal commissioners in the 1790's forbidding the building of dwellings of less than three stories lest the new capital look mean in consequence, law a century later put an upper limit upon private buildings in order to prevent the rise of skyscrapers that would dwarf public edifices and darken the streets.[11]

Most of the streets were better kept than those in other American cities. "Carp," as Frank Carpenter signed his columns in the Cleveland *Leader*, observed in 1883: "Washington's streets . . . are kept clean by a patent twig brush run by horses. This sweeps them daily, and the thousands of fine carriages and hundreds of bicycles, which go spinning along them, are kept shining like black enamel and polished silver." Although the 65,000 carefully tended trees bordering the streets and avenues were little more than saplings, citizens took pride in them. When in 1882, ten years after the city first witnessed a demonstration of electric lighting, the commissioners contracted for the installation of a few arc lamps, public safety dictated a ruling that all wires must be laid underground, but

[11] 25 *Stat.* 451; 27 *Stat.* 532; 30 *Stat.* 922; Comrs Rpts, 1894, pp. 15-16, 1900, I, 31.

a by-product of the decision was the preservation of the trees. During an experimental display on Pennsylvania Avenue in the fall of 1881 a dynamo belted to an engine in an old sawmill nearby had fed power to lamps suspended from guy wires strung from housetop to housetop; at the click of a switch the sudden splutter of light from the Capitol to the Treasury had delighted the onlookers, but the danger of fire had been undeniable. While the cost of underground wires prevented the rapid replacement of gas lamps, before 1890 Washington boasted 181 arc lights and added seventy-five to a hundred yearly thereafter.

The battle for underground wires soon involved other utilities. Overhead telegraph lines had strung along Washington's streets since 1845, and that "selfish octupus," the Western Union, a particularly powerful corporation in a city where newspaper correspondents kept wires busy, continued to plant its "uncouth poles at will in front of any man's premises without his consent." After 1878 the new Chesapeake and Potomac Telephone Company also erected poles and wires, and in the 1890's, when street railway companies began to replace horse-drawn cars with trolleys, the traction interests entered the fight. The struggle intensified when Congress denied the commissioners authority to grant permits for new underground installations. Yet little by little public opinion won the day. By 1900 not only did Washington enjoy telegraph and expanding telephone service, electric street lighting, and electric street railways, but within the city limits more than half the wires ran underground. The principal exceptions were the lines running into private houses from poles placed in alleyways at the rear.[12]

[12] Cleveland *Leader*, 5 Jan 1883; *Patriot*, 22 May 1872; *Star*, 20 Oct 1881, 22 Jan 1883, and summaries, 1896, 1898; *Post*, 1 Mar 1887; Comrs Rpts, 1882, pp. 10, 140-41, 1885, p. 172, 1889, pp. 260-62, 296; Nevil Monroe Hopkins, "The United States Electric Lighting Company of Washington, D.C., and its New Equipment," *The Electrical Engineer*, XXVI, 425-33.

MUNICIPAL HOUSEKEEPING

In scores of American cities of the 1880's and 1890's, utility and transit companies, their franchises secured to them by local political bosses, were exploiting the public mercilessly. In the capital, where Congress granted the franchises, the issue was not outright graft but the companies' disregard of local wishes. Indignant citizens believed the commissioners unduly subservient to these corporations. "Do the commissioners," inquired a newspaperman, "govern the District, or do the street railway companies govern the commissioners?" The sins of the "traction moguls" were everywhere evident: T-tracks projecting above the level of the pavements made the streets hazardous for horses and carriages; the space adjoining the rails was not kept clean, a particular affliction as long as the cars were horse-drawn; the cars were stuffy and cold in winter, dirty and overcrowded the year round; service was slow; tax evasion was frequent, and the fifteen separate companies operating in the city and suburbs produced confusion rather than wholesome competition. The commissioners themselves protested at these abuses. When the campaign against overhead trolley wires within the city limits met with sudden success in 1895 the commissioners were able to exact other reforms. Ground rails flush with the pavements supplanted the projecting T-rails, and express cars running at speeds up to ten miles an hour improved service.

Consolidation of competing lines provided the financing essential for these changes. When the Rock Creek Company bought out the Washington and Georgetown in 1895 to form the Capital Traction Company, $12,000,000 went into new equipment and a power house on 14th Street below the Avenue. In 1900 thirteen other independent lines merged to become the Washington Traction and Electric Company. The merger, effected with congressional blessing, several million dollars of new capital, and reportedly generous watering of stock, included the United States Electric Light and the Potomac Electric Companies. A congressman from Jersey City took charge.

51

No one at the time found it improper for a member of the House of Representatives to direct a huge public utility business in Washington while he served his term in Congress. The local public derived immediate advantages. Use of transfers whereever allowed cut costs for passengers, better heated and ventilated cars added to comfort, and more frequent runs reduced waits.[13]

The city's struggle with the Baltimore and Ohio and Pennsylvania Railroads followed a different and far less satisfactory course. Again public safety and urban aesthetics were the main points of argument, but the question of what to do and how to do it was complicated by sharp differences of opinion in Congress and by the awe in which public officials held the great railroad corporations. The safety campaign centered around the elimination of grade crossings within the city where the B & O tracks and those of the Pennsylvania's subsidiary, the Baltimore and Potomac, crossed the public ways at street level. Statistics assembled by the Board of Trade proved that fatal accidents or serious injuries to pedestrians at these crossings averaged about thirty a year. The most feasible of the proposed remedies called for sinking the rails into cuts below street level along part of the right of way and, along the remainder, elevating the tracks on embankments under which cross streets would tunnel. To obviate the hazards on the Long Bridge new construction would be necessary, for trains puffing over the narrow causeway and the railroad bridge set up vibrations in the shaky spans of the adjoining highway bridge, frightened horses, caused runaways, and made it generally unsafe for pedestrians and horse-drawn vehicles. Citizens declared, moreover, that

---

[13] Comrs Rpts, 1879, p. 7, 1886, p. 35, 1894, p. 40, 1898, p. xxii; *Star*, 28 Oct 1879, 16 Aug 1881, 3 May 1883, 13 Jan 1887, 1 Jan 1896; *Chronicle*, 10 Mar 1895, 10 Jul 1897; ptns, S49A-H14, 1886, H54A-H7.3 and S54-J21, 1894, and hundreds more; *Post History*, pp. 244-46; Nevil M. Hopkins, "The Displacement of the Cable by the Underground Trolley in Washington," *Electrical Engineer*, xxiv, 526-27; "The Open Conduit Electric System of the Capital Traction Company," *The Electrical World*, xxxii, 707-15.

the Baltimore and Potomac illegally used the streets in south Washington for freight yards and car sidings, while the B & O similarly exploited northeast Washington; as a result large areas of the city no longer had residential value. Finally, inasmuch as Boss Shepherd, while removing the Washington and Alexandria Railroad tracks at the foot of Capitol Hill, had not touched the B & P rails crossing the Mall to the Gothic stone station on the present site of the National Gallery of Art, the Pennsylvania Railroad dominated the public domain in the very heart of the national capital.

Seemingly more powerful than Congress itself, the railroad corporations expressed willingness to abolish grade crossings and build freight terminals provided the public pay most of the cost, but they fought every proposal to move the Baltimore and Potomac depot from its commanding position on the Mall or to erect a union station for all railroads entering Washington. For twenty years angry citizens watched the District commissioners yield to cavalier railroad officials and permit the collapse of every scheme for relocating tracks and terminals. The engineering problems were formidable at best. No plan found universal favor. Permanent residents opposed further railroad intrusions upon public property, but businessmen hesitated to support any scheme that would mean long wagon hauls from freight terminals on Washington's outskirts. Throughout the city taxpayers objected to shouldering the costs of safety measures that they believed the railroads could well afford to finance. Year after year Congress, in turn, reached no consensus. Bills were offered, debated, and shelved. Railroad officials stated that a bill of 1893 requiring the B & O to eliminate grade crossings would force the road into receivership. Congress dropped the idea. The B & O went into receivership anyway. Then, seven years later the Senate District Committee and all but two members of the House District Committee endorsed two astonishing proposals.

The first and the more obnoxious to Washingtonians offered to the Pennsylvania Railroad as inducement to change its grade crossings a gift of fourteen acres on the Mall and, for freight yards and sidings, twelve acres of Garfield Park southeast of the Capitol; the United States government and the District together would pay over some $1,644,500 to cover damages to private property and the cost of approaches to the right of way where streets would pass over or under the tracks; and appropriation of $568,000 for a highway bridge over the Potomac would leave the railroad in sole possession of the Long Bridge and causeway. The Pennsylvania was to build a huge new $1,500,000 station on the Mall, and public funds would create an imposing plaza opening out into B Street on the north. The train sheds would project southward into the Mall, and the tracks elevated on an embankment would slice diagonally across the park toward the Long Bridge. A new thoroughfare, "West Capitol Street," would pass under the embankment by means of a fifty-foot archway. Symbolically and bodily members of Congress would bow their heads to the railroad as they went to and from the Hill. Senator McMillan, whose name would later be associated with large plans for beautifying the capital, defended the scheme: "Indeed so far as sightliness is concerned, the proposed changes will add greatly to the beauty of that portion of the Mall."

The concessions tendered the B & O were less generous. Its freight yards and roundhouses were to be moved beyond the city limits, the Metropolitan branch and Washington-Baltimore branch lines were to be combined and rerouted within the city proper, and the company was to receive a free gift of the square north of the present Senate office building on which to erect a new passenger depot; tracks elevated on an embankment across lower land to the northeast would enter the new station at ground level. Thus one railroad would share the Hill with the Capitol; the second would occupy the central stretch of the park between Capitol and White House.

Congressmen William Cowherd of Missouri and Thetus Sims of Tennessee of the House District Committee had from the first labelled the entire scheme shortsighted and preposterously generous to the railroads. The Chief of Army Engineers and the federal Commissioner of Public Buildings and Grounds decried the folly of abandoning the very core of L'Enfant's original plan. One senator declared the two bills yoked together by "an interdependent mutuality of greed." Every citizens' association, the Washington Businessmen's Association, and the Single Tax Club voiced outrage, while the Board of Trade emphatically restated its ten-year opposition to any alienation of the city's public parks. Possibly the commissioners' unfortunate statement that the plan was the best the District could hope for encouraged illusions in Congress. Congressional leaders pronounced the bills satisfactory to "ninety-nine out of one hundred" Washingtonians, a misinterpretation of local sentiment which, Representative Cowherd remarked, showed the handicaps under which unrepresented citizens labored in trying to make their wishes understood. In February 1901 Senate and House passed both bills and President McKinley signed them.[14]

While the commissioners' deference to the railroad corporations offended citizens, they objected even more strongly to threats of interference with the school board. Admittedly the commissioners must appoint the board, but the vocal public felt that the trustees, once appointed, must have full authority over the school system. For, despite frequent squabbles about the disposition of funds and about appointments, particularly to teaching posts in the colored schools, the board generally functioned in keeping with citizens' wishes. The one insuperable problem was obtaining enough money to enable the schools to keep pace with the expanding population and with the de-

[14] S Rpt 1398, 56C, 1S, Ser 3895; *Rpt B/Tr*, 1898, p. 17; *Post History*, pp. 248-49; Comrs Rpt, 1885, pp. 9-10; H Rpts 2026 and 2036, 56C, 2S, Ser 4212; *Rec*, 56C, 2S, pp. 1801, 2104-06, 2180, and App. pp. 181-82.

mands created by temporary, non-taxpaying residents. Yearly, to taxpayers' wrath, the commissioners pared the figure the trustees estimated necessary, and yearly Congress, though appropriating more than the commissioners asked for, voted less than the trustees requested. Consequently a passionate outcry greeted the commissioners' announcement in December 1885 that they were taking over the duties of the school board because quarrels had destroyed its usefulness. At a mass meeting citizens asserted that the change would strip them of "the last that was left to them of popular government." Congress, besought to intercede, debated a school reorganization bill only to drop it. But the commissioners, obviously startled by the storm they had stirred up, quietly backtracked; the school board carried on, its membership later enlarged to include one white and one colored woman.[15]

Fortunately in 1885 the appointment of William Bramwell Powell as superintendent of the white schools suddenly pumped vitality into the system. The new superintendent inaugurated a whole series of innovations similar to the changes in educational approach later attributed chiefly to John Dewey. Brother of the famous head of the Geological Survey, Powell added to the curriculum courses in science and nature study, started manual training in the elementary grades, and dispensed with the rigid formality that had formerly ruled the classroom. Convinced that memorizing lessons was not good enough, he introduced field trips and demonstrations that, by relating book-learning to everyday life, awakened pupils' intellectual curiosity. In carrying out his program he fired ill-trained and uncooperative teachers, many of whom owed their jobs to members of Congress who considered the District's public schools part of their political

[15] *Star*, 13 Feb 1879, 10 Jan 1881, 12 Sep 1883, 23 Jan, 27 Mar 1886, 27 Dec 1887; *Rec*, 48C, 1S, p. 4225, 49C, 2S, pp. 121-30, 2516, 2546; *Sentinel*, 26 Jun, 11 Dec 1886; ptns, H50A-D1, n.d., and 2 Feb 1888; 27 *Stat.* 536; *Report of the Board of Trustees of Public Schools of the District of Columbia*, 1880, pp. 14-16, 151-52, 1886, pp. 6-7, 1892, pp. 36-81; Comrs Rpt, 1882, p. 7.

patronage. He thus won enmity on the Hill and, accused of sacrificing the three R's to frills, was dismissed in 1900. But despite the controversies he stirred up, in the intervening years he made Washington's school system one of the two or three best in the country.[16]

Yet much of the school story repeated earlier history—too little space, underpaid teachers, and always the school board quandary of choosing between expanding the primary schools and providing better for older, advanced pupils. In 1879 an arrangement with the trustees of the Myrtilla Miner Fund, a fund raised by private donors for Negro education, enabled the superintendent of the colored schools to open a colored high school, but until 1882 the nearest approach to a white high school was a scheme Powell's predecessor devised in 1881; he selected the best students in the eighth grades, put them into the third-floor rooms of one building and called the group a high school. The next year the white trustees insisted upon using the principal of the school fund that had been accumulating since 1826 to build a white high school. Unusually large appropriations for new schoolhouses lessened overcrowding in the lower grades during the late eighties, but scarcely was a new building opened than a new generation of school children overflowed it. Washington, observed the Board of Trade, was the only city in the country which allowed non-residents to attend her schools free of charge. By 1899, with enrollments 50 percent higher than in the mid-eighties, 68 white and 14 colored first grades held morning sessions only; second grades used the rooms in the afternoon. Night schools for children who worked during the day, a few summer "vacation schools," and kindergartens, first opened in 1898, put further pressure upon

<hr>

[16] S Mis Doc 72, 49C, 1S, Ser 2343; William H. Darrah, *Powell of the Colorado*, pp. 325-26, 388; John W. Cook, "Memorial to William Bramwell Powell," National Education Association of the United States, *Addresses and Proceedings*, 43rd meeting, pp. 361-65 (hereafter cited as *NEA Addresses*); *Star*, 27 Jun 1900; Charles Zueblin, *American Municipal Progress*, 134-38.

limited budgets. And parental clamor mounted yearly for a high school course that would qualify graduates for college entrance. Yet the city yearly spent a million and a quarter dollars on public education.

Complaints from white and colored parents and teachers, principals, trustees, Superintendent Powell's political enemies, and sometimes complaints directed at the complainants, led the Senate to investigate. The outcome was an administrative reorganization spelled out in the appropriation act passed in 1900. It increased the school budget by a quarter-million dollars, left to the commissioners control of expenditures and the power to appoint a new seven-member Board of Education, and gave the board, instead of the superintendent, final say in hiring and firing teachers. A single superintendent was to have overall direction with two assistant superintendents under him, one for the white schools and a second for the colored schools. With Powell out of the picture, the Board of Education revised the curriculum "to make it more practical and to reduce the amount of home study." As the larger appropriation provided money for new schoolhouses, public agitation about the school system largely evaporated.[17]

Free public education ended in the two normal schools, although Washingtonians continued to hope for a national university. Howard University received a small federal appropriation annually, but Georgetown, Columbian, and the National Universities drew their support from private sources. A fifth institution came into being in 1889. One hundred years after John Carroll founded Georgetown Seminary, the Roman Catholic hierarchy celebrated its centennial in America with the opening of a theology school as a first unit of the new Catholic

[17] Comrs Rpts, 1887, pp. 5, 14, 1890, pp. 842-43, 1891, p. 8, 1895, p. 8, 1899, pp. 9-10, 1900, I, 9; *Sentinel*, 12 Mar 1892; S Rpt 825, 52C, 1S, Ser 2914; S Rpt 174, 54C, 1S, Ser 3362; S Doc 107, 54C, 1S, Ser 3350; *Rpts B/Tr*, 1898, p. 80, 1899, p. 89; S Rpt 711, 56C, 1S, Ser 3889; 31 *Stat.* 564.

University of America; schools of philosophy and science followed in the 1890's. Shortly afterward Methodists also took steps to establish a university. In 1891 Bishop John Hurst and a number of influential Washingtonians formed a board of trustees, raised $100,000, and purchased a beautiful stretch of wooded land above Georgetown. The energetic Bishop at once made overtures for a merger with the National University, hoping that the name *National*, reinforced by Methodism, might induce Congress to support an institution such as George Washington had willed his shares of Potomac Canal Company stock to found. The proposed merger fell through, Congress appropriated no money, and the Methodist trustees, choosing the name American University, erected Hurst Hall on the new campus in 1898. Building and campus stood unused for nineteen years. Meanwhile, the law school, the small medical school, and even smaller dental school that made up the National University set a pattern that later became standard in Washington: night classes enabling young men to get professional training while they earned a living in daytime government jobs. As none of the local universities had much scholarly prestige, Washington was richer in quantity than quality of higher education; but within the community the vision of the city as the future seat of American learning gained strength.

Interest in education, civic pride, and religious feeling apparently combined to inspire Charles Glover to propose to fellow Episcopalians that they establish a national cathedral foundation in Washington "for the promotion of religion and education and charity." Glover organized the campaign for funds and in 1893 obtained a charter from Congress, while Henry Satterlee, Bishop of Washington, selected Mt. St. Albans for the site on which the Cathedral of St. Peter and St. Paul should rise. There within the close the Phoebe Hearst School, later the National Cathedral School for Girls, opened in 1894. Four years later the Foundation completed the purchase of the entire hilltop with its commanding view of river and city.[18]

While the Cathedral Foundation, the universities, and other organizations lying outside the realm of the commissioners' and congressional responsibility contributed to Washington's distinction, Americans came to regard her local government as the best in the United States. Far from labelling the autocratic municipal administration a contradiction of republican principles, visitors and people who knew the city only from hearsay and from the pages of popular magazines joined with the chorus of prominent Washingtonians in praising the arrangement. In 1900 the *Atlantic Monthly* published a panegyric on Washington—on the honesty, efficiency, and economy of her administration, the courtesy of her police, her low taxes, model schools, splendid care of public health, and admirable protection of the indigent and sick; Alexander Shepherd, in redeeming the city's streets, "unconsciously rendered an even greater service to his beloved city and gave to his people an object lesson in the benefits to follow from a pure autocracy." At Washington's centennial celebration the address of Commissioner Henry Macfarland reflected that widely held view of the system: "Its greatest virtue is that it is distinctly a government by public opinion. The unusually high intelligence of the citizens of the District, and their remarkable interest and activity in the conduct of its affairs, make them its real rulers, under the constitutional authority of the President and Congress."[19]

[18] *Star*, 2 Jun 1879, 24 May 1888; *Post*, 13 Nov 1889; Federal Writers Project, *Washington, City and Capital*, pp. 466-67 (hereafter cited as *WPA Guide*); S Mis Doc 222, 52C, 1S, pp. 25-26, Ser 2907.
[19] A. Maurice Low, "Washington, City of Leisure," *Atlantic Monthly*, LXXXVI, 769; Henry B. F. Macfarland, *The Development of the District of Columbia*, p. 13.

CHAPTER IV

ONLY FOR THE WORTHY, 1879-1901

THE wave of humanitarianism that swept the western world in the second half of the nineteenth century reached Washington in the late 1870's. It was largely a secular movement. A dozen charities, it is true, sprang up under denominational aegis—Episcopal, Lutheran, Congregational, and Baptist; Washington's seven hundred Jewish families unobtrusively and efficiently cared for their own; and, as in the past, the Roman Catholic Church maintained an impressive array of eleemosynary institutions ranging from St. Ann's Infant Asylum to a home for the aged and the Providence Hospital. Yet the impelling spirit was not primarily religious; the sense of civic obligation seemingly transcended feelings of Christian and "guild" fellowship. Regardless of his church affiliation, the Washingtonian of recognized standing in the community expected as a matter of course to dedicate time, energy, and money to some charity, and usually to more than one. As enlightened self-interest heightened his sense of public duty, so duty forbade indiscriminate giving: only the "worthy poor" should receive help. Acceptance of that concept, rare in the ante-bellum city,[1] was linked in the last quarter of the century to a rising belief in the teachings of "social Darwinism," a conviction that selection of the fit must operate in the community.

Of the significant features of Washington's philanthropy the most immediately noticeable was the expansion of charitable institutions and relief agencies and the amount of money that was poured into them. During the 1880's prosperity enabled people in the upper brackets of society to give large sums of

[1] E.g., *Proceedings of the Sixth Annual Meeting of the Female Union Benevolent Society of Washington City and the Report of the Managers, 1844.*

money without great sacrifice, but in the hard times of the nineties contributions to charity shrank surprisingly little and far exceeded those recorded in the 1870's. For example, whereas a citizens' committee in the severe winter of 1878-1879 managed to raise $3,000 to supply fuel, food, and clothing to the poor, a similar committee in 1893-1894, another depression year, collected nearly $50,000. It is improbable that the later generation was intrinsically more generous; the difference in results doubtless sprang from the greater social pressures and better organized campaigning of the nineties. The contrast in effectiveness is nonetheless startling. A growing population explains some of the proliferation of charities, but, while population rose from about 175,000 to 277,000 souls between 1879 and 1901, the number of institutions doubled, and tax money spent for their support and for direct relief increased almost five-fold. Before 1879, Congress had resorted every winter to emergency appropriations for direct or "outdoor" relief, that is, for persons not in institutions; thereafter the District's annual budget included from $13,000 to $20,000 for outdoor relief. Public officials, like private citizens, accepted gradually broadening responsibilities toward the city's needy.[2]

Children were, above all, the beneficiaries. Just as the Washington City Orphan Asylum had been the first organized charity in the city, so orphanages and "child saving" institutions enlisted wider interest and stronger financial support than any other form of philanthropy; by 1899 they were receiving eight times as much money as in 1879. In the late nineties Washingtonians were maintaining eight non-sectarian homes for children in addition to three Roman Catholic orphanages and St. Rose's Industrial School for Girls. When the refusal of most of these institutions to accept any colored child over six created

[2] *Star*, 30 Jan 1879; Comrs Rpt, 1895, pp. 139-40, 153; S Doc 185, 55C, 1S, Joint Select Committee to Investigate the Charities and Reformatory Institutions in the District of Columbia, "Part i—Hearings," p. 157, Ser 3565 (hereafter cited as Ch Hrgs).

an acute problem, two more came into being—the Hart Farm School for destitute and delinquent Negro boys, and a temporary home for colored children sponsored by the Board of Children's Guardians.

The Board of Children's Guardians, itself, was an outgrowth of the mounting concern for child welfare. The board's predecessors, the Guardian Society of the early 1860's and a children's branch of the Washington Humane Society in the 1880's, had lacked both the authority and the resources to institutionalize neglected and abused children. In 1892 Congress accordingly created the Board of Children's Guardians, empowering it to place out or itself to support any child whom the courts committed to its care. Under the selfless and public-spirited leadership of William Redin Woodward, a Washington attorney, real estate broker, and title insurance company executive, the board staunchly advocated placing children in private homes instead of institutions, for, as Woodward pointed out, life in a private family would give a child its best chance to develop "a stalwart individual character." Woodward, a man of exceptionally keen mind and deep humanity, carefully studied the findings of the National Conference on Charities and Corrections in order to give Washington the benefit of the experience of other communities. He was able to report in 1901 that, of the 720 children permanently under the guardianship of the board, 534 were living in private homes where they were "bound out," boarding, or on probation. For white children the scheme was a pronounced success.[3]

Medical charities won only slightly less generous support. Private funds equipped and staffed a dozen new dispensaries, while most of the District budget for poor relief went into medicines, fees for the physicians to the poor, and free clinics. Hos-

[3] Comrs Rpts, 1879, pp. 55-56, 1892, pp. 194-97, 1895, pp. 139-40, 1900, i, 104, 290, 1901, 485, 500-01; S Rpt 700, 55C, 2S, Joint Select Committee on Charities and Reformatory Institutions, "Part ii—Report," pp. 200-02, Ser 3565 (hereafter cited as Ch Rpt); Ch Hrgs, pp. 101, 146, 451, 455, Ser 3565.

pitals, no longer considered purely eleemosynary, had many more charity than paying patients, but the six institutions of 1880—the Washington Asylum, the Government Hospital for the Insane, Providence, Freedmen's, the Children's Hospital, and the Columbia Lying-in Asylum—grew to fifteen in the 1890's. Doubts arose about the wisdom of maintaining so many, but just as the Garfield Hospital chartered in 1882 as a memorial to the martyred President "made a stronger and more successful appeal to the charitable people of Washington than any other like institution has ever made," so citizens in advocating efficiency still believed medical charity should be "the last to be denied or . . . deferred." When a well-informed public official stated in 1897 that no other city in the United States could match Washington in provision for the sick and injured, he referred not only to the number of facilities but to the quality of service. At the Asylum Hospital, that catch-all for the helpless, conditions were appalling, the service "little above that of the primitive county poorhouse of an earlier day." But most of the public hospitals offered effective care, and two eminent physicians from the Johns Hopkins Hospital in Baltimore and Philadelphia's Pennsylvania Hospital pronounced the nursing and medical care at Freedmen's Hospital excellent, despite primitive sanitary facilities and a general aspect of "suffering and squalor."

For indigents stricken with contagious disease, alcoholics, drug addicts, the "mildly insane" and the chronically or incurably ill, on the other hand, provision was totally inadequate. Hospitals were unwilling to risk exposing patients to contagion and, until congressional threats in 1899 to cut off appropriations persuaded the staffs at Freedmen's, Garfield, and Providence to accept government subsidies and build isolation wards, all contagious cases had to be treated at home or in the smallpox hospital at the Asylum. A Home for Incurables founded in 1889 took a few patients, and a private hospital occasionally accepted one or two, but all medical institutions preferred to concentrate upon curable cases of a routine nature. Until 1900 and the opening of a small privately financed home, the indigent blind could go only to the almshouse. The aged or chronically ill, the "inebriate," the drug addict, and the mentally disturbed usually ended up at the Asylum Hospital, where the physician in charge had to make a place for them in the general wards. "It may be imagined," reported the Asylum commissioner, "the crowding, the bad air, and the consequent slow and poor progress towards recovery in many cases; when, besides, we take into consideration that all classes of patients, surgical cases before and after operation, chronic ulcers, syphilitic, acute and chronic diseases of all kinds, have to be treated in the same wards and in close proximity, it is a matter of surprise that the death rate is as low as it is."[4]

Help for women in distress, particularly those innocent of blame, was a third rapidly expanding charity. Although it rarely extended to colored women, it slowly reached out to include "fallen" white women despite public doubts about the wisdom of lowering the wages of sin. Before 1885 the Roman Catholic House of the Good Shepherd and the Episcopalian House of Mercy were accepting not only girls in need of "preservation" but also unmarried mothers, and in 1888 the Women's Christian Temperance Union set itself to join in salvaging girls "ruined" before they were nineteen years old. The WCTU Hope and Help Mission assisted them to become self-supporting while keeping their children with them, but the number of applicants soon outran capacity. In 1897 the mission came under the auspices of the National Board of Florence Crittenden Missions. Largely through the efforts of

[4] Comrs Rpts, 1880, p. 178, 1881, p. 146, 1882, pp. 267-68, 1890, p. 188, 1892, pp. 180, 662, 1894, pp. 102-07, 1896, pp. 113, 137, 160, 183-93, 227, 391, 1897, p. 266, 1899, i, 104, 297, 303-04, iii, 20, 1901, i, 414, 500-01, 560-69; *Rpt B/Tr*, 1899, p. 40; Ch Hrgs, pp. 113-14, 208-13, 376, 380, and Ch Rpt, p. 56, Ser 3565; S Rpt 781, 55C, 2S, Joint Select Committee on Charities and Reformatory Institutions, "Part iii—Historical Sketches," pp. 56, 57, 59-61, Ser 3565 (hereafter cited as Ch Hist).

various Protestant churches, homes for aged women also began to multiply, a badly needed service in a community which in the 1870's had only the almshouse, the Catholic Home for the Aged run by the Little Sisters of the Poor, and the Louise Home for a small carefully selected group of impoverished gentlewomen. Several organizations, furthermore, followed the example of the Women's Christian Association, which had opened a home in the 1870's and offered systematic assistance to transient women stranded in Washington without friends or work. Private subscriptions supplied the bulk of the funds for these women's institutions.[5]

While the tremendous growth of charities was the most dramatic feature of Washington's philanthropy, a second and equally significant characteristic was its lopsidedness. Besides the gaps in the program of medical charities, the community slighted services for needy men and for all Negroes. No agency, public or private, stood ready to assist the able-bodied unemployed male except during severe winters, and as soon as the weather moderated that help ceased. In an endeavor to save the city money by reducing the number of tramps who moved into the District in late fall and slept in the police station houses, in 1892 the commissioners opened a Municipal Lodging House and Wood Yard, where "professional vagabonds" could earn three days' keep by splitting fire wood for the schoolhouses. The establishment soon deteriorated into a variation of the workhouse. The aged male got scarcely more consideration than the unemployed. Although the Asylum housed some old men, and the Catholic Home for the Aged took a few, the aged male, like the unemployed, was expected to fend for himself. Public funds for all homes for the aged were virtually non-existent. Finally, the generous help given white women and children was conspicuously meagre for colored.

[5] Comrs Rpt, 1895, p. 102, 1897, pp. 467-68, 1898, pp. 277-79, 1899, I, 291-92, 1900, I, 474; Ch Hrgs, pp. 143, 290-96, 301-06, 387-91, 394, 398, 404; and Ch Hist, pp. 144-48, 150, Ser 3565.

The clinics and hospitals admitted Negroes to segregated wards and gave as good care to colored patients as to white, but usually only St. Ann's Infant Asylum and the National Colored Home accepted Negro children. The St. John's Parish Orphanage very occasionally took a Negro child, and in the early nineties the Newsboys' and Children's Aid Society accepted some colored boys but reversed its policy in 1898 when Congress refused to make a grant for a separate building for the colored. Catholics and Protestants shared the view of the Directress of St. Rose's Industrial School: "It would not be supposed we could mix them [Negro girls] with our young girls who are mostly orphans from good families." The difficulties of placing colored children in private homes led the Board of Children's Guardians in 1897 regretfully to request the courts to commit to it as few colored charges as possible, since it would have to crowd most of them into its temporary home. The restricted resources of the Home for Destitute Colored Women and Children, largely tax-supported, obliged the managers to limit the admission of children to those between the ages of three and ten. As "no householder will take into his family a colored child except as a servant and with the intention of getting a full equivalent for what he gives," Negro ten-year-olds, when turned out of the Home, usually wound up at the workhouse and the almshouse. "Because the world affords them no other place," said the commissioner of the Asylum, "at the end of their terms they constantly importune me to allow them to remain." A Home for Friendless Colored Girls founded in 1886 practically collapsed for want of support. Launched by a Negro woman when she discovered two little colored girls eating out of a garbage can, this was Washington's first Negro-sponsored charity. Yet the "band of worthy colored women" failed in their attempts to elicit funds from well-to-do Negroes, and the prominent white women whom Mrs. Grover Cleveland interested in the Home raised only $150 for it in two years of soliciting.

The story of help for colored women was much the same. A few found a refuge in the National Colored Home, and nearly fifty, thanks to the Little Sisters of the Poor, became inmates of the Catholic Home for the Aged. Otherwise before 1900 there was nothing but the Asylum and the Reform School for Girls, an institution more nearly penal than charitable. In 1900, greatly daring, the Hope and Help Mission, in collaboration with its "colored mission" in Alexandria, undertook to extend services to unmarried colored mothers. Triumphantly the director reported that "it has been proved that these colored girls can be cared for more easily and at less expense than the average white girl. As a rule, they are better trained for work, and more capable of earning their own living in a shorter time."

The Negro, as William Redin Woodward told a congressional committee in 1897, was "a race not yet recovered from the effects of slavery, practically without resources for the private support of necessary institutions for the protection of its own dependents, and for whose benefit wealthy citizens of the District of Columbia neither left large bequests nor contributed any considerable sums."[6] In most nineteenth-century cities, large gifts from wealthy individuals were a mainstay of charity. W. W. Corcoran, for forty years Washington's single most generous donor to good works, endowed the Corcoran Gallery and the Louise Home, gave large sums to Columbian University and the local orphanages, and on one occasion contributed $1,000 to St. Luke's Negro Episcopal Church, but upon his death in 1888 he left no bequest to any colored institution. Nor did other charitable Washingtonians. As whites tended to regard Negroes as an inferior breed of human being generally given over to indolence, the race

[6] S Mis Doc 93, 50C, 2S, Ser 2615; Comrs Rpts, 1882, p. 260, 1894, p. 101, 1896, pp. 347, 355, 1900, i, 290, 1901, i, 332; Ch Hrgs, pp. 100-01, 155, 197, 310-17, 396-97, 402, 554; Ch Rpt, p. 42, Ser 3565; Amos G. Warner, "The New Municipal Lodging House in Washington," *Charities Review*, ii, 279-82.

suffered from the prevailing philosophy that stressed charity only for the "worthy." The question remains why that philosophy first took strong hold here in the eighties.

That it had little currency in the ante-bellum District was probably due to a widespread assumption that public obligation ended with caring for orphans and providing emergency relief for needy adults in winter. Before the war the derelicts produced by the industrial system and the commercial competitiveness of the North were a rarity in Washington, in spite of the yearly inflow of "transient paupers" seeking government aid. Indeed, these transients had ordinarily escaped the label "undeserving." Slaves were a responsibility of their masters, and free Negroes concealed their needs as best they could, lest the workings of the black code expel them from the District. Hence, because most of the visibly needy appeared to be worthy, charity for the rest did not loom large. The workhouse could take care of them. When the flood of contrabands swept in during the war, the Army and northern abolitionists bore much of the burden, and in the late 1860's Mayor Bowen's make-work scheme, which seemed to his political enemies to pander to deadbeats, sidetracked indignant taxpayers' attention from the basic problem of how far public duty should reach. Reexamination of that question was further delayed by the confusions of the territorial regime and then by the panic and depression. While migrant workers, attracted by the District's comparatively mild climate, continued to pour into the city every winter, the plight of the non-resident was a side-issue, primarily a problem for Congress.

It was apparently the enormous prosperity of the 1880's in the upper ranks of Washington society that brought into the open a philosophy of justification. Rooted perhaps in subconscious feelings of guilt and fed by the writings of Herbert Spencer, adapter of Darwinian theories to social evolution, the belief took hold among the city's intellectuals that discrimination in giving was essential to human progress, certainly to community progress. The spread of that point of view and the resulting determination to establish standards of worthiness was the third characteristic of the city's philanthropy.

The idea once well sprouted flowered quickly and lasted longer in Washington than in cities where industrial strife ploughed deep and unsettled men's earlier premises. Conscientious Washingtonians carried into the twentieth century the conviction that poverty sprang from the flaws in the character of the individual rather than from weaknesses in the social structure. As the moral regeneration of the poor must be the first aim of charity, public-spirited citizens, instead of giving in to sentimental sympathy for suffering, must bend every effort to teach the poor to develop habits of frugality, industry, temperance, cleanliness, and chastity. In 1882, a year after Washington followed the example of London and some sixteen American cities in organizing an Associated Charities, a set of formal "Suggestions to Friendly Visitors" included the following instructions to volunteers:

1. Give no money . . . because your chief object is to lift the idle, ignorant and dependent, out of pauperism, to make them self-supporting and self-respecting and to prevent their children becoming beggars.

2. Inform the idle and squalid of the sanitary laws of the District and show them that misery and suffering are the inevitable results of idleness, filth and vice. Make kindly suggestions concerning ventilation, clothing, digestion and household cleanliness.

3. Take a gift of a plant or picture or some other tasteful suggestive object of beauty, to each wretched home.

4. Write out a wholesome economical bill of fare, and show how a little saving and constant thrift will provide against illness and misfortune.

5. Ascertain what each member of a family can do . . . and see that every one over 12 years of age is engaged in some useful occupation looking toward permanent self-support.[7]

Whatever the reception accorded to the free advice and the gift of a "suggestive object of beauty," the volunteers assembled information about Washington's deserving poor which enabled the Associated Charities to establish a useful file of case histories. Otherwise the organization accomplished disappointingly little. It had envisaged itself as a clearing house which would eliminate duplication of services, halt indiscriminate charity, and introduce efficient methods to relieve distress. Before 1896 its volunteer part-time staff undertook to solicit funds and disburse them itself and, in so doing, added one more agency to the several already engaged in direct relief. Aware of the confusion over who was to do what and troubled by the lack of specific information about community needs, a group of citizens in the mid-nineties organized a Civic Center patterned upon Chicago's Civic Federation. The Center conducted a valuable fact-finding survey of alley dwellings but contributed little else to solutions of welfare problems. In these years of trial and error, competition between the Associated Charities and other organizations ran strong over who was to distribute the money raised yearly by an official citizens' relief committee. The committee, after years of using the police as its sole disbursing agents, in 1894 released part of its funds to the Associated Charities and in 1897 determined to drop the police and use the Associated Charities exclusively.[8]

Efficient and economical administration of philanthropy was a constant goal. Since the Associated Charities was unable to bring order out of the confusion, in 1890 Congress, acting upon the pleas of the District commissioners, created the office of Superintendent of Charities to supervise the work of all publicly

[7] *Star*, 8 Jun 1881, 12 Apr 1882.
[8] *Ibid.*, 12 Jan 1884; Comrs Rpts, 1892, p. 204, 1894, p. 107; Ch Hrgs, pp. 19-23; Ch Hist, p. 174, Ser 3565.

aided agencies in the city. By law a presidential appointee, the Superintendent was to be brought in from outside, obviously to ensure an unprejudiced view of the local picture. Amos G. Warner, former head of Baltimore's Charity Organization Society, was the first incumbent and the first professional social worker to hold office in Washington. His high national standing, heightened in 1894 by his textbook on social work, gave his words weight. His primary objective was to reverse the trend of the 1880's whereby private agencies obtained public money and used it as they saw fit. In 1892 medical charities drew 58 percent of their income from the public treasury, the Industrial Home School and reformatories nearly 90 percent, children's charities 65.5 percent, and temporary homes over 70 percent.

Warner, his two successors, and leading local citizens believed blanket subsidies to private institutions should cease and a central board should set the standards for admitting applicants to all institutions and allot any public money on a basis of a fixed sum per inmate. The system supposedly would limit institutional care to the deserving and, by applying similar rules to outdoor relief, end the waste of money and effort spent on impostors, paupers who drifted into the District from states which ought to support them, and people whose moral shortcomings left them beyond hope of redemption. At a time when well-to-do Virginians facetiously but with some truth called the District "Virginia's poorhouse," the argument for introducing rigid rules denying help to non-residents had considerable force.[9] (See Table II.)

Every penny saved by intelligent management naturally meant more money for desirable objectives, but it was not shortage of funds that inspired the campaigns for efficiency and economy. Year after year the citizens' relief committee

---

[9] Comrs Rpts, 1887, pp. 384, 393-94, 1892, p. 169, 1897, pp. 258, 279-82; Ch Hrgs, pp. 13, 21, 332, 459, Ser 3565; *Rpt B/Tr*, 1897, p. 27; Frank Bruno, *Trends in Social Work, 1874-1956*, p. 101.

limited the amount allotted to any one family to about two dollars and came out every spring with an unexpended surplus of funds, in some years as large as the total spent. More lavish spending, the committee felt, would simply encourage pauperism. The committee secretary, a man trained in the new profession of social work, asserted in 1897 that a large permanent relief fund would be dangerous once the poor, particularly indigent Negroes, got wind of its existence. "You go to the house and see absolute destitution. The money is there for relief purposes and has to be granted. By having such a fund you take all the backbone out of these people." When asked whether they would not starve if not given help, he replied they would then go to work.

Herbert Lewis, who became Superintendent of Charities in 1897, took a slightly different position. He opposed the subsidy system because it fostered sentimentality and permitted private agencies to devote themselves exclusively to "the hopeful, promising and pleasant, leaving without sufficient consideration the idiotic, defective and crippled for whose care it is increasingly difficult to procure sufficient funds." He put his finger on the crucial weakness of Washington's charities: the almost complete exclusion of colored children from institutions that provided excellent care for white children. While he was unable to alter that, he managed to substitute the so-called District supply system, namely payment in goods, for the old arrangement of turning over lump sums of public money to private charities. In 1900 after a long investigation, Congress dropped a half dozen sectarian institutions from the list of the publicly subsidized and created a Board of Charities to establish uniform rules for organizations receiving public money. By 1901, with centralized financial control thus ensured and with trained social workers in charge of the Associated Charities' ten branch offices, a new era of professionalism in welfare work was dawning in Washington.[10]

[10] *Star*, 19 Apr 1884; Comrs Rpts, 1896, p. 115, 1897, pp. 267, 277,

Throughout the 1880's and 1890's the theories of professionals and laymen coincided closely. But laymen found theory hard to put consistently into practice. Reginald Fendall, R. Ross Perry, and Simon Wolf of the citizens' relief committee reported defensively in 1884: "That some have been relieved who were not worthy of relief, in one sense, is probable. Abstractly considered, a man or woman who will not work ought to starve or freeze, but it will not do to enforce this abstract proposition. That such ought to be forced to work is evident, but until the law empowers us to enforce this work we must not let them starve or freeze. . . . The man who can comfortably eat a hearty dinner when he knows that another man is starving near him, and yet does nothing to relieve him, is at heart a murderer. Such men do not make good citizens, nor are they safe guides to follow. . . . But even should these chronic cases be left to their fate, what shall be done with their wives and children?. . . . We must help them. There is no other way out of it. By so doing we doubtless increase poverty, but by refusing to do so we hurt ourselves, our community, our nation." The quandary would be painfully familiar to Washingtonians of the 1960's.

Like the committee, rejecting the abstraction, the sanitary officer of the police force felt obliged to provide for non-residents who arrived in Washington sick, "without a penny in their pockets. . . . It would be inhuman to turn them away." In defiance of the tentative congressional stand that these people were no responsibility of the District, he hospitalized sick and helpless strangers along with local cases, all told 3,890 persons in 1896 alone. Private citizens responded similarly when confronted with human misery. Charles Glover, who repeatedly served on the citizens' relief committee and presumably subscribed to its doctrines, gave unhesitatingly

---

287, 1899, I, 285, 300, 513, 1900, I, 85; Ch Hrgs, pp. 1-2, 13, 21, 24-25, 332, 459; Ch Rpt, pp. 172-74, Ser 3565; *Rpts B/Tr*, 1897, p. 27, 1901, p. 46.

what the colored press described as "large sums" to his butler to distribute to the poor daily during a blizzard in 1899.[11]

The launching of the Sanitary Improvement Company in 1897 is the clearest evidence that intelligent citizens were beginning to understand that the moral weaknesses of the poor might not be solely responsible for the wretchedness and disease and crime that infested parts of Washington. Hard-headed business men sponsored the new scheme. Their primary purpose was to lower the city's disgracefully high death rate by providing the occupants of the noisome alleys with decent low-cost housing. The project was at once an investment in faith and a business proposition: stockholders were to receive 5 percent on their investment. By the autumn of 1898 the company had erected eight small double houses of four rooms each, equipped with a bath, gas, hot and cold water, a range, and a cellar, all renting from $9 to $12.50 a month. A month's rent was remitted to every tenant who kept his premises in good repair for a year. Three years later the company reported it had 162 dwellings occupied by workingmen's families, a large part of them Negro; tenants appeared to observe company rules, repairs were kept to a minimum, and company assets had risen to nearly $200,000. As a practical venture in instilling habits of cleanliness, thrift, and industry the enterprise could be labelled a success. The results, however, were less astonishing than they at first seemed, inasmuch as the original plan of transplanting alley-dwellers into the new houses had quickly given way to renting to "the better class of wage-earners," in the belief that "in work of this character it is always best to begin at the top."

"Character-building" organizations, as a later generation would call the YMCA and the Women's Christian Association,

[11] Comrs Rpt, 1884, p. 76; Ch Hrgs, pp. 231, 238, Ser 3565; *Bee*, 4 Mar 1899. For Wolf's philosophy see *Third Annual Report of the Charity Organization Society of the District of Columbia*, 1886, pp. 21-23.

were never regarded as full-fledged charities, although the WCA, in undertaking to help women adjust to life in a strange city, was sometimes accused of acting as a relief agency. During the 1880's both associations lost much of their one-time religious character. The YMCA gradually relegated Bible classes and prayer meetings to a secondary place and built up its membership by emphasizing sociability and the opportunity to use the gymnasium in the new building on New York Avenue. When the Young Women's Association appeared in 1884, the managers followed the same general course insofar as the lack of a gymnasium permitted.[12]

The charity organization movement, originated in London and Berlin, spread rapidly in the latter part of the nineteenth century. Orderly philanthropy might in fact be called a by-product of swift urbanization. While the capital was caught up by the challenge more slowly than bigger American cities, in the 1880's and after, humanitarianism ran strong in Washington. Despite the limitations earnest citizens imposed upon it, the vigor with which white people on the upper social levels threw themselves into reducing pauperism and want in the community was a distinctive feature of Washington's life of the day.

[12] *Rpts B/Tr*, 1897, pp. 28-29, 1898, pp. 42-43, 1899, p. 48, 1901, p. 44; Kober, *Housing Movement*, p. 31; *Post*, 11, 15 Nov 1889.

CHAPTER V

EVERYDAY LIFE IN THE WHITE
COMMUNITY, 1879-1901

THE capital from the end of the 1870's to the turn of the century was more nearly a city of leisure than any other in America. "Compared with New York or Chicago," wrote an English visitor, "Washington, although it is full of commotion and energy, is a city of rest and peace. The inhabitants do not rush onward as though they were late for the train or the post, or as though the dinner hour being past they were anxious to appease an irritable wife." Another Englishman spoke of her air "of comfort, of leisure, of space to spare, of stateliness you hardly expected in America. It looks a sort of place where nobody has to work for his living, or, at any rate, not hard."[1]

By mid-twentieth-century standards, people did not work under high pressure. In reassuring her brother about her new job in the dead letter branch of the Post Office Department, Virginia Grigsby wrote in 1883: "We are fixed with every convenience, long desks, easy revolving chairs, footstools, plenty of servants and no specific amount of work to be done . . . There are all ladies in this room, and therefore they do as they choose, most of them bring dressing sacques and put them on to work in. Some even take off their corsets. You know Mama *never* wears any at home, perhaps she may be able to do all this in the Land Office." The "servants," that is government messengers, seldom hurried. Only common laborers, artisans, clerks in shops, and domestics worked long hours. Office workers breakfasted at eight or nine, at noon had a cup of coffee, a "dairy lunch" or a sandwich, and at four o'clock, when government offices closed, went home to hearty dinners or dined

---

[1] The Very Reverend S. Reynolds Hole, *A Little Tour of America*, pp. 309-10; G. W. Steevens, *The Land of the Dollar*, p. 92.

at a restaurant. "The lunch rooms of Washington are a characteristic of the city," wrote "Carp" in the early 1880's. "I know of no place in the world that has their like. They are found in every block and usually keep excellent coffee and delicious rolls." A dairy lunch room opposite the Treasury much frequented by government clerks served coffee in "pint shaving mugs"; customers helped themselves to sugar from two "holy water basins chained to the wall" and then relaxed in the wicker chairs about the room while they ate the sandwiches they had brought with them.

Save in the closing days of a congressional session, the pace of life was equally leisurely at the Capitol, "a little city in itself," peopled by "the busiest, wittiest and brainiest men" in the United States. In the House of the 1880's members talked and laughed, frequently with their feet propped on desks above the ever-present cuspidors, in an atmosphere as easy as that of a hotel barroom. Along the ground floor corridor leading from the House to the Senate, the chief street of the miniature city, stood small shops selling photographs, candy, and newspapers, a telegraph office ticking out messages, and at one end invariably a crowd of lobbyists, politicians, strangers, deadbeats, and bogus pension lawyers. The favor seeker knew that undue haste was self-defeating; his best opportunity might well come during an evening of billiards at one of the hotels, where congressmen played or watched "as though they were Monte Carlo gamblers." Early in the nineties the shops and stands were cleared out of the Capitol, and the House subjected itself to greater decorum, but representatives and senators, who always made a point of behaving with punctilio, took their time over their business and pleasures.

Some congressmen still lived in boardinghouses, but more of them, unable to afford to bring their families with them, patronized hotels and ate at restaurants, although "thirty-five or fifty cents is the least for which one can get a passable breakfast or dinner." The choice of places to dine was wide; some of the most famous were still popular in mid-twentieth century—the formal dining room opening off the Willard Hotel's Peacock Alley, the Ebbitt House, Harvey's Fish House, and Hall's near the river front, where a magnificent bar surmounted by a huge painting of a nude Venus added a special attraction. "Carp" informed his Cleveland readers "it would take the best part of a Congressman's salary [$5,000] to pay his board and whiskey bills, if he did not take a high room [above the second story] and leave his family at home. One New York congressman paid $600 a week for his rooms at one of the hotels." The pinch of hard times in the 1890's cut down that kind of extravagance.[2]

As "private board" at a minimum of $5 a week seemed high to most government employees, boardinghouses remained a Washington institution. At the end of the century, generals' and statesmen's widows ran many of the most select. Though these did not necessarily serve the best food, the seating arrangements followed rules of precedence as carefully as would the White House at a state dinner. Young men and women on their way up in the world occupied lowlier places than the eminent "has-been," and the lady in charge of the establishment exercised scrupulous judgment about who outranked whom in between top and bottom. Table mates, if frequently boring or slightly pompous, at least exposed the newcomer in Washington to a conic-sectioned view of the city's inhabitants ranging from salesmen to people "in office," as government clerks described their status.

The public market, patronized by society matrons as regularly as by boardinghouse keepers and economical housewives, was another Washington institution. On market day elegant ladies descended from carriages driven by stove-pipe-hatted

[2] Virginia Grigsby to Hart Grigsby, Jul 1883, Gibson-Humphreys Mss (SHC); Cleveland *Leader*, 22 Dec 1882, 5 Jan, 3 Apr, 29 Jun, 23, 30 Nov 1883; A. Maurice Low, "Washington, City of Leisure," *Atlantic Monthly*, LXXXVI, 759-71.

"darky" coachmen and, trailed by a retainer carrying a basket, made the rounds of the stalls at the Centre Market to select the fresh fruits and vegetables, the eggs and chickens, or the woodcock, wild duck, and other special delicacies of the season. There rich and poor rubbed elbows while chatting with the vendors and remarking on the weather to acquaintances. The true Washingtonian regarded marketing in person as much part of well-ordered living as making calls or serving hot chocolate to morning visitors.

For the government clerk with a family to raise, life was likely to be less eventful than for the temporary resident. "We rarely go to the theatre or to concerts," regretfully remarked a federal employee with a wife and three children to support on his $1,600 salary. With a monthly rental $30, the wood and coal bill $8, the gas bill $1.50, milk $2.30, groceries $15, perishables bought at the market $25, and the servant's wages $8 a month, he had little left over for entertaining guests or for expensive amusements. Thousands of families were in a worse position, since $1,600 was a handsome salary even in 1900 and placed a man well up in the ranks of government service. The man who earned $2,000 expected and was expected to give occasional formal dinner parties complete with soup, fish, game, roast, savory, and appropriate wines with each course. Although government pay rates remained at the levels set in the 1870's, any hardship caused by rising living costs was mitigated by the fact that everyone knew exactly what his neighbor earned and therefore what the proprieties demanded of him.[3]

As suburbs cut off city-dwellers from the fields and streams that had once made hunting, fishing, and picnicking universal pastimes, other diversions appeared. Bicycling on Washing-

[3] Louis Brownlow, *A Passion for Politics*, pp. 336-40; Mary S. Logan, ed., *Thirty Years in Washington*, p. 525; Moore, *Picturesque Washington*, p. 259; *Star*, 4 Dec 1884; *Official Register of the United States*, 1886; Carrie Angell Collier, Day Book, in possession of the author.

ton's smooth asphalt pavements had an early and long-lasting vogue. Bella Lockwood, the first woman lawyer to be admitted to practice before the Supreme Court and the only woman ever to be a party nominee for President, created a mild sensation when, with an unconcerned showing of her bright red stockings, she pedalled down Pennsylvania Avenue at ten miles an hour. More conservative ladies arrayed in elaborate cycling costumes soon took up the sport. When smaller wheels replaced the high front-wheeled models, a male dare-devil made sporting history by riding down the long flight of stone steps from the Capitol to the Mall. People of all ages played croquet, tried archery, and went boating on the "silvery Potomac." The Columbia Boat Club turned itself into the Athletic Club in 1887 and opened tennis courts, a running track and a lacrosse field on Analostan island. After 1891, thousands of people used the new public bathing beach on the river. Among the well-to-do, golf became fashionable when links opened at the country club in the late eighties. Amateur football, however, awakened more general enthusiasm. In professional sport interest divided almost equally between prize fights and baseball until the National League cut its teams to eight, and the Senators, who for years had ended the season at the bottom of the League, dropped out of sight.[4]

Custom, meanwhile, had not staled Washingtonians' pleasure in Saturday afternoon gatherings in the White House grounds: "Then the lawn is filled with a well-dressed crowd as cosmopolitan as you will find anywhere and the big Marine Band, one of the best in the world, clad in their flaming suits of red and gold, give forth the finest music. . . . Among the crowd you will find the best dressed and finest looking Negroes in the world; you may bump against a treasury clerk or a cabinet officer, and you may discuss the toilet of Frau Van

[4] *Star*, 30 May 1879, 18 May 1880, 1, 26 Jan 1889, Summaries, 1894, 1901, "Rambler," 27 Mar 1921; Comrs Rpts, 1899, p. 10, 1901, p. 494.

Nirgends, the chief lady of a foreign legation, or of pretty little peachy Miss Smith whose father is a messenger in the Treasury, and then the nature, the flowers, the trees and the long stretch of beautiful scenery away on the Potomac beyond the big white monument, make a combination of which any country may be proud."

National celebrations, moreover, periodically enlivened the everyday routine. Most memorable was the dedication of the Washington Monument on February 21, 1885, a day for which old inhabitants had waited thirty-six years. While children skated on Babcock Pond to the north of the Monument, shivering adults cheered Senator John Sherman's opening announcement that men might keep their hats on during the formal exercises; bitter weather reduced the prayer of the rector of Christ Church to a mere ten minutes. That night fireworks reflected by the snow covering the city made a magnificent spectacle. Every fourth year increasingly elaborate presidential inaugurations created a holiday mood. For President Garfield's inaugural parade grand stands for the first time lined the Avenue, and the newly finished National Museum, scene of the inaugural ball, resembled "a crystal palace," its rotunda and dome sparkling with "the whiteness of electric lights" while the rest of the building glowed with "the yellowness of the thousands of gas burners." In brilliant sunshine on March 4, 1885, nearly 100,000 people watched Grover Cleveland take the oath of office as the first Democratic President since James Buchanan. Men climbed to the roof of the Capitol and into the lap of Horatio Greenough's statue of Washington, and afterward, as a 25,000-man parade marched up the Avenue, "even the flags and streamers seemed to be affected by the general contagion which filled the air." Still larger crowds welcomed the next two Republican Presidents. A downpour of cold rain obliged President Harrison to stand under a dripping umbrella as he gave his address, but President McKinley in 1897 had the "Cleveland weather" that a snow storm had denied the Democrat at his second inaugural.[5]

Washingtonians on their own staged several impressive celebrations, notably an elaborate welcome for Alexander Shepherd when he returned on a visit in 1887. The demonstration had curious overtones; hundreds of people had been sharply critical of the Boss only fifteen years before. But it was good advertising for "the city which he plucked from the mire and set as a jewel in the sight of men," and most of his former enemies, their anger quenched by the prosperity of the immediate past, now greeted him as a symbol of "the new Washington." Fireworks on Pennsylvania Avenue brilliantly illuminated an hour-long evening parade. The entire District militia turned out, and in the wake of "mounted marshals with white sashes charging about" came some five hundred muddy-booted, overalled workingmen representing the street department. Behind them rode two hundred men on bicycles rigged with wire frames on which hung lighted Chinese lanterns. Every section of the procession carried "transparencies" with inscriptions such as "Population 1871, 80,000; 1887, 250,000," or "Washington suggested; Congress sanctioned; Shepherd made it."

Again at the end of the Spanish-American War when the District regiment of the National Guard returned from Cuba, flags and bunting draped from "windows, doors and sashes and even chimney tops" set the scene for a "reception that surpassed anything of a similar character ever before known in the history of the District of Columbia."

Two years later the city outdid herself in honor of her centennial. One innovation marked the parade from the White House to the Capitol: the Governor of Rhode Island and his staff rode in automobiles. Following the formal procession came "a number of real centennial-looking vehicles, manned by

[5] *Star*, 28 Feb, 5 Mar 1881, 4 Mar 1885, 9 Oct 1889, 4 Mar 1897; Cleveland *Leader*, 30 Sep 1883, 11 Apr, 5 Sep 1884, 4 Mar 1885.

the inevitable darky, with 'Express for Hire' scrawled in white chalk over the sides of the forlorn wagons, and in them the weary found repose for 'Only 10 cents, lady.' " At the Capitol, the "Avenue entrance to the [House] gallery was lighted by a suspended device, bearing the words, 'Capital Celebration, 1900,' in blazing incandescent lamps." Beneath this was a mammoth American flag in colored lights, mechanically contrived to pale and brighten to give Old Glory the appearance of waving. The celebration played up the theme of miraculous change: a city, for years a grubby village unworthy of the United States, now the embodiment of national greatness, a place of absorbing interest to every American.[6]

Although the lengthening roster of government officials gradually necessitated a stricter observance of the canons of rank, "official society" remained an elastic term. In the 1880's, according to a good-naturedly derisive journalist, it stretched to include "residents of Washington, strangers, and visitors." Any well-mannered white person, in short, who could afford servants and who meticulously followed the "cast iron" rules about making calls could be a part or hover on the fringes of Society. How far he and his wife got beyond the circumference was only partly a matter of rank. When Senator H. A. W. Tabor, the Vermont stonecutter who had struck it rich in Colorado silver mining, cast off a first wife and in a sumptuous wedding at the Willard Hotel married a glamorous little blonde, neither his senatorial office, his ostentatious spending, nor President Arthur's presence at the wedding enabled the groom and his bride to cut a swathe during his brief term in Washington. Distinguished family connections helped open doors, but distinction rested less upon ancient lineage than upon post Civil-War achievement. And a politician's social status, particularly after the Civil Service Act and repeal of the last sections of the Tenure of Office Act cut in upon his patronage,

6 *Star*, 10, 22 Sep, 7 Oct 1887, 2 Jan 1899; *Sentinel*, 25 Feb 1888; *Bee*, 15 Oct 1898; *Post*, 11-13 Dec 1900.

might depend almost as much on his wife's social skills as upon his own place in the governmental hierarchy. "Society women," remarked the acidulous Emily Briggs, "have politicians for husbands, but not all politicians have society wives."[7]

If the character of politicians did not change, at least observant wives learned that a display of wealth was a poor substitute for rank, and rank without suave manners might be a bruised reed upon which to lean. Non-alcoholic state dinners disappeared after Mrs. Hayes left the White House, but the days of eighteen to twenty toasts at formal dinners did not return, and the quiet tastes of succeeding first ladies helped to emphasize elegance rather than lavishness in entertaining. The rich outsider intent on becoming an insider discovered the uses not only of the *Elite List* and the *U.S. Register* but also of Mrs. Dahlgren's *Etiquette of Social Life in Washington*. Madeleine Vinton Dahlgren, daughter of a congressman, widow of a distinguished admiral, and from the early 1880's till her death in 1898 the self-appointed doyenne of Washington society, doubtless saved many a parvenu from unforgivable blunders. "No dinner," she warned, "however superb in prandial show, can be agreeable if the *convives* are dullards. . . . No sordid computation of dollars can buy or measure the Promethean light of conversational effect." Even proper Bostonians or Philadelphia gentlemen welcomed reminders of how to address a Russian count or her Britannic Majesty's minister to the United States.[8]

Forty years later a cultivated American who knew European capitals well declared the Washington of President Arthur's time the most delightful city in the world. If visitors to the

[7] *Star*, 13 Jan 1879, 18 Nov 1881, 25 Feb, 15 Mar, 14 Nov 1882, 31 Dec 1884, 16 Mar 1885, 11 Dec 1888, 26 Jan 1889; Cleveland *Leader*, 5 Sep 1884; *Sentinel*, 6 Mar 1886, 29 Dec 1888; *Olivia Letters*, p. 413.

[8] Marian Gouverneur, *As I Remember*, pp. 371-72; Low, "Washington, City of Leisure," pp. 773-74; Madeleine Vinton Dahlgren, *Etiquette of Social Life in Washington*, 5th ed., 1881, p. 50; Rudolph Keim, *Society in Washington, Its Noted Men, Accomplished Women, Established Customs and Notable Events*, 1887.

President's private quarters were astonished to find his bedroom redecorated in pale pink with blue brocade hangings, all Washington was pleasantly surprised by the social graces of the affable host in the White House. When his successor brought a twenty-year-old bride to the capital in 1886, again Washingtonians found the warmth radiating from the White House singularly agreeable. The wife of Senator Foraker of Ohio indicated that that charm endured: "The opening nineties saw the old *regime*, Anglo-Saxon, conservative, making its last stand at the White House. The Harrisons gathered around them a fine best-families group; women who could give all their time to social perfections undistracted by suffrage, divorce, interior decoration or other extraneities . . . We still exchanged recipes, had not yet begun to discuss diet, except as a delight, changed our dresses exhaustingly-often during the day, and were, altogether, as conventional as a sideboard. It was a nice period."

By the standards of London or St. Petersburg or Vienna or Berlin, ceremony in Washington was thin, scarcely greater than in Grant's day when the President's casual attire and off-hand manner had scandalized the newly arrived Danish minister. But changes began in 1894 when Great Britain and France acknowledged the growing importance of the United States in world affairs by elevating their legations in Washington to the rank of embassies. In 1897 Italy followed that example, and at the end of the Spanish-American War the emergence of the United States as a prospective colonial power hastened the process that gradually turned the city into a sophisticated as well as an agreeable capital. Senators, conscious of the new prestige attaching to the men who ratified or rejected international treaties, abandoned the broad-brimmed felts and string ties of yesteryear and adopted high silk hats and frock coats as standard daytime attire. Foreign diplomats came to look upon a tour of duty in Washington as only a little less desirable than assignment to one of the five or six great courts of Europe, while wealthy Americans as never before wanted a taste of Washington society. Not every debutante could marry a Lord Curzon as had Levi Leiter's daughter, and the growing dearth of bachelors all but put an end to balls, but sipping tea, horseback riding and dining with titled foreigners added dazzle to the social round. New York's Four Hundred could rarely produce more eligible lords in a season than could Washington hostesses. Moreover, as improved printing techniques enabled magazines to publish photographs of silk-hatted big-wigs and everyday scenes in Washington, popular interest in the life of the capital heightened. It took on simultaneously a visible reality and a new romantic aura that encompassed not only political personages but everyone privileged to live in the city.[9]

The relationship between "resident" and "official" society often confused new arrivals, particularly if they recalled tales of local aristocrats' disdain of officialdom during and after the Civil War. Readers of Henry James' story *Pandora* saw in Mr. Bonnycastle, a character actually based on Henry Adams, a portrayal of the Washington blue-blood of the 1880's when he suggests to his wife that for once they ignore the social niceties in preparing their guest list: "Hang it . . . let us have some fun—let us invite the President." But even in the Grant era with all its bitter partisanship and vulgarity, the line separating families firmly rooted in the community from the temporary office-holders had not been drawn sharply, and in the course of the next decade it faded out almost entirely. Mrs. Dahlgren explained that "in real solidity of social importance, the resident society must . . . be classed as of the very elite." She added, "the old families of Washington have an

[9] Mrs. Reginald De Koven, *A Musician and His Wife*, pp. 51-82; Logan, *Thirty Years in Washington*, p. 519; Festus Summers, ed., *The Cabinet Diary of William L. Wilson*, pp. 9-10, 198; Mrs. Joseph Foraker, *I Would Live It Again*, pp. 185-200; Mrs. William Howard Taft, *Recollections of Full Years*, p. 27; Louis A. Coolidge, "On the Streets of the National Capital," *Cosmopolitan*, XXVIII, 365-76.

interest for us which none other in the land may claim, for their social life has gone hand in hand with that of the nation."

But how old was old? By the end of the century the distinction was blurred. Third-generation families who from the first had had the cultivation and money to move in upper-class circles were extremely few, and, in striking contrast to cities such as Philadelphia and Boston, Washington and Georgetown together could muster scarcely eighty well-established second-generation families. The prominent Washingtonian of the 1890's was as likely to be a native of a northern state as of the District of Columbia. Although by 1900 four out of every five native American whites in the District were born below the Mason-Dixon line, in the upper social brackets southern background had ceased to weigh heavily. (See Table III.) Washington's first *Social Register* contained the names of about 2,100 families in 1900. Some 820 were those of Army and Navy officers, high-ranking departmental officials, members of Congress, foreign diplomats and Americans listed in one of the five other *Social Registers* who chose to transfer to Washington for the season. Among the twelve-hundred-odd others named were people who had lived in the city at intervals for twenty to thirty years without identifying themselves as Washingtonians—Henry Adams, for example, and the diplomat John W. Foster, Secretary of State under Benjamin Harrison and grandfather of a later Secretary. Over four hundred of the fixed residents listed were widows or single women. Of all the permanent residents included, perhaps two-thirds had been relatively new to the capital when Mrs. Dahlgren wrote of "the very elite."

Yet the omissions from the *Register* of 1900 illustrate as well as the inclusions the uncertainty and flexibility of social status in Washington. The cultivated Ohio-born John Joy Edson, a Washingtonian from his Civil-War school days, head of a dozen civic enterprises, and president of the Board of Trade in 1900, was left out; Brainard Warner was admitted, although

TABLE III

POPULATION OF THE DISTRICT OF COLUMBIA, 1870-1950*

	1870	1880	1890	1900	1910	1920	1930	1940	1950
TOTAL	131,700	177,624	230,392	278,718	331,069	437,571	486,869	663,091	802,178
% increase in 10 years	75.4	34.9	29.7	21.0	18.8	32.2	11.3	36.2	21.0
WHITES	88,278	118,006	154,695	191,532	236,128	326,860	353,914	474,326	517,865
% increase in 10 years	40.1	33.7	31.1	23.8	23.3	38.4	8.3	34.0	9.2
Native	72,107	101,026	136,178	172,012	211,777	298,312	323,982	440,312	478,368
% native to D.C.	53.9	55.4	52.1	48.5	46.7	38.0	39.6	33.2	31.4
% native to all southern states	25.0	24.2	25.9	28.9	29.6	31.4	33.7	34.7	32.1
% native to South exclusive of Md. & Va.	1.7	2.9	4.1	5.4	5.7	9.4	10.1	14.6	15.6
% native to North and West	20.9	20.5	20.9	22.3	23.0	29.5	25.8	31.2	33.5
Foreign-born	16,171	16,980	18,517	19,520	24,351	28,548	29,932	34,014	39,497
% of total population	12.3	9.7	8.1	7.2	7.5	6.7	6.3	5.3	5.5
% of white population	18.3	14.3	11.9	10.2	10.3	8.7	8.5	7.2	7.6
NEGROES	43,404	59,596	75,572	86,702	94,446	109,966	132,068	187,266[a]	280,803[a]
% increase in 10 years	203.2	37.3	26.8	14.7	8.9	16.4	20.1	41.9	49.9
% of total population	32.9	33.6	32.8	31.1	28.5	25.1	27.1	28.2	35.0
% native to D.C.	31.0	41.6	41.9	41.9	42.8	42.4	39.8	39.4	40.4
% native to Md. & Va.	65.7	54.1	51.9	50.8	46.3	42.3	35.4	27.3	20.9
% native to South exclusive of Md. & Va.	1.9	2.4	3.4	5.2	7.3	11.3	20.2	28.9	32.1

a Negroes only; the nativity percentages are computed from subtotals which include all non-whites other than Negroes was negligible.
* Compiled from U.S. Census, Ninth through Seventeenth.

his career in the capital was no longer or more notable and his bank account probably little larger than Edson's. Since the publication of the *New York Social Register* in 1884 and of later counterparts for Philadelphia, Boston, Baltimore, and Chicago, socially ambitious Americans had come to look upon a *Social Register* listing as a key to the pearly gates on earth; family position, fortified by money but untouched by scandalous notoriety, was at least theoretically a prerequisite. But inasmuch as expediency necessitated naming all high-ranking officials in the capital, including every senator irrespective of his forebears, the rules of selection in Washington lost some of their rigidity. The hope, however illusory, of exploiting that flexibility to squeak through the sacred portals drew to Washington people who knew they could not successfully storm the doors elsewhere.[10]

To newcomers Washington and Georgetown seemed one and the same, as officially they indeed were. But old Georgetowners, while sharing many of Washington's pleasures, felt themselves differentiated by their longer history and closer family ties. The sense of dignified antiquity which prevailed beyond the debris-strewn bank of Rock Creek was fortunately not a divisive factor in the larger community; residents of the city on one side of the creek admired the eighteenth-century houses of those on the far side without resenting their air of detached superiority. If Georgetowners preferred Sunday afternoon visiting with each other to mingling with the throng which promenaded along Connecticut Avenue to the accompaniment of a dozen different languages, Washingtonians enjoyed the cosmopolitan atmosphere of the capital nonetheless.

If few people considered Washington a center of creative

[10] Henry James, "Pandora," *Stories Revived*, i, 105; F. E. Mathiessen, ed., *Henry James' Notebook*; Low, "Washington, City of Leisure," p. 777; Dahlgren, *Etiquette*, pp. 33, 49. The figures on "old families" are based on a 20 percent sampling of the *Washington Social Register* of 1900 checked against the *City Directory* of 1846. See also Marietta Minnigerode Andrews, *My Studio Window*, pp. 101-02.

art, fewer still found her barren of opportunity. Nowhere else in the United States could sculpture be seen in such profusion— at the Capitol in the Hall of Statuary, in the Senate chamber adorned after 1886 with a growing array of busts of former Vice Presidents, in the Corcoran Gallery of Art, and in L'Enfant's spacious circles and squares, where equestrian bronze or stone generals and marble statesmen on imposing pedestals looked out over the city. Except for Vinnie Ream Hoxie's statue of Admiral Farragut in Farragut Square, none of the sculpture was the work of local artists. Most of it fell short of great art, but very little of it was patently inept, and when Henry Adams' memorial to his wife was unveiled in Rock Creek Cemetery in 1891, the beauty of St. Gaudens' simple tranquil figure, which Adams called "The Peace of God," led connoisseurs to declare it the finest sculpture in America. William Wetmore Story, the American expatriate whose statue of John Marshall stands on the Capitol grounds and who supposedly was Hawthorne's original for the sculptor in *The Marble Fawn*, remarked upon the rapid improvement in Americans' aesthetic taste when he lectured in Washington in the 1880's. The trustees of the Corcoran Gallery, impressed at the steadily increasing number of visitors, were themselves astonished in 1897 at the results of an experiment in opening the gallery on Sunday: a long queue of "wage-earners" formed at the entrance long before the doors opened, and few left before the closing bell sounded. The painting "Charlotte Corday" and Hiram Powers' "Greek Slave" commanded most attention.

Meanwhile the enthusiasm of the amateurs who flocked to the gallery to copy its pictures and to benefit from the free tutelage of Eliphalet Andrews led the trustees to offer a gold medal for the best piece of work and, in 1887, to pay Andrews a small salary to conduct classes such as he had taught as a volunteer for nearly a decade. The Corcoran School of Art came formally into being in 1888, for upon W. W. Corcoran's death in February a memorandum came to light among his papers setting aside $100,000 for an art school to be attached to the gallery. Plans for a new building on 17th Street therefore included spacious studios for classes. When the new white marble gallery opened in 1897, Andrews was able to persuade the artists who had been teaching paying students at the Art League to join him and his assistant at the Corcoran. By the end of the century the consolidation had secured the city an art school that would in time rank with Boston's and Chicago's.

Much of the local public preferred the ornate Renaissance style of the newly finished Library of Congress to the classical lines of the new Corcoran Gallery, while changes in taste rated Federal period domestic architecture below the heavy solidity of the Romanesque exemplified in the houses H. H. Richardson built on Lafayette Square for Henry Adams and John Hay. Formal schools of architecture were few in the United States. Young men learned the profession by serving virtual apprenticeships in the offices of established firms, just as a generation earlier young men read law in the offices of older men as preparation for the bar examinations. For aspiring young architects the buildings of the capital served as a kind of case book. If, like General Sheridan, they regretted that the red brick mass of the Pension Office was fireproof, awful examples of Washington's public architecture as well as her fine still served a useful purpose.[11]

In music Washington lagged behind other big American cities. A week or at most a fortnight of opera presented by companies on tour was her quota for the season. Occasionally a well-known instrumental soloist gave a concert, but professional performances were few. Like performing artists, composers were discouraged by the lack of a public concert hall.

[11] Teunis S. Hamlin, "Historic Houses of Washington," *Scribner's Magazine*, XIV, 475; Charles E. Fairman, *Art and Artists of the Capitol of the United States of America*, pp. 251 ff (hereafter cited as Fairman, *Art*); *Star*, 8 Jan 1879; Cleveland *Leader*, 23 Jan 1884; *Post*, 1 Mar 1897; Stanley Olmsted, "The Corcoran School of Art," Ms in possession of Corcoran Gallery.

The organist and later the pastor of the Congregational Church, however, composed a number of hymns, and John Philip Sousa, leader of the Marine Band, won local fame for his *Washington Post March*. He conducted the first performance in 1890 for a gathering of the Washington Amateur Authors' Association on the Smithsonian grounds. Later played at the Chicago World's Fair and at European courts, the gay *March* came to be known the world over. Unhappily for Sousa, before then he had sold the score for $35 to a Philadelphia publisher, and, unhappily for Washington, he left the Marines in 1892 to start his own band in New York.

Gifted amateurs could only partly fill the gap created by the absence of professional talent. The Georgetown Amateur Orchestra, starting in 1882 with thirty-one instruments, worked up to a hundred before 1901, and several churches, notably the Asbury and St. Luke's Negro Churches and the Congregational Church, had exceptionally well-trained choirs. For a number of years the German Saengerbund gave an annual *Lieder* concert, and the Washington Choral Society in the 1890's sang oratorios, including on one occasion the *Elijah a capella*. Beginning in 1886 a group of women with some leisure and a serious interest in music formed the Friday Morning Music Club, meeting at each others' houses to study and give private concerts. By the end of the century, the Club had begun to achieve professional stature. In 1897 some twenty talented Negro women organized the Treble Clef Club along similar lines. In an era when Edison phonographs and recordings were still an expensive innovation, most people had little chance to discover that listening engendered a taste for music. The city as a whole remained luke-warm to the art.[12]

[12] John Philip Sousa, *Marching Along*, pp. 115-17; *Post History*, pp. 339-40; *Post and Times Herald*, 3 Jul 1958; Frank Metcalf, "History of Sacred Music in the District of Columbia," Columbia Historical Society *Records*, XXVII, 175-202 (hereafter cited as CHS *Rec*); *Star*, 15 Dec 1879, 12 Apr 1882; Cleveland *Leader*, 2 May 1884; *Post*, 3 Nov 1889, 4 Mar 1897; *A Brief History of the Friday Morning Music Club of Washington, D.C.*, and programs filed under heading "Washington" in Music Div, L.C.

Literature, however, occupied an important place in Washington's life. The newspapers made much of the city's literary lights, perhaps partly because some of them were journalists who turned out an occasional novel or play in addition to their regular columns. Since dozens of independent newspapers had their own correspondents in the capital, numbers as well as talent kept reporters much in the public view. In 1889, having offended the Administration and thus somewhat weakened their own position, the leaders of the fraternity organized the Gridiron Club dedicated to giving an annual dinner for three or four specially invited, politically powerful guests. Yearly thereafter an anonymous skit, its authorship carefully concealed, neatly roasted the guest of honor, and members' secrecy about what went on was sufficiently well-kept to enable the victim to laugh with his tormentors. Public uncertainty about who wrote the "scorchers" for the Gridiron endowed all correspondents with a reputation for Rabelaisian wit.

While congressmen and retired generals penned memoirs and treatises on politics and the Civil War, a flood of verses, essays, short stories, and sketches of life in the capital poured out of Washington into the pages of popular magazines. Most of it left little permanent mark. Even Joaquin Miller, whose *Songs of the Sierras* and tales of the wild West seemed to ensure him lasting fame, might have dropped out of memory, had his log cabin on Meridian Hill not survived as a physical landmark long after he had departed. With a host of writers ready to participate, "literary evenings" became part of the social routine. The Shakespeare Club, the Circle des Precieuses Ridicules, the Unity Club, and a dozen others held readings, while the exercises conducted within the "enchanted circle of the Brain Club," as the Baroness Hegermann-Lindencrone had named the Literary Society in the 1870's, lost much of their former pretentiousness.[13]

[13] Theron C. Crawford, "The Special Correspondents at Washington," *Cosmopolitan*, XII, 351-60; Richard V. Oulahan, "Literary Bookland, the

By no means all of Washington's literary figures were dilet-
tantes. Government scientists turned out enormously valuable
studies, some of them rivalling in interest John Wesley Powell's descriptions of the Colorado River valley. In 1883 Lester
Frank Ward published his epoch-making *Dynamic Sociology*,
much of it written at his desk at the Geological Survey. The
work of a distinguished, albeit still relatively obscure, paleo-
botanist and paleobiologist, Ward's presentation of the case
for a planned society and his insistence that "ideas rule the
world of men" struck with telling force; in the 1890's his
Psychic Factors in Civilization and the *Outline of Sociology*
further developed his social philosophy. Simon Newcomb, head
of the Naval Observatory, produced not only lucid expositions
of complex scientific problems but two books on political economy and, for good measure, a romance.

Historians made wide use of the archival materials in the
Library of Congress, over which the bibliophile, author, and
scholar Ainsworth Spofford presided until 1897. While the
octogenarian George Bancroft completed his last book, from
Henry Adams' study nearby at 1603 H Street came the anonymously published novel *Democracy*, a satirical commentary on
Washington society, and in 1890 his history of Jefferson's and
Madison's administrations. Next door Adams' intimate friend
John Hay took time out from his collaboration with John Nicolay to write the *Breadwinners*, a novel attacking organized
labor as he had seen it in Cleveland during the railroad strike
of 1877. After Nicolay's and Hay's monumental ten-volume
Abraham Lincoln: A History appeared, Hay confined his writing to letters and a few pieces of verse, and, while Adams wan-

---

Gridiron Club of Washington," *The Bookman*, XXIII, 146-52; *Star*, 8 Jan
30 Jun 1881, 6 Feb, 12 Apr, 1 Nov 1882, 9 Jan, 27 Feb 1883, 20 Jan,
25 Nov 1884; *Post*, 4 Nov 1889; "Literary works in progress," Cleveland
Leader, 3 Mar 1884; Lillie Hegermann-Lindencrone, *The Sunny Side of
Diplomatic Life*, pp. 16-18; Helen Nicolay, *Sixty Years of the Washington Literary Society*.

dered over the South Seas and Europe, the houses on H Street ceased to be a source of distinguished literature.[14]

The number of literary women in Washington frequently astonished visitors. "One of the lions of the capital" was the petite auburn-haired Frances Hodgson Burnett, who, in creating *Little Lord Fauntleroy*, imposed black velvet knee breeches and lace collars upon a whole generation of rebellious small boys. James G. Blaine's sister-in-law, the short, stout, rather homely Abigail Dodge, still using the pen name Gail Hamilton, in the 1880's was still producing widely read columns on politics and politicians. The sketches and stories of Mary Clemmer Ames, best known for her *Ten Years in Washington*, Emily Briggs' *Olivia Letters*, Kate Field's witty pieces appearing under the title "Kate Field's Washington," and the writings of half a dozen other newspaperwomen in turn commanded respect. Forty years of turning out saccharine tales had shrunk Mrs. Emma D. E. N. Southworth's literary standing, but in the nineties the works of newer women novelists in Washington had not yet obliterated the little Georgetown widow's books from memory. Her little frame cottage on the bluff above the Potomac remained a "literary landmark." Younger authors frequently followed Mrs. Dahlgren's example in drawing upon knowledge of Washington society for background. If Grace Denio Litchfield's poems and the plays and stories of Jennie Gould Lincoln, wife of an eminent Washington physician, sold the better for being the products of society matrons, the quality of what they wrote mattered less to the community than the recognition they won from the rest of the country.

Feminists, pointing to the successful professional careers of women in the capital, called Washington "a special center of women." In 1890 wives, mothers, daughters, and sisters who believed the "Dawn of Woman's Era" at hand organized the

[14] A. Hunter Dupree, *Science in the Federal Government: A History of Policies and Activities to 1940*, p. 205 (hereafter cited as Dupree, *Science*); Ralph H. Gabriel, *The Course of American Democratic Thought*, p. 207.

"Wimodaughsis," a society which hoped to open a building for meetings of the National Woman Suffrage Association, the WCTU, the Red Cross under Clara Barton, the Women's National Press Association, and the like. The project made scanty headway; attractive young government clerks preferred to spend their leisure in the company of the bachelors with whom their jobs or the "dairy lunches" brought them in contact, and older women, such as Virginia Grigsby's mother with or without her corsets at the Land Office, were generally too tired at the end of the day's work to care about elevation, while ladies established in the social world of the capital inclined to look askance at the "career woman." Yet women of all conditions and kinds could lead a fuller life in Washington than in almost any other American city of the time.[15]

Among men it was the scientists and scholars above all who found Washington congenial and who added most to the variety of the city's intellectual interests. While generals and bankers gravitated toward the Metropolitan Club, notables in a dozen fields of learning gathered at the Cosmos Club in the house where Dolly Madison spent her last years. Founded in 1878 largely by the men who had organized the Philosophical Society seven years before, the Cosmos Club was the rendezvous of some of the most interesting men in America; and, after the remodelling of the house in the mid-eighties, usually also the meeting place of the city's learned societies. Faculty members of the Columbian and National Universities made up part of the group, but scientists in government service were its backbone.

For in spite of some congressional opposition and even more from university scientists such as Alexander Agassis of Harvard who, imbued with laissez faire doctrines, objected pas-

[15] Cleveland *Leader*, 4 Aug 1883; Etta Ramsdell Goodwin, "The Literary Women of Washington," *Chatauquan*, xxvii, 579-86; *Wimodaughsis*, leaflet in Bowen Mss; Susan Grigsby to Sarah Humphreys, 4 Aug, 5 Oct 1884; Gibson-Humphreys Mss.

sionately to a wider government role in research, programs of the federal bureaus expanded steadily during the eighties. Under imaginative leadership, basic research not infrequently became the accepted accompaniment of the search for solutions to practical problems. The challenge of the work possible in the Washington bureaus attracted brilliant men: geologists and paleontologists at the Geological Survey; marine biologists pursuing oceanographic studies for the Fish Commission, geneticists, plant and animal pathologists, and chemists in the Department of Agriculture; mathematicians and astronomers at the Naval Observatory; meteorologists working at the Weather Bureau under "Old Prob" Cleveland Abbe, so nicknamed for his reliance on "probably"; and in the 1890's bacteriologists, Captain Walter Reed among them, brought together by Surgeon-General George Sternberg in his reorganization of the Army medical service. At the National Museum George Brown Goode carried on a many-faceted program that inspired the men he trained in research to call the era before his death in 1896 "a golden age of natural history." Partial reversal of congressional policies clipped the wings of some of these agencies in the last decade of the century, but new regulations and reduced budgets did not put an end to much of the work.

The intellectual vigor of these men permeated the community. Their versatility was in itself stimulating. John Wesley Powell, a bluff, daring, one-armed, red-haired giant, was not only the first white man to traverse the length of the dangerous Colorado canyon, an able geologist, and the author of the famous report on the arid lands of the West, but was also so well versed in Indian languages and tribal mores that in the 1890's, as head of the Smithsonian Bureau of American Ethnology, he laid the groundwork for an expanding science of cultural anthropology in America. Simon Newcomb, the most eminent American astronomer of his day, combined personal charm with scientific erudition; the initiator of a new system of computing the position of the stars and the mass and motion of the planets, he was also an inspiring lecturer and teacher. The gentle Spencer Baird, in the 1880's secretary of the Smithsonian, initiated and directed the Fish Commission's extraordinary program of marine research and was the mentor of a group of gifted younger naturalists known in Washington as "Bairdians." At his death, the secretaryship of the Smithsonian passed to Samuel Langley, whose measurements of the radiant heat of the sun were of major importance to astrophysicists and whose aeronautical experiments stirred the public imagination even while doubting Thomases ridiculed the idea of human flight. At the same time in the attic of the Department of Agriculture Building, a new field of science was emerging. From under the microscopes of a six-man staff came revolutionary discoveries about the nature and transmission of plant and animal diseases such as Texas cattle fever and wheat rust. There two twenty-year-olds, Walter Swingle and David Fairchild, began careers that made them in their early thirties the foremost "plant explorers" in the world.[16]

From these men and a half-hundred equally famous associates came the spark that brought into being six additional learned societies in Washington before 1894. Unlike the Philosophical Society, which aimed at investigation of "the positive facts and laws of the physical and moral universe," several of the newer societies were concerned primarily with popularizing science. Yet eminent members of the Philosophical Society and other academically trained men were not above joining the Anthropological or the National Geographic Society, which made no pretense of nurturing erudition. Indeed the enthusi-

---

[16] Dupree, *Science*, pp. 149-270; *Star*, 11 Feb 1879, 30 Jun 1881, 27 Feb 1883; "Scientific Research and the National Government," *The Dial*, XXII, 73-75; Simon Newcomb, *The Reminiscences of an Astronomer*, pp. 123-27, 216-23; Paul H. Oehser, *Sons of Science*, pp. 61-106; John W. Powell, "The Personal Characteristics of Spencer Fullerton Baird," *Anl Rpt Smithsonian*, 1888, pp. 746-52; David Fairchild, *The World Was My Garden*, pp. 18-27. See also *Dictionary of American Biography*.

astic participation of laymen in the affairs of the new societies bound much of upper-class Washington into an informal intellectual fellowship. Published transactions extended the influence of these societies into cities where no similar organizations existed. In order to pool resources for publication and public lectures, in 1888 a tentative federation evolved from which the Washington Academy of Sciences sprang ten years later. Significantly its first president was Gardiner Hubbard, a man of great cultivation and an exceptionally well-informed student of the physics of acoustics and aeronautics, but an amateur, not a professionally trained scientist. Hubbard, who was the financial genius behind the Bell Telephone Company, and his son-in-law, Alexander Graham Bell, in founding the National Geographic Society set out to promote scientific exploration and, through the pages of a non-technical, profusely illustrated magazine, to educate the American public about remote parts of the earth.

The swelling ranks of gifted and fascinating men thus gave life in Washington its peculiarly satisfying quality. The brilliance of the far-ranging conversation to be heard at dinner parties astonished newcomers prone to think politics the capital's only interest. Here was an urbane community appreciative of the arts, albeit with little creative artistic genius, a city in which hundreds of temporary residents on government assignments usually wanted to stay and often did. The slow pace of life left people time to enjoy it. "We live," remarked Dr. John Billings, "in a fortunate time and place—in the early manhood of a mighty nation, and in its capital city, which every year makes more beautiful, and richer in the treasure of science, literature and art."[17]

[17] *Bulletin of the Philosophical Society of Washington, 1874; Report of a Committee from the Geological Society on the history of the Joint Commission of the Scientific Societies of Washington; The Cabinet Diary of William L. Wilson*, pp. xix-xx, 180, 198, 215, 233; Dupree, *Science*, 230.

CHAPTER VI

COLORED WASHINGTON, 1879-1901

FOR Negroes the satisfactions of life in the capital diminished steadily after 1878. Between white and colored people such tolerant friendliness as had survived the seventies slowly disappeared. White citizens forgot that Negro leaders had formerly commanded respect and, by their behavior, had encouraged belief in the possibility of building an intelligent bi-racial community. In 1888 the Washington *Elite List* carried the names of five or six Negroes; by 1892 they had been dropped. The white press, increasingly critical of Negroes' "shiftlessness" and the high rate of crime among them, gradually reduced other news about colored people to an occasional facetious comment on a colored social gathering. Exasperation or disgust blotted out compassion for the great mass of blacks, while white people's interest in the careers of gifted Negroes became so condescending as to be insulting, the more so as the condescension was often unconscious. By the mid-nineties a reader of the white newspapers might have supposed Washington had no colored community, let alone three virtually separate Negro communities. White people, in short, in the course of the twenty-odd years resolved the problem of race relations by tacitly denying its existence.

Concurrent with the loss of recognition from whites was a progressive loss of cohesiveness within the three-tiered Negro community and a widening of the gulf between the upper-class group composed of people of predominantly white blood, the middle-class mulattoes, and the blacks. Except as seen in all Negroes' search for "*whiteness*—the ability to pass unnoticed in the crowd, the power to avoid humiliation and abuse,"[1] a community in the sense of a group of people united by common

[1] Pauli Murray, *Proud Shoes, The Story of An American Family*, p. 53.

aspirations and cultural identity had ceased to exist well before 1879. The biological accident of pigmentation, so far from supplying a basis for group accord, created growing resentments which colored people directed at each other more bitterly than at whites. By the end of the 1880's Negroes in the District were adhering to the social pattern common in the deep South: conflict within the caste and compliance with or carefully concealed hostility toward the white group outside.[2] Washington Negroes at the end of the Civil War had shown signs of escaping that mold of behavior. Intelligent colored men, without attempting to halt the swift growth of elaborate class differentiations, had striven to prevent a destructive divisiveness and to develop mutual helpfulness and respect within a single enlarged Negro community; for a time they had seemed to make headway. The tragedy of the last decades of the century was the withering of this earlier promise as the men who had worked to make Washington a center of American Negro civilization in its highest form, a city where all Negroes might live in dignity, abandoned the struggle.

The discouragements besetting the District's colored people undoubtedly contributed to the decline of their public spirit. Indeed the basic cause may have been the growing racism of whites. But cause and effect were intertwined. As time went on, the failure of the bulk of the city's black population to evince any sense of responsibility disillusioned whites who had once held high hopes for the race. That disillusionment fed racial hostility as surely as racial discrimination undermined Negroes' determination to help themselves. The result was a vicious spiral. Whites concluded that most Negroes would never make good citizens, and Negroes, feeling themselves steadily shoved further into a corner by prejudice, ceased to stand up for each other and let the fight degenerate into one of each man

[2] See John Dollard, *Caste and Class in a Southern Town*; Allison Davis and G. and M. Gardner, *Deep South*; and W. Lloyd Warner, "American Caste and Class," *American Journal of Sociology*, XLII, 234-371.

for himself. The exceptions were too few to alter the large picture. Gradually over the years any person known to be "tainted" by so much as a drop of Negro blood found himself stripped of incentives to self-improvement. The ensuing frustration, manifested in every aspect of Negro life in Washington, forms the central theme of Negro history of the period.

For upper-class Negroes civil rights were the key to progress. The nibbling away at those rights began early in the Hayes administration. Colored men here, though disturbed over the President's conciliation of southern Bourbons, still counted on the local anti-discrimination laws for protection: the municipal ordinances of 1869 and 1870 were still in force within Washington's city limits, the territorial civil rights acts still applied to Georgetown and county as well as to Washington, and a congressional act of 1875 was added insurance. After 1878 violations of these laws occurred with mounting frequency, but for a time they were apparently either too trivial or too skillfully cloaked to lead to court action. The *Peoples Advocate*, in 1879 Washington's only colored newspaper, urged Negroes to concentrate on fair play: instead of suing white proprietors for refusing them accommodation, first file complaints against Negro barbers who refused to serve other colored men. Two years later the editor was no longer sure of the wisdom of those tactics. "A respectable colored lady or gentleman, unless it happens to be a man like Frederick Douglass, John F. Cook, or Register Bruce [former United States Senator from Mississippi], is not readily accommodated, if at all, in the eating establishments, no matter how genteel he may be in appearance or in manners." The result was "more or less friction between the keepers of these saloons and a class of our citizens rapidly growing in wealth and intelligence." Still Washington Negroes relied upon patience to destroy prejudice.

In the summer of 1883 a Negro visitor from Connecticut sued a Washington restaurant owner under the criminal section of the federal Civil Rights Act. Newspapers throughout the country discussed the case, partly because it was only the second suit to be brought under the act of 1875, partly because the argument for the defense had an ominous logic: a government which sanctioned separate colored schools could not reasonably require a restaurant proprietor to seat boisterous unwelcome Negroes in a dining-room with whites; he had offered to serve the colored man in the pantry. The judge reviewed all earlier decisions in local civil rights cases, noted that several verdicts had been adverse to the plaintiffs, but in this case found against the defendant and fined him $500.

It was at best a Pyrrhic victory. It strengthened white animosities and inspired pronouncements that the judge's interpretation of the law would force restaurant owners either to accept an exclusively black clientele, or see their businesses ruined, or both. Negroes native to the District were ironically rewarded for their past forbearance by repeated statements citing their eight-year failure to sue under the federal law as proof that the color line was unobjectionable to them. Two months after the decision of August 1883, the United States Supreme Court declared the Civil Rights Act unconstitutional in the states, although still binding in the District of Columbia and all United States territories. Educated Negroes in Washington were angry, and the ignorant were badly frightened, expecting to see the whipping post brought back at any moment. The most optimistic view was that the Court would in time recant and in the meantime District laws would suffice. But no one favoring racial legal equality pretended that the decision was not a blow.[3]

[3] *Peoples Advocate*, 5 Jul, 15, 29 Nov 1879, 10 Jul 1880, 6 Aug 1881, 25 Aug 1883 (hereafter cited as *Advocate*); Washington *Bee*, 4 Aug, 8 Sep 1883 (inasmuch as the local colored press carried in practically every issue items discussing the topics dealt with in this chapter, specific citations of the *Advocate*, 1878-1834, and the *Bee*, 1882-1901, are hereafter confined to direct quotations and occasional fact or comment not found easily elsewhere); *Star*, 7, 13, 16, 18, 24 Aug, 17, 24 Oct 1883; *Chronicle*, 21 Oct 1883; *Sentinel*, 3 Nov 1883; Cleveland *Leader*, 23, 26 Oct, 26 Nov 1883.

During the next two decades local colored men filed a dozen or more suits; some were dismissed, others won, such as the case against a lunch room proprietor who had not posted a price list and had overcharged a Negro outrageously by demanding 50¢ for three eggs, some biscuits, and a cup of coffee. In the 1880's bar rooms generally served colored customers, but lunch rooms and ice cream parlors usually excluded them, a source of particular irritation to "genteel" Negroes. Yet the "genteel" clearly indicated their readiness to have vulgar blacks denied service. Petitions submitted to Congress in 1886 asked for stronger local laws extended to areas not covered in the municipal and territorial acts, but new laws seemed unlikely to improve white tempers. Congress dismissed all proposals for racial legislation, on the one hand bills forbidding miscegenation, and, on the other, those demanding a change in the District Medical Society's discriminatory rules. In the fall of 1900 a suit against the owner of the Opera House for refusing to let a colored man occupy the orchestra seat he had paid for netted the plaintiff damages of one cent.[4]

Nor were Negroes guiltless. A number of Negro-owned barber shops and some hotels and restaurants run by colored men would not accept Negro customers. A circular of 1888, for example, announced: "Preston's Pension Office barber shop, first class in every particular. Devoted *Strictly* to *White Trade*. The rumor that this shop has been serving any Colored Trade is false in every particular." The white press called attention to such incidents. "The refusal is based, of course," remarked the *Star*, "not on color prejudice, but on the business consideration that the best paying class of customers can be retained only by excluding those who for any reason are objectionable to their fastidious notions."[5] After the founding of the short-

[4] *Star*, 8, 22 Nov 1884, 4 Feb, 10 Dec 1887, 18 Feb 1888; *Rec*, 47C, 1S, pp. 1408-10, 1839; ptn, S49A-H12, 18 Jan 1886; *Bee*, 1884-1899, 24 Nov 1900; S Rpt 1050, 52C, 1S, Ser 2915.
[5] *Star*, 12 Dec 1887; *Bee*, 21 Jul 1888.

lived Afro-American League in 1890, a Washington branch sent delegates to its national conventions, but disunity, lack of a positive program to combat racism, and the magnitude of the problem stripped the organization of effectiveness. Its successor, the Afro-American Council, which came into being in 1898, was largely controlled by Booker T. Washington, whose seeming subservience to whites alienated Negro militants. As Jim Crow laws began to multiply in the southern states, Negroes in the District realized they were far better off than most of their race; but they saw that the local anti-discrimination laws had come to be more honored in the breach than in the observance.

Chance, moreover, played into the hands of segregationists. In 1901 Congress accepted the first part of a codification of District law but left "the second or municipal part" to be revised and adopted later. Although Congress specified that existing police regulations, unless expressly repealed, should continue in force—a stipulation that meant the civil rights laws were still valid—the fact that the published code contained no mention of the anti-discrimination ordinances probably encouraged white men to risk ignoring them.[6]

Washington's old, well-established colored families like the Cooks and the Wormleys had reason for a time to believe that they and distinguished newcomers such as Frederick Douglass, Blanche K. Bruce, and Dr. Augusta could enjoy some rights not specifically protected by law. Good manners, professional status, and money made them acceptable residents of any locality provided they did not obtrude themselves socially upon white people. But cultivated Negroes, even those

[6] *Colored American*, 9 Apr 1898; *Bee*, 16 Nov 1889, 27 Aug 1898; August Meier, "Booker T. Washington and the Negro Press," *Journal of Negro History*, xxxviii, 85, n; *Rec*, 56C, 2S, pp. 3497, 3586, 3603; Walter S. Cox, "Attempts to Obtain a Law Code for the District of Columbia," CHS *Rec*, iii, 127-32; Phineas Indritz, "Post Civil War Ordinances Prohibiting Racial Discrimination in the District of Columbia," *Georgetown Law Journal*, xlii, 196-201.

who looked almost white, discovered that each passing year made it harder for them to purchase or rent comfortable houses without paying exorbitant prices; by the 1890's, they could rarely buy at all in a conveniently located, orderly neighborhood. Mary Church Terrell's *A Colored Woman in a White World* tells of endless humiliations in the course of her househunt. Yet her husband was a *cum laude* graduate of Harvard, a respected lawyer, and after 1896 a member of the Board of Trade, and she herself was a graduate of Oberlin and one of two women before 1900 to be appointed to the school board.

Rising rentals hastened the exodus of Negro householders who in the seventies had lived along 16th Street a few blocks above Lafayette Square and out beyond Scott Circle. As the real estate boom in northwest Washington gained momentum, colored people moved farther from the center of the city. Whether sheer economics or, as rumor had it, combinations of real estate agents kept respectable Negroes from moving into desirable localities, the result was the same. It did not mean that clear-cut solid black belts arose outside of which Negroes could not find housing; some intersprinkling of white and Negro dwellings continued down into the 1930's. But by 1900 the barrier of caste, seemingly collapsing in the late 1860's, had become stronger than ever. The one notable exception lay in the Board of Trade: James T. Wormley was a charter member, and Dr. Charles Purvis, Washington's leading colored physician, George F. Cook, superintendent of the colored schools, and Robert Terrell were elected in the mid-1890's.[7]

Disregard of civil rights as a rule affected only upper-class Negroes. The workings of the criminal law, on the other hand,

[7] *Advocate*, 8 Sep 1883; *Star*, 4 Feb 1887; Edward Ingle, *The Negro in the District of Columbia*, in *Johns Hopkins University Studies in Historical and Political Science*, 11th Series, nos. III and IV, pp. 50-51, 90 (hereafter cited as Ingle, *The Negro in D.C.*); Coroner's maps in Comrs Rpts, 1882, p. 508, 1890, p. 826, 1900, p. 826; Joseph W. Moore, *Picturesque Washington*, p. 139; Mary Church Terrell, *A Colored Woman in a White World*, pp. 113-19; membership lists in *Rpts B/Tr*, 1897, 1899; *Colored American*, 26 Mar 1898; *Bee*, 1898-1901.

touched the lives of countless blacks living on a bare subsistence level. Of those some were undoubtedly vicious; and some, though vaguely well-intentioned, took to thieving, drunkenness, and disorderliness as the easiest way to blunder through a world that offered them at best very little. In a city where only one person in three was colored, the number of Negro arrests exceeded the number of white every year after 1889. People as ignorant of their rights as of their obligations were, to be sure, in some measure at the mercy of the police, and police brutality was all too common. The *Bee* asserted that policemen, particularly the Irishmen on the force, frequently clubbed Negroes savagely when arresting them, and the dark-skinned man was always the first suspect when a crime occurred. Officers "took delight in arresting every little colored boy they see on the street, who may be doing something not at all offensive, and allow the white boys to do what they please." The individual prejudice of police court justices was likely then to determine the severity of the sentences imposed. Perhaps the number of Negroes charged with misdemeanors and felonies was as much an index of white men's aversion to colored as a reflection of Negroes' criminal tendencies. Calvin Chase, editor of the *Bee*, as a boy having seen his father shot down in cold blood and his white assailant go unpunished, was vitriolic about Washington police methods. But more temperate men than he believed that racial equality before the law had largely disappeared by the end of the century.[8]

Despite the decline of Negroes' legal position, political preferment for colored men fell off surprisingly little. It is true that after 1880 a Negro rarely received a federal post of any importance, and after President Garfield and President Arthur failed them, colored men ceased to talk of appointments to the

[8] *Star*, 15 Mar 1882, 27 Oct 1887, 1 Jan 1897; *Chronicle*, 10 Mar 1895, 7 Jun 1896; *Sentinel*, 15 Oct 1892, 25 Nov 1893; *Bee*, 6 Aug 1887; Ingle, *The Negro in D.C.*, pp. 100-101; William J. Simmons, *Men of Mark, Eminent, Progressive and Rising*, pp. 118-19; Elizabeth M. Chapin, *American Court Gossip, or Life at the Nation's Capital*, pp. 36-40.

Cabinet. But before the depression of the 1890's Negroes held as many minor clerkships and custodial jobs as they had formerly. Frederick Douglass, though shorn of some of the one-time dignities of the Marshal of the District, kept that post through President Hayes' administration, while the lucrative position of District Recorder of Deeds continued to go to Negroes. President Garfield, moreover, appointed ex-Senator Bruce of Mississippi Register of the Treasury, a place that would be filled by a Negro for the next thirty-two years. Both before and after the introduction of competitive civil service examinations, colored men feared for their jobs when a new administration took over, but even the shake-up anticipated during Grover Cleveland's first term did not cut the number of Negroes on the federal payroll; on the contrary, scrupulous fairness in grading examinations enabled more Negroes than ever before to enter government service. In 1891 out of 23,144 federal employees in Washington, nearly 2,400 were colored; they held 337 of the 6,120 jobs in the Interior Department, and 127 ranked as copyists, "transcribers," and clerks. Once appointed, Negroes rarely encountered overt hostility from fellow white employees. Negroes got far less consideration from the District commissioners. In 1879 one appointment out of fifty to the police force was colored, none to the fire department. Later policy gave Negroes some of the jobs but never established a stable ratio of colored to white. Outside the colored school system, in 1891 Negroes held only 25 District positions above the rank of messenger and day laborer.

Cleveland's second administration, troubled as it was by country-wide unemployment, saw a drop in Negro preferment and the dismissal of "surplus" Negro clerks. Republican prosperity, launched with the election of William McKinley, failed to restore the earlier proportion of colored employees in spite of the liberal attitude of Secretary Lyman Gage and his assistants in the Treasury Department. The falling off in other departments, if less pronounced than white men expected, was at once a bitter disappointment to Negroes and a gloomily foreseen development in keeping with trends in other areas of American life.[9] Negro pride was badly hurt, moreover, when the new president of Howard University filled seven out of nine faculty vacancies with whites, and when General George Harries refused to enroll any of the all-Negro Washington Cadet Corps in the District regiment sent to Cuba in 1898.[10]

The collapse of earlier hopes for political and legal equality might have distressed Negroes less had their economic opportunities widened consistently. With the District's colored population growing from the 57,000 of 1880 to 90,000 twenty years later, Negroes trained in the professions seemingly should have found abundant openings. Besides several hundred colored teachers, Washington in the 1890's had about one hundred qualified physicians, somewhat fewer dentists, over ninety ministers, and scores of lawyers. Negro doctors, barred from the District Medical Society, formed the Medico-Chirurgical Society in 1884, the first Negro medical association in the United States. But except for the pastors, including those without much schooling, colored professional men faced hard sledding. About ten applicants for every teaching post in the school system created intense competition. Relatively few Negroes could afford to pay doctors', dentists', and lawyers' fees no matter how modest, and a discouragingly large proportion of the colored people of means preferred to deal with white men. The *Colored American*, in 1898 the *Bee*'s new competitor, observed that colored people in Washington went to a colored doctor "only when we wish to run a bill we do not intend to pay." Dozens of law-

[9] Laurence John Wesley Hayes, *The Negro Federal Government Worker, A Study of His Classification Status in the District of Columbia, 1883-1938*, pp. 22-25 (hereafter cited as Hayes, *Negro Govt Worker*); Cleveland *Leader*, 7 Nov 1884; *Nation*, xcvii, 114; *Sentinel*, 10 Apr 1880; *Advocate*, 3 Dec 1881; *Bee*, 1882-1901; *Star*, 9 May 1883, 2 Feb 1887; Ingle, *The Negro in D.C.*, pp. 48-49; Rpt Sec/Int, 1895, p. 724, Ser 3383; Summers, ed., *The Cabinet Diary of William L. Wilson*, p. 96.

[10] Capt. George W. Evans, "The Militia of the District of Columbia," CHS *Rec*, xxviii, 95-105; *Bee*, 3 Jul 1897, 13 Jan 1900.

yers, in a frantic scramble to find clients, hawked their services about the Police Court.

Colored business enterprises also suffered from Negroes' reluctance to patronize men of their own race. The failure of the Freedmen's Bank in 1874, although due primarily to white exploitation, had shattered confidence in their capacity to handle finances. A colored savings bank opened in 1888 increased the list of its depositors yearly, but for commercial purposes Negroes used white banks. As in other American cities, Negro merchants had enormous difficulty in competing with white for the colored trade and could rarely cater successfully to both races.[11] The career of John A. Gray, a restaurant owner, illustrates some of the hazards. "He kept one of the first houses in the city," reported the *Bee*. "He first opened it for white people and was having a success until the Negroes kept clamoring for a respectable place to go. He opened his house to the high-toned colored people and in less than a year they broke him up." Undeterred by the refusal of white merchants to employ Negro help, colored families persisted in trading at white shops. Perhaps credit was easier there or the selection of goods better, but a pettier motive, some Negroes believed, was more basic: in the city's colored business world the "great impediment has been jealousy and a dislike to see each other succeed."

Caterers were one of the few groups able to avoid the complications of seeking mixed or purely colored patronage, for the business, unique to Washington, depended solely upon a white clientele. Unlike the modern term, catering in the capital

[11] *Colored American*, 14 May 1898; W. Montague Cobb, "Washington, D.C.," in Dietrich C. Reitzes, *Negroes and Medicine*, pp. 193-94; Walter L. Fleming, *The Freedmen's Savings Bank*, pp. 53-99, 129-30; W. E. B. DuBois, ed., *The Negro in Business, The Report of the Fourth Conference for the Study of the Negro Problems, held at Atlanta University*, May 30-31, 1899, pp. 13, 28-29, 56-61 (hereafter the special studies and the reports of the proceedings of the conferences sponsored by Atlanta University every May from 1896 to 1900 are cited only by title, conference number, and date); *Advocate*, 30 Aug 1879; *Bee*, 31 Jul 1886; Ingle, *The Negro in D.C.*, pp. 91-92; John H. Harmon, Arnett G. Lindsay, and Carter G. Woodson, *The Negro as a Businessman*, pp. 34, 51-55.

of the 1880's and 1890's meant delivering hot meals twice a day to people living in rented rooms who wished to escape from the restaurant or dismal boardinghouse table by breakfasting and dining in their rooms. The best caterers charged from $25 to $30 a month per person. Those with fast teams of horses could deliver well-cooked dishes in the specially constructed double-racked tin containers before the food cooled. A skillful caterer with a hundred clients could clear a considerable sum in a year, despite the decline of his business in the months between congressional sessions. Since the enterprise, however profitable, smacked of menial service, white men rarely competed.

A few Negroes, it is true, made money in fields considered wholly dignified, notably real estate, building, and selling life insurance or shares in benefit and relief associations. James Wormley, owner of the famous Wormley House, left an estate of over $100,000; his sons, after nearly doubling their inheritance, so gossip said, by betting on President Harrison's election in 1888, put the family fortune into the construction business. Negroes who had owned local real estate before the war and had hung on to it through the disasters of the Board of Public Works era and the Freedmen's Bank failure might be very well off indeed, although the number whose holdings were ever extensive was certainly small. District Tax Collector John F. Cook, himself said to be the largest taxpayer of his race, reported in 1887 two local colored men worth $100,000, two worth $75,000, a flour merchant worth $50,000, and some forty men with property valued at a figure between $10,000 and $25,000.[12]

While the lack of racial solidarity hurt the Negro professions and business enterprises, the increasing hostility of white workingmen and the bars erected by labor organizations severely

[12] *Bee*, 22 Oct 1887, 17 Nov 1888, 12 Jan 1889, 12 Jul 1890; Cleveland *Leader*, 5 Jan, 7 Apr 1883; *Star*, 23 Oct 1884, 18 Apr 1926; Simmons, *Men of Mark*, pp. 249-50; Harmon et al., *Negro as Businessman*, p. 91.

handicapped the lower-class Negro. An analysis of 1881 attributed the troubles of Philadelphia's colored workmen to foreign immigrants: "Southern cities were built by colored mechanical labor. In this city twenty years before the late war, it was no unusual thing to find a majority of colored mechanics engaged in all the leading trades. . . . But Irish emigration was destined to strike a blow at the colored mechanic, from which it will take years for him to recover." Negroes in Washington looked upon Irishmen as enemies, but foreign immigrants in the capital were too few in the last decades of the century to be a determining factor in the local labor market.

In the early eighties the local carpenters' union drew no official color line, and one of the two mechanics' unions had mixed membership, but white mechanics made life for their colored fellows miserable in a dozen minor ways, and, by refusing to accept colored apprentices, the unions gradually excluded all Negroes. A colored lodge of the Knights of Labor, organized in 1884 as the Thad Stevens Assembly, fell apart even before the Haymarket tragedy in Chicago two years later undermined the national brotherhood. In 1886 a Negro waiters' union appeared, but within a decade colored men found that occupations "which by common consent were regarded as belonging to them, such as waiters and the like, are now being monopolized by the whites." Booker T. Washington's exhortations to Negroes to think less about political equality and more about acquiring competence as workers fell on sterile soil in the District; here economic independence appeared to be unattainable merely by hard work.[13]

To combat trade union discrimination, "the curse of which has more than any other, fettered the energies of the colored people," and to recapture civil rights, non-segregated schools seemed to some Negroes the first essential; only early association of the races would induce a "more generous spirit" in white

[13] *Advocate*, 21 Apr 1882; *Bee*, 1 Jan 1897, 8 Oct 1898; *Star*, 26 Jul 1885; Simmons, *Men of Mark*, pp. 270-72; *Sentinel*, 30 Mar 1889.

men. Unfortunately for the proponents of mixed schools, the opposition of other Negroes strengthened as the colored school system expanded and the number of teaching posts grew. The opening of a colored high school in 1878, two years before a white high school was established, weakened the integrationists' contention that the white schools invariably provided a quality of education superior to anything available in the colored schools. In actuality the Miner Fund, not tax money, supported the colored high school as well as the Negro normal school. The question of mixed schools came to the fore in 1881 and 1882 when the school trustees allowed two or three very light colored children to attend white schools. While Negro advocates of separate systems insisted that more money and Negro trustees less prone to toady to whites and less ready to show favoritism would correct every shortcoming in the colored schools, the *Star* declared school integration a "purely sentimental" notion:

"There is a small sprinkling of colored children in the white schools, but for the most part the colored people prefer to have their separate school organization with a superintendent and teachers of their own race; just as they prefer to maintain their own . . . benevolent and social associations. The colored schools get their full share of school moneys; and in proportion to numbers are supplied with better school accommodations than the whites. For various reasons the colored children get on better in schools of their own. One is that they are spared the disadvantageous competition with white children of their own age who have had greater opportunities at home and elsewhere for advancement in their studies. Again were the schools to be merged it would necessarily throw 165 colored teachers out of employment, as it could not be expected that the white school population of the District—outnumbering the colored about two to one—should give up their teachers to make room for colored teachers."

". . . Better let well enough alone."[14]

The comparative census figures on adults unable to write suggest the handicap under which the children of hundreds of Negro parents labored:

	1880	*1890*	*1900*
White	5.4	2.67	1.86
Colored	59.3	39.4	30.47

From the mid-1880's onward one group of colored people argued that vocational training was a wiser goal for the Negro schools than a more literary education; a curriculum like that of the white schools should wait until the economic level of the average colored family had risen enough to enable Negro children to benefit from academic courses. In the 1890's Booker T. Washington, by then head of Tuskegee Institute in Alabama, began to popularize that thesis among white people who saw in it a way to create a permanent, docile working class. In Washington dissidents, although believing the plan equivalent to giving up the fight for racial equality and accepting a position of inferiority for decades to come, gradually abandoned the campaign for integrated schools. After 1900 that issue dropped out of sight for forty years.

Meanwhile Negroes, anxious to develop an independent school system as good in every particular as the white, vigilantly watched the school board, particularly its colored members. Salaries were nearly 10 percent lower and teaching loads heavier in the colored than in the white schools. At an annual salary of $750 a colored high school teacher earned $74.54 less than his white counterpart, and the differential for grammar and primary grade teachers was as great or greater. In 1890, white classes averaged forty-one children to a teacher, the colored forty-seven. Otherwise the two systems ran generally

[14] *Advocate*, 25 Feb 1882; *Star*, 14 Sep 1881, 22 Feb 1882; *Bee*, 30 Dec 1882; *Rpt School Trustees*, pp. 29, 33, 67.

parallel. In spite of Negro complaints about favoritism in teaching appointments and incompetence on the part of George F.
Cook, superintendent since 1870, the Negro schools made a
good showing. Somewhat lower standards obtained in the
colored grade schools than in the white, but in examinations
given all high school students in 1899, the colored high school
scored higher than either the Eastern or the Western High
Schools. Still when Congress reorganized the entire system in
1900, most Negroes evidently concluded their schools would
gain more in efficiency than they lost in prestige by having a
white superintendent put above the colored assistant superintendent.[15]

Unhappily, relatively few Negro children stayed in school
beyond the fourth grade, and of those who finished the eighth
grade, still fewer, especially of the boys, went on. "There are
inducements to keep white children in the white High School,"
remarked the *Bee*. "Our colored citizens should see to it that
some effort be made to keep their boys in the schools." Quite
apart from their poverty, the seeming futility of acquiring more
than an acquaintance with the three R's deterred many Negro
families from making the effort. They saw well-educated girls,
barred from suitable occupations by an inflexible caste system,
drift into the life of the *demi-monde* and Negro college graduates forced for want of something better to take jobs as waiters
and hotel bell boys. It is not surprising that 325 of the 367
students at Howard University in 1898 were enrolled in its
secondary school; as none of the 42 taking the college course

[15] Williston Lofton, "The Development of Public Education for Negroes
in Washington, D.C., A Study of Separate but Equal Accommodations,"
pp. 164-87 (dissertation, American Univ, hereafter cited as Lofton, "Sep-
arate but Equal"); *Tenth U.S. Census*, 1880, *Population*, pp. 916-25;
Twelfth U.S. Census, 1900, *Population*, II, Pt II, 22-23, 424-25, 434-35;
Bee, 11 Feb 1888, 20 Aug 1897; ptns, S54A-J19, n.d., S56A-J14, 6 Apr
1900; *Rpts School Trustees*, 1890, 1892, pp. 153-202, 1899, pp. 273-97;
S Rpt 711, 56C, 1S, pp. 1-4, 125-26, 195-96, 230-31, 296-97, and
Supplemental Rpt, Pt 2, p. 14, Ser 3889; Booker T. Washington, *Up From
Slavery*, p. 91; Ingle, *The Negro in D.C.*, pp. 34-37, 103.

were white men, the original ideal of a bi-racial institution vanished.[16]

Long before the Negro intelligentsia saw that public schooling in itself was unlikely to elevate greatly the general level of Negro society, Washington's colored aristocrats had begun to detach themselves from the Negro rank and file; for their own reassurance they must sharpen Negro class distinctions whether or not white people recognized them. Educated colored men in other cities also defended the thesis that the social equality of all Negroes was a concept destructive to racial progress. In 1880 a letter to the *Advocate* declared that Frederick Douglass, John F. Cook, and others to whom the community had once looked for leadership "have shown conclusively how little they care whether other colored men sink, as long as they swim." Calvin Chase of the *Bee*, not himself one of Washington's "first families" but occupying a place in the upper stratum of the rank just below, alternately defended the "exclusive set" and attacked it for a snobbery that he believed originated in the determination of the Lotus Club after 1863 to force contrabands to keep to themselves. Later societies heightened that snobbery. "The Monday Night Literary is a cast organization," wrote Chase. "There is more intelligence excluded than there is in the association . . . there are few holding clerkships who belong." Members had ceased to give New Year's Day receptions because they did not want to meet "objectionable upstarts."

The Negro press repeatedly insisted "There is more discrimination among the colored people than there is among the white against the colored." A petition complained to Congress in 1896 that only daughters of "the favored few" were admitted to the colored normal school. "The would-be leaders . . . John

[16] *Rpts School Trustees*, 1880, p. 152, 1886, p. 13, 1892, p. 17; *Rpt B of Education of the District of Columbia*, 1901, pp. 140-43 (hereafter cited as *Rpt B/Ed*); *Bee*, 14 May 1887; W. E. B. DuBois, ed., *The College-Bred Negro*, (Fifth Atlanta Conference, 1900), p. 16.

M. Langston excepted, have taken no interest in the general welfare of the masses of our people; political office by all means, after that, their wish is total exclusion from their race and to be white." Yet most of that small group composing the highest circle of Negro society were indeed nearly white, and many of them had personal distinction as scholars, office-holders, and professional men. They were certainly culturally closer to the white community than to the lower-class Negro. In displaying an ungenerous attitude toward their inferiors, they were behaving little differently from most self-made white men who reached positions of eminence in the face of enormous obstacles.[17]

The *Sentinel*, Washington's German-American newspaper edited by a former abolitionist, presented the tolerant white man's view of the Negro's position in 1883: "The colored people of Washington enjoy all the social and political rights that law can give them, without protest and without annoyance. The public conveyances are open to them, and the theatres, the jury box, the spoils of party power are theirs. Many of these men are wealthy. . . .

"But the color line is rigidly drawn in what is known as society. Wealth, learning, official place, give no colored family the right or privilege of entering the best or the commonest white society on terms of equality or endurance. In this respect the colored race lives as separate and exclusive a life as in the days of slavery, and as a drop of African blood was once held to make a man a negro, so now it taints him and makes an immutable barrier against social recognition.

"[Ex-Senator] Blanche K. Bruce, [formerly of Mississippi but now Washington's leading Negro,] lives in a handsome house that he owns on M Street. It is richly furnished . . . Mrs.

[17] *Advocate*, 4 Dec 1880; *Star*, 11 May 1880; *Bee*, 10 May 1884, 18 Sep 1886, 18 Sep 1887; ptn, H54A-H7.6, 2 Jun 1896; see cuts accompanying the articles on Washington Negroes in Simmons, *Men of Mark*; Richard Bardolph, "The Distinguished Negro in America, 1770-1936," *American Historical Review*, LX, 527-47.

Bruce is a handsome woman, with not a suggestion of her race in her face, and whose manners are regarded as the consummation of ease, grace and courtesy. She dresses as richly and handsomely as any woman in the city. In official circles Mr. Bruce is received in courtesy and as a political equal, but there the line is drawn."

Envious Negroes, averred the *Sentinel*, considered this exclusive set not good enough for whites and too good for its own race, but the next lower rank of Negro society was equally detached from the class below. Government clerks formed the basis of the second stratum. "They are well dressed, seem to prosper and are happy. For the great bulk of the colored population—the servants, laborers and the poor—they have sympathy, but have no more social relations than a white family would." Those at the base of the social pyramid "in the main are thriftless, living from hand to mouth; happy if they do nothing, happy if they get a job. Their social instincts are gratified by the organization and maintenance of societies of all sorts, benevolent, patriotic, social and economic. There are nearly one thousand of these organizations, supported almost entirely by the laboring colored people."[18]

That portrayal, if in any degree fitting the Washington of 1883, was too simple and too cheerful in tone to describe the Negro community a decade or more later. Before the end of the century the class structure resembled a pyramid less than a truncated cone capped by a needle. From the strata below, the Negroes who danced on the point of the needle appeared to be, not angels, but scarcely more accessible than heavenly creatures. Of the District's 700 octoroons and 1,100 quadroons, those who had, in addition to light color, the qualifications of antiquity of family, money, education, and honorable occupation belonged to the aristocracy; "honorable occupations" included the professions, political posts of more than trivial importance, banking, real estate brokerage, and businesses not

[18] *Sentinel*, 22 Dec 1883.

tinged with menial service. Washington's Negro "Four Hundred," as the *Bee* dubbed the aristocrats, probably numbered not more than sixty or seventy families.

The middle class in the 1890's apparently derived mainly from the District's 18,000 mulattoes. Only less fully than the Four Hundred with their very light skins and generally non-Negroid features were the mulattoes conscious of gradations of color: those of "doe-nut or ginger-cake color . . . said those blacker than themselves should be ignored." Yet the relative flexibility of the middle class permitted the occasional acceptance of exceptionally able, ambitious, full-blooded Negroes. Minor government employees still formed the core of this group, but even a government clerk, if a newcomer to the city, could not hope for immediate entree to upper-middle-class circles. Whether the barber, the caterer, the livery-stable man, the oyster-house owner, or the proprietor of any other small business was acknowledged as upper or lower middle class evidently depended upon the extent of his business success as well as his nativity and his complexion. Warnings frequently appeared in the *Bee* about unsuitable marriages between scions of established families and those of doubtful antecedents who wormed their way into the "social circle" by joining a "tony" church, by enrolling for a few weeks in one of Howard University's professional schools, or by making a specious show of great wealth. Differentiations among the "masses," that is, chiefly the city's thousands of full-blooded Negroes, were not a topic the press bothered to explore.[19]

From 1884 to 1898 Washington's Negro press was the *Bee*. It prided itself on its sting aimed at the shoddy and evil. Yet back-biting and destructive jealousy of one class and one Negro toward another became a striking feature of the paper. Let anyone get his head ever so little above his associates, and his

[19] *Bee*, 30 May 1885, 8 Jun 1889; W. E. B. DuBois, ed., *The Negro in Business* (Fourth Atlanta Conference, 1899), pp. 13, 19-20; *Eleventh U.S. Census*, 1890, *Population*, I, 397.

individual accomplishments and former services were forgotten in vitriolic attacks upon his real or imagined self-seeking. Instead of applauding a colored man who won recognition, especially from whites, his fellows at once set to work to belittle him and accuse him of sycophancy and putting on airs. The *New National Era* had eschewed that line, and the *Peoples Advocate*, which ceased publication in 1884, pursued it very little. The *Bee*, without wholly abandoning a crusading point of view, indulged in more sweeping condemnations of individual Negroes and organizations the longer it ran. Perhaps its publisher found it sold better when it concentrated upon scandal and malicious gossip. A comment on a problem affecting Washington as a whole was a rarity.

Booker T. Washington, after some months at the Baptist Wayland Seminary in 1878-1879, decided that Washington was no place for a Negro who wished to dedicate his life to helping his race; here false standards and selfishness predominated. Among immigrant minorities and among the Jews in the District, a sense of group solidarity produced mutual helpfulness. Not so among Negroes. The pressures of caste which kept the gifted colored man from going as far as his talents would otherwise permit split colored Washington into jealously competing fragments, with results damaging to every Negro. Congress, noted a Philadelphia journal, was naturally disinclined to do anything for Washington's colored people, because their squabbling made them ridiculous: rivals claimed "that this one's father was a horse thief, that one doesn't know who his father was, another is too black, another is too light and therefore does not represent the race, another does not belong to the best families and still another is an interloper." Bitterly the *Bee* asked in 1887: "Who of our so called colored representative men can point to a single thing of a public character beneficial to the colored people established and fostered by them? To their shame and to the humiliation of the race the record is a blank, and with all our boast about our wealthy . . . men the race is dependent upon the charity of whites." Yet if "you talk to our people about an excursion down the river in August, or a cake walk in December, they will listen to you and will no doubt purchase several tickets." And a large part of the funds of the mutual benefit societies, in which much of the social life of working-class Negroes centered, went for elaborate funerals rather than help for the living.[20]

The assertion that well-to-do Negroes never lifted finger for the needy was, of course, an exaggeration. John F. Cook, for years an active member of the citizens' relief committee, was also a trustee of the Home for Destitute Colored Women and Children, while a dozen public-spirited Negro women served on the board of manageresses. The woman who founded the Home for Friendless Girls also organized an Aid Society at the Berean Baptist Church. About the same time, two or three Negro women opened a free kindergarten and day nursery for the children of working mothers, and in the 1890's the newly organized Colored Women's League expanded the program. Although Alexander Crummel, rector of St. Luke's Episcopal Church, was more concerned with developing character in his people than with their material progress, he raised a large sum of money for the Episcopal Freedmen's Aid Society by sale of copies of one of his speeches. In 1887 the Colored Baptist Home Mission Society was "putting shoes on the feet of the poor, clothing on them, and giving immediate aid," but $95.72 represented the total sum collected in the course of several months from Washington's thirty-five colored Baptist churches and the members of the society.

During the worst of the depression of the nineties Negro volunteers worked with the Associated Charities, and the "Hill

[20] Jesse Lawson to Booker T. Washington, 6 May 1902, Booker T. Washington Mss (L.C.); Washington, *Up From Slavery*, pp. 88-90; *Congressional Globe*, 41C, 2S, p. 842; Ingle, *The Negro in D.C.*, p. 109; Philadelphia *Odd Fellows Journal* quoted in *Bee*, 23 Feb 1901; *Bee*, 15 Jan 1887, 12 Nov 1898.

Group" on 6th Street, moved by the suffering of the poor at the foot of the hill, distributed food and fuel in that neighborhood. Probably a good many relatively well-to-do individuals gave help without working through any organization, just as desperately poor Negro families often took care of the children of even poorer neighbors. From a mother-child center, opened in 1895, came the Southwest Social Settlement, and that year Miss Amanda Bowen, assisted by funds from the Metropolitan African Methodist Episcopal Church, launched the Sojourner Truth Home for Working Girls. Three years later the Colored Women's League undertook "Rescue Work" among young women. A study prepared for a conference on Negro problems held in Atlanta in 1898 listed thirty-eight Negro churches in Washington which spent $4,300 for charity, contributed to the support of eighty-three benevolent and missionary societies, and supplied twelve workers in the slums and the jail. The individual generosity of Professor William Hart of Howard University made possible the Hart Farm School for colored boys. And in 1900 a colored woman started the Stoddard Baptist Home for aged Negroes.

Yet when everything was added together, the record of Negro charities while not "blank" was distinctly thin, thinner than during the Civil War and Reconstruction, if accounts of that period be trustworthy. The impressively long list of welfare projects at the end of the century was deceptive, for most of the undertakings were small-scale and short-lived unless white people came to the rescue. And the uncooperativeness of well-to-do Negroes chilled the ardor of white philanthropists. "We all know," a white woman told a congressional committee, "that a good deal of what was good in the race has gone and they are now in a state of transition." What exasperated whites failed to take into account was that the social pressures that fostered philanthropy in the white community could not operate effectively among people who felt their precarious position in the city's over-all social structure progressively and inescapably weakening further. And white people probably attributed larger resources to prosperous Negroes than they actually had.[21]

Negro pastors and Negro churches, which in earlier years had not only provided spiritual leadership but taken an active part in lightening parishioners' material distress, apparently lost sight of both goals as congregations vied with each other in building big, costly edifices. Between the worldliness of the sophisticated churches and the excessive otherworldiness of those wedded to a somewhat primitive, highly emotional religion teaching that only heaven or hell in the hereafter mattered, the efforts of the handful of selfless civic-minded Negroes met with defeat. Proposals to turn over to the National Colored Home the proceeds of Emancipation Day celebrations fizzled because the money from ticket sales went into the pockets of "sharks" or for the rental and elaborate decoration of floats for the parades. Lack of funds threatened to close the Sojourner Truth Home three years after it opened. A small indebtedness, which modest gifts could have wiped out, shut down the colored YMCA. According to one critic of his people, when Negroes contributed to any good works their motive was notoriety, not Christian charity. Such behavior was characteristic of the *nouveaux riches* the world over, but the disturbing fact remained that the generosity that had once distinguished Washington's upper-class Negro society was rarely in evidence at the end of the century.[22]

[21] Katherine Hosmer, "What Women Have Done in Washington City Affairs," *Municipal Affairs*, ii, 514; W. E. B. DuBois, ed., *Some Efforts of Negroes for Their Own Social Betterment* (3rd Atlanta Conference, 1897), pp. 14, 36-37, 57-59; *Bee*, 14 May 1887; Cleveland *Leader*, 29 Feb 1884; *Advocate*, 5 Feb, 20 Nov 1881; Ch Hrgs, p. 56, Ser 3565; *Anl Rpt of the Home for Destitute Colored Women and Children*, 1891; Inabel Lindsay, "Participation of Negroes in the Establishment of Welfare Services, 1865-1900, with special reference to the District of Columbia, Maryland and Virginia," pp. 124, 129-30, 137-55, 159, 164, 170-73 (dissertation, Univ. of Pittsburgh, hereafter cited as Lindsay, "Negro Welfare Services").

[22] Lindsay, "Negro Welfare Services," pp. 105-08, 112, 115-18, 133; *Advocate*, 5 Apr 1884; *Bee*, 1887-1901; Ingle, *The Negro in D.C.*, pp. 95-100, 107; Carter G. Woodson, *The History of the Negro Church*, pp. 224-30.

Negroes with means could scarcely plead ignorance of the want existing about them, for destitution was nearly as widespread as in post Civil War years. In the early nineties, amidst the enormous prosperity of much of the city, 16,000 persons, the great majority of them colored, were without visible means of support; in 1870 the number had been little greater. Until 1897 the police were responsible for reporting cases of destitution and illness and for distributing relief, but although Negro distrust of the police was an obstacle, the health department defended the system on the grounds that it hastened investigations of complaints and relieved the doctors of "the untidy class," presumably malingerers. The police found Negro families eking out existence by picking spoiled food from garbage cans and dumps. Households in the Negro slums were ridden with illness; a report of 1891 described a one-room shanty in which beside a dead infant lay five adults and six children stricken with influenza. Four-fifths of the patients at the Freedmen's Hospital were indigent Negroes; of the 17,048 persons to whom the District's seven public dispensaries ministered in 1891, over 12,000 were colored. The most conscientious physician could do little more than palliate momentarily the miseries he encountered daily.

In twenty years the colored death rate dropped to 28.12 per thousand from the 40.78 of 1876, but Negro mortality always greatly exceeded and in most years was double that of whites. Infant mortality, high for whites, ran in 1890 to 338.5 per thousand for Negroes and in 1900 to 317. The occasional charge that Negro "ignorance and indifference" was to blame was a part-truth. A larger cause, the health officer noted, was the foulness of the alley tenements in which thousands of Negroes lived.[23]

[23] *Star*, 15 Mar 1882; Comrs Rpts, 1887, pp. 16-17, 1889, p. 14, 1890, pp. 639, 756-57, 845-47, 1895, pp. 9-13; H Ex Doc 1, 51C, 1S, p. 94; *Chronicle*, 11 Sep 1899; *Eleventh U.S. Census*, 1890, *Population*, I, Pt. II, 20; *Twelfth Census*, 1900, *Population*, Pt. II, 22; W. E. B. DuBois, ed., *Mortality among Negroes in Cities* (1st Atlanta Conference, 1896), pp. 8, 18-19, 20-28.

Neither poverty nor illness, however, prevented Negroes from enjoying themselves at times. The gift of laughter, that capacity to create and delight in moments of gaiety in the midst of suffering and want, is a Negro characteristic that down to the present day confuses and baffles white people. As W. E. B. DuBois sardonically put it, "that we do submit to life as it is and yet laugh and dance and dream is but another proof that we are idiots." With a light-heartedness that sober-sided white Washingtonians called irresponsible, colored families not always able to feed themselves joined in church sociables and in club and fraternal society celebrations. The lower down the economic ladder, the more pleasure members of a society apparently took in giving it a high-sounding name, such as "Grand Ancient Order of the Sons and Daughters and Brothers and Sisters of Moses of the USA and the World at Large." A funeral, always an occasion, usually called for lavish spending on carriages and clothes. Noisy picnics complete with bands to furnish music took place on Sundays, in the 1880's frequently at the "Manor," once the John P. Van Ness house and grounds, where the National Red Cross Headquarters now stand; when a proprietor of the beer hall there closed the place in 1887, colored picnickers were allowed to use the Schuetzen-verein park. Mutual benefit societies arranged excursions down the Potomac until the steamboat lines, adopting the pretext that every boat was already chartered, refused to sell Negroes tickets.

For lower-class Negroes the great event of the year was the annual District Emancipation Day parade on April 16th. Every colored organization in the District usually took part. Despite a downpour of rain, in 1883 the procession was a mile and a half long; among the scores of societies parading in dress array were the Chaldeans, the Knights of Moses, the Osceolas, the Galilean Fishermen, the Sons and Daughters of Samaris, the Solid Yantics, the Lively Eights, and the Celestial Golden Links. White onlookers, watching the elaborately decorated floats and the thousands of Negroes marching on foot to the accompaniment of twelve brass bands, were impressed, amused, or indignant at the money poured into the display. Sophisticated Negroes sensitive to white ridicule protested now and again that a church service would mark the day more fittingly. "The thought is already gaining ground," wrote Frederick Douglass in 1886, "that tinsel show, gaudy display and straggling processions, which empty the alleys and dark places of our city into the broad day-light of our thronged streets and avenues, thus thrusting upon the public view a vastly undue proportion of the most unfortunate, unimproved, and unprogressive class of the colored people, and thereby inviting public disgust and contempt, and repelling the more thrifty and self-respecting among us, is a positive hurt to the whole colored population of this city. These annual celebrations of ours . . . should bring into notice the very best elements of our colored population." But until the school board voted in 1899 not to dismiss the colored schools for the day, the parade on the 16th of April was more important to most of colored Washington than the 4th of July and Christmas and New Year's combined.[24]

Few middle-class Negroes were in a position to carp at the extravagances of their social inferiors, for display was an essential ingredient in most of their own pleasures. Below the thin top crust all Negro society was as intent upon keeping up with the Joneses as were ambitious, socially insecure whites. Booker T. Washington spoke with dismay of seeing "young colored men who were not earning more than four dollars a week spend two dollars or more for a buggy on Sunday to ride up and down Pennsylvania Avenue in, in order that they might try to convince the world that they were worth thousands." Plug-hatted "dudes" carrying canes swaggered about the streets

---

[24] W. E. B. DuBois, *Dusk of Dawn*, p. 147; Ingle, *The Negro in D.C.*, p. 106; Cleveland *Leader*, 19 Apr 1883, 28 Sep 1884; *Advocate*, 28 Apr 1882; *Bee*, 21 Apr 1883, 24 Mar 1888.

to impress their fellows. Clothes were all-important. At a club party "young gentlemen and ladies in and just leaving their teens, assembled, dressed in full reception style, the young gents in full dress suit, the ladies in every ornamentation art or fancy could give. One lady of family remarked, 'they are all plebians, too!'" Plebeians as well as aristocrats still attended the theatre occasionally, but, as time went on, evening parties at home or concerts at the churches became a more customary form of entertainment. Athletics had not yet begun to loom large, although Negro bicycle clubs appeared in the eighties, and in the nineties colored cyclists held races at the Park Cycle Track.

After the Lotus Club disappeared, for several years the Monday Night Literary Society embraced the most distinguished of the Negro intelligentsia. Later the Bethel Literary and Historical Society, founded in 1881 by Bishop Payne of the Metropolitan Methodist Episcopal Church, overshadowed the older clubs. The younger not only explored literature and philosophy but, more important, supplied the principal forum for enlightened discussion of race problems; the most notable colored men in America addressed the group. Business and professional men also valued membership in the Cosmas Club, organized in 1900. If the choral groups were less exclusive than the literary societies, the Treble Clef Club was as selective as the white Friday Morning Music Club and undertook equally ambitious programs.

The Negro newspapers gave a great deal of space to high-class weddings; the list of presents with the donors' name attached might fill over a column. The gowns, "a Worth dress of canary silk," or a "crimson velvet entrainee," were described in the same detail with which white society reporters wrote of the costumes at White House receptions. Even after discounting the braggadocio of the Negro press, the evidences of Negro wealth were startling—beautiful jewelry, handsome clothes, well-furnished houses tended by Negro servants, and expensive summer holidays. Every June the exodus began with "Saratoga trunks" packed for Newport, Harpers Ferry, and Cape May. In 1886 the *Bee* reported: "Mr. Richard S. Locke of Washington who spends his summers at Nonquitt Beach [Massachusetts] has sold his beautiful yacht; Mr. Locke is the only gentleman of color that ever owned a yacht at Nonquitt." By and large, the higher a Negro's social standing, the more exactly his diversions corresponded to those of white people of similar position.[25]

At the opening of the twentieth century Washington Negroes whose memory stretched back into the late 1860's had no cause for optimism. Since the days when colored men had shared in governing the city and the territory and the wall of caste had appeared to be crumbling, their bright prospects had darkened and then vanished in the shadows of a new and mounting racism. Frederick Douglass and his associates of the *New National Era* had marked 1870 as the high point for the Negro community and saw the shrinkage of its horizons as beginning with the creation of the territorial government. Witnessing the inexorable narrowing of their world after 1874, the wisest colored people doubtless knew that the splintering into mutually jealous groups had further reduced the elbow room for all contestants and had multiplied the difficulties of combatting white prejudice. Washington's revived racism was the harder to fight because the white community, increasingly oblivious to the existence of any other, recognized no opponent. "As long as the flat surface of color remained the lone dimension of a human being," from the standpoint of a white man a duel was impossible for lack of a human adversary. The few white Washingtonians who admitted that the city contained Negro citizens

[25] Cleveland *Leader*, 7 Apr 1884; Washington, *Up From Slavery*, pp. 88-89; *Advocate*, 1880-1884; *Bee*, Apr 1883 and 1884-1901; Francis Cardozo, Jr., to Booker T. Washington, 8 Aug 1902, Booker T. Washington Mss (L.C.); *New National Era*, 25 Jun 1874; Mrs. E. T. Williston, "History of the Treble Clef" appended to program, *Treble Clef Club*, 16 May 1923 (Music Div., L.C.); *Post*, 3 Aug 1902.

were prone to dismiss the possibility of any injustice by declaring the capital "the colored man's paradise."

The very light-colored Negro with three-fourths or seven-
eights white blood might find an answer for himself by con-
triving to pass permanently into the ranks of whites. Miscegenation, not unlawful in the District of Columbia and perhaps far more common than most people realized, eased the
process for the stranger, but for a member of any well-known
local family passing was difficult. In any case, it left the larger
problem unsolved: how Negroes were to live with dignity in
a white world. Frederick Douglass speaking in 1883 urged
assimilation rather than isolation; he himself married a white
woman a few months later, but presumably he was advocating
the ideal of social rather than biological assimilation. Voluntary
isolation might protect individuals from some humiliations
but would scarcely ensure economic progress for the race. Preoccupation with these questions stripped colored Washington
of interest in the well-being of the city as a whole.[26]

In 1901 for white Washingtonians the future stretched out
in an ever-widening vista of prosperity and orderly living in a
beautiful city whose national and world importance could only
expand. The difference between that picture and what perceptive Negroes could envisage for their own people was
heightened by the contrasts between their status then and that
of a quarter century before. True, some families had made
money in the interval, and others had achieved a modicum of
financial security. Those who held government clerkships, while
perpetually fearful for their tenure in office, usually enjoyed
civil, if impersonal, treatment. Moreover, a careful unobtrusive-
ness permitted well-dressed Negroes to hover in the background
at the reception celebrating Washington's centennial. But sensitive men and women found that concession a poor substitute

[26] *Advocate*, 5 Jun 1880; *Bee*, 18 Sep, 2 Oct 1886, 15 Dec 1900;
New National Era, 20 Feb 1873; Murray, *Proud Shoes*, p. 88; *Star*,
17 Apr 1883.

for friendliness. Fortunately they could not foresee that events in the next fifteen years would force colored aristocrats and middle-class Negoes into a psychological ghetto along with irresponsible blacks.

While the most easily observed factor in the progressive disintegration of Washington's Negro world was the failure of economic opportunity to keep pace with the growth of the colored population and with the spread of education, that material loss was itself rather a manifestation than a cause of the change. The wealthy Negro knew all too well that financial security provided no safeguard against endless humiliations and frustration. The deterioration of Negro status sprang from a complex of causes, but the common denominator was the steady paring down of incentive. With the dwindling of the attainable external rewards for continuing the struggle, only the strongest individual able to draw upon deep inner resources could withstand the ceaseless battering of his self-respect. That the number of Negroes possessed of such spiritual fortitude would not increase rapidly in the bitter years ahead was a logical development.

CHAPTER VII

THE CITY BEAUTIFUL, 1901-1916

WHEN word reached Washington of President McKinley's assassination in Buffalo in September 1901, Secretary of State John Hay, shocked into immobility, shut himself into the study of his home on Lafayette Square and left his subordinates to notify foreign governments and arrange for the swearing in of Theodore Roosevelt. Yet, if here and there Americans counted the toll of three Presidents shot down in thirty-six years as evidence of national political instability, the vigorous "Teddy" quickly dispelled their fears. Within a matter of days Washington was turning to the future with greater enthusiasm and optimism than ever.

The city had reason to call herself blessed. She was known for her cultivated society. Alone among big American cities she had escaped and would continue to escape the social adjustments of assimilating thousands of non-English-speaking immigrants. The capital in 1901, and indeed in 1910, contained the largest Negro population of any city on earth, but the declining ratio of colored inhabitants to white was reassuring to the handful of whites who were faintly troubled about race relations. For most of white Washington, colored Washington existed but was of no real significance. The meagreness of industry in the city spared her the afflictions of more or less open warfare between labor and capital; her working classes were not subject to conditions such as Upton Sinclair would shortly portray in *The Jungle* describing Chicago's stockyards. While sensitive citizens realized that Washington's alleys were the local counterpart of the slums of New York and Chicago, the reform spirit that had stirred in the city since the late 1890's encouraged faith in the community's capacity to redeem those evils. President Roosevelt's extraordinary capacity to awaken idealism in young people strengthened Washingtonians' belief that they could make the capital in every respect the model for the rest of the country. In aiming at that goal, they assigned importance to beautification of the city.

When Senator James McMillan persuaded his colleagues to appoint an advisory Park Commission in 1901, the "city beautiful" movement in America was still in infancy. Born at the Columbian Exposition of 1893 in Chicago, where architects and artists had created the exquisite White City from a swamp on the Lake Michigan shore, the movement had a vigorous start. "Make no little plans," Daniel Burnham, chief architect of the Fair, had counselled, and city-dwellers throughout the country, excited over the miracle he and his associates had brought about, adopted the slogan. But the long depression of the 1890's had cooled the first ardor and delayed the appearance of a new profession of city planning. The return of prosperity had reawakened interest in recapturing for future generations neglected natural assets like lake and river fronts and in mapping out the form later city expansion should take. By the turn of the century Boston had purchased 5,000 acres of outlying lake- and wood-land for a vast urban recreation area, and Cleveland had given thought to a municipal lake-front development. But otherwise no big American city had drafted an over-all plan, let alone engaged experts to prepare it.

Upon this body of tentative ideas the proposals of the Park Commission for the national capital burst with powerful effect. It was intensified for Washingtonians by the realization that the plan, if accepted, would reverse the congressional decision of February 1901 to turn over a central piece of the Mall to the Pennsylvania Railroad. Popular magazines publicized the plan by publishing maps, artists' projections of what the national capital would look like, and photographs of the gardens, fountains, and the architectural splendors of European cities which Washington's beauties would one day surpass. The fame of the members appointed to the commission added

133

weight to their recommendations; every American concerned with the "city beautiful" knew of the architects Daniel Burnham and Charles McKim, of the sculptor Augustus St. Gaudens, and of the son of Frederick Law Olmsted, the landscape architect who had laid out New York's Central Park and the grounds of the Capitol. The dimensions of the plan for the public domain in the national capital, moreover, stirred the most sluggish imagination. Americans who had never set foot in Washington or studied L'Enfant's original layout were suddenly eager to see it revived and elaborated. Thus, as the details became known, the project for Washington gave impetus to city planning throughout the country.[1]

When the Park Commission report appeared in January 1902, Washingtonians gratefully scrutinized it. The basic features of the grandiose plan were L'Enfant's with a few modifications and extensions into areas beyond the limits of the eighteenth-century city. Local citizens knew that they had prepared the way for the enlargement by prevailing upon Congress to impose restrictions upon suburban subdivisions, to purchase the land for the zoo and for Rock Creek Park, and to create the Highway Commission in 1893 empowered to supervise the orderly expansion of the city into the county. The publicists of the so-called McMillan plan were unfamiliar with its late nineteenth-century local antecedents; outside the District of Columbia people assumed that Washingtonians had contributed nothing and would merely reap the benefits of other men's aesthetic concepts. In fact magazine articles frequently contrasted the beautiful city that would emerge under Park Commission guidance with the dreary community in which the

[1] S Dis Comee, 58C, 1S, Hearings, "The Mall Parkway," pp. 23-24; Charles Zueblin, "Washington Old and New," *Chautaquan*, XXXIX, 156-67, and *A Decade of Civic Development*, pp. 60-62, 92-99; Frederick Law Olmsted, "Beautifying the City," and Carroll D. Wright, "The Embellishment of Washington," *Independent*, LIV, 1870-77, 2683-85; H. B. F. Macfarland, "The Rebuilding of the National Capital," *The American City*, I, 3; American Institute of Architects, *Of Plans and People*, p. 10; *Rpt B/Tr*, 1902, p. 11.

natives had supposedly been content to live until, in spite of themselves, Boss Shepherd in the 1870's had briefly shaken open their pocketbooks. Washingtonians themselves were unconcerned about who got the credit for the new project as long as it won congressional endorsement.

The members of the Park Commission declared their function to be the preparation of "a well-considered general plan covering the entire District of Columbia," so that when Congress provided for new buildings and parks, it would have a blue print to follow instead of resorting to the former "piecemeal, haphazard and unsatisfactory methods." Forty years later the phrase "general plan covering the entire District of Columbia" would baffle city planners who recognized the comprehensiveness of Burnham's ideas for Chicago, but could find nothing comparable in the scope of the proposals for the capital. Instead of including the business district and residential sections in the Washington plan, Burnham and his three associates viewed their mission as limited to a layout of parks in suitable relationship to public buildings.

For any city, consistency in sticking to a plan was more important, Frederick Olmsted insisted, than the adoption of any particular plan. The placing of the Treasury and the Library of Congress where they interrupted the sweep of Pennsylvania Avenue and the location of the State, War and Navy Building blocking off New York Avenue from the White House were departures from L'Enfant's original layout which the commission felt obliged to accept as irretrievable. It was also patently impossible to move the Washington Monument several hundred feet to the point where L'Enfant's east-west axis intersected the axis running south from the White House. And for unexplained reasons the commission recommended clustering all the executive office buildings about Lafayette Square. Otherwise the proposals were aimed at reviving the essentials of the original plan.

Museums and public galleries should line the Mall above

and below the Smithsonian. Edifices related to the legislative and judicial branches of the government should face upon the Capitol grounds. Restoration of the Bulfinch fence and gates at the foot of the Hill and a waterfall cascading from fountains on the western terrace into a lake at First Street would add to the grandeur of the Capitol itself. At the far end of the Mall a new memorial to Abraham Lincoln should rise, with a bridge across the Potomac beyond leading to Arlington Cemetery. A sunken garden, fountains, and a canal or reflecting pool should give dramatic emphasis to the drop in elevation from the base of the Washington Monument to the temple to Lincoln. Statues commemorating other national heroes should occupy some of the triangles formed by the radial avenues and the gridiron of streets. Fountains as magnificent as those at the Villa d'Este should refresh the eye in a dozen spots.

Remarking that the "dearth of the means of innocent enjoyment of one's leisure hours is remarkable in Washington, the one city in this country where people have the most leisure," the commission proposed to convert the area south of the Washington Monument into recreation grounds. Ball fields could be laid out on the long spit of made land forming one shore of the Washington Channel, while the Tidal Basin above, with its controlled flow of tidal water, "should have the most ample facilities for boating and for wading and swimming in summer, as well for skating in winter." Parks and boulevards like those already marked out on the Highway Commission's maps should encircle the city from Rock Creek to the Soldiers' Home and on to the Anacostia. The swamps bordering the Anacostia should be drained, the upper reaches of the stream made into a "water park" like Belle Isle in Detroit, and eventually the lower stretches treated like the quays of the Seine with a boulevard along the top and stone wharfage at the water's edge. Above Georgetown, drives and lookout points along the palisades of the Potomac up to and including the Great Falls would complete the ring of parks and boulevards.

Since the "government gardens" stretching from the Capitol to the Potomac were a vital element in L'Enfant's scheme, the park commissioners early realized that they must either abandon the Frenchman's plan or persuade the Pennsylvania Railroad to remove its tracks, train sheds, and the heavy-towered stone depot from the Mall. As the law passed in February 1901 had authorized the company to enlarge its holdings there and to erect a huge new station at 6th Street, the task of inducing the corporation to relinquish that valuable land promised to be difficult, if not impossible. In August 1901 Daniel Burnham, at the end of a Park Commission tour of European cities, sought out Alexander Cassatt, president of the railroad, in London. Unexpectedly Cassatt volunteered to withdraw from the Mall and to collaborate in building a Union Station, provided that compensation be made for the cost of the change and that proper approaches be ensured "worthy of the building the railroads propose to erect." That about-face made possible what Senator McMillan blandly called "a modification of the project of last year." The Union Station would "give a complete, adequate, and monumental treatment of the railroad terminals" and make it "in reality the great and impressive vestibule to Washington."[2]

Neither the Senate nor the local public greeted all the recommendations of the commission with undiluted enthusiasm. Some features of the over-all plan seemed visionary, and even with its execution spread out over decades the estimated cost ranging from $200,000,000 to $600,000,000 gave more than one official pause. Objections arose to moving the Botanical Garden from the foot of Capitol Hill, where the greenhouses had stood for sixty-odd years, and to locating new federal office buildings in Lafayette Square. When the commission placed on exhibit at the Corcoran Gallery plaster models of the

[2] S Rpt 166, 57C, 1S, pp. 3-50, 91-97, 105-16, Ser 4258; "The Embellishment of Washington," *Municipal Affairs*, v, 911-16; S Rpt 982, 57C, 1S, Ser 4261; S Doc 220, 57C, 2S, Ser 4430, a compilation of all canal and railroad legislation for the District, 1800-1903.

future city stretching westward from the Library of Congress, residents of east Washington feared they were again to be slighted. In spite of the recommendations for drives along the Potomac palisades and a reservation in the wooded valley of Foundry Run, the Glover-Archbold Park of today, Georgetown proper also received relatively scant attention. For her the most significant proposal lay in the plan to clear the banks of Rock Creek of the rubbish accumulated over the years and to lay a narrow ribbon of parkway along the creek to link Potomac and Rock Creek Parks.

The House as a body completely ignored the plan, for Senator McMillan had made the politically egregious error of not obtaining the concurrence of the lower chamber to the appointment of the commission. Touchy representatives consequently professed to think the work of the Senate's creature no concern of theirs. When "Uncle Joe" Cannon became Speaker in the autumn of 1903, his hostility, Charles McKim explained to the President, presented a major obstacle to obtaining congressional approval of any part of the plan. Furthermore, after Senator McMillan's death in the summer of 1902, none of his colleagues undertook to see that copies of the report received adequate distribution within the government. Inasmuch as the members of the commission had given, gratis, nearly a year of their time, the plan, McKim contended, should at least be considered on its merits. Interested as he was in the "Mall Park," President Roosevelt did not intervene. He appeared to be more anxious to see McKim complete the authorized additions to the White House than to prod Congress about action on the "city beautiful" as a whole. It was the founding of the American Civic Association in 1903 that kept the project alive after the first public excitement had worn thin.[3] Despite congressional delays in implementing the plan,

[3] *Rpts B/Tr*, 1902, pp. 52-53, 1905, pp. 7, 59-60, 1909, p. 30, 1916, p. 62; *Star*, 13 Mar 1903, 1 Jan 1908, 4 Aug, 30 Nov 1909; *Times*, 5 Dec 1906, 1, 2, 14 Nov 1907; *Post*, 30 Jan 1902, 5 Jan 1910; S Doc 89, 58C, 2S, Ser 4588; Frederick Law Olmsted to Daniel Burnham, 10 Aug

Glenn Brown of the American Institute of Architects later averred that it came to exercise "great moral force." When the time came to vote money for new buildings or new bridges or other public works, a majority of Congress accepted the principle if not the details of the Park Commission's recommendations.

Other than purchasing the land for the Union Station on Massachusetts Avenue and voting the railroads the compensation promised earlier for the elimination of grade crossings within the city, the first congressional measures relating to the commission plan authorized new government buildings rather than additional parks. As the railroad companies began to erect the elaborate new station and the tunnel under the Hill to carry the tracks underground across government property, work started on six new edifices: the long awaited District Building at 14th Street on the former site of the Capital Traction Company powerhouses, offices for the House of Representatives and the Senate on the Hill, a new building for the Department of Agriculture and a new National Museum flanking the Mall on the south and north respectively, and an imposing home on Arsenal Point for the recently organized Army War College. Except for the huge domed National Museum, all these buildings were finished and in use by 1908. They immediately added to the city's aura of dignity. It was heightened by the clearing of the Mall of the railroad tracks and depot in 1909 and the grading of the plaza in front of the new Union Station where Larado Taft's Columbus Memorial Fountain was unveiled three years later. On Mt. Vernon Place the District Public Library, built with money given by Andrew Carnegie, opened in 1903. The spring of 1910 saw the completion of Continental Hall erected by the Daughters of the American Revolution, and adjacent, on the site of David Burnes'

1903, to Charles Moore, 6 Oct 1903, and 14 Jun 1904, and Charles McKim to Theodore Roosevelt, 10 Feb 1904, copy, Charles Moore Mss.

farmhouse, the Hall of the American Republics, architecturally a skillful blend of Spanish and French Renaissance styles. As the "Marble Palace," headquarters of the American National Red Cross, began to rise nearby, lower 17th Street promised to present an unbroken phalanx of imposing structures.[4]

The return to neo-classical architecture for government buildings pleased a public tired of the vagaries of the preceding half-century—the romantic red sandstone Norman castle of the Smithsonian, the mansard-roofed Department of Agriculture building, the "architectural infant asylum," as Henry Adams had labelled the State Department building, the heavy square-towered Post Office on Pennsylvania Avenue, and the ornate Italian Renaissance Library of Congress. Uniformity of style and the use of marble and pale gray granite became the rule, with the exception of the red brick War College and the officers' quarters built on Arsenal Point. Stanford White's design for the War College and grounds illustrated the restoration of another late eighteenth-century canon of city planning, namely the creation of long vistas wherever possible. Thus White placed the building at the tip of Arsenal Point where the Anacostia would serve as backdrop and an unimpeded half-mile sweep of tree-bordered lawn stretching along the Washington Channel would provide a magnificent approach; he located the new Officers' Club and the line of officers' houses with their big white columns well to the right of the entrance gates in order to keep the War College the focal point of a unified design. The day he discovered that the War Department had refused to tear down the obstructing old arsenal buildings and the grim four-

---

[4] *Rec*, 57C, 1S, pp. 2648-61, 2730, 57C, 2S, p. 1350; Glenn Brown, *Memories: A Winning Crusade to Revive George Washington's Vision of a Capital City*, p. 270 (hereafter cited as Brown, *Memories*); Comrs Rpt, 1903, p. 11; *Rpts B/Tr*, as in n. 3 above, and 1912, p. 21; *Star*, 25 Mar 1903, 1 Jan 1915; *Times*, 11, 15 Feb 1914; International Bureau of the American Republics, *The Report of the Director to the Fourth Pan American Conference Held at Buenos Aires, Argentine Republic*, Jul 1910, pp. 46-51; *Annual Address, President James F. Oyster to Chamber of Commerce*, 14 Jan 1913, p. 13, Woodrow Wilson Mss (L.C.).

square red brick prison in which the conspirators involved in Lincoln's assassination had been hanged, the outraged architect turned on his heel and never again set foot in the grounds. Yet government officials generally strove to act upon the Park Commission thesis that landscaping of the areas adjoining new buildings and the approaches to bridges was as important as the architecture itself.

Unlike the purely utilitarian bridges of nineteenth-century Washington, those built after 1905 had harmonious proportions and decoration. An ugly but sturdy iron trestle "highway" bridge, to be sure, replaced the ricketty seventy-year-old Long Bridge across the Potomac, but in 1908 the magnificently engineered "Lion Bridge" spanning Rock Creek valley was adorned with placid stone creatures at the Connecticut Avenue approaches. Several other new bridges involved extraordinary feats of engineering, notably the skillful use of concrete to encase the old water mains that carried the Pennsylvania Avenue bridge over Rock Creek and the graceful strength of the arches of the Q Street bridge guarded by bronze buffaloes. The Park Commission plan included a memorial bridge as an extension of the Mall to Arlington Cemetery, but, although members of the Grand Army of the Republic laid a cornerstone for the bridge in May 1902, not until 1913 did Congress appoint a special commission to choose a site and a design. And work would not begin until the mid-1920's. A million-dollar appropriation meanwhile for a replacement of the old Aqueduct Bridge promised to improve the looks of the Potomac River front at Georgetown.[5]

As the conviction deepened that harmony must obtain between public buildings and space, Congress created a permanent Fine Arts Commission in 1910 to advise "upon subjects within the domain of the fine arts." The Park Commission, never recognized by the House of Representatives, ceased to

[5] *Rpts B/Tr*, 1902, p. 28, 1905, pp. 8, 19-20, 1907, pp. 15, 120, 1909, pp. 42-43, 1916, pp. 41-43; Comrs Rpts, 1909, p. 46, 1915, p. 45; Engineer's Office, D.C., *Washington's Bridges*, 1945.

exist after submitting its report in 1902. The new body, like its predecessor, had no authority. The architects, sculptors, painters, and landscape gardeners composing the new commission had no chance to oppose the rewriting of the Height of Buildings Act, by which Congress permitted fire-proof business blocks to rise twenty to fifty feet higher than the law of 1899 had allowed. Members of the commission objected in vain to the 18th Street location and characterless design of the Interior Department building erected in 1916, but, more often than not, Congress followed their advice. In the face of vigorously pressed counterproposals they chose the site and design for the Lincoln Memorial and selected the architect, Henry Bacon, and the sculptor, Daniel Chester French. Virtually the executors of the plan of 1901, they fought for simplicity of line in new buildings and particularly for heights and cornices that would correspond to those of adjacent structures. Before World War I the Fine Arts Commission had made itself the arbiter of public taste in the capital.

A serious conflict developed in 1916. Secretary of the Treasury William McAdoo insisted that economy dictated placing a new government power and heating plant at the head of the Washington Channel near the Bureau of Engraving, where, the Fine Arts Commission contended, four huge smoke stacks cutting the sky line would not only mar the view of the city when approached from the south but compete with the Washington Monument and the Capitol seen from any angle. While a citizens' committee joined in the protest, an unconvinced Congress let excavation begin. Glenn Brown of the American Institute of Architects then led the fight. When engineers sent up a balloon from the power plant foundations to mark the height to which the smoke stacks would rise, Brown hastily got a photographer to take pictures showing the balloon slicing across the shaft of the Monument and blotting out part of the Capitol dome. Prints sent to every member of Congress and published in the *National Geographic Magazine* failed to halt

1. Dedication of the Washington Monument, February 21, 1885

2. Flood on Pennsylvania Avenue, 1889; the result of an inadequate storm sewer system

3. Tourists at the Capitol, 1880, from *Frank Leslie's Illustrated Newspaper*

4. Riggs National Bank on the right with the late W. W. Corcoran's office building on the left ca. 1890. Newspapers and commercial firms rented part of each building

5. View of Virginia Avenue in 1894 showing in the foreground a race track and the John Van Ness house

6. View of Virginia Avenue in 1944 showing in the foreground the Munitions Building, the Hall of the American Republics, Continental Hall, and "New Interior"

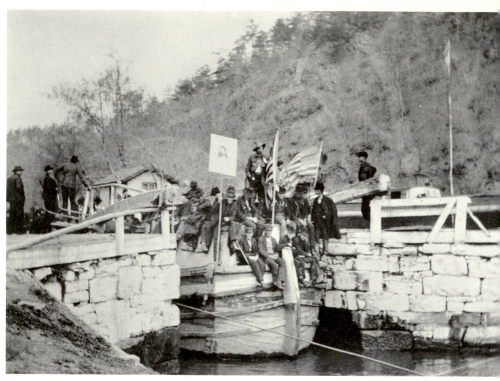

7. Some of the "Army of the Unemployed" arriving by C & O Canal Boat, 1894

8. Members of Coxey's Army

9. The plant pathologists of the Department of Agriculture, ca. 1890

10. G. Browne Goode, ca. 1889

11. Samuel Langley and his "Aerodrome" with his mechanic on the left

12. School children visiting the Smithsonian Institution, 1899

13. School children visiting the Library of Congress, 1899

14. Three views of the Park Commission Plan of 1901: top, the Mall looking west toward the Potomac; center, the Mall looking east toward the Capitol; bottom, the "South-North Axis" from the river to the White House

15. Extension of the White House, 1903

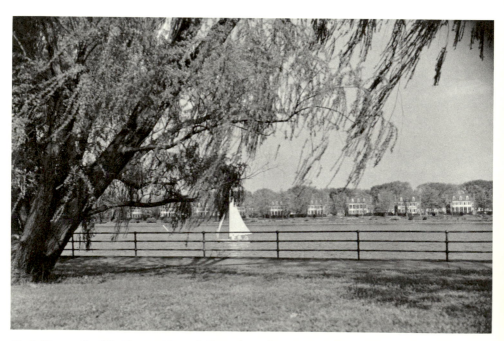

16. Sailing on the Washington Channel. Beyond stands the line of officers' houses built by Stanford White on the grounds of the Army War College

the work. Brown then engaged a sign maker to paint sandwich boards, one board depicting the eighteenth-century plan of the city under the caption: "The Past—A Heritage from Washington," the other marked: "The Present—McAdoo's Smoke Stacks" portraying the city after the completion of the new power plant. Dressed in a long white robe, bare feet in sandals, and his face covered by a black mask, Brown wore the sandwich boards to a Beaux Arts ball given at the Willard Hotel to raise money for the children of French artists killed in the war against Germany. The only person with masked face, he walked back and forth, saying no word but letting everyone study the contrasting pictures. Overnight McAdoo became a laughing stock. Congress agreed to the Fine Arts plan of enlarging the existing power plant on low-lying land to the south of the Capitol, and the "Heritage from Washington" was saved.[6]

For thirty years before the appointment of the Fine Arts Commission statuary had been multiplying in the circles and triangles formed by the intersections of the avenues and streets. Once an organization had obtained permission from Congress to erect a memorial on the public domain, only the group commissioning the work or the sculptor executing it passed upon its suitability and artistic merit. Few people admired the towering Daniel Webster on his granite pedestal at Scott Circle, or the all too appropriately motionless equestrian figure of General McClellan at the head of Connecticut Avenue, or the already nearly forgotten Albert Pike, the Confederate general who had enlisted Indians in the fight against the Union and whose effigy now rose near the old City Hall. Public subscription had paid for the bronze of Boss Shepherd in front of the new District

---

[6] 36 *Stat.* 371; H Rpt 1294, 62C, 3S, Ser 6335; "The Proposed Lincoln National Memorial," *Harper's Weekly*, LVI, 21; *Post*, 19, 20 Jan 1913; *Rpts Fine Arts Commission*, 1913, pp. 15-18, 1914, 22-23, 35, 1915, pp. 5, 15-16, 27-28, 1916, pp. 12-14, 16, 19-22, 34-37, 52-53; Brown, *Memories*, pp. 301-03; *An Appeal to the Enlightened Sentiment of the People of the United States for the Safeguarding of the Future Development of the Nation*, March 1916.

Building, the one example in America of a politician portrayed with his hand behind him, but consensus labelled the memorial undistinguished.[7] Hence the community welcomed the new requirement that the Fine Arts Commission approve in advance the design and location of every new piece of sculpture proposed. Decisions as to who was to be commemorated in bronze or marble still lay with Congress, but that question would not trouble the public until mid-century.

Meanwhile the decorative planting of the public grounds and the voluntary elimination of billboards along the streets commanded public interest. Inasmuch as enforced removal of the unsightly billboards from scores of privately owned vacant lots meant interference with the sacred rights of the property owner, the campaign against hoardings proceeded slowly. But pleasure in seeing well-tended stretches of lawn and flowerbeds of pansies, tulips, and the traditional red cannas about the public buildings was an incentive to private property-owners to demolish eyesores. Washingtonians were especially caught up by excitement over the landscaping about the Tidal Basin when the plan took form in 1911 to ring the basin with Japanese cherry trees. David Fairchild, whose travels as a plant explorer justified his calling the world his garden, had brought back several flowering cherries in 1905 and successfully naturalized them in the woods about his home in Bethesda. The Department of Agriculture consequently could draw upon his experience when the mayor of Tokyo presented two thousand trees to Mrs. William Howard Taft, which she then gave to the city. She planted the first tree with her own hands. The discovery that several hundred trees were diseased necessitated burning the entire lot and replacing them with healthy stock, but by the spring of

[7] Macfarland, "The Rebuilding of the National Capital," *American City*, I, 8-9; Comrs Rpts, 1903, pp. 23-24, 1909, pp. 15-16, 1912, pp. 51-52, 1915, p. 46; *Rpts B/Tr*, 1909, p. 30, 1910, pp. 9-10, 61-62, 1913, 62-70, 1915, pp. 56-57, 62, 1916, pp. 59-62; "A National Monument to Columbus," *Harper's Weekly*, LVI, 17; *Post*, 3, 5 Mar 1913; *Times*, 19 Aug 1907, 21 Jan 1909, 16 Mar 1911; *Star*, 2 May 1909.

1915 the beauty of the delicately pink blossoms was breath-taking.[8] The "Speedway" along the river nearby and out on to Haines Point along the Washington Channel became the Washington equivalent of the Champs Elysée.

In the years ahead Washingtonians had occasion to wish that the Park Commission in 1901 had undertaken not only to emulate the surface beauties of St. James Park, the Champs Elysée, and the Bois de Bologne but also to adopt plans for a subway like the London "Underground" and the Paris "Métro." But horseless carriages were a novelty on the streets of the capital at the opening of the twentieth century. People walked to and from work, and fewer than 300,000 inhabitants in the entire District of Columbia made the growth of a metropolitan area of two million souls within a lifetime seem unthinkable. To spend money on placing a transit system underground appeared to be sheer folly in 1901. Furthermore, laws imposing any but sanitary restrictions on the use of privately owned land would have raised an outcry. The limit placed on the height of buildings was acceptable because Washingtonians were not yet ready to build higher than the law of 1910 allowed. But all Americans were wary of any measure smacking of "collectivism" or "socialism." Members of the Park Commission urged extensive purchase of land while it could still be bought relatively cheaply, but they confined their specific recommendations to the treatment of the public domain. Fifteen years before the first municipal zoning act in the United States went into effect in New York City, planned and controlled land-use affecting private as well as public property was an unpopular notion rarely discussed.

Today a careful examination of the plan of 1901 may induce a sense of disappointment that waterfalls tumbling from the west terrace of the Capitol to a pool at the foot of the Hill, a sunken garden below the Washington Monument, and boulevarded quays at the river's edge above and below the Navy Yard

[8] *Post*, 20 Jan 1913; Helen Taft Manning to the author, 4 Dec 1958; Fairchild, *The World Was My Garden*, pp. 254, 410-13.

have not come into being, and that bands of concrete highway and parking lots now occupy space designed for shady lawns and fountains. Still the concept of the "city beautiful" evolved at the turn of the century left its mark not only upon Washington but upon other American cities. In 1949 the American Institute of Architects labelled the proposals of 1901 "obsolete" at the time they were offered, a sign of an enduring "cultural colonialism" as disastrous for America as, in Louis Sullivan's opinion, the Chicago World's Fair had been in stifling all originality in native American art. Yet without a long-term plan and its partial execution before the first World War, skyrocketing real estate prices in Washington thereafter would almost certainly have stopped Congress from acquiring the land essential to any large-scale, orderly scheme, however faulty. City planning throughout the United States might well have suffered a setback, for the results visible in Washington at the end of 1916 kept alive the vision of the "city beautiful" in communities that had not yet taken constructive steps.[9]

[9] Montgomery Schuyler, "The New Washington," *Scribner's Magazine*, LI, 129-48; American Institute of Architects, *Of Plans and People*, pp. 10-12; "A List of American City Planning Reports," *American City*, XI, 1914, pp. 490-97.

CHAPTER VIII

THE REVERSE OF THE COIN: SOCIAL BETTERMENT, 1901-1916

AS MONEY poured into the adornment of the capital, a disturbing one-sidedness in the program troubled conscientious citizens. In 1901 the Associated Charities and the Central Relief Agency, speaking also for Washington's churches, begged the Park Commission "in formulating plans for the systematic beautification of our city to give especial consideration to its poorer neighborhoods." In the heart of Washington, behind the substantial houses that faced the streets bounding some 276 of her large squares, lay a warren of stables, shanties, and noisome tenements housing a few score of horses and thousands of human beings. The lack of playgrounds and the ramshackle condition of schoolhouses in poorer sections contrasted sharply with the landscaped grounds and architectural elegance of new federal buildings. Appropriations of $600,000 for new parks in northwest Washington and $275,000 for the bridge over Rock Creek at Q Street seemed out of all proportion to the $100,000 for reclamation of the malarial swamps near the mouth of the Anacostia and the $75,000 for making a playground out of the "notorious Willow Tree Alley" in the square later occupied by the federal Health, Education, and Welfare Building. At a national conference in 1910 speakers pointed out that city planners everywhere, captured by "a superficial quest for beauty," had paid too little attention to overcrowding in vital residential areas; consequently "from a social and hygienic standpoint" a community might continue to be undesirable "though outwardly it may be 'the city beautiful.' "[1] In Washington the bright face of the

[1] *Star*, 22 Aug 1901, 16 Jul, 2, 4 Aug 1909; *Times*, 5 Dec 1906, 18 Mar 1911; *Post*, 24 Jul 1904; *Rpts B/Tr*, 1904, p. 16, 1905, pp. 8-9; Max West, "Room for Improvement," *Outlook*, LXXIX, 625-26; George B. Ford, "Second National Conference on City Planning and Congestion,"

coin bore the clear imprint of the Park Commission plan; the reverse was blurred by shadowy indications of evils no one wanted to contemplate.

Indeed, a major difficulty in convincing Congress and the influential public of the existence of these evils within a stone's throw of the Capitol and within two blocks of millionaires' houses about Dupont Circle lay in the inadequacy of words to convey a vivid picture of Washington's inhabited alleys. No other city in America had their like. It meant little to say that "each 'alley' comprises a set of several streets which branch and turn about the center of the great city blocks"; that often six to twelve persons lived in a single room of an alley tenement with one water faucet to a floor of a dozen rooms; that leaky roofs and no gutters turned dwellings and the clay ground around them into foul morasses in wet weather; that lack of cross ventilation in summer made infernos of the closely packed houses and shanties; and that in winter newspaper wadded into cracks of the outer walls and about broken window panes kept in the bad air without warming it. Photographs taken among the shadows of those interior courts revealed a very small part of the misery and human degradation they enclosed. Neither words nor pictures reproduced the overpowering stench pouring out of doorless sheds lined with rows of uncovered wooden privies, rising from lidless barrels sunk in the ground, and pervading alley houses where each floor, occupied sometimes by as many as thirty families, was equipped with a single water closet in a windowless cubby hole.

From the street, a square containing a segment of the fetid, hidden slum world frequently appeared to be an ordinary respectable residential block. A diagram published in 1906 showed a typical layout: fifty-six brick and eight frame houses fronted on the four sides of the square and hid its interior; three

---

Survey, xxiv, 293-98; S Doc 247, 64C, 1S, "Fiscal Relations of the United States to the District of Columbia," pp. xlvi-xlviii, liii, lix, Ser 6915 (hereafter cited as *Fiscal Relations*).

openings led into an inner maze of courts formed by seventeen spacious stables and seventy narrow habitations and their accompanying outhouses. Bad as those physical features were, the secretary of the Associated Charities believed that the secret walled-off quality of alley life was its most destructive characteristic. A person who had never ventured down the alley openings could scarcely believe the tales of what he would find. The publicity social workers attempted to give to these conditions sounded like over-dramatized fiction to citizens who preferred to play ostrich rather than face such unpleasant facts.[2]

By 1907 the completion of the pumping station and sewage disposal plant, the water filtration system and enlargement of the District water supply relieved the District budget of the heaviest demands upon it and seemingly left funds available for playgrounds, roomy fire-proof school buildings, and a concentrated attack upon the great blight of the capital, the alley dwellings. But powerful members of Congress, having permitted the District to finance its costly public works by deficit spending, insisted that taxes must go first of all toward reducing the funded debt and next to repaying with interest the sums advanced from the United States Treasury for sewers and the water supply. The legislation of 1892 had prevented the building of additional shanties in narrow alleys but had not restored to District officials the authority exercised by the Board of Health under the territorial government to condemn and raze unsanitary tenements. Yet if Washington was to become the magnificent capital to which she aspired, the city must wipe out her slums.[3]

That task, as civic-minded people were coming to see, could not be achieved simply by the moral regeneration of alley

[2] Charles Weller, "Neglected Neighbors," *Charities*, xv, 762-67.
[3] *Times*, 17 Apr 1908; George S. Wilson, "Municipal Indebtedness, Washington, D.C.," *Annals American Academy of Social and Political Science*, xxv, 628-29, and Daniel E. Garges, "Washington, D.C.," *ibid.*, xxx, 157-60; S Rpt 943, 57C, 1S, Ser 4261; Comrs Rpt, 1906, p. 49; *Rpts B/Tr*, 1905, pp. 6, 9, 68, 1907, p. 127; *Star*, 24 Aug 1912.

dwellers. The reorganization of the Associated Charities in 1896 had started the process of changing Washingtonians' ideas about the battle against pauperism, and in the next dozen years the philosophy dominant in the 1880's and 1890's shifted considerably. Reduced to its simplest terms the change lay in a growing acceptance of the idea that environment might be as important as inherited character in making good citizens, and thus a good city. If "moral uplift" alone could not win the fight against the degradation of poverty, the campaign must be broadened to include provision for decent living conditions and wider economic opportunity for the city's poor. The "social betterment leaders," as the language of the day called them, continued to rely heavily upon education and persuasion to evoke cooperation, but they early realized that new legislation was also essential to the success of their enlarged program.

Among the leaders in this movement a half-dozen stand out as men of exceptional vision and tireless vigor. John Joy Edson is the best single example. His kindly, undistinguished face, partly hidden by untrimmed mustachios, showed little of the extraordinary force of his personality; he looked more like a small-town businessman than the powerful big city banker and the deeply religious, selfless social reformer that he was. He repeatedly refused appointment as a District commissioner, but for more than three decades he played a major part in every significant civic project, for twenty years shouldered the thankless task of heading the District Board of Charities, and blazed a new trail in penal reform. The contributions of Dr. George Kober of the Georgetown University medical faculty were equally valuable and, through his published articles, better known outside Washington than Edson's. Kober was at once a scientist, a gifted teacher, and a philanthropist initially concerned chiefly with sanitation and housing problems. Years of serving on the Board of Charities widened his interests; upon his seventieth birthday in 1920 grateful fellow citizens would acclaim him one of Washington's chief benefactors. Closely associated with him in the campaign against the alley slums was ex-Surgeon General George Sternberg, the distinguished bacteriologist who had reorganized the Army Medical Corps. Sternberg, with his military bearing and the prestige of his rank, carried enormous weight in the community and became the city's foremost authority on sanitary housing.

Washington also owed much to three successive secretaries of the Associated Charities. George Wilson more than any other man gave new direction to its work in the late 1890's, and his informed humane ideas continued to have great influence when he became the first secretary of the newly created public Board of Charities. Wilson's successor was Charles Weller. In 1900 still a man under thirty, he brought to Washington the experience he had acquired in five years' work with Chicago's Associated Charities. His insights and his youthful confidence that once Washingtonians fully comprehended the local problem they would find solutions gave him peculiar persuasiveness. In his eight years of directing the Associated Charities he trained hundreds of volunteers and taught them by example the meaning of constructive social service. Under his inspiration the Monday Evening Club, organized in 1898 by professional social workers anxious to learn about each other's work, became a vital force in the community. As the club expanded to include laymen, it turned into "an educational lyceum" on Washington's civic needs and gradually became virtually "a standing conference" on charities and corrections. Weller's cloak descended upon Walter Ufford in 1908. A Congregational minister before he took a Ph.D. degree in sociology at Columbia and undertook settlement work in New York, Ufford was a mild-looking man of forty-nine whose unimpressive appearance belied his gifts. Like Weller, he gave more than one well-intentioned Washingtonian a new concept of social work and philanthropy.

151

Scarcely less important were the contributions of several women, although, true to Victorian standards of lady-like behavior, they kept out of the limelight. The charming Elizabeth Brown Ufford, before her marriage herself an experienced social worker, supplied her innately conservative husband with his more forward-looking ideas. Older and outwardly more formidable, Mrs. Archibald Hopkins, who had grown up in Washington, had a warm feeling for Negroes and from the 1890's onward was a staunch behind-the-scenes campaigner for slum clearance. She incessantly prodded and encouraged the men who took charge. Similarly, Mrs. Whitman Cross, without ever letting her name appear, succeeded in launching reforms in a dozen seemingly hopeless areas. "When you wanted to get something constructive done in Washington," a contemporary later said, "you went to John Joy Edson or to Mrs. Cross."[4]

The attack upon alley dwelling, begun in the early 1890's, resumed with new earnestness after Charles Weller's arrival. Acting on his suggestion, in 1902 fifty prominent Washingtonians organized a Committee on the Improvement of Housing Conditions. Men of the stature of Sternberg, Kober, Episcopal Bishop Henry Y. Satterlee, and S. W. Woodward, president of the YMCA, headed the group. While the committee sponsored lectures, distributed circulars, and prepared notices for the press and for the local churches, Weller inaugurated the use of visual aids, a series of stereoptican slides, to show existing conditions to Washingtonians and members of Congress. The committee's invitation to Jacob Riis of New York to investigate Washington's alleys and describe what he found proved to be particularly effective. Riis, widely known for his

---

[4] "Anniversary Tribute to George Martin Kober . . . by his friends and Associates, March 28, 1920," *American Journal of Physical Anthropology*, III, 217-83; *American Biographical Directories: District of Columbia*, 1908-09; *Times*, 7 Jun 1911; Dupree, *Science*, pp. 253-57, 260, 263-67; Associated Charities, *Reports*, 1902, p. 5, 1905, pp. 10-11 (hereafter cited as A.C. *Rpts*); "How the Associated Charities has Recruited the Social Forces of the Capital," *Charities*, xv, 816-19; *Survey*, xxiv, 197-98.

book *How the Other Half Lives*, testified before a joint session of the House and Senate District committees that Negro alley dwellers in the capital lived under worse conditions and "one-room families" were more numerous than in the grimmest slums of New York City. President Roosevelt's message to Congress in 1904 pointed out that the death rate in one-room tenements averaged twice that in two-room, four times that in three-room, and eight times that in four-room tenements. The combined pressure of Riis' findings, the President's appeal, and the demands for remedial action pouring in upon Congress from constituents promised to produce the legislation for which Washingtonians had begged in vain for more than a decade.

With a new law in prospect empowering the District commissioners to demolish alley dwellings, in 1904 Dr. Sternberg and Dr. Kober launched a second housing company patterned on the then seven-year-old Sanitary Improvement Company, but with a 4 instead of a 5 percent limit on dividends, in order to have inexpensive housing available to the families that would be rooted out of the alley slums. In 1906 after several disheartening delays Congress created a board vested with authority to condemn unsanitary buildings. Within a year, 203 houses were razed and 53 more repaired, while the District commissioners ordered the opening up of twelve narrow alleys. Unhappily early in 1907 the Supreme Court ruled a key clause of the 1892 alley-opening act unconstitutional; assessing the costs upon property-owners would be legal only where a jury found the accruing benefits equal to the costs assessed. Thus all attempts to convert the alley ways into streets came to a halt, the Board of Condemnations had to limit its activities, and, in spite of the President's appointment of a Homes Commission, the campaign to wipe out alley-dwelling slackened. With only a 4 percent return and a sense of public service as bait, the Sanitary Housing Company attracted few investors. Unless public funds supplied money to build hundreds of cheap houses, the eviction of families from the alley shanties would mean doubling up in tenements on the streets. And Congress, particularly members from rural communities and primarily agricultural states, rejected the very idea of public housing.

While admitting the existence of the slum menace, a considerable body of white Washingtonians clung to belief that "alley evils are simply due to the racial traits of their principal inhabitants—the colored people." Move them out of the interior courts, and they would take their ignorance and shiftless habits with them to produce new slums in plain sight. How could a change of locale lessen the danger of Negro slum-dwellers' spreading disease to white households where hundreds of them worked as domestic servants by day? When Weller pointed out that "conditions in a typical white alley, inhabited by white people exclusively and nearly all of them native-born Americans," duplicated those in Negro-filled alleys, race prejudice again supplied an answer: Negroes set alley standards that then corrupted their white neighbors. Under such circumstances, President Roosevelt's Homes Commission perhaps deliberately chose to omit from its report specific comments on racial problems in housing.[5]

Although the report of the President's Homes Commission, published in 1908, produced no tangible results, it was not without significance. The commission's specific proposals stressed the futility of small-scale individual efforts, but its analysis of the causal relationship between low wages and alley dwellers' miseries helped to destroy lingering illusions that pauperism was due solely to the moral weaknesses of its victims and could be cured by moral uplift. Nor did the commission wholly subscribe to the Associated Charities' thesis that

[5] *Post,* 14 Apr 1902; *Rpt B/Tr,* 1902, p. 33, 1907, p. 3; A.C. *Rpts,* 1902, pp. 5, 9, 15, 1903, pp. 18, 32, 1905, p. 43; Jacob Riis, "Backing up the President," *Charities,* xv, 754; Charles F. Weller, "Neglected Neighbors," *ibid.,* pp. 764-777; Grace Vawter Bicknell, *The Inhabited Alleys of Washington, D.C.,* pp. 8-12; *Star,* 28 Dec 1903; H Rpt 2478, 58C, 2S, Ser 4583; 34 *Stat.* 157; Comrs Rpt, 1906, pp. 7, 29.

moving people out of the hidden alleys into the open light of the streets would effect a remedy. The recommendations indicated a new awareness that fundamental faults in the economic and social structure of the community contributed to the ills of which alley-dwelling was only a symptom.

The diverse backgrounds of the commission's fifteen members make their report the more remarkable. All served without compensation. No member was a trained social worker, and only General Sternberg and Dr. Kober qualified as professional housing experts. S. W. Woodward, philanthropist, tight-laced Puritan, and successful merchant, presumably looked at some problems from a different standpoint from that of the former cigar maker or the livery stable man on the commission; Attorney Frederick L. Siddons, confirmed single-taxer, doubtless differed at times with the Negro real estate broker; the ideas of George W. Cook, Negro dean of Howard University, perhaps troubled some of his associates; the two women members, Miss Mabel T. Boardman and Mrs. Thomas Gaff, both decidedly of the city's wealthy social elite, may have thought questions of wage rates beyond the competence of a Homes Commission or any non-employers, even those who had studied the Bureau of Labor *Bulletin*, which traced statistically the links between dependency and destitution in Washington and unemployment or annual wages of less than $600. Yet the commission's common concern to locate the "causing cause" and to suggest feasible remedies for the wretchedness of thousands of Washington families resulted in a penetrating and thought-provoking report.

Some of the proposals called for legislation—partial public financing for opening alleys and establishing playgrounds, government loans at low interest to enable "business philanthropy," like the Sanitary Housing Company, to build low-rental houses, an anti-usury law, a District Bureau of Labor, workmen's accident insurance, provision for more vocational training in the public schools, and better pay for government employees, which would include not only the unskilled but also the clerical force whose salary scale had remained unchanged since 1853. In an appeal to community conscience and enlightened self-interest, the commission also urged private employers to raise wages to ensure a minimum standard of living below which no family, irrespective of its morals or its wage-earner's skills, need exist. The one basic problem that the commission ignored was the effect of race prejudice upon the ability of nearly a third of the city's population to help itself.[6]

If Washingtonians were disappointed that the report failed to inspire action on the Hill, optimists persuaded themselves that past accomplishments were sufficient to meet the needs of the immediate future. Those accomplishments were in fact impressive. Congress yielding to community pressure had created a juvenile court, appointed a Prison Commission to study penal reform, passed a "non-support" act compelling fathers to contribute to the support of their children, enacted school attendance and child labor laws, established an Industrial Home School for Colored Children, replaced the almshouse with a new Home for the Aged and Infirm, opened a model tuberculosis hospital, and appropriated several small sums for public playgrounds. Groups of private citizens had raised money for additional playgrounds and summer outings for children; the Board of Trade had organized a free legal aid service; the Associated Charities staff had served as employment agents, and voluntary gifts had increased the charity fund fifteenfold within a few years. Perhaps still more noteworthy, though less well-known, Negroes had started an educational campaign against tuber-

---

[6] George M. Kober, "Report of Committee on Social Betterment," *Reports of the President's Homes Commission*, pp. 3-9; Weller, "Neglected Neighbors," pp. 761-94; *Times*, 3 Jan 1908; U. S. Department of Commerce and Labor, Bureau of Labor, *Conditions of Living Among the Poor*, 1906, pp. 593-698, and *Charity Relief and Wage Earnings* (prepared by Samuel E. Forman), 1908, pp. 876-922; ptn, U.S. and D.C. employees to the President, 19 Dec 1916, Wilson Mss.

culosis, organized an Alley Improvement Association, and founded a Children's Temporary Home.[7]

Unhappily the dedicated zeal that had made that record possible faded as citizens concluded they could no longer look for help from official Washington. A four-year lull set in when President Taft succeeded Theodore Roosevelt. As the White House ceased to provide initiative, new District commissioners settled into a do-nothing regime. The turnover in Congress occasioned by the elections in 1910, moreover, gave control of the District committees to men more concerned with attacking real estate speculators and the utility interests in Washington than with helping her poor. The one forward-looking local measure passed during an administration determined to check the spread of socialism in America was an act accepting most of the recommendations of the Penal Commission of 1908 and appropriating funds to carry them out.

The ensuing penal reform was primarily the fruit of the humane and courageous thinking of John Joy Edson, the commission chairman. Not content with spelling out the obvious need for a parole system, suspended sentences, and an expanded physical plant to relieve the shocking over-crowding at the workhouse and jail, Edson and his associates boldly advocated a totally new method of handling first offenders and minor misdemeanants: help them to rehabilitate themselves under watchful but unrestrictive supervision, instead of locking them up with hardened criminals in the penitentiary or with "the mass of derelicts" at the Asylum workhouse. Because the ladies of the Mt. Vernon Association objected to having a penal institu-

[7] *Times*, 16 Feb 1908; *Star*, 24 Nov 1909; A.C. *Rpt*, 1902, pp. 8-10, 1903, p. 23, 1905, pp. 5, 10-11, 26-28, 1909, pp. 8-9; William H. Baldwin, "Making the Deserter Pay the Piper, The District of Columbia Plan of Paying Prisoners' Wages to Their Deserted Wives," *Survey*, XXIII, 249-52; 31 *Stat.* 822; 33 *Stat.* 386; 34 *Stat.* 73, 86, 219, 482; 35 *Stat.* 303, 420; *Rpts B/Tr*, 1902, pp. 31-32, 1905, pp. 47-48, 1907, p. 64; Comrs Rpt, 1912, pp. 17-18; Henry S. Curtis, "The Playgrounds of Washington," *Charities*, xv, 830-31; Bicknell, *The Inhabited Alleys*, pp. 24-25.

tion adjacent to a national shrine, in 1912 Congress transferred to the War Department the site at Belvoir, Virginia, which had been purchased in 1910 for the reformatory for the "more hopeful" class of adult offenders. The change of location delayed the opening of the Lorton reformatory until November 1916; and legislation authorizing indeterminate sentences and parole had to wait till the 1920's. But the opening in 1911 of the new workhouse at Occoquan, Virginia, initiated a revolution in penal administration. Here was a large institution without bars, bolts, or other means of physical restraint, night or day. The inmates worked on the farm or at the brick kilns that by 1914 were supplying all the brick for the District government's building and repair work. Officials from every section of the United States and from Europe visited Occoquan to observe the astonishing success of a system that combined minimum custody with wholesome outdoor employment.[8]

While the pace of civic uplift slowed after 1908, interest in public health prevented its coming to a halt; the cleanliness of the city, like a lowered death rate, was as important to business promoters as to social workers. When a "clean-up week" sponsored chiefly by the *Evening Star* resulted in the collection of thirty-three wagon loads of rubbish from a single block, a "clean city" committee set itself to teach thoughtless citizens the principles of sanitation. By 1912 the Board for the Condemnation of Insanitary Buildings, though grumbling that "a school of good housekeeping" was the chief need of alley dwellers, had ordered the demolition of over 1,500 buildings. At the same time philanthropists, aroused to the plight of aged people, provided some seven new homes, chiefly under

[8] H Rpt 825, 61C, 2S, Ser 5592; S Doc 989, 62C, 3S, Ser 6364; *Times*, 9, 15 Jun 1907, 10 Apr 1908, 17 Jan 1909, 28 Feb 1913; Comrs Rpt, 1909, p. 28, 1915, p. 38; *Report of the Board of Charities of the District of Columbia*, 1917, pp. 9, 85 (hereafter cited as *Rpt B/Ch*); George Kober, "Charitable and Reformatory Institutions in the District of Columbia," S Doc 207, 69C, 2S, pp. 51-62, 69-73, Ser 8702. Kober's summary contains a history of penal administration and reform in D.C., 1865 to 1927.

denominational aegis, while private contributions continued to flow also into medical and children's charities. And, contrary to all logic, during these years of parsimonious appropriations for health and building inspection, for proper enforcement of the compulsory school attendance law, and for staff for the Board of Children's Guardians, Congress granted generous subsidies to private hospitals.[9]

Out of this curious situation grew a struggle that focused Washingtonians' attention for several years on administrative procedures. The fight lay between directors of private charities and the Board of Charities, that public body created to prevent overlapping services and to provide for needy people whom private institutions did not reach. The five-man Board of Charities felt strongly that public money should go only to public institutions; private resources could adequately support private philanthropies. But socially prominent Washingtonians resented that plan as belittling their own pet charities. Board arguments urging the economies of building a general municipal hospital financed by public funds and administered by public officials met with fierce resistance. The sanctity of custom and the prestige of its defenders defeated a recommendation of 1909 in which such influential men as John Joy Edson and Dr. George Kober proposed closing Emergency Hospital and denying the public Columbia Hospital $300,000 for a new building, since both institutions tended to spend their government monies on better care for pay patients instead of enlarging service to the poor for whose benefit the grants were intended.

The shortcomings of public institutions, it is true, were all too obvious. Meagre appropriations for the new almshouse, renamed the Home for the Aged and Infirm, forced economies in construction and a prison-like sparseness of furnishings and

[9] *Star*, 4 Apr, 27 Jun 1909, 8 Sep, 2 Oct 1912; Comrs Rpt, 1912, pp. 18, 47; Bicknell, *The Inhabited Alleys*, pp. 23-25; S Doc 422, 61C, 2S, Ser 5656; A.C. *Rpts*, 1903, pp. 18-19, 1913, pp. 12, 15; S Doc 207, 69C, 2S, pp. 22, 118, 131, 149-56, 167, Ser 8702.

facilities—neither screened porches, assembly rooms, chapel, diet kitchen, nor private rooms for the desperately ill or dying; the scanty funds allotted for running the home with its 130 inmates in need of 24-hour care kept the staff to 13 attendants. The provision for the education of colored children in the new Industrial Home School was equally thin; they received some training in domestic work, gardening, farming, and good habits, but no industrial or vocational schooling, and the physical plant was grossly inadequate. This public institution, which supplanted the Hart Farm School after 1906, was little improvement over that older subsidized private charity. On the other hand, the tuberculosis hospital opened in 1908 showed that a carefully planned, well-run public institution could perform services no private organization could equal.[10]

Apparently it was the presidential election campaign of 1912 that revitalized the city's interest in the substantive features of social betterment; for Woodrow Wilson's "New Freedom" promised far-reaching social as well as political changes. Moreover, Washingtonians realized that the admirable laws passed between 1905 and 1908 had become virtually dead letters for lack of appropriations with which to work; and the needs of a growing population in the interim had outrun what the earlier acts were designed to supply. Public charity was still sharply limited in scope; private philanthropy had widened its field very little; and urgent wants within the community still fell betwixt and between. Other than several old buildings at the Asylum, the District still had no place in which to care for the chronically ill or for drug addicts, alcoholics, and the "mildly insane." The program of the Board of Children's Guardians for placing

[10] *Post*, 5 Mar 1904; *Rpt B/Tr*, 1907, p. 87, 1912, Walter C. Clephane, "Public and Private Hospitals and Charities in the District of Columbia"; Comrs Rpts, 1902, p. 299, 1915, p. 39; *Rpts B/Ch*, 1907, p. 7, 1909, pp. 355-74, 1917, p. 231; George S. Wilson, *Supervision of Private Charities*, p. 4; *Star*, 1 Feb 1912; "Municipal Hospital for the Capital City," *Survey*, xxvii, 1924-25; S Doc 207, 69C, 2S, pp. 12, 15-16, 22, 109-117, 166-68, Ser 8702; *Times*, 22 Sep 1907; D.C. Village, *Fifty Years at Blue Plains, 1906-56*.

its wards with private families was imperilled by the smallness of the staff of inspectors assigned to visiting the widely scattered foster and boarding homes—only one inspector to 340 children, compared to 85 to 100 in most American cities. Over 700 feeble-minded children got no care at all. And the unwillingness of white people to give more than token sums for Washington's nearly 1,500 destitute colored children multiplied difficulties. No observant resident of the capital regarded Washington in 1912 as a model municipality.[11]

Yet when the new drive for social improvements began, it again centered on alley-dwelling. The most enlightened Washingtonians adopted the creed: good homes make a good community. Tacitly the creed implied that good housing might make responsible citizens out of Negroes. While members of the Monday Evening Club, the spearhead of the new campaign for legislation, prepared a directory of inhabited alleys, the Associated Charities, the Woman's Welfare Department of the National Civic Federation, the Men and Religion Forward Movement, and the Social Service Conference of the Episcopal Diocese of Washington studied the problem. A Central Housing Committee enlisted the cooperation of the press, church groups, and business associations in a united appeal to Congress for a federal housing commission with authority to act.

Help came from an unexpected quarter the following spring when Mrs. Woodrow Wilson began a tour of Washington's alleys and settlement houses. The daughter and granddaughter of slave-owners, Mrs. Wilson explained that her upbringing had taught her to accept work in behalf of Negroes as her Christian duty, a point of view Negroes themselves found objectionably condescending. During her first weeks in the White House she attended Associated Charities conferences and threw herself into the welfare work of the Civic Federation with such

[11] Comrs Rpt, 1915, p. 39; *Rpts B/Ch*, 1909, pp. 336, 360-61, 1917, p. 210; S Doc 207, 69C, 2S, p. 236, 327-31, Ser 8702; *Fiscal Relations*, p. lviii.

energy that, as one associate noted, "people flocked to our standard and everybody wanted to help in the alleys. It was laughingly said that no one could move in polite society in Washington who could not talk alleys." Debutantes formed a Neighborhood House Auxiliary to do kindergarten work in the settlements, and by May 1913 "Automobile tours of our best people, by way of 'studying the conditions' and 'helping' the poor, are now established as socially correct." While some of this activity was useless and essentially frivolous, citizens were aroused over alley-dwelling as they had not been since Charles Weller first showed his stereoptican views of Washington's slums.

By June 1913 women had raised $8,500 for the Sanitary Improvement Company, Senator Works of California had submitted a bill to establish a federal housing commission, bills in both House and Senate proposed the conversion of two of the worst alleys into parks, and a new citizens' committee had undertaken to draft a housing measure acceptable to businessmen and large taxpayers. At this point the Senate requested a tabulation of ownership of alley property. The forty-page list revealed more than a thousand different owners, most of whom had only a lot or two, many of whom were women, and a few of whom themselves lived in the alleys. Realty companies owned very little alley property. A disconcerting discovery was that title to six lots was vested in the Washington City Orphan Asylum. Hence the battle could not be fought against a mere handful of villains or a few unwitting exploiters.[12]

The plan that eventually emerged from the citizens' committee made no mention of public housing but called for conversion of alleys into minor streets or parks by drawing on the District's

[12] A.C. *Rpts*, 1911, p. 12, 1912, p. 15; Wilbur Vincent Mallalieu, "A Washington Alley," *Survey*, xxviii, 69-71; Bicknell, *The Inhabited Alleys*, pp. 16-17, 20, 23-28; and "The Home Maker of the White House, Mrs. Woodrow Wilson's Social Work in Washington," *Survey*, xxxiii, 19-22; *Post*, 17 Apr, 20 May 1913; *Times*, 20-31 May, 1 Jun 1913; S Doc 120, 63C, 1S, Ser 6536.

general fund over a ten-year period. The proposal reached Congress early in 1914; by then popular excitement had died down and congressional opposition to spending federal money in the capital had grown. Nothing stirred on the Hill until mid-August. Then Congress learned that on the last morning of her life Mrs. Woodrow Wilson had told the President she would rest happier if she knew the alley bill had passed. Two months later what would soon prove to be a curiously unrealistic measure became law. It forbade after July 1, 1918, residence in any alley not converted to a minor street, but it provided no machinery and no funds and ignored the problem of where evicted families were to live. Shutting their eyes to the weakness of the new law, most Washingtonians elatedly assumed that the alley problem would now solve itself, inasmuch as a survey showed a decline in the alley population from the 19,076 of 1905 to 11,400 in 1912, and fewer than 8,500 still there in 1915. With the new Ellen Wilson Homes Association preparing plans for low-rental houses on the streets, concern about the families remaining in the alley slums dropped. No one foresaw in 1916 that within a year the demand for housing in the war-ridden capital would consign the alley act to limbo.[13]

Social betterment in other realms, notably child care, fortunately made more lasting progress. Infant mortality, on the decline since 1900, had dropped to one in ten by 1917. Thanks in considerable degree to a Children's Council formed in 1911, day nurseries, child welfare centers, public playgrounds, summer camps, and classes and clubs at the settlement houses multiplied in endeavor to check juvenile delinquency before it began. The Juvenile Court, to be sure, proved disappointingly ineffectual: it had only two probation officers, had to function as a criminal rather than a domestic relations court, and its

[13] *Times*, 22 Oct 1913, 27 Jan, 19 Feb, 25 Aug, 21 Sep, 1914; Bicknell, "The Home Maker of the White House," pp. 21-22; "Washington Alleys; A Half-way Measure," *Outlook*, CVIII, 240-41; 38 *Stat.* 716; *Rpt B/Tr*, 1916, pp. 104-05; H Dis Comee, 63C, 2S, Hrgs, "Certain Alleys in the District of Columbia," pp. 12, 22; Comrs Rpt, 1915, p. 189.

policy of making short-term or temporary commitments of children to the Board of Children's Guardians forced the Guardians to place an increasing number of their wards in institutions
instead of private homes. Yet the Guardians succeeded in providing better care for colored children than was possible earlier,
for, while the number placed with private families was pitifully
small, the quality of the homes was higher. On the other hand,
whereas good private homes had been available at the turn of
the century for four out of every five of the white children, by
1916 the Board had to put more than half into institutions,
since white families were reluctant to take temporary boarders,
chances of adoption accordingly diminished, and after 1914 policy dictated abandoning all placement by indenture. The institutions were on the whole better run and more numerous than
in the 1890's, but an institutional atmosphere hung over the
best of them, even the new Episcopal Home with its spacious
grounds beyond the Anacostia where the children were housed
in groups of eight to ten on "the cottage system."[14]

More significant than the recurrent dissatisfaction with child
placement was the growing realization that the most efficient
handling of a social problem after it had developed was no substitute for prevention. In 1914 the president of the Board of
Guardians, B. Pickman Mann, a Patent Office examiner and
son of Horace Mann, studied the background of the board's
1,500 charges in an attempt to identify and find ways of eradicating the social forces that brought them into its custody. He
concluded that two obstacles stood in the way of a constructive

[14] *Times*, 9, 11 Sep 1914, 8, 23 Jun, 15 Nov 1915, 17, 27 Oct 1916;
Rpts B/Ch, 1912, pp. 358-59, 1914, pp. 352-65, 1915, pp. 312-15, 1916,
pp. 239-45; A.C. *Rpt*, 1912, p. 14, 1913, pp. 10-15; Hastings Hart, *Child
Welfare in the District of Columbia*, pp. 3-14, 72, 77, 117-123, 130-132
(hereafter cited as Hart, *Child Welfare*); Louis G. Weitzmann, *One
Hundred Years of Catholic Charities in the District of Columbia*, pp. 120-
25, 142-48; S Doc 207, 69C, 2S, pp. 234, 236, Ser 8702; Emma O.
Lundberg and Mary E. Milburn, "Child Dependency in the District of
Columbia," U. S. Department of Labor, Children's Bureau Publication
No. 140, 1924, p. 67 (hereafter cited as Lundberg, *Child Dependency*).

attack upon delinquency and dependency in Washington, namely race prejudice and the lack of any means of keeping a family together when long illness, unemployment, or the desertion of the wage earner caused a domestic crisis. Mann had no panacea for racial antagonisms, but he believed extensive recourse to mothers' pensions, a plan the Associated Charities had followed as best it could since 1906, would cut the roots of many problems of child care. A law passed in 1914 limiting to eight hours the working day of women in mercantile and manufacturing establishments had had some beneficial effect, but in a non-industrial, generally non-commercial city, where jobs in factories and shops were few and virtually never open to colored women, the act did little to preserve family life, least of all among colored people, whose children yearly swelled the ranks of delinquents. Chiefly at Mann's instigation but with the co-operation of the judge of the Juvenile Court, the Children's Council, and other child welfare groups, in 1916 the Children's Protective Association came into being to carry on Mann's study of how to rectify the social maladjustments that underlay delinquency and dependency.[15]

An enlightened segment of the community began at the same time to take a new look at adult unemployment and its consequences. The fluctuations were confusing: the number of unemployed, homeless men who sought temporary refuge at the Municipal Lodging House rose from 6,800 in 1914 to 9,900 the next year and again dropped to 6,800 in 1916, when munitions plants in other parts of the country opened up jobs for the able-bodied. Although the Lodging House was designed for "tramps," the Monday Evening Club put a new, better-equipped Lodging House high on the list of civic needs. The ups and downs of employment for permanent residents troubled thought-

[15] *Rpt B/Ch*, 1909, pp. 322-23, 1913, pp. 424-38; Hart, *Child Welfare*, p. 124; "LaFollette-Peters Eight-hour Bill Enacted into Law," *Survey*, xxxi, 689; H Doc 1461, 62C, 3S, Ser 6460; *Times*, 15 Nov 1915; Consumers' League of D.C., *Third Anl Rpt*, 1915, pp. 4-5.

ful citizens even more. Because of the seasonal character of the building trades, unemployment rose alarmingly in severe winters, but its decline in a mild winter had long encouraged public reliance on stopgaps. Yet in the winter of 1914, if the superintendent of the Gospel Mission appeared to be making a moral judgment when he labelled most of Washington's 15,000 unemployed men "deserving," charitable citizens were too concerned with the basic facts of want to consider moral criteria. The Chamber of Commerce urged an immediate start on all public works for which there were appropriations; Walter Ufford wrote 3,000 letters to householders who might have jobs to offer, but he remarked: "What Washington really needs is an employment bureau under Government auspices, without the tinge of charity."[16]

Ufford went much further, for he advocated old age, sickness, accident, and unemployment insurance for all wage earners and minimum pay of $2.00 a day for common laborers. At the time, $1.50 to $1.75 was standard, despite findings that $720 a year was below a subsistence wage for a family of five. Ufford's thinking far outran that of most citizens and indeed would have little impact until the 1930's. Even the Consumers' League put its major emphasis on getting Congress to pass a women's minimum wage law. The Associated Charities felt obliged to continue to work on a finger-in-the-dyke basis that left little energy or time to plan far-reaching social reconstruction. In early 1916 Congressman Nolan of California, in response to a flood of petitions from government clerks, introduced a bill setting a minimum pay rate of $3 a day for all federal and District government employees. The proposal seemed unthinkably extravagant, particularly as seven hours constituted the normal day in government offices. Repeated pleas of government clerks for a pension system got even less attention. By and large, the

[16] *Times*, 21 Jan 1911, 13 Feb 1913, 22, 31 Dec 1914, 18 Nov, 15, 23 May, 7 Dec 1916; *Rpts B/Ch*, 1914, p. 393, 1915, p. 347, 1916, pp. 265-66; A.C. *Rpt*, 1915, pp. 4, 13, 1916, pp. 9-10.

American public at the height of the Progressive era still believed that laws of supply and demand, not federal legislation, must regulate wage rates and individual thrift and foresight must provide for "the rainy day."[17]

Theories of self-sufficiency notwithstanding, both philanthropy and public welfare services widened. Private gifts opened two new homes for the aged, one of them sponsored by colored people; and, under the leadership of Mrs. Archibald Hopkins, the Home for Incurables got more support. The long debated question of a municipal hospital, furthermore, appeared to be settled in 1914 by an appropriation voted for a building in northwest Washington. Bitter opposition from property owners who were unwilling to have a "pauper" hospital in their neighborhood caused a three-year delay, but a change of location back to the old Asylum grounds on the Anacostia disposed of those objections, and a politically adroit proposal of District Commissioner Brownlow won over reluctant members of Congress: the institution was to be named Gallinger Hospital in honor of the former chairman of the Senate District Committee.[18]

Sentiment, meanwhile, had been mounting to force the closing of the houses of ill fame in the triangle below Pennsylvania Avenue near the Treasury. Known as "Joe Hooker's Division" since Civil War days when General Hooker's determination to keep prostitution within bounds had led to a semi-official demarcation of a few squares along the Avenue, the red light district had spread until in 1913, according to investigating "suffragettes," it stretched from within two

[17] S Doc 422, 61C, 2S, Ser 5658; H Rpt 825, 61C, 2S, Ser 5592; A.C. *Rpts*, 1913, p. 7, 1916, pp. 7-9; Consumers' League, *Third Anl Rpt*, 1915, pp. 7-15; *Star*, 23 Mar 1916; H Dis Comee, 64C, 1S, Hrgs, "Resolution Authorizing the Department of Labor to Inquire into the Cost of Living in D.C."; *Rpts B/Ch*, 1902, pp. 207-08, 1916, p. 244; ptns and ltrs in D.C. file, Woodrow Wilson Mss; *Times*, 9 Apr 1911, 30 Apr 1913, 17 Jan 1914, 29 Jan, 22 Mar, 16 Apr, 25 Nov, 7 Dec 1916.

[18] *Bee*, 10 Apr 1915; *Rpt B/Ch*, 1916, pp. 225-27; *Fiscal Relations*, pp. lii-liii; Brownlow, *A Passion for Anonymity*, p. 101.

blocks of the White House to the edge of Capitol Hill. A tale indicative of the open acceptance of vice in the city told of a madame brought into court who, when asked whether she pled guilty, responded, "Your Honor, everybody knows I run the second-best house in the city." "Second best?" queried the judge. "Certainly," came the answer, "the Treasury runs the best." As the establishments advertised the city's vicious aspects to tourists, in 1914 Congress passed the so-called red light bill, but President Wilson refused to sign it until some provision was made to care for the prostitutes. The Florence Crittenden Mission thereupon undertook the task and the bill became law.

The new importance of women in the "civic uplift" movement, illustrated in the suffragettes' battle against vice, was also reflected in the non-political activities of the Women's Welfare Department of the National Civic League and in the anti-saloon campaign. Women made little headway in fighting the liquor traffic, particularly as the District Excise Board, established by law in 1909, did not relish their missionary zeal. If earnestness devoid of humor was a handicap, still they increasingly made their ideas count. In 1913 one writer said of the war against alley dwellings: "Never before have the women of the capital risen in a body"; the victory was theirs. Women's clubs were not the mainstay of volunteer social service as they were in other big cities. The National Professional Women's League, the Woman's Suffrage League, and the District Federation of Women's Clubs had in view either political objectives or professional advancement. Otherwise "club life" tended more to sociability than to public service. Ladies attended current events lectures at the Washington Club but carried on their civic activities through the churches and charity organizations.[19]

---

[19] Washington *Herald*, 21 May 1907; *Star*, 15 Feb 1912; "Washington's Red Light District Attacked," *Survey*, xxxi, 314; *Times*, 28, 31 Jan, 2 Jul 1914, 16 Feb 1916. S Rpt 391, 63C, 2S, Ser 6552; S Doc 981, 63C, 3S, Ser 6775. The story of the madame was told me by a former Secretary of State who heard it from a former judge.

In many parts of America women with leisure at their disposal first learned about community service when war work drew them into it. In Washington the sense of obligation came much earlier, doubtless partly through the skillful appeals of Charles Weller and later through the example set by women with the social prestige of a Mrs. Hopkins, a Mrs. Whitman Cross, a Mabel T. Boardman, and Mrs. Woodrow Wilson. While Dolly Madison and Frances Folsom Cleveland each had participated in her day, neither First Lady had played so direct a part in Washington's charities as Mrs. Wilson, and neither had occupied the White House in a period when social guilt ran strong in the upper ranks of American society. Mrs. Hopkins and Mrs. Cross indicated by precept and deed that for women the one justification for unearned wealth and leisure lay in good works. Miss Boardman, after serving on President Roosevelt's Homes Commission, began teaching Washington debutantes through the District chapter of the American Red Cross that their privileged place in the world put upon them a debt to society that they could best pay by personal service in worthy causes. Debutantes quickly learned that they could combine charitable activities with the gaieties of the social season and, after the founding of the Washington Junior League in 1914, a disciplined pursuit of the former was likely to enhance the latter, especially for young women of slightly insecure social background.[20]

City-dwellers the country over, spurred on by the muckrakers and preachers of the social gospel, were seeking solutions to urban problems as diligently as were Washingtonians. They rarely questioned their capacity to succeed. In 1916 District Commissioner Oliver Newman told the Monday Evening Club that Washingtonians had a wider interest in community affairs than he had seen in any of the other nine cities where

[20] Edith Elmer Wood, "Four Washington Alleys," *Survey*, XXXI, 182; *Times*, 3 Nov, 17 Jul, 10 Sep 1914.

he had lived.[21] Perhaps nowhere was the optimism that characterized American reformers of the time so marked. If naïve and somewhat shallow, it nevertheless suffused the city with a golden warmth of hope.

[21] *Times*, 18 Jan 1916.

CHAPTER IX

THE BOARD OF TRADE AND PUBLIC AFFAIRS, 1901-1916

"OH, my sister cities of the land, harken to me . . . Young and strong, fair of body, clean of mind, I have kept our faith. I live and grow, in beauty and power, in the strength of the spirit that makes for good. . . .

"I am the Capital and blood kin to our Mecca of the East. Day by day, year by year, century by century, I will grow. . . . It shall be mine, by the example that I teach, to put order in thy houses, where disorder now reigns. It shall be mine to teach thee cleanliness of body and of mind, and honesty and the municipal faith. It shall be mine to teach thee the meaning and show thee the soul of the beauty that lies within and the beauty that shines without." So bragged the *Evening Star* in a eulogy of the capital in 1909.

In only less fulsome phrases presidents of the Board of Trade voiced similar complacency; occasional reminders that no one must rest on his oars scarcely interrupted the flow of self-congratulation over "the grandeur of our city." In addition to a "delightful climate," a magnificent physical layout, an ample supply of pure water, efficient local government, and moderate taxation, Washington offered "superb commercial and manufactural probabilities" and exceptional educational advantages through her universities and schools, art galleries and libraries.[1] "Is it any wonder," former District Commissioner Henry West asked rhetorically in 1913, "that during recent years there should have been attracted to Washington a most desirable class of residents—people . . . who are glad to live in a city which is attractive and well kept, where the society is cosmopolitan, where peace and order reign with freedom from polit-

[1] *Star*, 1 Jan 1909; *Rpts B/Tr*, 1905, p. 5, 1906, p. 37, 1910, pp. 13-14, 1912, pp. 5-6, 1913, pp. 33-44; S Doc 420, 63C, 2S, p. 11, Ser 6593.

ical disturbance, and where the constant march of progress is unchecked?"

Land prices mounted steadily. Row houses rose in the vicinity of Lincoln Park and in Mt. Pleasant, apartment houses adapted to families who could afford only one servant multiplied in more central areas, and the expanding "millionaire colony" about DuPont and Sheridan Circles was making the "City of Magnificent Distances" also the "Home of Palatial Mansions." Wall Street depressions had little effect upon banking or building operations in the District; real estate, on the contrary, attracted outside capital, and during the panic of 1907 one realtor boasted that Washington grew faster in two months than she had in twelve during the 1890's. As office buildings and stores took over the area immediately to the north and east of the Treasury, real estate brokers developed new residential sections along upper 16th Street, about Chevy Chase Circle, and, for people of very modest means, along the eastward extension of Rhode Island Avenue. Uneasiness about the attitude of the new administration in 1913 and then the outbreak of war in Europe lessened the volume of transactions; but, although over 4,700 houses stood vacant in early 1915, prices held up, and later that year the building of apartment houses again accelerated.

Built-up blocks interspersed with an ever diminishing number of vacant lots stretched for a mile or more north of Florida Avenue by 1907, making the formal city limits a limit only in name. Prophecies ran that within a decade Washington's suburbs would reach into nearby Maryland. By 1910 the area outside Washington contained a quarter of the District's total population. Trolley lines passing over the Aqueduct Bridge hastened the growth of Roslyn on the Virginia shore and inspired so many real estate ventures there that in 1909 a District commissioner argued that the federal government would soon have to negotiate for reannexation of the southern third of the original ten-mile square: Washington would need that area for factories and homes for her poor. The reannexation question never got beyond vague talk among Washington promoters, and by 1920 the creation of Arlington County would kill hopes that the Commonwealth of Virginia would relinquish so valuable a region.[2]

Building and loan associations financed most small householders' home-building, while the city's big national banks handled larger enterprises—entire suburban subdivisions, new office buildings, and the extension of utilities. Before the Wilson administration embarked on banking reform, the government itself treated the powerful Riggs National Bank with deference. For years the president of the bank, Charles Glover, kept a desk in the main Treasury, where he would be the first to hear of impending developments in official monetary policies. In 1915 when the Comptroller of the Currency, John Skelton Williams, invoked the authority of the new Federal Reserve Act to stop what he characterized as the improper practices of the Riggs Bank, its officers chose to defy the Treasury. Glover, by then denied his desk at the Treasury and incensed at charges which he labelled vindictive misrepresentations, hit Williams over the head with a walking stick when the two met by chance in Lafayette Square, and was summoned before Congress to make public apology. But once the courts had declared the bank's monetary transactions legal, Riggs' stature in American financial circles rose to new heights.[3]

In spite of virtually unbroken prosperity, the Chamber of Commerce, an offshoot of the Board of Trade started by small

[2] Because newspaper pieces on business progress, taxes, and District administration ran to thousands, I have limited specific citations to a mere sampling: *Post*, 6 Apr 1902, 13 Mar, 25 May 1913; *Rpts B/Tr*, 1903, p. 16, 1908, p. 23, 1910, pp. 13-14, 1912, p. 17; *Star*, Summaries, 1908-1916; *Times*, 9 Jun 1907, 28 Feb 1913, 18 Jun 1915; Comrs Rpt, 1906, p. 41, 1912, p. 57, 1915, p. 50, 1919, p. 575; *Rec*, 59C, 2S Index, p. 267; H. B. F. Macfarland, "The Rebuilding of the National Capital," *American City*, I, 11-12; S Doc 489, 64C, 1S, Ser 6954.

[3] Interview, Louis Brownlow; "The Riggs Bank Row," *Literary Digest*, L, 939-40; "The Riggs Bank Case," *Outlook*, CIX, 953-54; *Star*, 23 May 1916; *Post*, 25 Jan 1913; *Times*, 11 Oct 1915.

business interests in 1907, advocated a campaign to attract industry. Proponents argued that industry would reduce seasonal unemployment and give Washington her proper place in the American business world. The Board of Trade, on the other hand, as a body committed to developing the city as a show place and residential center, shied away from a proposal sure to antagonize Congress: "It is entirely unlikely," announced one representative, "that Congress could tolerate manufacturing districts here, with the massing industrial population, the danger of strikes, boycotts, lockouts, etc." And attempts to enter into industrial competition with other American cities, *Scribner's Magazine* contended, would cost "the spoiled child of the republic" the favors she enjoyed. The squeeze caused by rising prices in a community where fixed incomes were the rule led the president of the Board of Trade to suggest in 1915 that factories in the suburbs might furnish the District with badly needed revenue without proving offensive to residents of Washington. In fact a munitions plant opened on the far side of the Anacostia in 1914 operated without Washingtonians' discovering that it was there. But the difficulty of harnessing the Great Falls, the area's one major source of power, and reluctance to risk offending Congress combined to halt tentative anglings for industry.[4]

All businessmen talked about expanding Washington's commerce by means of improved railroad freight service, a shipping canal from the Anacostia to Chesapeake Bay to be built with federal subsidies, and the construction of a huge auditorium for conventions. None of these proposals, most of them bolstered by arguments familiar since the 1840's, produced

[4] *Rpt B/Tr*, 1902, pp. 39-46, 1905, p. 50, 1910, pp. 10-11, 1915, pp. 7-8; *Post*, 7 Jul 1906; *Herald*, 14 May 1907; *Times*, 29 Jun, 25 Aug, 10 Nov 1907, 23 Jan 1911, 9 Jan 1914; "Made in Washington," *Harper's Weekly*, LVI, 15 Jun 1912, p. 30; speech by Walter F. Fowler, D.C. Budget Officer, to Bankers' Association, Apr 1959, Ms in possession of Louis Brownlow; Montgomery Schuyler, "The New Washington," *Scribner's Magazine*, LI, 131-32; *Fiscal Relations*, p. 25, Ser 6915; *Star*, 6 May 1916.

results. Congress ignored the appeals for $250,000 of District tax money for a convention hall, and a National George Washington Memorial Association, which supposedly would raise $2,500,000 for it, failed to materialize. Not until the 1950's would plans for a "Washington Cultural Center" receive any encouragement. Yet yearly the flood of visitors ready to spend money in the capital rose. By 1908 Washingtonians were learning to recognize the arrival of spring less by the appearance of crocuses and daffodils than by the fleet of victorias and sightseeing wagonettes manned by megaphoned guides which lined up near the White House. By 1916, next to government business and real estate, the tourist trade ranked as Washington's chief financial asset.[5]

The Board of Trade meanwhile ceased to exercise the enlightened leadership that had originally distinguished it. In 1903 the president over-stated the case very little when he said that once a board committee, the directors, and the full membership endorsed any proposal, it immediately commanded "public attention, public respect and the support of all good citizens" as well as serious consideration in Congress. Thereafter a growing tendency to regard the welfare of the city as identical with that of the thin top layer of society gradually stripped the organization of its representative quality. Unlike the older, most of the younger generation of directors took little active interest in local philanthropies. Possibly the increasing professionalism of social welfare work accounted for part of that change, but it had the effect of divorcing board policy-makers from close associations with the social betterment leaders. The citizens' associations did not fill the gap, since they increasingly concentrated upon their own neighborhood problems to the exclusion of city-wide concerns. When

[5] *Star*, 2 Jan 1905, 2 May 1909, 28 Feb 1912; *Rpts B/Tr*, 1905, pp. 10-12, 51, 114, 1907, pp. 150-53, 1908, p. 40, 1910, pp. 13-14, 31, 92-98, 1912, p. 8; *Times*, 17 Jun 1908, 19 Mar 1911, 15 Sep 1915; George Fitch, "Seeing Washington through a Megaphone," *Ladies' Home Journal*, Aug 1907, p. 22; *Times*, 15 Sep 1915.

the Federation of Citizens' Associations was incorporated in 1911, it usually presented only the sum total of its members' complaints.

The *Times*, Washington's nearest approach to a left-wing paper, observed in 1911 that the Chamber of Commerce "represents the most advanced and most progressive thought of the community." From it came recommendations on questions the Board of Trade now bypassed—utility rates, milk inspection, and similar matters important to the rank and file of humble citizens. Unhappily, the Chamber carried less weight than its parent organization. After 1907 neither included any colored men. Never admitting that it no longer spoke for the city as a whole, the Board of Trade after 1910 devoted itself to city finances and the protection of the "half-and-half" principle from congressional inroads. The board of directors, men linked with the great real estate companies, the big banks, and the utilities, continued to have enormous influence, particularly as long as some members of Congress looked upon investment in Washington as a sure road to fortune. The comment of one congressman indicated that here and there that view still obtained in 1915; he assured Louis Brownlow in congratulating him on his appointment as District commissioner that a term in the District Building should net him at least $1,000,000.[6]

Irrespective of any incidental, albeit potentially sizable, financial benefits that might accrue to a commissioner, the post was sought after as an honor. But as an incumbent could affect the course of the city's development, the inner circle of the Board of Trade expected to name the civilians whom the President would appoint. President Roosevelt was not wholly amenable to that arrangement. He kept in office Henry Macfarland, whom one Washingtonian later described as "a nice

[6] *Reports of the President's Homes Commission*, p. 212; *Times*, 8 Jan, 26 May 1911, 17 Dec 1913; *Rpts B/Tr*, 1902-1906 inclusive, especially 1903, p. 6, and 1916, pp. 37, 94-96; *Star*, 2 Dec 1909.

piece of bric-a-brac," and, in the face of protest in 1902, appointed Henry West, another journalist. "It is not in human nature," Theodore Noyes wrote the President, "that the *Star* should view with any complacency the appointment to local municipal control of the employee and representative of a rival newspaper of democratic proclivities." Although bitter quarrels between West and Macfarland interfered with their functioning, both men served until late 1909. The retired general and the hardware merchant whom Taft appointed were more to the liking of the Board of Trade.

Board of Trade satisfaction turned to alarm in 1913 when Woodrow Wilson selected two former officers of the Monday Evening Club, Oliver Newman, an experienced newspaper correspondent, and Frederick L. Siddons of the District Bar.[7] Admittedly swayed by a judgment confided to him that the District government had been "controlled by men with connections in speculative real estate, a triangle of profit and power manned by a triumvirate," the President had made clear that he wanted no commissioner tied to the local real estate "ring."[8] In the eyes of powerful business interests both men named were tainted with radicalism. Resentment ran so strong among the old guard that one of the group brought a suit contesting the legality of Newman's appointment on the grounds that he was not a *bona fide* resident of the District; the plaintiff lost. Another blow awaited the former kingmakers in 1915. President Wilson elevated Siddons to the District Supreme Court, and chose as his successor thirty-five-year-old Louis Brownlow. In time to come "Brownie" would be recognized from coast to coast as an authority on public administration. In 1915 he was known in Washington as a competent reporter for a big news

[7] D. H. MacLedan to Albert Burleson, 3 Apr 1913, Wilson Mss; Henry Cabot Lodge to Theodore Roosevelt, 30 Jul 1902, Theodore W. Noyes to Roosevelt, 11 Aug, Crosby Noyes to Roosevelt, 15 Aug, and Mark Hanna to Roosevelt, 20 Aug 1902, Theodore Roosevelt Mss (L.C.).

[8] Quoted in Herbert Janvrin Browne, *Assessment and Taxation in the District of Columbia, and the Fiscal Relation to the Federal Government,* 1915, p. 64; *Post,* 7 Jan 1910, 28 Jan 1913.

syndicate, a friend of muckrakers such as Robert Wickliffe Woolley and, doubtless a source of special uneasiness to ultra-conservatives, a son-in-law of Congressman Thetus Sims, the old warrior of the House District Committee who for years had fought special privilege in the District.[9]

If Macfarland was smug, West easy-going, and Taft's appointees unimaginative and intellectually timid, those shortcomings were more than offset by the qualities of Siddons, Newman, and Brownlow. The engineer commissioners, moreover, one after the other set a high record of efficiency. All told, the successive boards of commissioners during the fifteen years preceding the United States' entry into the war achieved a standard of public service not again equalled in the District until the 1950's.

The commissioners' job was no sinecure. Ideally it meant maintaining and improving the appearance of the capital and simultaneously meeting the community's less immediately visible needs out of the funds Congress was willing to appropriate. It meant balancing the wants of one group of citizens against those of another and providing for intangibles, such as public health and police protection, without curtailing public works. And always it meant, after the administrators had mapped out what they considered the wisest allotment of money, a struggle to persuade the House Subcommittee on District Appropriations that the figure for each item was justified. The prohibition on borrowing in itself created a never-ending quandary even early in the century when Congress authorized Treasury advances at interest for enlargement of the water distribution system and construction of the sewage pumping station. The list of public works the commissioners

[9] *Star*, 13, 14, 18 Nov 1909; interview, Louis Brownlow; *Times*, 14 Nov 1909, 15 Jul, 22 Oct 1914, 31 Jan, 21 Jun 1915; memorandum for Edward C. Becherer, Mar-May 1913, and Elijah Knott to Woodrow Wilson, 19 May 1913, Wilson Mss; Brownlow, *A Passion for Anonymity*, pp. 1-12.

labelled urgent in 1909 and the estimated cost of each suggests the dimensions of the problem of meeting such needs out of current income:

Project	Cost
Reclamation of the Anacostia flats, a measure vital to the city's health	$2,552,320
Improvement of Rock Creek valley from its mouth to Massachusetts Avenue, most of the stretch still an unsightly and insanitary dumping ground	$4,750,000
Improvement of the harbor front	$2,880,000
Purchase of additional land for parks	$5,000,000
New buildings for the reformatory and workhouse	$1,000,000
Installation of a high-pressure fire protection system	$ 750,000
Extension of suburban trunk sewers, a project to be spread out over 12 years	$2,000,000
Extension of trunk water mains to the suburbs	$ 800,000
Enlargement of public hospital facilities	$ 150,000
Elimination of dangerous railroad grade crossings outside the city limits	$ 400,000

The total of some $20,282,000, even if spread over several years, would leave nothing over for new services, let alone the expansion of old, in a rapidly growing city whose local revenues had never reached $7,000,000. Then and later, some men on the Hill, like many Washingtonians, would have preferred less emphasis on physical embellishments and more on higher salaries for school teachers, additional school nurses and dentists, sanitary inspectors, larger staff for the Board of Children's Guardians, and a bigger, better paid police force. But critics on the floor of Congress rarely succeeded in redistributing funds in the District budget as it came from committee; at most they cut the over-all figure.[10]

Before 1910 the commissioners' programs got fuller support from Congress than did their successors'. Congressional constituents approved of expenditures for beautifying the capital, and the laws enacted to promote social betterment involved relatively little money. Furthermore, the financial interests of District Committee members pled Washington's cause. Stories, never denied, ran that Senator Arthur Gorman made $1,000,000 and Joseph Babcock, chairman of the House District Committee for some years after 1895, cleared $400,000 in Washington real estate and utility stocks simply by using their advance knowledge of which sections of the city were to get funds for improvements and what privileges were to be allowed the utility companies. And there were others. Congressional decisions to maintain high utility rates and occasional evasion of the 1878 commitment on sharing District expenses were annoying, but the friendliness of the "plunderers of Washington" brought some benefits to the entire community. The *entente cordiale* was undoubtedly more useful to the well-to-do few than to the impecunious many, but humble citizens were gratified that Congress heeded their pleas for a compulsory education law, the removal of an upper age limit for night school students, additions to the fire and police departments, and minor increases in the allowances for charities.[11]

But the honeymoon was over. Indications of growing ir-

[10] Comrs Rpt, 1909, pp. 57-58; Max West, "Room for Improvement," *Outlook*, LXXIX, 625-26; H. B. F. Macfarland, "The Needs of the National Capital," *Outlook*, LXXXIII, 518-21; *Star*, 6 Dec 1909, 15 Feb, 24 Aug 1912; *Times*, 29 Nov 1911; *Survey*, XXVII, 1591; S Doc 422, 61C, 2S, p. 19, Ser 5658; *Fiscal Relations*, p. liii, Ser 6915; *Rpts B/Tr*, 1906, p. 20, 1908, p. 28, 1909, p. 34.

[11] Robert Wickliffe Wolley, "The Plunderers of Washington," *Pearson's Magazine*, XXII, 631-35; *Times*, 30 Nov 1907, 18 Jan, 20 Mar, 9 Aug 1908, 9 Sep 1911; *Star*, 10 Jan 1903; *Rec*, 63C, 2S, p. 4536; Comrs Rpt, 1906, pp. 25-26; *Rpt B/Tr*, 1905, p. 80; Alonzo Tweedale, "The Budget for the District of Columbia," *Proceedings of the Cincinnati Conference for Good City Government*, 1909, pp. 273-83.

ritation in Congress over the half-and-half arrangement appeared in a law of 1909 which required the commissioners thenceforward to submit their annual budgets, not as in the past in the form of estimates of needs, but as statements of expected revenues from District taxes and matching federal funds. Although the innovation precluded long-term financing of major public works, the act at first looked innocuous, simply a way of tailoring the suit to fit the cloth. But new leaders in Congress were soon snipping away at the federal share of District expenses by reducing over-all appropriations. Thus when the commissioners estimated District tax revenues for 1913 at $6,477,000, Congress appropriated $10,531,000, of which less than $4,054,000 was federal money, more nearly a third than a half the total. While working on schemes to shift to the District the entire cost of street maintenance, the House dug into thirty-year-old records and exacted some $1,800,000 from local taxpayers for such items as interest on bonds of 1877 and 1878 and deficiencies in payments for services for which no bill had ever been rendered.[12]

Viewed from the perspective of half a century, three facts are clear about the fight that came out into the open in the early months of 1910: first, the congressmen who launched the attack believed they were engaged in a righteous battle with that monster, special privilege; second, they frequently used battering rams where fly swatters would have served; and, third, many of Washington's self-styled financial experts unwittingly undermined her defenses by shifting ground or by taking positions they could not fortify with incontrovertible figures. Promoters talked of the city's "moderate taxation" when they were trying to attract new business enterprise but insisted to Con-

[12] *Star*, 22 Sep 1909, 15 Jun 1912; *Fiscal Relations*, pp. 1628-39, Ser 6916; *Rec*, 60C, 1S, p, 1908, 60C, 2S, pp. 8, 818-19, 859-74; *Post*, 15 Jun 1910; Comrs Rpt, 1913, p. 97; Laurence Schmeckebier, *The District of Columbia, Its Government and Administration*, pp. 52-54; S Doc 403, 63C, 2S, Ser 6593; *Rpt B/Tr*, 1912, p. 14, and "Financial Relations of the District of Columbia and the Federal Government from 1871 to 1912."

gress that per capita taxes here were higher than in other like-sized cities and that any added burden would be ruinous. Confused thinking and much misinformation in Congress about District laws and practices complicated the struggle. Even members of long standing rarely understood the Treasury's accounting methods in handling District funds. Attendance during debates on District affairs was always slim. Congressmen periodically indulged in preposterous statements, asserting, for example, that the United States defrayed the entire cost of running the schools and paving the streets. Under these circumstances ill temper and a sense of outrage developed in both camps.[13]

The changed attitude of the congressional majority sprang partly from the increasing size of the commissioners' requested budgets: for fiscal year 1901 $7,657,773 was asked for, $7,532,519 voted; for 1910, the last year in which estimates of need determined the amount requested, $16,176,356 was asked for, $10,528,292 appropriated. If the city could manage on $7,500,000 in 1901, irate congressmen argued that more than twice that sum for 1910 was nonsense; they kept the appropriation below $12,880,000 for the next six years.

In the second place, when for unknown reasons the men in control of the House and Senate District committees ceased to invest heavily in Washington real estate and utility stock, they began to advocate economy and the cancellation of a fiscal arrangement that they felt enabled the city's millionaires to batten on the taxpayers of the rest of the country. Reformers from urban constituencies inclined to believe that only financially powerful exploiters of lesser citizens benefitted from the existing system. And senators and congressmen from agrarian districts were determined to hold the line against the march of

[13] *Fiscal Relations*, pp. 266, 296, 367-69, 930-69, Ser 6915, and 1742-44, Ser 6916; "A Square Deal for Washington," reprints from *Star* in Wilson Mss; *Times*, 14 Feb, 13, 27 May 1911, 14 Dec 1913; *Post*, 26 Jan 1913; *Rec*, 61C, 2S, pp. 200-01, 2923-24, 61C, 3S, p. 1597, 62C, 2S, p. 1226, 63C, 2S, p. 1014; *Rpt B/Tr*, 1911, p. 14.

"socialism," that insidious threat creeping out of teeming cities to engulf robust American individualism.[14] Fear of socialism took odd forms. A God-fearing, earnest representative from a farm district in Michigan fought tooth and nail against appropriations for public playgrounds in Washington because to him they represented a socialistic perversion of public obligation.

Conflict between rural and urban interests in Congress, sectional controversies, the admission of three western states between 1907 and 1912, the widening recourse to direct primaries, and after 1914 the popular election of senators, all affected the balance in both houses and bore upon attitudes toward the District of Columbia. Party politics and the constantly mounting pressure of legislative business for a nation grown to a world power pushed local affairs further and further into the background. The minority party usually opposed majority-sponsored District bills, and both parties postponed "District days" with increasing frequency. Compared to the spate of constructive local acts passed between 1902 and 1908, the measures enacted in the next decade were few and relatively insignificant. Badly needed social legislation sneaked through, if at all, only by the skills of its supporters in tying it to an appropriation bill.[15]

Still, by 1916 the community's fiscal condition was encouraging. The money borrowed from the Treasury in 1901 and after had been fully repaid and the funded debt reduced to $4,000,000. More equitable real estate assessments that

[14] *Letter from Secretary of Treasury Transmitting Estimates of Appropriations*, 1901-1917; "What the States Pay towards the District of Columbia's Municipal Expenses," *American City*, VIII, 119-20; *Rec*, 60C, 2S, p. 1832, 63C, 2S, p. 1162; H Rpt 937, 63C, 2S, Ser 6560; *Rpts B/Tr*, 1914, p. 9, 1915, pp. 10-12; *Times*, 13 May 1911, 17 Dec 1913.

[15] *Rec*, 60C, 1S, p. 4353, 4383-85; *Star*, 9 May 1909, 28 May 1911, 25, 26 Aug 1912; Louis Ottenberg, "Fatherless Children of the National Capital," *Survey*, XXXIV, 459-60; *Times*, 19 Dec 1913, 15 Jul, 6, 12 Dec 1914, 7 Jan, 18 Apr 1916; *Fiscal Relations*, pp. 963-66, Ser 6915; *Rpt B/Tr*, 1916, pp. 10, 13.

added $40,000,000 to over-all valuations cooled the heat of critics in Congress, and a law imposing a local tax on intangible personal property promised to catch up with "malfactors of great wealth." A newly created District Public Utilities Commission, made up of the three District commissioners, obtained authority to fix rates and control the sale and emission of utility stocks and securities. The difficulty of arriving at just valuations of the companies' property, the basis of the rates to be set, delayed final rulings until after the war, but the essential first steps in protecting consumers had already been taken. Still more important, the principle of some federal sharing of District expenses survived lengthy congressional hearings held late in 1915.[16]

The fiscal hearings revealed the intricacies of the problem and the strengths and weaknesses of both sides of the argument. Senator Gallinger pointed to complications arising from the long established custom whereby Congress authorized federal officials not responsible to the District commissioners to spend local funds voted "in the sundry civil and legislative appropriation acts, in deficiency acts," and others. Some of the data presented by both sides contained outdated figures and faulty comparisons with the taxes of other cities, but the testimony, if occasionally colored by passion, was illuminating to committee members who had never before examined the tangle of interrelated obligations. Several witnesses reverted to the arguments of the Southard report of 1835 setting forth the pledge implicit in the government's eighteenth-century agreement with the original proprietors of the land. Other men spoke of the paucity of manufacturing plants and great commercial houses such as supplied the bulk of taxes to other big cities and stressed the loss of revenue from the extensive tax-exempt federal holdings. Agreement that the national government should pay

[16] H Rpt 937, 63C, 2S, Ser 6560; *Rec,* 63C, 3S, pp. 1335-37; *Rpt B/Tr,* 1910, pp. 57-58, 1916, pp. 7-8; Brownlow, *A Passion for Anonymity,* pp. 90-91.

something left the main question of how much and by what method.

Local taxpayers opposed a sliding scale of federal payments on the grounds that it would mean constant uncertainty about how much money would be available in any given year. The two civilian commissioners favored a scheme by which the government would foot all the bills but would collect from District property-owners levies equal to, but not in excess of, those paid by residents of other like-sized cities. Louis Brownlow believed that plan sounder than the "legislative fiction" of half-and-half; he demonstrated the impossibility of separating the costs of services to the local public from those primarily benefitting the national government. In spite of Brownlow's convincing exposition, the committee, after decreeing half-and-half sharing no longer feasible or necessary, concluded that District taxes should be used solely for the District, and all local revenues be spent before drawing upon the United States Treasury. Congress took no action on the report, but it left the door open to future readjustments which, Senator Works remarked, should provide for the restoration of some authority to the community over its own expenditures and relieve Congress of some of its aldermanic responsibilities.[17]

Local self-government and "half-and-half" were so tied together by the Organic Act of 1878 that, quite apart from uneasiness over Negro suffrage, influential Washingtonians were still loath to contemplate an elective city government lest it kill all federal financial aid. Full voting representation in Congress, on the other hand, got increasingly wide support from 1909 onward. At a public dinner given for President Taft in May 1909 Chief Justice Stafford of the District Supreme Court made an eloquent plea: "Strip men of the ballot and you take away from society the most powerful inducement that

[17] Rec, 63C, 3S, pp. 143, 160-61, 1113-16, 1348, 4864-65; Bureau of the Census, Statistics of Cities Having a Population of over 30,000, 1907, pp. 330-33; Fiscal Relations, pp. i-lix, 43-44, 406-07, 963-80, Ser 6915, pp. 1639-40, 1742-57, Ser 6916.

can prompt selfish human nature to educate and elevate its helpless and its poor." In a scarcely veiled attack on white fears of Negro voting, he asked: "Shall we say we fear the suffrages of ignorance and vice . . . that could not last a generation if we did our duty by our fellow-men? . . . Never until the men of wealth and education have spent their last surplus dollar and exhausted the ingenuity of their brains in the effort to make their fellow-men worthy to be sharers in the government, never until then will they have a right to hide behind an excuse like that."[18]

The President derided Stafford's arguments, but a straw vote conducted the next year by the newly organized District Suffrage League polled 10,816 ballots favoring local suffrage to only 944 against. By 1915 the Board of Trade also decided the city had more to gain than to lose from a modification of the Organic Act. Residents felt little dissatisfaction with the administration of commissioners Newman, Siddons, and Brownlow, but the disadvantages of rule by congressional committee were emerging with unmistakable clarity. To much of the local public the surest remedy seemed to lie in having an elected District senator and representatives on the Hill, although some opposition to accompanying that change with an elected city government continued. Congressmen who discussed the matter at all inclined to think well of a watered-down home rule under congressional supervision, but they were more than doubtful about giving the District virtual statehood.[19] In short, what the community believed most beneficial was what Congress was least likely to grant. Yet at the end of 1916 confidence ran strong that city and Congress together could work out a mutually satisfactory solution.

[18] *Star*, 9 May, 23 Nov 1909; S Doc 684, 60C, 2S, Ser 5408; S Doc 1138, 62C, 3S, Ser 6365.
[19] *Star*, 15 May 1909, 1 Jan 1911; *Times*, 29 Apr, 8 Dec 1913, 14 Oct 1914, 26 Oct 1916; Archibald Butt, *Taft and Roosevelt*, pp. 29-31; *Post*, 16 Feb, 4 May 1913; *Rec*, 63C, 2S, p. 1161; *Rpt B/Tr*, 1916, pp. 13-16; S Dis Comee, 64C, 1S, Subcomee Hrgs on D.C., pp. 10, 21, 55-71.

CHAPTER X

THE CITY OF CONVERSATION, 1901-1916

IN Lafayette Square pigeons strutting, children playing Prisoners' Base while their governesses and nursemaids gossipped, men reading their newspapers in the warm sunshine and glancing across to the White House lawn to admire the reds of the tulips in the big round bed before the portico; open carriages drawn by well-groomed horses rolling along the Avenue; silk-hatted dignitaries and ladies in sweeping skirts and picture hats mounting the stone steps from the Mall to the Capitol terrace and nodding to the bandannaed colored women offering passers bunches of violets and daffodils; in the alleyways pickaninnies jostling for room for games of hopscotch or marbles under the clothes lines hung with rich people's wash,—spring-time in Theodore Roosevelt's Washington. In Rock Creek valley horse-back riders followed the paths through woods scarcely touched since Henry Adams found enchantment there in the 1860's; flat layers of white dogwood blossoms showed near the thickets of chestnut trees where, come fall, boys armed with sticks and pillowcases would be collecting the prickly bursting burrs. Frequently accompanied by the French ambassador or some other panting notable, the President, advocate of the strenuous life, often clambered about the ravines in Rock Creek Park and sometimes, after a vigorous walk, with a gusto equalling John Quincy Adams' eighty years before, stripped off his clothes for a swim in the Potomac. Delighted Washingtonians long talked of the day when J. J. Jusserand followed his example, only to have the President call back to him from midstream, "Look at your hands!"; the courtly ambassador had forgotten to take off his gloves.

Hot weather brought men, women, and children to the bathing beach on the Tidal Basin. When the basin froze,

187

"the clerks and shopgirls of the city skated over the ice shoulder to shoulder with cabinet officers and their families and with important members of foreign embassies and legations."[1] And there was the zoo now accessible by trolley and now populated not only with buffaloes and elephants but also lions, tigers, and bears, exotic birds, fearsome looking reptiles, and, on pleasant days, thousands of the human species equipped with picnic baskets and bags of peanuts to share with the monkeys. The nineteen new municipal tennis courts were in constant use, while boys and young men played ball on the diamonds on the White lot, the Monument grounds and in Potomac Park. When the American League, organized in 1901, admitted the Nationals', Washington's baseball fever rose rapidly; the home games drew crowds seemingly untroubled at repeated defeats. When the Griffith Stadium opened in 1912, President Taft set the precedent of tossing out the first ball from the bunting-draped box in the grandstands. The first game of the season thenceforward became a state occasion lightened by a special camaraderie. During the summer of 1916 the excitement in much of Washington caused by the Nationals' standing for the first time within reach of the pennant largely blotted out concern over torpedoed shipping and the stalemate of trench warfare in Europe.[2]

"More and more," wrote a London newspaper correspondent, "Washington becomes the Mecca of the United States." Brides and grooms, now eschewing Niagara Falls, chose to honeymoon on the Potomac, high school students chaperoned by their history teachers came every spring by the trainload and, as automobiles ceased to be costly luxuries, entire families made the hegira by car. On spring and summer mornings, licensed guides, most of them Negroes, lay in wait for their prey in Lafayette Square. One man with a flair for the dramatic always

---

[1] *Times*, 4 Jun 1908; *Post*, 13 Jan 1910.
[2] Comrs Rpts, 1906, p. 35, 1909, p. 41, 1917, p. 19; *Times*, 17 Jul 1915; *Post*, 20 Jun 1904; *Star*, 26 Mar 1905, 28 Jun 1909; Souvenir Program, 1901-1951, *The Nationals of the American League*.

assembled his audience first at the bronze group commemorative of General Lafayette and, with a wave of the hand toward the sketchily draped figure kneeling at the hero's feet and extending a sword to him, announced: "Great General! He not look at naked woman. She say: 'General, you give me back mah clothes and ah give yo back yo s-ward.'" Commenting on "the vastness and variety" of Washington's floating population, an Englishman called her "at once the most and the least American city in America, the most American because there, if anywhere, one feels oneself assisting at the great composite panorama of American life."[3]

European visitors generally admired the public architecture and the layout of the capital which Charles Dickens sixty years before had ridiculed as "The City of Magnificent Intentions." The Honorable Maud Pauncefote, daughter of the British ambassador in 1903, thought "the red brick town" surrounding the white government buildings unprepossessingly ugly, but she considered Washington's cosmopolitanism and good manners a chief attraction, one not duplicated by the wealth of New York, or the blue-stocking atmosphere of Boston and Philadelphia. H. G. Wells, on the other hand, was not beguiled by Washington's easy-going amiability. In 1906 seeking to understand "the future of America," he found the capital an "anti-climax," a place not wholly "alive to present and future things."[4]

Henry James, by 1906 as British as he was American, wondered about "the 'real' sentiments of appointed foreign participants . . . before phenomena which, whatever they may be, differ more from the phenomena of other capitals and other societies than they resemble them." Struck by the "extraordinar-

[3] A. Maurice Low, "Washington, the American Mecca," *Harper's Weekly*, LVII, 11; Sydney Brooks, "Washington and the White House," *The Living Age*, CCLXXVII, 69-70.

[4] The Honorable Maud Pauncefote, "Washington, D.C.," *The Nineteenth Century and After*, CCCXII, 280-81; Montgomery Schuyler, "The New Washington," *Scribner's Magazine*, LI, 135; H. G. Wells, "The Future in America, Washington as Anticlimax," *Harper's Weekly*, L, 1420.

ily easy and pleasant" quality of life in Washington, he disagreed with Americans who thought politics always omnipresent; on the contrary, he noted a bewildering absence of "political permeation." In this capital, in contrast to the "social ubiquity . . . of the acceptable MP" in London, not more than "half a dozen members of the Lower House and not more than a dozen of the Upper" were part of the social scene. To him Washington presented two faces, "the public and official, . . . the Imperial part," and that of "a group of people engaged always in conversation." Her properest name was "City of Conversation." What did people talk about? Washington—almost nothing else. Unlike the rest of America, here men were "solidly, vividly present" as part of civilization outside "the market." Yet despite her differences, James thought the city the embodiment of the American spirit.

One anonymous "English Visitor" to the chief "legislative foundry" of the United States remarked upon what he labelled the very limited range of society. Besides the diplomatic corps, Cabinet members and the high-ranking military, the only people that counted were "distinguished scientists in government service," Supreme Court justices, a handful of senators and congressmen whose social position at home made them acceptable in Washington, a "few dozen old residential families," and a small selection of the recently arrived *nouveaux riches*. The fabric of society resembled a small piece of "exquisite embroidery overweighted by a fringe that is neither small nor exquisite. . . . The fringe in question is composed of Negroes, who form a third of the population, the shopkeepers and retail traders, the clerks in the government offices, about nine-tenths of the Senators, including their wives and daughters, and of course the entire army of trippers."[5]

The exclusion of most congressmen from the ranks of "soci-

---

[5] Henry James, "Washington," *North American Review*, CLXXXII, 662-68, 673-75, 905-07 (later published in *The American Scene*); "The Social Stride of Washington's Elite," *Harper's Weekly*, LV, 9.

ety" frequently distressed newly arrived congressional wives. Forgetting that the twentieth-century capital was no longer a small town in which a Dolly Madison would make them feel at home, and unaware that rich New Yorkers following "T.R." to Washington had endowed high society with a new sophistication, women from rural communities turned into "social tragedies." "While the ramparts are theirs to stroll around, the citadel itself is as securely barricaded against them as though it were the Austrian court." The Women's Congressional Club founded in 1908 probably lightened their loneliness and disappointment, but tea and committee meetings in the house on McPherson Square were a poor substitute for the "superb" dinners given within the "innermost stronghold." "When a young girl comes out," Maud Pauncefote noted with amusement, "she is called a Bud." But buds sprung from congressional stock were rare, and the cost of raising one in a Washington hothouse forbade families not to the manor born from attempting it.[6]

Yet touches of small-town simplicity remained. As the President had persuaded Congress to vote funds for a wing of executive offices at the White House, small Roosevelts and velocipedes took over the upper floors of the house while on Saturday mornings their father shook hands with visitors touring the mansion, his famous grin particularly warm for mothers trailed by a string of children. Almost any well-mannered white person could still wangle an invitation to a White House reception except during the weeks of preparation for the marriage of "Princess Alice" to Speaker of the House Nicholas Longworth. In fact, the character of official entertaining changed very little before 1913, although Mrs. Taft put footmen into livery at the White House, in order to spare visitors the discomfort

[6] Mrs. Henry T. Rainey, "The Women's Congressional Club," *New England Magazine*, n.s., XL, 265-71; Roberta V. Bradshaw, "The Congressional Club," *Good Housekeeping*, LVI, 27-30; *Times*, 13 Oct 1907; "What It Cost Me to be a Prominent Man," *American Magazine*, LXXI, 84-85; Pauncefote, "Washington," p. 281.

of mistaking a fellow guest for a servant. Sheer numbers of officials required such a tightening of the rules of precedence that one man mournfully found himself the dinner partner of the same woman thirty times over a single season. Public appetite for news about social doings was so keen that in 1910 a weekly magazine, *Washington Society*, began publication of every gleanable detail of who squired whom where, how Senator Henderson's wife, after getting 16th Street renamed "Avenue of the Presidents," served vegetarian fare to guests at "Henderson Castle," and who introduced the fashion of the large Sunday dinner parties that made the McKinley's hymn-singing Sunday evenings seem part of another age.

As a heavy sleet and snow storm during the night of March 3, 1909, held up trains filled with guests and made Washington's streets all but impassable, President Taft's inauguration lost much of its splendor, but that deprivation heightened the eagerness of citizens four years later to stage an elaborate inaugural celebration. To the consternation of local promoters, President-elect Wilson, having concluded that inaugurations were being commercialized, refused to allow an inaugural ball. Washingtonians and the 200,000 visitors had to content themselves with the formal ceremonies at the Capitol and a parade that disorderly suffragettes attempted to break up. "Society" received a further shock when the new President, professing lack of time for golf, declined membership in the Chevy Chase Club, which he obviously looked upon as a hotbed of unwholesome social standards nurtured by people with more money than good sense. Annoyance increased at his playing nine holes now and again at the unpretentious Congressional Country Club. For the first time since the founding of the Metropolitan Club in the 1870's, its officers extended no invitation to the President of the United States to join that select body.[7]

[7] Taft, *Recollections of Full Years*, pp. 27, 280-81, 372-73; "Spectator," *Outlook*, LXXXV, 305-06; A. Maurice Low, "Sundays at the Capital,"

To the group that prided itself on keeping "society and trade . . . divided by a gulf as broad as that which separates them on the other side of the water," the socialistic notions and puritanism of the erudite former professor in the White House were as offensive as a background of trade itself could have been. His disapproval of everything "undemocratic," according to a friend of the old regime, merely meant that instead of the former "well-ordered dignified affairs" held in private homes, now "state receptions and dinners were given in hotel parlors and dining rooms." Criticism of such lack of savoir faire found another outlet shortly after the death of old ex-Senator John Henderson; for his teetotaling widow smashed every bottle of his famous cellar so that the gutters of 16th Street below Henderson Castle ran red with vintage wines. The marriages of two of the President's daughters and in 1915 his own remarriage, one woman observed maliciously, at least "gave society plenty to talk about."[8]

The city's social structure, meanwhile, irrespective of political realignments, had undergone change. In 1905 Bishop Satterlee expressed an uneasiness shared by old families: "A new type of residents are [sic] gathering in Washington, who, while they bring wealth, magnificence and luxury to the capital of the country, are, as a rule, actuated by no sense of civic, moral or religious obligation regarding the welfare of the community, and it is a very serious question whether the material advantages that they bring are any compensation for the atmosphere of careless irresponsibility which they create." Self-protectively the descendants of the group Mrs. Dahlgren had called the "very elite" began to draw away from much of

Harper's Weekly, LVI, p. 9; *Post*, 7 Jan 1906, 30 Jan, 27 Nov 1910, 2, 27 Feb, 16 Mar 1913; Butt, *Taft and Roosevelt*, pp. 48, 189; *Star*, 7 Jan 1906; *Times*, 23 Feb, 9 Mar 1908, 3-5 Mar 1913; Mrs. John King Van Rensselaer, *The Social Ladder*, pp. 256-59; *Washington Society*, I-V, 1910-1915.

[8] Helen Nicolay, *Our Capital on the Potomac*, p. 454; Isabel Anderson, *Presidents and Pies, Life in Washington, 1897-1919*, pp. 167-68.

official society and its hangers-on. High-ranking government officials without independent means were themselves troubled at the growing elaborateness of the entertaining expected of them, but Washington and Georgetown bluebloods were seldom office-holders and in social matters thus had freedom of choice. That freedom gave birth to the "cave-dweller." The name was new; the phenomenon was not. Resentment of brash newly arrived politicians and their protégés had perhaps laid the groundwork for cave-dwelling as early as President Jackson's day. But neither that first breach nor that created by the distaste of dignified old families for the wealthy social carpetbaggers of the Reconstruction period had endured. The twentieth-century manifestation lived on into the 1950's.

Inasmuch as Washington society of the Roosevelt era had an undeniable brilliance, more than one observer believed that cave-dwelling arose from lack of money to keep pace. But some cave-dwellers had ample fortunes, and the non-intercourse policy apparently stemmed not only from rejection of the ostentatiously rich but also from dislike of the snobbery of rank. Furthermore, the constant turnover among officials discouraged attempts to winnow the chaff from the grain. Yet, in setting themselves apart, cave-dwellers wrapped themselves in an exclusiveness that socially ambitious outsiders longed to break in upon. Few people agreed at any given time about who was and who was not a cave-dweller. Some included New England-born-and-bred Henry Adams, and somewhat later the Leiters and McLeans, new to the capital in the 1890's, would claim to be part of the select group.[9]

Yet even had the voluntary withdrawal into their caves never occurred, the eminent old families of Washington and Georgetown must have played a progressively smaller part in the social life of the capital. As the international responsibilities

[9] *Star*, 26 Mar 1905; Henry Loomis Nelson, "The Capital of Our Democracy," *Century*, LIV, 39; Maria Columbia, "Washington: Its Cave-Dwellers and Its Social Secretaries," *Delineator*, LXV, 248-53.

of the United States multiplied and government functions widened, the new complexity of governmental operations began to create a compartmentalization that slowly affected social intercourse itself. The lengthening list of high-ranking federal officials also tended to shrink the importance of a local aristocracy dwindling in relative if not in absolute numbers. For forty-odd years sons had been leaving Washington to build careers wherever larger opportunities offered. Daughters stayed behind to marry or, by ill chance, to remain maiden ladies; but marriage itself took many young women away. A genealogical tracing of the native belles who married into the military services would, it is true, doubtless reveal a considerable group who departed but returned now and again and, upon their husbands' retirement, resumed permanent residence in Washington or Georgetown; nevertheless as Army and Navy wives they no longer represented the deeply rooted local tradition of their forebears. That steady drain upon the community's human resources had profound, albeit subtle, consequences, denying Washington, as time went on, a core of influential families conditioned by generations of devoted service and interest in local affairs.[10]

Experienced globe-trotters, captivated as they were by a pervasive charm that endured in spite of social climbing and occasional outright vulgarity, still observed in Washington a curious cultural provincialism. It contrasted sharply with the catholicity of taste and many-faceted artistic talents to be found in European capitals. Henry James implied that Washington's self-absorbed conversation at best touched very lightly on the creative arts. The anonymous "English Visitor" declared that the city had "no influence over the arts and letters of the American people. The day is infinitely distant and in all probability will never come at all when every American artist, author,

---

[10] Based on a sampling of the Washington *Social Register*, "Married Maidens," 1901-1916; Barry Bulkley, *Washington Old and New*, pp. 108-09; Schuyler, "New Washington," *Scribner's*, LI, 135.

dramatist, and musician will turn instinctively toward Washington."

Reporters covering the current American political and society news found Washington a happy hunting ground. The Gridiron Club dinners were still gala occasions for the men privileged to attend the "cannibal feast." But the novels, poetry, and essays turned out in Washington were fewer and of lesser quality than in the 1880's. No American poet worthy of the name deliberately chose to live in the capital. Symbolically as well as materially Joaquin Miller's log cabin stood empty on Meridian Hill until in 1912 the shell, minus poet, was moved to Rock Creek Park. Henry Adams, John Hay, Theodore Roosevelt, and Senator Henry Cabot Lodge formed a quartet of literary lights at the opening of the twentieth century, but John Hay soon left Washington for good, Adams was in Washington only intermittently thereafter, official duties increasingly dimmed the purely literary brilliance of the other three, and Hay died in 1905. Gaillard Hunt edited the letters of Margaret Bayard Smith and later wrote a charming social history, *Life in America One Hundred Years Ago*, while Thomas Nelson Page, before he became ambassador to Italy in 1913, turned out new tales of "Ole Virginia." Washington's literary colony, however, steadily dwindled; professional writers other than journalists, scientists, and a handful of historians bound to the capital by the demands of their work rarely lingered long in the city. J. J. Jusserand, the French Ambassador and British Ambassador James Bryce managed to write distinguished books while they were here, but Americans apparently found Washington distracting. Lord Bryce suggested that the federal system itself militated against having a single city at once the political, financial, and literary capital of the country.[11]

[11] "The Social Stride of Washington's Elite," p. 9; Richard V. Oulahan, "Literary Clubland, the Gridiron Club of Washington," *The Bookman*, XXIII, 151; Francis Weston Carruth, "Washington in Fiction," *ibid.*, XV, 451-63; Paul Wilsbach, "Literary Landmarks of the National Capital," *ibid.*, XLIII, 486-94; Anderson, *Presidents and Pies*, p. 26.

Popular plays at the National Theatre and the Lafayette Opera House, later renamed Belasco Theatre, generally drew fair audiences for matinees, but skimpy crowds for evening performances. Vaudeville flourished at theatres no longer able to support plays, and the three or four burlesque houses had a still larger clientele, of which Supreme Court Justice Oliver Wendell Holmes was probably the most notable individual. Movies, though not yet a recognized form of art, by 1910 were cutting in upon every other type of entertainment.[12]

In 1903 the public was still unaware that the Smithsonian Institution included a potential National Gallery of Art. When fire in 1865 destroyed the two hundred-odd Indian paintings of John Mix Stanley and William Bird King which had hung in the Smithsonian's art exhibition hall, the regents had loaned the remaining paintings and prints to the Corcoran Gallery and the Library of Congress. Reclaimed thirty years later but, for lack of a place, not put on display, the pictures had remained a secret nucleus of a national collection. In 1903 Harriet Lane Johnston, belle and hostess of the White House in her uncle James Buchanan's day, bequeathed her collection of old masters to a National Gallery when one should come into being. A friendly law suit followed which ended with a court decree that a National Art Gallery was already in existence. "Valuable as were the paintings," wrote an officer of the National Museum in 1909, "the real gain was in the stimulus given to art as a feature of the national collections, in the example set that the government might be trusted as a custodian of art for the people." The immediate result was an offer from Charles Freer of Detroit to give the National Gallery his paintings, largely canvasses by American artists, notably James McNeill Whistler, and a still uncompleted collection of oriental art, all to be housed in a special building; two years later William T. Evans of New York gave the gallery his collection of modern Amer-

[12] *Star*, 26 Mar 1905, *Times*, 28 Jul 1907.

ican paintings. When the new National Museum on the Mall opened in the spring of 1910, the central hall was hung with the nation's old and new art treasures.

In the interim local citizens organized the National Society of the Fine Arts and within a year or two affiliated with the country-wide American Society of the Fine Arts. While the Society's lectures and annual conventions held at the New Willard Hotel further quickened public interest, Washingtonians were disappointed in their hopes of seeing the city become not only "the foremost art center in the western world" but also the home of a distinguished school of American painters. Of sculpture the story was much the same. Daniel Chester French, Gutson Borglum, Lorado Taft, and other eminent sculptors commissioned to execute pieces for the government maintained their studios outside Washington.[13]

Fostered by the volume of building in the city and influenced by the taste emanating from the Octagon House, which the American Institute of Architects rescued from demolition in 1902 and made its own headquarters, architecture, at once a craft, an art, and a profession, supplied more native talent than appeared in other fields. While New York firms designed most of the new government buildings, a growing number of local architects commanded attention. The originality of a Frank Lloyd Wright, it is true, never materialized in the churches, office buildings, and expensive houses put up in these years, but construction was solid, proportions were usually well balanced, and the ornamentation was seldom offensive.

The beautiful and cultivated Mrs. Reginald De Koven rue-

[13] Richard Rathbun, *The National Gallery of Art*, Smithsonian Institution, U.S. National Museum *Bulletin*, No. 70, Reprint 1916, pp. 18-19; "National Gallery of Art," Rpt, Smithsonian Institution, 1910; the National Society of Fine Arts, *Articles of Incorporation, Constitution and Bylaws*, 1906; "Art in Washington," and "The Best Art in America," *Art and Progress*, III, 532, and IV, 1007-09; Leila Mechlin, *Works of Art in Washington; Star*, 2 Dec 1905, 1 Jan 1912; *Times*, 24 Nov 1913; Anderson, *Presidents and Pies*, pp. 2-3, 167; Marietta M. Andrews, *My Studio Window, Sketches of the Pageant of Washington Life*.

fully observed that Washingtonians cared less about sym-
phonies than about tea. When Reginald De Koven and his
wife moved to Washington, they believed that the city would
support a professionally trained orchestra. His name was well
known. His successful light opera *Robin Hood* had won him
acclaim both abroad and at home, and his lyric "Oh Promise
Me" became a standard addition to the Lohengrin and Men-
delssohn marches at American weddings. Having persuaded
several wealthy Washingtonians to underwrite the cost of six
concerts, he assembled sixty qualified instrumentalists and
launched a first concert in April 1902 with Paderewski as
soloist. The *coup de grâce* was dealt the struggling new Washington Symphony Orchestra the next autumn, for scarcely had
De Koven scheduled a series of Friday afternoon concerts for
the 1902-1903 season than word came that the White House
had chosen Friday afternoons for the official teas over which
Mrs. Theodore Roosevelt would preside. Evening concerts
were virtually out of the question because halls were not available at night, and society was dining out. After giving the six
guaranteed performances, each well received by the critics,
the orchestra disbanded.

That failure silenced the newspapers, which from time to
time had talked of Washington's increasing dedication to
music. In 1907 and again in 1910 and 1912 the Music Art Society of Washington vainly attempted to revive the local symphony. And yet in 1914 a Bostonian, who had expected to
starve for lack of concerts in the capital, found "a veritable
feast of music." Played chiefly by the Boston, New York
Philharmonic, or the Philadelphia orchestras, afternoon performances confined audiences to people of leisure. Talented
amateurs and professional musicians played for the Friday
Morning Music Club, but the general public had a narrower
musical choice: a limited selection of phonograph records, a
week of opera every winter, church music, including the sing-
ing of the boys' choir at the open air services in the close of

the National Cathedral, concerts given by the amateur choral societies or by the Marine Band, overtures before curtain-rising at the National and Belasco theatres, minstrel show rag-time and cakewalks at the vaudeville houses, and the pianos at local movies.

Colored people were usually refused admission to white concerts, but Negroes to whom good music in some form was all-important set high standards for their own choral societies. Negro church music excelled anything to be heard in white churches, and white people not infrequently edged their way into evening services of Negro congregations to hear the choirs. In 1904 a bi-racial audience considered the great musical event of the year the rendition of Samuel Coleridge-Taylor's *Hiawatha*, conducted in person by that gifted British Negro and sung by the Negro choral society named for him. The Marine Band supplied the orchestra.[14] Later the growing barrier between the races interfered with a repetition of that success.

As the government widened its fields of scientific investigation, every year brought more scientists into federal service. In spite of the continuing hold of William Graham Sumner's laissez-faire teachings upon industrial America, the scientific needs of industry itself led to new demands for answers which federal bureaus might supply. At the same time growing public concern over conservation of the nation's dwindling natural resources and over preservation of citizens' health put pressure upon government agencies to expand research. Thus between 1901 and 1905 alone, four new bureaus came into being in Washington—the National Bureau of Standards in 1901, the Bureau of Mines, and a separate Bureau of the

[14] De Koven, *A Musician and His Wife*, pp. 204-05; Washington Choral Society *Bulletin*, I, 55, v, 191; *Post*, 28, 29 Apr 1902; Sunday *Star*, 20 Nov 1932; *Times*, 27 Nov, 22 Dec 1915; *Program of the Eighth Concert of the Rubenstein Choral Club*, 1911-1912, Cuno Rudolph Mss (L.C.); miscellaneous programs and Notice of Samuel Coleridge-Taylor Choral Society (Music Div, L.C.); Elbert F. Baldwin, "An American Cathedral Close," *Outlook*, LXXX, 288.

Census in 1902, and in 1905 the Forestry Service. The century-old Marine Hospital Service, enlarged in 1902 and again in 1908, became the Public Health Service in 1912, and, in the meantime, units in other federal departments took on new scientific functions. The National Advisory Committee for Aeronautics, created in 1915, supplied the capstone of the impressive government structure.

Mounting stress upon applied rather than basic research, it is true, lost to government service brilliant men who preferred the disinterested, cloistered search for pure knowledge to the routine of seeking answers to practical problems. The universities took over most of the fundamental research which John Quincy Adams had believed the federal government should pursue. But if no Joseph Henry, no Simon Newcomb, and no George Brown Goode now represented the United States government in the ruling circles of science, and if "bureau builders," like the conservationists Gifford Pinchot and James R. Garfield, and Charles D. Walcott, Secretary of the Smithsonian, preached that scientific investigations "on the part of the Government should be limited nearly to utilitarian purposes evidently for the general welfare," the achievements as well as the broadened reach of federal scientific activities worked as a yeast in the community.

The successes in applying science to urgent public problems were stimulating. When Major Walter Reed and his associates in Cuba proved that the "Aedis Egyptae" mosquito was the carrier of the yellow fever bacillus, the work of the Army Medical School, which Major Reed directed from the dispensary at Arsenal Point until his premature death in November 1902, inspired fresh confidence in the value of government programs. Investigations begun in the 1890's under Harvey Wiley of the Department of Agriculture's Bureau of Chemistry not only informed the American housewife of the dangers of adulterated food stuffs and brought about passage of the Pure Food and Drugs Act of 1906, but also heightened interest in chemical research. Physicists at the Bureau of Standards were employing cathode-ray tubes and radio-active minerals before 1916, and the presence of the bureau's scientific staff generated a kind of electric current that linked Washingtonians to an exciting unknown universe. Forgetting the ridicule once heaped upon "Professor Langley's bird," during 1909 and 1910 citizens travelled by trolley across the river to Fort Myer to watch the performances of the Wright brothers' heavier-than-air plane. Even uninformed people expected great things from the National Advisory Committee for Aeronautics and its newly opened experimental laboratory.

Although the studies of Indian culture that John Wesley Powell had initiated in the Bureau of American Ethnology appeared to serve no immediately utilitarian purpose, the findings and the carefully ordered collections at the National Museum drew anthropologists to Washington. Data feeding in from the Geological Survey and the Department of Agriculture turned the National Museum of the Smithsonian Institution into a research center in anthropology, zoology, and botany, while the reports stemming from the oceanographic explorations of the Bureau of Fisheries' ship "Albatross" had perhaps as much significance for the student of evolution as for the American fishing industry.[15]

Nor was scientific work in twentieth-century Washington confined to the government. Andrew Carnegie's gift of $10,000,000, which launched the Carnegie Institution in 1902, restored to the city an important role in the realm of pure science. Of the Institution's eleven divisions, only the Department of Geophysics, the Department of Terrestrial Magnetism, and the Department of Historical Research carried on their programs in the capital, but the contributions of the

---

[15] Dupree, *Science*, pp. 182, 252, 268-97, 385; O. Edward Anderson, *The Health of a Nation; Post*, 20 Mar 1904; *Times*, 8 Aug 1911; *Proceedings of the U.S. National Museum*, XXXVIII; "Celebration of the One-Hundredth Anniversary of the Organization of the U.S. Coast and Geodetic Survey," *Journal of the Washington Academy of Sciences*, VI, 260-68.

"earth scientists" caught the attention of the entire world, and the work of the historical unit enabled American historians for the first time readily to locate essential archival materials. Explorations sponsored by the National Geographic Society, moreover, exposed Washingtonians vicariously to scientific adventure in remote parts of South America and Alaska. At the dinner celebrating the Society's twenty-fifth anniversary in 1913, seven hundred members and guests heard Professor Hiram Bingham tell of his expedition into the Inca country of the high Andes and then, crowning moment of the occasion that British Ambassador James Bryce declared had no parallel in all history, the distinguished audience watched Rear Admiral Robert Peary, "discoverer" of the North Pole, award the National Geographic Society gold medal to the Norwegian Captain Roald Amundsen for his feat in reaching the South Pole.

Social scientists and historical scholars were less in the public eye than the men working in the exact sciences, but the Cosmos Club provided a common meeting ground. There exchange of ideas might occur naturally between men of widely divergent intellectual interests—between, for example, the witty and dedicated pure food expert, Harvey Wiley, and the urbane and learned Herbert Putnam, Librarian of Congress; between the elderly economist and statistician Francis Walker and Walter Swingle, the plant explorer, or the young ichthyologist Austin Clark, whom the Swedish government would later decorate for his work on forms of marine life; General George Sternberg might talk easily with George Burgess of the Bureau of Standards or with J. Franklin Jameson of the Carnegie Institution and editor of the *American Historical Review*. Similarly the Library of Congress Round Table luncheons, which Herbert Putnam inaugurated and presided over, daily brought together eight or nine gifted men from many walks of life; Judge Wendell P. Stafford or Supreme Court Justice Oliver Wendell Holmes might lunch beside the engaging Gaillard Hunt, or Secretary Charles Walcott of the Smithsonian, or some still obscure young scholar engaged in research at the library. No university campus in America offered more varied intellectual nourishment than the "city of conversation."[16]

Conversation, after the German torpedoing of the "Lusitania" in May 1915, turned with mounting intensity to the question of American intervention in the war in Europe. For months "business as usual," meaning concentration upon domestic politics and the accompanying "social game," continued to be a widely accepted motto in Washington. The resignation of Secretary of State William J. Bryan in June and the appointment of Robert Lansing made a stir, but one cynic later argued that it arose not from hopes for a more aggressive foreign policy but from relief that the prohibitionist Bryan could no longer urge upon diplomats the virtues of grape juice. While State Department policy-makers both before and after that change spent anxious hours drafting notes to the Central Powers about the rights of neutrals, the League for the Enforcement of Peace won strong support, especially among older people in Washington. The German background of several influential families such as the Kauffmanns, chief owners of the *Evening Star*, had bearing upon attitudes. Clifford Berryman's cartoons in the spring of 1916 portrayed the mood of both the *Star* and the isolationist Washington *Post*: in March the figure of "D.C." stood rake in hand amid a litter of papers reading "Blockade Trouble," "Pursuit of Villa," "Armed Ships Question" and "Submarine Issue," while "D.C." said: "Can't let troubles stop my spring work"; in May, while the bloody campaign on the Meuse was under way, "D.C." armed with a fly swatter and a

[16] *Proceedings* and *Journals of the Washington Academy of Sciences,* 1901-1916; *Annual Reports of the Carnegie Institution of Washington,* 1910, 1916; Elizabeth Donnan and Leo F. Stock, eds., *An Historian's World, Selections from the Correspondence of John Franklin Jameson,* pp. 90-91; "Amundsen and Peary," *National Geographic Magazine,* XXIV, 113-30.

banner inscribed "Destroy the Fly" announced, "Forward March! Now's the time for a spring drive." But as war reached out into the mid-Atlantic, the younger generation of Washingtonians took the position that national dignity and morality demanded taking up arms in defense of American principles.

Shortly after the Beaux Arts ball held for the relief of French war orphans, a National Service School opened a "military encampment" at Chevy Chase to teach women to shoot rifles. Most of the six hundred trainees enrolled at the "Ladies Plattsburg" in April 1916 were ardent interventionists, although they reportedly explained that they liked "to get back to nature"; and, in spite of the rule forbidding jewelry, few of them saw any incongruity in "wearing heavy three-stone diamond earrings with a khaki suit that cost $10.50." When law authorized the tripling of the National Guard, the commanding general of the District militia emphasized the need of serious military preparedness. The District National Guard filled its quota. A "Preparedness Day" parade in June drew requests from scores of organizations to take part. For the first time in history, the President of the United States himself marched on foot the entire way. Preparedness, however, was not war, and, like countless other Americans, a great many Washingtonians apparently thought military training was designed chiefly to enable the United States to bring Mexican insurgents to heel. The reelection of President Wilson in November persuaded the capital that the even tenor of her ways would continue.[17]

Thoughtful people have often sought to explain the powerful attraction that Washington before the first world war held for almost every American who ever lived there. The knowledgeable Helen Nicolay, daughter of President Lincoln's secretary and biographer, described "a rambling, self-satisfied community with some of the characteristics of a watering place and

[17] Anon., *Mirrors of Washington*, pp. 214-16; *Star*, 13 Mar, 2, 5, 16, 18, 24 May, 21 Jun, 5 Oct 1916; *Rpt B/Tr*, 1916, pp. 76-78. The paucity of newspaper comment on possible American involvement in war is at least negative evidence of local attitudes.

some of a village, and more still of a thriving county seat. Precedents and prejudices and conventions hedged it about." Other cities were as friendly and less wedded to a rigid etiquette; the natural beauty of many places was more spectacular; creative art had wider scope in other communities, and the intellectual climate of the great universities was quite as kindly to scholarship and intensive research; the rewards of a business career were greater in American financial and industrial centers; the incessant jockeying for national political power in the capital was frequently disillusioning, and the perpetual shift in the city's *dramatis personae* could be disconcerting to the person who valued stability. Wherein, then, lay Washington's peculiar enchantment? As was true a hundred years earlier and in the late nineteenth century, the infinite variety of background and talent of the people living there or coming and going gave her social life unique fascination. "In Washington," wrote Mrs. Larz Anderson, "there is always something new under the sun."[18] Temporary residents left with regret, and uncounted men and women who called themselves temporary stayed on for twenty and thirty and forty years to see changes that heightened their affection for the relatively uncomplicated "city of conversation" they had known before the war.

[18] Nicolay, *Our Capital on the Potomac*, p. 512; Anderson, *Presidents and Pies*, p. 1; Nelson, "The Capital of Our Democracy," *Century*, LIV, 39.

CHAPTER XI

THE BEGINNINGS OF ORGANIZED NEGRO PROTEST, 1901-1916

THE optimism that warmed white Washington rarely penetrated the clouds hanging over the colored community. In the Deep South the exclusion of Negro voters from the polls in state after state had progressed inexorably, beginning with South Carolina in 1889 and, by 1901, extending to nine others. Determination to establish white supremacy on an immutable basis had multiplied Jim Crow laws and confined Negro education largely to the vocational and manual training deemed suited to a servile labor force. From Texas through the Gulf states and up into North Carolina, lynchings of Negroes had grown in frequency during the 1890's. Washington Negroes had not faced lynchings or overt intimidation. Here the black masses at the bottom of the heap were little worse off in 1901 than in the early eighties; in fact, with luck on jobs, consistent good health, and three or four years of schooling, hard workers might rise a peg into the ranks of the Negro lower middle class. It was the upper middle class and the aristocrats whose status and pride had suffered and from whom either courageous leadership or corrosive despair must emanate. During the preceding twenty years their role had become increasingly negative. Yet colored Americans throughout the country still looked to the privileged members of that group to act as standard bearers for them all.

Contrary to later, often quoted Republican claims, the position of Negroes continued to worsen during the Roosevelt and Taft administrations, although subtle changes rather than admitted shifts in official policy marked the decline. As President Cleveland's first Civil Service Commissioner, Theodore Roosevelt had exercised scrupulous fairness in putting the merit system into effect in government, but the Colonel of the Rough

Riders had deeply offended colored men by belittling the heroic services of the Black Cavalry at San Juan hill during the Spanish-American War. As President, the vigorous "Teddy" for a time seemed to colored Washington to be a staunch friend: one of his first acts was to invite Booker T. Washington to dine at the White House to discuss Negro appointments to office. Hopes built on that unusual gesture quickly shrivelled under the hot blast of arch-conservative Republican wrath. Within six months the Washington *Bee* was speaking of "the Negro political decapitation dinner."[1] The President stuck by his guns to the point of winning Senate concurrence in several Negro appointments, and he retained a number of colored men McKinley had put into office, but thereafter he made no further overtures. On the contrary, in 1906, when Negro troops in Brownsville, Texas, were involved in a brawl in which a white man was shot, presidential severity in approving the dishonorable discharge of the entire battalion for refusing to identify the guilty person alienated Roosevelt's colored supporters. His appointment of two Negroes to the Homes Commission in 1908 won him no applause since all members of the commission gave their services.

President Taft stirred up fewer animosities than his predecessor. Avowing belief in the Tuskegee philosophy of Negro economic advancement before enlargement of Negro political power, Taft declared himself unwilling to appoint colored men to posts in the South, where white resentment would create friction. But he selected colored men for several "offices of essential dignity at Washington," on the principle that it was better to give "large offices to well-equipped Negroes of the higher class" than to scatter "a lot of petty ones among the mass of their race." Rather apologetically he wrote to Robert

[1] E.g., Republican National Committee, *Republican Campaign Textbook, 1912*, p. 278; *Bee*, 15 Oct 1898, 19 Oct 1901, 8, 22 Feb 1902, 5 Aug 1905; Hayes, *Negro Govt Worker*, p. 22; Monroe N. Work, ed., *Negro Year Book, An Annual Encyclopedia of the Negro, 1912*, pp. 75-76.

Terrell: "I have not done all I ought to do or all I hope to do in the matter of the recognition of colored men, but positions are hard to find. Nobody resigns and nobody dies." However sound his reasons, Taft's policies offered the city's colored people meagre encouragement.[2]

Up to a point colored Washingtonians rejoiced at any Negro's receiving a responsible federal post, but they were dismayed at the President's consistently passing over well-qualified local Negroes even for the office of Recorder of Deeds for which local taxes paid half. The profound respect in which all colored Americans held Washington's upper-class colored community heightened the grievance. Upon Booker T. Washington's recommendation, President Roosevelt appointed Robert H. Terrell to a municipal judgeship, but colored Republicans from the states won the other six major federal assignments in the capital, namely the posts of Register and Deputy Register of the Treasury, Assistant District Attorney for the District of Columbia, Auditor of the Navy Department, the District Recorder of Deeds, and Chief Surgeon at the Freedmen's Hospital. President Taft added two more, the office of Collector of Customs at Georgetown and, still more gratifying, the position of Assistant Attorney General of the United States, a plum which fell to a prominent colored lawyer from Boston. At those nine, Negro preferment stood till 1913.

The significance all Negroes attached to those nine offices seems at first out of proportion to their number or their intrinsic importance. But between 1901 and 1913 they represented far more to colored people than sops to racial ambition. For, during the first dozen years of the twentieth century when no colored man sat in Congress, Negro civil service employees

[2] As in chapter VI, citations of the *Bee* are reduced in this chapter to a small sample, since relevant comments appear in almost every issue. *Bee*, 17, 24 Sep, 31 Dec 1904, 17 Mar, 21 Apr, 1, 8 Dec 1906, 4 May 1907; William F. Nowlin, *The Negro in American National Politics*, pp. 114-15; *Negro Year Book, 1912*, pp. 30-31; *Star*, 20 Jun 1909; President Taft to Judge Robert Terrell, 2 Mar 1910, Mary Church Terrell Mss (L.C.).

came to depend upon the President's Negro appointees to serve as their bulwark against injustice. In the 1880's and 1890's Negro congressmen had filled that role, or at least so colored departmental clerks believed. Now they must look elsewhere for help in getting merited assignments when civil service rules swayed precariously in the winds of a stiffening racism. In 1910 a Negro journalist jokingly called Taft's nine principal Negro appointees "the Black Cabinet." The name stuck, and with some reason: although their intervention was not always successful, it sometimes had the desired effect.[3]

Nevertheless the civil service held fewer opportunities for intelligent Negroes than in the 1880's and 1890's. The commission's rules had always allowed a department or division chief a choice among the three top candidates whose examinations qualified them for a vacancy, but after the turn of the century that latitude, Negroes believed, increasingly came to be a weapon of racial subjugation. Certainly promotions became fewer and fewer for Negroes; more often white associates of lesser education and experience and therefore presumably of lesser competence were pushed ahead of them. By 1908 not more than three or four colored men had advanced into supervisory positions and all colored federal employees in Washington had dwindled from the 1,537 of 1892 to 1,450, about 300 of them clerks, the rest messengers or common laborers. Until 1909 the State Department had no colored employee ranking above a messenger, and the lone Negro who then attained a clerk's rating achieved it, he later explained, because his personal friend, the incoming Secretary of State, insisted that the merit system recognize merit. While Republican campaign literature of 1912 claimed that the federal government then had more than 4,100 colored employees in Washington earning

[3] *Bee,* 19 Apr 1909, 23 Feb, 25 Mar, 11 Sep 1911, 29 Mar, 12 Apr 1913; William McKinley Clayton to Woodrow Wilson, 19 Mar 1915, Wilson Mss; *Negro Year Book, 1912,* pp. 70-71; Hayes, *Negro Govt Worker,* pp. 26-27, 32-35.

over $4,000,000 a year, those figures were manifestly exaggerated and in any case made little impression upon educated Negroes, who knew that the color of their skins would keep them in the bottom grades of government service.

In the District government civil service rules did not apply at all. The wishes of members of the House or Senate District committees might determine who was hired or promoted and, when congressional patronage did not interfere, the preferences of individual commissioners or their immediate subordinates were the deciding factor. The *Bee* insisted that the engineer commissioners never approved of Negroes in any but menial jobs, and of the civilian commissioners only Henry West displayed no "colorphobia." In 1908 out of a clerical force of 450 in the District Building, only 9 were Negroes; among 731 policemen and 498 firemen 39 and 9 respectively were colored; 79 clerks and 55 mail carriers were colored out of 881 city Post Office employees; 460 colored school teachers selected chiefly by the Assistant Superintendent completed the list of the District's Negro employees in white collar jobs. The pay scale put the yearly income of all but a very few at less than $1,000. Four years later a city containing some 94,000 colored inhabitants and 20,000 colored taxpayers had about 900 Negroes on the payroll, nearly half of them rated as unskilled laborers at wages of $500 or less a year.[4]

At the same time jobs open to Negroes in other fields, especially domestic service, shrank in number. Judge Terrell put the blame for householders' shift to white servants upon his own people; for too often, he said, they skimped their work

[4] Hayes, *Negro Govt Worker*, pp. 125-30; *Republican Campaign Textbook, 1912*, pp. 71-72; Osceola Madden, "A Color Phase of Washington," *The World Today*, XIV, 549-52; *Bee*, 22 Jul 1905, 11 May, 16 Nov 1907, 2 Oct 1909, 4 May 1912, 20 Feb 1915; Kathleen Dudley Long, "Woodrow Wilson and the Negro, 1912-1916," (M.A. Thesis, Bryn Mawr College, 1956), pp. 14-17; H Committee on Reform in the Civil Service, 63C, 2S, "Hearings on Segregation of Clerks and Employees in the Civil Service," pp. 4-5; Sherman's *Directory and Ready Reference of the Colored Population of the District of Columbia, 1913*, pp. 388-417.

while making unwarranted demands upon their employers. He viewed the refusal of Negroes to work for other Negroes as particularly serious in a city where he estimated a tenth to a fifth of the colored people were jobless; he told the National Negro Business League in New York of a colored woman who, having advertised for a washwoman, was informed by a colored applicant: "Lady, I can't work for you; I'm in society myself." The overcrowding of the professions in colored Washington, pronounced in the late nineteenth century, now intensified. In spite of the efforts of the local branch of the newly organized Negro Business League, and in spite of a few isolated examples of modest success—an insurance company, a shoe store, and several drug stores—Negro business enterprises made no progress. In 1903 Washington's one Negro Savings Bank failed; attempts to organize another came to nothing. While the *Bee* improved its appearance, gave better news coverage, and adopted a more dignified tone, the *Colored American*, which Booker T. Washington had largely financed, ceased publication in 1904 after a losing six-year struggle for existence. The *Bee*, in turn, ran into financial difficulties in 1908 when a rival, the Washington *American*, appeared. Calvin Chase's repeated attacks upon Mr. Washington's "Uncle Tomism" notwithstanding, the educator came to the *Bee*'s rescue, for he considered a vigorous Negro press an important weapon in the fight for advancement, and the national capital above all must have Negro newspapers.[5]

Accompanying the growing economic pinch was a gradual tightening of the cordon excluding Negroes from any slight share in a common social life in the city. The one exception was the children's annual Easter Monday egg-rolling contest on the White House lawn when for a few hours white and

[5] *Star*, 20 Aug 1905; *Bee*, 26 Aug, 25 Nov 1905, 27 Mar 1909, 15 Feb 1913; *Rpt B/Ed*, 1910, pp. 207-08; Booker T. Washington to Judge Robert Terrell, 19 Feb 1906, B. T. Washington Mss; *Negro Year Book, 1912*, pp. 170, 175; August Meier, "Booker T. Washington and the Negro Press," *Journal of Negro History*, xxxviii, 68, 88-89.

colored children intermingled, "all beaten up as it were in a social omelette. Eggs of every color are rolled back and forth . . . and there are just as many shades, if not as many colors, of skin as of egg shell." The rest of the year race prejudice seeping down from parents poisoned the relations between white and colored youngsters. As Joe Gans, the Negro prize fighter, won fame in the ring, whenever a championship bout was scheduled, a boy of either race who ventured alone into Washington's streets beyond his own immediate neighborhood risked a beating up from a gang of the enemy intent upon upholding the honor of Gans or his white rival. One very light-colored, red-haired Negro boy faced double jeopardy, since colored contemporaries outside the Negro section of Foggy Bottom took him for a white, while white boys pounced on him as a Negro. Jack Johnson's victories over Jim Jeffries later made matters worse. Athletic prowess, which in post-World War II years would begin to bridge racial cleavages, merely widened the gulf.

The rapidity with which the breach developed in the first decade of the century is astonishing. In 1902 the Washington *Post*, with an unusual display of interest, devoted a half column to praise of the city's upper-class Negro society, "the Negro scholar in silk hat and frock coat," the well-to-do Negro lawyer, the half-dozen colored members of the Washington Board of Trade, the colored women graduates of Wellesley, Smith, Oberlin, and Russell Sage, the Treble Clef Club, "organized for the study of classical music," the Samuel Coleridge-Taylor Oratorio Society with its 225 voices, and the church choirs which "won golden opinions." Two years later the *Post* was deploring the unseemly ambition of Washington's colored leaders to get "the ballot, recognition, admission to theatres and restaurants, monopoly of the public parks and other like prerogatives," instead of pouring their efforts into establishing colored vocational and manual training schools as Negroes in the Deep South were doing. White residents overlooked the steady decline of illiteracy among Washington's adult Negroes; in 1910 it stood at less than 17 per cent. The *Star* suggested that white people should not draw the color line in giving Christmas charity; but otherwise, save for an occasional friendly notice in the Washington *Times*, after 1903 the city's white press confined its favorable comments on Negro activities to applauding Booker T. Washington's Tuskegee program with its implied acknowledgment of Negroes' inherent racial inferiority. By 1908 a dispassionate appraisal of race relations in the capital led a magazine writer to conclude that in Washington "the separation of the races is more nearly complete than in any other city of the Union. The better class of white and colored people know absolutely nothing of each other."

Intelligent Negroes were painfully aware of what was happening. An anonymous article entitled "What It Means to be Colored in the Capital of the United States" listed for readers of the *Independent* some of the new manifestations of racism: in January 1906 the Columbian Debating Society at George Washington University debated the question: "Resolved that a Jim Crow law should be adopted and enforced in the District of Columbia"; the affirmative won; a few months later a bill for Jim Crow street cars was introduced into Congress with a citizens' association endorsement; until 1900 the colored schools had had colored directors of music, art, cooking, sewing, manual training, and physical culture; now all were white. "For fifteen years," wrote the author, "I have resided in Washington, and while it was far from being a 'paradise for colored people' when I first touched these shores, it has been doing its level best ever since to make conditions for us intolerable."[6]

Mounting white antagonism had its effect: from 31 percent

---

[6] Mrs. R. Kent Beattie, "Easter Egg-Rolling," *Crisis*, XI, 313-14; *Bee*, 19 Feb 1916; *Post*, 3 Aug 1902, 9 Jan 1904; *Star*, 14 Dec 1903; Madden, "A Color Phase," p. 549; "What It Means to be Colored in the Capital of the United States," and "Our Washington Letter," *Independent*, LXII, 181-86, 1012.

of the total population in 1900, colored Washington dropped to 28½ percent in 1910 and would be only 25 percent by 1920. Knowing themselves unwelcome, the colored members of the Board of Trade resigned. At the request of the local chapter of the Women's Christian Temperance Union, Negro women withdrew in 1908 to form a Jim Crow unit. While the severity of sentences imposed on colored misdemeanants increased, white supremacists talked openly of reestablishing the whipping post to check Negro crime or of forcing all "niggers" out of the District. Even generously disposed northerners fell easily into the habit of using only the Christian name in speaking of or to a Negro, no matter how distinguished he might be. In her published *Recollections*, so kindly a person as Mrs. William Howard Taft alluded to her indebtedness to Arthur Brooks, a major in the colored unit of the District militia; but, perhaps because he was also a messenger in the War Department, she wrote of him as "Arthur," never "Major" or "Mr. Brooks"; every white person mentioned, except the Taft children and the uneducated Irish coachman, was dignified by his surname and title. Such minor slights were unimportant save as never-ending reminders to colored people that they had won scant respect from whites.

Probably a better gauge of the strengthening of the caste barrier lay in the attitude of white churchmen. At the Congregational Church, which had welcomed Negro members in the 1870's, a congressman from Maine received an ovation when he stated that colored men should never have been enfranchised *en masse*, but rather one by one as each proved himself ready. Episcopal Bishop Henry Satterlee went further. Giving Negroes equality through suffrage when they were not in fact equal, combined with the growth of the Negro population, he said, had promoted racial hostilities. Although he supported Christian missions for colored people, he thought Negroes "morally and intellectually a weaker race, and . . . even if they should

215

become great landowners, men of wealth and of education, race antagonism would only become stronger and more sharply defined." Washington's Negro intelligentsia no doubt saw some truth in these pronouncements, but the Bishop's repudiation of education, wealth, and political power as means of closing the gap between the races and his statement that a solution must depend upon every Negro's winning for himself "a strong, robust Christ-like character" were profoundly discouraging. Seemingly, white men could remain devils, but colored must become saints. Told by white men year after year of the virtues of Booker T. Washington's subservient philosophy, Negro aristocrats listened without enthusiasm to the sage of Tuskegee when he informed them at the colored YMCA that the eyes of the world were upon them and they must set an example by ridding the city of loafers, drunkards, and gamblers.

Perhaps the most deadly blow the city's white churches dealt their dark-skinned Christian brethren came in 1910 with the assembling in Washington of the sixth World Sunday School Convention. The local committee on arrangements refused to seat local colored delegates or permit them to march in the parade because they were not members of the District Sunday School Association although they belonged to the World Association and had taken part in earlier conventions. The *Star* reported all "wrinkles . . . smoothed out" by a vote of the organization to make Booker T. Washington a life member, but as Mr. Washington represented "Uncle Tomism" to many local Negroes, the *Star*'s account smacked of belittling the issue.[7]

More alarming to colored Washingtonians were the multiplying instances of racial segregation in government offices. A "Jim Crow corner" first appeared in 1904 in the Bureau of

[7] *Rpt B/Ch*, 1901, p. 269; *Bee*, 11 Feb, 10 Dec 1905, 8 Feb 1908; *Post*, 18 Apr 1904, 7 Nov 1910; *Star*, 11 Jan 1905, 10 May, 20 Jun 1909, 20, 24 May 1910; Mrs. William Howard Taft, *Recollections*, pp. 279-80; *Times*, 14 Jul 1907; *Rpt B/Educ*, 1905, pp. 105-15.

Engraving and Printing. The *Bee* noted in 1905 " a systematic effort inaugurated to Jim Crow the Negro. The fever is spreading. . . . The Negro is afraid to complain." Race prejudice, having once gained a foothold under a Republican regime, quickly widened its reach. Before 1909 separate locker and washrooms and separate lunchroom accommodations had become the rule in several sections of the Treasury and the Department of the Interior, and, although the scheme did not spread far during the next four years, the administration made no move to check or forbid it.

What Republican officials saw fit to allow set the pattern for private concerns. In 1910, at the invitation of the Federation of Citizens' Association, ten recently organized Negro neighborhood groups attended a meeting, only to have their hosts then vote to exclude them from federation membership; the Negroes thereupon took the name Civic Associations and formed their own federation. The local civil rights acts still stood unrepealed, but restaurants, barber shops, and hotels now barred Negroes as a matter of course, theatres admitted them only to "nigger heavens," and railroads and buses carrying passengers into the District from Virginia and Maryland enforced Jim Crow seating. As a suit, if won in court, meant at most token damages for the plaintiff, Negroes ceased to invoke the law.[8] Indeed a good many of them obviously shrank from public complaint lest it feed fuel to the campaign to repeal the laws. White extremists might persuade Congress not only to destroy the last flimsy legal safeguards against racial discrimination in the District of Columbia but to make segregation mandatory.

From 1907 on, bills for Jim Crow cars in the District came up in the House of Representatives at intervals. While a new congressman from Georgia announced his determination to force all Negroes out of government service, agitation for a District anti-miscegenation law made headway. In February

[8] *Bee*, 3 Sep 1904, 11 Feb 1905, 7 May 1910, 4 May 1912.

1913 the House passed the bill in less than five minutes; only Senate inaction stopped it. When the Negro Register of the Treasury and a colored guest lunched in the House Office Building restaurant, five congressmen threatened a boycott that would close it down if such an affront to white manhood ever recurred; the manager assured them it would not. With lynch law rampant in the Deep South, Negroes in Washington had some reason to think the moment inopportune to protest the curtailment of their own civil rights. Possibly only a few men understood the seriousness of the trend in the capital; before the summer of 1913 perhaps the rank and file were not apprehensive for themselves. But over a ten-year span the evidence the *Bee* assembled and published periodically indicated clearly that Washington Negroes, although spared lynchings, were already subject to most of the discriminations imposed upon colored people elsewhere in America.

The city's upper-class Negroes, however, reacted with growing militance to the accelerating racism of white Washington. Booker T. Washington kept many close friends in the capital, but educated colored people who accepted his program of "racial solidarity, self-help and economic chauvinism" increasingly rejected his methods and his disregard of political action. His conciliatory policies, his anxiety to avoid friction with whites, and his stress upon patience led to a break between him and a group of Negro radicals in 1906 when some twenty-nine "rebels" headed by the brilliant, young W. E. B. DuBois of Atlanta University and William Monroe Trotter, editor of the Boston *Guardian*, launched the so-called "Niagara Movement" with a manifesto of Negro rights and aims. Four Washington Negroes took part in the first Niagara conference. Inspired by that example, leadership long dormant in colored Washington began to reassert itself.

Kelly Miller, professor of sociology and later dean at Howard University, George W. Cook, Treasurer of Howard, the Reverend Samuel Carruthers of the Galbraith AME Church, Francis J. Grimké of the 15th Street Presbyterian Church, three or four other local pastors, Mary Church Terrell, the first president of the National Association of Colored Women, Calvin Chase of the *Bee*, and a score of other men and women who commanded prestige now abandoned the tactics of suffering indignities in silence and began a campaign of outspoken protest against social injustice. Few of them openly criticized Booker T. Washington, and Mrs. Terrell, while serving on the Board of Education, rebuked a Negro newspaperman for objecting to the "Tuskegee idea" of Negro education, although she herself advocated giving the colored child in the District the same schooling as the white. But irrespective of their feelings about Mr. Washington, all of the group joined in publicizing the fact that colored people were not content to be hewers of wood and drawers of water and that whites were deluded if, like the New York *Times*, they thought "the Negroes of the United States are doing very well."[9]

Although Washington's Negro militants constantly gained adherents, the city was not initially in the front of the fight, perhaps because the District's voteless status gave political leadership to New York, Boston, and Chicago, perhaps also because colored people in the largest Negro city in the country, having escaped the excesses of "lily-white" agitation that the Deep South was experiencing, were wary about forcing an issue locally lest it boomerang violently. If, as one scholar avers, Booker T. Washington's greatest ascendency, which spanned the first decade of the century, "coincided with the period of greatest oppression Negroes have faced since the Civil War,"

[9] H Rpt 8072, 59C, 2S, Ser 5065; *Star*, 14 May 1909; *Herald*, 21 May 1907; *Post*, 11 Feb 1913; *Crisis*, v, 270-71; Hayes, *Negro Govt Worker*, p. 33; W. E. B. DuBois, *Dusk of Dawn*, pp. 88-89, 92-95; August Meier, "Booker T. Washington and the Negro Press," pp. 75, 79, 80-81; *Bee*, 25 Nov 1905, 25 Apr 1906, 26 Nov 1910, 29 Jul 1911; Mary Church Terrell to H. G. Pinkett, 9 Sep 1906, Terrell Mss; New York *Times*, 18 Apr 1913.

the birth of the National Association for the Advancement of Colored People in New York City in 1909 must be recognized as marking the beginning of the slow march upward. Started by a handful of earnest white people, the association from the first was intended to be bi-racial. But of its national officers and staff only W. E. B. DuBois was a Negro, and radicals such as William Trotter of Boston distrusted it too deeply to join or work with it. In Washington, caution and inertia apparently combined to delay until the spring of 1912 the organization of a local branch of the NAACP. Within a few months, it was one of the largest in the country and counted 143 dues-paying members, among them so distinguished a white man as Chief Justice Stafford. But, unlike the New York group, white members were few. Here the most able of the upper-class Negro community took charge, bending their first efforts to providing legal aid for Negro victims of discrimination.[10]

Grim as things looked for all American Negroes in 1912, gleams of hope were visible in Washington. They derived principally from the changing point of view of the city's professional social workers and the volunteers they trained as visitors in the slums. First-hand exposure to the conditions under which honest hard-working colored families had to live taught fair-minded investigators a good deal about the obstacles confronting the city's Negroes. The report of the President's Homes Commission and the United States Labor Department's eye-opening study had presented evidence that starvation wages and destitution were directly related. Businessmen occasionally talked as if lowering the Negro death rate was important only because high mortality interfered with favorable advertising for the city, but few men sounded as sure as once they had that Negro "shiftlessness" lay at the root of the problem.

[10] Meier, "Booker T. Washington," p. 88; *Negro Year Book, 1912*, p. 134; *Third Annual Report National Association for the Advancement of Colored People*, p. 23 (hereafter cited as *Anl Rpt NAACP*); Flint Kellogg, "Villard and the NAACP," *Nation*, CLVIII, 137-40; *Crisis*, VI, 190.

Furthermore, white assumptions that upper-class Negroes lacked civic-mindedness received a jolt when a compilation of scattered data revealed that Negroes had initiated and carried on several projects for their people, notably a day nursery for infants of working mothers. Of the $50,000 collected in Washington for a colored YMCA, colored people contributed $27,000. Conferences between Negro workers at the colored Southwest Settlement House and white philanthropists came to be "remarkably free from race consciousness, the one thought on both sides being the common welfare." Negroes thus brought into touch with whites active in Washington charities could feel the lightening of the atmosphere of censoriousness.[11]

Inasmuch as white men's respect, not their charity, was the goal of Negro leaders, any sign that a segment of white Washington was ready to work with them for the common good assumed importance. Reform was in the air throughout the United States as the presidential election of 1912 approached, and, noting the fervor with which white muckrakers and Progressives talked of the far-reaching social and political changes that must come, thoughtful colored men dared think reform might extend to race relations. None of the candidates made explicit promises, but while Republicans pointed to President Taft's record of Negro appointments and Theodore Roosevelt denounced "brutal" Democratic and "hypocritical" Republican racial policies, Woodrow Wilson preached the "New Freedom" with its guarantees of "fair and just treatment" for all. The *Bee*, wary of trusting any Democrat, urged its readers when the election was over to have faith in the assurances of Wilson's influential colored supporters that the incoming President would not countenance continued discrimination and segregation.[12]

[11] A C *Rpt, 1903*, p. 23; *Crisis*, III, 51; *Rpt B/Tr*, 1910, p. 8; *Times*, 5 May 1911; Sarah C. Fernandis, "In the Making," *Charities*, XVI, 703-05; *Bee*, 13 Apr 1907, 17, 24 May, 5 Jul 1913; Washington *Sun*, 12 Feb, 14 May 1915.
[12] Long, "Woodrow Wilson and the Negro," pp. 14-32; *Republican Campaign Text Book, 1912*, p. 238; Theodore Roosevelt, "The Progres-

Negroes in the capital waited eagerly for word of new appointments and measures that would wipe out the Jim Crow sections in government offices. March and most of April 1913 came and went. Confidence in the "New Freedom" gave way to uneasiness. Then piece by piece the world of colored Washington fell apart. Within the next few months the President dismissed all but two of the Negroes whom Taft had appointed "to offices of essential dignity at Washington" and replaced them with white men. He nominated a colored lawyer from Oklahoma for Register of the Treasury with the intention of making the Register's section an all-Negro unit, but when the nominee, intimidated by fierce opposition in the Senate, withdrew his name, Wilson appointed an American Indian. The District Recordship of Deeds, a colored preserve since 1881, went to a white man in 1916. By then the only Negro to hold an appointive position in Washington was Robert Terrell, confirmed in April 1914 for another term as a municipal judge. Disillusioning though these snubs were, they were pin-pricks compared to the segregationist policies officially sanctioned in government departments in the summer of 1913.

"Segregation," reported a white officer of the NAACP, "is no new thing in Washington, and the present administration cannot be said to have inaugurated it. The past few months of Democratic Party control, however, have given segregation impetus and have been marked by more than a beginning of systematic enforcement." As soon as the Virginia-born President was installed in the White House, a group of Negro baiters calling themselves the National Democratic Fair Play Association had undertaken to stir up trouble in order to get Negroes out of the civil service, to restrict them to menial jobs, or at the very least to keep white and colored workers separate. A Fair Play committee busily poking about in various offices

---

sives and the Colored Man," *Outlook*, ci, 909-12; *Journal of Negro History*, xxxii, 90; *Bee*, 12 Dec 1912.

had elicited complaints from "Democratic clerks and other white employees of the government who are inimical to the Negro," and had obtained the backing of office-seekers who declared it intolerable for white people to work in proximity to Negroes, let alone under their supervision.[13] The President, apparently convinced that racial friction was rife in the executive departments, was anxious to check it if only because it might imperil his legislative programs.

In view of the southern background of Postmaster General Albert Burleson, Secretary of the Treasury William McAdoo, and Secretary of the Navy Josephus Daniels, perhaps segregation would have become standard throughout their departments without the impetus supplied by outside agitation and the shocked disapproval of Mrs. Woodrow Wilson at seeing colored men and white women working in the same room in the Post Office Department. There the change, by whomever inspired, had gone into effect before the end of July 1913, and by autumn the Treasury, after cautiously watching public reaction, had consigned the colored employees of most divisions to separate rooms and forbidden all Negro employees to use the lunch tables and the toilet facilities that for years past they had shared with their white fellows. Similar rules applied in the Navy Department as well as in all federal offices where segregation had obtained under Republican rule.

"The effect is startling," the NAACP report noted. "Those segregated are regarded as a people apart, almost as lepers." White clerks, seemingly without personal convictions, now said they approved. To endorse the new arrangement had become "the thing to do." Yet ever since President Cleveland had quashed every proposal of segregation, the *Bee* pointed out,

[13] *Bee*, 29 Mar, 26 Jul, 25 Oct, 15 Nov, 6 Dec 1913; *Nation*, XCVII, 114; *Crisis*, VI, 9, 60-63, XII, 198; New York *Times*, 19 Feb, 25 Apr 1914; L. H. Pickford to Joseph Tumulty, 12 Jun 1916, Wilson Mss; *NAACP Report*, 13 Aug 1913, and "Segregation in Government Departments," *NAACP Report of an Investigation*, 1 Nov 1913, Wilson Mss (hereafter cited as *NAACP Rpt*, 1 Nov 1913); *Post*, 30 Apr 1913.

"Afro-American clerks" had worked side by side with white in "peace and harmony." In the summer of 1913 Booker T. Washington wrote a friend: "I have never seen the colored people [of Washington] so discouraged and so bitter as they are at the present time." Many of them refused at first to believe that the author of "The New Freedom" knew what was afoot, but in late October when a delegation led by William Monroe Trotter of Boston begged him to intervene, the President's evasive answer dissipated doubts: Jim Crowism in the federal government had his approval. A mass meeting to protest "the officializing of race prejudice" overflowed the Metropolitan AME Church, but for the moment Negroes in the government service dared go no further lest they precipitate a drastic change in the civil service law which would extend segregation into every federal department and be far harder to rescind then the word-of-mouth orders of departmental chiefs.[14]

Local leaders of the NAACP realized that "almost every man employed by the government and by the schools risks his position when he stands on our militant platform," but they believed that only a united front could stop the spread of racial discrimination. In November they organized a speakers' bureau to go from church to church, society to society, and lodge to lodge, "to arouse the colored people themselves to their danger, to make them feel it through and through, and at the same time to make them willing to make sacrifices for the cause." The response was "nothing short of a miracle." In a city notoriously rent by "all sorts of factions," Archibald Grimké, president of the Washington NAACP branch, almost disbelievingly saw "school teachers whom you would not believe cared for anything but pleasure, society women, young men," join in the

[14] *Post*, 2, 20 May 1913; Ralph Tyler to President Wilson, 12 May, Booker T. Washington to Oswald Garrison Villard, 10 Aug, enclosed in ltr, Villard to Wilson, 18 Aug 1913, and Villard to Wilson, 29 Sep 1913, Wilson Mss; *Bee*, 10, 17 May, 26 Jul, 6 Sep, 15 Nov 1913; Arthur Link, *The New Freedom*, pp. 245-54; *Crisis*, vi, 220, 289-99, vii, 89; *NAACP Report*, 1 Nov 1913.

campaign. At the M Street High School a group of exceptionally inspiring teachers passed on the torch to their students;
for them W. E. B. DuBois became a symbol of liberty. By the
early months of 1914 the Washington NAACP had over seven
hundred dues-paying members and had sent nearly $4,000 to
national headquarters.[15]

Personal letters from influential white men pleading with
the President to alter his course and indignant articles in the
liberal magazines and newspapers failed to persuade Mr. Wilson to reverse his position. On the contrary, his resistance stiff-
ened. When a second Negro delegation, again led by William
Monroe Trotter, reminded him of his earlier promise to see
justice done, Wilson lost his temper and told the delegation he
was not to be high-pressured. The remonstrances, however,
were almost certainly instrumental in preventing the wholesale
adoption of segregation throughout the government. In March
1914 when the House Committee on Civil Service Reform held
hearings on two bills calling for mandatory racial separation
of government employees, a Louisiana sponsor of the bills
argued that to put a member of "this inferior race" in a position
of authority over Caucasians was unrighteous. By the stamp of
color the Lord had decreed a lowly place for Negroes. When
Congressman Martin Madden of Illinois asked: "Who can say
the Almighty decreed it?" the Louisianan replied: "History,
experience, and first-hand knowledge." Northern representatives
killed both bills in committee.[16]

In the meantime a Supreme Court ruling that the federal
Civil Rights Act of 1875, which had long ago been declared

[15] *Crisis*, VII, 192-93, VIII, 32-33; Dr. Rayford Logan to the author,
9 Mar 1960.

[16] O. G. Villard, "The President and the Negro," *Nation*, XCVII, 114; Vil-
lard, "The President and the Segregation at Washington," *North American
Review*, CXCVIII, 800-07; "Race Segregation at Washington," *Independent*,
LXXX, p. 275; *Washington Herald*, 16 Nov 1914; *Times*, 13 Nov 1914;
Crisis, IX, 119-27; *Negro Year Book, 1914-15*, pp. 34-36; H Comee on Reform
in the Civil Service, 63C, 2S, *Segregation of Clerks and Employees in the
Civil Service*, 6 Mar 1914, pp. 3, 7.

unconstitutional in the states, was invalid also in federal territory opened the door to new discriminatory laws in the District of Columbia. But fresh attempts to exclude Negroes from government service, District anti-miscegenation and Jim Crow street-car bills, and a segregated residential bill patterned on a Baltimore ordinance of 1913 all met with defeat. Pressures in fact eased slightly in 1915 when the Supreme Court in an unforeseen reversal of earlier opinions refused to allow nearby Maryland to write a "grandfather clause" into her constitution.

"More than seventy-five per cent of the present segregation," the *Bee* reminded its readers in 1915, "was transmitted to President Wilson by the Republicans," and the editor noted more Negro promotions in the civil service than in years past. But although the transit companies were not allowed to introduce Jim Crow cars, other District corporations and individual white citizens interpreted the administration policy to mean that short of open violence they could carry discrimination virtually as far as they chose. Informal agreements between sellers and buyers effectively strengthened the residential color line. In 1914 an eminent Boston lawyer persuaded the American Bar Association to rescind its recent ruling that no Negro could be elected to membership, but the substitute provision that applicants must state their race served the same purpose. While not all white Washingtonians shared the prevailing colorphobia and Chief Justice Wendell Stafford fought it in the District Supreme Court, most of the white community took it for granted that colored teachers should be excluded from a teachers' lecture series held in the Congregational Church and that Negro civic organizations should not be invited to join with the fifty-six white groups in planning better correlation of the city's recreational activities.[17]

[17] *Crisis*, VII, 117, 142, 169, 252-53; *Negro Year Book, 1914-15*, pp. 30, 34-35, 39; *Times*, 3 Dec 1914; *Bee*, 4 Oct 1914, 27 Feb, 5 Mar, 15 May 1915; *Sun*, 26 Mar, 30 Apr, 25 Jun 1915; H Rpt 1340, 63C, 3S, Ser 6766; H Dis Comee, 64C, 1S, Hrgs, "Intermarriage of Whites and

The attacks and the disheartening indifference of white people, however, had the effect of maintaining the new solidarity in the Negro world. In Washington's triple-tiered colored community a sense of cohesiveness, lacking for thirty years, had begun to emerge before 1911; it strengthened extraordinarily during the crisis of 1913 and 1914. Although, as the struggle against race prejudice dragged on, the failure to make headway might well have dissolved the new bonds, they endured. In northern cities also, upper-class Negroes, the "talented tenth" upon whom W. E. B. DuBois pinned hopes for the race, saw they could not remain detached from the lower-class black, no matter how superior they knew themselves to be and no matter how uncongenial they found his society. But the growth of "group-identification" among all classes of Washington Negroes had special significance, both because elaborate class distinctions were older here than in most of the United States and because all colored people recognized Washington as the center of Negro culture in America.

The new attitude of the *Bee* supplies an index to this change. Where the paper had once carried scathing accounts of Negro discrimination against Negro and had sneered at any colored man who achieved distinction, the editorials and news articles gradually took on a constructive character. The addition to the editoral staff of the wise, public-spirited George H. Richardson gave the *Bee* new dignity; his opinions carried weight. Calvin Chase, whose attacks on Booker T. Washington had stopped in 1908, lashed out periodically at W. E. B. DuBois, arch opponent of Mr. Washington's subservient teachings, but after the death of the Tuskegee leader in November 1915, those explosions ended. Chase and Richardson saw fit to needle colored men who sought their own advantage at the sacrifice of principle. Editorials called attention to the destructive selfish-

---

Negroes in the District of Columbia, and Separate Accommodations in Street Cars for White and Negroes in the District of Columbia."

ness of Negro candidates for office under the proscriptive Democratic regime. "Woody," one article declared, "believed his segregation policy was approved by the black gentry because so many of them were anxious to serve under him, segregation or no segregation." Sarcastically the *Bee* observed that no local colored men had had the courage to ask the President in person to define his position on race questions as William Monroe Trotter of Boston had twice obliged him to do, first in November 1913 and again a year later. Yet in taking cowards and the mean-minded to task, the *Bee* also accorded praise to colored men of firm convictions and larger vision. Scoldings at Negro short-comings became progressively fewer and turned instead into exhortations to push on with the noble work of establishing a self-respecting, self-sufficient Negro Washington within the larger community.[18]

Four other Negro publications were appearing regularly in Washington in 1914 and 1915—the short-lived *Sun*, put out by a talented but erratic protégé of Booker T. Washington, the *American*, the *Odd Fellows Journal*, and the *National Union*, organ of a Negro insurance company. In 1915 the *Journal of Negro History* began its long and useful career. The *American*, an uninspired, rather shabby sheet, and the ably edited *Sun* pursued the same line as the *Bee* in less bellicose language: buy colored, support colored charities and colored civic enterprises, take pride in Negro achievements, and don't be "Jim Crowed" by patronizing places where Negroes are segregated. The fourfold program, already familiar, put novel emphasis on Negro successes won by Negro cooperation. Gradually business firms and non-profit groups began to advertise what Negro solidarity had accomplished. They pointed out that the Howard Theatre, upon reverting to colored management after two or

[18] *Negro Year Book, 1914-15*, pp. 43-45; Arnold M. Rose, *The Negro's Morale, Group Identification and Protest*, pp. 57-95; *Bee*, 21 Nov 1914, 27 Feb, 5 Mar 1915; Colonel Campbell C. Johnson to the author, 9 Jun 1960.

three years of white, provided good entertainment—some plays, more minstrel shows, and musical hits like those of the "Black Patti Troubadours"—and by renting the premises for amateur performances now and again served as a kind of community cultural center; at the *Majestic* vaudeville theatre and two new Negro movie houses colored audiences never had to face Jim Crowism. Le Droit Park's 5,000 colored residents could enjoy a similar freedom by giving their custom to the Negro-owned grocery store.

The *Sun*, remarking that the local Negro Business League had gone "to sleep" in 1913, began in 1915 to carry a directory of reliable Negro business firms in the city. A colored department store in a building on 14th Street employed only colored help and met a long-felt want. U Street in northwest Washington was becoming the colored Connecticut Avenue. In southwest Washington the new Douglass Hotel offered colored tourists and conventions comfortable accommodations. The Negro press now insisted on use of the capital *N*, and after 1914 frequently capitalized "colored" also; doubtless in the interest of racial harmony, colored newspapers practically dropped the term "black." Despite the militance of the new propaganda, it was refreshingly free of the braggadocio that had formerly accompanied attempts to encourage Negro enterprise.

Indeed, there was more in which to take pride, as the social disorganization that had long characterized colored Washington began to yield to community effort. Progress, begun even before the disasters of the Wilson era added impetus, was particularly noticeable in the realm of charities and civic undertakings. By the spring of 1913 the recently opened colored YMCA, built brick by brick by Negro workmen, was able to meet its first year's operating costs of $8,200 and show a 56-cent balance. "The fraternal spirit existing between the Y and the local ministry is happily shown in the use by a number of the churches of the great swimming pool for baptismal purposes." As a true community center, the Y became the meeting place of the local branch of the NAACP, the Public School Athletic League, the Christian Endeavor Union, the Federation of Civic Associations, the Negro Medical Society, and other organizations. The colored YWCA expanded its program and paid off all but a small indebtedness during 1913. While public-spirited Negroes admitted that too few well-to-do families contributed to charity, a new determination to carry on without white philanthropy went far toward obliterating their earlier attitude: let the whites shoulder the burden, since they are responsible for the colored man's plight. Roscoe Conkling Bruce, Assistant Superintendent for the colored schools, reminded the audience at the annual meeting of the Colored Social Settlement in December 1913 that Dr. John R. Francis, Washington's leading colored physician, had launched the center "about which many and various efforts for social uplift are organized." In appealing for generous support of this primarily Negro-sponsored charity, Bruce pleaded also for teaching colored children about the great men of their own race; only thus would the younger generation escape being overwhelmed by white prestige and avoid impairment of colored initiative. In much the same vein the newly organized Oldest Inhabitants Association (Colored) of Washington announced its purpose to be the fostering of Negro civic pride.[19]

It would be untruthful to picture colored Washington in 1915 and 1916 as a unified community free of the old divisive jealousies and destructive backbiting, its individual members now single-mindedly working all for one and one for all. Leaders faltered, quarrels persisted—particularly over teaching appointments and promotions in the school system—and self-contempt, shown in the sheer meanness of Negro to Negro, continued to

[19] *Bee*, 17 May, 6 Dec 1913, 2 Oct 1915, 25 May 1916; *Sun*, 8 Jan, 12 Mar, 23 Apr 1915; *Crisis*, xi, 90-94; John H. Paynter, *A Souvenir of the Anniversary and Banquet of the Oldest Inhabitants Association (Colored) of the District of Columbia, April 16, 1914.*

interfere with the important task of raising the economic level of all classes. The *Sun* argued that the cost of racial disunity was as high for the light-colored Caucasian-featured person as for the black-skinned Negroid-looking, but few of the former were willing to discard class distinctions based largely upon degree of color. Moreover, the tightening of the net drawn by strengthened white hostility, while binding courageous colored people together in a common purpose, strangled the will of the weak and timid; circumstances that awakened a fighting spirit in some of the race stripped others of the capacity to hold up their heads at all. Nevertheless the energy with which Washington's Negro leaders fought lynching in the South and racial discrimination everywhere was impressive.[20]

W. E. B. DuBois later wrote of the early years of the Wilson administration: "Quite suddenly the program for the NAACP, which up to this time had been more or less indefinite, was made clear and intensive." The Washington branch forestalled adverse legislation, got a few Negroes reinstated in government jobs, and induced Congress to continue appropriations for Howard University and its 300 college students. Besides a vigorous separate University chapter, by 1916 the Washington branch of the NAACP, with 1,164 members, was the largest in the United States, and, according to national headquarters, constituted "really a national vigilance committee to watch legislation in Congress and lead the fight for Negro manhood rights at the capital of the nation."[21]

Differences of opinion inescapably arose over both long-term strategy and more immediate local tactics. For example, in which direction should Washington Negroes lean when the

[20] *Sun*, 12, 26 Feb 1915; M. C. Terrell to Robert Terrell, n.d., Terrell Mss. Practically every issue of the *Bee* carried some complaint about Negro school administrators' injustices.

[21] W. E. B. DuBois, *Dusk of Dawn*, pp. 235-36; *Sun*, 15 Jan, 12 Mar 1915; *Crisis*, IX, 217, XI, 35, 256, XII, 197; see also list of Washington members at the 1916 conference at Amenia, New York, *Programme*, Terrell Mss.

discussion of District Home Rule revived in 1916? At one time the colored press had argued that voting in municipal elections was essential to the progress of the city's Negro community. But as Henry West and Frederick Siddons had always treated Negroes with exemplary fairness and Oliver Newman and Louis Brownlow showed no racial prejudice, might not colored people be better off under the rule of commissioners like those than under officials chosen by a two-thirds white electorate? Most colored men side-stepped the question; if white citizens persuaded Congress to restore the franchise, then would be time enough for their colored neighbors to seek their share of local political power. Again, what was the wise course to pursue when "The Birth of a Nation" began its long run in Washington movie houses? Some men, seeing it as an incitement to race hatred, wanted to demand that the commissioners ban the picture, just as they had barred the prize fight film of Jack Johnson beating Jim Jeffries; other colored people believed that a petition for censorship would merely advertise the offensive D. W. Griffith film more widely.

While in the national arena Negro leaders examined alternatives as the presidential campaign of 1916 opened, in the voteless capital the question about working with whites for "national preparedness" caused uncertainty. In June 1916 the colored men who marched in a big preparedness parade were "Jim Crowed with a vengeance" and two days later were greeted with a formal segregation order from the War Department. At the request of a New Jersey congressman whose reelection hung in the balance, the order was later rescinded, but before the end of October the all-Negro battalion of the District National Guard was on the Mexican border. Six months later the United States' declaration of war upon the Central Powers would force upon all American Negroes a decision of whether to be Americans first and Negroes second or to let white Americans carry on without voluntary help from the people they treated as second-class citizens.[22]

Still, every Washingtonian daily rubbed elbows with or at least was aware of the presence of people not of his own race. Scores of Negroes were as acutely concerned with municipal taxation, civic betterment, and artistic growth as were their white-skinned neighbors. Whether they would or no, some give-and-take resulted. An experiment of 1913 in publishing a Negro city directory was not repeated. Colored Washington, largely separate and wholly unequal in status, was still part of the over-all community.

[22] *Bee*, 14 Nov 1908, 1 Apr 1916, 17, 19 Jun, 9 Sep, 21 Oct 1916; *Sun*, 9 Apr 1915; Rose, *The Negro's Morale*, pp. 38-39; *Seventh Anl Rpt NAACP*, 1917; *Crisis*, XII, 194, 268; W. E. B. DuBois to Woodrow Wilson, 10 Oct 1916, and Memorial, Boston Branch Negro Equal Political Rights League, 20 Apr 1917, Wilson Mss.

CHAPTER XII

THE GREAT CRUSADE AND ANTICLIMAX, 1917-1918

JANUARY and February 1917 came and went in Washington amid uncertainties about what President Wilson would consider sufficient provocation from Germany to force America into war. On January 22nd, the President spoke to the Senate of his hope of seeing "peace without victory" in Europe. Nine days later the Imperial German Government informed the United States that unrestricted submarine warfare, halted after the sinking of the "Lusitania" in 1915, would resume at once. On February 3rd the President broke off diplomatic relations by dismissing Ambassador von Bernstorff and recalling the American ambassador from Berlin. That done, the President appeared to be unwilling to go further than to obtain authority to arm American merchantmen. While the Central Committee of the American National Red Cross instructed its regional offices to prepare for war, the Council of National Defense, created by Congress in 1916, asked the recently organized National Research Council of the National Academy of Sciences to act as its scientific research unit. The "city of conversation," meanwhile, talked with more passion than urbanity.

The first week of March saw the mustering out of the District National Guard regiments returned from the Mexican border, the passage of a local prohibition act to take effect on November 1st, and President Wilson's second inauguration attended by a large, undemonstrative crowd. As the grandstands along Pennsylvania Avenue came down and visitors departed, the city returned to normal routines. Then on March 18th word of the torpedoing of three unarmed American merchantmen reached the capital. People who had watched unhappily the mounting anti-German feeling in Washington now agreed: "If the sinking of these ships is not war, it inevitably means war," but everyone reassured his neighbor and himself: "This will only be a war on paper or at most a war at sea."

During the next fortnight the capital burst into frenzied, if at times slightly ridiculous, activity. Bellhops at the New Willard drilled daily on the hotel roof. Two thousand boy scouts prepared to mobilize at thirty minutes' notice "for first aid work, police and detective duty." Superintendent Thurston introduced daily salutes to the flag in the public schools, and the Board of Trade met to condemn "German militarism," each member waving a flag to show that "there is no hyphen in the citizenship of Washington." While the War and Navy Departments increased the guard about government property, stationed infantrymen at bridge heads, and placed cavalry along the road to the reservoir, the District naval militia readied itself for a call to board "fighting ships" within twenty days, and recently mustered out national guardsmen prepared to return to active duty. Young men flocked to the enlistment stations opened in various parts of the city. The President requested Congress to convene in special session on April 2nd "to receive a communication concerning grave matters." As rumors spread about impending arrests of disloyal German-born citizens, the Chief of Police refused to permit a loyalty or a peace parade. But when David Starr Jordan, President of Leland Stanford University, and other pacifists hurried to Washington to plead with the President and Congress, serious disorders threatened; members of the District National Guard daubed yellow paint on the headquarters of the Emergency Peace Foundation and talked of "smashing the building." Throughout the city tensions rose.[1]

The weeks of soul-searching and waiting ended dramatically

[1] For a running account of events, see Mark Sullivan, "Over Here, 1914-1918," *Our Times*, v, 248-50, 256-66; Foster Rhea Dulles, *The American Red Cross, A History*, pp. 138-39; R. M. Yerkes, ed., *The New World of Science and Its Development During the War*, pp. 13-16 (hereafter cited as Yerkes, *New World of Science*); *Star*, 1, 11, 16, 19, 25-30 Mar, 1 Apr 1917; *Bee*, 17 Feb 1917.

on the evening of April 2nd. Over the city fell "a soft fragrant rain of early spring; the illuminated dome of the Capitol stood in solemn splendor against the dark wet of the sky," as the President, escorted by cavalry to save him possible annoyance from pacifists, drove to the Hill. The great chamber of the House of Representatives was crowded to the doors. "To every person present," wrote an eye-witness, "from members of the Cabinet and the Justices of the Supreme Court in the first row, to observers in the remote seats of the gallery, that evening was the most-to-be remembered of their lives." Among the diplomats seated behind the Cabinet expectancy reigned. "The present German submarine warfare," the President began, "is a warfare against mankind." Chief Justice Edward D. White nodded his head in assent. As the stirring words denounced the "war against all nations," eyes in the audience turned toward the Chief Justice. When the President declared the United States incapable of choosing the path of submission, White, "without waiting to hear the rest of the sentence, sprang to his feet, his action a cue for the entire Senate. His face worked almost convulsively. Great tears rolled down his cheeks. From that moment to the end he was vigorously applauding." Four days later Congress declared war upon Germany.

The declaration of war somewhat sobered the most loudly belligerent elements in the city, but it was the signal for a chorus of high-sounding, earnest pronouncements of the sort a cynical later generation would deride: "Our war is of the kind which God sanctions. . . . The call to arms in such a war hardens and strengthens the muscles, inspires the spirit and thrills the soul of every loyal American." Virtually overnight, Washingtonians long accustomed to the placidity of the prewar capital were caught up in turmoil. "Life seemed suddenly to acquire a vivid scarlet lining," wrote Helen Nicolay. "Old prejudices gave way to passionate new beliefs. Old precedents were wrecked in an endeavor to live up to the duty of the hour. The one invariable rule seemed to be that every individual was found doing something he or she had never dreamed of doing before. The rule worked even in those somnolent parts of Georgetown that seem under the spell of a Rip Van Winkle sleep."[2]

With decentralization of the government still a novel concept, the capital bore the brunt of the confusions attending the creation of a war machine, setting it in motion, and keeping it running. In the process the city lost most of her identity as a community and became a national war center. People eager to be useful poured into Washington during the first week of the war, and the flow did not lessen until after the Armistice in November 1918. Here were the headquarters not only for the armed services but also for the Liberty Loan drives conducted by the Treasury, for the Food Administration headed by Herbert Hoover, the War Trade, the War Industries, and the Shipping Boards, the Fuel Administration, the American National Red Cross, and, when the United States government took over the railroads in December, the railroad administration. At Fort Myer, across the Potomac, 1,200 student officers at a time were in training, and several hundred engineer trainees occupied the long-empty buildings of the American University; within a radius of 25 miles some 130,000 soldiers were stationed, most of whom spent their leaves in Washington. Foreign missions and uniformed representatives of all the allied nations came and went, for, as an Englishman remarked, "this newest and rawest of the capitals, which, yet in some sense in these straining times becomes the chief capital . . . is the fountain of capacity for war and victory." A city of some 350,000 inhabitants in April 1917 acquired about 40,000 new residents before autumn, and a year later estimates based upon street-car fares raised the total to over 526,000. These and the uncounted

---

[2] Sullivan, *Our Times*, v, 272-74; *Star*, 6 Apr 1917; Nicolay, *Our Capital on the Potomac*, pp. 512-13.

transients strained the facilities of the District to the bursting point.[3]

"Everyone," remarked Alice Roosevelt Longworth, looked for an "excuse" to come to Washington. Viewing the city not as a dedicated old resident like Miss Nicolay but as Society's "Princess Alice," she observed: "People . . . never seemed as solely occupied with 'war work' as they were in other places." Not unnaturally "it pleased the Washington that went to and gave dinners to feel that entertaining the representatives of the Allies had a recognized part in 'winning the war.' Anyway it was a far pleasanter form of war work than canteens, Red Cross classes and Liberty Loan drives!" Journalists made fun of the deprivations some of these "war-workers" complained of— for example, after prohibition went into effect in the District on November 1, 1917, the sacrifice of cocktails before dinner and only Pol Roget, 1904, to serve with every course. Young women imported to file mountains of War Department forms doubtless felt little kinship with women who "did their bit" by knitting diligently as their chauffeurs drove them along the Avenue in their Pierce Arrows. But a "war job" in Washington, whatever its nature, held a fascination for people in all walks of life and from every part of the country.[4]

Besides the thousands of obscure, relatively uninformed typists and clerks crowded into government offices, colorful personages of the American business and professional world thronged the city. In hot little cubicles in "emergency" buildings powerful industrialists such as Charles Schwab of the United States Steel Corporation and the one-time Wyoming cowboy, Alexander Legge of the International Harvester Com-

[3] Comrs Rpts, 1917, pp. 5-6, 1918, pp. 6, 26; Theodore Tiller, "Washington in War Time," *Review of Reviews*, LVI, 629-32; Richard Oulahan, "Washington of Today," *Country Life in America*, XXXIV, 36; *Star*, 1 Jul 1917; Henry Leach, "The Charm of Washington," *Living Age*, IX, 597.

[4] Alice Roosevelt Longworth, *Crowded Hours*, pp. 258-62; Jesse Lynch Williams, "Country Life in War Time," *Country Life in America*, XXXIV, 41-42.

pany, worked long hours as government "dollar-a-year men," while in other cubby-holes brilliant but impecunious college professors such as the economist Edwin Gay of Harvard and Walter Tower, economic geographer of Chicago, earned their modest salaries many times over in a single day. Not everyone stayed longer than was necessary to learn where and how he could most usefully serve, but the nerve center of the nation at war lay here. In the thick of frustrating delays, overlapping efforts, and exhausting hard work, the challenge of the job to be done endured, and the influx of talents and ideas left permanent marks upon the city: when the tide receded with the coming of peace, Washington would discover that these war-workers had endowed her with new goals, new institutions, and some gifted new residents.[5]

Generals and admirals, disturbed by the alarming shortages of conventional arms to equip a million or more fighting men, were equally alarmed at the gaps in military equipment for which no prototype had as yet been developed—listening gear to enable ships to locate submarines, aerial cameras to serve "as the eyes of the army," wireless communication systems for both aircraft and ground use, American-made optical glass to replace German imports, improved range finders for big guns, and a dozen more. In answer to the call of Robert A. Millikan of the University of Chicago, newly appointed executive of the National Research Council, physicists, chemists, and medical research men left their university classrooms and laboratories and, accompanied by a few men trained in industrial research, joined forces with scientists already in government employ or at the Carnegie Institution of Washington. Occasionally "finds" came from unlikely sources: in the spring of 1917, for example, an unknown electrician from Salem, Massachusetts, walked into an office at the Navy Yard with a package under his arm containing his design of an underwater mine; later produced

[5] Sullivan, *Our Times*, v, 380-88; Herbert Heaton, *A Scholar in Action, Edwin F. Gay*, pp. 98-138.

as the Mark VI, this almost casually tendered innovation proved the means of screening off from submarines the stretch of sea from northern Scotland to the Norwegian coast. But scientists enlisted by the National Research Council collaborating with the military and with industry planned the programs and conducted most of the work. As the Army and Navy took over the projects one by one and put civilian scientists into officers' uniforms, most of the actual research was transferred to new installations in other parts of the country, but Washington remained the clearing house for all scientific work underway.

Because fighting a world war required far more than military hardware, medical research reached out to devise new techniques of surgery and prevention of epidemic diseases in training camps and overseas, while psychologists developed intelligence and special aptitude tests for classification of draftees in a citizens' army. The government turned also to social scientists and historians. In the six months preceding the United States' entry into the war, several federal bureaus had benefitted from a few studies undertaken by political economists at a newly founded, privately financed Institute for Government Research, but the role of the inexact sciences widened in the spring of 1917. In April the British and French missions to Washington explained to the President that, if Germany were to be kept from overpowering western Europe, the United States would have to supply its hard-pressed allies with food, oil, and iron, as well as munitions and men. The undertaking would tax America's resources to the utmost and demanded, in the words of an eminent economist, "a new ordering of [national] life." The emergency boards and commissions that quickly proliferated in Washington contained a sprinkling of experienced government administrators but were manned chiefly by businessmen and college professors trained in assembling factual materials and interpreting their significance.[6]

[6] Yerkes, *New World of Science*, pp. 20-30, 291-350; Dupree, *Science*, pp. 308-23; Benedict Crowell and Robert E. Wilson, *The Armies of Industry,*

As federal census reports in the past had focused primarily on data needed to reapportion representation in Congress and to draft tariff legislation, the lack of precise information available in Washington about the character and extent of national resources posed an enormous problem, for, without accurate knowledge of the nature and quantity of national assets, planning could not proceed logically, and, without planning, the task of imposing restrictions upon the civilian economy was impossible. Hence the importance of the work undertaken by Edwin F. Gay and his "cabinet" of economists in the Shipping Board's Planning and Statistics Division. Similarly, since Americans would not accept interference with the sacred free enterprise system unless they understood the reasons, the Committee on Public Information drew upon scholars to educate the public about what was at stake and why drastic measures were necessary. The endeavors to effect "a new ordering" of national economic life ended with the cessation of fighting in Europe, but government officials and private citizens in the interim learned a good deal about the value of exact information and efficient procedures. Washington would feel the lasting effects of this hard-won wisdom.

"Scholars in the human sciences," Frederick Keppel of Columbia later noted, "did not dominate the situation as did scholars in the physical sciences," but the voluntary "mobilization of the history men" began in late April at a conference called by J. Franklin Jameson of the Carnegie Institution's Department of Historical Research. Eager to put "historical scholarship" to immediate use, a National Board of Historical Service enlisted lecturers, writers to prepare pamphlets on "war issues," and "Four-Minute-Men" to speak at Liberty Loan

---

I, 319; *Autobiography of Robert A. Millikan*, pp. 142-99; The Brookings Institution, *Institute for Government Research, An Account of Research Achievements*, pp. 4-18; Allyn A. Young, "National Statistics in War and Peace," *Quarterly Publications of the American Statistical Society*, March 1918, p. 2.

rallies. The board strove also to ensure the preservation of valuable wartime records and prepared background materials that might assist in the eventual negotiation of a just peace. Later sometimes accused of performing as propagandists rather than judicious scholars, historians in and out of Washington vigorously pressed the case for improving the quality of history teaching and textbooks in school systems throughout the country. Scholars' insistence on the importance of records was instrumental in creating historical branches in the State, War, and Navy Departments during the war and, a dozen years later, in persuading Congress to vote money for a public record repository—the National Archives. Out of the interest in better teaching came the American Council on Education in 1918, "an organization of organizations" in which school and college administrators joined with historians in an effort to raise the standards of American education. While undertaking to recruit 10,000 students for nurses' training, the council's directing heads in Washington soon realized that their chief tasks would lie in the postwar world. With a full-time director appointed after the Armistice, the council began its major work in 1920.[7]

Washingtonians occupied few important posts in the hastily established emergency agencies. A non-industrial city had no businessmen of the stature of Charles Schwab to take charge of shipbuilding, or of Henry Dennison of the Dennison Manufacturing Company, expert on business administration, or of Bernard Baruch whose spectacular lone-wolf career in the stock market made him a power to reckon with and a logical choice for head of the War Industries Board. Four or five professors of the "dismal science" at the local universities and a number of experienced men whose long service in Washington made them "permanent temporary" residents had responsible jobs with the federal wartime boards, and members of the Library

[7] American Historical Association, *Annual Report*, 1919, I, 131-89; *American Council on Education, Its History and Activities*, pp. 1-5.

of Congress staff and scholars attached to other federal offices volunteered assistance. But the civil service system of making appointments on a quota basis to citizens of the states kept local people out of war jobs until the housing shortage in Washington called attention to the desirability of employing qualified local talent.[8] Life acquired its vivid scarlet lining for most Washingtonians because they believed fervently in the "great crusade," and here where mighty events moved forward they felt themselves an intimate part of it. They served as the Marthas of the capital, the people who carried on the humdrum thankless chores of supplying as best they could the wants of the newcomers.

Yet the local community made distinct if little recognized contributions to the winning of the war. The foresight of District Commissioner Brownlow and several federal officials who believed some form of military conscription inevitable enabled the city to set an example to the rest of the country in drafting men for the armed services: the draft forms for the District were in print, and maps showing registration stations were ready for posting several days before the National Selective Service Act passed Congress on May 18, 1917; run by volunteers among the District government's employees, registration then moved so swiftly and smoothly that on September 4th the President himself underscored the achievement by leading a parade of the District's "citizens' army" up Pennsylvania Avenue. Although agitation about "rounding up slackers" went on for weeks thereafter, Washingtonians were proud of having 10,000 inductees and nearly 7,000 voluntary enlistments before the Armistice, in addition to the 2,000 men in service when war broke out.

Given a quota of $8,500,000 in the first Liberty Bond drive, the city raised more than twice that amount; in the second drive four months later she raised nearly $23,000,000 and oversub-

[8] H Dis Comee, 65C, 1S, Hrg, "Housing in D.C."; *Star*, 25 Oct 1918.

scribed her quotas in every later campaign. Some of the subscriptions came from temporary dollar-a-year men, but the local response was remarkable inasmuch as the spiraling costs of living in the overcrowded capital by 1918 had reduced by about 30 percent the purchasing power of federal and District employees, who even in 1916 were shockingly underpaid. Nor did householders escape acute privations: 5,000 families were without heat in sub-zero January weather when the city had less than a day's coal supply on hand even at strict ration levels. Volunteers appointed to a District Council of Defense cheerfully took charge of projects they "had never dreamed" of before; some five thousand war gardens produced over $1,000,000 in foodstuffs during 1918; a group cooperated with the Traveller's Aid in assisting newcomers to find places to live, and women made surgical dressings under Red Cross direction, organized camp entertainments, and manned canteens. As American troops began to move overseas, Washington, like every city and village on the continent, saw "tears and cheers; sudden marriages and sudden farewells. . . . And endlessly there was the suspense of waiting for the next war news."[9]

War, moreover, imposed unique problems on the District government, perhaps none more troublesome than keeping order in the war-swollen capital. In the spring of 1917 the national government had scanty machinery to provide for its own protection—a small Secret Service attached to the Treasury department to keep track of counterfeiting and three or four men assigned to the White House, a Capitol police force composed largely of political appointees, and the Federal Bureau of Investigation, which, established in Theodore Roosevelt's day to prevent fraudulent transactions in public land, had only two or three men located in Washington. In 1915 and 1916 Louis Brownlow, the District commissioner responsible for the police

[9] Brownlow, *A Passion for Anonymity*, pp. 44-82; Comrs Rpts, 1917, pp. 5-6, 1918, pp. 5-8, 1919, pp. 9, 557-67; *Star*, 15, 21 Jun, 12 Aug, 2, 28 Oct, 9 Dec 1917, 9, 28 May, 11, 17, 20 Oct 1918, 12 May 1919; *Rpt B/Tr*, 1917, p. 11.

department, and its newly appointed chief, Major Raymond Pullman, had taken the first steps to forestall German espionage. Not until the war was five months old did a new Emergency Division in the Department of Justice begin to handle all matters touching alien enemies, sabotage, and espionage; in the interim the local police carried much of the load. The force was always below authorized strength, partly because of Army enlistments, but even more because pay rates, set by Congress in 1916, stood at about half the figure offered by private employers. The *Bee* suggested the time ripe to add colored officers to the department, but either Negro candidates failed to qualify or Major Pullman was unwilling to risk antagonizing whites. At Brownlow's insistence, however, the department enlisted several policewomen, an innovation that initially scandalized conservatives.

One episode that assumed some international significance illustrates policing problems. As the first Allied missions began to arrive in Washington, militant women suffragists chose to picket the White House; their banners labelled the President and the administration more tyrannical than Kaiser Wilhelm or the Romanoff Czar. As infuriated clerks pouring out of the government buildings every afternoon tore down the offensive banners, street riots greeted the eyes of foreign emissaries. Commissioner Brownlow finally ordered the arrest of the leading pickets, all of them socially prominent women, and, upon their refusal to pay the court fines, sent them to the Occoquan workhouse. The President, unwilling to create martyrs, promptly issued pardons. The daily street riots resumed. Unfortunately, as enemy newspapers in Europe interpreted them as pro-German demonstrations, they hurt Allied solidarity. Without seeking presidential approval, which Wilson would probably not give, Brownlow then put some thirty of the most obstreperous women into a freshly painted, newly furnished, separate building of the District jail in cells without lockable doors. The new inmates at once went on a hunger strike. So the Commissioner had two stoves installed in the corridor and engaged three eight-hour shifts of cooks to fry ham night and day. The ham went to charitable institutions. Defeated by the fragrance of frying ham, the hunger strikers voluntarily left the jail, and the campaign of militant abusiveness collapsed.

While the police force, at times reduced to fewer than 700 men, struggled with a mounting volume of crime, President Wilson's passion for vaudeville added to troubles. Every week, in war as in peace, he attended Poli's Theatre on 15th Street, and crowds gathered nightly at the entrance in order to buy tickets for the performance that he chose. Lincoln's assassination at Ford's Theatre fifty-odd years before stood as a painful warning. The worried manager of Poli's fell in with Commissioner Brownlow's suggestion to reserve the entire balcony for reliably patriotic people whenever the President was to occupy his box. The manager cut a doorway through the theatre wall into the alley at the rear so that the White House limousine accompanied by a Secret Service man could deposit the President unobtrusively there whence a back stairway led to his box. But the President never decided when he would go until the morning of the day; then Brownlow would telephone the theatre to sell no balcony tickets for that night, and he himself issued free passes to people known to be trustworthy. President Wilson, unaware of these elaborate arrangements, later remarked cheerfully that the crowded balcony showed that at least Poli's profited from his patronage.

Other units of the local government also faced almost insoluble problems. Before the autumn of 1917 the experienced engineer commissioner, Major Kutz, and Commissioner Oliver Newman left for active Army service. An able but physically frail retired Brigadier General, John G. D. Knight, replaced the former, and W. Gwynne Gardiner, a Washington attorney, a little reluctantly succeeded the latter. For the next two and a half years, as Gardiner spent less and less time in his office, Louis Brownlow ran the District almost single-handedly. Short and slightly rotund, the sharp intelligence and humor in his snapping brown eyes partly concealed by gleaming pince-nez, Brownlow at the age of 37 looked more like an insurance salesman than an imaginative, widely read, forceful public servant. But neither experience nor energy could ensure adequate transportation on the overburdened, privately owned, street railway system, or, at the wage rates allowed, hire hands for vitally necessary public chores, or enlarge the public water supply.

The maximum safe capacity of the city reservoir and filtration plant was 65,000,000 gallons of water daily; by the summer of 1918 daily consumption at times exceeded 75,000,000 gallons. As private industry drew away the men operating the District sewage pumping station, where the pay scale ranged from $900 downward to $540 a year, only Brownlow's personal appeal to President Wilson obtained from the President's emergency fund the $8,000 needed to keep the sewage system in operation; the President filled out the forms and signed the requisitions in his own hand. When the contractor who collected the city garbage, after months of losing money, threw up the contract, Brownlow undertook to extract a deficiency appropriation from Congress to enable the District to make the collections and run the garbage reduction plant. When he presented a carefully figured cost estimate to the House subcommittee, the chairman immediately barked: "There is not one bit of use coming up here and asking us in time of war to start off the District government on a lot of socialistic experimentation." Fortunately, Congressman Vare, the Republican boss of Philadelphia who had made millions as that city's garbage and trash collector, persuaded his fellow committee members that the request was reasonable. The appropriation passed.[10]

Far worse troubles followed. Early in September 1918 the

[10] Interviews, Brownlow, and John Lord O'Brian, head of Emergency Div., Justice Dept, 1917-19; *Star*, 18 Aug 1917, 1 Jan, 8-10, 12 Jun, 8 Aug 1918; *Bee*, 17 Nov 1917; *Rpts B/Tr*, 1917, pp. 70-71, 1918, p. 81; Comr Rpts, 1917, p. 22, 1918, pp. 25-26, 1919, p. 26.

former District health officer who was now health commissioner of Boston, wired Brownlow to warn him that several cases of virulent disease called Spanish flu had occurred in Boston and to urge him to require Washington physicians to report any suspected cases. Prompt action on that advice failed to head off the plague; by September 21, it had hit the overcrowded capital with a force that broke down the reporting service and swamped doctors with desperately ill and dying patients. Both Commissioner Gardiner and General Knight were stricken. Brownlow and the new health officer, Dr. Fowler, closed the theatres, the movie houses, the churches, and most of the shops, persuaded the school board to close the schools, and, with the cooperation of the Visiting Nurses Association, the Red Cross, and a volunteer motor corps, opened nursing centers in four or five schoolhouses. But the epidemic spread. Physicians and nurses caught the disease. Every hospital bed in the city was filled. At one point George Washington Hospital, one of the largest, had every bed occupied and not a single nurse on duty. With half the trolley motormen on the sick list, street-car service was utterly disrupted. And as the death toll mounted, there were neither coffins nor gravediggers enough to meet the emergency.

In mid October, Brownlow later wrote, "it seemed that we had come to the end of our resources. There was a dreadful Saturday." That day he enlisted through the White House the help of every federal agency and arranged for a high-level meeting at the office of the War Industries Board on Sunday morning. A scrutiny of the records filed by war workers revealed people with nursing skills or medical experience. Judge Edwin B. Parker of the War Industries Board virtually commandeered a building just vacated by a division of the Army, and contractors and union representatives were told to ready the building for hospital use, while merchants assembled bedding. By eight o'clock Sunday night a seven-hundred-bed hospital was equipped, and a skeleton staff of doctors and nurses, brought together by Army and Navy medical officers, the Public Health Service, and Dr. Fowler, was ready to receive patients. Volunteer ambulance drivers worked through the night. By two o'clock in the morning every bed was filled. In the interval Secretary of the Navy Daniels ordered marines from Quantico, Virginia, to Washington to dig graves, and, on Judge Parker's instructions, two carloads of coffins in the Potomac railroad yards consigned to Pittsburgh were transferred to the city hospital, where Dr. Fowler took charge of distributing them at a fixed price. Thus the dead were buried, and the worst ravages of the plague halted. By November 4th the emergency was over. Official records showed 35,000 cases reported and 3,500 deaths in those six weeks, but no one could tally the unreported cases, and deaths resulting from later complications ran into hundreds. Only magnificent cooperation supported by unlimited authority rescued the capital from one of the worst disasters in its history.[11]

If the behavior of the local community during the crisis won it commendation, during most of the war outlanders held Washingtonians up to opprobrium as "rent sharks" and "profiteers." The commissioners' report of 1919 tells the essentials of the story:

"Not since the journeying of St. Ursula with her 11,000 virgins to their martyrdom at Cologne, some 1,500 years ago, has there been such a pilgrimage of young women as that which moved toward Washington after the beginning of the war in 1917.

"Many of the young women who were attracted by the relatively large salaries offered had never been away from home before, and in the nostalgic reaction . . . everything different from what it was at home was apt to seem objectionable. It had not occurred to these pilgrims that the expenses must also be figured on a new basis, and that the advantages of life at home

[11] Brownlow, *A Passion for Anonymity*, pp. 69-73.

in a small place could not be expected in a crowded city. This
. . . led to a great many undeserved criticisms of Washington
people who had never had outsiders in their homes before, but
who were admitting them then from a patriotic desire to help
share with them in this way the burden which war imposed."
In most cases, said the report, rents were not raised exorbitantly,
and congressional hearings indicated fairly clearly that sub-
rentals accounted for the worst abuses; house-owners and real
estate companies were relatively seldom party to them. But who
bothered to read or weigh the facts presented in long official
reports? The public image of the housing squeeze in Washington rested on magazine stories of extortionate charges, for example, the $30,000 a year rental paid by a dollar-a-year man.[12]

In the summer of 1917 square wooden boxes, called "tempos,"
began to rise on the Mall to provide temporary office space for
war agencies that overflowed the business blocks the government commandeered. But not until January 1918 did federal
authorities accept any responsibility for finding living quarters
for incoming government clerks. A War Department grant
then supplied money to furnish and open some unoccupied
houses, but, as informed people acknowledged, without the
intelligent planning and vigorous work of Mrs. Archibald Hopkins, head of the women's committee of the District Defense
Council, that official scheme would have brought few results.
In May 1918 alarming statements of the Civil Service Commission that half of its appointments were refused on the
grounds that the pay was insufficient to meet the high cost of
living in Washington led Congress to act. It passed a resolution
aimed at preventing rent profiteering, appropriated several
million dollars for building government dormitories, and, in
order to avoid adding eight thousand alley dwellers to the

[12] Comrs Rpt, 1919, i, 569-71, 576; Clara Savage, "On to Washington,"
Good Housekeeping, LXVI, 158; H Dis Comee, 65C, 2S, Hrg, "Housing
in D.C."; Subcomee H Dis Comee, 66C, 1S, Hrgs, "The High Cost of
Living in D.C.," pp. 807-17; *Star*, 8, 19 Mar, 9 Apr, 29 May 1918, 1 Jan
1919.

throng of homeless, waived the requirement of the Alley Dwelling Act of 1914 that called for evacuation of all alley houses by July 1, 1918. In September the Housing Corporation of the Department of Labor relieved the District Defense Council of the task of locating, inspecting, and listing available rooms, and commandeered a few private homes, but none of the government dormitories on the Union Station Plaza were ready before the Armistice. Consequently, the District commissioners observed, by and large "the problem of caring for incoming government employees was met by the citizens of Washington."[13]

Those citizens, aware of having stopped many gaps for the federal government, were indignant at hearing themselves excoriated as "profiteers." In spite of shortages of goods and higher tax assessments, business concerns almost without exception had made money, but so had business firms elsewhere. "That madman Ben Johnson," as Louis Brownlow forty years later dubbed the city's chief enemy on the Hill, led the attacks in Congress. Two weeks before the Armistice Theodore Noyes of the *Star* wrote angrily: "The last summer has been full of bitter days for the people of Washington; gloriously bitter in the cheerful endurance of necessary patriotic war sacrifices with other good Americans; humiliatingly bitter through discriminating, slurring, hurtful legislation, unnecessarily imposed or threatened, and through the slanderous vilification of Washingtonians which has accompanied it.

"Mr. Johnson denounces the property owners and landlords of Washington as the most unpatriotic people in the whole world. He poses as peculiarly the protector of the boys in the trenches and of the civilian war workers.

"Mr. Johnson's Washington constituency has sent more boys to the trenches to give their lives to win the war . . . has furnished more civilian war workers . . . [and] has put up more

[13] Comrs Rpt, 1918, p. 6, 1919, I, 576, 582-83; "Living in War-Swollen Washington is a Serious Problem," *Literary Digest*, LVII, 65; *Star*, 3, 6 Jan, 30 Mar, 25 May 1918.

money . . . in donations through the Red Cross and otherwise, in Liberty Loans and in war taxes, than his Kentucky constituency." When underpaid clerks who worked long hours of overtime protested at an increase in their hours without any increase in pay, some members of Congress condemned them as slackers.[14]

Unlike other American cities, Washington underwent crises not in periods of business depression but amid the booming activities of wartime. The War of 1812 had nearly extinguished the city; the Civil War and its aftermath had subjected her citizens to wholesale charges of disloyalty; the war against the Central Powers brought down upon her patriots the hostility of their countrymen. Yet as long as the world war continued, most Washingtonians were too absorbed in their war jobs, in the rush of business created by the swelling population, and in coping with the difficulties of running their households to be deeply disturbed by outlanders' complaints. Philosophical, long-time residents could recognize the harsh criticism as part of a hysteria born of overwork and anxieties they themselves shared. Conscious of doing their best, even at the sacrifice of local charities and other civic interests, they generally submerged their irritation at their detractors in belief that peace would restore sounder judgment to their critics. Unhappily, time would show that the attacks, coupled with the failure to forestall others, severely damaged community morale for a decade to come. Indeed Washington never fully regained her former faith in herself.

When the Armistice came, the capital celebrated less boisterously than cities whose responsibilities had been lighter. Since the commissioners requested postponement of a great victory parade until after the formal signing of a peace treaty, jubilation found expression chiefly in talk rather than, as in New York, in

[14] *Rpt B/Tr*, 1917, pp. 40, 42; Comrs Rpts, 1917, pp. 11-12, 1918, pp. 10-12; *Star*, 23 Sep, 8 Oct 1917, 7 Apr, 29 Oct 1918; H Rpt 288, 65C, 2S, pp. 3-4, Ser 7037.

flinging ticker tape from the windows of skyscrapers. At noon on November 11th the President rode down Pennsylvania Avenue through cheering crowds to deliver official confirmation of the thrilling news to Congress. That night forty-nine bonfires on the Ellipse lighted the sky from the Monument to the river. A day or two later, dollar-a-year men triumphantly began emptying their brief cases into office waste baskets, filling them with reports and regulations that need now be nothing but paper.

In the next weeks, however, the expected rapid exodus of the rank-and-file of war-workers did not occur; in fact, the demand for housing and the prices for all essentials continued to rise. While local business showed no signs of falling off, Washingtonians' zeal for good works waned rapidly. Only large contributions from government employees enabled the city that had met every earlier wartime challenge to raise her $800,000 quota for the "war chest" upon which the YMCA, the National Catholic War Council, the Jewish Welfare Board, the Salvation Army, and several other organizations depended in caring for servicemen. The drive for Red Cross members in December 1918 was close to a complete failure; Washington did about a third as well as the national average. Perhaps still more indicative of the community's spiritual exhaustion, the annual campaign to raise money for the Associated Charities fell $2,000 short of its modest $8,800 goal.[15]

The one project that appeared to evoke universal enthusiasm among Washingtonians was the drive for a constitutional amendment giving the District voting representation in Congress and the electoral college. In May and June 1917 resolutions offered in House and Senate and referred to the Judiciary committees had proposed a diluted version in the form of an amendment authorizing Congress whenever it saw fit to grant Washingtonians representation. The war relegated all District affairs to the background. Now with the fighting war over,

[15] Sullivan, *Our Times*, v, 520; *Star*, 14, 21 Nov, 16-17, 23-26 Dec 1918.

citizens with a singleness of purpose new in the District's political history set out to win the status which recent experience had convinced them was their surest safeguard against future injustice. Carefully laid plans included an educational campaign to enlighten congressional constituents throughout the United States about the handicaps under which residents of the capital suffered.

In January 1919 the undertaking got off to a good start. A citizens' committee had laid the groundwork in 1916 by visiting other cities to assemble data on their tax structure, so that a nucleus of organization was already in existence. The impressive feature of the new Citizens' Joint Committee on National Representation for the District of Columbia, headed by Theodore Noyes and John Joy Edson, was the all-inclusiveness of the white groups participating—the Chamber of Commerce, the Board of Trade, the Merchants' and Manufacturers' Association, the Central Labor Union, the Federation of Citizens' Associations, the Oldest Inhabitants Association, the Bar Association, the Monday Evening Club, the Real Estate Brokers Association, the 20th Century Club and a half dozen more—in short, every significant civic and business organization in white Washington. The local press carried long accounts of progress; out-of-town correspondents for metropolitan papers gave the program good notices. Local business firms attached to their out-of-town correspondence red stickers informing recipients that the District, with 400,000 inhabitants, paid taxes, obeyed federal laws, and went to war, but was voteless. The response was surprisingly quick and encouraging. Offers of support flowed in from many parts of the country where people expressed astonishment at learning that Washingtonians were disenfranchised or paid taxes in any form. Not a dissident note sounded for weeks. But neither did anything happen on the Hill.

Some opposition from Congress was to be expected, for, although the 1918 election had put Republicans in control of both houses, objections to a partly Negro electorate in the capital seemed likely, and hostility to the community still sounded on the Hill. "Washington," remarked one senator, "has more profit-eers and grafters than any city in the United States." Give them representation and their demands for free gifts would allow Congress no time for anything else. But in early March the leader of the House reportedly said Congress was "making a mess of the job" of "long-distance" governing of the District, and when a conference of one hundred city mayors and state governors endorsed suffrage for Washington, prospects for early success looked rosy.[16]

While Congress, ostensibly waiting for completion of the peace negotiations at Versailles, delayed action on the District's appeal, the New York City press launched upon criticisms di-rected chiefly at Washington's modest tax rate and reliance on federal contributions. The New York *Post* declared that until the creation of the territory in 1871 "there had been no taxes in the District"; debts had accumulated only under territorial rule. Newspapers elsewhere picked up the theme of a greedy city. Unfortunately, local campaigners, for all their careful or-ganization, had not devised a method of presenting an accurate picture of the incidence of taxes. Repeated statements that the District paid more in federal income and internal revenue taxes than did sixteen states did not provide fool-proof figures that would satisfy out-of-town inquiries about how the levies on Washington business firms compared with those of other cities. An exact, easily understandable comparison was, to be sure, impossible because of the intertwining of federal and District costs and services, but lengthy, involved explanations tended to raise as many doubts as they settled. Nor did the publicity drive home the basic difficulty of persuading Congress to sanc-tion the use of District taxes for such acute needs as higher

[16] *Rpts B/Tr*, 1917, pp. 14-17, 1918, pp. 59-68; *Star*, Summaries, 1918, 1919, 17 Feb 1919; clippings and letters in J. D. Kaufman, Scrap-books on Washington Home Rule, Jan-Mar 1919; *Times*, 4, 11 Mar 1919.

salaries for school teachers and new schoolhouses. Neither friend nor critic remarked on colored Washington's aloofness from the campaign.

By the time the 66th Congress convened in May 1919 and turned over new resolutions on a constitutional amendment to the Judiciary committees, Washingtonians' solid front was showing cracks. The Board of Trade advocated only representation in Congress and perpetuation of an appointed commission for local government. The Chamber of Commerce stood for securing a place in Congress before considering home rule. The labor unions, on the contrary, urged immediate substitution of elected local officials for the commissioners. Louis Brownlow had also reached the conclusion that home rule offered the only answer: "Because the membership of Congress was overwhelmingly rural in background, it was frequently impossible to get the necessary legislation or the required appropriations of funds to enable the District to keep up with the constantly increasing demands of American urban life." Even two District senators and two or more representatives in the House would not ensure parochial concerns attention from a body whose national and international responsibilities were mounting with every passing year. If aware of that probability in 1919, business leaders still preferred to take their chances on dealing with Congress to risking the rule of an electorate in which propertyless voters might predominate. Even had all Washington united in asking for full-scale enfranchisement, a favorable response was unlikely from a Congress still disgruntled about the city's supposed war record. But whatever chance of success the suffrage campaign had had early in 1919 vanished in July, when a flare-up of violence in the city's race relations chilled white ardor and obliterated Negro interest in political change.[17]

[17] New York *Post*, 29 Mar 1919, and other papers, Kaufman Scrapbooks; *Rec*, 66C, 1S, pp. 25, 1013; *Rpts B/Tr*, 1917, p. 15, 1918, p. 51, 1919, pp. 11, 128; *Times*, 9 Feb 1919; *Star*, 12 Feb, 9 Dec 1919; Brownlow, *Passion for Anonymity*, p. 100.

Civic lethargy enveloped most of the city for the next eighteen months. Postwar upheavals in other cities, Chicago's race riots, Seattle's general strike, Boston's police strike, and fear of worse to come in other places failed to arouse Washington from her apathy. Citizens' associations added members without producing constructive action. Local charities continued to limp along with little support. In October the campaign for representation in Congress resumed in tepid fashion when the Board of Trade issued a call to work for "that prized American privilege and power we so much desire and which the capital . . . so greatly needs." Out-of-town newspapers occasionally commented on war-workers' resentment of Washingtonians' touchiness and lack of cordiality, and an Arkansas paper urged cave-dwellers to take to their bosoms the congressmen's wives whose exclusion from "the local social set" engendered a bitterness that then infected their husbands. But neither self-exhortation nor advice from outsiders restored to Washingtonians their earlier enthusiasm and confidence.[18]

Several depressing aspects of life in postwar Washington contributed to a drying up of local pride. The resignation of nearly 150 of the most gifted white public school teachers who had taken better-paid jobs had stripped the school system of its chief asset; at the present salary scale the superintendent could not engage others. The very look of the city had changed for the worse. The Mall was a clutter of tempos; to the east of the Smithsonian a string of them stretched from B Street south to B Street north, another ugly cluster stood beyond the Monument, and near the center two great chimneys cut the skyline. From the Union Station to the Senate Office Building on the Hill starkly utilitarian barracks for government clerks occupied most of the Plaza. Residential sections also had altered in appearance. "Old Washington vanished never to return," wrote Helen Nicolay, "when its skyline changed from one of dormer

[18] *Rpts B/Tr*, 1919, p. 11, 1920, pp. 70-71, 131; *Star*, 1 Jan 1920; *Syracuse Journal*, 12 Feb 1920; *Little Rock Gazette*, 23 Oct 1919.

windows and aspiring chimneys to the great impersonal apartment houses of tile and light-colored brick, with their square outlines, and the private houses of French Renaissance or modified colonial types, also light in color, that have replaced the deep-red brick beloved of Mr. Corcoran and his contemporaries."

Even the character of the bookshops changed. Washingtonians no longer dropped in to browse and chat socially; "expensive knickknacks and cheap postcards by the acre" diluted the stock. Strangers were everywhere. "Most of the women wear fur coats and the latest cut of shoes, and the latest shade in face powder. It is a crowd such as could not have been in Washington ten years ago, or even five." Photographs of debutantes and hostesses never seen before the war filled the rotogravure sections of the newspapers. Washingtonians had trouble feeling at home in Washington.

The gates to the White House grounds, closed before the United States entered the war, remained shut, giving strange lifelessness to the very heart of the city. Old residents had looked forward to the moment when all would be as before. For a brief time after the Armistice prewar festivities had seemed about to resume, but early in January the *Star* regretfully reported: "As the New Year reception of the White House will never again be witnessed in its old form, the one day of the year when the representatives of kings and the humblest citizen might shake hands with the President and wish him good luck, so the cabinet day of old when the drawing rooms of cabinet homes were thronged with any who wished to call has gone the same way." For the first time since John and Abigail Adams had occupied the Executive Mansion, the American President was away from Washington for long periods—in Paris during the spring of 1919, in the autumn taking the League of Nations issue before the country. However much the old guard of Theodore Roosevelt's and Taft's day disliked the social attitudes of Woodrow Wilson, his absence in official society was rather like

Hamlet without Hamlet. Vice President Marshall had to review the parade of the First Division led by General Pershing. The President's illness upon his return to Washington had a further dampening effect in spite of the elaborate entertainment arranged for the visits of the King and Queen of Belgium and the Prince of Wales.

Above all, Washington's new impersonality troubled old residents. They could recognize it as the inevitable price of bigness and, indeed, could perceive the advantages of a country-wide awakening to "the possibilities of doing things on a national scale, of adapting the mechanism of national life to fit national ends."[19] But a sense of loss remained. As it became clear in the early months of 1920 that the intimacy of the leisurely old Washington was gone, a feeling of oppressive uncertainty engulfed the city.

[19] Comrs Rpt, 1919, IV, 11-13; Nicolay, *Capital*, pp. 515-20; *Star*, 17 Nov 1918, 5, 12 Jan, 14, 28 Sep, 12 Oct, 12 Dec 1919; Anderson, *Presidents and Pies*, pp. 237-38; Brownlow, *Passion for Anonymity*, pp. 86-88; Young, "National Statistics in War and Peace," p. 11.

CHAPTER XIII

THE AFTERMATH OF THE COLORED
MAN'S WAR, 1917-1919

UNLIKE colored radicals in several northern cities in 1916, Washington Negroes had not seriously considered putting race before country. On the contrary, they early came to look upon the war as their opportunity to win recognition as loyal Americans and the inevitable postwar readjustments as a unique chance to establish themselves permanently in a sound economic position. The relative stability of the local colored population heightened the chances of success. Whereas industrial cities like Detroit and Chicago were inundated with southern Negroes who moved north to take jobs in war plants, Washington faced no comparable colored immigration. The intelligent local Negro community, consequently, was not submerged by a wave of ignorant blacks from the rural South. The Washington branch of the NAACP declared that patriotism did not require colored men to put up with injustice or to remain silent about lynchings in the South and unprovoked attacks such as those in East St. Louis, Illinois, but, from early 1917 till the return of colored troops of the AEF two years later, complaints about racial discrimination in Washington dwindled. The local Negro press underscored every instance of fair behavior from whites and exhorted colored people to make the most of the new openings which wholehearted cooperation would bring. However flimsy the foundations of that counsel of hope, colored Washington built on it.

Thus the District's colored candidates for officer training swallowed their dismay at being sent to an all-Negro camp at Des Moines, Iowa; there they at least might have a better chance to prove their worth than in a mixed camp. George Richardson of the *Bee* warned colored servicemen not to write home about every slight they endured; their record would plead their cause eloquently upon their return. Signs of white recognition seemed to be multiplying: Herbert Hoover appointed a Negro science teacher from the Dunbar High School to head the colored bureau of the Food Administration; Secretary of War Newton Baker made Emmett J. Scott an assistant in the War Department, and the local chapter of the Red Cross asked Scott to serve on the finance committee; the Labor Department assigned George Haynes to a responsible position, and Secretary of the Treasury McAdoo proposed to send fifty colored men across the country to explain national war aims to Negroes. Even the arch conservative Oldest Inhabitants' Association invited the Oldest Inhabitants' Association (Colored) to visit the white headquarters in the old firehouse at 19th and H Streets northwest.[1]

Yet proofs of lingering white antagonism were also numerous: new congressional proposals for residential segregation and other Jim Crow bills, which, though not passed, were a slap at the Negro war effort; the three-year sentence imposed by court martial on a Negro sentry for shooting a white man who disobeyed the command to halt; the failure of government offices to hire colored people qualified by civil service examinations and of the District police department to take on colored patrolmen; the refusal of the street railway companies to employ Negroes to fill some five hundred operator jobs; and Red Cross segregation of colored volunteers from white. District officials and Congress rejected a housing plan for alley-dwellers when Negro builders proposed a loan to enable them to put up low rental housing. When the president of Howard University retired, the trustees again elected a white man; and during the war for the first time Negroes heard themselves called "darkies" in a District courtroom.[2]

[1] *Crisis*, XIV, 4, 304, XVI, 217-19, XVII, 182-84, 194; *Bee*, 14, 21 Apr, 26 May, 2, 30 Jun, 28 Jul, 25 Aug, 1, 15 Dec 1917, 13 Apr, 4, 11, 18 May, 7 Sep 1918; *Star*, 21 Oct 1917, 1 Oct 1918.
[2] *Star*, 3 Sep, 25 Dec 1917, 3 Jan, 18 Jul 1918; *Bee*, 3, 10 Nov

Negro leaders knew that some white Washingtonians, like those who joined the local branch of the NAACP in 1918, deplored the continuing discriminatory practices and fully appreciated what Negroes were doing for their country. The best element in the colored community clung to hope that the perceptive element of the white community would insist upon racial justice in the postwar world. So the handsome Archibald Grimké, able head of the Washington NAACP and president of the American Negro Academy, told the academy in December 1918: "I am glad to say that associated with us . . . are a number of leading white men. We do not have to fight this battle alone." About the same time John R. Hawkins of Howard University presented to the Washington NAACP fourteen points, paralleling President Wilson's famous fourteen points for world democracy, which alone would give meaning to the word in the United States. While Mary White Ovington, one of the white founders of the National Association, wrote in the *Crisis* that "the last place to which the returning colored soldier can look for justice is Washington, the very foundation of the government he has so faithfully served," she added: "The power of numbers, but *organized* numbers, is the power that wins the battle. Every oppressed group . . . is engaged in a separate struggle to secure something of value for itself in the chaos that comes at the close of a great war. Now . . . while systems are fluid, before the structure of society becomes rigid again is the opportunity to win the reality of democracy."[3]

Colored Washingtonians won a first minor victory in January 1919 when Commissioner Brownlow established an all-Negro platoon in the fire department, an arrangement that

---

1917, 2, 9, 23 Feb, 9, 23, 30 Mar, 28 Sep 1918; *Crisis*, xiv, 139, xvii, 116; H Rpt 420, 65C, 2S, Ser 7304.

[3] Corcoran Thom to Mary Church Terrell, 25 Nov 1918, and Jane Ogle, to M. C. Terrell, 3 Dec 1917, Terrell Mss; *Star*, 26 Dec 1918; Mary White Ovington, "Reconstruction and the Negro," *Crisis*, xvii, 169-70, 172; *Bee*, 16 Nov 1918, 4, 18 Jan, 15 Feb, 21 Jun 1919.

ensured promotions for the department's four colored veterans of twenty years' service and gave new appointees a chance to prove their competence under men of their own race. Equally helpful to colored morale were several articles in the *Star* describing the valor of the District's "famous old 1st Separate Battalion" in action in France. Of the battalion's 480 Washingtonians, 25 had been awarded the Croix De Guerre, and the officers of the French regiment to which the battalion was attached had nothing but highest praise for the entire unit. The *Star* correspondent remarked that the city would surely want to stage a homecoming demonstration for these troops, for "every citizen of Washington—in fact of the United States—should feel proud of them." And the chief secretary of the national Salvation Army said he had "a pretty complete record" of the conduct of the colored soldiers and that "something ought to be done to show their courage and fidelity were appreciated." He had rented a building in the capital to house them when they returned late in March 1919.[4]

That was the last expression of general good will in Washington. The parade of returned white soldiers, led by President Wilson, took place before the 1st Separate Battalion reached home. As if alarmed by the praise already meted out to the colored heroes, after February 1919 Washington's white newspapers had nothing more to say of them or of Negroes' part on the home front. By late spring the *Crisis* reported that influential Americans were repeating comments supposedly originating with high-ranking officers of the AEF to the effect that "the Negro officer is a failure" and the behavior of colored troops in France had been cowardly in battle and improper in social contacts with French people. W. E. B. DuBois, after three months in Europe spent in collecting facts for a "History of the Black Man in the Great War," concluded that "no person in

[4] *Star*, 18 Jan, 14, 15, 17, 28 Feb 1919; *Bee*, 8, 22 Mar, 14 Jun, 19 Jul 1919.

an official position dare tell the truth" about the shabby treatment the American Army had accorded colored soldiers.[5]

While most of colored Washington was smarting with indignation over the seeming white conspiracy of silence about their war service, a group of colored parents launched a prolonged fight with the school board over its refusal to dismiss Assistant Superintendent Roscoe Conkling Bruce. The Parents' League, representing perhaps six or seven hundred colored parents, accused Bruce of favoritism in making teaching appointments and, worse, lack of vigilance in what came to be known as the "Moens affair." Armed with a recommendation from the Dutch embassy, which the president of the school board had forwarded without comment, Bruce had given a Dutch anthropologist by the name of Moens permission to photograph some of the city's colored school children for purposes of comparative anthropological data. Moens, so the stories ran, had then taken advantage of innocent children and indulged in indecent behavior with one of the colored teachers. White members of the school board and Mrs. Coralie Cook, a Negro member, upheld Bruce and inclined to regard the tales about Moens as gross, if unwitting, exaggerations or lies. But Negro women picketed the Franklin School week after week, whenever the school board met at its offices there. Only a small minority of the Negro community took stock in the lurid rumors about the Moens' affair or shared the view of the Parents' League that here was fresh evidence of white indifference to Negroes' good name, but lily whites insisted that the agitation proved all Negroes emotionally unstable and lacking in judgment.[6]

Still more important in increasing racial tensions in the first half of 1919 was the outbreak of a crime wave more serious than any since the 1850's and the Civil War. White newspaper

[5] *Crisis*, XVII, 111-12, XVIII, 9-11, 63-67; *Bee*, 14 Dec 1918, 15 Feb 1919.

[6] *Bee*, 29 Mar, 12, 26 Apr, 28 Jun 1919; *Star*, 10 Jun 1919, 1 Jan 1920.

accounts of street robberies and attacks upon women generally conveyed the impression that Negroes alone were responsible. At one point the *Post* accused the Negro press of "a plot" to stir up race hatred. By July a series of sex crimes, most of them, later evidence established, committed by a single colored man, had whipped the city into a fury of alarm and rage. While a Negro bishop assured whites that colored people would join in the manhunt, the *Bee*, aware that the temper of white Washington might lead to punishment of innocent colored people, insisted that the criminals were not local men and that an all-Negro precinct in the undermanned police department would be useful in bringing the assaults to an end. At the same time the local NAACP warned the city's white dailies that further "inflammatory headlines and sensational news articles" would encourage race riots. Hundreds of servicemen stationed in and about Washington roamed the streets during those hot July evenings and added to the pervasive sense of restlessness. In a situation already explosive their presence served as a fuse requiring only a minor episode to trigger violence. Military police had been withdrawn from Washington in June.

The "Red Scare," moreover, which was sweeping the entire country, had already assumed huge proportions in the capital. In June a bomb set in the house of the new attorney general convinced conservative citizens that "bolsheviks" were about to destroy the entire fabric of American society. "It is unsafe," announced the *Star*, "to wait for specific proof of individual criminality. It is dangerous to delay until jury-proof cases can be found." Although no one came out flatly with the accusation that colored Washington was one of the "red centers" in the United States, anxieties lest radicalism eat its way into Washington's working classes, at the bottom of which stood the city's black masses, undoubtedly increased racial animosities.[7]

[7] *Bee*, 16 Feb, 12 Jul 1919; *Crisis*, XVIII, 242. From mid-April to the end of July practically every issue of the *Star*, and, all during July, the

The first overt acts of race warfare occurred on a Saturday night, July 19th: "Men in Uniform Attack Negroes" announced the Sunday papers. "As a climax to the assaults on white women . . . a band of more than a hundred soldiers, sailors and marines last night invaded southwest and beat several colored persons before they were finally dispersed by a provost guard, a detachment of marines and reserves from three police stations." Worse followed. On Monday morning the Washington *Post*, after describing Sunday's fighting, carried an alarming article under a huge headline, *Scores are Injured in More Race Riots*:

"It was learned that the mobilization of every available service man stationed in or near Washington or on leave here has been ordered for tomorrow evening near the Knights of Columbus hut, on Pennsylvania Aveune between Seventh and Eighth streets.

"The hour of assembly is 9 o'clock and the purpose is a 'clean-up' that will cause the events of the last two evenings to pale into insignificance.

"Whether official cognizance of this assemblage and its intent will bring about its forestalling cannot be told."

If, as Commissioner Brownlow wrote later, "these white ex-service men were frauds, paid to provoke the trouble they began," and if the Washington *Post* deliberately fanned the fires, the wicked and malicious scheme succeeded. "That night, the race riot swept over Washington. If it had not been for the good work of police and soldiers who kept the large mobs from contact, the city would have been a shambles. During the week the race riots in Chicago and Knoxville followed and the month of July ended with a feeling of apprehension and disturbance."

In Washington colored people, convinced that the time for meekness had passed, fought back. Guns brought from Baltimore and distributed at 7th and T Streets provided weapons

Post, carried stories on Negro crime; equally frequent items on the bolshevik threat began in February 1919.

for men trained to their use by war service. Colored men then and later believed that it was the killing of whites by Negroes that brought the riot to an end within five days. Reinforcement of the police by some four hundred cavalrymen from Fort Myer and four hundred marines from Quantico unquestionably helped. But the restoration of outward order at the end of the week did not cool Negroes' anger, for, although every eye-witness of the opening fights testified that white men had been the aggressors, only eight or nine of the hundred-odd persons arrested were whites, and of those only one was convicted for carrying a concealed weapon. Soothing words in the white press to the effect that the "colored residents of Washington are law-abiding people, good citizens and dependable in all crises" came too late to allay bitterness.

Commissioner Brownlow felt sure that the riot had been a put-up job skillfully arranged by two or three outwardly respectable, unscrupulous men, who were determined to make trouble for the police and force him and Major Pullman to resign. The 1918 increases in tax assessments and Brownlow's refusal to exempt from the law persons who had long considered themselves entitled to special privileges had won the commissioner enemies, among them individuals not above employing any weapon, including a race riot, to undermine his authority and thus escape prosecution under the Mann Act. The inflammatory article of July 21st with its allusion to "official cognizance" of an "assemblage" that no one had heard of until the paper announced it lent some plausibility to the conspiracy theory. The *Survey* tentatively attributed the trouble to anti-prohibition forces which "welcomed and to some extent, planned a 'crime wave' in the nation's capital to illustrate the appalling consequences of the bone-dryness since July first."[8]

[8] *Post*, 21-23 Jul 1919; Brownlow, *Passion for Anonymity*, p. 84; Comrs Rpt, 1920, I, 223; Rayford W. Logan to the author, 9 Mar 1960; *Star*, 20-25, 27 Jul 1919; *Bee*, 26 Jul 1919; Edgar M. Gray, *The Washington Riot, Its Cause and Effect*, (mcf pamphlet, Arthur A. Schomburg

Colored leaders displayed extraordinary restraint. A week after the first night's outbreak Judge Terrell and Dr. Emmett J. Scott, former special assistant to the Secretary of War, issued a statement to Negro newspapers in the rest of the country pointing out that, whereas white servicemen were to blame for the Washington riots and Negro retaliation was natural, the most important fact was that "white and colored citizens freely counseling together in the interest of law and order" had successfully reestablished peace and that henceforward all efforts must be directed at preserving the "gains of mutual war-time sacrifices." James Weldon Johnson, the NAACP investigator sent down from New York, shared Brownlow's private opinion that the Washington *Post* had had a large part in fomenting the violence. His report in the *Crisis* contained humorous touches: the city editor of the *Post*, assuming that Johnson had come to tell Washington Negroes "to be good," had welcomed him cordially but had then suffered near-panic upon discovering that the NAACP might ask the Attorney General to bring action against Washington's white newspapers, the *Post* above all, for inciting to riot. Johnson averred that Negro courage had saved the day in Washington. By fighting "in defense of their lives and homes" instead of running, they had prevented Washington's being "another and worse East St. Louis." Indeed, he concluded, bad as things had been, white shame over the shocking events in Washington and Chicago "mark a turning point in the psychology of the whole nation regarding the Negro problem."

That note of encouragement, if overly optimistic in the long run, appeared justified in the months immediately following. Washington's white press, perhaps frightened by the consequences of its earlier propaganda, ceased to harp on Negro criminality. In December at a meeting called to raise money for

---

Negro Collection, New York Public Library); "The Darkest Cloud," *Survey*, XLII, 675.

a war memorial to colored heroes, white response was heartening. Secretary of War Newton D. Baker and Secretary of the Navy Josephus Daniels both spoke, and "the tabernacle quaked from the acclamation of approval" when Judge Stafford challenged the crowd: "Cite me a case of a Negro traitor"; "show me a Negro anarchist"; "let me see a Negro bolshevist"; "the only red rag the Negro ever carried was when his shirt was stained crimson by the sacrificial blood he gave for America."

The single most penetrating analysis of the Negro problem in Washington and in Chicago came from the pen of George E. Haynes, director of Negro Economics in the United States Department of Labor. His article entitled "Race Riots in Relation to Democracy" recognized the role of sensational journalism in contributing to racial hostility but pointed to three other, equally significant factors. First was the lack of mutual understanding that resulted from the loss of contact between the races: "The lack of contact has increased with the years. Older residents of Washington and Chicago tell you of the growing racial antagonism with the growth of separation. Only a few weeks before the riots in both cities, some leading people of Washington were discussing the fact that in former years the white and colored representatives of various philanthropic and community agencies were accustomed to meet more frequently than now for the exchange of views and plans on matters of community interest. The holding of such meetings has grown more difficult and less frequent." Second was the new Negro militance. Years of seeing the unequal enforcement of law had led the colored man to believe "his safety demands that he protect himself and his home," a conviction strengthened by a new conception of liberty which accompanied the higher standard of living that war had brought to thousands of colored families. Although well-to-do, well-dressed Negroes had been a familiar sight in Washington for forty years past, other observers than Haynes remarked upon white irritation at Negroes' improved economic status: "Everywhere one can hear expressions of disgust at the expensive clothes of successful Negroes, their owning automobiles, etc." The third factor was the realization by both white and colored Americans that the United States as a great world power was now "face to face with the problem of dealing with the darker peoples of Asia, Africa, Central and South America." Those peoples would judge the United States by the treatment white Americans accorded darker-skinned citizens within its borders. That an Abyssinian mission had been in the national capital during the riots was an uncomfortable reminder that race relations here had a wider bearing than a purely domestic local question.[9]

While much of the colored community benefitted from better paid jobs during and immediately after the war, school teachers and government clerks, who composed the backbone of the middle class, had suffered, like their white counterparts, from the pinch of rising living costs and minor or no salary increases. And even at the peak of employment the number of appointments to professional or clerical posts in Washington fell far short of the number of Negro candidates qualified either by graduation from the Miner Normal School or by civil service ratings. Assistant Superintendent Bruce, while fighting to get better salaries for colored teachers, implied in 1919 that those willing to leave Washington now had larger opportunities than formerly because of the prosperity the war had brought to Negroes in other cities. The opening of a colored Industrial Savings Bank on U Street and a new well-built, well-furnished Negro hotel indicated that, in spite of inflation, Negro business enterprises here also had enjoyed some success, and the wider support of charitable projects suggested that many Negro families had more financial leeway than ever before. But the

[9] *Star*, 27 Jul, 16 Dec 1919; *Crisis*, XVIII, 241-43; *Bee*, 2 Aug 1919; "The Darkest Cloud," and George E. Haynes, "Race Riots in Relation to Democracy," *Survey*, XLII, 675-76, 697-99.

NAACP and the *Bee* repeatedly reminded colored people that racial solidarity was essential to a continuing advance.[10]

In the autumn of 1919, while colored Washingtonians strove to believe they had gained more than they lost by the race riots, white business leaders betrayed brief uneasiness lest the outburst seriously injure the city's good name. On top of the accusations of wartime profiteering, a reputation for uncontrolled racial violence and for being a hotbed of Negro radicalism could do Washington infinite harm. But a large part of Washington soon ceased to think about the local riots at all. Senate ratification or rejection of the Versailles treaty, plans, quickly quashed, for a District policemen's union affiliated with the American Federation of Labor, wage strikes that threatened Washington's white building trades, and the intensifying conflict throughout the United States between capital and industrial labor preempted local attention. Although, like Americans everywhere, people here were frightened by the bogey of red infiltration into the ranks of organized labor, in a predominantly white-collar city fear of a red-infected local black proletariat had relatively little to feed upon.

In early October 1919 a National Industrial Conference, with Secretary of the Interior Franklin K. Lane in the chair and the level-headed Secretary of Labor William B. Wilson acting as special adviser, met in the Pan-American Union building to discuss workingmen's rights to collective bargaining and to find a formula for settling a nation-wide steel strike, by then at the stage of open warfare in the Midwest. Washingtonians, conservatives and liberals alike, awaited the outcome with interest but with considerable detachment. The A.F.ofL. repudiation of any connection with reds failed to win support for labor's cause; when Samuel Gompers walked out of the conference, workingmen silently acknowledged defeat. Neither

[10] Comrs Rpts, 1919, iv, 238, 1920, iv, 323-39; *Star*, 19 Mar 1920; *Crisis*, xiii, 168, 174-76, 280, xiv, 89, xvii, 116, xviii, 154; *Bee*, 29 Mar, 26 Apr 1919.

the local business community nor federal officials linked Washington's race riots to labor radicalism. Although nine men had lost their lives in the street fights and more than thirty men later died from injuries, Congress saw no cause to investigate. Thus reassured, white Washingtonians determined to Americanize the foreign-born in their midst but banished from memory the uncomfortable events of July: they represented no more than an unfortunate episode best forgotten as quickly as possible.

Yet the wish to forget the unpleasantnesses of "the intense, restless, disturbed year," as a Board of Trade committee described 1919, had long-lasting consequences; it reinforced white prejudices, deepened the obliviousness of much of white Washington to the needs of a bi-racial city, and for nearly two decades defeated the attempts of an enlightened minority to seek closer cooperation with Negro citizens. The unyielding attitude of influential white people was an important factor in crippling endeavors to revive a vigorous community spirit. Just as country-wide reaction against the Red Scare in 1920 heightened Americans' longing for "normalcy," so Washingtonians' desire to return to a less troubled past undermined their will to examine its weaknesses and build better for the future.[11]

[11] *Rpt B/Tr*, 1919, p. 128; *Star*, 28 Nov 1918, 29 Jul, 29 Sep 1919, 1, 3 Jan 1920; Brownlow, *Passion for Anonymity*, pp. 84-89; Robert K. Murray, *Red Scare, A Study in National Hysteria, 1919-1920*, pp. 148-256; Gray, *The Washington Riot* (Schomburg Collection). Further evidence of local whites' unconcern about race relations derives from interviews with people living here in 1919 and from the disappearance of newspaper items about local Negro radicalism and all Negro ideas.

CHAPTER XIV

BUSINESS INTERESTS AND NATIONAL CITY PLANNING, 1920-1929

IF, as Senator Blair prophesied in the 1890's, long-enforced political irresponsibility bred in Washingtonians apathy about governing themselves, their indifference never extended to the outcome of a national election, for that was likely to affect every taxpayer, every wage-earner, and, by enlarging or shrinking the clover fields, every social butterfly in the District of Columbia. In 1920, irrespective of their convictions about the League of Nations and other national issues, adults in Washington first and foremost wanted an end of turmoil. With the collapse of the Red Scare in midsummer, that desire appeared to be more attainable than it had earlier. Wages in the building trades were still at wartime levels—as, unhappily, was the meagre pay-scale of permanent civil service employees—and, despite reductions in the federal payroll after the dismissal of some 16,000 temporary war-workers, business had not yet suffered. Still apprehensiveness endured.

The District commissioners managed to carry out essential services for a city approximately 25 percent more populous than the Washington of three years before and indeed effected several innovations. While Commissioner Gardiner practically withdrew from participation, Commissioner Brownlow and General Kutz, again made engineer commissioner in 1919, acted *ex officio* as a Public Utilities Commission and, after prolonged negotiations with corporation officers and lawyers and a fight in the courts, succeeded in establishing an acceptable cost basis for each utility company and then fixed rates. A more extraordinary feat—the two men drafted and won acceptance for a zoning ordinance. Thanks to frequent consultations with white citizens' and Negro civic associations while the maps were under preparation, the zoning ordinance satisfied everyone, even real estate firms from whom fierce opposition had initially seemed inescapable. Furthermore, although congressional hearings held in December 1919 limited the federal share of District appropriations to 40 percent instead of the theoretical former 50 percent, the new fiscal act provided for a sliding tax rate that permitted the commissioners later to lower the then rate of $1.95 on every $100 of assessed valuation.[1]

A controversy unhappily arose in the spring of 1920 over the refusal of the Board of Education to reappoint the well-meaning but ineffectual superintendent of schools and over the retention of Assistant Superintendent Roscoe Conkling Bruce in the face of demands from the Negro Parents' League for his ouster. The school fight involved the question of who was to succeed Gwynne Gardiner as District commissioner after his resignation at the end of 1919. In May the Senate refused to confirm President Wilson's nominee, Dr. John Van Schaick, a former president of the Monday Evening Club, suspect for its "radicalism," and president of the school board at the time of the Moens affair. Whatever the Senate's reasons in this case, Republican rejection of all President Wilson's nominees for all offices left the Board of Commissioners minus one man. A more serious loss befell in September: Louis Brownlow resigned to become city manager of Petersburg, Virginia, a city of 30,000, where he would receive double the $5,000 salary allowed the administrative head of a city of 437,000 and the capital of the nation. One of his last acts as commissioner was to appoint an interracial committee of eminent citizens to explore

[1] Comrs Rpts, 1919, p. 5, 1920, i, 5-7, 11, 29, 226, 1921, p. 48; *Star*, Summaries, 1920, 1921; Brownlow, *Passion for Anonymity*, pp. 90-99; *Rec*, 66C, 2S, pp. 1444-54; *Rpts B/Tr*, 1920, pp. 73-74, 113-15, 183-86, 1921, p. 21; H Dis Comce, 66C, 2S, Hrgs, "Fiscal Relations between the U.S. and D.C.," pp. 3, 117-18, 134-51, 247-73; Paul H. Douglas, *Real Wages in the United States*, p. 376; Schmeckebier, *District of Columbia*, pp. 52-58.

ways of improving communication between white and colored Washington; the committee fell to pieces after his departure.

Since the Senate was not in session that autumn, two interim appointees, Miss Mabel Boardman and J. Thilman Hendrick, accepted office as commissioners. Miss Boardman, a rather over-powering-looking woman whose high pompadour added to her Victorian mien, in 1920 was best known as the chief organizer of the Women's Volunteer Services of the American Red Cross; Hendrick was a stockbroker scarcely known at all outside the city's financial circles. Under the two inexperienced new officials a stalemate obtained in District affairs. Meanwhile, in a bedroom at the White House an ailing President—how ill scarcely a dozen people knew—awaited with dreadful anxiety the decision of November 4th. "A feverish uncertainty, a reluctant looking for a something that every man and woman hoped might never come, has been the condition attendant upon the passing days of the year," wrote a Board of Trade official. "We are looking forward to the happy time, when, under new and settled conditions, the business and pleasures of our people, their thoughts, hopes and aspirations may once more be along normal lines; and unrest and I.W.W.-ism may become unknown in the universal endeavor to upbuild our industries and manhood, and curtail our all too large national debt."[2]

The election of Warren Gamaliel Harding snapped much of the tension in the capital. If knowledgeable Republicans had secret misgivings, no one voiced the opinion Mrs. Longworth later expressed: "Harding was not a bad man. He was just a slob." As the winter wore on, all classes of society, white and colored, appeared to relax visibly and, with the approach of the inauguration, an air of almost forgotten festivity settled over

[2] *Star*, frequent entries Feb-Jun 1920; *Bee*, 17 Jan, 13, 20 Mar 1920; S Dis Comee, 66C, 2S, Hrgs, "The Nomination of Dr. John Van Schaick, Jr., to be a Comr of the D of C," pp. 5-9, 56-59, 80, and *passim*; Comrs Rpt, 1920, p. 5; *Rpt B/Tr*, pp. 54, 131.

the city. It was dampened but not extinguished by an "economy howl in Congress," which persuaded the President-elect and the inaugural committee to cancel plans for an elaborate parade and an inaugural ball. The business slump and the consequent drop in employment that had struck most of the country had not yet affected the capital; gratitude for that reprieve—escape, the unwary called it—heightened Washington's enjoyment of the golden sunlight flooding the city on March 4, 1921.

Shock at sight of the wasted figure of Wilson seated beside the well-fed, handsome Harding when the presidential limousine rolled down Pennsylvania Avenue silenced the on-lookers momentarily, but pity and regret yielded quickly to interest in what lay ahead. The new President's inaugural address contained nothing startling unless it were his statement that "the Negroes of America . . . have earned the full measure of citizenship bestowed; that their sacrifice in blood on the battle-fields of the Republic have entitled them to all freedom and opportunity, all sympathy and aid that the American spirit of fairness and justice demands." Negroes were elated; lily-whites were not disturbed. That night, while colored society celebrated at a large reception and a dance at "Convention Hall," two other non-official balls took place, one a benefit for the Child Welfare Society sponsored by the wife of newly deposed Vice President Thomas Marshall, the other a private dance given for some six hundred GOP merrymakers by "Ned" McLean, chairman of the inaugural committee. If on that occasion Mrs. McLean wore the famous Hope diamond, its reputed evil powers may have seemed to the superstitious to account for the ills that two years later overwhelmed several of her guests. Mrs. Harding herself, an arch believer in the clairvoyants she consulted periodically, apparently had no forebodings.

Springtime in Washington, along whose tree-lined streets in 1921 people still walked for pleasure, exercised peculiar charms that year. For the first time the war receded into the distant past. The very sight of the open gates of the White House grounds inviting the world to walk and drive in and out lightened the atmosphere; on Easter Monday children and Easter eggs again dotted the lawns. "Balloon men," wrote a senator's wife, "with their rainbow-colored balls floating lightly above them in great clusters, and vendors of flowers stand on every corner; the Japanese cherry blossoms, a mass of fragrant blooms, border the basin and speedway above the Potomac River; the starry dogwood scatters its petals in Rock Creek Park; and wisteria, drooping and feathery, hangs over doorways and porches, and clouds the rotunda at Arlington." Newly appointed federal officials took up their duties with leisurely zest, while with still greater enthusiasm wives new to Washington society set about mastering the mysteries of etiquette in the capital.

Nor did the pervasive gaiety entirely vanish when the country-wide business depression reached Washington in the early summer. "National Music Week" in June brought together on the Ellipse an assembly of school children such as the city had not seen since the homecoming welcome for the Army of the Potomac in May 1865. The chorus of more than 50,000 children's voices carrying the strains of the *Star-Spangled Banner* from the elm-bordered rim of the Ellipse to the flag-draped grandstand near the Monument moved everyone, from the dignitaries surrounding President and Mrs. Harding to the humblest parent on the outskirts of the audience. Week after week the baseball diamonds and tennis courts on the Ellipse and the Monument grounds and the nine-hole golf course in East Potomac Park were filled with light-hearted, light-skinned players; the dark-skinned, by order of the North Carolina-born commissioner of public grounds, were allowed to play only on Tuesday afternoons and were never permitted to use the equally popular bathing beach at the Tidal Basin. But few people, white or colored, were ready to plunge into the arduous task of remaking the city's social order. Official Washington, in delighted dedication to normalcy, embarked that autumn upon a whirl of parties abnormal even by standards of the Roosevelt and Taft eras. In fact in the upper echelons a pleasurable acceptance of things as they were survived the shock of the Teapot Dome scandals, President Harding's death in 1923, and every succeeding slight disruption before the autumn of 1929.[3]

The business slump, it is true, in mid-1921 halted building, brought unemployment, and, coupled with unexpectedly severe cuts in District appropriations recommended by the newly established federal Bureau of the Budget, caused anxiety to Harding's appointees to the District Board of Commissioners, but the depression ran a relatively short course. By the early autumn of 1922 a revival was in full swing, marked, as usual in Washington, by an expansion of private building—apartment houses, luxury hotels, office buildings, a high-shouldered auditorium in Foggy Bottom intended to attract the convention trade, and private houses built wholesale by contractors who bought entire blocks of lots and sprinkled them thick with undistinguished but salable dwellings. In 1925 alone, investment in building reached the unheard-of total of nearly $63,-000,000. Two sides of Lafayette Square changed character completely. On Jackson Place the philanthropist Robert S. Brookings put up an office building to provide revenue for a recently founded center for economic research. Nearby on the site of the old W. W. Corcoran mansion rose the new headquarters of the United States Chamber of Commerce, constructed, the Board of Trade noted approvingly, under "the

[3] *Bee*, 5, 12 Mar 1921; Sullivan, *Our Times*, vi; Longworth, *Crowded Hours*, pp. 322-25; *Star*, 6, 9, 28 Mar, 4 Jun, 20 Nov 1921; Frances Parkinson Keyes, *Letters from a Senator's Wife*, pp. 191-259; Comrs Rpt, 1921, pp. 19-21; Washington *Tribune*, 16 Jul 1921.

American plan . . . on the basis of the open shop."⁴ Next door the red-brick houses Richardson had built for Henry Adams and John Hay gave way to the stone Hay-Adams Hotel towering above Latrobe's "Church of the Presidents" across the way.

The Board of Trade took credit for much of this burgeoning growth. While the mounting demand for office space was probably due chiefly to Secretary of Commerce Herbert Hoover's far-ranging programs, which encouraged national trade associations to set up headquarters in the capital, Board of Trade advertisements of Washington's special advantages for investment offered counter-attractions to the New York stock market. A convention bureau reaped a first disconcerting harvest in the summer of 1925 when 25,000 hooded white-robed Ku Klux Klansmen gathered in Washington and staged a showy parade and a ceremony on the Monument grounds. A more satisfactory advertisement of the city was a pageant held in the spring of 1927 when the Japanese cherry trees around the Tidal Basin were in full bloom; the success of that first Cherry Blossom festival made it an annual event thereafter. Slum clearance and District representation in Congress dropped out of sight as younger and less civic-minded men replaced the older generation of board directors, but the organization's secretary proudly pointed "to the rapidly growing friendliness on the part of Congress toward the District of Columbia, especially when its needs are presented to them by representatives from the Board of Trade."

Indeed congressional hostility to the city largely evaporated after House and Senate fixed the federal contribution to annual District expenses at a flat $9,000,000. After that scheme went into effect in 1925, District taxes alone met over 70 percent

⁴ Comrs Rpts, 1922, 47-48, 1925, p. 55; *Star*, 15 Aug 1925, 31 Dec 1927; 42 *Stat*. 1488; *Rpt B/Tr*, 1928, p. 64. Board of Trade reports, 1922-1929, deal exhaustively with the questions under discussion in this and the next three paragraphs and are therefore not cited in detail.

of the budget, but meanwhile a new ruling vested in the commissioners the authority to set the tax rate and thus to raise additional revenue by increasing the rate if they judged acute municipal needs warranted it. With the bonded indebtedness of 1878 paid off in 1921, with private property values rising, and with consumer purchasing power improved by a new federal pay scale that increased civil service salaries about 10 percent in the upper brackets and as much as 50 percent in lower, District finances were less crippled than taxpayers had expected. Loss of income from liquor licenses and the mounting cost of trying to stop bootlegging were annoyances, but the major difficulty was still the old one of persuading Congress to let the District government spend the city's taxes on the projects important to the community, albeit of no interest to congressional constituents.

Still, during the seven fat years of the 1920's, appropriations were big enough to enable successive engineer commissioners to reduce the backlog of badly needed public works that had accumulated during and after the war. As seen from the District Building everything ran smoothly. The Board of Trade expressed its wishes, Congress authorized larger expenditures of local taxpayers' money, and the commissioners acted. They increased the police force, in 1925 started a five-year school building program, enlarged the water supply by completing the Dalecarlia reservoir and a second conduit, gradually extended the sewage system not only into rapidly building-up sections of the city but also, by using money paid in by the Washington Suburban Sanitary Commission, into suburban Maryland. One commissioner, when asked thirty years later to name the District's chief problems during this era, replied: "There were no problems. Everyone was perfectly gentlemanly."[5]

Gentlemanly behavior, however, failed to dissipate traffic

[5] Comrs Rpts, 1924, pp. 26, 57-59, 1925, pp. 1-2, 61, 1926, pp. 20, 60, 1928, p. 28, 1929, p. 52; interview, Proctor L. Dougherty.

congestion. In 1921 and 1922 many people still walked to and from work, but, as population spread farther and farther, more people drove or rode. Gas fumes and the menace to life and limb from the rush of moving vehicles took most of the pleasure out of walking. In spite of a new regulation requiring applicants for driving permits to pass an examination, the installation of additional traffic lights, and somewhat stricter enforcement of the 22-miles-an-hour speed limit, "vehicular casualties" mounted. The nearly 9,400 accidents of 1925, to be sure, fell to 4,138 in 1928, but in the interval motor vehicle registrations rose and by 1930 topped 173,600, not counting commuters' or tourists' cars. Drivers unable to find legitimate parking spaces in the heart of the city left their cars all day on the Ellipse below the White House, on the Mall about the tempos, or in a fenced-off area of Potomac Park. "The entire Mall," protested the Fine Arts Commission, "has become an open-air garage; in the Department of Agriculture grounds automobiles are parked on the grass." The competing trolley and bus lines afforded inadequate service. In 1929, only 34.3 percent of the people who rode to work in downtown Washington used public conveyances; in Kansas City and Milwaukee, cities with the next smallest number, the figures stood at 45.5 and 50.3 percent, respectively. What the Board of Trade called the "best municipal government" in the United States was unable to provide an answer.[6]

Traffic itself was instrumental in persuading Congress to modify its postwar determination to reduce the national debt before investing money in expensive public works in the capital. While some citizens fumed about postponement of land purchases necessary to carry on the Park Commission's plan,

[6] Comrs Rpts, 1921, I, pp. 26-27, 212, 1925, pp. 28-30, 1928, pp. 7, 12, 31, 1931, p. 9; M. O. Eldridge, "Making the National Capital Safe for Motorists and Pedestrians," *American City Magazine*, XXXIII, 129-32; *Rpt Fine Arts Comm*, 1929, p. 31; *Civic Comment*, No. 15, 1 Sep 1927; Roderick McKenzie, *The Metropolitan Community*, p. 282; S Dis Comee, 66C, 3S, to 71C, 2S, "Hearings on Merger of Street Railways in the District of Columbia," (bound volume in S Dis Comee Room, S Office Bldg.).

members of the Fine Arts Commission announced in 1921 that they were not "concerned with the rate of progress; they are vitally concerned that the progress shall be always toward the goal set in 1792 and again in 1901." But they, too, recognized the dangers of delay. "All sorts of suggestions are being made for improvements and changes. Many of these new projects are based on the desire of individuals to exploit themselves. Others are due to ignorance of the existing plan and the progress of work being done in accordance with it." Three years after the Armistice the commission was first and foremost eager to see the execution of the plans for the long-talked-of bridge across the Potomac beyond the still unfinished Lincoln Memorial. "The Highway Bridge connects Potomac Park with a little race track, with marshes lately used as the city dump, and with Agriculture Department barns, so designed and constructed as to thrust their ugliness upon one's attention with all the insistence of a spoiled child at table. Through this variegated area a narrow, tortuous, dangerous road winds its uncertain way to Arlington National Cemetery. The bodies of the Nation's dead take this path to their last resting place." A traffic jam on Armistice Day in 1921 sharpened that picture.

Government officials had planned a solemn ceremony to mark the interment of the Unknown Soldier in Arlington Cemetery. From the Capitol, where the flag-draped casket lay in the Rotunda, a formal procession was to accompany the symbol of all American heroes to the great mausoleum across the Potomac. But at the approach to the river a traffic tie-up occurred, immobilizing for two hours and more the cars carrying important guests, among them foreign statesmen gathered in Washington for the opening of the Naval Disarmament Conference. A number of dignitaries did not reach the cemetery at all. Late that afternoon the Fine Arts Commission met to recommend immediate enactment of the legislation necessary to start work on the new bridge.

The formal dedication of the Lincoln Memorial on Decoration Day in 1922 intensified public interest. Where gulls had once swept over the marshy land bordering the Tidal Basin and the river front, the nation's personages now assembled before a marble temple from which the figure or statue of the Great Emancipator looked out over a pool reflecting the shaft of the Washington Monument. Impressive as was the setting, everyone present could see how much it would gain from bridging the Potomac at that point and landscaping the shore line. Congress voted a preliminary appropriation a fortnight later. As the bridge was an integral part of the Park Commission plan for the river end of the Mall, Washingtonians committed to the "city beautiful" ideal drew a deep breath when Congress accepted the designs submitted in 1924: a stone bridge of simple flowing lines placed slightly below the Lincoln Memorial, above it a water-gate for boats and a plaza with parkways radiating from it, and on the far shore a second bridge over the Virginia channel and the intervening Columbia island to an imposing entrance into the cemetery.[7]

Yet a magnificent approach from the Virginia side of the Potomac was not enough to make the capital a place of sheer beauty. Successful application of Washington's new zoning ordinance notwithstanding, private enterprisers were gobbling up land needed for parks and erecting buildings that threatened permanently to scar the looks of the city. As a first move to check architectural aberrations, in 1923 an advisory council of the American Institute of Architects collaborated with a Board of Trade committee and District officials to revise the District building code. Then, at the request of the commissioners, the council offered suggestions on design free of charge to appli-

[7] Rpts Fine Arts Comm, 1921, pp. 21-22, 37, 1925, pp. 45, 59; Forty Years of Achievement Commemorating the 40th Anniversary of the Establishment of the National Commission of Fine Arts, 1910-1950, p. 25 (hereafter cited as Fine Arts Comm, Forty Years); Star, 13 Nov 1921; Charles Moore, "The Transformation of Washington," National Geographic, XLIII, 583-666; S Doc 95, 68C, 1S, Ser 8240; Rpt B/Tr, 1923, p. 109.

cants for building permits. A few months later, from the recently formed Washington Committee of One Hundred on the Federal City came a revolutionary proposal: the creation of a board of trained architects empowered to regulate all private buildings in the District. Few members of Congress at that time would have dared suggest so "socialistic" a scheme, and in fact it was never adopted except for buildings adjacent to public edifices; but the committee, one of fifty organized in various parts of the country by the American Civic Association to promote the artistic and orderly development of the national capital, contained people eminent in public life. Weight attached to the recommendations of a body that included Secretary of State Charles Evans Hughes, Secretary of Commerce Herbert Hoover, William H. Holmes, director of the Smithsonian National Gallery of Art, several of the best-known artists and architects in Washington, District officials, and a score of well-to-do businessmen.

The preliminary report of the Washington committee pointed out that the Park Commission of 1901 had not provided for city planning as the term had since come to be understood. Urban planning in the 1920's must take transportation, recreation facilities, and over-all land use into consideration. In hammering away at the urgency of extending the District park system before construction companies obliterated the natural beauty of areas like Klingle Valley and sewage polluted every stream, the committee made itself heard. Six months after its preliminary report appeared, Congress established the National Capital Park Commission vested with authority to acquire land for parks, parkways, and playgrounds in the District of Columbia and in nearby Maryland and Virginia, subject only to the approval of the Fine Arts Commission on the sites selected. Half the purchase price was to come from the federal government, the other half from local taxpayers.

Here was progress, or so it seemed. Unhappily, authority to

buy did not provide cold cash. Because Congress voted less than a third of the expected appropriations, the new commission was all but helpless. Enlightened private citizens did what they could. One group bought land to hold until the Park Commission had money available; Charles Glover and Mrs. Anne Archbold gave outright a stretch of woodland along Foundry Run above Georgetown. But individual efforts could go only so far. Indignation stirred in the American Civic Association, already distressed at the ravages the steam shovel and the ax had wrought during the preceding five years. The District highway department had cut shade trees right and left in the process of widening downtown streets and building arterial thoroughfares. By 1925 devastation threatened every section of the District of Columbia.[8]

"Only a remnant of the Klingle stream was left," the *American Civic Annual* reported, "and the parkway connection [was] absolutely blocked by cutting, grading and building. The beautiful Broad Branch and Piney Branch valleys are now but pitiful stubs adjoining Rock Creek Park. Their waters are confined to underground sewers. Their wooded banks are laid desolate. Rectangular house lots take the place of shady slopes. Rows of shoddy, uninteresting houses perch precariously on the deep fills of yellow clay which flank the axial boulevard of 16th street. The stately Tiger Bridge, erected at great cost to span the stream, is now nothing but a street extension over a dry culvert. These tragedies . . . cannot be remedied. Nor can much be done about the acres of land which, since the war, have been plastered over with the wrong kind of houses set in the wrong kind of lots, served by the wrong kind of streets."[9]

[8] *Preliminary Report by the Washington Committee of One Hundred on the Federal City to the American Civic Association*, 3 Jan 1924, *passim*, especially pp. 2-5, 11-14, 27, 35-36; 43 *Stat.* 463; *Rpt B/Tr*, 1924, pp. 68-69; *Civic Comment*, 8 Jun 1924, p. 8; Comrs Rpts, 1924, p. 47, 1925, p. 52; *Herald*, 10 Apr 24; *Star*, 18 Mar 1926.

[9] Harlean James, ed., "The Federal City Committees of the American Civic Association," *American Civic Annual*, 1929, I, 66-68.

The one body with sufficient influence throughout the country to bring order out of laissez-faire anarchy appeared to be the American Civic Association. Founded in the heyday of the muckrakers, the association had set out to awaken a sense of public duty in citizens whose wealth, social standing, and artistic perceptions qualified them as leaders in their own communities, men and women willing to share in wresting control of municipal affairs from unscrupulous and ignorant political bosses and then ready to introduce efficient city government and a systematic program of civic improvements. Chicago had been one of the first places to feel the force of the planning mystique, but neither Chicago, where political reform had met with meagre success, nor any other city had as yet carried out more than a fraction of an over-all plan. Washington seemingly needed little political house-cleaning, but she obviously must have "external aid" if the plan of 1901 were to be expanded to cover the now very much larger city and if a modicum of public control over the use of privately owned land were to safeguard public interests.

The committees on the federal city from the first set their sights on the creation of an official body farsighted and strong enough to develop and carry out "a comprehensive, consistent and coordinated plan for the national Capital and its environs." It was an undertaking that ought to concern all, a Boston landscape architect averred, for if "our Federal City shall become an inspiring example of sustained interest and intelligent action in city planning, the benefits will spread in some measure to every city in the land." As the modest hopes pinned on the National Capital Park Commission proved vain, in the autumn of 1925 Frederic A. Delano, president of the American Civic Association and by then a resident of Washington, arranged a series of conferences between representatives of half a dozen national professional societies and federal and District officials anxious to evolve a planning bill with teeth in it. Forty years later, Washingtonians exposed to frequent pronouncements on the wrong-headedness or provincial backwardness reigning in the District of Columbia would marvel at the fervent interest other Americans displayed in perfecting the capital. In the mid-twenties zeal was both country-wide and, up to a point, effective. It brought into being the National Capital Park and Planning Commission.

The act establishing the new commission authorized the President to appoint for six-year terms four civilians to serve with the federal and District officials of the former commission and greatly enlarged the responsibilities of the new body; not only was the commission to prepare plans for orderly growth in the District but also, in cooperation with Maryland and Virginia authorities, to map out a scheme of harmonious development for Greater Washington that would forestall the pollution of the streams and preserve the region's natural beauties. But the law left the new commission with no more power than its predecessor to ensure acceptance of its recommendations. Its purchasing powers still depended upon uncertain congressional appropriations. State legislatures might or might not collaborate.[10]

Recognition of the regional aspects of planning nevertheless was a long step forward. Maryland set up a Maryland National Capital Planning Commission in 1927, and, although Virginia failed to take effective action, officials of Arlington county were ready to cooperate. In the opinion of Lieutenant Colonel U. S. Grant, III, grandson of President Grant and the federal commission's first secretary, the legal powerlessness of the planners was in fact a minor handicap; inasmuch as the federal executives and members of the Senate and House District committees who were in a position to reject or drastically amend every proposal were either themselves members of the commission or represented thereon, plans adopted in conference usually had an excel-

10 *Ibid.*, p. 69; Arthur A. Shurtleff, "Guiding the Growth of the City of Washington," *American City Magazine*, XXXIII, 40; 44 *Stat.* 1330.

lent chance of receiving congressional blessing, if not large appropriations. The big stumbling blocks to action were the stipulation that prices paid for land never exceed its assessed valuation by more than 25 percent, the less than $4,000,000 available to the commission in its first four years, and its inability to borrow in order to buy land while it was relatively cheap. In the 1950's thoughtful people would sometimes regret that a Washington Metropolitan Regional Authority had not come into being before the depression of the 1930's cut off funds and chilled public interest in so drastic a political innovation. But in 1926 and 1927 responsible men believed they must first draft a detailed regional plan and only then seek the power to carry it out.[11]

The progress achieved before 1930 was due in considerable degree to Frederic A. Delano. An aristocrat imbued with a strong sense of civic obligation, an admirer of Daniel Burnham, and an active participant in launching the Chicago as well as the New York Regional plans, Delano, though a railroad executive and a financier rather than a landscape architect, had the background, the enthusiasm, and the persuasiveness to make him an invaluable member of the commission; in 1930 he became its chairman. He himself always denied that he contributed anything beyond a ready ear to other men's ideas, but his associates felt the force of his personality, visible in his commanding figure and the character in his strong patrician features. On every job he undertook, and they were many even when he was in his seventies, he gathered about him "top technical talent." His "modus operandi" consisted "of bringing men together—frequently at Cosmos Club luncheons— to pool their talents, even when their views and their interests

---

[11] Lt. Col. U.S. Grant, III, "Washington Looks Ahead," *American Civic Annual*, i, 69-74, and "Governmental Jurisdictions in the National Capital," *ibid.*, ii, 90-91; Charles W. Eliot, II, "Planning Washington and Its Environs," *City Planning*, iii, 177-93; *Rpts National Capital Park and Planning Commission*, 1928, p. 28, 1929, p. 29, 1930, p. 45 (hereafter cited as *Rpts NCPPC*).

were in opposition. Antagonisms faded out in his presence and never a tart rejoinder was spoken in his direction." His tact, his personal charm, and his social prestige were as great an asset to the planning cause as the authority represented by Army engineers and the special skills provided by the commission staff.

Still, without the insights and, on some measures, the initiating force of key members of the House and Senate, much of the program would have netted scant attention, and, without the unflagging support of constituents, the congressional majority might well have remained indifferent. In both houses the chairmen of the District committees, the Public Buildings committees, and the subcommittees on District appropriations were strong advocates of improvements for the capital, and a score of other men worked hard to get the necessary appropriations, while Congressmen Louis Cramton of Maryland and R. Walton Moore of Virginia pushed for federal and state legislation helpful to plans for Greater Washington. The Capper-Cramton Act passed in 1930 enabled Maryland to borrow from the federal Treasury for extension of the District park system into Montgomery and Prince George's Counties. When the planning commission presented its first formal "Progress Report" in January 1930, members of Congress, the Secretary of the Treasury, the governors of Maryland and Virginia, the legislature of Virginia, notables from the rest of the country, and Washingtonians nearly filled Constitution Hall. If, as Colonel Grant believed, the approaching bi-centennial of the birth of George Washington stimulated interest in the city whose original layout he had overseen lovingly, probably an even stronger impulse sprang from the growing awareness that sensible solutions to the manifold problems of expanding metropolitan areas must depend upon intelligent advance planning.[12] The capital was a logical place to begin.

[12] "Frederic A. Delano (1863-1953)," Vignette the Thirty-fourth, *Cosmos Club Bulletin*, VII, No. 2, pp. 2-5; Grant, "Washington Looks

Because the Planning Commission had to buy land piecemeal at constantly rising prices, developments dependent upon purchase moved more slowly than the beautifying of property already part of the public domain. While acquisition of the strip of land between Potomac and Rock Creek Parks permitted building and landscaping that parkway, several other major projects made no headway at all. Particularly disappointing to Delano and to humbler citizens in time to come was the gradual abandonment of an early plan for "a system of neighborhood centers," each designed to encompass a twenty-acre site containing a school, a library, a playground, and park facilities. Only three small playgrounds materialized. The parkways skirting both sides of the Potomac as far as Great Falls and the circumferential drive connecting sites of the twenty-four Civil War forts that ringed the District would still be under discussion in the late 1950's. The improvements taking form along the Mall, however, and the $50,000,000 federal building operations launched in 1926 lessened impatience at the relative slowness of park development.

The magnitude of the building program might well have proved self-defeating; scores of departmental executives, members of Congress, the Planning and the Fine Arts Commissions, and a host of architects, private citizens, and real estate firms had an immediate interest in it. It was able to move forward with astonishingly few hitches by reason of the federal Public Buildings Commission, which Congress had created in 1916 but which had had no opportunity to function during and after the war. The composition of the commission went far toward ensuring cooperation between the legislative and executive branches of the government; the minority as well as the majority

Ahead," *American Civic Annual*, i, 74, and Frederic A. Delano, "Progress Report," *ibid.*, ii, 83; *Star*, 31 Dec 1926; Maj. Gen. U. S. Grant to the author, 16 Apr 1960; *Rpt B/Tr*, 1928, pp. 51-57; *Rpt NCPPC*, 1930, pp. 70-71; Eliot, "Planning Washington and Its Environs," p. 181; *Star*, 3 Apr 1927.

party in House and Senate was represented and shared in every decision; the commissioner of public buildings, the architect of the Capitol, and the supervising architect of the Treasury supplied administrative and technical knowledge and, through the Secretary of Treasury, access to the President. Even so, conflicts and costly delays seemed all too probable. Yet the record of the building commission in the late 1920's, in the words of one official, "affords an example of how coordination of action . . . can be and was achieved."

Buildings for the Bureau of Internal Revenue and the Commerce Department began to rise below Pennsylvania Avenue late in 1927, and government purchase of virtually the entire stretch of land from the Treasury to the foot of the Hill between the Mall and the Avenue foreshadowed the location of additional departmental offices in the "Federal Triangle." A Board of Trade housing expert warned against overcrowding the triangle with massive government structures, but the tentative plan published early in 1927 showing open park-like spaces between each building allayed anxiety on that score. Milton B. Medary, president of the American Institute of Architects, proposed the method adopted in developing the triangle: a board of experienced architects to draft a harmonious composition and each man to design one building of the group in order to avoid monotony in treatment. Since by law the supervising architect of the Treasury was responsible for the designs, the Medary proposal became feasible only because Secretary of the Treasury Andrew Mellon contrived the necessary legislative authority.[13]

The Fine Arts Commission pointed to other work afoot in mid-1929: the removal of the World War I dormitories from the Union Station Plaza and the landscaping of the terrain, plans for a new Municipal Center, the relocation of the Botanic

[13] S Doc 240, 69C, 2S, Report of the Public Buildings Commission, pp. 1-5, and plate facing p. 8, Ser 8707; Grant to the author, 16 Apr 1960; *Rpt B/Tr*, 1926, pp. 56-57, 1928, pp. 13, 54-57, 64-65; *Star*, 31 Dec 1927, 1 Jan 1930; Fine Arts Comm, *Forty Years*, pp. 25-26; Herbert Hoover, *Memoirs*, II, 250.

Garden and the beginning of the Arboretum, a new Department of Agriculture building adjoining the old, extension of tree-lined drives along the Mall, and the selection of a site for a Supreme Court building facing the Capitol. Not since the early years of the century had old residents seen so much permanent federal construction. If a few citizens would have preferred greater emphasis on land purchase as a safeguard against further despoliation, and if some hearts stood still at the felling of trees along B Street preparatory to making it a "great ceremonial avenue," Washingtonians by and large were elated at the new outward grandeur the city was attaining.[14] That they themselves had not produced most of it, that it was rather an expression of national pride in the capital, did not matter. Indeed by 1930 few people differentiated between a Washingtonian and any American temporarily living in the District of Columbia.

[14] H. G. Dwight, "The Horrors of Washington," *Harper's Magazine*, CLII, 64-72; Kenneth L. Roberts, "Nobody's Capital," *Sat Eve Post*, CIC, 20; Eliot, "Planning Washington and Its Environs," pp. 178-81; Louis C. Cramton, "Congress and the Federal City," *American Civic Annual*, I, 75-79; *Star*, 3 Jan 1930; *Rpt Fine Arts Comm*, 1929, pp. 4, 31.

CHAPTER XV

THE INTELLECTUAL AND SOCIAL CLIMATE, 1920-1929

A DECADE called in contemporary and later writings the "Age of the Golden Calf," the "Era of Wonderful Nonsense," the "Jazz Age," the "Hardboiled Era," and the "New Era" of science and technology was a period of contradictions that produced the distinctive literature of the "lost generation," a disillusioned rejection of everything serious, and at the same time a faith in the wonder-working powers of science that reached the point of "superstition in another guise."[1] No one in the capital produced a *Farewell to Arms*, or a *This Side of Paradise*, or a *Main Street*, and flag-pole sitting and dance marathons bypassed Washington, but most of the wonderful nonsense and the hard-boiled selfishness characteristic of the 1920's was in evidence here, and perhaps nowhere else in the country did dedication to research bite deeper.

Thoughtful Americans had realized before the Armistice that the United States could no longer draw upon Europe for the discovery of new basic scientific principles or for fresh approaches to the study of social phenomena. And the United States was ill-prepared to fill the gap. A coordinating body to direct and abet research on a nation-wide scale in both the natural and the humanistic sciences seemed the logical answer, an organization like the National Research Council of the National Academy of Sciences but not under government control or dependent on government money. The upshot was that shortly after the war Congress amended the Academy's charter authorizing a membership of three hundred and complete independence of the government. Private funds thenceforward sup-

[1] Henry F. May, "Shifting Perspectives on the 1920's," *Mississippi Valley Historical Review*, XLIII, 405-27; Frederick L. Allen, *Only Yesterday*; William F. Leuchtenberg, *The Perils of Prosperity*, p. 2.

ported the Academy and its operating agent, the Research Council. Consensus was general that Washington was the most suitable location for its headquarters. Financed by a gift of $5,000,000 from the Carnegie Corporation, a handsome new building rose on north B Street across from Potomac Park, where a permanent staff took charge. Through awards of fellowships and grants-in-aid in eleven fields, ranging from anthropology, psychology, and "Educational Relations" to geology, physics, and medicine, the National Research Council gradually supplanted the Smithsonian as the prime mover in American scientific research. For although the older institution still acted as a clearing house of scientific data and a series of popular books published from 1926 onward served to disseminate knowledge, an insufficient endowment and the growth of the National Museum had gradually transformed the institution's main function from exploration of new scientific frontiers into guardianship of the past.

Several of the federal bureaus also suffered in the postwar decade. Distaste for everything military cut War and Navy Department research. Although the Navy in 1923 got appropriations for a laboratory whence came radar in the late 1930's, and the Public Health Service under the aegis of the Surgeon General managed to carry on some investigations in the control of venereal disease and developed a vaccine for Rocky Mountain spotted fever, even the famous Army Medical Library fell upon hard times. Congress allowed funds for Weather Bureau research, and the Interior Department conducted some small-scale scientific programs, but only the Departments of Agriculture and Commerce succeeded in expanding their research. The achievements of the plant explorers who had introduced to the United States crops such as avocados, dates, and soy beans, and the progress made in the realm of plant and animal pathology and chemistry ensured continuation of that work; and the country-wide prestige of Secretary of Agriculture Henry Wallace, himself responsible for developing hybrid corn, enabled him to get congressional endorsement of a Department of Agriculture Graduate School. Opened in 1923 in a department building, the school offered evening courses in some twenty fields, by no means all limited to agriculture; anyone could enroll for a nominal fee. Secretary of Commerce Herbert Hoover, wedded as he was to private enterprise, also widened research in the bureaus under his control. In order to establish simplified labor-saving practices and commercial standardization in all American business, he instituted a cooperative program at the Bureau of Standards where representatives of private firms worked alongside government employees. He hoped to see industrial corporations contribute $20,000,000 to a national fund for basic research, but, while waiting vainly for that to materialize, he encouraged strictly utilitarian government projects. Scientists in government service thus played a lesser national role than they had in the 1870's and 1880's, but the value of their work in the 1920's was far from negligible.[2]

Research in the social sciences, intensified by the troubles of wartime agencies in assembling precise information, received further impetus after the war from dollar-a-year men who had seen the need of a clearer understanding within the federal government of the principles of political and business economy. Robert S. Brookings, a wealthy St. Louis manufacturer who had served on the War Industries Board, took the lead. In 1919 a slim, handsome, white-haired, trimly bearded man of 69 whose formal education had ended when he was 16 but whose intellectual interests had deepened as his fortune grew, Brookings virtually singlehanded raised the money to prevent the threatened demise of the privately supported Institute for Govern-

[2] Millikan, *Autobiography*, pp. 199-201; Dupree, *Science*, pp. 322-43; Frederick A. Ogg, *Research in the Humanistic and Social Sciences, Report of a Survey Conducted for the American Council of Learned Societies*, pp. 168-69; *Rpts Smithsonian Inst.*, 1923, pp. 6, 12-13, 23, 1924, pp. 2-3, 15-16, 1925, pp. 2-3, 16, 1927, pp. 2, 12, 1928, pp. 2, 5; *The Graduate School of the Department of Agriculture*, 1961.

mental Research. From the institute's dispassionate factual studies came the recommendations that Congress wrote into a law of 1921 creating an executive accounting system and the federal Bureau of the Budget. Under the direction of William F. Willoughby, formerly a Princeton University Professor, abetted by his twin, Wester W., an expert in international relations, the institute then moved on to prepare other useful monographs. The best known of these, an examination of the government's handling of Indian affairs, brought about the reorganization of the Indian Service.

Brookings meanwhile concluded that the economic problems facing the world—war debts, reparations, and labor questions—demanded the scrutiny of "trained scientists, avid of facts, suspicious of assumptions and detached alike from personal prejudice and from any obligation to score points in the name of Patriotism." So, with Carnegie Corporation funds and generous contributions from his own pocket, he founded the Institute of Economics in 1922 and persuaded Harold G. Moulton of the University of Chicago to head it. The outwardly domineering "manufacturer-turned-educator" promised Moulton that he and his staff would not be subject to interference, and the trustees, men of the calibre of the paleontologist John C. Merriam, president of the Carnegie Institution, and Frederic A. Delano, also pledged themselves to give free rein to every scholar participating in the institute's work. It was a commitment of more than ordinary importance to American intellectuals. For while the public, despite Tennessee's rejection of evolution at the Scopes trial, was ordinarily ready to accept the tenets of natural science, studies in the human sciences, especially of touchy economic questions, still seemed to most Americans to be matters of opinion. The independence given the men at the Institute of Economics heightened their responsibilities but also enormously strengthened the case for academic freedom throughout the United States.

Moulton, a round-faced, strong-jawed extrovert, an athlete who had once considered a career in professional baseball, was at the same time a scientist intent on getting at the truth and seeing it presented in lucid non-technical language. He gathered about him a distinguished group of men. Their findings laid the analytical foundation upon which the Dawes Plan for German reparations was built and so molded public opinion that a settlement of allied war debts to the United States became possible. The long postwar agricultural depression led to Edwin G. Nourse's thought-provoking studies, *The Legal Status of Agricultural Cooperation* and *The Cooperative Marketing of Livestock*, practical guides to new forms of economic organization. Whenever a new institute monograph appeared, Moulton invited congressmen, federal executives, and independent scholars to a formal dinner at the Brookings headquarters, where the author of the study outlined his central thesis and answered questions about it. As a result quotations from the book, duly accredited, not infrequently found their way into the *Congressional Record* and government reports.

Eager to ensure a constant flow of young scientific experts into government service, in 1924 Brookings raised money to open a graduate school where hand-picked students were to be exposed to the practical workings of the government as well as book-learning. But as most of the students, instead of apprenticing themselves for careers in civil service and statesmanship, prepared for teaching posts, a plan to consolidate the school with the Institute of Governmental Research and the Institute of Economics took form in 1927 which brought about the chartering of the Brookings Institution "devoted to public service through research and education in the social sciences." Perhaps the hard-headed economists and political scientists who carried out the research and writing and schooled younger scholars in their own exacting methods considered Brookings' dream overambitious when he envisaged the institution of the future as "a kind of cap-stone to the educational arch of the country." Nevertheless by 1929 the trustees and the staff believed the experiment had abundantly proved its value.[3]

The American Council on Education, meanwhile, periodically brought together in Washington leading figures in American higher education. The council worked on the principle Woodrow Wilson had once enunciated: "Find out what you want in a college graduate and let the ways of getting it work themselves out"—that is, through the initiative and efforts of local communities rather than by government fiat bolstered by federal subsidies. By means of *The Educational Record*, prepared by committees and the small headquarters staff in Washington, the council's influence reached into every university and college in the country. In serving the teaching profession, the government, industry, and occasionally foreign universities, the council undertook various tasks. For example, the *Record of Usage*, a study of the manifold duties of foreign service officers, indicated what instruction colleges should give men training for these careers; the factual basis of the study was the day-by-day notations kept, at President Coolidge's request, by some three hundred foreign service officers. Another analysis examined the teaching of foreign languages in American colleges and outlined methods of improving it.

The American Council of Learned Societies Devoted to the Humanistic Sciences in turn contributed to the city's scholarly standing and gave new vigor to the local universities. The primary purpose of this federation of fifteen independent societies was to lay the groundwork for interdisciplinary research in archeology, history, philosophy, modern European and Oriental languages, and other special fields of knowledge. Like the National Research Council, the Brookings Institution, and the

[3] The Brookings Institution, *A Consideration of the Application of Research in the Social Sciences to the Problems of Modern Civilization*, 1931, pp. 8-14, 16; Herman Hagedorn, *Robert C. Brookings, A Biography*, pp. 21-22, 252-69, 289; Dexter M. Keeger, "Making The Social Sciences Sociable," *Survey*, LV, 80-82.

Council on Education, the humanists drew upon foundations for financial support. Among the early projects of the ACLS was a series of conferences on "the gifted student," a topic that stirred a response from the general public only thirty years later. But full recognition of the council's services followed upon the publication in 1928 of the first volume of that invaluable scholarly tool, the *Dictionary of American Biography*. Another contribution lay in awakening American scholars to the importance of oriental civilization.[4]

Above all, the Library of Congress drew scholars in the humanities to Washington. For Herbert Putnam looked upon the collection in his charge as a national library rather than a legislative tool, although, in establishing the Legislative Reference Service in 1915, he provided an efficient system for furnishing Congress with exact information. Over the years he had won the complete confidence of Congress by the temperate character of his requests; when he asked for funds the House Appropriations Committee accepted his word for the need. He had built up the accessions by drawing upon his exceptional knowledge of books and manuscripts in many realms of learning and by exercising intuitive judgment about those he did not know; his decision was final. In the opinion of his subordinates he seldom made a mistake. Autocratic though his manner toward them was, his high standards of performance and his never-failing sense of justice robbed his rebukes of any sting. No library in America had so devoted a staff or such rich materials in so many fields.

The Chinese collections and the way the Library of Congress acquired them are a case in point. First credit goes to Walter T.

[4] David A. Robertson, Assistant Director American Council on Education, 1924-1930, to the author, 15 Apr 1960; *The Educational Record*, I, No. 1, pp. 33-36, No. 3, *passim*, and III, No. 10, *passim*; Ogg, *Research in the Humanistic . . . Sciences*, p. 161; *Bulletins of the American Council of Learned Societies*, I-X, 1920-1930, especially No. 4, Jun 1925, p. 25, No. 5, May 1926, pp. 43, 52, No. 7, Apr 1928, pp. 60-61, No. 9, Dec 1928, p. 29 (hereafter cited as *ACLS Bulletin*).

Swingle, plant pathologist and plant explorer of the Department of Agriculture, for, in the course of his travels to collect seeds and cuttings in remote lands of the East, he learned of rare books dealing with oriental agriculture, Chinese philosophy, and Chinese literature. From 1913 onward he wrote long, detailed descriptions of these finds to Putnam, and Putnam unhesitatingly acted upon Swingle's advice to buy them. Neither man could himself read any oriental language. Swingle accepted the judgments of learned Chinese friends; the librarian accepted Swingle's, even to the point of paying $1,000 for a unique 1590 edition of a Chinese herbary, huge volumes of ideograph that scarcely fifty men in the United States could read. A colored man, Armstrong Claytor, who unpacked the shipments of orientalia, taught himself enough Chinese to identify and catalogue the materials, while the courtly and persuasive Swingle induced the Department of Agriculture to employ a scholar to translate the books so that students of agriculture as well as historians could benefit. So distinguished had the Library's Chinese accessions become that in 1928 Putnam obtained appropriations to establish a division of Chinese literature headed by the gentle and learned sinologue Arthur Hummel. Japanese and Tibetan materials also multiplied, while the Freer Gallery, under the wing of the Smithsonian, furnished magnificent examples of oriental art. In that fashion Washington became the one place in the western world where the student of oriental civilization could find the resources he needed.

Indeed, the Library of Congress came to be virtually a national cultural center which private donations constantly enriched. In 1912 a bequest from Mrs. Gardiner Hubbard had created a fund for annual purchases of engravings and etchings, but not until 1925, after Mrs. Frederic Shurtleff Coolidge had offered an endowment that would build an auditorium and provide for chamber music concerts, did Congress create a Trust Fund Board to administer similar gifts and bequests. At the newly completed Coolidge Auditorium a chamber music festival first took place in October 1925. Mrs. Coolidge, herself a talented musician, had explained her wish that the concerts be considered "national and professional" events, and since "fashion is an enemy to art," guest lists omit "the fashionable element as such . . . if it has no musical qualifications." Abetted by the "Friends of Music in the Library of Congress," founded in 1928 and headed by Speaker of the House Nicholas Longworth, the annual festivals opened up to discriminating audiences musical opportunities rare in any city. Other gifts permitted the Library to establish "chairs" of American history, the fine arts, aeronautics, and, with funds from a new Hispanic Foundation, a chair in Spanish and Portuguese literature.[5]

Radio broadcasting and new concert series widened the city's interest in all music. In a single week of 1925, for example, Louise Homer sang at the Washington Auditorium, Marian Anderson, the already famous young Negro contralto, at the First Congregational Church, and Sophie Breslau at the National Theatre, the New York symphony played at Poli's, the American pianist Charles Cooper and the Davison Glee Club performed at the Masonic Auditorium, and the organist Henry Seibert at the Washington Auditorium. At morning musicals sponsored by Mrs. Lawrence Townsend, herself a composer of some note, leading artists made their Washington debuts. Although most of the symphony concerts were still day-time affairs, the Knights of Columbus opened an Evening School of Music, and societies such as the Arts Club and the United Art Society offered Sunday concerts.

In colored Washington music was a cultural cement. Negroes excluded from white concerts provided their own. Until the demise of the *Bee* in 1922, the paper regularly devoted a half-page to events "In The World of Music," and the *Tribune*, born

[5] *ACLS Bulletin*, No. 10, Apr 29, pp. 33-58; *Rpts, Librarian of Cong*, 1928, pp. 1-2, 6-7, 272, 287-316, 1946, "The Story Up to Now," pp. 202-14.

301

in 1921, for years followed much the same course. Here was a realm in which the Negro community knew it excelled. The Snowden Diamond Jazzologists, Duke Ellington's, and other bands made the city "known for its syncopation," even if as innovators they did not rank with New Orleans' musicians. In the 1950's Washington would proudly claim among her native sons jazz artists of the fame of Louis Armstrong. Nor did the colored community neglect classical and church music. Upper-class Negroes cultivated all music as an art and trained their children in its practice. Unknown to most white Washingtonians, least of all to the "smart set," the Mus-o-lit Society occupied a very special place in the life of what the *Crisis* came to call the "Secret City."[6]

While increasing enrollment in the Corcoran Art School and streams of visitors to the Freer and Corcoran galleries indicated a growing appreciation of the fine arts, informed Washingtonians realized that neglect was restricting the potentialities of the National Gallery. The pictures were crowded into a few rooms of the National Museum, where only part of the collection could be displayed and lack of space forbade accepting new accessions. "We are the only civilized nation that has not risen to a realization of the real value of art and of important functions of a National Gallery," wrote the Secretary of the Smithsonian in 1922. "No important art work has, for art's sake pure and simple, ever been purchased with the approval of the United States Government. The Nation has received as gifts and bequests, art works amounting to more than ten millions in money value, and has expended on their acquirement and care possibly one two-hundredth part of that amount." Unless Congress were to meet the cost of erecting a new building, only private sub-

[6] Programs, 1920-1929, Washington file (Music Div, L.C.); *Star*, 8 Nov 1925; *Bee*, 19 Feb, 12 Mar 1921; *Tribune*, 21 May 1921, 21 Jan 1922; *Crisis*, xxxix, 185. Issues of the Sunday *Star* in October and November, when the concert season opened, carried yearly full notices of what was to come.

scription could give the national collection a suitable gallery and opportunity to expand, since the endowment of the Smithsonian was no longer adequate even for its scientific programs. Faced with that dilemma, several Washington business firms and the regents of the Smithsonian campaigned for a bigger endowment, while a committee of fifteen leading citizens arranged a special loan exhibition to promote interest in the gallery. By 1929 the Secretary could report: "The year has been gratifyingly and unexpectedly rich in progress. . . . The National Government and many friends of the Institution have added materially to its income—Mr. John Gellatly, of New York, has made the gift of his extensive collection comprising classic American and European paintings, outstanding specimens of jewellers' art, tapestries, furniture, and oriental art, valued altogether at several million dollars, . . . for eventual exhibition in the National Gallery."[7]

Meanwhile belief that "the sense of well-being and enriched capacity for living which art can give" should be "a privilege of the many as well as the technically trained and sensitive few," inspired Duncan Phillips, a discriminating private collector and art critic, to open to the public in 1920 what one admirer called an "Art Gallery for Delight." Housed in two rooms of the family residence, the paintings—an occasional sixteenth-century piece, some French impressionists, some Whistlers, and a few twentieth-century American artists—were regrouped periodically to illustrate particular ideas and themes. The Phillips Gallery came to be known to connoisseurs the world over. At intervals after the founding of the Washington Chamber Music Society in 1924, private concerts took place at the gallery.[8]

[7] *Star*, 3 Jul 1920; *Rpt Fine Arts Comm*, 1921; *Rpt Smithsonian*, 1921, p. 16, 1922, pp. 6, 49, 1923, pp. 6, 19, 1924, pp. 3-4, 1925, pp. 18-19, 1926, pp. 3-4, 7, 24, 1927, p. 25, 1929, p. 2; *Exhibition of Early American Paintings, Miniatures and Silver, Assembled by the Washington Loan Exhibition Committee, December 5, 1925-January 3, 1926*; Frederick P. Keppel and R. L. Duffus, *The Arts in American Life*, p. 67.

[8] Duncan Phillips, "Art and Understanding," *Art and Understanding*,

While science, scholarship, and a deepening interest in the arts thus took possession of much of Washington, an innovation aimed at strengthening the influence of religion brought the College of Preachers into being at the Cathedral of St. Peter and St. Paul. In a building erected in the Cathedral close in 1924, Episcopal rectors in groups of fifteen to twenty from parishes all over the country gathered for post-ordination "refresher" courses and discussions of how the church could widen its reach. Relatively few people knew anything about this college, but its very existence and growth during the Age of the Golden Calf pointed to a richness and variety in Washington's life that newcomers rarely expected.

If frequently startled to find such diversity, the discerning newcomer was invariably struck by Washington's persistent village-like quality. Its unexpectedness entranced most people. Here was a bucolic Cleopatra whose wiles seduced the good home-spun citizen. World capital though she was, "the chief official personages who people the scene are villagers with a villager's outlook and a villager's background." The sense of intimacy, which in 1920 Washingtonians had feared lost forever, again pervaded all strata of white society. When the Senators won the World Series in 1924, people of all sorts and kinds celebrated together at street dances in a dozen neighborhoods. Years later one man recalled a spring evening when, as he and his wife boarded a trolley, the long fringe of his wife's Venetian shawl caught on the conductor's sleeve button; instead of yanking it free the conductor followed her into the car and, slowly disengaging the strands, said very courteously: "Madam, you certainly have me on the string tonight." Even the critic who considered the city "rootless" and "without ambition," a place in which "material barrenness . . . [is] matched by its own cultural barrenness," admitted that a "dance is a

---

I, 1; "Art Gallery for Delight," *Weekly Review*, III, 611; programs Washington Chamber Music Society, 1924-1932 (Music Div, L.C.).

pleasanter place than a factory or a laboratory or a study; conforming travelers on the broad path are easier on their fellows' elbows than angular men of ideas and purposes."[9]

The picture of Washington that emerged from the popular press for the great American public was of a city given over entirely to dances, teas and dinner parties, incessant social climbing, and, as a way to the top, jockeying for political preferment. The canvas was narrow; the arts occupied little space, the world of learning even less. Political commentators, including radio broadcasters, talked of responses in Washington to national and international problems, but in the new Babylon, once the scandals of the Harding administration had blown over, politics as such generally netted less attention than Society with a capital S, although the farmer's son in the White House was not only "agin sin" but agin extravagance and disliked social functions. Month after month women's magazines carried descriptions of what the well-dressed senator's wife was wearing or what etiquette demanded in the capital; metropolitan dailies seized upon Washington gossip. The raw material lent itself admirably both to derisive and reverential treatment.[10] Bathtub gin and bootleg whiskey, sleek sports cars, backbiting and competition over precedence, short skirts and Zulu-like, bushy permanents on nine debutantes out of ten held the limelight.

The local newspapers, in adopting a worshipful tone toward high society, presented a one-sided view of the city's life. The *Times*, which ten years before had championed civic causes deserving public support, had changed hands and now swung far to the right. In the opinion of the crusading Oswald Garrison Villard of the *Nation*, the *Times* became a "noisy and insincere" paper, while the *Herald*, which had once promised substantial

[9] Robertson to the author, 15 Apr 1960; Edward G. Lowry, *Washington Close-Ups, Intimate Views of Some Public Figures*, pp. 7-9; John W. Owens, "A City Without a Main Street," *Nation*, cxx, 513-14.

[10] Nearly a quarter of the entries under the heading "Washington" in the *Reader's Guide to Periodical Literature* from 1920 to 1929 consists of articles about "high society."

fare, offered a bland diet only occasionally spiced with biting, politically loaded comments. Newspapermen despised the Washington *Post*, a "poison sheet" without moral integrity. The *News*, of which the courageous and gifted Lowell Mellett was the backbone, carried valuable items on its inside pages but spread trivia like the "Marble Championship" across its front page. The *Star*, one of the biggest moneymakers in the newspaper business, trod such a wary path lest an editorial or news item offend Congress or an important advertiser that every column appeared swathed in cotton wool. Readers naturally were happy to learn that Mrs. Herbert Hoover made history: for the first time "the wife of a President has operated a car while in the White House." Non-controversial items and homey "small-town gossip" were safer than opinions, even those well right of center, and kept for the *Star* a large local public. For, as Villard noted, there is "no such hide-bound conservative in all the world as your retired civil official or retired army or navy officer," and Washington was full of them. People who wanted to follow public affairs other than the "shifting social pageant" read the New York *Times*, the Baltimore *Sun*, or the *Christian Science Monitor*.[11]

Ridicule of the city's most publicized element came chiefly from outsiders. In this "most temporary Society in America," wrote a New Yorker, the native aristocracy often had a background of only two or three generations of residence. Hovering upon the borders of "that august group" was "a swarm of widows." The comment that, when a millionaire went to heaven, his wife took up residence in Washington, overlooked the scores of widows, wealthy and otherwise, who had originally come as wives of generals and admirals and stayed on because the rootlessness of military life made the capital the place where they

[11] Oswald Garrison Villard, "Washington: A Capital without a Thunderer," *Nation*, cxvii, 232-35, and *Some Newspapers and Newspapermen*, p. 175; *Star*, 4 Apr 1929; [Robert Allen], *Washington Merry-go-Round*, pp. 322-58.

felt most at home. Theoretically anyone "in trade" was anathema, but by 1923 the Chevy Chase Club had slipped so far as to lower the bars several times, leaving only the Grasslands Country Club and the fifty-member Alibi Club untainted. No Jew was allowed even as a guest in the country clubs. "A shrine for the non-political world of fashion" was the Massachusetts Avenue house of the three Patten sisters. Emphatically not cave-dwellers and with only one generation of moderate wealth behind them, they had set out before the war "to rule Washington by giving great tea parties at which one's presence was the sign manual of society. Their tireless energy in unearthing obscure facts raised gossip to the plane of research." In the popular phrase, the way to spread the news in the city was "telephone, telegraph, or tell-a-Patten." Their omniscience was simultaneously terrifying and fascinating. Social climbers, minor functionaries of the diplomatic corps, and gay young married couples yearned to be invited to Sunday afternoon teas that might furnish stories on which to dine out for the rest of the season.[12]

In colored society snobbery took slightly different form, since color itself entered into social gradations. But cave-dwelling had come to be as firmly established in Negro Washington as in white. A long line of Washington ancestors, non-Negroid features, and very light color were more decidedly marks of distinction in the 1920's than at the turn of the century. Colored ladies spent afternoons playing bridge and five hundred, their husbands took flyers in the stock market and bought expensive cars, and all the well-to-do gave select evening parties in their homes to which the cultivated Negro newcomer could not hope to be invited. Like whites, Negroes also made some obeisance to wealth. "When Washington Society 'Turns Out'" described that aspect of the colored city's life to readers of the *Tribune*: "There are two events in the District of Columbia which attract

[12] Mrs John King Van Rensselaer, *The Social Ladder*, pp. 248-72, 289; Dixon Wecter, *The Saga of American Society*, p. 418.

307

the undivided support of the 'well-known' and 'exclusive' Washington society. They are the Howard-Lincoln football game and the annual cadet corps drill. Just as the 'pretty school marms' exhibit their raccoons, chinchillas and sable skins at the gridiron classics, so the cadet drill occasions the display of the choicest most elaborate and scantiest spring frocks." When Washington's and Baltimore's "smart set" barred darker-skinned Negroes from the summer colony which Frederick Douglass had founded in the 1880's at Highland Beach, Maryland, the ensuing feud equalled in intensity the battles in white society.

At the end of the 1920's Langston Hughes, great-nephew of colored Washington's idol of the 1870's and 1880's, lashed out at the city's high yellow elite. Poems sketching the porter "climbing a great big mountain of Yes Sirs," the "Black Gal" crying "I hate them rinney yaller gals," and the "loud laughers in the hand of Fate" had won him some literary fame, but the disregard of his Washington neighbors angered him. They overlooked talent; they objected to Jean Toomer's *Cane* and Rudolph Fisher's *City of Refuge* because the main characters in both books were so "black." Many of the "best people" were newly rich, and many were not cultured at all. A true picture would reveal their "pseudo-culture, their slavish devotion to Nordic standards, their snobbishness, their detachment from the Negro masses and their vast sense of importance to themselves."[13]

As the Jazz Age was nearing its end, angry criticism of the shallowness of high white society also sounded. The anonymously published *Washington Merry-go-Round* described the bungling of the welcome prepared for the "Lone Eagle" as an illustration of the city's ineptness: the dinner in Charles Lindbergh's honor wound up with a recording of "They're Hanging Danny Deever in the Morning." In this "humdrum capital,"

[13] *Tribune*, 22 Apr 1927, 26 Oct 1929; Langston Hughes, *Fine Clothes for the Jew.*

where the diplomatic corps was "starched futility," "boiled bosoms" served as the brittle front for the emptiness of society leaders. "One of the most charming things about Washington is that it is almost never without a social, diplomatic or matrimonial war." Society was divided between "those who want to get their names into the papers and those who want to keep them out." And the heavy drinking of party-goers in a supposedly dry capital made them the more boring. Yet in being well supplied with bores and over supplied with bootleg liquor, Washington differed little from other American cities of the period.

Neither the adulatory nor the derogatory descriptions of Washington hinted at any complexity in the social structure, and over-simplification postulated a fixity in the white social order that did not obtain. The personable unattached male was still much in demand irrespective of his rank. If no agreeable young bachelor in a minor government post in the 1920's could successfully emulate James MacNeill Whistler's debonair scheme of pinning up his frock coat into tails and then sallying forth to captivate Washington hostesses, still seventy years later the presentable young man able to rent a dress suit might find himself invited to debutante balls. Rumor ran that, when asked what "book" he was listed in—the *Social Register*, the *Green Book*, successor to the *Elite List*, or *Who's Who in the National Capital*—one man replied: "The telephone book." While the label "cave-dweller" was increasingly sought after, some of that group had gone to seed and some kept to their caves as the only way of concealing the meagreness of their personal attainments. Georgetown, in particular, contained a number of odd characters, products of intermarriages within their own small circle, eccentrics whose status hinged upon aloofness from everyone without local antecedents going back into ante-bellum days. Yet the interpretation of Washington's social hierarchy as built upon "wealth and an imported aristocracy either directly or indirectly political" left out of account the variety of individual talent in the city and the ease with which doors barricaded against the social climber opened to genuinely gifted new-comers. The new arrival whose accomplishments and good manners qualified him for membership in the Cosmos Club received a cordial welcome that sometimes astonished him.

During an era in which business enterprise rode high in America, Washington's businessmen commanded curiously little social prestige, although the heads of several banks, fortified by years of controlling the credit of people ostensibly more powerful, were listed in the *Social Register*. While enjoying "Coolidge prosperity" Washingtonians, old and new, like thousands of other Americans, poked fun at the President's occasional gaucheries, just as they later delighted in grossly exaggerated apocryphal tales of the "elbowings" of Dolly Gann, the Vice President's stout, red-haired sister and hostess, in her successful efforts to see her brother officially outrank the Speaker of the House. But pontificaters on precedence and status-seekers alike tacitly admitted that they could not deny position to the city's intelelctuals.

President Hoover's "business administration" leaned heavily upon the scientists and social scientists in Washington. The President's zeal to put everything on a businesslike, scientifically efficient basis thus gave unexpected importance to men versed in research. He wanted no traditional folderol to interfere with scientific management, although neither did he want science that failed to produce the formulae he anticipated. He objected, for example, to some of the monographs prepared by the Brookings Institute of Economics which, he contended, had cost the economy of the United States a million dollars yearly.[14] Yet he

14 *Washington Merry-go-Round*, pp. 10-33, 50, 85-87, 100-12, 262, 285; Longworth, *Crowded Hours*, pp. 313-17, 328-30, 336-37; interviews, especially Ralph W. M. Shoemaker of Georgetown, 1878-1961, and Edwin G. Nourse. See also Rowland Berthoff, "The American Social Order: A Conservative Hypothesis," *Am Hist Rev*, LXV, 499-514.

inaugurated during his first months in office the studies that culminated in the many-volumed *Recent Social Trends*, an invaluable detailed analysis of American resources and modes of life. In attempting to act upon his conviction that government was a task for specialists, he strengthened the position of the expert in Washington. Unwittingly he paved the way for the New Deal brain-trusters.

CHAPTER XVI

CIVIC CONSCIENCE, 1920-1929

A P H Y S I C A L L Y beautiful city in which some of the most interesting and many of the most talked-about people in the United States lived naturally had an aura of glamor. As the postwar depression lifted, well-to-do residents inclined to see little amiss in their surroundings. Life had its seamy side everywhere; that for several hundred Washington families there was no other side was an uncomfortable notion that only the sensitive conscience could entertain. And "the Hardboiled Era" did not encourage sensitivity. Philadelphia, Cleveland, Rochester, and several other cities, according to informed social workers, succeeded in maintaining a sense of community responsibility. But if a generations-old tradition of civic obligation enabled "Philadelphia gentlemen" to expand their philanthropies, and if the "quest for quality" similarly inspired Clevelanders and Rochesterians, in much of the United States the civic betterment movement of prewar days slowed or came to a halt. H. L. Mencken, once the high priest of the literary avant garde, struck a note congenial to many Americans disillusioned after the war: "If I am convinced of anything, it is that Doing Good is in bad taste."

Difficult as it was in other cities to enlist support for charities, let alone to arouse interest in the underlying causes of poverty and wretchedness, in Washington the problem was heightened by the steadily declining proportion of "old families," the group ordinarily readiest to acknowledge *noblesse oblige.* Householders who voted and paid taxes in other localities to which, often mistakenly, they expected to return were disinclined to concern themselves about Washington's well-being; that was a task for local citizens. Few of these, however, possessed large means; most of the fortunes in the city belonged to residents who considered themselves temporary. The constant turnover of intelligent people of widely varied experience, the very element that gave the capital much of its fascination, was a deterrent to the nurturing of civic spirit.

A more fundamental obstacle rested upon citizens' political impotence. A "city council" composed of outlanders who were rarely swayed by local wishes had to approve every measure involving public action or the spending of local taxes. As it happened, Congress during much of the 1920's was more responsive to District needs than at any time since 1906, but the necessity of begging for every constructive law and every appropriation still had a chilling effect upon the community. A life-time of participation in civic undertakings led one Washingtonian to aver in 1959 that from the moment Congress voted the first penny for a local project to the day when citizens could call its realization assured generally ran to five years.[1] But to get that first penny might take four or five years of patient persuasion, often took ten, and sometimes a full generation. The struggle for a municipal hospital and a home for feeble-minded children are cases in point. In other cities when local feeling ran strong about any needed service, elected municipal functionaries were prone to respond. Here when the nearly twenty-year-old campaign to rid the city of alley dwellings had reached fever-pitch in 1913, it took the death-bed plea of the President's wife to induce Congress to enact a law; and, because of the intervention of war, postwar exigencies, and the unacceptability of anything so radical as public housing, execution of the act of 1914 then had to wait another two decades. Small wonder that only the stoutest-hearted had the fortitude yearly to renew the welfare fight.

The sense of helplessness, moreover, blurred perceptions

[1] Minutes of the Board of Managers of the Associated Charities, 1921-1929, especially 11 Jun 1924, p. 4, 13 Oct 1925, p. 5, 13 Jan, 10 Mar, 12 May, 13 Oct 1926, *passim*, and 9 Mar 1927, pp. 1-3, typescript in possession of the Family and Child Services of Washington, D.C. (hereafter cited as Min As Ch); Mrs. Henry Grattan Doyle, statement at panel on Washington Problems held at the American University, April 1959.

about what welfare should encompass. Clevelanders, say, or Philadelphians could project an orderly scheme of community services, putting responsibility for matters of city-wide concern upon tax-supported agencies and leaving privately financed organizations to handle the rest. Washingtonians' inability to carry out a rational, comprehensive plan made its mere formulation an unrewarding exercise to be abandoned before seriously attempted. A clear over-all picture consequently did not emerge. Philanthropists, seeing only bits and pieces, focused their attention upon areas in which their efforts might count. Hence even while doubts mounted about the adequacy of private charity, the public-spirited tended still to look upon charity societies and church groups as the city's mainstay. Most Washington residents shrugged their shoulders.

Just as the Civil War destroyed long-established patterns of behavior and brought nearly two decades of confusion to the city, so World War I bequeathed to Washingtonians a nine-year legacy of bewilderment and apathy. The extent of community disorganization was not immediately evident. On the contrary, in 1920 several signs pointed to a strengthening of civic vitality. Intent upon keeping alive "the spirit of cooperation that characterized the communal life of Washington during the war period," a group of high-minded citizens first of all launched Community Services, Inc., with the purpose of opening neighborhood centers which, unlike the segregated units started in 1917 under school board aegis, whites and Negroes could enjoy together. Later in the year social workers in public and private agencies formed a bi-racial Council of Social Workers; it included employees of the police department, the Juvenile Court, the U.S. Public Health Service, the Visiting Nurse Association, the Associated Charities, the white and colored YMCA's, the NAACP, the Boy Scouts, Community Services, Inc., and half a dozen more. Members planned to exchange ideas and experiences over the lunch table and, in the process, improve race relations. As white restaurants would not serve Negroes, the first meeting took place at the Phyliss Wheatley colored YWCA. Shortly afterward, at the instigation of the energetic Mrs. Whitman Cross, laymen representing some twenty-five private charities, Protestant, Roman Catholic, Jewish, and non-sectarian, founded the Washington Council of Social Agencies to examine common problems, agree upon major objectives, and collaborate in achieving them. And in the last weeks of the Wilson administration, Vice President and Mrs. Thomas Marshall brought the secretary of the Boston Council of Social Agencies to Washington to draft a code of welfare laws for the District.[2] Each of these promising undertakings either collapsed completely within a matter of months or slid gradually into prolonged ineffectiveness.

The rift between the business community and do-gooders was partly responsible for that debacle. The split, first discernible about 1910, widened rapidly after the war. In 1920 businessmen who had been active participants in the civic betterment movement counted on seeing the prompt restoration of the old social order. Still smarting from accusations of war profiteering and indignant at the perpetuation of rent controls in the District, they wanted no further "socialistic" measures imposed upon the city. From conservatism a growing proportion of Board of Trade members soon swung into the ranks of reaction. With the Red Scare commanding newspaper headlines, Community Services, Inc., early became suspect. Despite the eminent respectability of its principal sponsors, it appeared to have the earmarks of a radical organization ready to back revolutionary changes. Since proponents of racially mixed recreational centers obviously must have left-wing leanings, a joint committee of the Board of Trade and the Chamber of

[2] *Rpt B/Tr*, 1920, pp. 199-210; Minutes, Council of Social Agencies, 14 Feb 1921, typescript in possession of Health and Welfare Council of the National Capital Area (hereafter cited as Min CSA); "The Hand of the Vice President," *Survey*, XLV, 621-23; Robert W. Kelso, "A Challenge," *ibid.*, XLVI, 151-53; *Bee*, 1 Jan 1921.

Commerce condemned the community center plan. Without the financial endorsement of businessmen the project could not survive, and after a flutter or two Community Services fell apart. When the Bostonian engaged by the Thomas Marshalls submitted his proposals for a District welfare code, the Board of Trades objected to his recommendations; a preoccupied Congress ignored them. Gauged by contributions to the Associated Charities, by 1925 the Board of Trade and the Chamber of Commerce had put themselves on record as having no interest in organized altruism; only 17 and 16 percent of their respective members subscribed to the charity fund, whereas 35 percent of Cosmos Club and Metropolitan Club members answered the appeal. The alienation of businessmen's sympathies was a severe blow to the cause of social welfare.

Faint uneasiness about the new professionalism of social workers for a time was a second, albeit minor, source of friction. Observable in other cities also, it was based upon belief that "social workers are . . . the worst sort of benevolent tyrant." The increasing emphasis upon case-work techniques and a psychiatric approach to social ills naturally bred in graduates of the new schools of social work a reluctance to use untrained help, and, as their assignments became more complex and time-consuming, their unwillingness to give the volunteer intensive training necessarily relegated the well-intentioned layman to a subsidiary role. Admirable and selfless though the aims of Washington's professionals were, in organizing the Council of Social Workers they set themselves apart from the volunteers whose support in the past had proved essential to the success of community undertakings. Here was a reversal of the course the Monday Evening Club had always followed. So far from strengthening cooperation, the new alignment threatened to erect fresh obstacles. The council, in actuality, early ceased to be a force of any kind, since a drifting away of white members within a year or two transformed the organization in essence into an ineffectual Negro body. Still, the feeling among lay members of charity boards that their services were unwanted except for money-raising weakened further an already thinning interest in civic and eleemosynary projects.

Certainly the decline of the Council of Social Agencies suggests a deepening sense of uselessness and defeatism among its directors. The monthly meetings during the first two years evoked some optimism: delegates examined the pros and cons of fund-raising through a community chest, drew up a list of the city's most pressing needs, and persuaded the District commissioners to borrow an expert from the Russell Sage Foundation to identify lacunae in services and assist a citizens' committee in drafting a public welfare code. But before the end of 1923 Newbold Noyes, son of Theodore and one of the few younger men to concern himself with civic matters, was voicing keen disappointment at the meagre attendance at council meetings. Colored delegates rarely came. Although the Associated Charities had two Negro districts, each headed by a trained colored worker, representatives of white philanthropies learned little about Negro needs, still less about Negro attempts to meet them. None of the twenty-eight objectives listed in 1921 and 1922 looked attainable without far more effort than the council's constituent organizations were supplying.[3]

The charity societies composing the Council of Social Agencies did not, it is true, embrace all volunteer groups intent on community service. The Washington Junior League and, under the guidance of Miss Mabel Boardman, the various corps of the American Red Cross Women's Volunteer Service undertook to direct Washington's yearly crop of debutantes into work helpful to the city. But the League, earnest as many of its officers were, had not yet fully evolved its training courses for "pro-

[3] *Rpt B/Tr*, 1921, pp. 50-51; Min As Ch, 8 Oct 1924, p. 6, 11 Mar 1925, p. 3; *Rpt B/Ch*, 1924, p. 2; *National Conference of Social Work*, 1929, p. 499; interview Col. Campbell C. Johnson; Min CSA, 1922-27, and Questionnaire of the Citizens' Chest Survey Committee, 1947, Appendix 5, "Résumé of Council Activities since 1923."

visional" members, and even thirty years later it would find itself unable wholly to escape the label of dilettantism attaching to any group in which membership hinged upon social position. The Red Cross corps, with their expensive uniforms and the faint air of aristocratic superiority with which Miss Boardman imbued them, fell even deeper into the category of very part-time ladies bountiful. For Miss Boardman, the quintessence of the Victorian lady, always immaculately and elegantly dressed, her hair coiffed in a Gibson-girl pompadour, looked upon professional social workers as a self-important, power-greedy lot most of whose duties intelligent society women could well handle as volunteers. Whether or not that thinly concealed hostility interposed difficulties, unquestionably the eighteen hours of service a year which the Volunteer Service stipulated was too little to have any perceptible effect upon Washington's welfare problems. Probably the chief value of both the Junior League and the Red Cross corps lay in preventing the total submergence of philanthropic impulses among young women caught up in the feverish gaieties of the Jazz Age.

Of more enduring importance was the work of the Voteless League of Women Voters of the District of Columbia. Made up initially of former campaigners for women suffrage, the Voteless League set itself to study legislation affecting the city. Because League committees made a point of sponsoring or opposing measures only after careful scrutiny, their recommendations were often slow to appear; but once they took form they represented an educated consensus. Members testified before congressional committees in behalf of stronger school attendance laws, mothers' pensions, minimum wages for women, and again and again for appropriations large enough to permit existing institutions to function efficiently. As members gained confidence with experience, they made League opinion count on every major issue.[4]

[4] Dulles, *American Red Cross*, pp. 238-41, 254-56; *A History of the League of Women Voters of the District of Columbia*, 1960.

Issues were all too numerous. A scathing article in the *Survey* entitled "Medieval Washington" described the primitive character of most of the city's services in 1923. A later study of the provisions for child welfare revealed that the facilities supported by private societies were by and large far less well managed than those in other cities. "The state of affairs in the public field," the specialist from the Russell Sage Foundation reported in 1924, "is illogical, wasteful, and intolerable, not only from the standpoint of the public which pays the bills but from the point-of-view of the neglected dependent clients whom this group of organically unrelated agencies and institutions attempts to serve." In the interim an open fight between the Board of Children's Guardians and the trustees of the Industrial Home School over placement of dependent children had brought on a congressional investigation. Although witnesses proved the Guardians guilty of highhandedness, testimony also showed that, in view of their limited funds and small staff, their record was surprisingly creditable. Nevertheless the hearings, the Russell Sage investigator's report, and the recommendations of the citizens' commission on a welfare code convinced Congress that a single board of public welfare should replace the three "organically unrelated" agencies, namely the Board of Charities, the Board of Children's Guardians, and the trustees of the Industrial Home School. The act went into effect in 1926.[5]

The centralization of responsibility for all public welfare and correctional institutions, except the National Training School for Boys, reduced the chances of friction with Congress and produced useful economies. The single, nine-man board appointed by the District commissioners and serving without com-

[5] Hart, *Child Welfare*, pp. 3-4, 22-23, 47-56, 102-03; Lundberg and Milburn, *Child Dependency*, p. 43; William Hodson, *Preliminary Report of the Commission on Public Welfare Legislation of the District of Columbia*; Mina C. Van Winkle, "Medieval Washington," *Survey*, L, 212-13; "They Guard the Past," *ibid.*, LI, 399-400, and *ibid.*, LII, 325; Jt Subcomee of S and H Dis Comees, 67C, 4S, Hrgs, "Investigation of the Bd of Children's Guardians," and 68C, 2S, Hrgs, "Establishment of a Board of Public Welfare in the D of C."

pensation included John Joy Edson, Mrs. Coralie Cook, and several others of recognized judgment and courage. The selection of George S. Wilson to head the staff was also a happy choice. With thirty years of experience, first with the Associated Charities and since 1900 as secretary of the Board of Charities, Wilson knew the city's problems intimately and how best to avoid administrative pitfalls. While he lacked breadth of imagination and seemed imperturbable in the face of miseries he could not end, he was far from indifferent to suffering. Hard-headed Scot that he was, he stood out against excessive cuts in the welfare budget. The District commissioners felt free, in their own phrase, to "leave it to George." In spite of closely trimmed appropriations, service to the needy and weak improved, and, in proportion as the welfare board did its job well, private charities were able to concentrate their efforts more narrowly. At the time no one objected to confining the public agency largely to the field of institutional care or foresaw that private philanthropy would stagger under an insupportable relief burden once depression struck.

Even in the flush 1920's serious gaps remained in the District's public welfare services. The Juvenile Court, still allowed only one judge at a salary a third smaller than that of other federal judges, needed expanded facilities and an administrative overhauling. Appropriations for the Board of Welfare were kept to a figure that meant an overworked staff paid at salaries below those offered in like-sized or smaller cities. Investigators for the Child Welfare division each carried at least 120 cases, twice the load recommended by professional organizations and considerably bigger than that customary elsewhere. The head of the division exhausted her energies in re-fighting the old battle against institutional care, instead of foster homes, for children. Public playground space, skimpy in 1920, fell far behind the growth in population, particularly in southwest Washington and in an area west of North Capital Street, already coming to be known as the "notorious second precinct." "Mildly" delinquent Negro boys were shoved into the overcrowded, shockingly ill-equipped Industrial Home School for Colored Children; delinquent small colored girls, if committed anywhere, had to go to the reform school intended for older Negro girls; no institution, public or private, would accept a Negro child under two years of age. Since Congress voted no money for inexpensive public housing, the Alley Dwelling Act of 1914 remained a dead letter; some 8,000 people, mostly Negro, continued to inhabit the alley slums.

Public health services taken for granted in most American cities were few in Washington and badly staffed before 1929. The tuberculosis hospital, twenty years earlier a source of community pride, was not only over-crowded but had a long waiting list and a woefully small corps of nurses and attendants. While the opening of a psychiatric ward in 1923 in the partly built Gallinger municipal hospital relieved some of the city's medical needs, until 1929 the old Asylum hospital had to suffice for general care, and only the generosity of Mrs. Anne Archbold provided the hospital with small, occupational therapy and social welfare departments. Fortunately the completion of Gallinger in 1930 gave the city a well-equipped, adequately staffed municipal hospital before the depression took its toll of public health.[6]

The basic weakness of the District's welfare system was its stress upon treatment rather than prevention. Like public administrators, the managers of the Associated Charities, the main source of direct relief to needy families, generally perceived the shortcomings of the finger-in-the-dike method of dealing with want. In 1928 a careful study showed that, of the $2,500,000 Washington raised for private charities, $1,269,000 was spent by hospitals for the cure of disease, $50,000 for pre-

[6] *Rpt B/Ch*, 1926, pp. xiv, 1-3, 91, 94; *Annual Report of the Board of Public Welfare*, 1929, pp. 3, 19, 1930, pp. 3, 88 (hereafter cited as *Rpt B/PW*); Lundberg and Milburn, *Child Dependency*, pp. 81-82.

vention, $270,000 for child welfare work, and $32,550 for handling juvenile delinquency. But to forestall poverty and despair born of periodic or chronic unemployment, of wages too small to support a family, of bodily illness, desertion, or death of the wage-earner—to name only the most frequent causes of destitution—demanded far-reaching social reforms that professional social workers could not initiate, conservative local citizens were loath to embrace, and more daring Washingtonians felt sure this bi-racial community would not support. In the earlier years of the century, when Washington was smaller and less heterogeneous, laymen such as John Joy Edson, S. W. Woodward, and B. Pickman Mann, together with professionals such as Charles Weller, Walter Ufford, and George Kober, had constantly sought ways of eradicating the underlying causes of social ills. Congressional inaction had blocked their programs. By the mid-twenties Weller had long been gone; Woodward and Mann were dead; Edson, Ufford, and Kober were old and tired. In the next decade women would gradually show initiative, but in the 1920's Mrs. Cross, the frail septuagenarian Mrs. Archibald Hopkins, and the other valiant fighters were handicapped by their sex, and the Voteless League of Women Voters supported but did not originate constructive proposals. Vigorous wide-ranging civic leadership had thus largely vanished.[7]

Whereas a considerable body of liberal local opinion before the war had urged social legislation upon unwilling congresses, in the 1920's successive congresses were ready to go further than was most of the articulate local public, especially the business community. As the decade wore on, the Monday Evening Club itself, once the advocate of measures so sweeping as to win it a reputation for dangerous radicalism, showed only lukewarm

[7] *Prelim Rpt Comee of 100 on the Federal City*, p. 60; *Survey*, LI, 387-88; *Rpt B/Ch*, 1923, pp. 6, 100, 1924; Min As Ch, 45th Anniversary Meeting, 22 Mar, and 12 Apr 1926, 14 May 1928; *Rpt B/PW*, 1927, pp. 6, 53-54, 56, 1929, pp. 19, 73; *Star*, 3 Mar 1926.

interest in new approaches to social problems. In 1920 Congress enacted a District minimum wage law for women, an act hailed by social workers throughout the country as a great forward step. The District Merchants' and Manufacturers' Association, which in 1917 and 1918 had endorsed the scheme, now protested at its application to mercantile establishments; and, ironically enough, it was a suit brought by the trustees of the Children's Hospital, Washington's most popular and widely supported private charity, that ended in the famous *Adkins* v. *Children's Hospital* decision declaring the minimum wage law unconstitutional. When Congress passed a District workmen's compensation act in 1928, the Board of Trade objected to its terms, although the obligations put upon employers were moderate compared to the provisions of some state laws.

In actuality the social legislation passed in the 1920's for the District of Columbia merely paralleled that already in force in many states: a new, more comprehensive child labor law and a strengthened compulsory education law, expansion of the school nursing corps and free dental and medical inspection clinics in connection with the public school system, and, perhaps most significant of all, a mother's pension act such as B. Pickman Mann had recommended in 1914. Furthermore, Congress voted appropriations for an institution for the feeble-minded and for a receiving home for children who were under Juvenile Court surveillance but not yet assigned to foster homes or institutions. If the larger proportion of representation for urbanized areas in House and Senate partly explained the changed temper of Congress, the social vision of the senators and representatives who held key positions on the District committees and appropriations subcommittee was more directly responsible. They were the same men who backed the National Capital Park and Planning Commission; they acted upon the principle Frederic A. Delano enunciated in 1924, that "in our desire to make the city *beautiful* we do not forget the multifarious needs of our population." The backsliding in popular local support presumably stemmed not only from the pervasive hedonism of the period and an accompanying disbelief in the reality of want in the midst of plenty, but also from large taxpayers' irritation at having Congress put new expenses upon them while it cut the federal share in District appropriations from 40 percent to 27 percent or less; if men on the Hill wanted to recast the District's social structure, let the Treasury help pay for it.[8]

The civic irresponsibility visible in Washington's affluent society troubled only a small group. Except where death had thinned its ranks, its nucleus was still the handful of men and women who from Charles Weller's day onward had led the fight to make the capital an ideal city. In the disorganized community of the 1920's public opinion was no longer a force in recruiting members of the younger generation. Chance brought Coleman Jennings into the struggle. A gay young bachelor about town, he had been oblivious to the city's problems until after his father's death, when Walter Ufford, a friend and admirer of the selfless older Jennings, gave the grief-stricken son a subscription to the *Survey* in his father's memory. Touched by that kindness, the young man began dipping into the journal. It opened his eyes to conditions he had not believed possible, led him to follow in his father's philanthropic footsteps, and brought him into close touch with the work of the Associated Charities. Together with a few contemporaries, notably Charles Carroll Glover, Newbold Noyes, and the somewhat older Edward Graham, Jennings threw himself into the task of awakening Washingtonians to the city's plight.

Although the 511 families on the Associated Charities' relief

---

[8] *Monday Evening Club Yearbook*, 1930; *Rpts B/Tr*, 1921, p. 62, 1926, p. 63, 1927; "District Minimum Wage Law," *Survey*, XLVI, 425, and XLVIII, 537; Florence Kelly, "Is the Minimum Wage Unconstitutional?" *ibid.*, L, 74; "The Fifteenth Compensation Law," *ibid.*, LX, 427; Elizabeth Brandeis, "Mercantile Wages in the District of Columbia," *Monthly Labor Review*, XV, 343-44; "Child Labor Law of the District of Columbia," *ibid.*, XXVII, 66-68; *Rpt B/PW*, 1927, p. 5, 1929, p. 3; Comrs Rpt, 1927, p. 2, 1928, p. 41; *Civic Comment*, No. 8, pp. 4-5.

rolls in 1927 represented only a small fraction of the District's 450,000 inhabitants, the fact remained that the help available to the destitute was always too little—generally half to a third less per capita than the sums spent in other cities. Furthermore, calls for direct financial aid were steadily mounting, in spite of Washington's outer mien of material abundance. While the Catholic Charities, organized in 1921, attempted to assist all Catholic applicants, and the Hebrew charities, as for years past, assumed responsibility for needy Jewish families, in a decade during which population increased about 30 percent and the cost of living about 18, Associated Charities' expenditures for direct relief more than tripled. The implications for the future were disturbing. But to persuade people secure in their own comfortable world to accept and ponder such unpleasant facts was hard at best and made immeasurably harder by the reluctance of white citizens to give any serious thought to colored Washington where want was concentrated. Unimaginative residents of white neighborhoods preferred not to hear anything about Negroes. And even the kindly disposed white who ventured into an impoverished solidly black area was likely to feel oppressed by its strange alien quality and shrink from taking any responsibility for improving it.[9]

In 1920 and early 1921 racial toleration had seemed to be regaining some of the headway lost after the Reconstruction era. Whether, as some colored men believed, Negroes' resistance to aggression at the time of the race riot of 1919 had won them grudging respect from whites and thus laid the basis of understanding, or whether the earnest endeavors of social workers before the war had at last begun to bear fruit, a new spirit of friendliness had appeared in the bi-racial Community Services and Council of Social Workers. Republican campaign promises

[9] Min CSA, 1921-29; Min As Ch, Joint Meeting with Citizens Relief Association, 12 May 1926, pp. 5-6, 13 Oct 1926, p. 3, 9 Mar 1927, pp. 1-3, 7, and 52nd Anniversary Meeting, 26 Feb 1934, pp. 2-4; interview Coleman Jennings; Douglas, *Real Wages*, p. 377.

and President Harding's inaugural speech had further encouraged hopes for a gradual revival of the attitudes of the early 1870's when, outside the schools and most of the churches, segregation had hardly existed at all. Those hopes were short-lived. By 1922 white acceptance of racial discrimination as a fact of life in the capital had become nearly universal. Some northerners doubtless deplored the consequences—the needless hurt to the pride of a distinguished colored man, the lack of care provided for the small Negro orphan, the persistent stifling of Negro ambition—but they, like native southerners, apparently thought the existing social order immutable.

If bootleggers and other elements of the underworld ignored color lines, the only places in the rest of the city where racial segregation did not obtain were on the trolleys and buses, at the Griffith Stadium, and in the reading rooms of the public library and the Library of Congress. When one of the "Senators" knocked out a home-run, white and black rooters in the stadium bleachers delightedly slapped each other on the back and together discussed the team's prospects. Although no colored player was allowed on the team, when Washington won the pennant in 1924, the *Daily American* wrote: "Long live King Baseball, the only monarch who recognizes no color line." In the libraries, Negroes might read and study in peace alongside whites, a circumstance, a Washington-born Negro scholar recalled, that alone had prevented his pursuing the path of a Richard Wright in his hatred of all white America.

Had the ratio of Negro to white inhabitants risen sharply during and after the war, the tightening of segregation in Washington might be easier to explain. Between 1910 and 1920 Chicago's and Detroit's colored populations had grown respectively nearly seven and six times as fast as their white, and the change had been only less pronounced in four or five other northern cities. All of them confronted an unfamiliar social and economic problem. For Washington a large Negro population was no novelty. Here, moreover, the proportion of Negroes to whites had dropped in a decade from the 28.5 percent of 1910 to 25.1, and, with the exception of 1920, the 27.1 percent of 1930 was below the figure shown in any census since the Civil War. White fears of being swamped in a black metropolis therefore had less validity than formerly. But Negroes' slightly improved economic position threatened to lessen the supply of cheap domestic and unskilled labor and, more important, by enlarging the Negro middle class, jeopardized the social status of lower class whites. Seemingly the best way for whites to minimize their discomfiture was to build an invisible wall about all colored Washington and then to forget about the inhabitants of that Secret City.[10]

Probably that walling off helped reduce overt white hostility to colored people. Certainly open friction tended to die down as Negro militance, weakened by frustration and fatigue, subsided. Negro crime and its obverse, police brutality, netted relatively scant space in the newspapers. The white press in 1922 allotted only two or three lines to the "silent parade" of 1,500 Negroes in wordless protest against southern lynchings, but the organization of a local Ku Klux Klan also failed to make a stir in the white city. While the showy parade of National Klansmen led by the Grand Kleagle and the exercises held on the Monument grounds in July 1925 caused the Negro community anxiety, white onlookers regarded the performance as merely a variation of the Shriners' convention held three years before. No white newspaper suggested any impropriety in permitting a formal gathering of the Klan in the capital. White Washington simply ignored Negroes as long as they did not get under foot.

Much of official Washington in November 1921 had watched Marshal Foch receive an honorary degree from Howard Uni-

[10] *Washington Daily American*, 9 Oct 1924, 13 Oct 1925; *Fifteenth Rpt NAACP*, 1924, pp. 21-23; Louise V. Kennedy, *The Negro Peasant Turns Cityward*, p. 34.

versity, "while scores of veterans of colored regiments who had served under the French military leader in the World War stood at attention." But the impressive ceremony had not inspired President Harding to appoint colored men to office. A year after his inauguration only three had received posts of any consequence; Negroes in civil service jobs were more fully segregated and all Negroes more rigidly excluded from the city's public recreational facilities than during the Wilson regime. Full realization of the situation came at the dedication of the Lincoln Memorial on Decoration Day in 1922. Dr. Robert Moten, president of Tuskegee Institute, had been invited to speak at the unveiling of the bronze of the Great Emancipator, but, instead of being placed on the speaker's platform, he was relegated along with other distinguished colored people to an all-Negro section separated by a road from the rest of the audience; and the language of the ill-tempered Marine who herded the "niggers" into their seats caused well-bred colored people as much indignation as the segregated seating itself. Chief Justice Taft's later explanation that the arrangement had not had official sanction failed to modify colored Washington's view: no Negro could hope to be treated as a full-fledged American citizen as long as the White House, Congress, and the overwhelming majority of the city's white residents looked upon him as a creature apart and inferior.[11]

That state of affairs underwent little change under the two succeeding Presidents. Only three colored men received desirable posts from Coolidge or Hoover, and one of those appointees, James Cobb, merely succeeded to the municipal judgeship that Robert Terrell held till his death. The federal commissioner of buildings and grounds who attempted to segregate the picnic places in Rock Creek Park and who sanctioned the Ku Klux Klan gathering on public property met with only one rebuke: when

[11] *Tribune*, 21 May, 25 Jun, 16 Jul 1921, 18 Feb, 27 May, 10, 13, 17 Jun 1922, 24 Jan, 14 Apr 1923; *Herald*, 9, 25 Jan, 16 Jul 1923; 4 Dec 1924; *Star*, 17 Nov 1921.

328

he barred Negroes from the public bathing beach at the Tidal Basin, Representative Martin Madden of Illinois, chairman of the House Committee on Appropriations, indignantly insisted that Congress cut off funds and close the beach altogether. At the end of 1926 the *Tribune*, by then Washington's principal colored newspaper, declared that segregation had "grown to the dimensions of a national policy." As a working arrangement it was in full force in the government departments, and "it remains only to observe that the Negroes themselves have about reached the stage of acquiescence in the practise." Colored civil service employees, fearful of losing their jobs, refused to lodge complaints, leaving NAACP officials without provable grounds for protest. The major gratification the colored intelligentsia had that year was the Howard University trustees' selection of a Negro president, Mordecai Johnson.

Uneasiness lest an organized Negro vote in the northern states put Al Smith into the White House led to a slight relaxation of departmental segregation rules in 1928, but civil service policies did not change. The Department of Labor published statistics contrasting the number of the government's Negro employees in 1928 and 1910: some 51,880 at salaries totalling nearly $64,484,000 compared to fewer than 23,000 paid less than $12,456,000. The *Crisis* promptly noted that laborers, charwomen, and messengers, earning on the average $1,243 a year, still made up the bulk of the list; well-paid jobs for Negroes were actually fewer than in 1910. When Oscar De Priest of Chicago was elected to the House of Representatives, colored morale rose a little; and it rose higher when Mrs. Hoover invited his wife to a White House reception with a small, carefully chosen group of other congressional wives. But otherwise the first Negro to be elected to Congress in twenty-five years could do little for the local community. In 1929 when at long last a published code of laws for the District of Columbia appeared, it did not mention the sixty-year-old ordinances and the territorial acts prohibiting racial discrimination, although those had never been repealed or declared unconstitutional. The NAACP's drive that stopped Senate confirmation of Judge Parker of North Carolina as an Associate Justice of the Supreme Court seemed to colored Washington a negative triumph, at best a block to new inroads upon civil rights.[12]

Outraged as were Washington's upper-class Negroes at segregated seating at concerts where Negro singers as famous as Roland Hayes performed, they regarded housing restrictions as peculiarly invidious. In 1926 the District Supreme Court upheld the legality of voluntary covenants among white property-owners aimed at preventing Negroes from purchasing or occupying houses in white neighborhoods. The battle against restrictive municipal ordinances had been won before the war; now voluntary compacts seemingly negated that victory and threatened to confine all Negroes to a true ghetto. As whites endorsing the covenants displayed as much passion as the Negroes who sought to halt them, ill-will between the races grew. Kelly Miller, professor of sociology at Howard University, contended that since white people were determined to prevent racial intermarriage, the "destiny of the Negro population in large cities is clearly foreshadowed. The Negro is to live and move and have his social being in areas apart from the whites." Yet, as Miller himself pointed out, tempting offers from colored men sometimes overcame white resistance: only a year after the Supreme Court verdict the "very block that was the subject of the test case in Washington is now occupied by negroes, in uncontested tenancy, although the court decision forbids persons of negro blood to buy or live in that block for a period of twenty-one years." Long afterward, Campbell C. Johnson, in the 1920's secretary of the colored YMCA, looked back upon

[12] *Tribune*, 2 Jul, 31 Dec 1926, 25 Jan, 14 Jun 1929; *Crisis*, xxxv, 337, 369-87, 418, 427, xxxvi, 298-99; Walter A. White, *A Man Called White*, pp. 110-11; Indritz, "Post Civil War Ordinances," *Georgetown Law Journal*, xlii, 201; William H. Jones, *Recreation and Amusements among Negroes in Washington.*

the fight against residential segregation as a constructive move, for the men who sued for their right to live wherever they could afford raised a banner around which other colored Washingtonians gathered; and when the court ruling made further litigation useless, their continued efforts to stop the spread of restrictive covenants contributed to reviving self-respect.[13]

If the housing controversy rekindled the sparks of racial pride, the embers had burned too low since 1921 to burst quickly into flame. Furthermore, as the covenants affected only well-to-do Negroes, the conflict did not reawaken in Washington's high yellow society its wartime zeal to "close ranks" with its social inferiors. On the contrary, civic-minded Negroes encountered among their educated fellows the same kind of indifference to the welfare of the black masses as public-spirited white people met with in high white society. By 1926 the Washington NAACP was no longer powerful. Some Negroes thought it too radical, others too conservative and too prone to appease; a good many gave it no thought at all. With a few rare exceptions, young men upon whom leadership might logically have fallen lacked the will or had lost faith in their capacity to win a respected place for their people. Negro real estate brokers and firms building Negro apartment houses made some money, and the National Life Insurance Company with three hundred employees in its home office on U Street paid a 10 percent dividend in 1928, but confidence in other Negro enterprises waned. When a Harvard graduate, after a distinguished but heart-breaking career in the AEF, became a convert to the necessity of never-ending Negro militance, he started the *Washington Daily American*, the second Negro daily in the United States; despite

[13] *Crisis*, XXVIII, 271-72, XXIX, 19, 27; *Tribune*, 1 Nov 1924, 9, 16 May 1925, 8 Jan 1926, 2, 9 Mar 1928, 18 Jan, 25 Oct 1929; Kelly Miller, "The Causes of Segregation," and Herbert J. Seligman, "The Negro Protest against Ghetto Conditions," *Current History*, XXV, 827-33; William H. Jones, *The Housing of Negroes in Washington, D.C.*; Bernard H. Nelson, *The Fourteenth Amendment and the Negro since 1920*, pp. 23, 31, 34; interview, Col. Johnson; "Housing of Negroes in Washington, D.C.," *Monthly Labor Review*, XXX, 972.

its excellence, the paper was unable to get enough advertising to survive. The *Tribune* absorbed it. Between the lines of newspaper exhortations to "buy Negro," give to Negro charities, and build up a self-sufficient community ran hints that calls for racial solidarity fell on deaf ears.

Upper-class families, tired of making common cause with needy blacks, washed their hands of every group but their own. Lightness of color was necessarily a bond, for where light-skinned people could move about in a white world with some freedom, the acceptance of a dark-skinned person into the group circumscribed the activities of all. It was a fact of life white people never had to face. Whites prone to think Negro social distinctions absurd lost sight of the obvious truth that the cultivated Negro had no more in common with the lower-class black than the white society leader with the white ditch-digger. The creed of the high yellow elite ran: let the uninformed masses applaud Marcus Garvey, "the Black Moses," or gather adoringly about "Papa Divine." Let the vulgar loaf on 7th Street, that "bastard of Prohibition and the War," where, sang Jean Toomer,

> Money burns the pocket, pocket hurts,
> Bootleggers in silken shirts,
> Ballooned, zooming Cadillacs,
> Whizzing, whizzing down the streetcar tracks.

All that need not touch the aristocracy. The very light-colored group, on the other hand, was frequently involved with "passing." Former associates of the person who chose to pass were at pains not to betray him; his success rarely provoked resentment: the joke after all was on the white folks. Morality was in no way involved. Tacit agreement among old friends decreed that each must decide what was right for himself. Passing was so common in the twenties that the National Theatre employed a black door man to spot and bounce intruders whose racial origins were undetectable by whites. And no Negro despised the door

man for earning his living in that fashion; a job was a job.[14]
Still, passing tended to disrupt the solidarity of the top level of
Washington's colored world.

Washington during most of the 1920's was thus more nearly
a geographic expression than a community. In addition to the
rigorously maintained separateness of whites and Negroes in
every lawful walk of life, seemingly unbridgeable gulfs yawned
between class and class, between clique and clique, and between
cave-dwellers and upstarts in both white and colored Washington. Self-styled Christians disliked association with Jews;
Jews were wary of Gentiles. Some 70,000 white men, so the
A.F.ofL. stated, were union members in good standing, but,
in this non-industrial city, working men's problems had no
reality for businessmen, politicians, and civil service employees.
Here labor meant the building trades whose walking delegates
dealt with contractors. The rumblings of trouble in the rest of
the country over wage-earners' pay rates, hours, and the occasional timid proposals for unemployment insurance sounded
faint in the District of Columbia. And, as always, a subtly
divisive factor was the uncertainty about who was a Washingtonian and therefore responsible for developing community
feeling, if indeed it were worth striving for. How so disorganized a city could achieve any sense of common purpose borders
on a historical mystery. Yet in 1928 the miracle began to take
form.

The awakening was primarily the cumulative result of the
patient campaign conducted by the remnants of the old guard
of the civic betterment movement and its few younger converts.
Little by little they convinced some of their neighbors that the
city's ills were not imaginary and that only a concerted attack
upon them could provide a remedy. A slowly growing realiza-

[14] *Tribune*, 11 Apr 1925, 12 Aug, 30 Dec 1927, 18 Jan, 9, 30 Mar
1928, 1, 25 Nov 1929; *Crisis*, XXXI, 11-16, XXXIII, 186-87, XXXIV, 193,
212, 224; Eugene Davidson, *Black Boy on a Raft*; interview Eugene Davidson; Jean Toomer, *Cane*, p. 71; Caleb Johnson, "Crossing the Color Line,"
Outlook, CLVIII, 526-57.

tion that everyone, not merely the poverty-stricken, benefitted wherever a neighborhood spirit could be nursed into life also had some effect, as the community centers under school board direction came into wider use for amateur theatricals and other group pastimes. Possibly the sheer passage of time brought about a desire for unity among people living in geographical propinquity. Whatever the reason, a nascent revival of community consciousness began to emerge in 1928. Although overburdened professional social workers made no attempt to teach classes of volunteers, laymen set themselves to examining problems they had long ignored or never thought about. If they were useless as case-workers, they could at least raise money. The Board of Trade, determined to have business efficiency directing enthusiasm, engaged Elwood Street, an experienced fund-raiser from St. Louis, to organize a Community Chest in Washington.

The effect of Street's arrival and the announcement of his plan of action was electrical. To the dismay of lily-whites, he stated that this must be a united effort of the entire city, not of white Washington working apart from colored Washington; representatives of both races must meet and participate as equals. Accordingly at the initial organizing luncheon, for the first time in the memory of most people present, prominent white Washingtonians sat at the table alongside leading colored Washingtonians. No one protested then or later. That in itself gave the undertaking an element of drama. Frederic Delano accepted the presidency of the Chest, Kelly Miller the vice presidency. Equally valuable in creating a sense of common purpose as preparations moved forward was the exchange of information that went on week after week among organizations anxious to join the Chest. The benefits of that give-and-take, far in excess of anything the Council of Social Agencies had achieved, long outlasted the fund-raising campaign. In a fashion perhaps incomprehensible to cities where periodic political campaigns gave electorates a common albeit hydra-headed

17. President Wilson addressing Congress, April 2, 1917, to ask for a declaration of war

18. War workers' dormitories under construction in the Union Station Plaza, October 1918

19. Eminent Washingtonians: top (left to right) Gardiner Hubbard, John Joy Edson, Librarian of Congress Herbert

Putnam; center, Commis Louis Brownlow; bottom to right) Archibald G Mary Church Terrell, fessor Kelly Mille

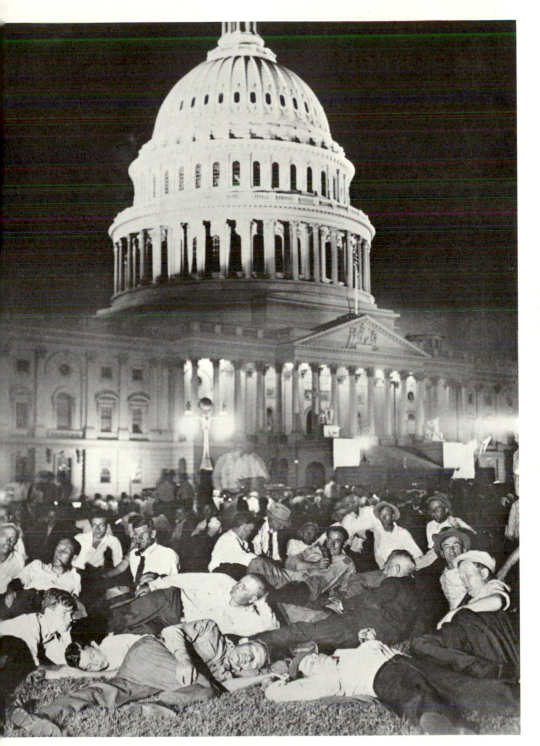

20. Bonus Army on the Capitol grounds, 1932

21. General Glassford inspecting Camp Marks

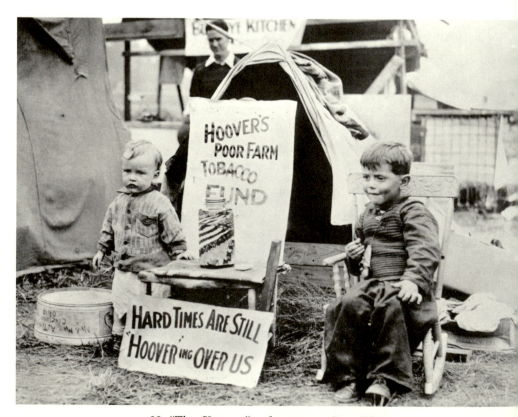

22. "Tiny Veterans" and posters at Camp Marks

23. Ku Klux Klan Parade, 1925

24. The Elder Lightfoot Michaux baptizing his sheep in water from the River Jordan, ca. 1938

25. Alley dwellings near the Capitol in Dingman Place, where four-room tenements with outdoor water taps and privies rented at about $15 a month each

26. Schott's Alley with the Senate Office Building in the background

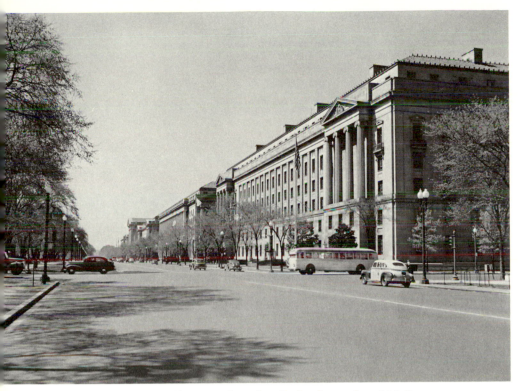

27. Federal triangle, looking west along Constitution Avenue from 10th Street

28. At the zoo

29. National Symphony Orchestra Concert at the Watergate, 1938

30. Art show in Lafayette Square, ca. 1938

interest, Washington found herself for the first time in more than half a century absorbed by a single community objective. Temporary residents joined with natives in the fund-raising. Although the first drive did not quite go over the top, the heady discovery that the city could unite even briefly was exhilarating.

The change, to be sure, was neither so sudden nor so profound as ill-informed optimists believed. Years of work by a dedicated few had prepared the way. The Associated Charities and the Council of Social Agencies from 1921 onward had maintained a narrow, somewhat insubstantial bridge between white and colored Washington; individuals had tried to widen it. In December 1928 two hundred delegates representing some eighteen social service and interracial organizations throughout the country met in Washington under the sponsorship of the Social Science Research Council to discuss the statistical data assembled on race relations by Graham Taylor of Chicago and Charles S. Johnson of Fisk University, but the sessions had ended without producing any positive scheme of action. In 1929 the managers of the Associated Charities were still not ready to act upon the long-debated proposal to elect Negroes to the board. Although the Washington Federation of Churches in 1927 had commissioned William H. Jones, a young colored sociologist, to prepare a study of that most controversial problem, Negro housing, the federation rejected the arguments of Canon Anson Phelps Stokes of the National Cathedral, Richard W. Brooks, Negro pastor of the Lincoln Congregational Church, William Jernegin of the Fifteenth Street Colored Presbyterian Church, and some eleven other ministers of both races urging the admission of colored churches to membership. At the gala dinner held at the Mayflower Hotel to wind up the first Community Chest campaign, Elwood Street bowed to local mores: Kelly Miller did not dine with his white associates but, accompanied by Mrs. Street, came in afterward to make his report. The Community Chest scored its chief triumph in pricking the conscience of white people and arousing in colored people a deeper interest in Negro charities, but the immediate effect of the campaign on interracial collaboration was slight.[15]

Too many white people merely displayed condescension in new form, marvelling at their own broadmindedness in recognizing human attributes in the Negro. That he might respond to the question "What do colored people want?" with the blunt answer "Get out of our way" was an idea well-meaning whites could not yet grasp. Six months after the first Chest drive ended, Richard Brooks summarized Washington's situation as he saw it: economic conditions were uncertain, morals "blatantly corrupt," and race relations marked by more mutual ill-will than ever.[16] Yet thirty years later wise men, both white and colored, averred that the launching of the Community Chest was a turning point; from that moment the gulf between the races began to close, and the end of the 1950's would find Washington more nearly genuinely integrated than any big city in the country.

[15] Min CSA, 14 May 1928 to 11 Nov 1929; Min As Ch, 1928-30; "Street Accepts the Challenge," *Survey*, LX, 507; "Local and National," *ibid.*, LXI, 429; William H. Jones, *Housing of Negroes*, Preface; *Tribune*, 18 Oct, 1 Nov 1929; *American Journal of Sociology*, XXXV, 902.
[16] *Tribune*, 15 Nov 1929.

CHAPTER XVII

THE ROLE OF THE PUBLIC SCHOOLS,
1920-1941

ODDLY enough, amid the disintegrative forces at work in the city of the 1920's, interest in the public schools survived to provide a bond among Washington's disparate elements—"oddly," because the school system itself was dual, because citizens had no real control over it, and because the good private schools in the city might well have diverted the attention of well-to-do parents from public to private education. The depth and enlightened nature of concern, it is true, varied from time to time and from social class to social class, but the remarkable fact is that, sophisticated or naïve, wealthy or financially hard pressed, Washingtonians continued to keep a hawk-like watch over public school developments.[1] Although that watchfulness often produced scanty results, it probably prevented the further erosion of community feeling by perpetuating in one realm a sense of common purpose. It even transcended the color line, separate though the white schools were from the Negro. Consensus about how to reach the common goal was as rare as concepts were various about what constituted an ideal school, but unanimity endured for more than a decade about the over-all civic objective: to secure for Washington the best system of public education human wisdom could devise. That the intensity of interest waned in the mid-thirties may be attributed partly to premature belief in a victory already assured, but was probably also a consequence of a draining of community vitality as national affairs submerged local.

A good many American communities, the federal Commis-

[1] See the comments of the committee on schools in *Rpts B/Tr*, 1920-1930, and the lists of contributors to school projects in "School Achievements in Ten Years, July 1, 1920 to June 30, 1930," *Rpt B/Ed*, 1930, pp. 83-84 (hereafter cited as "School Achievements," 1930).

sioner of Education had implied in 1910, had come to take their public schools for granted. A statistical sampling he presented that year indicated that more than half the students enrolled in normal schools came from families in the middle and upper economic brackets of society and hence, inferentially, from home environments friendly to "that culture which should characterize the teacher." But, the commissioner warned, unless school boards raised teachers' salaries above the average of $57 a month and insisted upon better professional training, the standards of public education would sink below a level already "lamentable" in a number of towns and cities. Whether meagre pay and an accompanying loss of social standing did notably lessen the calibre of public school teaching in the course of the next generation is not susceptible of proof; that the public believed that a decline set in is clear from the chorus of dismay which arose with the discovery in the 1920's that gifted college graduates were no longer willing to embark upon school-teaching careers.[2] Some later comments suggested that the post-1910 proliferation of state requirements of courses in methodology preliminary to teacher certification, so far from raising standards, acted as a deterrent in the recruitment of able candidates. In most big cities, furthermore, as the impersonality of metropolitan life spread, tenuous evidence pointed to a loss of close collaboration between parents and teachers; the former tended to consider their responsibility ended where that of the latter began—at the school threshold. Wherever that change occurred, school questions took on meaning to the rank and file of citizens only when a crisis led them to conclude that they were paying a high price for an inferior brand of education for their children. In Washington that kind of inattention to the school system had not existed since the early 1870's.

From 1874 onward District citizens had had little say about school policies, and still less about expenditures. The Organic

    [2] *Report, U.S. Commissioner of Education*, 1910, II, xxvi, 677; Bureau of Education, *Biennial Survey of Education*, 1920, p. 50.

Acts of 1874 and 1878 forbade bond issues; schoolhouse building, like all other public projects, stood on a pay-as-you-go basis; Congress fixed every detail of the budget. In 1900 the Board of Education won the right to choose the superintendent and the white and the colored assistant superintendents, and in 1906 a new law vested in the judges of the District's Supreme Court the appointment of the board's nine members, by custom, six white and three colored. But while the board thereafter set educational policies within budgetary limitations, its executive authority remained slight. Private citizens had no direct power at all. Yet their impassioned protests over any suspected neglect of the schools had had effect more than once. The reorganizations of 1900 and 1906 had grown out of popular demand for administrative changes. Over the years, despite the legal handicaps of the District's voteless residents, they had exerted enough influence to give some substance to their belief that the schools were their creation.

Although the city was the headquarters of the federal Office of Education, the National Education Association, and, after 1919, the American Council on Education, nothing suggests that Washingtonians as a whole were more knowledgeable than other Americans about curricula, teaching methods, physical plant and equipment, or the intangibles calculated to give every child a chance to develop his potentialities to the utmost. Nevertheless here parents, childless taxpayers, teachers, administrators, and clerks, all had opinions on these subjects. Perhaps financial impotence intensified interest, for as long as Congress decreed how much local tax money should go for any purpose, everyone could indulge in sensible or crack-pot suggestions without risking the consequence of having them put to the test. More probably criticisms of the school system in curious fashion served as an outlet for civic impulses that in other cities found expression in local politics.

Pride in what they had accomplished reinforced Washingtonians' proprietary attitude toward the public schools. Thanks to Superintendent William Bramwell Powell, at the opening of the twentieth century the capital's schools had attained an excellence that justified pride. Powell's three immediate successors had undertaken few significant changes except for emphasizing vocational training, a development that Congress had encouraged by appropriating money to build the white McKinley Technical High School and the colored Armstrong High School in 1902 and to enlarge the former in 1912. While fuming about congressional parsimony that severely limited new schoolhouse construction and necessitated half-day sessions in many elementary grades, parents and members of the Board of Education had on the whole continued to feel satisfied. Parents who would have preferred to forego private schooling for their small children sometimes had succumbed because of the doubling up in the public school primary grades, but in the higher grades patronage of private schools dropped rapidly. Teaching was reportedly unusually good at the long-established coeducational Sidwell Friends School, the much younger St. Alban's Episcopal School for boys, and the well-staffed expensive boarding- and day-schools such as the Convent of the Visitation, Miss Madeira's and the National Cathedral School for girls, but the number of local children enrolled in private schools had remained small.[3] In the 1950's old Washingtonians in looking back on the years before World War I would insist that "everybody went to the public schools in those days."

Colored people, to be sure, resented an arrangement whereby their children not infrequently were accommodated in somewhat dilapidated school-houses which, originally built for whites, were converted to Negro use when population shifts changed the racial character of neighborhoods. In fact, Washington Negroes looked upon the entire system as more separate than

[3] *Rpts B/Ed*, 1902-1914. Tables in the *Biennial Survey* show year after year that private school enrollments, including parochial schools, declined progressively above the primary grades.

equal, but that very fact heightened their gratification over the achievements of their own schools. They faced little competition from private or parochial schools. At the M Street High School, the principal, Dr. Winfield Scott Montgomery, a Phi Beta Kappa of the class of 1878 at Dartmouth, had gathered together an extraordinarily inspired and inspiring group of teachers; before 1916 scores of their students had gone on to Howard University or to good northern colleges and thence in some cases to pursue professional careers. No other single colored school in the country had turned out so many promising graduates. Ambitious Negro families occasionally had moved to Washington solely to enable their children to attend there. The Paul Dunbar High School, which replaced it in 1916, had also made its mark. While elementary schools had a less outstanding record, performance had at least equalled that in any other city that maintained a racially segregated system.[4] For two generations pride in the schools had gone further than any other social force in cementing colored Washington into a community. The prestige commanded by Negro public school teachers fortified the class structure but at the same time offered incentive to the gifted, industrious, lower-class Negro child to qualify for the honored position of teacher.

World War I had cost the white schools more than the colored. Both had suffered from inflation and from congressional disregard of local needs as long as there was a war to be won, but the relatively high-salaried war jobs that had stripped the white schools of a number of competent teachers had not siphoned off Negro teachers. Furthermore, although a considerable part of the war influx consisted of single women and men unaccompanied by their families, between 1917 and 1919 enrollment in the white schools, built to accommodate about 36,000 pupils, had jumped to over 44,300, whereas the colored schools had lost about 800. In casting about for ways of shoring

[4] *Crisis*, xxxv, 376; Dr. Rayford Logan to the author, 14 Jun 1960.

up the educational structure, Superintendent Thurston had encouraged the formation of parent-teacher associations, while the Board of Education, with the backing of the other civic organizations, had sponsored the use of school buildings and grounds as community recreation centers. The latter scheme, rather elaborately worked out with representatives of the citizens' associations in the neighborhoods involved, had served the transient adult population well, but had not lessened the difficulty of educating an increasing number of children in badly understaffed white schools, taught by discouraged, under-paid teachers. A parental rebellion probably explains why 1919 had found over 18 percent of Washington's school population entered in parochial and other private schools; a decade before the figure had stood below 10 percent. Thurston had tried to stem the tide by introducing junior high schools, an innovation that promised, in addition to other benefits, to reduce the congestion in the grammar grades and the four-year high schools. But the opening of one white and one colored junior high school in 1919 had slight immediate effect, and in the meantime "Americanization" classes for aliens started on a small scale that summer added another item of expense. By 1920 citizens were up in arms over the deterioration of the educational system.

An outraged public blamed Superintendent Thurston and Assistant Superintendent Bruce for most of the shortcomings in schools long starved for appropriations. Unjust though some of the criticism was, Thurston's timidity, coupled with charges that he lacked intellectual grasp, and Bruce's maladroit handling of human relations convinced the Board of Education that both men must go, the superintendent at once, his assistant somewhat later. Thurston's successor, Frank W. Ballou, former Assistant Superintendent of Schools in Boston, came with his eyes open. The Board of Education had warned him that he would inherit a large backlog of financial problems, would have to deal with congressional committees in solving them, might encounter some animosity from Thurston's friends, and in any case would have to establish a working relationship with an assistant superintendent of the colored schools and satisfy colored Washington. Gradually Ballou would prove himself able to clear every hurdle but the last. White people would look back upon his twenty-three year superintendency with gratitude; Negroes would merely state tersely that, among colored people, Ballou came to be the most hated man in the District of Columbia.

Short in stature, his slightly round face lengthened by a close-clipped black imperial, his rather protuberant eyes shadowed by heavy brows, Ballou looked like Mephistopheles in modern dress; but his outer mien gave little hint of his immovable determination to rebuild an antiquated school system into an effective educational machine. A Ph.D. in education from Harvard, years spent in responsible posts in the Cincinnati and Boston schools, and money inherited from a first wife had imbued him with a self-confidence that bordered on arrogance. He was as ready to contradict an ill-informed congressman at a school appropriation hearing as to rebuke an inept subordinate or to belittle the wisdom of a member of the Board of Education who disagreed with him. But his very imperviousness to criticism, his open disdain of stupidity, and his disregard of other people's feelings were assets to him in a tough job. His experience, particularly in the field of educational testing, was wide, his knowledge of educational theory extensive—and he charted his course on the basis of both. People who disliked him acutely as a person admitted that he was capable. And recognition of his competence revived their faith in the school system.[5] He waited till he had studied Washington's problems thoroughly before presenting his analysis of what was basically wrong. In 1922 he appended

[5] Comrs Rpts, 1917, i, 20, 1918, i, 19, 1919, i, 20-21; *Rpts B/Ed*, 1918, p. 11, 1919, p. 186, 1921, p. 101, 1922, pp. 36-39; *Rpt U.S. Comr Ed*, 1910, ii, 670, 677, 703; *Biennial Survey*, 1920, pp. 50, 126, 144; Frank W. Ballou, "Junior High Schools in Washington," *NEA Addresses*, LXII, 416-17, 423.

TABLE IV

School Enrollments, 1920-1955*

	1920	1927	1931	1935	1937	1941	1944	1948	1950	1955
Total	77,355	80,882	92,706	106,876	107,723	109,345	103,780	109,198	112,810	124,754**
White										
Non-Cath. Private		2,258	1,907	1,565	1,549	2,287	2,448	2,508	2,682	
R. Catholic		7,713	9,599	11,224	11,822	13,410	12,971	14,088	13,851	
Pub Welfare						46	95	120	76	
Public	45,775	46,865	53,175	59,582	58,793	55,777	49,500	47,801	46,736	38,165**
Total		56,836	64,681	72,371	71,164	71,520	64,919	64,440	63,351	
% pub sch of all wh enrlmt	79.1	82.4	82.1	82.3	82.6	77.98	76.17	74.17	72.19	
Colored										
Non-Cath. Private		54	82	86	72	63	75	146	117	
R. Catholic		621	969	777	691	917	1,018	1,182	1,226	
Pub Welfare				144	171	179	188	172	136	
Public	19,523	23,371	26,974	33,498	34,625	36,666	37,768	43,264	47,980	68,877
Total		24,046	28,025	34,505	35,559	37,825	38,861	49,758	49,459	
Consolidation										
Non-Cath. Private		2,312	1,989	1,651	1,621	2,350	2,513	2,648	2,799	2,325
R. Catholic		8,334	10,568	12,001	12,513	14,327	13,989	15,193	15,083	14,241
Pub Welfare				144	177	225		292	212	543
Public	65,298	70,236	80,149	93,080	93,418	92,443	87,268	91,065	94,716	107,042**
% change in wh pub sch enrlmt		2.38	13.4	12.04	−1.32	−5.13	−11.2	−3.43	−2.22	−18.34

% colored of all pub sch enrlmt	29.89	33.4	33.6	35.9	37.	39.66	43.27	47.60	49.60	64.34
% non-Catholic prvt sch of pub sch enrlmt	18.45	3.29	2.48	1.77	1.73	2.54	2.89	2.90	2.95	2.77
% R. Catholic sch of pub sch enrlmt		11.8	13.1	12.89	13.39	15.49	16.02	16.68	15.92	13.30
% R. Catholic sch of all sch enrlmt		10.3	11.4	11.22	11.61	13.10	13.47	13.91	13.37	11.45

* The 1920 figures derive from the *Comrs Rpt*, 1920, I, 20 and from U.S. Comr of Ed, *Biennial Survey of Ed*, 1920, pp. 50, 126, 144, in which private school data are estimated. The rest of the tabulation is from the official records of the Statistics Dept. of the D.C. public schools. Roman Catholic includes parochial and private Catholic schools. In 1950 school records show 263 children in Hebrew and 96 in Seventh Day Adventist schools and in 1955, 317 in Hebrew, 88 in Seventh Day Adventist schools, who are shown here as entered in private schools. The Board of Public Welfare entry refers to schools at centers maintained by the board for children in its care.

** Exclusive of 603 white students in Americanization classes.

to the report of the school board a section entitled "Why Educational Progress in Washington is so Slow."

Any Washingtonian who had persuaded himself that all that was necessary to restore the public schools to their former high standing was to get larger appropriations and install a new superintendent must have felt shock upon reading that summary. It included the testimony of the United States Commissioner of Education before a congressional committee: "I could go on, as I started, about buildings and teachers' salaries, . . . because any tyro could see the many defects which exist," but even immediate big appropriations would not redeem the schools under the existing administrative system. Overhead organizations so fettered the superintendent that he was practically impotent. "I would not take the job," said the commissioner, "at two or three times the salary." The *Cyclopaedia of Education* noted: "The confusion existing is hardly credible. Authority and responsibility are hopelessly tied up with red tape" unfurled in the District commissioners' offices, the courts, and the United States Treasury. Congress in passing on appropriations could and did change basic policies. "Board of Education" was a misnomer for a board of school visitors. "Education conditions in Washington are among the worst to be found in any city in the Union" from an administrative standpoint. "Until Congress can be made to realize that it is incompetent properly to administer such an undertaking and will give the Board of Education the power and control which should belong to it there is little hope of a good, modern school system for the District of Columbia." Ballou's text spelled out the details.

A recent rigmarole over procuring pens for handwriting classes illustrated one kind of impediment to efficiency. By law, before the District purchasing officer could advertise for bids, the District general supply committee had to ascertain whether any government installation listed a surplus of the wanted item. As the Brooklyn Navy Yard reported an oversupply, the requisition had to go there while the penmanship teachers waited; when the consignment at last arrived, it contained only stub pens useless for instruction of children in the art of Spencerian script. Building repairs, whether requested as "urgent," "necessary," or merely "desirable," had to be approved by the District engineer commissioner, the District health officer, and the fire department before the men in the District repair shop could start; meanwhile roofs might continue to leak, furnaces blow coal gas into classrooms, and decrepit plumbing break down. Repairs to playground equipment, limited by decree of the District auditor to $45 a year for each of the seventy-eight school yards that had such luxuries as swings, seesaws, or backstops for ball games, had to receive the endorsement of the District recreation department. The issuance of work permits fell to the child labor office, the follow-up to the police department. Funds from the school budget paid the salaries for school doctors, nurses, and dentists, but the District health officer supervised their work. Such a minor matter as opening a corrective speech class required an act of Congress. Equally hampering was the authority vested in the Comptroller General, the General Auditing Office of the Treasury, and, by custom, the District auditor, which enabled two or three men to delay or prevent payment for a program already approved by Congress. They even exercised their power to decide which teachers were entitled to the "advanced standing" pay designed for those with special experience and training.

Frustration frequently drove members of the Board of Education to resign. Of the nine who were members when Ballou came in 1920, only three were still acting in 1922; the superintendent did not mention that one man had resigned because of congressional criticism of his connection with a local business firm that advertised its readiness to furnish children with school essays at stipulated prices. The turnover of officials at every level, in fact, interfered with planning and made a consistent educational policy impossible. The District had had seven different commissioners within two years. The Bureau of the Budget, only a year old in 1922, was shortly to get a new director. Three of the five members of the House Subcommittee on District Appropriations were new, and four of the nine members of the Senate District Committee.

Ballou climaxed his report with a recapitulation of the process of obtaining the school appropriation for the fiscal year beginning July 1, 1922. Fifteen months in advance, every principal had prepared a written list of his needs; the superintendents then held hearings to determine which items were indispensable and in July sent the Board of Education a detailed estimate; finding only essentials included, the board transmitted it to the District commissioners, who returned it with orders to cut it by 24 percent. The superintendents reworked the data, and the commissioners, without consulting the school board, sliced off an additional chunk before submitting the request to the Bureau of the Budget. There officials reduced the sum further, and, because the law expressly forbade publication of the figures before they reached Congress, until the House Subcommittee opened hearings on the school budget, private citizens had little inkling of what it contained or what had dropped out. By then time was too short to organize public opinion effectively, despite the strong feeling in the community that teachers' salaries must be raised and several million dollars spent for new buildings. The House pared 10 percent from the Budget Bureau's proposal and, after a compromise with the more generous Senate, voted approximately two-thirds the amount school officials had considered an absolute minimum.[6]

Without attempting to cast off completely the "legislative strait-jacket," as Ballou called the school act of 1906 with its manifold binding restrictions and procedural detail, the superintendent concentrated in 1922 on getting teacher salary in-

[6] *Rpt B/Ed*, 1922, pp. 136-37; *Star*, 1 Jan 1923.

creases, a fixed salary schedule instead of specified amounts in yearly appropriations acts, a revised promotion system, a new compulsory school attendance law with provisions for continual school censuses that would make it enforceable, and free high school text books. Cures for the ills of divided authority and classroom shortages he hoped would follow. Certainly the need for new buildings was obvious. A voluminous congressional report of 1908 had recommended immediate expenditure of $8,880,000 for school sites and buildings. Ten schoolhouses condemned at that time were still in use in 1922, although elementary grades had spilled over into 71 portables, 152 rooms were used in double sessions, classes of forty and fifty children were the rule, and, for lack of other space, pupils were jammed into basement rooms, converted offices, and storerooms in rented buildings. The $6,186,000 appropriated in driblets over the past fourteen years, so far from making up arrears, had not sufficed to keep pace with the growth in the school population; and, in the interim, building costs had risen from 17 cents to 50 cents a cubic foot. In short, school administrators, like the Red Queen, had to run faster and faster to stay where they were.

A good many men on the Hill distrusted local judgment, particularly when any federal money was involved, but fortunately a dozen members of both houses were as intent as school officials on raising Washington's educational standards. Hearings lasted for months. While waiting for Congress to act, PTA's and the District Public School Association, born in 1923, fostered patience, and the Teachers' Institutes, one for white and one for colored, supplied professional self-help through monthly discussions and seminar sessions. When Superintendent Ballou got permission in 1923 to establish a research department in both the white and the colored schools, educational testing and studies of ways to better instruction held out new hope for improvements. Still the legislative mill ground slowly. Not until June 1924 did a bill pass raising teachers' salaries, setting a uniform rate for elementary school teachers similar to that in the high schools, and so ending the cumbersome and wasteful system of the past, whereby a first-grade teacher could get higher pay only by assignment to a second grade, a second-grade teacher only by moving to a third grade, and so on. In contrast to the former top teaching salary of $2,250, the average after 1924 for principals, supervisors, and teachers was $2,350. That rate, together with later adjustments to retirement pay, boosted morale, enabled Ballou to recruit fresh talent, and opened the way to requiring more intensive professional training.

A few months later a rewriting of the school attendance law extended its application to all children between the ages of 6 and 16 and placed supervision of work permits, annual school censuses, and truancy under a school attendance department. And early in 1925 Congress authorized the long-wanted five-year building program that, at an estimated cost of $20,185,000, would supposedly wipe out by June 1930 the accumulated arrearages, ensure space for the yearly increase in enrollment without resorting to double shifts and half-day instruction, cancel dependence upon rented buildings, flimsy portables, and ill-lighted, ill-ventilated rooms, and safeguard against a pupil-teacher ratio of more than forty to one. Elation swept the community. As pride in the school system reached new heights, an overwhelming majority of "non-residents," that is, people who kept their state citizenship and paid taxes elsewhere, followed Washingtonians' example in sending their children to the public schools.[7]

The next five years saw several changes directed chiefly at introducing a moderate "progressivism." "Special" classes multiplied—atypical classes for mentally subnormal children, fresh

[7] Ballou, "Introducing Educational Research into Washington Public Schools," *NEA Addresses*, LXIII, 783-85; Subcomee H and S Dis Comees, 68C, 2S, Jt Hrgs, "Schools and Playgrounds in D.C."; Comrs Rpt, 1925, IV, 56-57, 66-67; *Rpt B/Tr*, 1925, p. 96; *Rpt B/Ed*, 1923, p. 25, 1926, p. 82, and "School Achievements," 1930, pp. 58-59.

air schools for tuberculars, ungraded classes for delinquents and truants, classes for the physically handicapped, night classes, vocational schools, and Americanization classes for adults. Unlike several cities where separate classes for unusually gifted children became a feature, Washington compromised. Standardized intelligence and achievement tests developed by the research department enabled principals to classify children according to capability and assign them to section X, Y, or Z, representing above average, average, and below average groups, respectively. Pupils behind in their work received coaching from "supplementary teachers." And when a research department study of teaching methods showed the wastefulness of repeated arithmetic drills, the Board of Education adopted exercise books that gave each child a chance to set his own pace. Here was an instance of a new flexibility that recognized the differing potentialities of every individual.

Neither Ballou nor the school board accepted the credo of the progressive extremists who twisted John Dewey's dictum, "freedom is achieved through the exercise of intelligence" into the opposite, "intelligence is achieved through the exercise of freedom," a freedom that rejected all discipline. The proof of the pudding was, of course, in the eating. Washington high school graduates who went on to college in the late 1920's found themselves far better prepared than students from most public school systems. Whether that gratifying record was due to superior pre-college teaching or to the richer cultural home background of Washington students did not come under scrutiny. The very fact that upper-class families in the capital sent their children to the public schools testified to a continuing confidence in their quality. Washington administrators believed that children whose education ended in high school or earlier also received as sound schooling as they could get anywhere. When Assistant Superintendent Garnett Wilkinson said that the District's colored schools were the best Negro schools in the United States, his statements stood unchallenged. The PTA's took credit for some of the achievements; others were due to experiments undertaken in Washington by national organizations, such as the National Research Council's Committee on Child Development.

Although Congress allowed the building program to lag and did nothing about physical education and medical care, some money was forthcoming for a few school libraries, and, when the "city council" authorized the conversion of the white and the colored normal schools to four-year teachers' colleges, the Board of Education made three, instead of two, years of professional training the prerequisite for a teaching post. Belief that "the progressive school of today cannot consider itself apart from the current of every-day affairs" inspired supervisors, principals, and teachers to direct instruction less at instilling facts into pupils and improving their skills than at encouraging initiative and independence of thought. The most noteworthy aspect of the decade of effort was the general feeling among school employees and citizens' organizations that they had all had a share in winning an important battle, that the single-minded strength of public opinion expressed repeatedly at congressional hearings had impelled Congress to act.[8]

Yet the most fundamental obstacles to further progress remained, namely divided authority and the iron grip Congress kept on the controls. Some citizens, among them taxpayers who disliked Ballou's methods, believed an elected Board of Education would remedy matters, but, as spokesmen for the Powell Junior High School PTA pointed out to a congressional com-

---

[8] *Biennial Survey*, 1928, p. 126; S Doc 58, 70C, 1S, pp. 4-17, 33, 43, 95-97, 126; *Rpt B/Tr*, 1929, p. 22; Boyd H. Bode, "The New Education Ten Years After," *New Republic*, LXIII, 63; Garnett C. Wilkinson, "Washington is Easily the Foremost Center of Negro Education in America," *School Life*, XI, 114; "Growing Children are Studied at the Washington Child Research Center," *ibid.*, XIV, 184-87, and Mrs. Giles Scott Rafter, "Social Hygiene Work of the Parent Teacher Associations," *ibid.*, pp. 15-18; Comrs Rpt, 1926, p. 20; *Rpts B/Ed*, 1922, p. 40, 1926, pp. 81-82, and "School Achievements," 1930, pp. 57-118.

mittee, the trouble lay not in the appointive character of the board but in its powerlessness to take needed action. Despite that reminder and the earlier warnings of the United States Commissioner of Education, Congress neither delegated any financial authority to the board nor cut the procedural red tape that enmeshed it.[9]

The first years of the depression threatened to destroy the American public school system. By late 1932 New York City had dismissed 11,000 teachers, Chicago had let a $28,000,000 arrearage in teachers' salaries accumulate, Alabama had closed 85 percent of her schools, and scores of cities had shortened the school year, cancelled building plans, and curtailed or dropped all special classes and services. At the same time adolescents unable to get work were pushing secondary school enrollments to a new peak. Angered at the neglect of education for which former supporters of American business ideals now blamed the "banker-power trust" and "the greedy manufacturer," the once conservative National Educational Association announced that only the public schools could save American civilization, and they must henceforward concentrate upon teaching social responsibility. In late 1933 and after, Public Works, Works Progress, and National Youth Administration funds helped revive school systems, and general economic recovery by 1938 resolved most of the difficulties caused by the financial crisis. But, contrary to expectations, the number of children entering high school continued to mount, and the percentage that graduated rose astonishingly: from the 16.7 percent of graduating age who finished in 1920 to 50.7 percent in 1940. Enforced attendance, the federal Office of Education noted, was not the sole reason; better teaching, courses of greater interest to students, and better transportation also contributed. While the long-run advantages to society of more schooling for young Americans appeared self-evident, sheer

[9] *Star*, 1 Jan 1930; Subcomee on Education, H Dis Comee, 71C, 2S, Hrgs, "Public School Ed in D.C.," pp. 10, 27-33, and 71C, 3S, pp. 5-6.

numbers of students inescapably complicated questions of how to recruit competent teachers and how to devise a scheme of education suitable for a political democracy in a world in which dictatorship was spreading and scientific discoveries were yearly widening the boundaries of knowledge.[10]

In Washington, reduced appropriations cut maintenance funds and salaries in 1933, but a capital outlay of about $4,490,000 in 1931-1932 had provided more new schoolhouses than in any one previous year in Washington's history; the sum, almost nine times that allowed in 1934, was twice the amount voted for any year thereafter until 1948. Moreover, unlike many cities, Washington, instead of losing, added teachers; the roster lengthened from the 2,764 of 1930 to 2,906 in 1935 and, with the restoration of pay cuts that year, the District's salaries ranked just below New York's and California's. By comparison with most of the United States, Washington was obviously well off. That reassuring knowledge, coupled with an easing of pressures on the schools, tended to induce a relaxation of vigilance in the community, for, while junior and senior high school enrollment continued to rise, the falling birth rate checked the yearly expansion of the elementary school population, and after 1937 the total number of pupils shrank.[11]

Meanwhile "character education" became a major topic of discussion. Apparently troubled by the disciplinary problems created by bored adolescents resentful of the school attendance law that kept them in school till they were sixteen, Superin-

[10] *Biennial Survey*, 1932, "State School Systems," p. 10, and 1940, II, "Statistical Survey," pp. 18-19; Doak S. Campbell, Frederick H. Baer and Oswald L. Harvey, *Educational Activities in the Works Progress Administration*, Staff Study No. 14; Merle Curti, *The Social Ideas of American Educators*, pp. 576-77; Robert E. Sherwood, *Roosevelt and Hopkins*, p. 57.

[11] *Rpts B/Ed*, 1932, p. 1, and 1940, "School Achievements, in Twenty Years, July 1, 1920 to June 30, 1940," pp. 16-17; Comrs Rpts, 1931, p. 26, 1933, pp. 35-37, 1934, pp. 56-65, 1935, pp. 26-35, 1936, pp. 32-41, 1937, pp. 30-39, 1938, pp. 32-41, 1939, pp. 52-62, 1940, pp. 50-60, 1941, pp. 52-63; *Biennial Survey*, 1940, II, "Statistical Summary," pp. 23-24.

tendent Ballou had appointed a teachers' committee in 1929 to prepare recommendations on curriculum changes and classroom techniques designed to develop in children cooperative attitudes and an eagerness to learn. In 1931 the committee reported that inasmuch as "the first aim of public school education should be training in character which will fit boys and girls for citizenship in a democracy," less emphasis must be placed upon academic subjects and more upon physical education and pupil participation in group activities. Parents, the community centers, playground directors, the churches, and social agencies should assist. While a citizens' advisory committee approved the proposal, until a Senate committee on racketeering and crime endorsed it, Congress hesitated. In 1934 an act appropriated money for a two-year experiment at one white and one colored school at every level from elementary through senior high school; a small corps of special teachers was to supervise the necessary changes in curriculum and teaching methods.

The scheme lapsed before it was well begun; in 1936, when a representative accused the staff of "teaching communism," Congress cut off funds. But the idea persisted that education must shift its focus. Superintendent Ballou appointed teachers' committees to plan a "Child Development" program for the public schools; the parochial schools under the leadership of Father John Ryan of Catholic University introduced social studies into their curricula; and before the end of the 1930's educators throughout the country endorsed the general concept that the function of the schools was to develop character which would then produce acceptable patterns of social behavior. Washington's avowed goal of ten years before, the nurturing of individual initiative and independence of thought in school children, was no longer all-important.[12]

The school board lay proud stress on the discarding of "sub-

[12] "Preliminary Report of the Committee on Character Education," *School Bulletin* 9, 1931; Curti, *Social Ideas of American Educators*, p. 578; "School Achievements," 1940, pp. 8-88; *Star*, 20 Oct 1935.

ject orientation" in favor of the new "child orientation" program. But in reviewing the achievements of the 1930's the board
passed lightly over the abandoning of the X,Y,Z plan of grouping children according to their intelligence and achievement
ratings. As parental objections grew, in 1932 the "three-track"
system had given way to not very sharply differentiated X-Y
and Y-Z units, corresponding generally to the A and B divisions
within a classroom which were traditional in grade schools the
country over. Since appropriations for the research department
had always been so meagre that it had to entrust most of the
administering and grading of the IQ and achievement tests to
teachers who already had their hands full, not improbably the
three-way placements had often been faulty. Financial pressures
during the depression wiped out special classes for gifted
children in every city school system except Cleveland's and
Denver's, and before the end of the decade the informed American public, bristling over Nazi Germany's "Heldenschule,"
emphatically rejected the concept as contrary to democratic
ideals. Not until the late 1950's would Washington's school
administrators, recognizing the wisdom of paying more attention to bright students, introduce the "four track" system into
the high schools.[13]

The Board of Education also took pride in the improvements
in physical care achieved during the 1930's, the classes for adult
illiterates, the units in vocational rehabilitation, the nursery
schools, which opened with emergency relief funds in 1934 and
disappeared in 1939, the cancellation of the so-called "Red
Rider" to the appropriation act for 1936, which had denied
salary to any teacher who "taught communism," and "the workshops and discussion groups democratically organized which
were . . . broadening teachers' horizons." In keeping with the

[13] *News*, 23 Nov 1932; *Biennial Survey*, 1932, "The Education of Exceptional Children," pp. 9-11; George D. Strayer, *Report of a Survey of
the Public Schools of the District of Columbia*, 1949, p. 428 (hereafter
cited as *Strayer Report*); "School Achievements," 1940, pp. 1-123; "Demonstrating Child Welfare," *Community Service*, ii, 5.

doctrine of equal opportunity for all regardless of ability, the widened reach of the junior and senior high schools, and, after the elevation of the vocational schools to the status of high schools, the granting of diplomas to graduates appeared to be further steps forward, since officials rejected any possible element of truth in the assertion of a mid-western high school teacher that "the gradual democratization of the American high school was lowering the scholastic standards of the secondary schools."

Within the Board of Education, however, faint apprehension was stirring before 1940 lest thoughtful parents lose faith in the public schools. The uneasiness arose not from the volume but from the source of the complaints, for they emanated from perceptive and discriminating citizens unlikely to carp at imagined grievances. Inasmuch as enlightened public opinion coupled with intense interest in the school system had always provided the Board of Education with such power as it had, withdrawal of that kind of support could undermine the schools for years to come. In the four years preceding Pearl Harbor school census figures supplied some statistical justification for that fear: white public school enrollments dropped by about 3,000, whereas parochial and other private schools added about 2,300.

Criticism of the quality of public education increased steadily from about 1937 onward. Emphasis on making children "happy," some parents felt, was leading teachers into an easygoing attitude toward home-work badly done or not done at all. Excessive attention to non-essentials, including high school athletics, left too little time for basic studies. A few people apparently thought teachers were no longer exerting themselves because financial security had robbed them of ambition. Parents were rarely aware of the new demands upon teachers who felt the superintendent's invitations to join in committee work amounted to "the Colonel requests." Time spent on drafting a new "Philosophy of Education" and evolving cirriculum changes to fit it could not be devoted to guiding the progress of individual pupils. In any case, performance proved something amiss, particularly in several schools where the socio-economic background of children was above average. Whereas high school graduates in the 1920's had entered reputable colleges without difficulty, in the late 1930's teachers now and again were informing parents that Johnny could not possibly hope for admission to, say, Harvard or Yale unless he had special tutoring. True, the fault might be Johnny's or parental failure to insist on home study, not a relaxing of teaching standards or an injudicious curriculum, but dissatisfaction continued to spread and in time to come would be a factor in the "flight to the suburbs."[14]

Logically, developments in the colored schools over the years should have paralleled those in white. Both systems were subject to the same rulings laid down by the bi-racial Board of Education; salary rates were the same for colored teachers as for white; and, from the early 1920's onward, in spite of pronounced inequities in congressional appropriations for athletic fields, classroom accommodations, and research staff, the dollar-and-cents equality of the separate systems was generally observed in budgeting for ordinary operating expenses: close to a third of the over-all revenues went to the Negro schools, which, until the late 1930's, embraced approximately 34 percent of the school population. Garnett Wilkinson, assistant superintendent for the colored schools, like the assistant superintendent of the white schools, came under the immediate supervision of Superintendent Ballou and received such briefing as Ballou thought necessary. Several times a year Ballou called white and colored supervisors and principals together to explain his plans, and

---

[14] Interviews, former teachers and Mrs. Henry Grattan Doyle, president of B/Ed 1935-1943; *Strayer Report*, pp. 406-07, 424-48, 497; Kathleen Brady, "The Depression and the Classroom Teacher," *Journal of the National Education Association*, xx, 263.

even in the 1920's he sometimes appointed one or two Negroes to teachers' committees. Yet the application of policies in the colored schools, or at least the results, diverged further and further from the white as time went on. The magnitude of the differences in some important respects would not be clearly revealed until racially integrated schools opened in Washington in the autumn of 1954. Wilkinson, a fine-looking, dignified, soft-spoken man, qualified for his post by an M.A. from the University of Pennsylvania, hewed strictly to the lines laid down by his superior, but in so doing, some of his own friends felt, he acted with a self-protectiveness costly to his people.

The separateness of the two systems in operation was so rigid that neither group of principals, supervisors, and teachers had first-hand knowledge of the programs and teaching methods employed in the other. For a white teacher to visit a colored classroom was virtually unthinkable, however unbiased he or she might be; such a step would have represented to the colored teacher an intolerable intrusion, an act of spying. Nor would a Negro visitor be welcomed in a white school. From the beginning of public schools for Negroes in the 1860's, the lack of communication had always obtained, but it became more costly to the colored schools once Superintendent Ballou launched research units to explore new ideas. At the suggestion of a representative of the Central Labor Union, in 1930 the Board of Education appointed a bi-racial citizens' advisory committee on vocational education, and thereafter white and colored teachers not infrequently sat on committees together. Still the joint discussions of particular problems failed to bridge the racial gulf.

If aware of the ten-year efforts of a white group that succeeded in 1938 in inaugurating vocational and educational counselling for white high school students, Negro teachers, cognizant of the racial restrictions on jobs, formulated no comparable plan for colored children. Negro principals, unlike white, apparently never dared introduce an innovation into the schools in their charge without first obtaining the explicit sanction of the assistant superintendent. Where white elementary school principals exercised a good deal of autonomy—perhaps an outgrowth of a widespread feeling that the elementary grades were "step-children" of the school system under Ballou—colored principals and their subordinates adhered to an autocratic chain of command. If that autocratic rule was frequently salutary, it nevertheless discouraged initiative in the lower ranks despite Negro teachers' curiosity about white teachers' experiments and achievements. The multitudinous voluntary associations that cropped up in the white schools—associations of high school principals and supervisors, of special teachers, of junior high school principals, and corresponding groups for the elementary grades—had few active counterparts in the colored schools. The staff of the latter saw no occasion to follow the lead of the former, even after bi-racial committees had begun to undercut the mutual isolation.

A second and ultimately more significant difference between the two systems lay in the tendency of the white schools to concentrate upon children of average or below average mentality and those with physical disabilities, leaving the unusually gifted to fend for themselves, whereas Negro school administrators believed their first obligation was to the upper strata of the colored school population measured in terms of learning capacity. To the distress of some members of the Board of Education, a good many colored principals and teachers appeared to take the position that truants, pupils who fell behind in their work or got into other trouble, the emotionally disturbed, and mentally retarded children were not entitled to special attention, for it would necessarily be at the expense of their more competent fellows. Since school resources were limited, and all Negro children faced discrimination in a predominantly white world, those able to make effective use of education must not be sacrificed to the less promising. While nothing in official reports openly acknowledged such a philosophy, it was a natural point-of-view in so class-conscious a community as colored Washington, where teachers, themselves occupying an enviable place in the social structure, would understandably want to preserve it intact.

Before World War II, only a very small unvociferous minority of Washington Negroes saw any advantage in school integration. On the contrary, a striking feature of colored school administration in the 1920's and 1930's was the jealousy with which it guarded its independence. Full recognition of its accomplishments and a larger, juster share of funds with which to better past records constituted the main goal. In 1933 when an official of the American Association of Teachers' Colleges gave Miner Teachers' College an "A" rating and declared that his survey had upset his settled conviction about the inferiority of Negro institutions, colored Washingtonians felt they had proved their ability to run their own show. Not improbably distrust of Superintendent Ballou, whom they considered tainted with racism, strengthened their determination to keep their schools free of white interference. The superintendent had approved the use of a white school building for a citizens' association meeting called in the 1920's to tighten restrictive housing covenants; he repeatedly, Negroes mistakenly believed, betrayed a dislike of colored people; and in 1939 when the school board was about to permit the famous colored contralto, Marian Anderson, to sing in the white Central High School auditorium, he had all but insisted that the permission be conditional on its not setting a precedent. Manifestly, observed the *Crisis*, if Washington's dual system were to be discarded, it would be at the insistence of economy-minded whites in the face of Negro opposition.[15]

[15] Robert Haycock, "The Capital's Unique School System," *School Life*, XVII, 102-03; *Tribune*, 25 Oct 1929, 5 Feb 1932; Lofton, "Separate but Equal," pp. 245-68; *Rpt B/Ed*, 1930, p. 36; *Crisis*, XXXIX, 39, XLVI, 170-71, and John Lowell, "Washington Fights," *ibid.*, 277.

The Negro intelligentsia, however, like the white, had begun to question the adequacy of the schools. "To some of us who got our schooling before the present-day reign of fads, futilities and 'activities' so-called," protested the *Tribune* in 1933, "it is no surprise to observe the shocking deficiency in the fundamentals—the three R's, if you please—of the present-day high school pupil." If school officials regarded wails about the "watered-down curriculum" and the lowering of teaching standards as merely the vaporings of fault-finders yearning for "the good old days," an investigation conducted by Dr. Howard Long of the colored school research unit eventually proved some of the fears justified. Starting with 1935, Long's meticulous study compared the Intelligence Quotient scores made by Washington's Negro school children year after year with the results of their achievement tests. His findings, first presented in 1943 to Assistant Superintendent Wilkinson, showed no loss in the IQ average but "a general downward trend in the achievement of pupils on all grade levels from the year 1935 to 1943," with the sharpest decline after 1937. While Long acknowledged that the large influx of Negro families from the deep South had bearing on the problem and explained that he "inclined to place a great deal of emphasis on the effects of cultural social-economic status of the pupils," he suggested that "ineffective instruction" was a contributing cause. His proposals of how to remedy the weaknesses failed to save him from bitter attack from colored Washington when mimeographed copies of his report reached the public in 1948.

Whether, as parental complaints implied, a comparable decline in achievement had begun in the white schools in the late 1930's is purely inferential. Not until outside experts submitted the Strayer Report to Congress in 1949 would a body of dispassionate evidence point to a lower record than the national norm in a number of Washington's white schools.[16] But before

[16] *Tribune*, 10 Mar 1933; Howard H. Long, "Intelligence and Achieve-

Pearl Harbor most of the local public was not alarmed. Washingtonians looking back over the preceding quarter century could see problems surmounted as well as some still unresolved. If school questions now occupied a lesser place in community thinking than in the 1920's, was that not a sign that successes in the interval had disposed of major troubles? Certainly in the autumn of 1941 Washingtonians by and large considered the school system among the least of their worries.

---

ment of Colored Pupils in the Public Schools of the District of Columbia," Parts II and III, mimeo, 1948; *Strayer Report*, pp. 417-18, 463-66, 552-53.

CHAPTER XVIII

BEFORE AND AFTER THE BONUS
MARCH, 1930-1933

F E W Americans in 1930, Washingtonians perhaps least of all, thought of the depression that followed the stock market crash of October 1929 as the beginning of a country-wide economic collapse. Not until midsummer of 1931, when unemployment had reached unheard-of dimensions and was still increasing, did the business world realize that here was more than a sharp downward dip in the business cycle that would soon reverse itself. Even then the possibility that old residents of the capital would again see, as in 1894, an Army of the Unemployed encamped in their midst seemed remote.

In Washington, where government activity shielded citizens from the full force of the national catastrophe, cautiously optimistic prophecies filled the pages of the local press. During 1930 plans for new wings to the Smithsonian's Natural History Museum received congressional approval, and the vast building program for the Federal Triangle and the Department of Agriculture across the Mall kept a host of workers employed. Private building operations dropped by some $13,000,000 from the nearly $48,000,000 of 1929, a number of small businesses failed, and toward the end of the year the appeals from the Associated Charities for help for destitute families took on a note of desperation. But the Community Chest drive for the first time went over the top, and in February 1931 Congress authorized an immediate start on an eight-million-dollar District public works project of new buildings, street paving, sewer and bridge construction, and extension of water mains. Not only did the public school system thus acquire several long-needed new schoolhouses, but unemployment, which had begun to mount alarmingly, shrank as nine to ten thousand men got work. The nearly $5,000,000 spent by the National Capital Park and Planning Commission during fiscal years 1931 and 1932 also helped the city. And when private subscriptions brought the National Symphony Orchestra into being in the autumn of 1931, delighted Washingtonians dared hope it meant that the business slump was ending.[1] They later learned that the musicians frequently had to play for love, since Conductor Hans Kindler could not offer them salaries.

District Commissioners Luther H. Reichelderfer, a retired physician, Herbert B. Crosby, a retired general, and Major John C. Gotwals, appointed by President Hoover in 1930, betrayed no sense of anxiety in their first two annual reports. As in every city in the country, relief rolls lengthened while want and nameless fears turned tempers edgy, but here complaints about public welfare measures were relatively few. The police department was the principal sore spot. Its scandals and outright incompetence impelled Commissioner Crosby to look for a new superintendent. Chance provided the answer in the person of Pelham D. Glassford, who had been the youngest general officer in the AEF. In the summer of 1931 at the age of 47 he had retired in order to spend the years ahead ranching with his father and painting in Arizona. When his father's death upset those plans, he returned briefly to Washington to manage the Armistice Day celebration and then yielded to the persuasions of his one-time commanding officer, General Crosby, to accept the post of Major and Superintendent of the Metropolitan Police.

Glassford knew Washington well. During a tour of duty at the Army War College in 1924 and then another in the office of the Chief of Staff, he had taken a roomy, shabby old house in Georgetown, where he felt free to decorate the walls

[1] *Rpts Smithsonian*, 1930, p. 1, 1931, p. 1; Comrs Rpts, 1931, p. 58, 1932, p. 42, 1934, p. 46; *Rpts/NCPPC*, 1930, p. 45, 1931, p. 44, 1932, p. 29; Min As Ch, 12 Feb, 19, 21 Mar, 18 Jun 1930, 12 Jan, 11 Feb, 8 Apr 1931; *Star*, 1 Jan, 11 Dec 1930, 4, 11 Oct 1931; "Washington's Chest Expansion," *Survey*, LXVI, 99.

with his own murals. There he imposed upon his four children a regime combining Bohemia and discipline that led his friends to dub the household "the Borneo Embassy." Doubts assailed the public about the suitability of a man without police experience for so difficult a job as head of Washington's police force. Might not a military man prove to be the worst sort of martinet? Relatively few people at the time realized that Glassford represented the very best of Army tradition. Brought up as an "Army brat" in western posts, he had a deep devotion to duty, a dedication to the public interest. He lacked all political ambition.

Within a month of his appointment Glassford captured public respect by his handling of the "Hunger March." In December 1931 about a thousand jobless men arrived in the capital to stage as violent a demonstration as they dared contrive against the government. The new police chief instructed his men to be watchful but not to interfere with the soap-box orators as long as they fired only words. To the surprise and intense relief of the city, a week or so of listening to each other's bitter harangues without provoking any attack from constituted authority sufficed to discourage the Hunger Marchers; they faded away. A second group, encountering the same sort of treatment, similarly disintegrated. Glassford's unorthodox habit of riding about the city on a big blue motorcycle while he checked on police performance earned him the label of "screwball," but by the spring of 1932 he had won a reputation for friendly, unobtrusive competence.[2]

At that point the Board of Trade began speaking with renewed confidence. For the first time since its founding in 1889 the directors had omitted annual reports in 1930 and 1931, but the informal typescript prepared by the president in April 1932, though lacking the customary impressive format, presented a triumphant picture of the preceding twelve months.

[2] Fleta Campbell Springer, "Glassford and the Siege of Washington," *Harper's Magazine*, CLXV, 641-48.

"In drab surroundings," ran the summary, "at a time when every other organization that I know of is compelled to retrench and curtail their activities, the Board of Trade is ending the record year of its history." Five hundred new members, fewer resignations and fewer delinquent dues than every before, double the usual number of bills tendered to Congress and defended at hearings, and the bringing to Washington of sixty conventions, a hugely increased tourist trade, and $10,000,000 in new business were outstanding achievements. Besides holding the largest clam-bake ever attempted, the board had sponsored a dinner in honor of Post and Gatty, the "Round-the-World-Flyers." The Aviation Committee had prevented the placing of two-hundred-foot towers on the new Arlington Memorial Bridge, the Municipal Art Committee was preparing "the usual award for meritorious building," the Law and Order Committee had held several talks with the commissioners, the Finance Committee had fought off bills injurious to local business, and the American Ideals Committee, the committees on national representation, schools, alley-dwelling, public health, traffic, and a dozen other problems had all worked diligently. If the board president was deliberately pumping courage into his associates, the record supplied him with power. Prospects for a mounting number of visitors looked bright.[3]

In late May an unexpectedly heavy flood of visitors did roll in upon the capital with one object in mind: a vote in Congress for immediate payment of the bonus that World War I veterans would not otherwise receive until 1945. Starting from Oregon, the Bonus Expeditionary Force, as its members wryly called it, hitchhiked, rode freight trains, and gathered reinforcements along the way, as jobless men, some of them driving battered old cars, joined the march on Washington. Word of their coming ran before them. General Glassford, recognizing the grave possibilities of trouble, sought out congressional

[3] Rpt B/Tr, 1931-32, typescript in possession B/Tr.

leaders to beg quick action on the bonus bill, for, as long as it was tied up in committee, the Bonus Army would continue to expand. Only prompt defeat or passage of the bill would halt the march before it reached overwhelming proportions. When Congress disregarded his plea, he hurriedly prepared for the impending invasion by finding billets for the veterans. Neither then nor later did he doubt that most of them, for all their unmilitary appearance, were ex-servicemen, not the communist trouble-makers the administration would in time depict. He got permission to house the first contingent in a vacant department store, induced the Assistant Secretary of the Treasury to let others occupy empty buildings scheduled for early demolition on lower Pennsylvania Avenue, assigned some men to empty sheds and warehouses in southwest Washington, and, as he was unable to borrow tents from the Army or the District National Guard, he helped the main body of bonuseers establish a camp adjoining the dump on the mud flats across the Anacostia, where they set up ramshackle huts made from old packing cases, odd bits of lumber, scraps of canvas, and tin cans.

Before the middle of June over 20,000 bonus marchers had collected in the District of Columbia. Glassford issued orders to his subordinates not to harry them. He persuaded the National Guard to lend its rolling field kitchens and elicited money from rich friends to eke out the rations with which sympathizers in every part of the country were supplying the commissariat of this strange, bedraggled army. Thus abetted, Walter Waters, the elected commander of the Bonus Army, and his lieutenants succeeded in maintaining discipline within its ranks. On the Anacostia the heavily populated "Camp Marks," named for a former police chief, ran with a semblance of military order. Bugle calls sounded Reveille and Taps, K.P. details prepared mess, the men stood in chow lines, dug latrines they called "Hoover Villas," and organized baseball games.

Similar if less exacting discipline held among the men encamped within the city proper. Washingtonians, moved by curiosity or benevolence to visit the various encampments, marvelled to see white men and Negroes amicably sharing quarters. Gifts of bedding, odd bits of furniture, utensils, and food multiplied, as residents of the capital observed the needs and the order-liness prevailing among these ill-assorted lobbyists. "The arrival of the bonus army," remarked John Dos Passos, "seems to be the first event to give the inhabitants of Washington any inkling that something is happening in the world outside of their drowsy sun parlor."

The House of Representatives passed the bonus bill on June 15th. President Hoover said he would veto it as class legisla-tion if it won in the Senate. Two days later, while Commander Waters vainly tried to see the President, the veterans collected on the Capitol grounds to await the Senate's decision. Thanks to Glassford, they were not arrested for walking on the grass, as "General" Coxey had been in 1894. They sat under the trees and on the Capitol steps or milled around restlessly. The afternoon dragged on and turned into twilight. Tension grew. At last the word came: the Senate had killed the bill. For a moment silence lay heavy, followed by some "boos" and a stir-ring of the crowd. Then Waters, prompted by a young woman reporter, called out: "Let us show them that we are patriotic Americans. I call on you to sing 'America.'" The song rang out. The men then quietly formed into platoons and walked back to their makeshift quarters on the Avenue, across the Mall, and on the mud flats of the Anacostia.

Neither the defeat of the bill nor the efforts of the adminis-tration to get the marchers out of the capital ended the story of the Bonus Army. While the Democratic convention in Chicago nosed it off the front page of the newspapers till after Franklin D. Roosevelt's nomination, the bonus marchers waited uncer-tainly. When the government offered them free rides home some of the men accepted; most stayed on, seeing nothing to be gained by returning jobless and penniless to homes that no longer existed. New arrivals, wives and children among them, swelled the army, for, until Congress adjourned in mid-July, hope for some constructive action lingered. An act passed cutting civil service salaries by 8⅓ percent and decreeing obligatory furloughs without pay for government employees, but such economy measures were of no help to unemployed veterans. While a band of fifty to a hundred avowed communists, ostracized by the rest of the bonus seekers, attempted to picket the White House, during the last days of the congressional session four hundred foot-weary "Death Marchers" shuffled back and forth in front of the Capitol for sixty hours to prove their determination to fight lawfully until they dropped; because the architect of the Capitol insisted that they not sleep on the grass and kept water sprinklers running night and day to discourage them, they napped occasionally on the lawn of the Library of Congress and, for relief of their necessities, used the library washrooms—indeed sometimes the ornately tiled hallways. The vigilant, kindly police chief saw to it that hot coffee lessened the rigors of the "Death March," and one night Mrs. Neddy McLean, divorced wife of the owner of the Washington *Post*, appeared at 2 a.m. with a thousand sandwiches. When an apprehensive Vice President called for a detachment of Marines to clear the approach to the Capitol, Glassford sent them back to their barracks with the statement that only the President could order out troops, and they were not needed. On the very last day of the session Congress voted a loan of $300,000,000 to be distributed to the states for unemployment relief. Gloomy veterans foresaw that it would take months to get into motion the massive machinery necessary to produce results.

Meanwhile General Glassford—"our friendly enemy," Waters called him—insisted that the men must go, since "the police department has not the means to continue much longer to provide for the thousands of veterans in the city." A solid core of the Bonus Army stood firm, reiterating its four-point rule: "Stay until the bonus is granted; no radical talk; no panhandling; no booze." Day after day smoke from the cooking fires in the city's parks and vacant lots drifted through the streets. The occupants of Camp Marks entrenched themselves doggedly, adding to the collection of pitiful huts they had put up earlier. Here and there tin cans planted with flowers appeared alongside, a reminder to visitors that this was becoming home to several hundred families. Half-buried garbage and summer heat bred flies and disease, and quarrels led with increasing frequency to fist fights that the omnipresent Glassford usually broke up with the admonition: "No fighting among veterans." With the flat decree that all must share alike, he quashed Commander Waters' plan to deny rations to the handful of communists who had collected about John Pace of Detroit. By their own count never more than a hundred in number, the communists found themselves thwarted in their every attempt to make the B.E.F. a tool of revolution, but they were a thorn in the gaunt flesh of the great body of men whose motto was: "Eyes front, not left."

Hunger had already become the major enemy. Foodstuffs and money had poured in from all over the United States, but by mid-July the Bonus Army's treasury was empty; the rations of mush, beans, and salt tripe on which the men had lived for days were running out. Glassford spent nearly $1,000 out of his own pocket to buy supplies; one $750 purchase furnished 1,000 pounds of coffee, 3,000 pounds of meat, 200 pounds of sugar, 200 pounds of salt, and some other staples. But when broadcasting companies stopped the radio appeals for food, voluntary contributions dwindled. To abide by the rule of no panhandling became increasingly difficult. The Board of Public Welfare was not in a position to draw for the benefit of non-residents upon the recently created emergency relief fund, and the over-burdened private charity societies could not feed 15,000 strangers, veterans or otherwise. If the families encamped on the Anacostia flats were to dig in permanently, who was to provide them with the necessities of life? At this juncture students of the past may have recalled the city's difficulties of the first decades of the nineteenth century when Congress year after year lifted never a finger to care for the throngs of "transient paupers" who collected in the capital.

President Hoover's refusal to see a delegation of the Bonus Army in June had disturbed a good many Americans, especially thoughtful Washingtonians who witnessed the direct effect. A month later, according to the recollections of a staunch local Republican, Hoover's "frozen-faced" dismissal of the wants of hungry American ex-soldiers baffled admirers of the "great humanitarian" who had taken charge of feeding starving Europe in 1918. B.E.F. Commander Waters contended initially that only non-veterans, derelicts who passed themselves off as part of the Bonus Army, resorted to panhandling, but it inevitably spread and sometimes took on a note of belligerence that timid householders found potentially ominous. In the heart of the business section from 7th Street to the Treasury, from Pennsylvania Avenue to G Street, idle, seedy-looking men stood about, not by and large soliciting openly, but by their mere presence creating vague apprehensions in passers-by. Businessmen came to feel they were under siege. At the same time grumblings began to be heard at the police for not enforcing the law requiring peddlers' licenses of the veterans who had set up soft drink stands and sold souvenirs on the streets. While the President and his advisers persisted in the view that the entire problem was purely a local affair, the District commissioners considered it a federal responsibility, the result of a national catastrophe; apparently the White House and the District Building concurred only in criticizing

Glassford for his "passivity." Temperate citizens, in spite of sympathy for the invaders, gradually reached the point of concluding that they must be persuaded to leave; the situation might soon become explosive.

Of the estimated 60,000 to 80,000 men who had joined the Bonus March at one time or another, not more than 10,000 were still in Washington by the last week in July. But official patience had run out. The Treasury demanded that the Pennsylvania Avenue buildings be vacated at once so that demolition could begin, and on July 21st the District commissioners instructed the police to have that area cleared of occupants within thirty-six hours, to have the squatters removed from all government property within the city proper by midnight of the 24th, and by August 4th to have everyone out of Camp Marks as well. Glassford, determined to avoid precipitating violence, promptly conferred with the commissioners; they rescinded the order, "pending the straightening out of certain legal matters." The police chief used the interlude first to extract from Waters and his lieutenants an assurance that the veterans would not resist eviction and, second, to hurry on an arrangement with Judge William Bartlett, who had tentatively agreed to let them set up a camp on his thirty-acre estate near Anacostia. During the next five days the ranks of the Bonus Army thinned perceptibly. The period of grace ended abruptly on July 28th.

That morning Glassford, acting on the commissioners' written orders, began the eviction of the veterans from the area near the tip of the Federal Triangle. As the police moved into the buildings, the men moved out, merely tossing a few mild curses at the "blues," while Waters and the police chief watched. Suddenly two new arrivals from Camp Marks tried to force their way into one building, and a brick hurled at a policeman set off a brick-heaving battle. It lasted for perhaps five minutes before Glassford and Waters, yelling the magic words "lunch" and "to Camp Bartlett," persuaded the combatants to halt the fight. With quiet restored, Glassford left to report to the commissioners. After the event, the commissioners declared he had then asked for federal help. This Glassford flatly denied; he had said the police could hold the section already cleared but warned that serious trouble would ensue if the commissioners insisted upon his moving further that afternoon. If force were to be employed, let federal troops, not the police, exercise it. He then returned to the "riot area." There everything was still quiet. Commissioners Reichelderfer and Crosby came to see for themselves and departed. A few moments later a scuffle originating no one knew quite how occurred in one of the buildings; a policeman drew his pistol and two veterans were shot and several men injured before Glassford got the trouble-makers under arrest and the situation again under control. Only then did the police chief learn from a reporter that the commissioners had already requested the President to call out federal troops. Glassford ordered the police lines back from the sidewalk so as to give the bonus seekers room to move. The veterans sat down along the curb to await developments.

Washingtonians, observing the final act of the Bonus Army drama, discovered that when men in power lose their heads, anything can happen. At three o'clock on that hot July afternoon word went out over the radio that troops called in from Fort Myer under General MacArthur's command were assembling at the Ellipse. Startled, incredulous spectators began to collect. A half-mile to the east the veterans sat patiently. They waited two hours. Then the march down the Avenue began—cavalry with sabres drawn, cavalry with sabres sheathed, infantry with bayonets fixed, tear bombs on belts, and an accompaniment of six Whippet tanks with hooded machine guns. In the lead rode General Douglas MacArthur, his medals shining on his immaculate uniform, his boots gleaming, his horse perfectly groomed. It was a magnificent sight. The bedraggled men sitting on the curb and the crowd gathered nearby watched with fascination. An order sounded, shattering the illusion of splendid make-believe. A screaming police siren scattered the on-lookers; the soldiers advanced; tear bombs drove the sitting men into a frantic scramble of retreat, and, while the cavalry couriers charged back and forth over the forty-yard stretch of "battleground," the squatters abandoned all attempts to salvage their meagre possessions. When every other encampment in the city had been similarly purged, the tanks, under command of Major Dwight D. Eisenhower, lumbered off to block the Anacostia Bridge, and about nine o'clock the infantry moved on to Camp Marks to drive its denizens out. The fires set to destroy their makeshift homes illuminated the riverfront; by 11 p.m. only embers, smoke, and rubble remained. Householders in Anacostia took in weeping, bewildered women and children and let the dazed remnants of the Bonus Army stretch out in their yards.[4]

Since the government "unsheathed the sword," wrote an indignant eye-witness, "the people . . . unsheathed the pen." Letters deluged the administration and the press. Most of the Washington newspapers avoided censoriousness, especially after official justifications began to appear from the Justice and War Departments. Attorney General Mitchell announced that the "extraordinary proportion of criminal, communist, and non-veteran elements among the marchers" had brought into the capital "the largest aggregation of criminals that had ever been assembled in this city at one time." General MacArthur assured the public that, had the President not summoned troops, "another week might have meant that the government was in

[4] Springer, "Glassford," pp. 645-55; Walter W. Waters, with W. C. White, *B.E.F., The Whole Story of the Bonus Army*, pp. 56, 63-64, 149-98; *Post*, 1, 3, 5, 8-10, 12-17, 21-29 Jul 1932; John Dos Passos, "Washington and Chicago," *New Republic*, LXXI, 178, *Star*, 27-30 Jul 1932; *News*, 1-29 Jul 1932; "The Human Side of the Bonus Army," *Literary Digest*, CXIII, 25 Jun 1932, pp. 28-30; Roy Wilkins, "The Bonuseers Ban Jim Crow," *Crisis*, XXXIX, 316-17; Irving Bernstein, *The Lean Years*, pp. 437-55.

peril." Secretary of War Hurley—"the Cotillion Leader," as the *Washington Merry-go-Round* had named him—declared that his instructions to the Army had read: "Use all humanity consistent with the direct execution of this order." If, as Democratic journals contended, Republican leaders in this election year had chosen to campaign on the slogan "Hoover vs. Radicalism," the Washington *Post*'s comment on the use of troops was to be expected: "The roster of the opposition," notably Norman Thomas and Fiorello LaGuardia, "is enough to confirm the good judgment of the President." It was merely a pity that General MacArthur had let his sense of drama run away with him.

The *News*, on the other hand, noted that of the hundreds of letters received from Washingtonians, not one in ten expressed anything but anger and contempt for the ruthless handling of the Bonus Army eviction. Citizens who opposed the payment of the bonus and who had been troubled by the presence of the marchers condemned the "brutality" with which the military machine had rolled down upon defenseless men; it was sheer luck that casualties numbered fewer than seventy. Anacostia householders passionately denied that they had ever regarded the men at Camp Marks as a panhandling menace or felt anything but sympathy for them. Thirty years later a conservative Washington lawyer remarked sadly that the late summer of 1932 had "scarred" the community.

The scars were deepened by subsequent official acts. While Army sergeants searched the streetcars for B.E.F. left-overs and Justice Department agents rounded up two hundred supposed "reds," the commissioners ordered the police to deport from the District all "alleged radicals" and stop the ingress of newcomers whose purposes were dubious. General Glassford wrathfully pointed out that such measures were not only impractical but of doubtful legality. He challenged the Attorney General's statement about criminals and subversives:

police records showed that, of 362 Bonus Marchers arrested during more than two months, only twelve were charged with any crime; except for eight arrested for soliciting alms, the rest had been picked up for petty offenses such as trespass, drunkenness, or making speeches without a permit. In fact, the crime rate in August after the expulsion of the B.E.F. considerably exceeded that for June and July. Glassford did not last long thereafter. When the commissioners refused to let him fire unreliable subordinates, he resigned. He returned to Phoenix that winter to devote his energies to setting up camps for the bands of homeless boys who, like the swarms of starving children in postwar Russia, had begun to migrate across the country. With his departure, Washington lost more than a colorful, humane police chief; for, although a number of citizens thought he had been too casual in his methods, his going stripped the community of a subtle élan.[5]

The autumn of 1932 was a profoundly depressing period throughout the country. The Democratic victory in November raised hopes in some quarters without dispelling deep anxieties or filling empty bellies. For the first time Washington felt the full force of the national disaster, for, as one journalist put it, the depression hit the capital on July 1, 1932. The District's chief industry, government, had not collapsed, but the slicing of federal salaries, the obligatory furloughs without pay, and the reductions in force in every government department directly affected one family in every three, wiped out life-times' savings, and crippled business. Four banks went into receivership. President Hoover's plan to cut another $700,000,000 from the federal budget for fiscal year 1934 spelled doom to the federal building program, Washington's economic mainstay during the pre-

[5] Springer, "Glassford," p. 655; *News*, 30-31 Jul, 1, 2, 9, 18, 27 Aug, 22 Nov 1932; *Tribune*, 29 Jul, 5, 12 Aug 1932; *Star*, 1 Jan 1933; P. V. Anderson, "Tear-Gas, Bayonets and Votes," and "Republican Handsprings," *Nation*, cxxxv, 138-40, 188-89; *Post*, 30, 31 Jul, 1 Aug 1932; T. J. Joslin, *Hoover Off the Record*, pp. 263-72; *Literary Digest*, cxiv, 24 Sep 1932, p. 12; *New Republic*, lxxii, 139-41, 316, 326, 359.

ceding two years. In August the District commissioners had pared $10,000,000 from the requests for funds submitted by the District departments, and experience indicated that the budget, when passed, would be considerably below that estimated minimum. The 72nd Congress in actuality adjourned on March 3, 1933, without voting any District appropriation for 1934.

In April 1932 Coleman Jennings, president of the Associated Charities, had begged the House Subcommittee on District Appropriations to include in the welfare budget the $600,000 the President had recommended for local relief. Although Hoover let the Community Chest canvass government offices, the Chest's $185,000 deficit had forced member organizations to curtail their services; unless tax-supported agencies could assume a share of the load, the city would face untold suffering. The House assigned the $600,000 to preparing plans for the Municipal Center, a building project that, as it happened, would not materialize until 1937. Fortunately the District budget finally voted for the fiscal year 1933 did include $350,000 for unemployment relief. The Welfare Board at once assigned five of its members to a new emergency relief committee to administer the fund. Within two weeks of the August 1st opening of the committee office, 4,891 applicants for work had appeared. Every week thereafter added several hundred. Most of the relief fund went into hiring men to clear up the debris at Camp Marks and improve the grounds of Gallinger Hospital. By December the money was gone.

Estimates of the number of people out of work ran as high as 200,000. In that crisis the Community Chest turned over to its employment committee $100,000 to stop the gap till Congress should act. Just before New Year's Congress voted the Welfare Board a $625,000 deficiency appropriation, but the demands upon it were so great that the year's allowance for a destitute family had to be limited to $100. The emergency relief committee was forced to exclude from public assistance some five categories of needy: all single men, all families with less than eighteen months' residence in the District, families in which the unemployed wage-earner was over 60, families with part-time earnings too small to support them, and all cases where other social problems complicated unemployment.[6] When some 3,000 new "Hunger Marchers" arrived to demand that Congress enact national unemployment insurance, a dejected community, all passion spent, listlessly watched the police bait them. Major Brown, the new chief, made it clear that he would not be "soft" like General Glassford. No one paid much attention to the few die-hards of the defunct Bonus Army who, under the unfortunate name of "Khaki Shirts," had returned to campaign for federal unemployment relief for all jobless Americans. The Khaki Shirts nevertheless set a useful example of self-help by obtaining their headquarters rent-free in return for undertaking repairs and renovations to the building, one of the forms of barter to which men in other cities also were resorting.

In response to an appeal from the Council of Social Agencies, one real estate firm located several house-owners and landlords who were glad to reduce or forego rent in exchange for free renovations, but, the *Monthly Labor Review* noted: "little cooperation had been received from the real estate group as a whole." Elder Lightfoot Michaux, a recently arrived Negro evangelist, arranged the largest single transaction: he got the use, rent-free, of a big building at T and 7th Streets, which his followers at the "Church of God" repaired, and there he installed some forty Negro families evicted from their former quarters for non-payment of rent. The Council of Social Agencies also helped along two or three other self-help schemes: vegetable gardens in vacant lots during the summer, clothes

[6] *News*, 13 Aug, 22, 26 Nov, 6, 7, 10 Dec 1932; *Post*, 10 Jul 1932; Comrs Rpt, 1932, p. 25, 1933, pp. 82-83; *Anl Rpt Comptroller of the Currency*, 1932, pp. 19-20, 505-12; Min As Ch, 9 Mar, 15 Apr, 12 May, 14 Dec 1932; interview, Elwood Street, director of the Washington Community Chest, 1928-1934.

conservation by engaging unemployed women to collect, mend, and distribute over 18,000 garments to the desperately needy, and the "Old Woman in the Shoe" cobbling service, which rebuilt and issued to 20,000 applicants badly worn footwear donated by better-heeled persons. The Community Chest drive, however, fell nearly $500,000 short of its goal, and angry complaints multiplied about solicitors' high-pressure methods, particularly in government offices, where the average annual salary had dwindled to about $1,560. The $975,000 of public money appropriated to the Welfare Board was too little to prevent under-nourishment and concomitant illnesses from adding some 3,000 patients to the year's total in the already overcrowded Gallinger Hospital.[7]

From Reconstruction days onward Washington had always taken on much of the coloration of each successive administration. After twelve years of Republican rule, the top level of society awaited the impending change with trepidation. Bad as things were in the winter of 1932-1933, conservatives doubted that newcomers to office would do better. In shutting himself up behind locked gates at the White House during the Bonus March crisis, had President Hoover not at least discouraged further demonstrations, and, in opposing federal subsidies to the unemployed, was he not following a precedent as old as the Union? Even angry critics of his policies came to feel a touch of pity for the embittered, defeated man in the White House. After the convening of the lame duck Congress, high society carried on outwardly much as usual. If some of the elite were piqued at not being invited to the President's grand diplomatic reception, which traditionally opened the

[7] Slater Brown, "Red Day in Washington," and Malcolm Cowley, "King Mob and John Law," *New Republic*, LXXII, 153-55, 263; *Nation*, CXXXV, 652-53; *News*, 4, 28, 30 Nov, 3, 6, 24, 30 Dec 1932, 9 Mar 1933; Min As Ch, 10 Feb, 12 Oct, 10 Nov 1932, 31 Jan 1933; *Monthly Labor Review*, XXXV, 1038; "School Achievements," 1940, p. 89; Comrs Rpt, 1933, pp. 83-84, 87; *Pictorial Review of the Church of God*, pp. 26-27.

season, chagrin lessened when the word went out that political obligations to social nobodies from the Sticks had left Mr. Hoover no alternative. But gaiety at official functions that winter bore a resemblance to the false cheer that had offended Margaret Bayard Smith in the last days of John Quincy Adams' presidency.

Still, bright spots lessened the gloom. Brenda Putnam's marble Puck poised lightly over the fountain on the grounds of the new Folger Shakespeare Library reminded passers-by "what fools these mortals be," and in January 1933, thirty-one months after the laying of the cornerstone of the handsome building on East Capitol Street, the library's directors opened the reading room to the "limited use" of scholars while the staff hurried on the cataloguing of the priceless manuscripts and folios. At the DAR Constitution Hall the National Symphony Orchestra, unlike its short-lived predecessor in 1903 and 1904, played on Sunday afternoons so that the working public could attend, and the Philadelphia Orchestra scheduled a series of evening concerts. The chamber music concerts at the Phillips Gallery, formerly invitation affairs, were now open to everyone; the Library of Congress concerts continued; and a choral society at the Epiphany Church delighted participants and audiences equally. As amateurs showed their paintings, the Art League enlisted new members. Russian ballet dancers performed at the Central High School in November.

Indeed, hard times had a unifying effect upon the community. In July and August dancers and theatrical companies had staged weekly entertainments at the Sylvan Theatre on the Monument grounds, where seats cost only 25 cents, and spectators on the grassy slopes beyond could watch for nothing. The George Washington University Cue and Curtain Club drew enthusiastic audiences, and at the community centers neighbors shared in diversions ranging from classes in French or ceramics to bridge parties and amateur theatricals and pageants. During the fall crowds thronged to high school football games, which the local newspapers reported upon in flattering detail. The Board of Trade and the commission in charge of the bicentennial celebration of George Washington's birth sponsored a Hallowe'en parade and a street dance to orchestra and band music on the pavement of the newly christened Constitution Avenue. Colored Washington danced on a block of T Street.[8]

The "secret city," it is true, still stood apart from the white capital. In fact, intensifying competition for jobs strengthened sections of the barrier. Contractors for the new British Embassy on Massachusetts Avenue had to abandon plans to hire some colored builders and workmen because the A.F.ofL. raised a row about the use of non-union labor. White waiters supplanted Negro at the House of Representatives restaurant, and business firms that had customarily employed colored people for menial work took on whites instead. Even under General Glassford only forty of the thousand-man police force were Negroes. While white directors of charities deplored Negro unresponsiveness to appeals, Negro social workers, denied admission to local universities' schools of social work, were unable to acquire the professional training demanded for important posts in the welfare agencies. Victor Daly's *Not Only War*, a new novel by the colored Washington real estate dealer who thirty years later would hold a key position in the United States Employment Service, touched on the all-too-familiar theme of the effect of race prejudice on the careers of educated Negroes doomed to look in vain for "the elusive altruism which they imagined they had found in college."[9]

[8] *Star*, 4, 11 Oct 1931, 20 Nov 1932; *News*, 24 Aug, 1, 6, 22 Nov, 16 Dec 1932; programs and notices of musical events, 1930-33 (Music Div., L.C.).

[9] *Tribune*, 17 Jan, 28 Feb 1930, 8, 15 Jan, 5, 19, 26 Feb, 11, 25 Mar, 1 Apr, 10 Jun, 15 Jul, 30 Sep, 2, 9 Dec 1932; *Crisis*, xxxix, 187, 234, 343-44, 362; Victor Daly, *Not Only War*.

Discrimination took all the old forms. Under the system of relief and mothers' pensions, the *Crisis* declared, white social workers set one standard for the budget of white families, another for colored. "The white visitors insisted on calling colored mothers by their first names, discouraged them in the education of their children, and suggested sleeping apartments in cellars." A Roman Catholic priest interrupted the prayers of a Negro woman kneeling in the white section of the Immaculate Conception Church and hustled her off to the gallery. A War Department regulation covering the pilgrimage of Gold Star mothers to Europe decreed segregated units, with the colored women assigned to converted cattle ships. With Congressman Madden safely in his grave, Colonel U. S. Grant, III, commissioner of public buildings and grounds, proposed in 1932 to revive segregation in picnic areas of Rock Creek Park. Congress and the school board earmarked 80.4 percent of the new building fund for white neighborhoods and part of the 19.6 percent for Negro schools for repairing the Business High School, a badly located building erected in the 1890's for white students. That only economy dictated this arrangement made it no less an affront to Negro dignity.

Yet the shock of the depression brought the Negro community a few positive gains, difficult though they were to perceive at the time. Carter Woodson, founder and director of the Association for the Study of Negro Life and History, spoke of the "blessings" of the economic disaster which was forcing every Negro to depend upon his own people and to "indulge in serious thinking." Some of that thinking found expression at a meeting called by Campbell C. Johnson, Secretary of the colored YMCA, at which Colonel West Hamilton, printer and publisher, J. A. G. LaValle, editor of the *Tribune*, Mary Church Terrell, and Lucy D. Slowe, dean of women at Howard University, and other leaders discussed Negro welfare services and methods of coordinating them. At the same time a newly formed Committee on Improving Industrial Conditions among Colored People in the District of Columbia undertook an educational campaign to combat the factors that interfered with Negroes' getting and keeping jobs: intractability, lack of skills, unreliability about reporting for work after Sunday and pay days, lack of cleanliness, and refusal or inability to work under Negro bosses. "Possibly for the first time in years," said a member of the new Associated Negro Press, "our local politicians, high-hatters, low-brows, schemers, and general hustlers found something that requires their attention to a greater degree that they have been faithfully and joyfully giving to their favorite pastime of trying to unload a President of Howard University or an assistant superintendent of the public school system." Common troubles were submerging the old divisiveness. The *Tribune*, to be sure, complained about the lack of a "representative militant organization": the PTAs had no drive, and "the civic associations are made up of pussy-footing government employees and scared school teachers." While the local branch of the NAACP was put to it to enroll 2,500 members, a delegation persuaded the Bureau of the Budget to transfer $315,000 from the white to the colored schools.

Breaches in the wall about the secret city, moreover, were beginning to appear. It was a matter of concern to some people that the first bi-racial dance to be held in Washington since President Grant's inauguration in 1873 was a party sponsored by the Young Communist League, but police officers noted nothing objectionable during the evening. Interracial social work conferences took place during 1931 and 1932, and the 19th Street Baptist Church was twice host to three white Baptist congregations at religious services. In 1932 the Associated Charities at last elected two Negroes to the board of directors, and at its fifty-first anniversary meeting Mordecai Johnson, president of Howard University, was the principal speaker. If Negro intellectuals who looked upon him as an untrustworthy self-seeker would have preferred to have some other Negro chosen, they concurred in his theme that, not free grocery slips, but jobs on public works with no racial strings attached would alone end the depression.

Colored Washington had observed with grim satisfaction that the 2,000 Negroes among the Bonus Marchers faced no Jim Crowism; white Washington had also noticed it. More astonishing in light of the hostility the police had often displayed toward colored people, there was no segregation at the annual metropolitan police Christmas party for Washington's needy. College alumni groups began occasionally to invite colored graduates to social gatherings. When the Supreme Court decreed a new trial for the seven Negro boys charged with rape in Scottsboro, Alabama, white people joined with Negro in a huge demonstration on the Capitol grounds to demand the freeing of the prisoners. The Scottsboro case promised to be as important in American history as the Sacco-Vanzetti; the outcome, many a Washingtonian prayed, would be different, although within the secret city perhaps only incurable optimists believed in that possibility. Still, the winds of public opinion in parts of the United States were obviously shifting slightly. National journals, particularly church publications and left-wing magazines, were giving race relations increasing attention and suggesting that white condescension was almost as destructive as overt racial antagonism. If the colored intelligentsia in the capital saw little basic change in the white city's point-of-view even when the National Theatre announced a "special" performance of *Green Pastures* on March 2, 1933, which would be "open to all," a white newcomer remarked upon an atmosphere so friendly to well-mannered

Negroes that the disappearance of racism in Washington seemed "just around the corner."[10]

[10] *Tribune*, 10 Jan, 14 Feb 1930, 5, 19 Feb, 1 Apr, 17 Jun, 23, 30 Dec 1932, 3 Mar 1933; *Crisis*, XXXIX, 187, 316-19; Min As Ch, 10 Dec 1930, pp. 4, 6, 50th Anniv Mtg, 12 Jan 1932, p. 7, 51st Anniv Mtg, 31 Jan 1933; *News*, 7 Nov 1932; *Negro Status and Race Relations in the United States, 1911-1946, The Thirty-five Year Report of the Phelps-Stokes Fund*, pp. 73-79. For typical exhortations about race relations, see *Christian Century*, XLVII and XLVIII, especially Hubert C. Herring, "An Adventure in Black and White," XLVII, 1526-29.

CHAPTER XIX

THE NEW DEAL CAPITAL IN WHITE AND BLACK, 1933-1940

A CHILL wind carrying a drizzle of rain swept across sullen skies above the Potomac on March 4, 1933. Anxiety rested heavy upon the crowd gathered on the Capitol grounds. Early that morning every bank in the United States had locked its doors, almost thirteen million Americans were out of work, and the means of relief seemed to have dried up in every city and hamlet across the continent. At noon, the President-elect, his son James at his elbow, walked out onto the East Portico. A cheer, then silence. Chief Justice Hughes administered the oath, and the new President began to speak. As the beautiful, resonant voice rolled out reassuring words, tension relaxed. Wild applause greeted his statement, "We have nothing to fear but fear itself." When he promised to act quickly to restore confidence to the nation, the crowd's ovation echoed across the plaza. As he concluded, the clouds lifted, and suddenly sunlight bathed the Capitol. Symbolically, the fulfillment of the promise had begun.

At the White House, Supreme Court Justice Benjamin Cardozo swore in the new Cabinet in the late afternoon. Twenty-four hours later, the radio announced that the President, exercising war powers granted President Wilson in 1917, was declaring a bank holiday and had summoned Congress into special session on March 9th. If fresh alarm struck here and there, a wonderful gaiety nevertheless took possession of Washington. That Sunday evening "Daisy" Harriman, National Democratic Party committeewoman, gave one of her famous supper parties. There General Douglas MacArthur shed benign charm on fellow guests who, like his hostess, had angrily criticized his treatment of the Bonus Marchers seven

387

months before; Junius S. Morgan of Wall Street and several other die-hard Republicans cheerily talked of the future with ardent Roosevelt supporters. Other Washington households also celebrated that evening, while lights burned through the night at the Treasury, where officials began hammering out an emergency banking bill to present to Congress eighty hours later.

The new week brought sobering reminders that words and a beam of thin March sunlight would not alone put the world to rights, but a sense of adventure took hold as businessmen and housewives set about learning how to manage without money. While three shifts working round the clock at the Bureau of Engraving turned out two million $1,000 Federal Reserve notes to have in readiness for a new banking act, pseudo-promissory notes circulated as scrip. On Wednesday President Roosevelt met with the press to discuss his ideas on the banking crisis. When reporters, hopeful of learning the outcome of a presidential conference with congressional leaders, gathered on the White House grounds that evening, a down-pour of cold rain impelled one of the Executive staff to invite the newsmen to stand in the shelter of the portico. "It was not long," reported the *News*, "before official members of the Roosevelt entourage accompanied by the correspondents were singing 'O Build Me a Home where the buffalo roam!' The White House cops stared and gaped, not realizing that serious business could be put to music without hurting either." Old Washingtonians, hardened to Herbert Hoover's curtness with the press, also gaped when they read of the incident.[1]

The emergency banking bill, presented to Congress shortly after noon on March 9th, became law before 9 o'clock that night. The act, which empowered the Secretary of the Treasury to release the newly printed Federal Reserve notes in exchange for

[1] Arthur M. Schlesinger, Jr., *The Coming of the New Deal*, pp. 1-21, 105, 182; *News*, 4, 6-9 Mar 1933. Throughout this and every succeeding chapter much of my most significant information derives from interviews.

currency and, under a system of licenses, to reopen the closed banks, brought gold and deposits flowing back into circulation. In the first of his "fireside chats" on the following Sunday evening the President talked to several million radio listeners about the act, making so complicated a subject as banking, Will Rogers said, understandable even to bankers. By March 14th, eight national banks, five trust companies, and seven savings banks in the District of Columbia were again transacting business. Over some protest, on March 20th Congress passed the Economy Act reducing veterans' pensions and cutting all government salaries 15 percent below the scale of nine months earlier. Before Congress adjourned in mid-June, it had enacted thirteen other major pieces of legislation and several of lesser importance.

While the speed of congressional action took Washington's breath away, the change in the social atmosphere was scarcely less astonishing. Days before the course of New Deal action became clear, the icy aloofness that had enveloped 1600 Pennsylvania Avenue gave way to a heart-warming friendliness. Herbert Hoover, tears sliding down his cheeks unobserved by the crowd at the Capitol, had left the city immediately after the inauguration. Grief and hopelessness seemed to vanish with him. A few hours, observed the head of the Secret Service, transformed the White House "into a gay place, full of people who oozed confidence." During that "renaissance spring," in Rexford Tugwell's phrase, the President "reigned in a splendid informality that shed its glow over all Washington." To the faint shock of society dowagers, Mrs. Roosevelt continued to write her newspaper column, "My Day," but she welcomed guests with a graciousness Dolly Madison herself could not have bettered. For, Alice Roosevelt Longworth explained to *Ladies' Home Journal* readers, her cousins Franklin and Eleanor "like people."[2]

[2] *News*, 13-15 Mar 1933; E. W. Starling, *Starling of the White House*, pp. 306-07; Alice Roosevelt Longworth, "Lion Hunting in the New Deal," *Ladies' Home Journal*, LI, 27.

"A good part of the national energy once bent on money-making animates the headquarters of the New Deal," wrote Anne O'Hare McCormick. College professors, lawyers, economists, social workers, some of them with "a passion for anonymity," some of them ridden by a cockiness congressmen and old Washingtonians found hard to stomach, the "brain-trusters" produced a ferment. Ideas were the currency of all the planners. And, as an old farm leader remarked rather sourly, like all uplifters they had "an unquenchable thirst for conversation. They were all chain talkers," from the brilliant economist, Rex Tugwell, and Secretary of the Interior Harold Ickes, the self-styled "Old Curmudgeon," to "Moley, Moley, Moley, Lord God Almighty," as the irreverent called political scientist Raymond Moley. Bright young men fresh from the universities and from offices without clients were soon pouring into Washington to man the new agencies created by congressional legislation. The first waves of New Dealers seldom doubted their capacity to establish a brave new world. "We were filled with a vast enthusiasm," one of them recalled, "although we didn't know exactly for what. And we didn't know what we were going to do. Most of us had to make work for ourselves."

The newcomers looked upon the city as theirs to use but not bother about and the aborigines as quaint at best, at worst a stuffy, negligible lot. The attitude was that of a sophisticated summer colony toward the natives. The natives' point of view also followed that pattern—irritation, touches of envy, thankfulness for material benefits, and anticipation of the day when the seasonal invaders would decamp, leaving the community to recapture its own. Yet within a year or two, the most supercilious of the New Dealers departed, and most of those who settled in learned little by little that not all the early settlers were dodos. And undeniably the new supply of red corpuscles enriched the bloodstream.[3]

[3] Thomas L. Stokes, *Chip Off My Shoulder*, pp. 362-63; Anne O'Hare McCormick, *The World at Home*, p. 231.

During most of 1933 immediate economic problems blotted out thoughts about the city's changed social climate. The "lurch into State socialism," almost universally welcomed during the "First Hundred Days," soon lost much of its appeal to Washington businessmen. As the Economy Act struck a blow at a city more dependent upon government payrolls than upon any form of private enterprise, the president of the Federation of Citizens' Associations foresaw a new low approaching on July 1st, when 17,000 Washington residents were to be "thrown off" the pension rolls. On top of the 15-percent cuts in federal salaries, a new ruling halved the already shrunken income of many a family, for, in effect, no one with a spouse in government employ could keep a government post; one to a family would spread the jobs. Places opening up in new federal agencies rarely fell to old-time civil service employees. Local bank deposits after rising slightly during the late spring shrank again during the summer. In October several of the District's savings banks were still in receivership, and depositors' prospects of reclaiming savings totalling some $12,500,000 were not bright.

A measure of the gloom was the listlessness with which baseball fans celebrated the Senators' winning of the American League pennant; nine years before, the capture of the World Series had people dancing in the streets. The day after the 1933 victory apparently no Washingtonian outside a small circle of scientists observed a brief newspaper notice telling of the discovery of heavy water. Householders feeling the economic pinch took little pleasure in hearing that the Turkish Ambassador, dean of the diplomatic corps, entertained 3,000 guests with champagne and caviar served by footmen in mulberry velvet on the very day the District tax assessor announced the impending sale of 28,000 pieces of real estate unless the $1,200,000 to $1,500,000 in back taxes were paid before Thanksgiving Day. As local building operations during the first year of the New

Deal dropped in value to less than half the $18,500,000 of the year before, financially hard-pressed residents tended to resent the accounts in metropolitan newspapers and magazines describing the exhilaration of living amidst the excitements of Washington.[4]

Yet by the end of 1934 journalists' picture of the capital was not over-painted insofar as it depicted the white business community. The Economy Act notwithstanding, the federal establishment in Washington grew steadily; the 63,000 government jobs of March 1933 expanded to about 93,000 before 1935, most of them filled by newcomers. Compared to salary reductions averaging 50 percent in other cities, the 15-percent federal pay cuts were slight, and 10 percent of the 15 was restored in July 1934, the rest the following spring. Months before the boarded-up shop windows along New York's Fifth Avenue ceased to be a commonplace, that index of business stagnation had disappeared in most of Washington. Mansions along Massachusetts Avenue, the Gold Coast of the 1920's, still stood empty, as former millionaires forewent the uncertain pleasures and the certain expense of spending the winter in the New Deal capital, but few smaller, unpretentious houses remained untenanted. The newspaper correspondents corps grew to five hundred, and, as the National Industrial Recovery Act demanded a framing of codes for every major industry, a stream of businessmen poured in month after month to sit around conference tables and later dilute their sorrows at hotel cocktail parties. Washington hotels that year, according to one report, took in $15,000,000. Concentrated campaigns of the Board of Trade enlarged the city's convention business; in 1934 the president estimated that the first formal Cherry Blossom Festival, with a beauty contest and the crowning of a queen, alone

---

[4] Oswald Garrison Villard, "Mr. Roosevelt's Two Months," *New Statesman and Nation* (new ser), v, 594; Comrs Rpts, 1933, pp. 37, 46, 49, 1934, p. 46; *Rpt Comptroller/Currency*, 31 Oct 1933, pp. 224, 229-30, 402, 590-92; *News*, 14 Apr, 22 Sep, 1, 2 Nov 1933; *Star*, 1 Oct 1933.

brought in over $500,000 of tourist money in a single week. While perhaps half the city's bankers, brokers, and real estate dealers joined the chorus which had begun to excoriate "that man" in the White House, the other half reminded them that as Washingtonians they had few valid grounds for complaint.

In describing Washington's business boom, Commissioner George E. Allen wrote that 40,000 people arrived daily at the Union Station in 1936. Though the city lacked heavy industry, he pointed to some $70,000,000 of "light manufactures," chiefly printing and bakery products, some of them doubtless far from light. The value of private building operations rose from the $7,000,000 of 1934 to about $24,000,000 within two years and within the next four reached $34,979,700. Still the nearly 1,800 new apartment houses, the more than 2,300 separate and row houses, and the 800 office buildings put up before 1940 fell short of demand. Every two weeks cash from the $8,500,000 in federal and the $1,000,000 in District government pay checks circulated in Washington shops and markets. "Effective buying income," asserted a magazine writer, averaged $3,782 in Washington, $2,000 in other American cities. It was easy to see why the *Star*'s advertising linage exceeded that of every other paper in the country. National unions, encouraged by New Deal friendliness to organized labor, began to set up permanent headquarters here. And, whereas the population of all other cities except Los Angeles declined during the decade, Washington's increased by 36 percent. Before midsummer of 1940, the federal payroll in the city swelled to about 166,000 employees.[5]

The public works program, briefly curtailed in 1933, soon expanded to embrace not only completion of the Federal Triangle, the massive Supreme Court, and the second House Office

[5] *Rpts B/Tr*, 1934-1936, *passim*, 1937, p. 10; *Star*, 21 Sep 1941; George E. Allen, "Washington, A Capital That Went Boom," *Nation's Business*, xxv, 32-33; Comrs Rpts, 1939, pp. 88-89, 1941, p. 78; Oliver McKee, Jr., "Washington As A Boom Town," *North American Review*, ccxxxix, 177-83; David L. Cohn, "Washington, The Blest," *Atlantic*, clxiii, 609-13.

Building but also construction of the Library of Congress Annex, new Department of Agriculture buildings to the south of the Mall, and beyond them a new central heating plant and a huge addition to the government warehouse alongside the railroad tracks. From the tip of the Triangle to the foot of the Hill, greensward and newly planted trees replaced the string of honky-tonk shops that had long been an eyesore along lower Pennsylvania Avenue. On the Constitution Avenue site of the old Baltimore and Potomac depot, the National Gallery of Art, gift of former Secretary of the Treasury Andrew Mellon, began to rise in 1937, while on Judiciary Square the Police Court building went up—the first unit of the long-talked-of Municipal Center. At the approach to the 14th Street Bridge, the new headquarters of the Bureau of Printing and Engraving looked out over the cherry trees encircling the Tidal Basin. "New Interior" facing the bulk of the "Old Interior" building across Rawlins Park and, beyond, a line of white marble edifices set in wide green lawns added dignity to the Potomac end of Constitution Avenue.

Although the neo-classical architecture for most of the new public buildings evoked occasional criticism, only the design and location of the memorial to Thomas Jefferson raised a storm of protest. When the specially appointed commission chose a site on the Tidal Basin and displayed John Russell Pope's model, one student of the eighteenth-century plan of the city insisted that a domed structure at that spot, by blocking the view from the White House southward over the Potomac River valley, would destroy a significant feature of L'Enfant's layout. Architects the country over denounced Pope's adaptation of Jefferson's design of the University of Virginia Rotunda, a "Roman Temple," singularly unsuited to a twentieth-century capital; they contended that the necessary cutting or transplanting of some of the Japanese cherry trees would further darken this "Twilight of the Gods." Not until the outcry of the 1960's over the projected "Stonehenge" in memory of Franklin Delano Roosevelt would popular indignation over architectural plans run so strong. The furor delayed construction of the Jefferson Memorial, and on the spring morning in 1939 when men and steam shovels arrived at the Tidal Basin to start digging the foundation, they found half-hysterical women chained to the cherry trees. Yet, when the building was at last completed in 1942, the columned, flat-domed temple, the bronze figure within, and the inscriptions from Jefferson's writings that ring the interior walls delighted the public.[6]

In guiding this huge public building program the Park and Planning Commission found itself playing a lesser role than formerly, first because instructions not to issue annual reports after 1932 meant dependence upon occasional newspaper articles to publicize proposals, and second because Congress omitted an appropriation until 1935 on the grounds that the $4,000,000 voted in 1930 and 1931 was to cover three years' expenditures. Fortunately Frederic Delano seized an unexpected chance to purchase a stretch of the Chesapeake and Ohio Canal; upon learning that the proprietors had applied to the Reconstruction Finance Corporation for a loan, he was able to buy at a bargain price the area from Rock Creek to the District line. The old tow path above the Aqueduct Bridge immediately became a favorite haunt of leisurely hikers, fishermen, and bird-watchers, and it encouraged the newly founded "Wander Birds" and the Capital Hiking Club to explore Potomac trails further. In 1935 when Congress again appropriated funds, it left the commission no discretion: the entire $800,000 was to go for the purchase of District playground sites. At the same time an organizational reshuffle enlarging the functions of the National Park Service diminished the

[6] Comrs Rpt, 1937, p. 68; Joseph Hudnut, "Twilight of the Gods," *Magazine of Art*, xxx, 480-81; Fred G. Vosburgh, "Wonders of the New Washington," *National Geographic Magazine*, LXVII, 457-88.

influence of the planning commission. While the Shipstead Act of 1930 required Fine Arts Commission approval of the architectural features of any new building or remodelling of old proposed on privately owned property adjoining or facing upon government buildings, and law broadened the Zoning Commission's powers to forestall construction that would intensify traffic, parking, or public health problems, the Park and Planning Commission largely turned into a land-purchasing agent for other government bodies.

Several of the planning commission's carefully thought-out proposals fell almost soundlessly into the void. Members and staff urged placing all buildings for the federal judiciary on the Hill in a cluster about a square east of the Supreme Court, which should be named in honor of the late Justice Oliver Wendell Holmes. Beyond the Folger Shakespeare Library on East Capitol Street a new building should go up to house the Surgeon General's Library. By extending federal construction eastward, the balance L'Enfant had intended would take form, and the beautifully planted, spacious Lincoln Park would assume the dignity designers had envisaged for the Hill 147 years before. After 1934, except for the Library of Congress Annex, no new government building would rise in that area until the mid-1950's. Fort Drive, projected in the 1920's as a scenic route encircling the city's Civil War forts, was shelved indefinitely.[7]

Meanwhile the creation of the Alley Dwelling Authority in 1934 promised the community more enduring benefits than new public buildings and parkways. Since 1917 the alley slums had worsened; now, under the direction of the able John Ihlder, eradication of those breeding spots of tuberculosis,

[7] Interview, Wm. McIntyre, Ntl Cap Planning Comm; *Star*, 2 Nov 1932, 18 Oct 1935, 15, 17 Apr, 1 May 1938, 5, 26 Jan, 18 Feb, 16 Nov 1939, 23 Mar, 19 Apr 1940; *Post*, 16 May 1941; *News*, 14 Aug 1935; David Cushman Coyle, "Frederic A. Delano: Catalyst," *Survey Graphic*, xxxv, 252-69; Coyle, "Washington Gets Broad Powers to Prevent Land Overcrowding," *American City*, LIII, 81.

juvenile delinquency, and crime within ten years looked possible. Unhappily the act came too late to be effective. Had it passed when drafted in 1930, Ihlder believed private builders would have cooperated in putting up inexpensive housing for the displaced "alley families," but by 1935 the building boom was in full swing, and projects on which profit would be narrow no longer interested contractors. They nevertheless opposed public housing. So the Alley Dwelling Authority had to spend most of its first two years fighting law suits aimed at stopping its acquisition of suitable sites. In that interval mounting prices limited the authority's purchasing power. The agency consequently sometimes cleared an area and sold the land instead of using it for new low-rental developments.

By 1937 some 9,000 houses were still lighted only by oil lamps, 7,000 multiple-family tenements were without inside water taps, and 11,000 families had no inside toilets. One of the worst slums stood within a hundred yards of the new air-conditioned office of the Federal Housing Administrator. Nor was the incredible squalor "behind the marble mask" of the capital confined to the alleys and Negro shanties. The tourist might drive along streets lined with what appeared to be respectable middle-class houses and never dream that behind the front doors fifteen to twenty families, white as well as colored, were packed into space designed for one. By 1940 construction of about 3,000 public housing units, including a 286-family Negro development on Benning Road, marked the total accomplishment of six years' work. Nine-tenths of the occupied alleys remained untouched.

Yet several forces combined after 1934 to shift population and ease housing for "the forgotten man" a notch above the bottom ranks of society. The Home Owners Loan Act, passed in the First Hundred Days, staved off mortgage foreclosures; the newer Federal Housing Authority guaranteed bank loans for private housing projects; and the Resettlement Administration, set up in 1935 under Rex Tugwell, undertook to open planned communities in the countryside beyond the congested areas of big cities. So Greenbelt, Maryland, a skillfully laid out town designed for about a thousand families in the middle-income bracket, began to rise within a half-hour's drive of downtown Washington; and in the spring of 1936 private enterprisers with some Housing Administration backing started in Clarendon, Virginia, a settlement of multiple-family dwellings, a pattern that spread as building and land prices in the area spiralled upward.[8] The outward push from Washington was hastened also by the business revival, the wish for play space for children, and the assumption that everyone above the pauper level would drive an automobile to work. Arlington, in 1920 set off from Alexandria under a county government, was one of the first suburbs to expand. Improved highways, the opening of the Memorial Bridge, the county's good public schools, and the comparatively modest cost of real estate in an agreeable semi-rural setting attracted scores of middle-class householders. The relatively well-to-do gravitated toward Chevy Chase in Maryland's Montgomery County, a much older, sophisticated region of roomy houses built on large lots in the vicinity of the country club. To the west the opening of two units of the National Institutes of Health encouraged a migration into Bethesda, while the overflow from the District pushed the growth of the small city of Silver Spring and began to affect Prince Georges County to the east.

The exodus from Washington was almost exclusively white. When the demolition of the curio shops along lower Pennsyl-

---

[8] *First Report of the Alley Dwelling Authority for the District of Columbia*, 15 Dec 1935; *News*, 15 Sep 1933; Rpt B/Tr, 1935, p. 11; John Ihlder, "Housing in Washington," *Council Bulletin*, I, Oct 1936, pp. 8-12; *Community Service*, I, Mar 1937, p. 9, May 1937, pp. 3, 6; "The United States and District of Columbia Housing," *ibid.*, Sep 1937, pp. 3-4; "We Can Get Rid of the Slums," *ibid.*, II, Feb 1938, p. 6, and "Alley People," *ibid.*, May 1938, p. 9; Comrs Rpt, 1938, pp. 173-74; NCPPC, *Washington Present and Future*, Monograph #1, 1950, p. 21; "Behind the Marble Mask," *Collier's*, CII, 3 Sep 1938, pp. 11-14; *Star*, 13 Oct 1935; Schlesinger, *New Deal*, pp. 370-71.

vania Avenue forced Chinatown to move, the colony of approximately one hundred Chinese families chose to locate on H Street on the fringe of the business district, but Negroes who would have preferred suburbia had no choice. Virginia and Maryland property-owners, real estate dealers, and builders stood fast against renting or selling to colored families irrespective of their financial resources; banks refused to make them loans. Hence a steady shrinkage in the percentage of nonwhites in the suburban population and a proportionate rise in the District of Columbia's followed. (See Table V.) And within Washington neighborhoods changed character.

TABLE V

Percent of Population Nonwhite in Suburban Jurisdictions of Metropolitan Washington and the District of Columbia 1930-1950

	1930*	1940	1950
Montgomery County, Md.	16.8	11	6
Prince Georges County, Md.	23.3	19	12
Arlington County, Va.	12.5	9	5
Fairfax County, Va.**	19.0	16	10
Alexandria, Va.	20.3	16	12
Falls Church, Va.	**	**	2
District of Columbia	27.1	28.2	35

* This was Negro only.
** Falls Church included in Fairfax County before 1950.

The most dramatic shift took place in Georgetown. Although a number of her beautiful eighteenth- and early nineteenth-century houses had been kept up over the years, a good many had fallen into disrepair before the turn of the century. In 1930 about half her inhabitants were poverty-stricken Negroes, most of them occupying substandard dwellings, some without running water or electricity. Yet the convenience of the location and the yeast of the abiding charm of the shabby little village had begun to work in the late 1920's. The remodelling started then had proceeded slowly during the depths of the depression

399

but about 1934 suddenly gained momentum. Impecunious young New Dealers moved into the cramped restored little houses. Tiny fenced-off patches of ground at the rear, recently littered with rubbish, again turned into gardens and patios with lilac bushes and crepe myrtle nursed back to vigor by pruning and feeding. Every rejuvenated spot inspired the redemption of others, while real estate brokers hastily played down their decades-old argument that once a neighborhood had become part-Negro, it deteriorated with inexorable rapidity. The "decoloration" of Georgetown would not be complete before the 1950's, but it had gone far enough by 1940 to intensify Negroes' housing problems.

Colored families usually were unable to resist the prices white dealers offered for Georgetown property or else could not afford the higher rentals caused by improvements to adjoining property. Since the acceptance of a bi-racial mode of life beyond Rock Creek failed to permeate the rest of Washington, relocation was difficult. Black ghettos became more tightly packed, and the complexion of some erstwhile white neighborhoods darkened, for example, the area around the Morgan School above Florida Avenue. Rows of gerry-built little boxes in remote stretches of northeast Washington began to fill with up-rooted colored tenants. Kelly Miller of Howard University observed that, far from easing after the climax of the fight against housing covenants in 1926, strict residential segregation had increased. And from 1933 onward, Negro in-migrants from the Deep South poured in, undeterred by the fact that hundreds of colored people native to the District were out of work. Thus, whereas the nearly 120,000 white newcomers of the New Deal era were generally well-educated upper-class citizens qualifying for government posts, a large part of the 55,000 colored people added to the population stood at the bottom of the socio-economic pyramid. The colored school records later showed that the IQ's of children born in the southern states averaged five points below the 97.31 median of school-children native to the city.[9]

Colored Washington had no share in the boom the white business world enjoyed. The depression killed traditional "Negro jobs," as white men asserted their superior claims to work they had formerly considered beneath them. After the upturn in white business, Negroes were seldom able to reclaim their places as waiters, bellhops, elevator operators, janitors, and barbers. The building trades unions kept Negroes out of skilled construction jobs, and colored men's brief hopes that the Capital Transit Company would hire Negro platform workers collapsed when the Transit Union threatened a walk-out if a single "nigger" were employed. Although thirty-five new Negro-owned retail stores opened between 1929 and 1935, the volume of business was too small and payrolls were too thin to take up any of the slack in the Negro labor market. Advertising in the *Tribune* shrank month after month till finally the paper merged with the Baltimore *Afro-American*.

Convinced that the boycott was the one weapon available to the colored community to check discriminatory employment practices, in the fall of 1933 a small group of men formed the New Negro Alliance to organize Negro consumers in the struggle. Their first move was to picket a U Street hot-dog stand whose owner employed only white men. A week or two without Negro customers persuaded the proprietor to hire colored help. The prospect of a similar boycott proved effective when members of the Alliance sought out the proprietors of the scores of small Jewish-owned shops in the neighborhood. By 1934 the A & P chain had taken on a few Negro clerks in its branches in colored neighborhoods. For a time Howard University intellectuals, notably Ralph Bunche, objected that the movement represented an unwholesome racism certain to

[9] Census Tracts, D.C., 1930, Bureau of the Census; Eunice Grier, *Understanding Washington's Population*, pp. 10-13; see ch. XVII, n. 16.

boomerang, but Alliance leaders insisted that "buy where you work" merely meant using Negro purchasing power to give qualified Negroes an equal chance with whites. Criticism subsided as small successes multiplied: by 1936 nearly 300 jobs filled by Negroes in stores formerly manned only by whites. Fifteen months of picketing the two branches of the Peoples Drug Store located in solidly Negro neighborhoods clinched the argument, for although the company held out against hiring Negro clerks and sidestepped the "sit-down" challenge by removing the soda fountains where Negroes asked for service, the heavy financial losses of the chain convinced the community of the utility of the "consumer strike." That Mary McLeod Bethune, President Roosevelt's special advisor on minority affairs, joined the picket line probably gave special significance to that particular campaign.[10]

Until Mrs. Bethune's appointment in 1936, and indeed after, the New Deal did less for colored people than they had expected. They got more and better posts in the executive departments, it is true. The District Recorder of Deeds, a municipal court judge, and the Minister to Liberia were colored men; William Hastie received the federal judgeship for the Virgin Islands; some forty-odd minor administrative posts in Washington went to eminent Negroes; and in 1935 forty got places in a new analysis section of the Labor Department. But in 1938, of the 9,717 Negroes in the federal service in Washington, 90 percent held custodial jobs for which the top annual pay rate was $1,260; only 9.5 percent had clerical jobs, and only 47 men had subprofessional rank. In the matter of promotions, the merit system was as inoperative as in earlier years. When the Resettlement Administration proposed to relocate colored families in Negro Greenbelts, the *Tribune* blasted the plan as a sign of a deliberate policy of cutting Negro Americans

[10] *Tribune*, 13 Jul, 5 Oct, 23 Nov 1933, 3, 31 May 1934, 6 Dec 1935; *Afro-American*, 28 Jan 1939; *New Negro Opinion*, Oct 1933-Apr 1936; *New Negro Alliance Yearbook*, 1939.

off from the main body of American life. Similarly, the hyper-critical wondered why the National Youth Administration should have a separate unit for Negro affairs instead of handling them as part of all youth problems.

Consensus, however, was general that Mary McLeod Bethune, former head of a colored girls' school in Florida, was the person to take charge of the NYA Negro division. Although nuances indicated a faint irritation among some of Washington's colored elite that she kept herself somewhat apart from the local community, they quickly realized that her breadth of knowledge, her perceptiveness, her political finesse, and her direct access to the President were invaluable to the Negro cause. In dealing with her white associates, as one young man recalled, her pronouncedly Negroid appearance in itself helped. With her deep-chocolate-colored skin, her heavy build, and rather prognathous jaw, she seemed like a product of darkest Africa—until she spoke. Then the exquisitely musical voice offering sagacious counsel in a perfect Oxford accent carried an impact that left no one in doubt that here was an extraordinary woman to whom any sensible person would listen with respectful attention.[11]

To some colored Washingtonians more important from the first than any political appointee or any New Deal agency was Elder Lightfoot Michaux and his "Church of God." Such confidence as they had in the President perhaps stemmed from the evangelist's assurance that Franklin D. Roosevelt was the Lord's chosen instrument. Not long after the Elder came to Washington in the depths of the depression, he managed, no one knew quite how, to get money for a daily radio program to tell listeners to lean on Jesus. Every morning at 7 o'clock the "Happy am I" preacher explained over station WSJV that W stood for willingly, J for Jesus, S for suffered, and V for

[11] Hayes, *Negro Govt Worker*, p. 104; John P. Davis, "A Black Inventory of the New Deal," and Abraham Epstein, "The Social Security Act," *Crisis*, XLII, 141-42, 334-38; *Crisis*, XLIII, 168, 204, XLVI, 271.

victory over the grave. His tub-thumping exhortations helped him quickly to collect a following as devoted as that of "Papa" Divine. Under the pastor's lead the little store-front Church of God on Georgia Avenue turned into a kind of institutional church that fed the hungry and housed the homeless. As a coast-to-coast network picked up the evangelist's broadcasts, one of his publications noted, "the people began to clamor for him to come out into the open and fight his War on the devil. Elder Michaux was himself eager to go directly to the front and boldly let the people eat right out of his hands the spiritual food they needed to keep the devil on the run." So the Elder organized the "Cross Choir" of 156 trained singers to stage elaborately executed programs of choruses and marches, usually at the Griffith Stadium.

The preacher won the ear of politically influential people. When the congregation of the Church of God elected five honorary deacons, District Commissioner George E. Allen, Dwight D. Eisenhower, "Steve" Early, personal secretary to the President, Clark Griffith, principal owner of Washington's baseball team, and Harry Butcher, vice president of the Columbia Broadcasting Company, all accepted the honor and a Bible each to seal the covenant. Upon hearing that a congressman, possessor of a race horse named "Not Worth Owning," was about to propose legalization of horse-racing in the District and revival of the old race track on Benning Road, the evangelist, pointing out that gambling was not pleasing to God, persuaded the congressman to drop his bill and sell Not Worth Owning. Having induced Honorary Deacon Allen to sell his horse also, Michaux then inveigled both men into helping him buy the race track at a bargain price. There in time to come he would put up Mayfair Mansions, a luxurious 596-unit Negro housing development. Until 1938 he engaged an excursion boat every summer to convey people awaiting baptism down the Potomac, but that year Honorary Deacon Clark

Griffith arranged to have a large canvas tank set up at the ball park, where the pastor, clad in a black robe, high rubber boots, and a black skull cap, baptized his sheep in water imported from the River Jordan. New Dealers prone to ignore all other local affairs and local citizens looked upon him as a personage, the one Washingtonian, white or colored, to excite their interest.

If nobody begrudged Elder Michaux his triumphs, neither were many colored Washingtonians willing to accept his brand of religious fervor or endorse his tactics. On the contrary. No doubt a number of white people were genuinely moved by his oratory and impressed by his good works, but the delighted amusement his methods provoked in much of white Washington contained the seeds of a derisiveness damaging to all colored people. The elements in American society that twenty years later would form the core of white citizens' councils naturally looked upon the Elder with favor as the epitome of the old-style camp-meeting Negro whose militance was directed at the devil, not in seeking equality with white men, a Negro to be patted on the back, helped when convenient, made use of, and ridiculed. Whether or not highly educated colored Washingtonians saw a potential threat in the racial image Elder Michaux presented, they looked for other paths than his to their goals.

The second half of the 1930's found much of the colored community groping. By 1936 the local chapter of the NAACP, unable to work with "the rowdy element," had faded out. The New Negro Alliance, however successful in opening up jobs, could not ensure fair wages, and colored Washingtonians were tired of waiting for whites to recognize Afro-Americans as more American than Afro. Hence when the brilliant and respected John Preston Davis, during NRA days executive secretary of the Joint Committee on National Recovery, issued a call to Negro organizations all over the country to evolve through a national Negro congress a national racial policy, the idea appealed strongly. But the conventions arrived at no plan of positive action, and in 1940 when Davis advocated the Communist party line, most of his followers repudiated him. The Congress fell apart. Meanwhile, in response to a proposal put forward by Assistant Superintendent of the Colored Schools Garnett Wilkinson, a handful of colored people turned to a new form of interracial conciliation by joining with a small group of earnest whites in founding the Washington Urban League. Chartered in December 1938, the league worked on the premise that persuasion was the only effective way to end racial prejudice and give Negroes economic opportunities. A gift from Canon Anson Phelps Stokes of the Cathedral provided funds for a first year, but the new organization made little headway. Ultra-conservative whites and, conversely, left-of-center Negro leaders considered the program of bi-racial conferences little more than talk and more talk. And talk opened no doors, not even to the movie theatres showing "Abraham Lincoln in Illinois" to which a colored man who had won a contest as the person looking most like Abe was refused admission.

Oddly enough, the most significant break in the color line to occur in Washington before 1939 occasioned little comment. Without any pressure, in 1937 the faculty of the graduate school of American University voted to admit Negro students. The unanimous decision came in answer to an application from an exceptionally well qualified candidate, a graduate of the Howard University Law School, who explained that she wanted to take a Ph.D. in political science; Howard neither offered sufficiently advanced courses nor conferred doctoral degrees. When the president and the most influential of the trustees endorsed the faculty vote, only one of the nearly 2,000 graduate students withdrew. Negro enrollment was not heavy. Some of the colored students found the standards of scholarship hard to meet, and professors were troubled now and again at having to give discouragingly low grades, but most of the candidates eventually completed the work for masters' degrees, and several won doctorates with distinction. Shortly after American University acted, Catholic University opened its school of social work to Negroes.

While this minor revolution went largely unnoticed, early in 1939 chance produced more dramatic results. The national limelight suddenly focused on racial discrimination in the capital when the DAR refused to allow the famous contralto Marian Anderson to sing in the DAR-owned Constitution Hall. When the Board of Education, after pondering the request for use of the white Central High School auditorium, hedged its permission about with a proviso that this was to be an exception, not a precedent, the furor aroused in the city and throughout the country exceeded any outburst of indignation within the memory of Washington's oldest inhabitants. Secretary of the Interior Harold Ickes immediately authorized the use of the Lincoln Memorial, and there on Easter Sunday afternoon the concert took place at the feet of the "Great Emancipator" before an audience of 75,000 people. No one present at that moving performance ever forgot it. It was the turning point, one man averred, in Washington Negroes' seventy-year-old fight against discrimination.

White people shed some of their condescension and more of their obliviousness, a revived NAACP chapter enlisted 2,500 members in a matter of months, and confidence in the future ran strong in colored Washington. Her 191 doctors, 72 dentists, 98 lawyers, and nearly 600 public school and university teachers upon whose "phenomenal culture" her name for distinction rested, in the opinion of the secretary of the new NAACP branch, in the past had sought white recognition too eagerly to heed their inferiors. Now a feeling of unity was emerging along with a belief that the New Deal was about to open the way for the "common man" of the Negro world, much as the age of Jackson had for white Americans a century before. In spite of the shortage of jobs, wrote Victor Daly, after six years of Roosevelt's administration colored people in Washington were better off "economically, socially and culturally" than anywhere else, and although custom perpetuated segregation in hotels, restaurants, and all places of entertainment, the concerted bi-racial movement fostered by the Marian Anderson episode promised to grow. The lessons of Nazi Germany's race doctrines were not wholly lost upon Washingtonians. Thus, before the American military build-up got under way in mid-1940, uninterrupted progress seemed assured.[12]

Social intercourse between the races was still rare. Distinguished colored musicians gave a few concerts at the White House; eminent Negroes occasionally attended official receptions or had tea with Mrs. Roosevelt; colored and white children shared the playgrounds in Georgetown parks; Negro graduate students met with white in university classrooms; and adults of both races periodically sat at conferences together. But during leisure hours the secret city of the 1930's was as remote from white Washington as in the 1920's. Cultivated colored people generally preferred it that way, just as they wanted separate, albeit truly equal, schools. Old families, though readier than in the 1920's to share in civic responsibilities, were, if possible, more than ever inclined to exclude the outlander from their social life. But neither were white cave-dwellers eager to take to their bosoms new arrivals brought to the capital by the government, institutions of learning, or business.

[12] *Church of God, A Pictorial Review*, pp. 6, 23, 26-27, 46, 51, 58, 60; Caroline Ware to the author, 21 May 1962; Address, Garnett Wilkinson at Twentieth Anniversary of the Founding of the Washington Urban League, 1958 (typesc in League files); *Tribune*, 22 Nov 1937; Victor Daly, "Washington's Minority Problem," and John Lovell, Jr., "Washington Fights," *Crisis*, XLVI, 170, 276-77; *Afro-American*, 7, 14, 21 Jan, 25 Feb 1939.

Formal white society itself underwent a considerable shakeup, for, apart from the diplomatic corps, official society, as Washington had known it from the 1880's onward, ceased to exist. It held little interest for New Dealers preoccupied with economic and social reforms; leading public figures now conversed on topics that ruled out the chitchat once heard at the dinner tables of sought-after hostesses or at the Misses Patten's teas. What newspaper correspondents regarded as news, furthermore, discouraged any attempt to restore the one-time glitter to "Society"; most of the columns from Washington in metropolitan dailies now dealt with such themes as the workings of the National Recovery Act, the new National Labor Relations Board, or the President's proposal to "pack" the Supreme Court. Only embassy parties retained touches of the old splendor, and those, too, lost some of their savor now that the press passed lightly over them. If sticklers for etiquette were aghast at hearing of a White House Cabinet dinner where the guests of honor were radio's "Amos and Andy"—in the flesh two personable young white men in white ties and tails—most Washingtonians merely wished they too could have been present. Perhaps a few *grande dames* of yesteryear deplored the disappearance of the formal afternoons at home, but the younger generation was glad to be rid of them. The great event of every winter became the annual Polio Foundation Ball. Otherwise, cocktail parties largely supplanted more elaborate entertaining. Even when Washington witnessed the largest crowd in her history on the occasion, in the commissioners' phrase, of the visit of the "King and Queen of Great Britain" in June 1939, the festivities in their honor lacked much of the pomp and circumstance that would once have attended them. Perhaps only the President and his royal guests at that moment were already hearing in imagination the rumble of tanks and the clump of army boots moving across Europe.[13]

[13] *Tribune*, 8 Feb 1934; *Afro-American*, 14 Jan 1939, 4 May 1940;

New attitudes born of the depression and a consequent reassessment of values were reflected also in larger church attendance, in an endeavor of the Washington Federation of Churches to widen its services, in the launching of the Roman Catholic Interracial Council, and possibly in the appearance in Washington of a small body of Black Muslims whose leader taught that white people were the source of all evil and only Mohammed's black followers would inherit the earth. But whereas heightened religious zeal was a foreseeable product of economic disaster, the tendency of the New Deal in its early stages to reject scientific research along with social frivolity and adulation of big business was an unexpected development. In 1933 and 1934 opprobrium attached to science as the source of over-production and, therefore, of the depression. Physicists and chemists, contended a writer in *Science*, had been travelling so fast that they had ceased to "heed or care what misapplications are made of their discoveries."

When the first New Deal Congress sliced the appropriations for military research, for the Bureau of Standards, and for the Census Bureau and the statistical branches of the Labor Department whose data were virtually essential to intelligent economic planning, alarm overtook the federal scientific bureaus. In 1933 a presidentially appointed Scientific Advisory Board headed by the physicist Karl Compton of the Massachusetts Institute of Technology drafted a blueprint for government cooperation in scientific work. But the President's closest advisers labelled the proposal extravagant, impractical, and overweighted in favor of the physical sciences. Secretary of Agriculture Wallace, on the other hand, unwaveringly advocated government funds for research, for, he argued, to charge it "with the responsibility for our failure to apportion produc-

---

Abell, George, and Evelyn Gordon, *Let Them Eat Caviar*, pp. 44-45, 191; Longworth, "Lion-Hunting," *Ladies' Home Journal*, LI, 27; Comrs Rpt, 1939, p. 121.

tion to need and to distribute the fruits of plenty equitably"
was folly. Better controlled use of science and engineering
would create more leisure and release more human energy
"to enjoy the things which are non-material and non-economic,
and I would include in this not only music, painting, literature
and sport for sport's sake, but . . . the idle curiosity of the
scientist himself."

Although appropriations for government research remained
small throughout the decade, Wallace's view, with its stress
on the social sciences and recognition of the value of basic
research—"the idle curiosity of the scientist"—largely prevailed
after 1935. At the President's request the National Resources
Committee in 1937 undertook a comprehensive study of the
"interrelation of government and the intellectual life of the
nation," which put to rest any lingering fears lest the government withdraw altogether from scientific exploration. *Research
—A National Resource* reviewed what had been done and what
must be done under federal aegis not only in the physical and
the social sciences but also in technology and education; the
report stated unequivocally that problems confronting the
federal government "ultimately compel the prosecution of
fundamental, or pure, research." Nevertheless, while the National Research Council continued to sponsor scientific investigations and the Carnegie Institution, unimpeded by governmental doubts about its utility, carried on pure research in the
fields of terrestrial magnetism and geophysics, during the
1930's Washington lost her dominant position as a center of
research in the natural sciences.

Decentralization took to the suburbs the Department of Agriculture's research headquarters, set up in 1936 at an experimental farm in Beltsville, Maryland, and the National Cancer
Institute, which the Public Health Service placed in Bethesda
in 1938 as a second unit of the National Institutes of Health.
Financial stringencies limited the work of the Smithsonian.

In the little building south of the red sandstone castle, Dr. Charles Abbot, secretary of the institution, pursued his studies in astrophysics assisted by Andrew Kramer, the instrument maker who had built Samuel Langley's aeronautical devices. There Abbott constructed solar-heat collectors that used the primal energy of the sun to run a small motor or to bake bread. "Who knows," he asked, "when he goes about an investigation to increase the bounds of knowledge, however remote his subject may be from the ordinary walks of life, what application the future may have in store for the results he gains?" Weekly nationwide broadcasts begun in 1936 presented "The World is Yours," dramatic non-technical accounts of what scientists through the centuries had learned about the universe, and the institution published some important monographs as well as an appendix to each annual report that constituted in essence a yearbook of contemporary science. But the big universities of the country conducted most of the fundamental research, and industrial laboratories, such as those of the American Telephone Company and DuPont, carried on much of the applied research.[14]

In the capital, research in the social sciences and the humanities, on the other hand, gradually took on fresh importance. Scholars made intensive use of the Folger Shakespeare Library, and many a jobless person spent hours in the Library of Congress learning while he could not earn. Foreigners accustomed to the red tape and rigid rules restricting the use of the great libraries of Europe were astonished at the ease with which anyone and everyone could draw upon the resources of this "storehouse of knowledge." In the general reading room, wrote James Truslow Adams, "which alone contains ten thousand volumes which may be read without even the asking, one sees

[14] Bureau of the Census, *Religious Bodies*, 1936, I, 395, 426-27; "Women's Department of the Washington Federation of Churches," *Miscellaneous Review*, LII, 546-48; Dupree, *Science*, pp. 344-68; Paul Oehser, *Sons of Science*, pp. 160-77; *Research—A National Resource*, I, 51, and *passim*.

the seats filled with silent readers, old and young, rich and poor, black and white, the executive and the laborer, the general and the private, the noted scholar and the schoolboy, all reading at their own library provided by their own democracy." The opening of the Annex in April 1939 added stack space for ten million books and made study rooms available both to American and foreign students engaged in research requiring constant use of the library's collections.

New gifts to the Trust Fund Board enabled Herbert Putnam to increase the number of library consultantships and chairs, while acquisition of the Joseph Pennell collection of Whistler drawings widened the resources of the Prints and Photographs Division. Still more gratifying to part of the local public was the enlargement of the concert program made possible by the Gertrude Clarke Whittall Foundation. In 1935 Mrs. Whittall, Nebraska-born widow of a prominent Massachusetts business-man, presented to the library her unique collection of Stradivari stringed instruments and Tourte bows and set up a fund to support additional chamber music concerts in the Coolidge auditorium, where the performers were to use the matchless instruments. When Mrs. Whittall offered to erect a "Putnam Pavilion" to house the instruments, the librarian gratefully accepted but told the donor: "You're a squandering squaw from Omaha! We'll call it the Whittall Pavilion." After 1938 the famous Budapest String Quartet became a resident orchestra and played regularly at the library.

Upon completing his 40th year as Librarian of Congress, Herbert Putnam retired in June 1939. President Roosevelt, acting chiefly on the advice of Supreme Court Justice Felix Frankfurter, chose a successor with characteristic speed and insistence. After unsuccessful preliminary negotiations with a reluctant Archibald MacLeish, the President summoned him to lunch at the White House. When the poet protested that he knew nothing about managing a great library, the President

replied: "Nonsense! You can run the library between the time
you wake up in the morning and the time you finish shaving.
You'll have the rest of the day for your own writing." In October,
a month after war broke out in Europe, MacLeish took up his
duties with a high sense of mission, for, he believed, "time is
running out, not like sand in a glass, but like the blood in an
opened artery," and Americans must learn to value and preserve
their inheritance lest "the nonculture, the obscurantism, the
superstition, the brutality, the tyranny which is overrunning
eastern and central and southern Europe" submerge the
United States also. Faith that understanding of the accumulated
wisdom of the past and awareness of the arts would save the
nation from disaster guided his policies. In 1940 he brought to
Washington the self-exiled French poet St. John Perse as a
consultant in French literature. Urging high school students
to use the library regularly, MacLeish strove constantly to
make it a tool of popular education. His concept was a departure
from Putnam's ideal of serving the world of learning, but the
younger man's associates felt in working with him that his
was "the brush of the comet."

Meanwhile, depression, New Deal, and the flight of scholars
from the spreading despotism in Europe benefitted the local
universities. As exceptionally able Washington high school
graduates unable to meet the expense of going away to college
entered local institutions, faculties expanded, curricula widened,
and prospective competition for jobs after graduation produced
a better quality of undergraduate work. Much the same se-
quence of cause and effect was observable in state universities,
but in Washington the challenge was the more immediate
because of the widening opportunities in the burgeoning government agencies. New federal bodies set up to handle problems
unfamiliar to old-line civil servants wanted people trained to
meet such novel responsibilities as assembling old age and
survivors' insurance data in the newly organized Social Security

Administration; in that case a course given at American University by a German political scientist with first-hand knowledge of European practices resolved the dilemma. At the Department of Agriculture Graduate School experts taught evening classes in as many as fifty different subjects, and at the American University's downtown "campus" in the string of Victorian houses on F Street west of the White House, graduate students with daytime jobs sat at the feet of specialists willing to teach at night. Besides economics, sociology, public administration, education, and fields of history that had direct bearing on government needs, law attracted students to graduate work. The listings in *Who's Who* of the 1950's and early 1960's show how many men eminent in public life had received their training in the Georgetown, George Washington, National, or Howard University Law School of the 1930's. And mounting world tensions as the decade wore on enhanced the importance of the Georgetown University Foreign Service School, where Father Walsh, its director, impressed students by his penetrating analysis of Russian communism.

As growing numbers of distinguished foreign scholars for whom Europe had become intolerable or unsafe accepted teaching posts in the American capital, the air of provincialism that had long clung to all Washington's universities disappeared. The famous physicist George Gamow of Copenhagen and Edward Teller, known twenty years later as the "father of the hydrogen bomb," added to George Washington's academic stature, and notable German economists and historians similarly increased the scholarly standing of the other universities. In 1940 Mr. and Mrs. Robert Woods Bliss' gift of their collection of Near Eastern *objets d'art* and Dumbarton Oaks, their beautiful old Georgetown house, to Harvard University for a museum and center of Byzantine studies opened out prospects of still further achievements in the world of learning. The foreign legations and embassies for 140 years had lent official society a cosmopolitan touch, but the savants who came in the 1930's to make their homes in Washington endowed the entire community with a new perception of Old World civilization. And their appreciation of what they found here, sometimes admittedly unexpectedly, deepened Washingtonians' sense of their own American heritage; that men who had spent their lives surrounded by the works of art and the traditions of a great past now preferred to live in Washington was at once an accolade and a challenge. Approximately 4,100 recently acquired foreign-born residents, a number of them artisans and shop-keepers rather than teachers and highly educated people, could not entirely reshape the attitudes and tastes of a city of more than 620,000 inhabitants. Yet the variety of languages to be heard on the streets and trolley cars gave people the feeling of being part of a world community. Thus with all her prejudices and grievances Washington attained a mellowness that no one could have anticipated in 1932.[15]

One gauge of that mellowness was the place music and drama assumed. Movies, ball games at the stadium, and trips to the zoo were still major diversions, but the uses to which people put leisure widened. Twice a week during the summer of 1935 the National Symphony Orchestra played from a barge anchored in the river at the Ceremonial Watergate, a tier of steps rising from the Potomac to Riverside Drive above the Arlington Memorial Bridge. There the Marine and the Army bands and after 1936 an independent musicians' cooperative played to audiences of about 12,000 people, working men's families, government officials, and Washington bluebloods alike seated on the steps or stretched out on the lawns adjoining, with the river flowing by at their feet, while couples listened from canoes drifting in the shallows. The WPA Music Project helped organize orchestras, choruses, and bands in a number of government

---

[15] "The Story Up to Now," *Rpt Lib/Cong*, 1946, pp. 212-22; *Dept/Agriculture Graduate School*, 1961; Mrs. Whittall herself tells the story of the "Putnam Pavilion."

departments; the fifty-man chorus at the Government Printing Office, to name but one, early acquired an enviable reputation for its performances. Amateur drama groups flourished at the churches and community centers, while the WPA Federal Theatre Project, in addition to sponsoring several lesser productions, staged *Pins and Needles* before a racially mixed audience. All these do-it-yourself forms of entertainment gave the city of over a half million souls a pleasant, small-town flavor.

Partly through government encouragement, interest in painting also spread. In 1933 a grant to the Treasury started the Public Works of Art Project, which engaged artists—at craftsmen's wages, to be sure—to decorate the new public buildings with murals. From that beginning came a permanent section in the Treasury Department for paintings and sculpture. George Biddle's murals in the Department of Justice building depicting "The Sweatshop" and similar themes, and Henry Varnum Poor's series on "Entrance into Prison," "Release from Prison," "Surveyors at Work," and a half dozen more were among the most admired products of this federal patronage. Before the decade was gone, the Corcoran Art School had some five hundred students enrolled, and the enthusiasm of the amateurs whom the gifted Law Watkins taught in evening classes at the Phillips Gallery led him to start a small daytime school. While waiting eagerly for the completion of the Mellon Gallery, Washingtonians looked with fresh eyes at the pictures in the National Museum which for thirty years had constituted the National Gallery of Art and now received the name National Collection of Fine Arts.[16]

Books, pamphlets, and magazine articles pouring out of Washington throughout the New Deal years testified further to the city's intellectual vitality. Some of the output was ephemeral, some was trivial, and some suffered from the weakness

---

[16] WPA *Guide*, pp. 139-42; *Newsweek*, VI, 27 Jul 1935, p. 30; "General Information," Ntl Gallery of Art, *Bulletin*, I, Mar 1941; *American Magazine of Art*, XXVIII, 204.

Mark Twain described in rebuking his wife's attempts to cure him of swearing by repeating some of his phrases: "You've got the words right, Libby, but you haven't got the tune." Still no earlier period had evoked so much published material of enduring value. Besides the commentaries and reminiscences of brain-trusters and their opponents, journalists' news stories and accounts of the news behind the news frequently attained literary distinction. A book such as Thomas Stokes' *Chip Off My Shoulder* would be as moving in the 1960's as in the thirties. Dos Passos and writers in the *American Mercury*, to be sure, implied that much of what emanated from Washington had a sycophantic tone deriving from an awed subservience to the "Radio-Voice from the Blue Room." But Brookings Institution economists attacked New Deal agricultural policies and other experiments in fashion that left no doubt that independent thinking had not stopped. Poetry and fiction, except that purporting to be solid fact, rarely appeared, for, despite new-found pleasure in the arts, simple diversions, and casual, friendly social occasions, to the New Dealer life was real and life was earnest. His was the role of the missionary. Had he had the genius, the engrossing business of remaking American civilization left him no time to transpose that experience into an epic poem or the Great American Novel.

Outsiders generally assumed that these changes, good and bad, if not actually foisted upon the local community, had at least occurred without its help. Disparaging critiques of the local press strengthened that notion: the *Star* still served up pure eye-wash; the slightly more perceptive *News* shied away from real issues; the *Times* and the *Herald*, merged in 1939, were pro-Americanism, pro-Hearst, pro-Marian Davies, and anti everything else; while the *Post*, which ex-banker Eugene Meyer purchased in 1933 and talked of turning into a liberal sheet, was merely a banking organ with a fascist slant.[17]

[17] Dos Passos, "Washington: The Big Town," *New Republic*, LXXVIII, 120-33; Marguerite Young, "Ignoble Journalism in the Nation's Capital,"

Characteristically such appraisals passed over the quality of reporting on significant local matters. For newcomers the city as an entity in her own right apart from the federal government did not exist.

To a degree never equalled before or after, the New Deal era subjected Washingtonians to an unconscious patronage that assigned them to the position of non-contributing beneficiaries of the progress wrought by new arrivals. Those New Dealers who stayed would discover later that they too had become part of that once faintly despised, indefinable body known as Washingtonians. Yet as generous-minded long-time residents knew, the brain-trusters imbued America with a new social consciousness and fresh intellectual curiosity that left a lasting imprint in the capital. The constant belittlement that the community faced had the virtue of undermining any latent complacency. Conscientious citizens anxious to do better for the city resented New Deal high-handedness only as it ignored local reform movements.

---

and Eugene A. Kelly, "Distorting the News," *American Mercury*, XXXIV, 239-43, 307-18.

CHAPTER XX

RUNNING UNCLE SAM'S COMPANY
TOWN, 1933-1941

SPECULATION about who would succeed Commissioners Reichelderfer and Crosby had begun in March 1933, but during the explosion of national legislation in the First Hundred Days Washingtonians reconciled themselves to waiting. Two days after the inauguration some indignation, reportedly shared by the President, had flared up at the metropolitan police for resorting to billy clubs, curses, and arrests in dispersing an unauthorized parade of some six hundred local unemployed—"mostly colored people under communist leadership," the commissioners explained airily—but, the politically wise realized, even new officials in the District Building would be unlikely to embark at once upon police reforms. In June a number of Hoover appointees were still holding various federal offices; obviously postponement of the exercise of the patronage left the President with a whip in hand. By midsummer, however, the local public was finding the delay "not only a mystery but also a source of some irritation." Then word circulated that the President was planning to reorganize the entire District government, substituting for the three-man commission a one-man rule like that of "Boss" Shepherd in the 1870's, minus a popularly elected legislature.

For several years past, national journals had been commenting on the ineffectualness of the District's government: it was an "Adventure in Autocracy" that subjected residents of the capital to indignities and endless inconveniences, including the ministrations of five separate bodies of police and a Public Utilities Commission that tolerated two mutually uncooperating transit systems and two gas companies in a city of fewer than 500,000 people. Let the city at least be under unified control;

the commissioners had become a "national laughing stock."
Here was an about-face from the position publicists had taken
in 1901 when they held up Washington's municipal government
as a model. Within the city dissatisfaction had been growing
as the depression deepened, but in the autumn of 1933 few
people took much stock in the rumors of a basic reorganization.
Still the Board of Trade, fearful of losing its influence in District affairs, was uneasy at reports that Roosevelt intended
to put in charge for a ten-year term a city manager who was
to be selected from the country at large rather than from the
ranks of local citizens. The plan would strip the community,
the board president contended, of its last vestige of local
representation. No comment came from the White House. As
October came and went, observers deduced that President
Roosevelt had little interest in the capital city and had delegated
decisions about the local government to one of his secretaries.
Not until mid-November did the newspapers announce that
Melvin D. Hazen and George E. Allen would be sworn in as
commissioners on the 16th.[1]

Hazen, a spare, athletic-looking, gray-haired man of sixty,
had been a District employee for forty years, city surveyor for
thirty, and consequently was familiar with the routines of
District business, but he had never had a hand in making
policy or in drafting a District budget. He owed his appointment, gossip said, not to his experience in public affairs, but
to his passion for horse-breeding and racing which had
cemented a friendship with Admiral Cary T. Grayson, head of
the Roosevelt inaugural committee and chairman of the
American National Red Cross. For years Hazen had spent
much of his time on his family estate in Virginia and avowed
a preference for country over city living. To choose for District

[1] *News*, 9, 13 Mar, 26 Sep, 15 Nov 1933; *Star*, 7 Jun, 16 Jul, 3, 11
Sep 1933; Comrs Rpt, 1933, p. 72; *Post*, 22 Jun 1933; *Herald*, 13 Jul, 30
Aug, 26 Sep 1933; J. Frederick Essary, "An Adventure in Autocracy,"
American Mercury, xx, 290; Rpt B/Tr, 1934, p. 7.

commissioner a man without intense interest in urban problems seemed odd to some of his subordinates and distinctly unfortunate to citizens who believed the moment ripe for vigorous leadership in the local as well as the national government. Allen's appointment came as a still greater surprise. Nine Washingtonians out of ten had never heard of him. Roosevelt himself had never laid eyes on him. A Mississippian born and bred, he had lived in Washington since 1928 when he became manager of the Wardman Park Hotel and other local hotel properties. He himself later explained that he had angled for a public office for which he had no known qualifications purely because he decided, as the depression denuded the Wardman Park of its patrons one by one, that he could benefit from the publicity of having his name thrown into the pot of candidates. His golf and bridge crony, Senator Pat Harrison of Mississippi, with the backing of Postmaster General James Farley, had quickly arranged matters, and the stocky, slightly balding 36-year-old hotel man had soon found himself ensconced in the District Building. Major Gotwals, the engineer commissioner, stayed on until August 1934.

Whatever discomfiture the local public felt at having its government entrusted to "a Virginian, a Mississippian and an Army officer," as the *Herald* characterized the trio, no one voiced open criticism until Hazen enlisted the help of the Chamber of Commerce in preparing his first District budget, a step which subjected him to derision and accusations of catering to business interests. His announced satisfaction with the police department dismayed people exasperated with its inefficiencies and periodic displays of ruthlessness. He disliked the very idea of change unless it were to enhance the authority of the commissioners. A dignified, slow-paced hack, reappointed three times over, he died of a heart attack at his desk in July 1941. George Allen, on the other hand, presented a facade of casualness, using camaraderie and humor, forced or otherwise, as his weapons. In the opinion of the then secretary of the Board of Commissioners, Allen did more for the District of Columbia on the golf course than in his office. As he became increasingly the boon companion of senators and congressmen and, somewhat reluctantly, took on the role of "court jester" at the White House, he was in a position to accomplish a good deal for his fellow citizens. A self-confessed show-off, he nevertheless convinced the tough-minded Harry Hopkins, head of the Federal Emergency Relief Administration, that Commissioner Allen was the person to direct the District relief program in the bitter winter of 1933.

People who had hoped that the President would appoint a Louis Brownlow to office watched the performance in the District Building for the next four and a half years with incredulity, resigned indignation, or pure cynical amusement. Not long after he was sworn in, Allen undertook to discover at first hand how other cities were handling relief. Donning his shabbiest clothes and posing as an unemployed waiter, he set off by bus for Cleveland, Detroit, Chicago, and Milwaukee. Refused a job twenty times over, thrown out of respectable hotels, and insulted by social workers, upon his return to Washington he told Harry Hopkins that he better instruct his staff "not to act like God Almighty." But Allen in turn could be both arbitrary and cocky. Impatient with what he considered the moribund procedures of the Board of Public Welfare, he by-passed the board, engaged a member of Harry Hopkins' staff to manage District emergency relief, and set about persuading Congress to transfer full control of welfare to the commissioners—in short, to him. That particular struggle ended when George Wilson, after thirty-eight years' service to the city's private and public charities, resigned, and Elwood Street, director of the Community Chest, became the executive of the Welfare Board. But Allen continued to inject himself into the picture in an attempt, as the new director of the Community Chest saw it, to pull the strings without putting himself to any trouble about the puppets' performance.

A generation later the hassle over welfare administration would seem to have been rather silly, inconsequential feuding. In the mid-1930's it was the foremost community problem. Among public-spirited Washingtonians resentment of Allen's easy-going methods and flair for self-advertising spread. Newspapermen found him "good copy" and played him up accordingly, even while they poked fun at a white collar project he instituted for jobless reporters: tabulating the record of race-track favorites to see how often the most heavily bet-upon horses won. Yet, in the curious backhanded fashion of political maneuvering, the publicity the local press gave him and his rather slap-dash propositions probably benefitted the city.[2] For while one civilian commissioner strove to perpetuate the old order, his younger associate stirred up controversy and perhaps unintentionally drew attention to the weaknesses of the District's entire governmental system.

Allen's career as commissioner had chiefly symbolic importance. Certainly he was not the first person to hold District office merely because he had friends on the Hill. When he resigned in the summer of 1938 to return to the more congenial world of private business, the attitude of serious-minded Washingtonians was revealed in their reaction to the tales told of a farewell dinner given for him. The party was "off the record," but stories leaked out of how the fifty-odd people there, many of them closely linked to the White House, used the occasion to twit the "presidential joker" about his performance as a public servant. The speeches of congratulation upon his resignation carried a note of the sadistic verbal horseplay which, Allen observed, had always characterized President

[2] *Star*, 16, 17 Nov 1933; *News*, 16, 23 Nov 1933; *Herald*, 15 Dec 1937; George E. Allen, *Presidents Who Have Known Me*, pp. 46-48, 58-68, 71-72; Rpt Public Assistance Division B/PW, 1934; *Herald*, 25-30 Mar 1934.

Roosevelt's dealings with him. The resigning commissioner responded by remarking that, when he was sworn in, the death rate and the cases of destitution in the city had stood at relatively modest figures, but he had taken care of all that: the totals had risen steadily during the last four and a half years. The facetious statement was greeted with roars of laughter from the listeners. Earnest Washingtonians considered the episode not only undignified but a measure of the indifference with which, in their eyes, the President and his appointee looked upon the well-being of the capital. Allen later remarked that the odd jobs the President asked him to undertake had turned him into a species of White House errand boy and thus, he implied, interfered with his official duties.[3]

Citizens nevertheless came to believe that Roosevelt invariably displayed a readiness to dismiss Washington's problems in a cavalier fashion strangely at variance with the concern he showed for the rest of the country; only Mrs. Roosevelt's active interest in the city could partly redeem the record. His staunchest admirers were never able to account for his aloofness. The most obvious explanation, the overriding importance of national affairs which left no time for those of the capital, was not wholly satisfactory, inasmuch as well-informed people felt that ten minutes of listening and perhaps fifteen spent in expressing his convictions to congressional leaders would have sufficed to settle questions that instead were passed over until they became virtually insoluble. One old friend of the President privately assigned his indifference to a distaste for all urban affairs engendered in part by his struggles as Governor with Tammany in New York City and, in part, by his addiction to rural life as the Squire of Hyde Park knew it. Perhaps Roosevelt assumed that, unlike many a provincial city, Washington contained enough brains to resolve her own

[3] Allen, *Presidents*, pp. 73-85.

difficulties without his help, provided the community cared enough to make the effort.

The person who carried most weight in the District Building was Daniel J. Donovan, the District auditor. Possessed of a photographic memory, an intimate knowledge of the laws affecting the District, and strong convictions about what was important, the dynamic Irishman reared on the outskirts of Swampoodle had arrived at his position of behind-the-scenes power by sheer incisive intelligence, inexhaustible diligence, and the force of his personality. He had begun his career in the District government in 1900, became auditor at the end of World War I, and, when the federal Classification Act brought into being the District Personnel Board, became director of that also. When he bellowed "Great Jehovah and the Continental Congress," everyone within earshot sat up and took notice, and to be labelled by Donovan "an unmitigated nuisance" was enough to persuade his staff to withdraw or modify an offending proposal. Once he had made up his mind he was hard to budge from his chosen position. While he could not fix the size of the over-all budget, he could advise upon changes in the tax rate, and his recommendations about the distribution of the general fund were, a federal Bureau of the Budget officer later said, generally "99 percent effective" in shaping the budget that went to Congress. The auditor thus controlled District spending more completely than did the commissioners themselves. As a permanent fixture for twenty-five years Donovan largely determined the policies of his ostensible superiors who came and went. His long experience and his devotion to his native city probably saved Washington from falling completely under the domination of big, self-seeking business corporations that had some congressional backing.

Hazen and two successive engineer commissioners carried on without a third member of the board from the time of Allen's resignation in August 1938 till June 1939, when Allen accepted reappointment. He again resigned two months later. His successor, John Russell Young, had long been a staff member of the *Evening Star* and since 1920 head of the White House correspondents corps. Possibly the nomination of another prima donna without administrative background, and a conservative Republican to boot, would have aroused opposition had the appointment come earlier, but by mid-April 1940 the Nazi invasion of Norway and drive into the Low Countries was absorbing most of the attention of every informed person in the capital.

Long before then the self-defeating complexity of the District's governmental structure had impressed itself upon people in and out of the District Building. By 1928 law had surrounded the Board of Commissioners with some twenty-five independent or partly independent agencies, and the New Deal increased the number until the maze of channels through which officials must find their way obstructed the transaction of the most routine business. Fiscal relationships were so intricate that only Daniel J. Donovan understood them. When at the request of the Senate, an assistant director of the Bureau of the Budget, the District auditor, and the Associate Corporation Counsel undertook to analyze the organizational tangles and recommend simplifications, the report required nine volumes of text and enough charts to paper the walls of a room.

A rule that held for one agency had no validity for the next. Over the presidentially appointed Public Utilities Commission, for example, the commissioners had no control of any kind after 1926. They passed upon the budgets of the National Capital Park and Planning Commission and the National Guard but had no supervisory power over the expenditures of either. Over the District highway department, on the other hand, the commissioners' fiscal control was all-inclusive, even after a vigorous campaign conducted by the Board of Trade induced Congress to allot to the District a share of the federal appropriations voted to the states for road building. In some realms federal contracting services gave the District help on a cost-of-care or cost-of-commodity basis. After 1934 the federal Bureau of Public Assistance matched District funds, just as it did for the states, and a division of the local welfare board ran the program, but in vocational rehabilitation District taxes paid half the costs while the federal bureau took charge of the work; in 1937 a new national act excluded Washington from the benefits given the states. Inconsistencies were everywhere. Civil service procedures applied to some District departments, not to others.

In asking for a detailed study of this cumbersome machinery, the Senate's major concern was to get a workable plan of streamlining District administration in fashion that would relieve Congress of the time-consuming business of acting as city council. Apparently few men on the Hill considered the effect on the local community. The bulky mimeographed "Organization Report" was never published, but in 1934, as descriptions of its contents began to appear in the press, Washingtonians suddenly saw prospects of a local political New Deal, even though the recommendations aimed chiefly at greater efficiency rather than a new democratic basis for governing the city. The principal proposal was to substitute for the board of commissioners a presidentially appointed legislative council on which two or more members of Congress should also sit, vest in it all powers now scattered among the commissioners and the numerous special boards, authorize it to appoint a city manager as executive, and give it full control of the District budget once Congress had appropriated the over-all total. To safeguard national interests, Congress was to have a veto over all local legislative acts. Washington citizens were to have the right to elect a non-voting delegate to the House and select in primaries a slate of men from whom the President should appoint the members of the council. The desirability of placing greatly enlarged fiscal responsibility upon a local governmental body seemed self-evident to a great many people. Primaries for naming council members, moreover, promised the city's rank and file opportunity to express preferences.[4]

The feature of the plan that troubled many Washingtonians was that it denied the people who paid 90 percent of the costs of running the city a voice in congressional decisions or any check on acts of the council after its appointment. Senator Capper of Kansas and Representative Mary Norton, in 1934 chairman of the House District Committee, agreed that local voting rights should extend to more than primaries and electing a delegate to Congress. William King of Utah, chairman of the Senate District Committee, rejected that notion. Washingtonians, he asserted, "shy away from responsibilities and though they may talk about their interest in greater control of their affairs, they do not want too great a degree of autonomy when it comes to a showdown." He never attempted to provide the showdown. Ready as he was to concentrate power in the Board of Commissioners or in an appointed legislative council, he failed to attribute local objections to distaste for a plan that would merely heighten the authoritarian character of the District government.

The Organization Report commanded much more attention in the community than in House and Senate, quite possibly because Congress disliked the very idea of weakening its own control of the city's purse. Newcomers to the capital found the subject confusing and boring, and men and women ridden by anxiety about getting and keeping jobs gave the matter scant thought, but much of the rest of Washington examined every aspect of the questions involved. Articles in the *Herald* explored every possible solution of the basic problem of federal

---

[4] Schmeckebier, *District of Columbia*; "Organization Report," 1934, ii-viii (Washingtoniana Room, Pub Lib); H Dis Comee, 80C, 1S, Subcomee Hrgs, "Home Rule and Reorganization of the Govt of D.C.," pp. 13-27, and "Preliminary Rpt," pp. 5-6; Rpt. B/Tr, 1934, p. 7; *Star*, 20 May 1932, 7 Jun 1933, 18 Feb, 25 Mar, 15 May 1934; *Times*, 24 Mar 1932, 4 Jan 1934; *Herald*, 7 Oct 1932, 21-30 Mar 1934.

and municipal relationships, and over a period of weeks the *Star* carried statements by officers of citizens associations and leading businessmen. All of them favored some change in the system.

Several men put particular emphasis upon removing the existing financial inequities and confusions, first, by a divorce of the local from the federal budget, second, by a release of District tax-money held without interest in the United States Treasury because Congress had not authorized the expenditure of the accumulated surplus, third, by permitting District officials discretionary power to transfer money from one project to another, and, fourth, by a reversion to the old arrangement that had fixed the annual federal payment for the city's routine expenses at a percentage of the total budget instead of a flat sum, which had dropped since 1928 from nine to five million dollars. Other statements insisted that only the election of District senators and representatives with full voting rights in each house would guarantee respectful attention from Congress to Washington's needs. A surprising number of articles took up the cudgels for home rule, since, its proponents contended, elected municipal officials would respond far more promptly and fully to local mandates than Congress ever would.[5]

Fifteen years earlier, Washingtonians had largely bypassed the home rule issue in their vigorous postwar campaign for national representation. After the collapse of that drive, a few valiants had carried on the fight but with mounting discouragement. In 1922 the Senate Judiciary Committee had reported favorably upon a joint resolution calling for the needed constitutional amendment, at intervals thereafter

[5] *Times*, 24 Mar 1932, 16 Apr 1934; *News*, 12 Apr 1934; *Herald*, 21-30 Mar 1934, 3 Jun 1935; *Star*, 23-26, 30 Apr 6, 8 May, 15, 22 Jul, 5, 12 Aug, 30 Sep 1934, 9 Oct 1935; Comrs Rpts, 1929, pp. 2-4, 1935, p. 7. See the collection of clippings on Home Rule and reorganization plans of the 1930's in Washingtoniana Room, Public Library.

Senator Capper had introduced a similar joint resolution, and some hearings were held. There progress had ended. By the mid-1930's although the Board of Trade still officially backed Capper's stand, many a Washingtonian had lost faith in its feasibility and was ready to settle for the "half-loaf" of an elected municipal council with taxing and ordinance-making powers. And alongside the "whole-loafers" and the "half-loafers" were ranged people anxious for improvements in the governmental machinery but prone to think that a few simplified parts and grease on the wheels would suffice. Between 1934 and the spring of 1940 a dozen plans of reorganization cropped up, some originating in Congress, some in the community.

For a time a referendum proposal interested Washingtonians by offering them a chance to express approval or disapproval of impending administrative or legislative acts and thus provide a guide to Congress and District officials. But as such polls would be expensive and have no binding force, the idea fell into the discard. Commissioner Hazen believed that the commissioners themselves could bring order out of administrative chaos once the powers of the bodies like the public welfare and school boards were cancelled or sharply curtailed. One of a committee of private citizens he appointed to work out that kind of reorganization plan later said ruefully that no member of Congress ever looked at the recommendations; the only observable result of the study was the transfer of Gallinger, Freedmen's and the T.B. hospitals from welfare board supervision to the health department's. At President Roosevelt's request, George Allen, after his resignation as commissioner, also tried his hand at drafting a reorganization bill. Its provisions, like those of several other bills, consisted mostly of a reshuffling of District departments and their duties. Attorney General Homer Cummings jocosely wrote the author that the one intelligible clause in the entire ninety-page document read: "The term District means District of Columbia."[6]

The amount of time and effort which civic organizations, individual citizens, and a score of legislators devoted to the problems of District government was astonishing even in an era of political and social ferment. But as one proposal after another wound up in congressional committee pigeon-holes, frustrated advocates of far-reaching change began to shift tactics. The thirty-year-old District Suffrage League concluded that the very multiplicity of proposals and comment had created an image in Congress of a community that did not know what it wanted. In order to test the strength of public opinion upon the basic issues, in April 1938 a Citizens' Conference representing 271 local organizations undertook to finance and conduct a plebiscite on two questions: do you want to vote for President and for members of Congress from the District of Columbia, and do you want to vote for officials of your own city government in the District? For three weeks newspaper and radio publicity, posters, and speeches before church and civic organizations advertised the purpose of the poll and the rules laid down for it. Since it lacked official sponsorship and the election machinery to be found in every village in the United States, the Suffrage League obtained the school board's permission to set up voting places in thirty-eight public schools. On the evening of April 29th, men and women dressed as Paul Revere's contemporaries paraded through the streets to remind the onlookers that government only by the consent of the governed had been an American creed for 170 years.

[6] Rpts B/Tr, 1934, p. 7, 1935, p. 20, 1936, p. 17, 1937, p. 15; *Herald*, 23 Mar 1934; *Rec*, 75C, 1S, pp. 80, 6298, and App, p. 639; Arthur Capper, "Washington City and the Rights of the People," CHS *Rec*, xl-xli, 63-77; *Star*, 15 Jan, 18 Dec 1935, 11 Mar 1936, 27 Feb, 1 May, 12 Jul 1937; S bill 2907, and H bill 8146, 75C, 1S; *Post*, 19 Jan 1935, 14 Sep 1936, 10, 13 Oct, 14, 15 Dec 1937; *Times*, 18 Aug 1937; Allen, *Presidents*, pp. 85-88; S bill 3425, 76C, 3S.

Reasoning that people who lived in the capital had an interest in it even if they voted and paid taxes elsewhere, the Suffrage League opened the polls to all adults irrespective of the state citizenship maintained by about half the city's residents. On April 30th, 95,538 people balloted. One Washingtonian reported that he had last exercised that privilege in 1874. Most of them had never voted before, and unfamiliarity with the procedures spoiled 804 ballots. When the judges of the District court who served as tellers announced the final tally, it showed a thirteen to one majority for seats in Congress, seven to one for home rule. Suffrage supporters were elated. In a city of some 627,000 souls, 95,500 represented less than 16 percent of the population, but according to political scientists that was an average turn-out for American municipal elections. Furthermore, careful calculation based on census estimates put the number of possible Washington voters, namely adults who did not exercise the elective franchise in any of the states, at 319,129 and thus raised the percentage taking part in the plebiscite to 30. Inasmuch as scarcely 56 percent of American voters had cast ballots in the 1936 presidential election, a suffrage leader pointed out, Washington's response to polling "on an abstract proposition with no candidates" was extraordinary. Here seemed to be the "showdown" that proved the error of Senator King's appraisal of Washingtonians' attitudes.[7] Only later would Suffrage Leaguers admit reluctantly that the evidence was anything but conclusive.

The House Judiciary Committee held hearings late in May on joint resolutions for national representation and a "Republican government" for the District, but the time allowed was short, much of the testimony was a rehash of familiar arguments,

[7] Clippings, Home Rule, 1938 (Washingtoniana Room); *Plebiscite News Sheet*; *Star*, 22 Apr, 6, 30 May 1938; *Post*, 1 May 1938; *Rec*, 76C, 1S, pp. 14864-65; *A History of the League of Women Voters of the District of Columbia*, pp. 76-77; S Judic Comee, 77C, 1S, Subcomee Hrgs on S J Resolution 35, "National Representation," pp. 226-30.

and committee members appeared preoccupied. Without explaining their reasons, they disapproved both resolutions. Lively hearings before the Senate committee had a similar ending. Yet the 74th Congress alone, one witness pointed out, had had to take time from national affairs to deal with 7 Senate and 3 House resolutions and 30 Senate and 138 House bills, 27 of which finally passed, all concerned solely with Washington. So far from killing discussion, the dismissal of the suffrage proposals inspired additional studies and a succession of new bills and resolutions. While the indefatigable Senator Capper again introduced his perennial resolution for a constitutional amendment authorizing District seats in Congress, and colleagues offered minor nostrums, two bills varying in details but fundamentally similar proposed an elective city council in which should reside all local taxing and ordinance-making powers, subject to congressional veto. The first bill was the more specific, but the second, prepared by the Suffrage League and submitted to the House in May 1939, had the twofold virtue of brevity and of furnishing a reminder to Congress that, if passed, the act would merely restore to the District its political status of 1871 without the superimposed appointed bodies that had wrecked the territorial government.

At this point William A. Roberts, the Washington lawyer who had written most of the Organization Report of 1934, spoke out sharply. The situation, he declared, had become critical. Washington was now the hub of a metropolitan area. Population growth had given new dimensions to civic problems, and the commissioners manifestly could not handle them. Theirs was "not a municipal government as such, but merely a jumbled and unassorted group of emergency departments." Six years of watching had convinced Roberts that a concentration of authority in any appointed body, be it legislative council or board of commissioners, would no longer answer. "Reorganization and suffrage," students of the question had come to agree, "go hand in hand and for practical purposes are inseparable." Washingtonians so far had not got the vote because they had been "too apathetic to fight for it." Of course "present District of Columbia officials have no real interest in suffrage, since it might affect the time of day they come to work or the horse races they like to attend." A *Handbook for District Suffrage* carried further the attack on the commissioners' "dismal failure" of the last ten years. "The commission government has swept problems under the bed till the rubbish caught fire and has done terrible damage to District health, welfare, education and municipal service." Let the disbeliever weigh Mrs. Roosevelt's evidence of the shocking conditions at the Home for the Aged and then judge for himself. The neglect of matters vital to the well-being of the community had reached a state where only a popularly elected city government could be expected to tackle the chore of clearing out the accumulated rubbish.[8]

Reasons for the mounting pressure for home rule are plain enough. The fear of losing the large federal payment toward District expenses, which for years had kept many Washingtonians out of the local suffrage ranks, no longer had bearing. Even when Congress boosted the $4,600,000 federal appropriation of 1934 to $6,000,000 for 1939, the higher figure amounted to scarcely 11 percent of the $44,000,000 District budget, every penny of which must be spent exactly as dictated on the Hill. The parsimony of the past decade underscored the need of an entirely new system. Furthermore, among the energetic newcomers whom the New Deal had brought to Washington were a number who considered her disenfranchised state preposterous; whether or not they stayed on in the capital, their indignation strengthened the self-government movement. And finally American horror at the spreading Nazi despotism in Europe gave new force to the contention that the

[8] H Judic Comee, 75C, 3S, Hrgs on H Resns, 232 and 564, "National Representation for D.C.," p. 63 and *passim*; H bills 6201 and 7095, 76C, 1S; S bills, 2776 and 3425, 76C, 3S; H bill 2984, 77C, 1S; Hrgs on SJ Res 35, pp. 52-53; *Star*, 5 Feb, 2 Aug 1940; *Post*, 12 Feb, 1939.

United States must uphold democratic processes throughout the nation, even in the capital.

The 76th Congress, troubled about the accelerating pace of the Nazi conquest and absorbed in the 1940 presidential election campaign, adjourned without acting on the District bills pending before it. But Washington's chances of achieving some political status improved that summer: after a bitter secret struggle, the platform committee of the Democratic Party inserted a plank pledging support for District suffrage. Probably because of that pledge the 77th Congress moved quickly to arrange hearings on a new three-part resolution calling for District representation in Congress, home rule, and a constitutional amendment granting District citizens the right to sue and be sued in the federal courts on an equal footing with citizens of the states. Opened in April 1941, the hearings before a subcommittee of the Senate Judiciary Committee commanded wider attention than those of three years before. At moments an air of solemnity filled the room. As a statute passed in 1940 seemed a sufficient guarantee of rights in the courts, the proposed amendment for that purpose dropped out of the discussion, leaving the floor to the representatives of some eighty local organizations and individuals eager to present their views on suffrage. Skillful though much of the argumentation was and useful as are the résumés of its historical bases, the chief interest of the volunteered statements lies in the sometimes deliberate, sometimes inadvertent, revelation of the sharpening conflict between the advocates of a new social order and the upholders of the old.

All power in Uncle Sam's company town rested ultimately in the company directorate—Congress. From the 1890's till the eve of World War I the most worldly of the directors had regarded a place on the House or Senate District Committee as a plum that, because of the advance information available there, offered a juicy bite of the returns on speculation in Washington real estate and utilities. After that era passed, the directors' "executive committee," while including some men genuinely interested in urban problems, contained also rural and small town representatives jealous of their prerogatives and wary of any group outside their own constituencies. As seats on the executive committee ceased to be sought after, any parochial-minded company director felt free to intervene in the management of company affairs. During the 1920's the struggle within the city to guide the hands pulling the strings had had to proceed, as never before, by elaborate indirection. Through a discreet word now and again at company headquarters and pointed suggestions to District commissioners impressed with the importance of big business, bankers, heads of large real estate firms, public utility executives, and the astute lawyers who furnished legal counsel to Washington's major business corporations had continued to exercise influence on the running of the town. But the depression with its accompanying distrust of all business introduced complications. Certainly the old methods would be unworkable in a community governed by popular elections where polls, not pocketbooks, would count and where the lean years had brought to the surface wants that would require large sums of money to satisfy—in short, higher taxes and probably bond issues.

Not every financially powerful Washingtonian shuddered at such a prospect, but the Board of Trade in the 1930's and after spoke for most of the city's big investors in opposing an elected city government. The local business boom evidently strengthened their determination to preserve the political status quo. Under the very nose of an administration intent upon bettering the lot of the "common man," they had tightened their hold upon the community's economic resources; at least the interlocking directorates among the biggest of the seventy-seven business corporations chartered in the District suggested a concentration of control in the hands of eighty to one hundred

men. In 1941 their adroit technique before the Senate committee consisted of bypassing the topic of municipal self-government by focusing the discussion on seats for the District in
Congress. No amount of maneuvering, however, could keep
home rule from the center of the stage. The men and women
who addressed themselves to that question represented a cross-
section of the articulate community: lawyers, salesmen, newspaper men, women absorbed in welfare work, Parent-Teacher
Association heads, and labor leaders. Despite an occasional
dissident, by and large they took the line that entrusting the
city's government to the rank and file was not only legal, just,
and in accordance with American democratic principles, but
would result in a better-run city. The committee room thus
ceased to be the scene of pleadings for a common cause and
turned into an arena in which the defenders of privilege fought
off their critics.

The most forthright attacks on the existing regime came
from men representing organized labor, an element rarely heard
from at earlier inquiries. The head of Washington's Central
Labor Union, with its 150 locals, bluntly characterized the
commissioners and their appointed underlings as a "company
union, organized and operated, and run by Congress." The
secretary-treasurer of the Maryland-District of Columbia CIO
informed the committee that, at the November 1940 convention of the Congress of Industrial Organization, delegates
representing 4,000,000 American workers had unanimously
endorsed suffrage for the District. "Local self-government is
the real McCoy on this suffrage proposition." The only objec-
tion, he asserted, came from people "who are satisfied with
their stranglehold on the status quo. It is obvious to the most
superficial and casual observer that the policies and interest
of certain powerful employer groups in the District of Columbia
are the dominant voice in our District government." They relied
upon "behind the scenes propaganda . . . accompanied by all

kinds of bogies catering to popular fears." While the White House concerned itself with democracy in Europe, friends of the President apologetically admitted they had been unable to get "the President of the United States to concern himself with democracy in the District of Columbia."

Of the "bogies catering to popular fears" Negro suffrage had long been the most omnipresent and the least talked about. Colored Washington took no active part in the suffrage campaigns, as Negro proponents knew their public advocacy would damage rather than help. Although some Negroes had voted in the 1938 plebiscite, and at the subsequent hearings Senator King had asked how the bi-racial city would behave if enfranchised, few white people had been willing to discuss the racial question openly. To do so had seemed to them futile, even obscurely dangerous. "Behind the scenes propaganda" portrayed a city under an irresponsible electorate, run by a local Tammany that would use Negro "bloc voting" as its most potent weapon. By 1941 home rulers concluded they must expose the falseness of that picture. When the head of the United States Government Employees and National Negro Council argued at the hearings that continued congressional rule was safest for his people, and a teacher at the Armstrong High School declared federal aid to Negro education in the South a necessary preliminary to any change in Washington's status, dedicated white suffragists undertook to analyze and explain the insubstantial character of those and all other obstacles to their cause.

The complex class structure of colored Washington, they said, made it inconceivable that all Negroes would vote as a solid racial bloc on any issue. Although some of the recent in-migrants from the Deep South lacked education, colored illiteracy in the District of Columbia in 1930 had stood below the national average of whites and Negroes together, and Washington's public school system could be counted on to transform illiterate newcomers into responsible voters. Nor was there cause to worry lest national interests suffer from allowing locally elected officials to run the capital. Citizens here were Americans first, Washingtonians second. Anxiety about "double voting" was equally groundless. Let federal employees hailing from other places cast ballots in their own state and national elections but have the right to vote in municipal elections in the city they recognized as home. "The solid half of them," said the head of the Citizens' Committee on Suffrage, "are old-time Washingtonians." Their participation in local affairs would benefit the city without injuring the national government.

In the late spring of 1941 Congressman Sumners of Texas, a relatively new convert to home rule, remarked: "If either the Senate or the House are given the opportunity to vote on this legislation, it will pass." The opportunity was not offered.[9] Thirty months later, when a new Senate committee again delved into the question, Senator McCarran explained that the 1941 hearings had convinced him and his colleagues that national representation meant the equivalent of District statehood and therefore clearly ran counter to the intent of the signers of the Constitution; the eloquent pleas for home rule notwithstanding, doubts that most Washingtonians wanted it had persisted. Since 1934 thirty time-consuming congressional investigations of local problems had netted the community little but disappointment. In 1941 when a District official growling about the folly of seeking popular self-government asserted that Washingtonians got fuller hearings on their wants than could people anywhere else in the country, nobody bothered to make the obvious retort: hearings had rarely produced action.[10]

[9] H Judic Comee, 75C, 3S, Hrgs; Comrs Rpts, 1935, pp. 1-7, 1939, p. 7, 1940, pp. 8-9; Hrgs, SJ Res 35, pp. 69, 99, 140, 166-69, 212-15, 234-35, 250-51; Daly, "Washington's Minority Problem," Crisis, XLVI, 139. The data on corporation directorates derive from charts in the possession of Dr. Caroline Ware which were compiled by an American University graduate student from the 1940 listings for D.C. in Poor's Register of Directors and Executives, United States and Canada.

[10] S Dis Comee, 78C, 1S, Hrgs on S. 1420, "Reorganization of the D.C. Govt," p. 7.

CHAPTER XXI

"PURELY A LOCAL AFFAIR," 1933-1940

WHEN the New Dealers swept into the capital in 1933 to remake the national economic and social system, Americans looking to Washington for help thought of the city as the most enviable and exciting place in the country. Although that point of view underwent modification in the next two years, the picture of a singularly privileged community generally endured outside the District of Columbia. By overlooking the "rubbish" accumulating under the bed, a number of local residents also accepted that interpretation. Tourists had no occasion to lift the dust ruffles. The greenness of the parks and the avenues that still boasted trees and the sense of space conveyed by the city's layout struck visitors as vividly and agreeably in the 1930's as in the 1920's, and, more fully than ever before, her air of intellectual vitality was almost palpable. Hence to a good many ears complaints about the meagreness of community services sounded empty, at most the product of perfectionists' disappointment at the capital's falling short of the ideal.

It was clear to critics of District administration that budgetary strangulation accounted for the most acute troubles. It had existed in the flush times of the 1920's, crippling, for example, the Juvenile Court and, despite the five-year building program, the school system as well. When the depression struck Washington in 1932, exigent need brought new demands on a shrunken public purse. No community could meet all the demands the economic collapse put upon it. Washington's per capita wealth, though not tabulated during the most critical period, was probably no smaller than that of other American cities, and for two or three years she managed as well as they. Yet when industrial recovery began to ease pressures and encouraged an expansion of public services elsewhere, problems here intensified, and appropriations in relation to the city's enlarging resources became increasingly parsimonious.

In 1933, although several million dollars of District taxes collected in earlier years sat idle in the United States Treasury, the first New Deal Congress, instead of authorizing the spending of the "surplus," sliced the proposed District budget by a fourth. With tax delinquence mounting and property values declining, the commissioners reduced the tax rate about 10 percent; when business revived, they kept the lowered rate for several years and then raised it only to the modest level of $1.75 per $100 of assessed valuation. The 73rd and succeeding congresses approved some Public Works Administration loans to the District but still forbade bond issues that would spread over five to ten years the cost of urgently needed capital outlays. If installment buying was not yet a standard procedure for private householders, certainly the national capital was the only big city in the United States that had to pay for every service entirely out of current account. As drastic cuts in the federal share of over-all appropriations for running the capital left Washingtonians footing most of the bills, the detailed specifications on the Hill about how local taxes should be spent deepened resentment. While supporters of the Washington Taxpayers Association opposed a tax increase, a solid segment of the community looked upon that as preferable to the protracted penny-pinching that left essential wants unsatisfied. Indignation, stirring in 1934, grew as the decade wore on.

"Organized civic Washington," bitterly observed the *Star* in 1935, "is just about as cheerful over its budget going to the Federal Budget Bureau as it is to hear that the body of a dear friend is at the District morgue." People in other parts of the United States would assume that the slashes in District estimates saved the Treasury substantial sums, but "the dear public would never suspect that the funds saved did not belong to Uncle Sam at all." Indeed outside Washington misunderstanding was almost universal about the distinction between federal money and local tax money collected from District property-owners for local purposes and then by law deposited in the United States Treasury. President Roosevelt himself appeared to share that confusion, for in regretfully setting aside Dr. Harvey Cushing's plea for a new $2,000,000 building for the Surgeon General's Library, the President wrote that "out of Public Works funds we must keep the District of Columbia somewhere within a reasonable ratio of expenditure compared with the population"; a new government office building, a sewage treatment plant, "very much needed, as my nose on River trips testifies," a modern T.B. sanitarium, and a stack room to house important current documents would have to come first. Here in a single list were two purely federal projects and two primarily local for which the District would have to pay most of the bills. Some $4,000,000 from PWA enabled the District sanitary engineers to start construction of the sewage treatment plant in 1935, but $2,800,000 of that sum was a loan which had to be repaid with interest.[1] Admittedly whether or not the rest of the country was aware of whose taxes paid for what was not of major importance, but the general misapprehension was irritating. And the usual response of outsiders that all this was a "purely local affair" rubbed salt in the wounds of impotence.

A budget, a Director of the Budget observed, by definition cannot be merely "a shopping list" but must entail choices. Federal analysts assigned to the District budget in the 1930's believed the community prone to forget that truth. Having been denied any responsibility for making the choices for two generations, Washingtonians came by complaints readily. Since law reserved the special water and sewer fees for those

[1] Daniel Garges, "The Government of the District of Columbia," *American City*, XL, 107-08; *Star*, 20 Oct 1935; F. D. Roosevelt to Dr. Harvey Cushing, 1933, quoted in Dupree, *Science*, p. 348; figures on PWA loan assembled by Sanitary Engineer's office.

two services and the gasoline tax for highway maintenance, only the general fund was subject to argument. With Auditor Donovan as adviser on District spending, the federal Bureau of the Budget ordinarily made a judicious allocation among the competing demands. At the end of the 1930's the bureau occasionally yielded to the requests of citizens' organizations to send representatives to the hearings held yearly with District department heads, but shifts in the disposition of money rarely followed, and the scheme was then abandoned, probably because local importunities made a difficult job still harder. By 1940 real estate taxes in the country's "Number One Boom Town" brought in $21,196,400, tangible personal property and gross earnings taxes $3,712,144, and, because of collection difficulties, the newly imposed District income tax less than $3,100,000 of the $5,000,000 expected. Loans and small grants from federal agencies supplemented the amounts available, but the paper total, including a carry-over from earlier years of $4,265,000 that Congress had not authorized spending, was too little to provide adequate services for a city grown in a decade from 487,000 to 663,000 inhabitants.[2] A 20-percent bigger budget had to be stretched to meet the needs of a 36-percent larger population. Which needs were to receive priority was a decision on which the people most directly affected had no say.

Perhaps the single greatest handicap under which the bureau and the city suffered was the stipulation of the law that the expected revenues for each year must determine the size of the budget sent to the Hill. Only additional taxable property, upward revisions of assessed valuations, or a higher tax rate could enlarge the figure. And, experience indicated, bigger assessments and hence larger municipal income were likely merely to add to the surplus held in the Treasury. The law

[2] Comrs Rpts, 1933, p. 1, 1940, pp. 5, 8-11, 1941, p. 7; interviews, Daniel W. Bell, Director of the Bureau of the Budget, and Frederick Lawton, Assistant Director, 1934-39.

enacted in 1878 to safeguard against a repetition of the reckless spending of Boss Shepherd's day forbade borrowing; the act of 1909, ostensibly only further insurance against municipal extravagance, was more crippling because it meant that Congress was never confronted with a realistic summary of the city's needs. If the necessity of a sewage treatment plant thrust itself on congressional noses as well as the President's, the consequences of neglecting equally serious if less blatantly unsavory problems were rarely self-evident. Busy members of Congress seldom thought of the predictable results, for instance, of allowing no money to the Children's Division of the welfare board for a preventive program directed at checking juvenile delinquency before it got started. Thoughtful Washingtonians inclined to believe that if the budget, however staggering the total, were to reflect the true picture of conditions, Congress would not disregard it or would at least forego further cuts in figures already fixed below an amount essential to the orderly functioning of a great city.

In view of Washington's record of 135 traffic fatalities in 1934, 115 the next year, and, throughout the thirties, the rapid multiplication of motor vehicles on her streets, Congress logically enough gave particular attention to transportation and traffic control. As automobile registration fees and gasoline taxes yearly produced between two and three million dollars of income, and the District got a share of federal funds under the national road-building act of 1935, the highway department together with the Park and Planning Commission mapped out a huge network of through-way and bridge construction. Overpasses and underpasses, especially a tunnel under Thomas Circle on Massachusetts Avenue, additional stop lights, and complicated traffic arrows gradually reduced traffic hazards, but not until law required strict driving examinations and periodic inspections of motor vehicles did the accident rate drop sharply. While a merger at last brought the streetcar and bus companies into a single transit system, the Board of Trade persuaded the highway department to widen F Street in front of the old Patent Office by shearing off the steps from William Elliot's replica of the Parthenon. Moving traffic was more important than static aesthetics. As the Washington airport was nearing completion, the Board of Trade also initiated a study of the feasibility of a subway system, but at congressional hearings arguments that so costly a measure was quite needless buried it.

Meanwhile parking troubles constantly worsened. A long report of 1930 prepared at the instance of the Park and Planning Commission, the metropolitan police, and a half-dozen business organizations had proposed the use of the interior courtyards of the Federal Triangle and under- and above-ground tiers of parking space at the rear of other office buildings, but in 1941 the downtown section of the city had only two or three big garages. Installation of additional parking meters and prohibition of leaving cars standing along much-travelled stretches of streets during rush hours made no dent on the problem. As long as twice as many people as in other big American cities persisted in driving their own cars into the business district, the chances of arriving at a solution looked dim. Only wartime gasoline rationing would provide a reprieve.[3]

Pointing out that directing traffic at rush hours daily took a third of the policemen on duty, the superintendent of the metropolitan police invariably attributed the shortcomings in his department to undermanning of the force. Special details frequently had to be assigned to watch over the comings and goings at official or semi-official parties, to keeping order at

[3] *Rpts B/Tr*, 1936, pp. 5-15; *News*, 25 Nov, 1 Dec 1933; *Star*, 20 Oct 1935; *Rec*, 75C, 1S, p. 6298; H Dis Comee, 74C, 2S, "Traffic Investigation"; Comrs Rpts, 1934, pp. 29-30, 1935, pp. 90-91, 1937, pp. 113-15, 1940, pp. 128-29, 1941, pp. 9, 133; Miller McClintock, *Report on the Parking and Garage Problem of the Central Business District of Washington, D.C.*, 1930.

parades, and, with the newly organized tear-gas squad standing by, forestalling trouble at demonstrations like those attempted by the Hunger Marchers. Consequently men walking beats usually had to patrol from twenty to sixty blocks instead of the six to ten the chief considered the maximum for adequate protection. The report of the Woman's Bureau in 1935 squarely presented the case for larger appropriations: "The police have always the unhappy duty of trying to deal with all the failures of the community. Conditions which the community, except for a small group, tolerates year after year have been greatly intensified in the last two years. . . . The increase in volume [of work] without increase in staff spells decrease in ability to do a thorough-going job in the field allotted to us. . . . This Bureau was set up to deal with human beings as individuals, not as job lots, but beyond a certain point this has become a physical impossibility, and it takes all that we have and sometimes more not to lose sight of even the minimum standards of service." Although Congress thereupon authorized an increase to bring the force up to 1,471 officers and five years later approved the addition of another 50, burglaries, larceny, and assault kept Washington in the category of a city of violence. The depression itself provoked lawlessness, but two congressional investigations brought to light several other sources of trouble.

Superintendent Ernest Brown, who had joined the force in 1896 and worked his way up without benefit of special training, had little sympathy with new-fangled notions of police education. In nearly twenty years only one subordinate felt impelled to avail himself of the FBI courses opened in 1921. So far from following General Glassford's method of supervising his men by riding around town on a motorcycle, Major Brown sanctioned tactics described in 1941 as "Gestapo." If the wiretapping that went on within the Chicago police department was not one of the devices employed, still the metropolitan police made use of an internal spying system that, conscientious officers testified, undermined the morale of the entire force. Recruits had to pass civil service examination, but promotions proceeded by recommendation, and favoritism, especially congressional influence, could make or break a man's career. Just as sanitary inspectors learned never to issue an order to a congressman's household demanding obedience to regulations aimed at controlling rats in rodent-infested neighborhoods, so the police rookie quickly discovered the wisdom of adapting his law-enforcement zeal to fit the rank of the offender. Unequal application of the law created an atmosphere of subtle corruption and tried the souls of citizens unable to claim the tacitly recognized immunity of federal officialdom.

If the high proportion of big-wiggery in the city, the endless streams of tourists, and the succession of marches on Washington ever since the Bonus Army invasion all constituted unique complications in policing the capital, the rise in juvenile delinquency during the depression was a familiar problem in every American city. In the autumn of 1933 Frank Jelleff, a Washington merchant whose knowledge of the community was exceeded only by his generosity, pointed out that in the District of Columbia one boy in every fifteen between the ages of 10 and 15 landed in the Juvenile Court and, of the age group of 17- to 20-year-olds, one in five was arrested. He proposed to get $200,000 from the Public Works Administration for a building where youngsters could gather under friendly, unobtrusive police surveillance for games, boxing, wrestling, playing records or the radio—a clubhouse boys could think of as their own where they would agree to rules to ensure the rights of every member. As PWA bypassed the plan, Major Brown picked up the idea and instructed uniformed policemen to solicit funds from house to house to start the Metropolitan Police Boys' Club.

The response of the thousand white boys who immediately

made use of the first clubhouse in southeast Washington led to the opening of a second in the Kenilworth section, a third in 1935 in the slums of southwest Washington, and the next year a club for colored boys. Every year patrolmen rang door-bells on their beats to collect cash for the clubs. As member-ship rose to 16,500, the effects appeared in police and Juvenile Court records: although a change in categories of cases pre-vented exact comparisons, in five years the number of juvenile arrests dropped startlingly, a decline to which the chances opened to 17- and 18-year-olds to enroll at Civilian Conservation Corps camps and the work of the National Youth Administra-tion undoubtedly contributed. Training courses and defense jobs made available in the autumn of 1940 lessened the im-portance of the boys' clubs, but men who had become interested in them regarded them as a vitally constructive force deserving public as well as private support.[4]

The ultimate cost to the community of cheese-paring ap-propriations, plain enough in the case of the understaffed police department and more so in the provision for penal and correc-tional institutions, was still heavier in the realm of public health and welfare. Needy people, as obscure as they were helpless, always tended to become statistics when tax expenditures were under discussion in the District commissioners' offices, at Budget Bureau conferences, and in committee rooms on the Hill. The overworked and underpaid medical and social work-ers of the District's public agencies never succeeded in portray-ing in compelling form the wretchedness they had to witness daily. Newspapermen trying to make the facts come alive merely earned the label "tear-jerker." Even comparative data made little impression. Testimony showed, for example, that other cities recognized an eight-hour day for hospital nurses;

[4] *News*, 8 Nov 1933; Comrs Rpts, 1933, pp. 71-74, 1934, pp. 89, 96, 1935, pp. 79, 84-85, 1936, p. 98, 1937, p. 105; H Dis Comm, 74C, 2S, "Investigation of Crime," *passim*, and 77C, 1S, "Investigation of the Metropolitan Police," pp. 2-7, 21-42, 66-88, 227-33, 382-405, 436-42.

at Gallinger they worked twelve. Built in 1929 to accommodate 300 patients, Washington's municipal hospital had a daily average of 691 in 1934 and 744 the next year. The cost of some social catastrophes could not be tallied statistically— the wasted potentialities of children, say, who got too little to eat and no care at home or who landed in run-down institutions and unsuitable foster families. While new concepts of social responsibility born of the depression brought fresh vigor to public welfare agencies in other cities, after 1935 Washington's had to mark time.

Why? Why above all in the capital, the nerve center of New Deal ideas and social experiment? The lag was certainly not due to the heartlessness of individual members of Congress or to the incompetence of the men and women in charge of the District programs. The principal reason is rather to be found in the remoteness of the men on the Hill, the decision-makers, from the problems of the city at their feet, and, besides the element of distance, the time dimension. Texans, Nebraskans, Indianians, and South Carolinians, however humane individually, could not be expected to feel and rarely showed profound concern for a community that was not their own; for them Washington's welfare was an abstraction when not an irritating chore foisted upon them at the cost of more rewarding assignments. Again and again months would slide by before preoccupied senators and representatives acted on an urgent local matter, and in the interim the situation changed, all too often for the worse. By the time Congress accepted a proposal originally put forward as an ounce of prevention, a pound of cure would no longer suffice. Members who served any length of time on the District committees generally came to understand the city's needs, but a single ill-informed or contrary member there or on the Appropriations Subcommittee or the Rules Committee might side-track a bill indefinitely. And southerners in Congress, loath to extend assistance to "niggers," let alone encourage Negro migration into the capital, were not above obstructionism. A second reason for delays and half-measures was the recurrent lack of community consensus about any particular remedy proposed. More than once well-intentioned citizens appeared at congressional hearings to fight against details of a plan carefully worked out by other well-intentioned people, with the result that everyone came away empty-handed, the entire project killed or indefinitely postponed. The history of Washington's health and welfare work thus became a constantly repeated record of too late and too little.

The District health officer optimistically ventured the opinion in 1940 that a recently-expanded public health program was at last redeeming the city's "adverse reputation." In 1934 her infant mortality rate of 66.1 per thousand was, with the exception of New Orleans, the highest of any big city in the country and a direct consequence, observers believed, of Washington's alley-slums; by 1939, new medical social services, the maternity and child care clinics made possible by grants from the U.S. Public Health Service and the federal Children's Bureau, and the demolition of some of the worst of the alley dwellings had reduced the rate to 48.1, lower than the national average. WPA help for several years kept the physical plant of Gallinger Hospital from irreparable deterioration, and in 1939 appropriations permitted the construction of several new buildings, but, as was the case also at Freedmen's and the T.B. hospital, too few nurses and doctors and a lack of equipment still made proper patient care an impossibility. In 1941 a reorganization and an enlarged professional staff held out hopes, unhappily ephemeral, that the institution henceforward could measure up to U.S. Public Health Service standards.[5]

The Board of Public Welfare functioned under still more

[5] Comrs Rpts, 1934, p. 134, 1935, pp. 128-29, 147, 1936, pp. 175-78, 1937, pp. 146-52, 1938, pp. 125-26, 149, 1939, pp. 143, 168-76, 194-208, 1940, pp. 139-42, 165-204, 1941, pp. 2, 5-16.

precarious circumstances. Until the summer of 1932, when the handling of the newly created $350,000 emergency relief fund fell to five of the nine laymen composing the board, its duties had been chiefly confined to periodic consultation with the executive director who supervised the District's public eleemosynary institutions. But, with the spread of unemployment and want, the unanticipated job of acting as almoner for tens of thousands of people became an overwhelming assignment. In every city and hamlet of America the foremost problem in 1933 was to get people back to work and in the meantime keep them from utter hopelessness and starvation. By midsummer 1933 Washington's emergency relief committee had spent $1,025,600 over and above the original $350,000 appropriation. During the next twelve months day after day despairing jobless men and women crowded the branch offices scattered through the city in old warehouses and shabby stores where a harried staff and flurried untrained clerical helpers tried to make pennies do the work of dollars. Some $10,658,000, four-fifths of it federal emergency funds, went into direct relief, wages paid through the short-lived Civil Works Administration, supplies, and social workers' salaries.

With such large-scale operations and such huge sums of money involved, inevitably confusions arose, and while George Allen fumed about inefficiencies, the administrative machinery geared to relatively simple tasks all but fell apart. The projects the emergency committee sponsored generally had long-term social value—community gardens, for one, for another the hot lunches for undernourished school children provided under school board aegis, and the nursery schools and adult classes frequently taught by women who had been dropped from the roster of regular teachers because they had close relatives on the federal payroll. Nevertheless cancellation of the federal Civil Works program in April 1934, when the number of families seeking help was still rising, called for a reorganiza-

tion of the entire relief scheme. The emergency relief committee of laymen serving without compensation accordingly
gave way to a professionally trained Public Assistance Division
paid out of welfare funds.

When Elwood Street accepted the post of welfare director
in June 1934, the highly qualified staff he put in charge of
public assistance furnished only a partial answer. Here, as
elsewhere, 1934 was a harder year than 1933. Eleven months
after the National Industrial Recovery Act had started pump-
priming, the Federal Emergency Relief Administration reported: "Industry is not absorbing the unemployed as rapidly
as the number of those whose resources are exhausted is increasing." Washington's major industry had expanded in the
interval, but as Secretary of the Interior Ickes kept a restraining
hand on public works in the capital, and most of the people
manning the new federal agencies came from other places,
few new government jobs opened up for Washingtonians. The
launching of the Works Progress Administration in the early
summer of 1935, creating jobs as it did for white-collar and
professional people as well as manual laborers, was all-
important for a city of office-workers. Men and women with
clerical training put school records in order and collected data
for special census tracts, artists catalogued paintings, and the
Federal Writers Project produced in 1937 the invaluable *WPA
Guide to Washington.*

Still neither WPA, nor its subsidiary the National Youth
Administration with its enlargement of the CCC program, nor
the widening scope of newly formed "trade and barter" co-
operatives disposed of Washington's relief problem. In 1935,
after 134 years of shoulder-shrugging, the federal government
undertook to care for the transients whom the Travellers' Aid
could not help, and that summer Street reported that the
number of families and unattached individuals on the relief
rolls had dropped from the 23,423 of the preceding year to

18,298. But costs for 1934 had come to more than $10,600,000, and, Street warned, "in many areas of activity increasing expenditures will be necessary because of the growth of the city, the increasing complexity of urban life and the inadequacy of many citizens by experience and ability to adjust themselves to that complexity." In June, however, passage of the national Social Security Act, with its multiple provisions for unemployment compensation, old-age assistance, and pensions for the blind, moved the Board of Public Welfare to speak thankfully of its "sense of the vast and enduring significance" of measures that "represent the acceptance of the principle that government is responsible for at least a minimum of economic security for all its citizens."

For Washington's public welfare the year 1936 marks a watershed. Difficult though relief problems had been since 1932, federal help and fairly liberal appropriations of District funds had enabled the public agencies to manage the load. Enactment of the social legislation of 1935 seemingly promised to reduce greatly the future burden, although the first monthly government payments would not begin until 1942, and meantime the extent of help to the aged would depend on the size of the budget earmarked for that purpose. The change for the worse brought about at the end of 1935 apparently grew out of congressional conviction that the emergency was now over, that the WPA could handle any vestigial unemployment problems, and that the District's Welfare Board no longer needed large sums of money. In November all relief payments were stopped until every family had undergone reinvestigation, in December grants were reduced 25 percent, and the following spring a hard and fast rule cut off all financial help to any family that included an employable person.

The full meaning of that rule was hard to grasp. Everyone agreed that its basis was sound: jobs would replace the "dole" and leave only society's physical and mental incompetents to receive relief. But did the public know, asked the Washington Council of Social Agencies, that "a family is classified as employable even if the only potential wage earner is an adolescent boy or girl who not only has no job but has had no training or experience to equip him for qualifying for a job?" Did the community realize that in the 4,138 families dropped from the local relief rolls in April 1936, "the employable persons actually were either unemployed or employed at a wage far below that required to provide minimum needs for their families, and that many of these persons could not be absorbed in private industry or in WPA jobs?" Technically these people, if certified, were eligible for WPA, but, unlike most of the states, the District had no agency to make certifications for employables not already known to the Public Assistance Division. Month by month the division's task grew in difficulty. By mid-1937 social workers were carrying case loads of 140 families each, and constant criticism of performance made recruitment of additional case-workers impossible.

Other units of the welfare service suffered equally. Maryland refused to permit further foster home placements from the District until the Child Welfare Division reduced the number of children supervised by one social worker from 104 to 65. In 1937 the appropriation for aid to dependent children was so small that less than 19 percent of those eligible could receive help. A single demonstration unit begun in one neighborhood with Children's Bureau funds proved "the potentialities of preventive individualized casework treatment for children who present behavior problems but whose delinquency has not become so much that they need to be considered by the juvenile court," but lack of money forbade the extension of that kind of service to other parts of the city. At the Industrial Home School for colored children vocational training embraced only a third of the projected program. When Mrs. Roosevelt visited the Home for the Aged and Infirm she was scandalized at the overcrowding, the understaffing, and lack of equipment.[6]

While one source of Washington's troubles was congressional disbelief that problems could be mounting here in the midst of a business boom, another factor was the reluctance on the Hill to provide "a minimum of economic security" to Negroes. It was common knowledge that in a community less than a third Negro, two-thirds of the people on relief were colored. It was also obvious that as long as Negroes were "the last hired and the first fired," unemployment among them would always run higher than among whites. But arguments that denial now of help to the family of an able-bodied jobless Negro would extend the problem to the next generation were useless. Pleas for a change in the rules and for larger appropriations merely turned the Board of Public Welfare into the *bête noire* of the budget-makers. The chief analyst for the District at the Bureau of the Budget insisted that all social workers thought that money grew on trees and testily suggested that people who could not support themselves look to the churches for help. Officials' irritation at citizens' repeated begging for bigger appropriations hurt every phase of the welfare program.

Anger at that point of view flared out in 1937 after the head of the Washington Taxpayers Association asserted that, in view of the business revival, widespread unemployment no longer existed and that the "howl" for more welfare money came solely from relief workers fearful of losing their jobs. Speaking indignantly for the Family Service Association, the new name for the Associated Charities, Canon Anson Phelps Stokes, Coleman Jennings, Carroll Glover, and Dr. Frederic Perkins,

[6] *Ibid.*, 1933, pp. 81-84, 95, 1934, pp. 111-16, 1935, pp. 121-25, 135, 1936, pp. 166-74, 1937, pp. 160-70, 1938, pp. 183-97; *Herald*, 28, 29, 30 Mar 1934; *Rpt, Division of Emergency Relief, B/PW*, 1934, p. 24; "Private Agencies are Still Needed in the Relief Field," *Council Bulletin*, I, Nov 1936, pp. 1-2; Schlesinger, *Coming of the New Deal*, 293-96; "Demonstrating Child Welfare," *Community Service*, II, Jan 1938, p. 5, and CSA, 17th Anl Rpt, "Research," *ibid.*, Apr 1938, pp. 2-5.

none of them professional social workers and all of them men
of property, testified that appeals for help in December 1936
had been more numerous and more urgent than in any month
since 1933: "Indeed we consider the situation so serious that
we would prefer to have our taxes increased if necessary,
rather than to encourage the permanent human wastage which
will almost inevitably result in hundreds of cases if promising
material for human rehabilitation is allowed to go unaided
this winter." While Jennings spelled out facts in letters to
every member of Congress, a committee explained to the Bureau
of the Budget that some of its data were faulty, especially on
Negro chisellers. Since the Board of Trade research staff had
reported $18,000,000 of public money spent that year on help
for the unemployed, the Family Service Association undertook
to prove that astronomical figure the result of charging a dozen
public services to relief. At a mass meeting, 1,500 people asked
for an additional $1,000,000 in welfare funds and revocation
of the edict forbidding help for unemployed employables. Congress yielded to the extent of waiving the rule for a three-
month period but then reinstated the restriction.

A special census early in 1938 showed forty-five out of every
thousand Americans totally unemployed, sixty out of every
thousand Washingtonians; fifteen out of every thousand Americans on emergency relief, sixteen Washingtonians. Here then
was no imaginary crisis; "First City—Worst City" cried Community Chest officers. The Welfare Board recommended a
general relief appropriation for 1939 of $3,247,750; the Budget
Bureau itself proposed $705,000 for old-age assistance. The
House, impervious to all urging, fixed upon $489,000 for the
aged and an over-all welfare total of $900,000. While the
bill was pending in the Senate, civic organizations, charity
societies, and white labor unions mobilized in support of the
original request; although the Board of Trade at first opposed
it, a subcommittee later endorsed it. At a meeting of a newly

formed Citizens' Committee on Unemployment and Relief, "interested organizations and large taxpayers gathered to protest their own right to pay for adequate relief to Washington residents who are in need." The House decision stood.

Later in the year as a result of congressionally authorized studies of District relief administration and child welfare agencies, the Children's Division netted an additional $30,120 for salaries and for extension of the "preventive individualized casework treatment" that the demonstration unit had found effective in forestalling child dependency and delinquency. In the meantime Elwood Street risked a direct appeal to Congressman Ross Collins of Mississippi, chairman of the House Subcommittee on District Appropriations. For several years past, 14-, 15-, and 16-year-old Negro girls, unaccompanied by their families, had been pouring into Washington from the South. Prepared only to live on the streets, many of them quickly landed in the colored unit of the National Training School for Girls. The school was overflowing; more space and more skilled supervisors were badly needed. Representative Collins, looking the social worker straight in the eye, said, "If I went along with your ideas, Mr. Street, I'd never keep my seat in Congress. My constituents wouldn't stand for spending all that money on niggers." Mississippi's racial views thus controlled correctional work in Washington. Shortly after that interview Street and his two most experienced assistants resigned.[7]

The efficacy of private charity inevitably depended in large measure upon the scope of the public agencies' work. Until

[7] *News*, 29 Mar 1933; Minutes of the Board of Managers of the Family Service Association, 13 Jan, 10 Feb, 10 Mar, 14 Apr, 12 May, 9 Jun 1937, 9 Feb, 9 Mar 1938 (hereafter cited as Min FSA); "Council Endorses Request for Deficiency Relief Appropriation," *Community Service*, I, Feb 1937, p. 6, and CSA, Anl Rpt, *ibid.*, Apr 1937, p. 20; "First City—Worst City," and "We Need Funds for Them," *ibid.*, Feb 1938, pp. 4-5, 11; "Everybody's Concern," *ibid.*, Mar 1938, p. 3; "Our Foremost Concern," *ibid.*, May 1938, p. 8; Comrs Rpts, 1938, p. 191, 1939, pp. 215-31, 1940, pp. 218-28.

1933 the Community Chest had carried almost the whole of the city's relief burden. Church charities, to be sure, lessened the load slightly. The Church of God, for example, ran a penny lunch room after the millionaire Bernarr McFadden, appalled by the pilferage from the establishment he had been financing, turned it over to Elder Michaux. The evangelist appealed to his radio audience for help, local people out of work gave their services and, when they got paying jobs, contributed money to the "Happy News Cafe," where thousands of hungry people were fed for a penny a meal. Still the city's organized charity societies, pledged to the Chest's single fund-raising campaign, could not adopt Michaux's method. Their "normal" functions of preventive work, rehabilitation, and health programs had to wait until the government recognized its obligation to provide food and shelter for the destitute. Seemingly that moment came with the expansion of the Welfare Board's duties and resources in 1934. That year the Associated Charities changed its name to the Family Service Association, appointed a successor to the elderly Walter Ufford, and joined with other social agencies in studying new approaches to community problems.

Thus, six neighborhood councils arose, each undertaking to abet and harmonize the activities of every organization concerned with dependency and delinquency in its area. Drawing upon sociologists at the local universities for surveys, the councils stressed that communities must pay in one of two ways "for the privilege of preparing the younger generation for future responsibilities. . . . The first way pays in both money and suffering through the delinquency and the crime which are the result of neglect. The second way pays by providing the suitable environment, including all kinds of opportunity for worthwhile activity, which remove the incentive and the occasion for abnormal conduct. Each community must decide how it prefers to pay." While an adult "Self Help Exchange" achieved some success, and the Voteless League of Women Voters worked for legislation, organizations such as the Legal Aid Bureau and the Washington Social Hygiene Society fought to cut the roots of particular social ills. Pioneering articles in the *Herald* were "the plow that broke the plains" in combatting public ignorance of the long-term consequence of 27,000 new cases of venereal disease every year. All the newspapers campaigned for funds for the summer camps sponsored by the Boy and Girl Scouts and a half-dozen child welfare societies. But in 1936, when Congress restricted public relief to families with no employable member, again the Council of Social Agencies had to man the breach at the cost of other services.[8]

Once past the fright of 1933 and 1934, affluent conservatives tended to revert to the view that public financing of welfare, whether through emergency relief, WPA, provisions of the Social Security Act, or public housing, ran counter to basic American principles. Granting that philanthropy was the logical alternative to tax-supported aid to the needy, much of the upper strata of society in the capital failed to act on that premise. As business recovered, gifts to the Community Chest shrank. Possibly former big contributors believed that tales of mounting want were fabricated by social workers. Perhaps some people considered generous help merely an invitation to irresponsible Negroes to milk soft-hearted whites. Whatever the reason, after 1935 the Community Chest fell short of its goal every year. "Defeat in our last campaign for financial support of private social work," stated the Chest's organ, *Community*

[8] Min As Ch, 10, 24 May, 14 Jun, 11 Oct 1933, 10 Jan, 26 Feb, 9 May, 13 Jun 1934; Min FSA, 11 Dec 1935, 8 Apr 1936; *Church of God, A Pictorial Review*, pp. 26-27; Herbert L. Willett, Jr., "Financing Washington's Welfare Work," and Thomas W. Gosling, "Neighborhood Councils," *Council Bulletin*, I, Oct 1936, pp. 2-5; "Skeleton of Relief," *Community Service*, II, Sep 1937, p. 5; "This Happened Here," *ibid.*, Oct 1937, p. 3; "Your Social Health," *ibid.*, Dec 1937, p. 3; Anne Geddes, *Trends in Relief Expenditures, 1910-1935*, Works Progress Administration, Monograph 10, pp. 91-93; *Forty Years of the Voteless League of Women Voters*.

Service, in 1938, "defeat in our battle for a more adequate relief appropriation from public funds, show that we have not yet succeeded in convincing the public of the value and necessity of our program." Catholic and Jewish organizations were free to canvass their own congregations, but Chest rules forbade non-sectarian societies to make independent appeals. Unable to find any other way to fill the gap in the relief program left by the public agencies, the Family Service Association repeatedly drew on the capital of its small endowment fund.

At this juncture the slow progress of slum clearance and public housing projects under the aegis of the Alley-Dwelling Authority and PWA inspired a new attempt to induce private builders to act. In an article in *The Nation's Business* entitled "A Philanthropy that Pays Dividends," a stockholder in the forty-year-old Washington Sanitary Improvement Company and the Sanitary Housing Company called attention to the fact that the former for many years had paid 6 percent dividends, the latter 5 percent, the original investments of $500,000 and $200,000, respectively, were now worth $1,120,000 and $340,000, and still the companies were able to maintain decent housing at rentals averaging $16.87 a month for tenants whose annual income was about $657. But even had the appeal convinced Washington building firms, an accelerated pace of demolition and rebuilding, one citizen observed sadly, would not in itself break "the dismal routine of slum living." The "individualized medical and social care required for the rehabilitation of slum dwellers," many of whom had occupied the same fetid shanties for more than a third of a century, would have to come both from public sources and private philanthropy.[9] Who or what was to awaken the government and Washingtonians collectively to the urgency of action?

[9] Min FSA, 15 Sep, 8 Dec 1937, 12 Jan 1938, 13 Dec 1939; "Do Your Part," *Community Service*, II, Oct 1937, p. 8; "Washington First and Last," *ibid.*, Nov 1937, pp. 8-9; "More and Better Publicity," *ibid.*, Mar 1938, p. 4; CSA, Anl Rpt, *ibid.*, Apr 1938, pp. 6-15; "Alley People," *ibid.*,

Contrary to congressional assumptions, 1939 brought more cases of need than had 1938, partly because the WPA ruled that no one could stay on its rolls for more than eighteen months, irrespective of whether he could find another source of livelihood. The rule applied in the states as well as in the District, but in the capital taxpayers' inability to increase the public welfare budget gave the edict particular harshness. Imposition of an arbitrary monthly maximum of $48 of public money for relief to any one family hastened the deterioration, the Family Service directors noted, "for which the community must ultimately pay." The summer camps for children had to cut their 1939 season from eight weeks to six. Despite the efforts of the minority, the community seemingly had decided to pay its obligations to the younger generation in the currency of neglect. As public and private agencies froze social workers' salaries below the sums paid in other cities, the turnover of experienced professionals, begun with Elwood Street's resignation in 1939, increased. Before the end of the New Deal era, the capital had the reputation within the social work profession of being the city where frustration and heartbreak would overtake the person of competence and vision more surely and quickly than in any other place in the country.[10]

Disappointing as was the accomplishment of seven years, "organized civic Washington" could see a few improvements in race relations. Certainly several white organizations had moved a considerable way toward recognizing colored Washington as an integral part of the community. Taken separately, the incidents that indicate a changing point of view are not impressive. The Associated Charities, after electing

May 1938, p. 9; Appleton Clark, Jr., "A Philanthropy that Pays Dividends," *Nation's Business*, XXVI, 21-22.

[10] Willett, "The Community Chest Buys Services from Its Member Hospitals," *Community Service*, I, May 1937, pp. 14-15; Min FSA, 30 Oct 1935, 14 Dec 1938, 8 Feb, 10 May, 13 Sep, 11 Oct 1939, 19 Jun 1940, 19 Feb 1941.

31. Inauguration of President Roosevelt, January 1945; the only inaugural ever conducted at the White House

32. "Press Conference," December 1941, drawing by Gluyas Williams for the *New Yorker*

33. World War II "tempos" and bridges over the Reflecting Pool on the Mall

34. The Jefferson Memorial

35. The National Gallery of Art with tempos in the foreground

36. Pentagon

37. Union Station, 1943

38. Queue at a shoe store just before a coupon was due to expire, 1944

39. Spectators at the Hancock statue waiting for the Civilian Defense Workers
Recruitment Parade, 1943

40. Franklin D. Roosevelt's funeral procession on Constitution Avenue en route to the White Hous...

41. Georgetown houses built in the 1840's

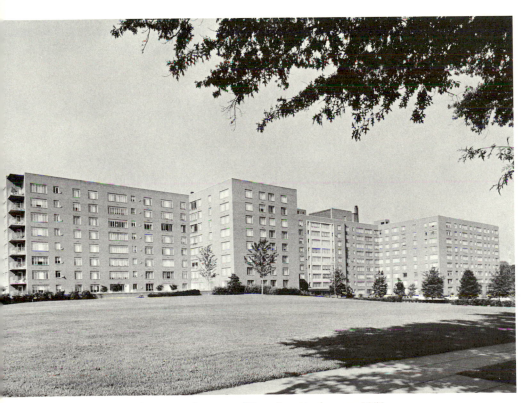

42. Apartment house on Massachusetts Avenue, 1956

43. St. John's Church and the AFL-CIO Building

44. Southwest Redevelopment Plan of 1955, later modified

two Negroes to the board of managers in 1932, went further by adding Campbell Johnson of the colored YMCA and electing Dean Lucy Slowe of Howard University to the executive committee. After seven years of backing and filling, in 1935 the Washington Federation of Churches invited Negro churches to join, and, not without some hesitation, four Negro congregations accepted, doubtless chiefly because its new bi-racial committee on race relations seemed likely to reach further into strongholds of local prejudice than other organizations could. Although Negro quotas in Chest drives were minuscule—$9,500 in 1933, less than $5,000 in 1934—money to run the three Negro settlement houses, the Stoddard Baptist Old Folks Home, St. Ann's Home, the Phyllis Wheatley YWCA, and the colored YMCA, all came from Chest funds, and on the whole ungrudgingly. The *Star*, which for fifty years had rarely printed any but derogatory or facetious stories about colored people, in 1933 carried a long account of a meeting of the Association for the Study of Negro Life and History and at intervals thereafter the white press published news items that implied, as a home ruler put it, that "Negroes are people."

In some areas bi-racial cooperation sprang up spontaneously. A racially mixed group inaugurated a self-help cooperative in northeast Washington in 1934, white and colored people together raised the money to open the Northwest Settlement House on M Street, and, in response to a plea from the *Tribune*, an interracial committee conducted a drive to combat the excessively high tuberculosis death rate among Negroes. As careful studies drew attention to the fact that Negro mortality from all causes was 70 percent higher than white and stressed the direct relationship between the incidence of fatal disease and the occupance of alley slums, Director John Ihlder of the Alley-Dwelling Authority and some of his associates urged the placing of less emphasis upon housing developments for medium income families and more upon building for the poorest—namely

Negroes. Condescension, to be sure, persisted among most well-meaning whites, whether donors to the Church of God who nevertheless dubbed Elder Michaux's devil-fighting "corny," or board members of the Family Service Association who as late as 1937 took segregated seating for granted at the annual luncheons. But with every passing year patronizing behavior lessened and Negro touchiness declined. When Dean Slowe died, the entry in the board minutes of the Family Service Association was as genuine a tribute to a rare person as the obituary of that gentle old crusader, Mrs. Archibald Hopkins.[11]

White House policies, if somewhat noncommittal, helped, and Mrs. Roosevelt's warm interest in colored people as people was reassuring. Secretary of Labor Perkins and the "Old Curmudgeon" apparently were equally color blind. And yet had the administration completely ignored race relations, the change in attitude that had begun to emerge in Washington early in Hoover's presidency would probably have spread. That the admission of Negro graduate students to American and Catholic Universities made no stir in itself suggests that racial toleration was growing without political forcing. The chief outside stimulus to a reexamination of second-class citizenship was the shock of observing the application of race doctrines in Nazi Germany.

In 1933 not more than two or three American cities had well-organized, comprehensive public health and welfare systems. Private charity, Edith Abbott noted, was "accidental, spasmodic, sporadic, and almost unbelievably inadequate." By 1940, however, a number of municipalities with state help had

[11] Min As Ch, 14 Mar 1934; Min FSA, 8 May, 8 Dec 1937; *Tribune*, 17, 31 Mar, 23 Nov 1933, 19 Jul, 13 Oct, 17, 24 Nov 1934, 6, 27 Dec 1935, 22 Nov 1937; Washington Federation of Churches, *Yearbook*, 1936; *Council Bulletin*, i, Oct 1936, p. 13; Mrs. William Kittle, "Fiftieth Anniversary of the American Social Settlement Movement," *Community Service*, i, Feb 1937, pp. 2-3; Paul B. Cornely, "Health Problems of the Negro in Washington," *ibid.*, May 1937, p. 5; *Star*, 22 Oct 1933; *Afro-American*, 14, 21 Jan 1939.

developed extensive, intelligently administered, tax-supported welfare agencies generously supplemented by philanthropy. In Washington, on the contrary, private charity had shrunk, and public services, though reaching out into realms formerly left to private enterprise, had neither expanded enough to fill the hole temporarily nor attained a firm basis for future growth. Public funds had built some low-rental housing and a dozen monumental government buildings, and, in the process, provided employment. Congress had investigated traffic and crime, enlarged the police force, and approved a highway construction program. But the spending for engineering projects vastly outran that for the intangibles. For school counsellors, for branch public libraries, for books and librarians with the time and skill to interest children in reading them, for well-equipped playgrounds in over-crowded areas off the tourists' beaten track, for decent care of the aged, in short, for all the human elements that could make Washington an inspiring place for humble people as well as notables, money was lacking.

"Bad though Washington was," wrote an authority on American community organization a quarter-century later, "and worse than more responsible cities, its particular badness was an elaboration of widespread basic badness, and conditions were plenty worse in a number of congressional districts."[12] Yet less hypercritical citizens than those who coined the phrase "First City—Worst City" could admit it more descriptive than "First City—Best City." In the spring of 1940 consciences were beginning to feel the prick of the implicit challenge. No one foresaw that within a few months civic reform was destined to be engulfed for half a decade as Washington became the wartime capital of the free world.

[12] Edith Abbott, "The Crisis in Relief," *Nation*, CXXXVII, 400-02; Caroline Ware to the author, 21 May 1962.

CHAPTER XXII

CAPITAL OF THE FREE WORLD, 1940-1945

IN SEPTEMBER 1939 the Nazi invasion of Poland had carried a warning to Washington that the United States might soon have to abandon its concentration solely upon domestic affairs. The creation of a War Resources Board to plan American industrial mobilization, the President's declaration of a "limited national emergency," and the start made on recruiting the Army up to full statutory strength had created a stir. But after the partition of Poland and the beginning of the "phoney" war abroad, public alarm had subsided along the Potomac. As modification of the Neutrality Act permitted shipment of munitions to belligerents on a cash-and-carry basis, and orders placed by the Anglo-French Purchasing Board after January 1940 sharply reduced unemployment in American industrial centers, the struggle in Europe had receded further into the background. In April the Nazi drive into Denmark and Norway shocked Americans, but the WPA was still carrying thousands of people on its rolls, and farm problems were still commanding congressional attention in late May when the German armies swept through Belgium and the British evacuation from Dunkirk began. The swift movement of events in June, however, destroyed all hope that the United States could go its own way uninvolved in the upheavals in Europe—the Italian declaration of war on Great Britain and France, the Russian move into the Baltic countries, and, on the 22nd, the capitulation of France and the signing of an armistice with Germany. Like the dropping blade of the guillotine, the fall of France cut off the life of the New Deal.

By July 1940 the build-up of military strength was already superseding programs aimed at providing Americans with peace-time jobs, housing, education, beauty, and recreation. Despite the neutrality campaign of America-Firsters, Congress appropriated not millions but billions for defense. Two Republicans, Henry Stimson and Frank Knox, accepted the President's proffered posts of Secretary of War and Secretary of the Navy, and at the request of the Council of National Defense Vannevar Bush, president of the Carnegie Institution, set up the National Defense Research Council to focus scientific research upon weapons and means of transporting them.

One unmistakable sign that a rapid development of industrial and therefore military might now overrode in importance every other objective was the reappearance of American business leaders as government officials. For seven years they had formed the core of resistance to the policies mapped out by "college professors playing anagrams with alphabet soup." Now the captains of industry, whom General Hugh Johnson in early NRA days had called "Corporals of Disaster," were again honored in Washington as well as in Wall Street. To them fell the task of organizing government purchasing and industrial production amid a constant reshuffling of boards and labels and responsibilities. Before the end of the year the multiplication of offices filled by important businessmen proclaimed that the United States, unlike France, had chosen guns instead of butter. While the creation of offices of price stabilization and consumer protection indicated a serious attempt to preserve a balance, people who suggested that a preference for butter showed a preference for civilized living over the barbaric violence of shooting found their voices growing steadily weaker. As 1940 was a leap year, for the only time in history a congressional session lasted 367 days, from January 2, 1940, to noon of January 3, 1941.

National and international news crowded most District affairs out of the local newspapers during the summer and early autumn. People sat with ears glued to the radio, anxiously following the course of the Luftwaffe's intensive bombing of Britain. Although that frightening drama sped the passage through Congress of the Selective Service Act and the exchange of fifty over-age American destroyers for British military bases in the western hemisphere, relief at the RAF victory in the Battle of Britain was partly offset by Germany's announcement of a ten-year Axis alliance with Italy and Japan. While American defense appropriations rose to over 12 billion dollars, and the drawing of names for the draft began, a universal sense of strain endured. It prevailed up and down the eastern seaboard but inevitably appeared in most acute form in the capital whence decisions on national action must come. A return of confidence followed upon the President's "Arsenal of Democracy" speech in late December and his proposal to Congress to enact a lend-lease bill to support the "Four Freedoms," namely freedom from want, freedom from fear, freedom of speech, and freedom of religion. After months of hesitating, the United States appeared ready to assert its convictions.[1]

The multi-billion-dollar defense contracts went to industrial cities, but the influx of administrators and clerical workers into Washington during the fall of 1940 created a demand for housing and office space that seemed likely to transform real estate brokers and building contractors into petty czars, efforts of the Defense Housing Authority notwithstanding. The draft, meanwhile, made inroads upon the surplus labor force. At the colored Armstrong High School and the Phelps Vocational School regular classes met from 8 in the morning till early afternoon; night school courses ran from 3 till 11 p.m.; and from midnight until 8 a.m. special defense classes began the training of Negro youths in carpentry and metal work. Applicants on the register of the District Employment Center dropped from the 62,000 listed fourteen months before to

[1] For the chronology of events abroad, the steps in the formulation of American policy, the measures taken to implement it, and the men placed in charge, see "The War Production Board and Predecessor Agencies, August 1939 to November 1945," *Historical Reports on War Administration, Misc Publication No 1*. In describing local responses, I have drawn chiefly upon interviews.

27,000, of whom 11,000, chiefly white-collar and totally un-skilled workers, were on the WPA rolls. By February 1941 all semi-skilled workmen in the city, the Family Service Asso-ciation reported, had found jobs. For the next four and a half years unemployment ceased to be a problem for able-bodied, mentally competent adults, although the work they under-took was not always congenial or paid at rates commensurate with their abilities.

During 1941, the pattern of move and counter-move was frightening and sometimes exhilarating: the German invasion of Yugoslavia and Greece, the President's announcement of a state of "unlimited national emergency," the closing of the German and Italian consulates, the organization of the Office of Scientific Research and Development with almost unlimited funds and authority over military research, unbeknownst to all but a very few top-ranking American and British officials and nuclear physicists the starting of the Manhattan Project, the German attack on Russia, Japan's occupation of Indo-China, declaration of her Greater Asia policy, and suspension of ship-ping with the United States, congressional extension of the life of the Selective Service Act, and, after a conference at sea between Roosevelt and Winston Churchill, announcement of the Atlantic Charter. Dollar-a-year men began to arrive in Washington in November to take charge of new units of what everyone still called "the defense effort." Every week swelled the number of defense workers in the city. Washington as a community was lost in the shuffle.

In a matter of months the very look of the capital altered. In the spring of 1940 the Park and Planning Commission was attempting to clear the Mall of World War I tempos; by autumn the War Department was demanding more, not fewer. The highway department, in full agreement with the Los Angelan who declared that all city planning must revolve around the automobile, set about felling of trees right and left to widen streets, while exhaust fumes blanketed whole areas of the city at rush hours. The opening of the National Airport in the summer of 1941 merely heightened the volume of traffic. Despite the fact that Congress voted the planning commission $1,300,000 for land purchases for highway extension and city parks, and the planners finally persuaded the War Department that its projected headquarters might better stand on the Virginia shore in the shelter of Columbia Island rather than upstream at the end of the Arlington Memorial Bridge, where a large building would interrupt the vista from the Lincoln Memorial to the cemetery entrance, Frederic Delano resigned. The planning commission, he explained to the President, no longer performed any planning functions; the government agencies to which it had to turn over the land purchased for them usually failed to put it to suitable use; even the city playground sites were unimproved. The President himself was reportedly intent on building a dramatic five-sided window-less fortress for Army headquarters; he agreed to windows only because munitions experts convinced him that a bombing that would demolish solid masonry walls would merely blow the glass out of windows piercing them.

Looking at the double line of barracks-like wood and stucco tempos erected along the reflecting pool between the Washington Monument and the Lincoln Memorial, Secretary of the Interior Ickes remarked: "Army officers, by the mere fact of their constantly changing assignments, are not in a position to be fully cognizant of the importance of adhering to long range programs prepared by competent planning agencies." Urban aesthetics were no concern of the men responsible for recruiting, training, and equipping a 2,100,000-man Army, a two-ocean Navy, and, with the enactment of Lend Lease, supplying the British with matériel. Silence greeted a suggestion that the solidly built brick dwellings of the slums in southwest Washington be remodelled for offices and defense workers' living quarters.[2]

Changes in ordinary routines accompanied the physical changes. Military phrases began to crop up as part of the city's everyday language. "Government issue," shortened to G.I., was not yet a term applied to enlisted men, but employees in offices and shops became "personnel," a commodity like raw materials and machinery. With restrictions imposed on civilians' use of such items as silk and an order to the automobile industry to cut production of passenger cars by a fourth, "priorities" and "quotas" were words heard everywhere; citizens who had never set foot in an industrial plant adopted terms like "mock-up," "stockpile," and "tooling up." To the men dominating the Washington scene, by the autumn of 1941 "getting out production" had obviously come to mean something more vital than getting into Heaven ultimately or into the Army-Navy and Metropolitan clubs sooner. The simplicity that had characterized social affairs in New Deal days dropped away. "Protocol" replaced what Washington for a century had called "etiquette." Hostesses competed to catch the most important-sounding new arrivals in the city—a railroad executive turned government transportation expert, a New York corporation lawyer now in charge of new federal tax regulations, or a British scientist come for consultation with his opposite numbers in the Office of Scientific Research and Development. Army and Navy officers, though still in mufti, recaptured the social prestige denied them since 1919. In crowded drawing rooms and hotel cocktail lounges dignitaries arranged troublesome matters difficult to settle over office desks. Talk, however, no longer centered on schemes for putting a chicken into every

[2] *Afro-American*, 12 Oct 1940; Min FSA, 16 Oct 1940, 15 Jan, 19 Feb, 11 Jun 1941; Comrs Rpt, 1941, pp. 2, 133; *Star*, 20 Dec 1940, 23 Mar, 18 Apr, 22 May, 1 Aug, 18 Oct 1941; *Post*, 3 Aug, 19 Nov 1940, 9 Jan, 16 May, 18 Oct, 15 Nov 1941; Coyle, "Frederic A. Delano: Catalyst," *Survey Graphic*, xxxv, 252-70.

pot, but on aluminum and rubber supplies, aircraft engines, ships, and trucks.

Angry protests at conditions in Washington sounded from time to time in the press. "Murder Capital," cried *Newsweek*, in June 1941. "In proportion to population there are 250 percent more murders in Washington than in New York City, 40 percent more even than in Chicago. Those who commit felonies . . . have a two-to-one chance that no one will be arrested . . . fifteen-to-one that no jail sentence will be served." Inasmuch as the Mafia had never moved in upon the District and organized crime had no permanent foothold in the city, those figures were doubtless a somewhat hysterical response to a peculiarly grisly unsolved murder of a young woman of a good family, but the addition of fifty men to the metropolitan police force that summer failed to halt violence. While the government put up rows of small houses near the Pentagon at Fairlington chiefly for Army and Navy officers' families and helped finance Park Fairfax, another big development across the Potomac, the Defense Housing Coordinator considered constructing residence halls in Washington for unmarried government workers; still the housing shortage reached a point more acute than that of 1918. In the once elegant mansions that had lined Massachusetts and New Hampshire Avenues in the 1920's, as many as six strangers frequently had to share a bedroom designed originally as a library or a reception hall. Small wonder that inexperienced young women from country towns sometimes got into trouble.

In April 1941 a new District Council of Defense set up committees of volunteers to coordinate private and governmental efforts in providing recreation for servicemen in the city and nearby camps, compiling rosters of people with special skills, and establishing a housing register and a rent complaint unit, but the 19,000 volunteers who immediately made themselves available had no power to impose regulations; the

District commissioners appeared to be unable either to delegate responsibility or to exercise effective control themselves. Upon Melvin Hazen's death in July 1941, Guy Mason, a well-known attorney, took his place, and when Colonel McCoach was assigned to active Army duty, 71-year-old Brigadier General George Kutz for the third time became the engineer commissioner. Mason, highly competent though he was, lacked experience in the new job, Kutz was tired, and, according to local critics, Commissioner Young manifestly found the District Building less congenial than the drawing-rooms of the cocktail circuit where his talents for mimicking high-flown political oratory delighted fellow guests when he performed as head of the "John Russell Young School of Expression."[3]

During the "defense period" Congress and the White House showed no more concern for the local community than they had during the regime of the "presidential joker." Predictions in the fall of 1941 set the District budget for the next fiscal year at the unheard-of figure of $54,000,000, but with an estimated growth in population from the 663,000 of April 1940 to over 750,000, the commissioners' problem of sufficiently expanding municipal services looked insoluble. As the trend of well-to-do whites to enroll their children in private schools or move to the suburbs did not offset the overload on the colored schools caused by Negro in-migrants, the Board of Education had to choose between transferring white school buildings to colored use, finding money to erect new Negro school houses, or renting additional space. Law enforcement and public health became increasingly hard to ensure in a city to which every month added at least 5,000 new residents. Only Daniel Donovan's steady hand at the helm in the District Auditor's office kept confusion from turning into chaos. In early December a magazine article

[3] *American Speech*, XVI, 160; "Murder Capital," *Newsweek*, XVII, 24-25; Josephus Daniels, "A Native at Large," and "Confusion on the Potomac," *Nation*, CLIII, 35, 118; Comrs Rpt, 1941, pp. 2-3, 1942, pp. 2-3; Donald Wilhelm, "America's Biggest Boom Town," *Am. Mercury*, LIII, 338.

entitled "Washington: Blight on Democracy" repeated the tale of shockingly inadequate accommodations for incoming government employees, steadily rising living costs, and a salary scale that kept the earnings of half the people on the federal payroll to less than $1,500 a year. But the author directed his frontal attack on the District government: only elected municipal officials, he argued, could lessen the city's racial antagonisms. "Negroes who have lived in many parts of the country say that nowhere else in America is there such bitter mutual race hatred."

If white people were startled at that judgment, colored Washingtonians knew it was sound. The confidence they had felt in the months after the Marian Anderson concert at the Lincoln Memorial had received several rough jolts as soon as the Army expansion began in June 1940. The *Afro-American* had at first argued that, War Department orders to the contrary, the United States could not and would not allow color bars to continue in the armed services. With Hitler master of Europe, "Uncle Sam needs every citizen, not merely every white citizen to do his duty." A few months later the Army was putting only white officers into command of colored draftees, the Air Corps and the Marines refused to accept any Negro, and in the Navy colored men could hope for nothing better than menial assignments. Memories of the humiliations Negro officers and troops had suffered in World War I fanned the anger of colored Washingtonians; the promotion of Colonel Benjamin O. Davis to the rank of Brigadier General seemed to them the merest gesture. Within civilian offices discrimination, far from withering away, as optimists had expected in 1939, strengthened with the appearance of new defense agencies. Doubtless the handful of colored typists and file clerks in newly organized offices sometimes imagined slights; few of them admitted that their more limited background and education might deny them equality with their white associates. But white supervisors intent on getting the job done generally felt justified in placing Negro typists in separate rooms and separate stenographic pools assigned to the least exacting work. By the end of 1940 Negro militants in and out of the capital concluded the time ripe to dramatize their demands for non-discriminatory treatment.

Early in 1941 Eugene Davidson pointed out to A. Philip Randolph, head of the Brotherhood of Sleeping Car Porters, that the New Negro Alliance picket lines had opened up several hundred jobs in Washington shops to Negroes during the depression. Now that the government and American industry were desperately in need of competent workers, the two men and NAACP leaders agreed that similar action on a national scale should produce wider results. Randolph sent out a call for 50,000 Negroes to march on Washington in July to present to the President and Congress colored Americans' protests at job discrimination. By April, as colored men throughout the country pledged themselves to march, high ranking government officials began to ask: "What'll they think in Berlin?" Still, apparently unable to believe that a Negro army bigger than the Bonus Expeditionary Force and possibly far more belligerent might actually descend upon the capital, federal department heads took no positive action. Plans for the march went on. In early June with the militants' move impending in less than a month, Mayor La Guardia of New York arranged a meeting between Negro leaders, Mrs. Roosevelt, and government representatives. The white men urged patience. Mrs. Roosevelt suggested that in the long run the march would heighten the racism of southerners in Congress and provoke disastrous retaliation. Randolph replied that, as the mere prospect of the march had already proved useful to the Negro cause, colored Americans preferred to chance revenge rather than drop the mass protest in exchange for mere promises.

Ten days later a conference took place at the White House. There Randolph, Davidson, and Walter White, executive secretary of the NAACP, faced the President, Secretary of War Stimson, Secretary of the Navy Knox, William Knudsen and Sidney Hillman of the Office of Production Management, La Guardia, and Aubrey Williams of the National Youth Administration. The upshot was a commitment from the President to set up a group to study the situation and recommend the ruling with the "teeth in it" that Randolph declared essential. But a study was not action; the Negro leader refused to cancel the march. Not until a second White House meeting on June 25th did a solution evolve: that afternoon an Executive Order on Fair Employment Practices went out over the President's signature, laying down rules of non-discrimination for all plants with government defense contracts as well as for all federal offices and installations; a committee within the Labor Division of the Office of Production Management was to check the observation of the rules, and the President, if given proof of violations, guaranteed that he would cancel the contract of the offending firm. For the first time since the Emancipation Proclamation of 1863 a President of the United States had issued an official order protecting Negro rights.

Satisfaction in colored Washington was tempered by events in areas to which the Executive Order did not apply. It did not touch the labor unions or private employers without defense contracts. When the stage production of *Native Son*, directed by Orson Welles, was opening at the National Theatre, Richard Wright walked into a restaurant in the company of one of the white producers and a white woman, only to be told that the management would serve the distinguished author in a car at the curb. Seemingly the Marian Anderson triumph might never have occurred. As the American Red Cross began to enlarge its professional staff and volunteers thronged into the District chapter offices to offer their services, colored women were given to understand that, provided someone could be found to give them the necessary preliminary training, they might be used as Canteen or Home Service workers or as nurses aides in connection with colored units. In fact, so far from ending Negro resentments, the Executive Order appeared, as time went on, to increase Negro hostility to much of white Washington. With some logic, colored people reasoned that since the administration was ready to recognize them as first-class citizens, all white Americans should do so; because they did not, Negro belligerence tended to mount.[4]

Yet the official non-discrimination policy had considerable effect in Washington. A story describing an inspection tour the President and Harry Hopkins made of the nearly completed Pentagon told of their astonishment at finding four huge wash-rooms placed along each of the five axes that connect the outer ring to the inmost on each floor of the building; upon inquiring the reason for such prodigality of lavatory space, the President was informed that non-discrimination required as many rooms marked "Colored Men" and "Colored Women" as "White Men" and "White Women." The differentiating signs were never painted on the doors. More astonishing in view of southern sentiment in Congress and the history of segregation in Washington during the preceding quarter-century, a law passed in May 1942 creating the District Recreation Board contained no racial restrictions; one of the four private citizens appointed to it by Commissioner Mason was a soft-spoken colored woman whose persuasiveness, joined with that of the ex-officio government representatives, led the board to approve bi-racial use of all city playgrounds except those forming part of the white and colored school yards. The influx of northerners to take government posts, furthermore, strengthened opposition to racism. Gifted colored men, ranked

[4] Alden Stevens, "Washington: Blight on Democracy," and Earle Brown, "American Negroes and the War," *Harper's Magazine*, CLXXXIV, 50-51, 545-52; *Afro-American*, 8, 22 Jun, 12 Oct 1940.

as government messengers in 1941, would gradually move up in grade and a few would eventually win the coveted "P" or professional rating. Ralph Bunche, formerly a little known Howard University political scientist, would become head of a policy-making section in the State Department. In the Office of the Price Administration where morale was consistently high no color line of any kind ever existed.[5]

White or black, long-time resident or new arrival, volunteer or paid worker, everyone in Washington found occasional compensations for the discomforts and uncertainties surrounding him. In March 1941, three months after workmen put the finishing touches to the pale, rose-white marble building on the Mall opposite the tip of the Federal Triangle, the National Gallery formally opened its doors to the public. Besides the paintings and sculpture of Andrew Mellon's collection, the old masters given by Paul Kress lined the walls of the well-lighted rooms. While connoisseurs pointed to the gaps, notably the lack of representative works of the eighteenth- and nineteenth-century French schools, appreciative crowds looked at the pictures with delight and admiringly walked around the fountain in the black-marble-floored Rotunda ringed by massive, highly polished deep green marble columns. Still larger crowds found relaxation at the zoo and in the racially segregated movie houses and theatres. And few people were impervious to the feeling that by merely living in Washington they were touching the fringes of history in the making.

The sense of being in the center of things did not immediately induce people to open their purses to the Community Chest. Inasmuch as the government was manifestly attempting to arrange for the well-being of defense workers, why, new arrivals asked, should they contribute to local charities? In 1941 the

[5] *Second Annual Report of the Citizens Committee on Race Relations, Inc.*, 18 Sep 1945; National Committee on Segregation in the Nation's Capital, *Segregation in Washington*, pp. 68-70.

Chest had to cut the allotment to the Family Service Association to scarcely half the $84,000 the board of managers had requested. In early December the association's case workers were dealing with over 400 families who were ineligible for public assistance and whose resources were too meagre to make them self-sufficient. "It is economic defense for the community," the board concluded," to provide service to these families, and private agencies need to be maintained for this purpose." Organizations such as the Boy Scouts, the Police Boys' Clubs, the YMCA and YWCA were similarly indispensable in meeting needs outside the sphere of legalized public expenditure. Rather unexpectedly the problem of financing diminished after the declaration of war brought a War Chest into being. In return for running the campaigns, Washington's central organization got a percentage of the money raised for British War Relief, the "China Relief," and other special causes. The arrangement ended arguments about local versus national and international giving, and, after Arlington, Alexandria, and Montgomery County joined with the District in a single War Chest drive, Washington's charities netted more nearly adequate funds than ever before—in one year as much as $4,500,000.[6]

In mid-November 1941, when a special Japanese envoy arrived to discuss with the President possible ways of reducing tensions between the United States and the chief power in "Greater Asia," Washington had settled into a state of half-readiness for war without really expecting it to come in the immediate future. Seemingly everything might go on as it was indefinitely. Embassy parties were gay, private parties even gayer, despite the scarcity of domestic servants. People worked hard but with a sense of having matters in hand. Such anxieties as pervaded the upper echelons of the government

[6] "General Information," *Bulletin, National Gallery,* Mar 1941; *Newsweek,* xvii, 24 Mar 1941, pp. 58-60, xviii, 14 Jul 1941, pp. 58-59; Min FSA, 12 Nov, 10 Dec 1941.

were well concealed. A Gallup poll of the city would probably have shown eight people out of ten preparing for a festive and relatively carefree Christmas.

On the afternoon of December 7th, Washington was relaxing over the Sunday radio programs and the newspaper stories of Saturday's Army-Navy football game when word of the attack on Pearl Harbor reached the White House. As the news spread, people talked of nothing but Japanese perfidy and the quick revenge the United States would mete out. Even a week later, after the formal declaration of war on Japan, the Japanese invasion of the Philippines, and, on December 11th, the German and Italian declaration of war on the United States, the emotional keynote in Washington was more nearly relief than fearfulness. "No one," wrote a careful observer, "showed much indignation. We are going into this war lightly, but I have a feeling that it will weigh heavily upon all of us before we are through." At least it should unite the country and put a stop to the anti-progressive, anti-labor agitation in Congress.[7] Confidence not unlike that shown in the city before the first battle of Bull Run endured for several weeks. Prime Minister Winston Churchill came and departed, men from every village and city in the United States applied in person or by letter for active military service, and, guided by the President with augmented powers, the creaking war machine moved into high gear.

For the next three and a half years Washington was like a city under siege. As the Japanese swept from victory to victory in the spring of 1942 and the German armies drove eastward upon Stalingrad and across North Africa into Tobruk, experienced and imaginative people in the American capital knew that life here was less precarious and that personal deprivations were far fewer than in the key spots of warring Europe and the Far East, but the realization that the fate of all depended upon

[7] *Star*, 7, 8, 29 Dec 1941; I. F. Stone, "War Comes to Washington," *Nation*, CLIII, 603.

decisions made and the speed of action taken in Washington imposed upon men in responsible posts here a burden that at times approached the unbearable. And they were not upheld, as in 1917, by belief that they were engaged in a holy crusade. The possibility of ultimate defeat was unthinkable, but with every passing month, as War and Navy Department telegrams beginning: "I regret to inform you that . . ." went out over the wires to American homes, the sombreness of spirit in high places in Washington deepened. It lightened in the early autumn of 1944, only to darken again during the Battle of the Bulge and the weeks that followed.

Washington's urbanity and vaunted southern charm shrank under the strain. In and out of government offices fatigue and fraying tempers found periodic release in snapping at anyone who commented on shortcomings in service: "Don'tcha know there's a war on?" While that phenomenon was by no means confined to the overworked, overcrowded, undersupplied capital, nowhere else on the continent, save perhaps in some of the mushrooming war production centers such as Willow Run, were living and working conditions more trying. Rent controls went into effect on January 1, 1942, without any protest from reputable real estate brokers who remembered World War I. But federal regulations that prevented monetary exploitation of newcomers did not provide them with housing, and many of them were aghast to discover that the legal rental of an "efficiency," a small room with bath and a kitchenette in a closet, ran as high as that of an entire house in their home towns. The residence halls put up for "white government girls" and Slowe and Carver Halls built for incoming Negro workers were soon overflowing. Tire and passenger car rationing, followed in the late summer of 1942 by gasoline rationing, brought hundreds of bicycles back onto the streets and so increased the difficulty of commuting that the suburbs lost most of their attraction. Thereafter, according to detective story writers, a tiny apartment in an old stable-turned-garage in a Georgetown alley became a pearl of price for which contenders might betray government secrets and involve themselves in murder cases. Office accommodations were equally meagre. Even a relatively high-ranking government functionary could feel lucky to have a desk in a pantry whence the butler had once dispensed champagne and fois-gras to the millionaire's family and guests.

Some war work was absorbing enough to blot out the day-by-day discomforts—for example research at the Bureau of Standards on target-seeking ammunition functioning by the so-called VT fuse, or the application of mathematics to the breaking of enemy codes, or the preparation of critical releases for the Office of War Information. Many assignments were deadly dull. While a government interdepartmental committee of personnel specialists arranged job transfers for the misfits and attempted to ease the personal difficulties of the homesick, the USO ran dances at the nearby Army posts with truckloads of delighted young women transported for the occasion from the blacked-out city. While a half-dozen national and local organizations clucked like mother hens over the young in government employ, according to magazine writers, most of the "government girls" were having the time of their lives. Even after the movement of troops to overseas stations accelerated, men outnumbered women in the capital, and the issue of marriage licenses reportedly went on at a rate to encourage any personable spinster under thirty-five. Still the turnover in government offices was huge, adding to municipal as well as federal problems.

Rationing, the blackout, the possibility of air raids, and the 48-hour or longer work-week curtailed the amenities. The National Symphony gave a few concerts, and the art galleries remained open, but the priceless collections of the Dumbarton Oaks museum were put into storage and the house turned over for the duration to the Office of Scientific Research and

Development. University enrollments dropped except for evening classes, and in those, some professors believed, standards of performance declined. Austerity marked affairs at the foreign embassies, and, with domestic servants unobtainable, food hard to buy, and fuel rationing so severe that well-to-do private householders shut off their drawing rooms to conserve heat during the winters, non-official dinner and cocktail parties became few and far between. Night clubs along G and H Streets flourished, and movie houses, USO lounges, and Red Cross canteens were crowded, but those resorts were frequented chiefly by transients, servicemen, and inexperienced newcomers unacquainted with the kind of dignified private entertaining that for sixty years had been a Washington hallmark. Indeed a cosmetic advertisement struck the dominant war-time note: in a black square the single phrase, "Beauty Can Wait."[8]

Local civic problems also had to wait except when they had direct bearing on national and international affairs. In June 1943 a race riot in Detroit sharpened memories of the summer of 1919 in Washington and brought into being a Citizens' Committee on Race Relations, headed by white ministers, lawyers, educators, laymen of the Catholic Interracial Council, and two or three prominent Negroes. Its purpose was to hold a watching brief and by factual publicity about sources of racial tensions reduce or eliminate them, whether springing from Negroes' anger at the segregation of Negro blood from white at Red Cross blood donor centers, from job and housing restrictions, or from white people's exasperation at Negroes' tendency to attribute their own inadequacies solely to white exploitation. The mere existence of the committee was useful, although it had to measure its wartime achievements in

[8] *First Report of the Rent Control Board of the District of Columbia*, Jun 1942, pp. 321-25; Charles Hurd, *Washington Cavalcade*, p. 282; Ernest K. Lindley, "Washington, Capital of the Allied World," *Newsweek*, xx, 7 Sep 1942, p. 40; "Social Doldrums," *ibid.*, 28 Sep 1942, p. 35; Helen H. Smith, "Uncle Sam's Seminary," *Collier's*, cx, 28 Nov 1942, pp. 18-19; and scores of other articles listed under "Washington" in the *Readers Guide*, 1942-1945.

terms of what didn't happen rather than what did. The Washington Housing Association, another volunteer organization, meanwhile hoped to make more and better living quarters available to colored families. Internal controversy over tactics proved an obstacle; one group advocated reliance on moral suasion to induce the Real Estate Board to abandon its transactions in "exclusive," that is, racially restricted, property, while another group wanted to stage an open fight both on that issue and over placing a Negro on the board of the National Capital Housing Authority, successor to the Alley-Dwelling Authority. One rabbi insisted that the association must take a strong stand against discrimination aimed at any minority, Negro, Jew, or other; a second rabbi passionately declared that to lump Hebrews with Negroes was to increase unwarrantably the handicaps under which Jews already suffered. Public housing for any but incoming federal workers made no progress at all. Elder Michaux, to the accompaniment of veiled charges that he was lining his own pocket, put up Mayfair Mansions into which nearly six hundred well-to-do Negro families moved in 1944, but of the 2,300 priorities allotted for low-rental Negro dwellings in 1943, private builders had undertaken only 30 by the end of the year and only 200 were finished in 1944. Obviously organizations without authority to force action could do little even if they had large memberships.[9]

That fact, together with the heavy demands the war put upon congressional time and the heightened confusions in the District Building after Auditor Donovan's death in 1943, apparently inspired the Senate Judiciary Committee that December to conduct hearings on a new bill for reorganization of the District government. Aware of the racial friction in the city, Senator McCarran opened the hearings with a plea for forthright discussion of Negro suffrage, a subject "which people often say you do not dare touch." One Negro witness deplored

[9] See n. 5; Dulles, *American Red Cross*, pp. 419-21.

"the injection of the race theme into the matter of local voting," but the inseparability of the two evoked outspoken objections to the bill from several people who regarded themselves as friends of both races. The gentle Clinton Howard, great-nephew of a founder of Howard University, argued that intensifying racial antagonisms in wartime Washington made the moment peculiarly unpropitious to talk of enfranchising "the under-privileged, illiterate, proletarian class who would at once possess the balance of power and, in the near future, a majority of the voting citizenry." In this, "the most southern city north of Richmond," where, he contended, the Negro population was permanent, the white largely temporary, "the law of fecundity" would rule. At his annual Christmas party in 1942 for all the children living in the square directly to the east of the Senate Office Building, there were no longer any white children in the houses adjoining his on northeast B Street, whereas in Schott's Alley at the rear were ninety-nine colored children, all of whom, scrubbed and well-behaved, came to his party. "Now that is Washington tomorrow. . . . The alley will dominate the avenue." By a touch of historical irony, within fifteen years the alley would have turned into a beautifully kept mews lined by small gardens and dwellings occupied chiefly by con-gressmen, while the marble mass of a new Senate Office Build-ing and a parking lot would dominate the traffic-packed avenue.

Suffrage advocates during the hearings flared out angrily more than once at the worshippers of "The God of Things as They Are." The president of the Federation of Citizens' Asso-ciations asserted that the federal Treasury was now paying less than 10 percent of the cost of running the city, Congress was giving less time than ever to her problems, and, in defending the existing regime with its petty corruption in the water depart-ment, the tax collector's office, and at Gallinger Hospital, the Board of Trade spoke not for its several thousand members but merely for its small self-perpetuating board of directors. The well-intentioned Clinton Howard, a labor leader explained, simply didn't know what he was talking about when he forecast disaster for a self-governing Washington. The Senate committee, sympathetic to local voting though it appeared to be, shelved the bill as untimely. It had aroused meagre public interest; most people in the wartime capital saw no direct connection between local suffrage and defeating the Axis powers. Home rulers would have to wait till the war was over.[10]

By the early spring of 1945 military victories in every theatre of war brightened the prospects for peace. But April 12th brought news that stunned the nation: Franklin D. Roosevelt was dead. In the streets of Washington people wept. At the White House Harry S Truman took the oath of office, while preparations moved forward to bring the former Chief's body back from Warm Springs to the capital. The funeral procession along Pennsylvania Avenue two days later perhaps stirred in very old men memories of the muffled roll of the drums and the black-velvet-draped hearse of Abraham Lincoln's funeral cortege. Then the war had been practically over; in April 1945 fierce fighting still lay ahead in pockets of Germany and in the Pacific. On the 25th, the day the United Nations conference opened in San Francisco, the United States and Russian armies converged at the Elbe River. The lynching of Mussolini, Hitler's death in the subterranean bunkers of Berlin, and Germany's unconditional surrender followed in swift succession.

Celebration of V-E day was restrained in Washington. The pressure of work in government offices eased only momentarily. Japan was still undefeated. But the release of some Army supplies of canned goods, the lifting of purchasing restrictions on several other items, and War Production Board authorization of partial resumption of passenger car and domestic wash-

[10] S Judic Comee, 78C, 1S, Hrgs on "Reorganization of the Govt of D.C.," pp. 7, 9, 141, 149-55, 169-73, 227, 243-56, 287-304, and *passim*; clipping files on "Housing," Washingtoniana Room, Pub Lib.

ing machine manufacture encouraged public faith that the end was in sight. And with the completion of a United Nations charter and the United States Senate ratification of it in mid-July, hopes for a peaceful new world order rose. When the atomic bombs dropped on Hiroshima and Nagasaki in early August, and Secretary of War Stimson spelled out the story of how and why the United States had developed and used that devastating weapon, shock mingled with relief in Washington. Suspense hung over the city for nearly a week. While rumors of Japanese capitulation set off a frenzied victory demonstration in New York, the capital forced itself to wait. For three successive days quiet crowds began to collect at dawn in Lafayette Square and drifted in and out until disappointment dispersed them late in the evening. On August 14th they were rewarded. From the White House President Truman announced the Japanese acceptance of the allied terms of surrender.[11]

[11] *Star*, 13, 14 Apr, 7-11, 14 Aug 1945.

CHAPTER XXIII

POSTWAR DESIGNS FOR THE
FUTURE, 1945-1950

V-J DAY made the steamy heat of a Washington August bearable. Bright lights streaming out over the capital at night revealed a beauty almost forgotten during the years of stress. Within a fortnight an official order cutting government employees' work week back to forty hours restored the luxury of free Saturdays. Everyone began to look forward to the return of the "boys" from overseas. Dollar-a-year men and high-ranking wartime officials were less precipitous than in 1918 about emptying their brief-cases into office wastebaskets and shaking the dust of Washington from their feet, but through September and October demobilization of the civilian work force proceeded, with the old, established government departments taking over the duties and some of the staff of the emergency agencies. Thanks to federal rent controls, rationing, and price stabilization, the city was emerging from the long strain without the spiritual scars World War I had inflicted; time and patient planning should erase the physical blights imposed by the military demands of the defense period and the war.

A lightheartedness unknown since 1940 enveloped the city during the fall. Householders who had taken in roomers as a public service reclaimed the privacy of their own homes, and the release of food stuffs long limited by rationing eased housekeeping. In the upper brackets of society mothers planned elaborate debuts for their daughters, and, as autumn moved into winter, the private dances and dinner parties hinted at a revival of that discard of 1932-1933, the Washington season. Gaiety born of the release from five years of tension permeated all social levels. Spring would allow the Cherry Blossom Festival to resume. Summer would revive the Watergate concerts, stopped by the wartime blackout, and open up to theatre groups the small outdoor stage in Meridian Park. In Rock Creek Park the Carter Barron outdoor theatre, given to the city several years before but unused during the war, would offer the pleasures of plays and ballet in a beautiful setting.

Yet uneasy thoughts of the more distant future stirred in the capital before the end of 1945. Demobilization officials prophesied that eight million Americans would be out of work in 1946. Even if industrial cities had to bear the initial brunt of that readjustment, a corresponding curtailment of governmental activities must eventually be costly to Washington. RIF's, that is, reductions in force, in the government had already cut deep. Scores of brilliant men attached to the Office of Scientific Research and Development had left the city by the end of the year, and drastic paring of government-sponsored research within a much discussed single Department of Defense might hamstring Washington as a scientific center. The talk of the dispersal of federal agencies into areas outside the District might soon turn into reality; it would save the city from further losses of taxable real estate but might cost her a number of more important assets.

Historical-minded residents could draw some comfort from thinking of the aftermath of other wars: a new federal city sprung up between 1815 and 1817; the years between 1866 and 1870 shadowed by fears about removal of the capital but succeeded by an era of extraordinary growth for the city; and after World War I, the transformation of uncertainty into fresh confidence and a multi-million-dollar burst of federal building. But now a new element was added: the competition of the suburbs. The resumption of passenger-car production and cancellation of tire and gasoline rationing opened the way to an exodus from the central city that could permanently undermine Washington's prosperity. She would unquestionably remain the nation's legislative center and keep the White House, the Supreme Court, the State Department, and the main units of the other executive departments; the foreign embassies were unlikely to move out of the District. All those, covering with other federal and District property about 46 percent of the land in Washington, were tax-exempt. What could the city draw on for funds if she neither had large tax-paying industries nor a long roll of residential property-owners subject to District taxation?[1] Washingtonians could only map out recommendations; the decisions would rest with Congress and the President.

Cleavages within the community had sharpened since 1943. The Board of Trade and the Real Estate Board, with its representatives from twenty-five banks, insurance and title companies, and building and loan associations, had defined their policy of tightening racial segregation and controlling the city's pattern of growth by every financial and political means at their command. Opposition to that formula had also mounted. In the ranks of its adversaries, ranged alongside all colored people, was a strangely assorted aggregation of whites—some wealthy individuals, a number of small businessmen, wage-earners, members of organizations such as the Urban League, the Catholic Interracial Council, and the recently formed Washington chapter of Americans for Democratic Action, most of the newspapermen reporting on city affairs, social workers, and a heavy sprinkling of the city's ministers and rabbis. Despite the disproportion of numbers on the left and on the right, the right-wingers had fended off change. The reluctance of officialdom to take any step to revamp the imbalance of power as long as the war was going on had strengthened their hands. In June 1945 the District Recreation Board had reversed its earlier non-segregation policy because the playground director had insisted that her staff could not handle mixed groups. A mass meeting

---

[1] "War Production Bd," *Historical Rpts . . . Misc Pub No. 1*; H & S Dis Comees, 80C, 1S and 2S, Jt Hrgs, "Home Rule and Dis Reorganization," p. 217 (hereafter cited as Home Rule Hrgs).

of protest held on V-J Day had failed to induce the board to rescind the order, but the defeat fanned resentment at perpetuation of oligarchic, discriminatory rule. In the autumn of 1945, with the peacetime future undetermined, Washingtonians in both camps prepared for a fight. On one side a compact body of powerful men set themselves to restore the old, solid-looking facade; on the other side stood people ready to demolish shibboleths and rebuild the city on broader social and economic foundations.

Still, the alignment of the opposing forces was not entirely clear cut. Some home rulers, the president of the Federation of Citizens' Associations for one, preferred to see segregation continue, and some believers in racial non-discrimination put little faith in an elected city government. People who vaguely disapproved of the local autocracy were frequently unwilling to campaign against it. The war had taken its toll of Washingtonians' energies; more than a few citizens felt the release from immediate anxiety too pleasant to sacrifice in a struggle in which the stand-patters had the backing of long-established custom. The unusually large number of high-ranking Army and Navy officers in postwar Washington also lent support to the extreme right, and their prestige had never stood higher. Although they avoided openly expressing opinions about District affairs, the arch conservatism of the armed forces, their unmistakable anti-Negro bias during the war, and the class tradition inbred at West Point and Annapolis tended to push them into the authoritarian fold. Many of the men who objected to basic change, moreover, were charming and cultivated individuals convinced that the city's economy would suffer from a fundamental social upheaval. Their friends disliked the idea of quarreling with them publicly. Wartime newcomers, who would later enter the lists with passionate fervor, in 1946 and 1947 rarely felt sufficiently informed about what was at stake to join in the battle. Because southerners as extreme as Theodore

Bilbo of Mississippi now controlled the District committees in Congress, an open fight involved the risk of skimpy federal appropriations for the District's schools, highways, and slum clearance. That threat, insubstantial though it proved to be, perhaps encouraged timid and lazy-minded citizens to stand on the side lines.[2] And probably not more than three people out of ten in Washington were aware of the conflict in the making. Congress was absorbed in federal reorganization.

Yet Congress had already showed interest in rescuing the capital from blight. A Redevelopment Act passed in May 1945 vested in the National Capital Park and Planning Commission authority to plan the rebuilding of all Washington's slum-ridden areas, to lay out a vast new highway system, to purchase land for additional parks and playgrounds, and to specify the sites for new public buildings. The program outlined by Lt. Gen. U. S. Grant, III, the commission chairman, awaited only detailed surveys and large appropriations. In the interim the demand for housing endured in spite of multiplying RIF's in government offices. While returning veterans and young couples with children looked for modest quarters in the suburbs, Washington real estate firms carried long lists of applicants for tenancy in the blocks of expensive efficiency apartments under construction. In order to rent anything more commodious, two years and more after the coming of peace would-be clients still had to grovel before lordly underlings in realtors' offices. Contrary to expectations, the sellers' market would last into the 1950's, and only the perpetuation of rent controls kept prices within bounds. Irrespective of rentals, houses or well-maintained apartments for new Negro families were all but unobtainable; they had to double up with relatives or acquaintances.

Amid all the discussion of redevelopment plans, a renewed

[2] Cit Comee on Race Relns, *2nd Anl Rpt*, pp. 8-9; National Committee on Segregation in the Nation's Capital, *Segregation in Washington*, pp. 82-84, and *passim* (hereafter cited as Ntl Comee on Seg, *Rpt*).

squeeze on Washington's colored residents had begun to gather force in the city. As if frightened by the slight inroads the New Deal and war years had made on the doctrine of white supremacy, avowed racists and, more numerous and more influential, men moved by an unemotional determination to keep Negroes to a servant class were busily perfecting schemes whereby all colored people would be housed in a geographical ghetto and their isolation reinforced by narrowed job restrictions. Now, while official redevelopment plans were going down on paper, was the time to fix the city's social pattern for generations to come. Washington's elected city councils had passed two non-discrimination ordinances during President Grant's administration; in 1947 his grandson announced that the National Capital Park and Planning Commission would see that "the colored population dispossessed by playgrounds, public buildings, parks and schools" was relocated in a remote section "in the rear of Anacostia." Segregation, explained a National Capital Housing Authority official, "is the accepted pattern of the community." Such statements staggered people who had dared think Washington's racial conflicts fading away. The challenge obliterated within the colored community the already weakened differentiations between light- and dark-skinned Negroes and the social distinctions linked to degree of color; the postwar threat, hitting every person with so much as a drop of Negro blood, closed the ranks.[3]

Inasmuch as a popularly elected municipal government would unquestionably induce changes in the leopard's spots, the question of local suffrage took on fresh importance. In 1945 the Washington *Post* had taken an informal poll of its readers; although responses were too few to represent city-wide opinion, 80 percent of the replies had favored District voting. A year later the Board of Trade organized a much-

[3] Ntl Comee on Seg, *Rpt*, pp. 35-47, 84-89; *Star*, 4 Sep 1946. As in Ch XXII, other data derive from a host of interviews and for the years after 1946 from personal observation and attentive reading of the daily press.

publicized plebiscite. The turnout was puzzlingly small; the results showed 70 percent of the adult participants supporting home rule—a more than 15-percent drop since 1938—and now nearly 60 percent of the white high school students, a scant 3 percent of the colored, against local self government. "Opposition to suffrage is on the increase," reported the *Times Herald*. The *Post*, commenting on the corrosive effect of deep-seated social ills, called Washington's disenfranchisement "a poisonous thing." Still a second poll conducted by the *Post* in February 1948 could count no more than 70 percent of the respondents anxious for change.[4]

Three developments of 1947 and 1948 nevertheless indicated that Washington was neither irretrievably sunk in political apathy nor committed to the racial containment program drafted by the real estate interests and endorsed by the head of the National Park and Planning Commission. First was the organization of the bi-racial Washington Home Rule Committee composed of well-informed, courageous residents. Taught by the mistakes of the now defunct District Suffrage Association, they limited their goal to the restoration of a popularly elected city government, prepared their every campaign with care, and for the next fifteen years refused to let repeated defeats sidetrack them; without ever winning acclaim, they came to represent the core of civic resistance to political impotence.[5] Second, and more immediately promising, were the joint House and Senate subcommittee hearings begun in July 1947 on District governmental reorganization. Third and ultimately most productive of results was the launching of a national committee of eminent Americans pledged to fight segregation in Washington. Their detailed report published in condensed form in November 1948 was probably the major force in the rout of aggressive racism in the capital.

[4] *Times Herald*, 6 Nov 1946; *Post*, 9 Nov 1946; Home Rule Hrgs, pp. 165-66, 392.
[5] Home Rule Hrgs, p. 271; files Washington Home Rule Comee.

The home rule bill of 1947 and 1948, named for its chief sponsor in the House, James Auchincloss of New Jersey, was in a sense the fruit of twenty-five years of congressional thinking, beginning in the early 1920's with Senator Capper's resolutions for District representation in Congress, moving on through the proposals of the 1930's for limited local voting, and followed by the home rule bills considered by the Senate Judiciary Committee in 1941 and 1943. But several circumstances, especially the fact that the Auchincloss bill reached the floor of the House, differentiated the postwar measure from the others. The hearings, opened at a time when the Real Estate Board was asserting its domination of the District's future, halted in July but resumed in February 1948 after an impasse had developed in the urban redevelopment program. The committee listened attentively to expressions of every shade of opinion, even to ideas on the management of the District dog pound. In content the home rule arguments were those of earlier years, but the tone revealed a conviction that a turning point had come. The protests at the "dual" voting provision that would give local suffrage to temporary non-tax-paying residents drew from the president of the Washington ADA the comment that, whereas once Americans had fought against taxation without representation, now the conflict appeared to be over representation without taxation.[6] Still most of the testimony concentrated on whether the community would benefit or suffer by regaining control of its purely local affairs.

From the first the joint committee's primary purpose was to design an act that would relieve Congress of the time-consuming chores of running the District; an efficient system responsive to local citizens' wishes was a secondary desideratum. Two years of intensive work on the part of an able committee staff produced a bill that met those specifications: Wash-

[6] Home Rule Hrgs, pp. 139, 146-47, 159-64, 195-99, 217.

ington residents, dual voters among them, were to elect a non-voting delegate to the House and a city council whose general legislation should come under the review of a joint Senate and House committee and be subject to presidential veto; the federal government was to pay the lesser of two amounts, either $15,000,000 or 14 percent of the city's yearly operating costs; all the special advisory boards were to be eliminated, leaving intact only the Public Utilities Commission, the Tax Appeal and Zoning Adjustment Boards, and the Redevelopment Land Agency of the National Capital Park and Planning Commission; otherwise all power was to be vested in the twelve-man council, four men chosen at large and two from each of the four geographical divisions of the city. The bill, approved by eight of the fourteen members of the House District Committee, reached the floor of the House in mid-May 1948.

For the first time in seventy years the lower house of Congress undertook to pass upon a revision of the Organic Act of 1878. The moment the debate opened, Representative Oren Harris of Arkansas, himself a member of the joint committee, demanded that the entire ninety-page document be read out word for word. So, hour after hour, the intoning voice of the clerk droned in the ears of representatives oppressed by the volume of legislation awaiting action before adjournment. At the end of two days the filibuster technique accomplished its purpose. An impatient majority shelved the bill. One perverse man, representing, Congressman Auchincloss estimated, the views of scarcely 50,000 citizens, had defeated the will of over 300,000 people.[7]

The blow to the hopes of the vast majority of Washingtonians intensified the determination of the National Committee on Segregation. Formed at the end of 1946 after the local com-

[7] *Ibid.*, p. 396, and App., pp. 429-30, 434-45; H Rpt 1876, 80C, 2S; Comee Recommendations on H 6227, 80C, 2S; interview George Galloway, comee staff director, 1946-1948.

mittee on race relations had dissolved, the national committee had opened headquarters in Chicago and engaged a competent research staff headed by an American University sociologist to pin down the facts of what Negroes in the capital were up against and to spell out the consequences for all America. Marshall Field, millionaire Chicago newspaper owner, Peter Odegard, president of Reed College in Oregon, Clarence Pickett, the Philadelphian who headed the American Civil Liberties Union, Hubert Humphrey, mayor of Minneapolis, Walter Reuther of the United Automobile Workers, Eleanor Roosevelt, and half a hundred other notables scattered from California to New York were not to be intimidated by a small, tight-knit, arch conservative group of men in Washington. Of the committee's ninety-odd members, only three of the thirteen who lived in Washington were Negroes. It was an impressive array of men and women without any personal ax to grind, intent only on reversing a trend that, left alone, they believed, would fasten a caste system upon the entire country. Over a period of eighteen months the staff collected a mass of irrefutable evidence. The findings condensed for publication by Kenesaw Mountain Landis, namesake of a former federal judge and czar of professional baseball, covered every phase of the pressures, old and new, which threatened to reduce Negroes in Washington to a servile status from which they could not escape without the help of energetic white people.[8]

Despite the impassioned language of the report and its overworked argumentation, a check on its sources forced the serious reader to conclude that here was an essentially truthful summary. Too painful, too shocking to become table talk, the report repeatedly emphasized that the pattern set in the capital would shape that of every community in the United States. The review of the steady degradation of Negroes from the 1870's on, if not news to thoughtful Washingtonians, worked

[8] Ntl Comee on Seg, *Rpt, passim.*

upon the consciousness and the conscience of people who would have preferred to forget. Although the report did not kill the anti-Negro movement in Washington, at least its force declined rapidly after November 1948. Within six years publicly authorized segregation would disappear, and the phrase "human relations" would begin to replace "race relations."

Contributing to that change was the publication early in 1949 of the Strayer Report on Washington's public schools undertaken at congressional request by George Strayer of Columbia University, a nationally recognized authority on public education. Assisted by a dozen other specialists, Strayer examined the strengths and weaknesses of the functioning of the Board of Education, the superintendent's and assistant superintendents' performance, and the quality of schooling provided at every level in both the white and the colored divisions. After analyzing the inadequacies in physical accommodations and the shortcomings in teacher recruitment and promotion, the experts discussed the work of the research departments and the areas in which pupils' achievements were above or below the national average. In general, the white high schools had a good record, in the junior high schools, a decade later labelled "the problem child of American education," pupils were a year behind the national norm in arithmetic but otherwise on a par, and the elementary schools varied from the excellent to those below the national standard. The colored schools, though as good as those in other cities with segregated systems, were definitely inferior to the white. Negro schoolrooms were more crowded, the pupil-teacher ratio disproportionately high, and equipment and teaching aids meagre. Although the investigators did not accept without qualification the interpretation that the head of the colored school research unit had put upon the IQ and achievement tests, the Strayer team observed the downward trend in colored children's achievements and attributed much of it to poor schooling in the regions from which Negro in-migrants came.

The matter-of-factness and lack of moralizing in the Strayer Report added to its impact. Praise as well as criticism dotted the 950-page text. But nobody studying it could fail to perceive the inequalities in the schooling offered the two races. The data verified a central thesis of the National Committee on Segregation, namely that the separate schools underlay the city's entire social structure. They formed the basis upon which the local universities built in maintaining racial bars. In 1948 only Catholic University had opened all its schools to Negroes. George Washington, Georgetown, the undergraduate college, though not the graduate school, of American University, the National University law and medical schools, all refused admission to colored students, and though Howard University did not exclude whites, only special circumstances occasionally led a white student to enroll there. Day by day association between young people of the two races thus never occurred.

If colored Washingtonians were glad to have outside authority validate their often repeated complaints, white people were dismayed at the new evidence of grave faults in the white schools, faults present in spite of the dropping enrollments that reduced the pupil-teacher ratio to a reasonable level. The flight of white families to the suburbs explained some of the decline in enrollments, but the increase in the entries in the city's private non-sectarian or church schools suggested a new parental rebellion at basic lacks in the public schools. (See Table IV.) "Wisely," the Strayer Report noted, the Board of Education had dispensed with the grouping of students according to ability. Counselling service, introduced in 1943, began with the 7th grade and was intended to give junior high school pupils guidance in their school work and help those with personality troubles, but the experts considered the number of counsellors too few and their consultations, therefore, too hurried to be of any real value. On the whole, teachers could feel they had come off well; criticisms were largely directed not at their individual frailties but at the system and the lack of the money with which to carry out teaching programs.

Educators who had followed closely the developments in American educational theory and practice of the preceding quarter-century could see that in several particulars Washington's public schools offered more than in the 1920's. But white parents, after skimming the report, tended to mourn gloomily for the good old days when the District's schools ranked among the three or four best in the country. Congress, on the other hand, took constructive action by voting larger appropriations for capital outlays in 1949 than in any year since 1931-1932.[9] Strong possibility exists, furthermore, that the survey laid the emotional groundwork on which a racially integrated system would rise five and a half years later, for, although not deliberately aimed at preachments on segregation, the findings revealed the monetary and social costs of the dual scheme. Certainly no other city where it had always obtained moved so quickly and effectively to discard it in 1954: four months after the Supreme Court ruling of May, all Washington's public schools opened on an integrated basis.

During the half-decade of postwar readjustment, national and international alarums and excursions distracted the city: the economic collapse of Europe, lightened but not fully dissipated by the launching of Marshall Plan aid, rumors of a far-flung Communist conspiracy within the government in Washington, Whittaker Chambers' testimony before the House Un-American Affairs Committee in August 1948 and the dramatic Hiss trial, the 1948 election, the outcome of which

[9] *Ibid.*, pp. 41, 46; Home Rule Hrgs, p. 191; *Strayer Rpt*, pp. 35-36, 414-16, 459-67, 497-98, 534, 550-52, 705-06, 940-41, 948, and *passim*.

startled everyone but journalist Louis Bean and Harry S Truman, and, slightly less than five years after V-J Day, war in Korea. In the interim, while retailers watched suburban shops cut in steadily upon business in the central city, the demand for down-town office space grew as the movement, begun with trade associations and learned societies of the 1920's and accelerated in the 1930's with the multiplication of headquarters of national planning groups in Washington, approached a crescendo that would make the political capital before the end of the 1950's the capital of all major American interests and aspirations. Throughout this confusing period of contraction and expansion, Washingtonians sought to reestablish a sense of community.

Stripped of the financial support of the War Chest, the Community Chest failed consistently to reach the quotas which would enable member agencies to maintain and extend their services, while the Public Welfare Department vainly endeavored to meet other needs of a city whose population, according to some estimates, had grown in seven years to over 900,000 souls, a third of them living at a bare subsistence level. If the term "population explosion" was not in common use before the 1950 census appeared, the dimensions of a future crisis were already visible in and about Washington. Private citizens ready to brave Roman Catholic opposition consequently organized Planned Parenthood to give advice and birth control information to clients wanting help. At the same time officials of the water department confronted the necessity of early construction of new reservoirs above the Great Falls to enlarge the city's water supply, a step that would involve vast expense and difficult negotiations with Maryland and Virginia. Simultaneously the ever-worsening pollution of the Potomac added to the troubles of the District sanitary engineers. Besides the rise in juvenile delinquency and new complaints about the dishonesty and inefficiency of law enforcement, the thickening traffic congestion harried the metropolitan police. At times Washingtonians felt caught in a tightening net, assailed by every quandary that could beset a geographically confined, racially divided, politically impotent area threatened by economic strangulation from the uncontrolled expansion of a surrounding megalopolis.[10]

The urban redevelopment program appeared to offer the best way out. Physical beauty unmarred by hidden slums and visible eyesores, convenience of access contrived by an improved highway system, and a new complex of cultural institutions and opportunities might give Washington a superiority over the outlying area that would ensure her domination of the entire metropolitan region. Few Washingtonians felt ready to define their ideas of urban beauty, convenience, and refreshment of the spirit, perhaps fewer still the relative emphasis each factor deserved. In 1946 and 1947 the Real Estate Board indicated that the first essential was a white metropolis with Negro servants' quarters in the rear. The District highway department, automobile salesmen, and doubtless householders living on the outer fringes of the District inclined to put chief stress on transportation. No one attempted to spell out the meaning of culture or how specifically to develop it for Washington's benefit. To the city's leading merchants and bankers the revitalizing of the downtown business center, however effected, was the foremost objective. Budget officers and big taxpayers never lost sight of the overriding importance of increasing District revenues. At every step congressmen, their constituents, and federal executives would probably have more say about developments than would Washingtonians.

Razing of the slums was by general consensus a necessary first move, particularly in the triangle of southwest Washington bounded by South Capitol Street, the Anacostia and the Wash-

[10] D.C. Welfare Dept, "Surveys of Income," 1947 and 1950 (mimeo); S Rpt 38, 86C, 1S, Final Report of the Joint Committee on Washington Metropolitan Problems, 1959, and Rpt Water Supply.

ington Channel, the main Department of Agriculture buildings and the Mall. The notorious "second precinct" adjoining North Capitol Street and Foggy Bottom beyond a new State Department building at 21st Street presumably should be the next. At that point agreement ended about use of the land when cleared. Instead of rebuilding with housing for the former occupants of the southwest area, General Grant implied that the National Capital Park and Planning Commission intended to turn most of it into parks and playgrounds, sites for public buildings, and highways to speed the traffic pouring in from and out to Virginia. If private contractors were disgruntled at the prospective loss of chances to erect expensive office and apartment buildings in the reclaimed space, Negroes were outraged upon hearing that the dispossessed were to be moved to remote sections of northeast or southeast Washington. In response to protests, in January 1948 the House Committee on Appropriations refused to grant the Redevelopment Land Agency the $3,400,000 needed to start operations; General Grant hastily declared that there had been a serious misunderstanding. Colored Washingtonians dared not count postponement as final victory but they believed white supremacists had at least received a rebuff. "Time," observed one wit, "wounds all heels."

The delay made Washington uneasy. While excavation of a Dupont Circle underpass destroyed old elms, slum clearance hung suspended. During the next two years every feature of official and private proposals for redevelopment underwent fresh scrutiny. Members of the American Institute of Architects issued diatribes against repetition of the "facadism" of the Federal Triangle, its "brutal stone masses" built in an eclectic style as boring as it was massive and unoriginal. Articles dealt with the ultimate cost of uprooting slum dwellers and relocating them in alien surroundings cut off from the life of the rest of the city. New York's experience in erecting huge apartment buildings to replace unsanitary old tenement houses pointed to the danger of substituting for the old a new and worse evil —impregnable and impersonal fortresses in which vice and crime and hopelessness extinguished every wholesome human impulse. Negro ghettos in the remotest section of the District might produce more ineradicable ills than those of the alleys. By 1950, moreover, some Washingtonians were beginning to wonder whether the projected many-laned highways were not likely to multiply instead of reduce traffic problems, to change pleasant, substantial residential sections into passage-ways for tourists' and commuters' cars, and to convert whole streets of small houses into blocks of apartment houses. And, irrespective of plans for the public domain, what of private development? Architecturally tasteless office buildings and residences could ruin the looks of much of the city, and exploitation of some sections for the benefit of others could reduce any over-all plan to meaninglessness.

Washington: Past and Future, the planning commission's first published report since 1932, set some fears to rest when it appeared in 1950, for it reflected a concern for the underdog and outlined a proposal that gave weight to human as well as financial values. Although work on a large scale would not start for another year, prospects brightened that the next decade would see a new Washington emerge embodying the best aspirations of an enlightened public. Demolition gangs and bull- dozers would wipe out every structure in southwest Washington except the government buildings flanking the Mall and at Fort McNair, two modern schoolhouses, two restaurants near the waterfront, and a beautifully proportioned brick row dating from about 1808 which lent itself to remodelling. In that wide expanse would rise some low-rental housing, a larger number of expensive apartments and town houses, a theatre, a shopping center, and an array of at least eight new government office buildings, all with extensive parking space. The architecture of the public buildings would abandon the neo-classical in favor of a modernized style using horizontal bands of windows interrupted by concrete grill-work to create an effect of screening, a style to be employed also for the brick apartment buildings; the lines of the town houses, flat-roofed and two-storied, would harmonize with both. Cutting across the area an elevated highway would run from a new bridge over the Washington Channel and Haines Point to a conjunction with an inner loop slicing through southeast Washington above the Navy Yard to Lincoln Park and thence northward.

Much of the elaborate plan seemed desirable, some of it disastrous—particularly the vague provision for families unable to afford even the lowest priced living quarters in rebuilt Southwest, not to mention the householders in Southeast who would be displaced by the demolition necessary to construction of the inner loop. The controversy encompassing changes undertaken in Foggy Bottom and elsewhere would continue into the 1960's. Thirty years had seen the District's share of the population of Greater Washington drop from the 72.2 percent of 1920 to 53.2 percent.[11] If no local Cassandra in 1950 was foretelling the further decline to 36.8 percent in the decade ahead, still the possibility remained that except for the public buildings the central city might become a series of concrete passage-ways lined by blocks of efficiencies, some expensive apartment houses, and warrens of cheap flats occupied, respectively, by single women and a few bachelors, well-to-do, elderly, childless couples, and Negroes.

Yet notwithstanding racial conflicts, political defeats, and wrangling over designs for the future, before midcentury Washington recaptured a charm as compelling as it is hard to explain. It was in fact more than a recaptured quality, for it had a com-

[11] Ntl Comee on Seg, *Rpt*, pp. 41, 46; Carl Feiss, "The Development of Washington," p. 15, *Washington Architecture, 1791-1957*, prepared by a Committee of the Washington Metropolitan Chapter, American Institute of Architects; NCPPC, *Washington: Past and Future*, 1950; editors of *Fortune*, ed., *The Exploding Metropolis*, pp. 106 ff.

prehensiveness that reached further than had that of the smaller, relatively uncomplicated community of the 1880's, or the sophisticated wealthy society of Theodore Roosevelt's and Taft's day, or the city of the New Deal era. The refusal of the Actors' Equity to play in a theatre that barred colored people forced the National, by then the only legitimate theatre left in the city, to close to stage productions in 1948. But other amenities widened in scope. Sociology and political theory did not enter into the pleasure householders of every complexion took in nursing their gardens and presenting trim lawns to the view of passers-by. While restoration of run-down houses in Georgetown moved forward rapidly, on Capitol Hill "Operation Bootstrap" began to take form, promoted by students at the Eastern High School who banded together as "Scrooch," Students' Committee for Redecoration of Old Capitol Hill. There residents, white and colored, set about sprucing up their neighborhoods with their own hands. If the amateur character of most of the performing arts and the naïveté of public appreciation of the visual arts denied the city a legitimate claim to being the "cultural center" of America, still a philistine spirit rarely marred Washingtonians' enjoyment of what was at hand.

In an old burlesque house opposite the Public Library the "Arena" opened, launched by a handful of Washingtonians interested in acting as an art and eager to try out a theatre-in-the-round. At Catholic University drama students presented plays ranging from *King Lear* to *Cyrano* with a finished skill that evoked the admiration of accomplished professional actors. Companies of dancers and vaudeville performers at the Carter Barron outdoor theatre added to the inexpensive diversions of summer evenings. Small private galleries opened displays of young painters' works, while accessions at the National Gallery put it into the front ranks of American collections. Nearly every evening offered a concert of an artistry that astonished

1947

1897

PUBLIC & SEMI-PUBLIC PROPERTY
BOUNDARY OF ORIGINAL CITY
URBAN DEVELOPMENT

the New Yorker prone to label Washington a cultural waste-land. The inclination of critics to poke fun at Margaret Truman's few public performances as a singer and at her father's piano strumming rather increased the secret pleasure of much of Washington in the musical interests of the White House. The city's home-spun quality was again in evidence.

Newcomers in turn felt the spell of Washington's magic. In the eyes of most of them it came solely from the streams of politically powerful and gifted personages who came and went; but even the most disdainful critics of the city's artistic provincialism spoke of this "fascinating city," the most "interesting place in America," and this "most beautiful capital in the world." No native dreamed of denying that her famous visitors and temporary residents endowed her with much of her fascination, or that a good deal of the rest grew out of the awareness that questions of world importance were part of the capital's day by day business. At least in roundabout fashion, the scholar, the lawyer, a labor leader at the Washington headquarters of an international union, or a scientist working with one of the recently founded research and development firms in the city might find himself contributing an iota to the formulation of significant policies. The humblest Washingtonian rarely escaped a faint sense of brushing against great events and great people. He could not stand on the White House grounds as part of "one democratic conglomerate," like B. B. French's contemporaries welcoming the Japanese mission in 1860, but the blackest little Negro boy in the mid-twentieth-century city might teeter on the curb as a parade went by and practically reach out to touch the Queen of the Netherlands, the British Prime Minister, or an envoy from Ethiopia.

At midcentury American urban problems were only beginning to command intensive national attention. Almost no one as yet had thought seriously of a cabinet post for urban affairs. People living in the countryside near big cities were not yet deeply alarmed by urban sprawl, and ideas of applying city planning to entire metropolitan regions were still novel. Washingtonians were frequently troubled by their own plight, but other Americans seldom saw it as it was, "A Tale of Two Cities." One of these, overwhelmed by financial difficulties, was a city of "slums, crumbling schools and hospitals, neighborhoods that are breeding places of preventable disease, unwanted children, juvenile delinquency, and a crescendo of crime on the streets," a community confronted by all the ills facing other metropolitan centers but, unlike them, powerless to check such miseries.[12] The other city was a beautiful capital of monuments and museums, green parks and tree-lined avenues, a place whose urbanity was heightened by its touches of provincialism. To dedicated Washingtonians the contrasts were ever-present: the distress and the frustration, and yet the delights. Far-sighted inhabitants of these two-cities-in-one perceived that the capital must enfold and redeem the lesser city if the Washington of the second half of the twentieth century were to become the symbol of American democracy at its best. In the early 1960's it was uncertain which pattern would prevail.

Yet the living testimony of two generations underscored the curious drawing power the dual city exercised. If the tendency in parts of the United States was to think of Washington merely as the center of an unwholesomely expanding bureaucracy that should be curbed, Americans who spent more than a brief time in the city rarely failed to experience an emotional response compounded of pride, pleasure, dismay, anger, and an intense interest in her future. Therein lay the hope for the years ahead.

[12] Washington League of Women Voters, *Washington, D.C.: A Tale of Two Cities*, p. 1.

GLOSSARY OF ABBREVIATIONS AND CITATIONS IN THE FOOTNOTES

ALL non-official manuscript materials cited are in the Manuscript Division of the Library of Congress unless other locations are specifically noted in the first mention in each chapter of papers elsewhere. Petitions, housed in the National Archives, are identified where they first appear by the record group number, but the number is not repeated, since all petitions to the House of Representatives are in R.G. 233, all petitions to the Senate in R.G. 46.

L.C.	—	Library of Congress
N.A.	—	National Archives
R.G.	—	Record Group
Ptn	—	Petition, if to the Senate listed as S, if to the House of Representatives, listed as H, in each case followed by numerals and letters identifying the Congress and general topic and by the date.
H Rpt __, __C, __S, Ser__	—	House of Representatives Report, followed by its number, the number and session of Congress, and the serial number of the volume in which the report is bound.
H Ex Doc	—	House Executive Document
H Misc Doc	—	House Miscellaneous Document
H __ Comee Hrgs	—	House Committee, identified by name and followed by the number and session of Congress, Hearings.
H Dis Comee	—	House Committee on the District of Columbia.
S Rpt __, __C, __, Ser __	—	Senate Report, followed by its number, the number and session of Congress and the serial number.
S Ex Doc	—	Senate Executive Document
S Misc Doc	—	Senate Miscellaneous Document
S __ Comee Hrgs	—	Senate Committee, identified by name, and followed by the number and session of Congress, Hearings.
S Dis Comee	—	Senate Committee on the District of Columbia

Rec	—	*Congressional Record*
— Stat. —,	—	*United States Statutes at Large*, with volume number preceding and page number following.
Comrs Rpt	—	*Report of the Commissioners of the District of Columbia* which, after 1935, is entitled, *Report of the Government of the District of Columbia.*
CHS *Rec*	—	Columbia Historical Society *Records*
AC *Rpt*	—	*Report of the Associated Charities*
Rpt B/Ch	—	*Report of the Board of Charities*
Rpt B/Tr	—	*Report of the Board of Trade*
Min As Ch	—	Minutes of the Board of Managers of the Associated Charities
Min CSA	—	Minutes of the Council of Social Agencies
Min FSA	—	Minutes of the Board of Managers of the Family Service Association

Sources for Washington's political and economic history after 1878 are in the main published materials. Some information is contributed by petitions to the Senate and House of the 1880's and 1890's located in the National Archives, some letters in the Theodore Roosevelt, Woodrow Wilson, and two or three other collections of papers in the Manuscript Division of the Library of Congress, and the typescript summaries of Board of Trade activities between 1932 and 1935 prepared by its presidents and housed among its records, but otherwise manuscript data are of negligible value. The sheaves of petitions that served to measure local aspirations in earlier years cease to be revealing after 1910 when appeals to Congress about matters of wide local interest usually found their way into print. I have cited all petitions in the Archives by the numbers they bore when I used them, before a recataloguing began a year or two ago; those for the Senate are in Record Group 46, for the House in Record Group 233. Published official records, newspaper reprints, letters to the editors, editorials, reporters' columns, some magazine articles, and, from 1890 down to the 1930's, the published annual reports of the Board of Trade provide the backbone of fact and opinion on the community's business progress and political aims.

The official records, however, are embarrassingly abundant and, up to a point, informative not only about the whats but the whys. The detailed annual reports of the District commissioners, before 1921 sometimes running to two or three fat volumes for a single year, spell out the workings of every department of the local administration. Economy limited the reports to one volume for several years after 1921 and, from 1926 onward, to the slimness of a pamphlet omitting the accounting of each separate unit. Copies of the reports from 1926 to 1932, no longer included in the congressional series, are to be found only in the Washingtoniana Room of the District Public Library. From 1936 onward they appear under the title *Annual Report of the Government of the District of Columbia*. As District concerns slide into the category of the routine, the *Congressional Record* and House and Senate documents dealing with the city's affairs contain less of interest to the student of Washington's history than do the debates and reports of the preceding decades. Published committee hearings, on the other hand, not only multiply but after 1915 illuminate local and congressional views on specific questions more fully than do any of the earlier records. Thus the hearings on federal-local fiscal relations held in 1915 are a mine of information on that controversial topic. Most of the printed hearings are housed in the Library of Congress, but some are to be found only in the House or Senate libraries in the Capitol. Laurence Schmeckebier's *The District of Columbia, Its Government and Administration*, published in 1928, gives an informative picture of the workings of all the District's complicated governmental machinery down through 1927.

School board reports vary greatly in usefulness. Those for 1879, 1880, 1886, 1892, and 1899 furnish the best clues to superintendents' and trustees' educational philosophy in the period before 1920. The report for 1922, that of 1930 which contains a ten-year summary of "Achievements," and a similar twenty-year statement, 1920-1940, review the later aims of the Board of Education and administrators. In determining Washington's comparative standing in the realm of public education, the reports of the United States Commissioner of Education and the *Biennial Summaries* are helpful. The Strayer Report of 1949 provides a critical appraisal of outside experts for the 1940's.

For the theme of city planning and the "city beautiful" movement, articles in architectural journals and popular magazines constitute a source only less important than congressional documents and reports of the successive commissions—namely the Park, the Fine Arts, and the National Capital Park and Planning Commissions. Furthermore, several letters of Frederick Law Olmsted and Charles McKim among the Charles Moore papers in the Library of Congress Manuscript Division explain some of the difficulties created by the coolness of the House of Representatives to the Park Commission plan of 1901. The plan as presented to the Senate is published as Senate Report 166, 57C, 1S, Serial 4259. The publications of the American Civic Association, the organization that inspired Congress to establish the National Capital Park Commission and its successors, contain the salient facts for the early 1920's. The annual reports of the Fine Arts and the Planning Commissions from their beginnings down to 1932 are informing, but from then to 1950 the omission of formal reports leaves a serious gap, only partly filled by summaries of their programs and plans published in midcentury and in the interim by newspaper pieces and comments from the American Institute of Architects. The Washingtoniana Room of the District Public Library fortunately has files of clippings on the subject.

In pursuing the "Social Betterment" movement, manuscript materials, notably the minutes of the Monday Evening Club, the Associated Charities, renamed Family Service Association in 1934, and the Council of Social Agencies, born in 1920, provide detailed running accounts of local philanthropic endeavors to resolve welfare problems. In addition, a Senate report of 1897 on District charities and their history, the findings of President Theodore Roosevelt's Homes Commission of 1907, and the first report of the Alley Dwelling Authority in 1935 throw light on the social planning of their time. After 1903 *Charities*, later the *Survey*, includes several articles analyzing conditions in Washington before the mid-twenties. The annual reports of the Board of Public Welfare, after it came into being in 1926, are disappointingly general; those of the Public Assistance Division of the 1930's, though much more specific, are diffuse and hard to use in constructing a clear-cut picture of social progress or deterioration. Between 1936 and 1938 the official organ of the Community Chest, *Council Bulletin* renamed *Community Service*, discusses the major questions. Convinced that the facts and ideas contained in these sources covered the field, I made no attempt to examine the records of particular organizations such as the Washington Orphan Asylum or its successor by self-denying ordinance of the late 1940's, the Hillcrest Children's Center.

Foreign visitors' descriptions of Washington, rewarding for the pre-Civil War years, add little to an understanding of the city after 1890. Frank Carpenter's pieces written for the Cleveland *Leader* over the signature "Carp" in the early 1880's contain a number of effective vignettes of every day life; these appear also in somewhat different form in Frances Carpenter Huntington's *Carp's Washington*. Mrs. Reginald DeKoven's *A Musician and His Wife* adds touches to the picture of President Arthur's Washington. Thereafter the flood of periodical articles, many of them in the twentieth century illustrated with photographs, supplants the collection of personal letters that supplied invaluable insights into the first three-quarters of the nineteenth century. Doubtless diligent search might have turned up private letters that would supplement the published commentaries, but the variety of the latter appeared to justify foregoing the time-consuming hunt for less guarded personal comments. At the same time, the nearer my narrative comes to the present, biographies and autobiographies useful for my purpose diminish in number; relatively few discuss the local scene. Fortunately, Louis Brownlow's *A Passion for Anonymity* tells of his years as District Commissioner, 1915-1920, in far from anonymous terms and contains a wealth of specifics about the troubled World War I era.

The role of science in Washington down to 1940 is admirably summarized in A. Hunter Dupree's *Science in the Federal Government*. That study, the publications of learned and scientific societies, and the reports of the Librarian of Congress and of the Smithsonian Institution enable the student to piece together the growth of the city's intellectual life. The 1946 report of the Librarian of Congress is especially useful inasmuch as the long section entitled "The Story Up To Now" reviews the history of the library from its beginning but gives particular attention to the steps by which services widened to encompass the arts. Scattered newspaper and magazine articles and the descriptions in the WPA Federal Writers' Project, *Washington, City and Capital*, published in 1937, tell the tale of mounting preoccupation with music, painting, architecture and sculpture.

The story of colored Washington, like that of the white community, derives first from the local press. The newspaper files in the Library of Congress include most issues; those of the *Daily American*, short-lived sheet of the mid-1920's, and *New Negro Opinion*, the mouthpiece of the New Negro Alliance of the mid-1930's, are in the possession of Eugene Davidson, the editor of both. Also indispensable are occasional monographs, reports like those assembled by W. E. B. DuBois on the Atlanta Conferences, 1896-1901, articles in the NAACP organ, *Crisis*, after 1910, and pieces in a considerable range of journals during Woodrow Wilson's first administration and after the mid-1920's. All these clarify the relationship between Washington's situation and that of colored communities elsewhere. Above all, interviews with colored leaders and followers have added factual details and deepened my understanding of the minority problems.

Interviews, indeed, constitute the single most important source for my account of local attitudes from 1930 onward. By trying to seek out people likely to take widely differing positions, I have endeavored to present a balanced over-all interpretation. Many of the questions I posed are still highly controversial. Hence to save embarrassment for my informants and to avoid cumbersomely long explanations of the special qualifications of each person to speak, I have ordinarily omitted their names from the footnotes except where the validity of my presentation would suffer sharply from preserving the anonymity of a person willing to be quoted. This method involved the danger of assigning undue weight to the ideas of a small minority, but the problem is inherent, I believe, in the task of attempting to analyze the recent past. The incorporation of data that, seen in the light of longer perspective, may not hold up or that further intensive research may modify is an occupational hazard that I have welcomed, for it should provoke additional historical studies of significant questions confronting urban America.

A listing of the materials I have used, category by category, follows.

BIBLIOGRAPHY

I UNPUBLISHED SOURCES

OFFICIAL PAPERS

Library of Congress Manuscript Division
  William McKinley Papers
  Theodore Roosevelt Papers
  Woodrow Wilson Papers
National Archives
  Petitions to the House of Representatives, 1879-1909, Record Group 233
  Petitions to the Senate, 1879-1922, Record Group 46

RECORDS OF SOCIAL AGENCIES AND BUSINESS ORGANIZATIONS

listed by location

Family and Child Services of Washington, D.C.
  Minutes of the Board of Managers of the Associated Charities of the District of Columbia, 1921-1934, continued as Family Service Association, 1934-
  Monday Evening Club Minutes, 1898-1929, and "Thirty Years Achievement," 1930
  Questionnaire of the Citizens Chest Survey Committee, 1947
Health and Welfare Council of the National Capital Area
  Minutes of the Board of Managers of the Washington Council of Social Agencies, 1921-1941
Washington Board of Trade, Reports of the presidents, 1932-1935
Washington Urban League, "The Founding of the Washington Urban League," statement of Garnett Wilkinson at Twenty-first Annual Meeting, April 1959

PERSONAL PAPERS AND LETTERS

In possession of Professor Charles A. Barker of the Johns Hopkins University, Sayles J. Bowen Papers, 1879-1892, cited in notes as Bowen Mss.
Library of Congress Manuscript Division
  Charles Moore Papers, 1900-1932
  Mary Church Terrell Papers, 1890-1940
  Booker T. Washington Papers, 1870-1915
University of North Carolina Library, Southern Historical Collection
  Gibson-Humphreys Papers, 1882-1886

MONOGRAPHS AND THESES

Lindsay, Inabel, "Participation of Negroes in the Establishment of Welfare Services, 1865-1900, with special reference to the District of Columbia, Maryland, and Virginia," Ph.D. Dissertation, University of Pittsburgh, 1959

Lofton, Williston, "The Development of Public Education for Negroes in Washington, D.C., a Study of Separate but Equal Accommodations," Ph.D. Dissertation, the American University, 1944

Long, Kathleen Dudley, "Woodrow Wilson and the Negro, 1912-1916," M.A. Thesis, Bryn Mawr College, 1956

Olmsted, Stanley, "The Corcoran School of Art," Corcoran School of Art, n.d.

II PUBLISHED SOURCES

OFFICIAL RECORDS

Annual Reports

    Alley Dwelling Authority for the District of Columbia, 1935

    Board of Charities of the District of Columbia, 1901-1925

    Board of Children's Guardians of the District of Columbia, 1893-1925

    Board of Education of the District of Columbia, 1901-1950

    Board of Public Welfare of the District of Columbia, 1926-1932, 1934-1950

    Board of Trustees of Public Schools of the District of Columbia, 1879-1899

    Commissioners of the District of Columbia, 1879-1935, continued as *Government of the District of Columbia*, 1936-1950, cited in the notes as Comrs Rpts

    Comptroller of the Currency, 1932-1935

    Fine Arts Commission, 1911-1932

    Home for Destitute Colored Women and Children, 1879-1892

    Librarian of Congress, 1928 and 1946

    National Capital Park and Planning Commission, 1927-1932

    Proceedings of the U.S. National Museum, 1911, 1916

    Public Assistance Division, Board of Public Welfare, 1934-1936

    Smithsonian Institution, 1879-

    Trustees of the Industrial Home School, 1879-1925

    United States Commissioner of Education, 1900-

Campbell, Doak S., Frederick H. Baer, and Oswald L. Harvey, *Educational Activities of the Works Progress Administration*, Staff Study No. 14.

Code of Laws of the District of Columbia, 1929, 1951

Congressional Record, 1879-

Congressional Serials, Bills, and Hearings, 1879-

    House of Representatives

        Bills

        Documents

        Executive Documents

        Hearings of committees, especially Committee on the District of Columbia, and on Reform in the Civil Service

Joint Hearings with Senate committees, especially House and Senate Committees on the District of Columbia, 80C, 1S and 2S, "Home Rule and Reorganization of the Government of the District of Columbia."

Miscellaneous Documents

Reports

Senate

Bills

Documents, especially Document 185, 55C, 1S, "Investigation of Charities and Reformatory Institutions in the District of Columbia," Serial 3565 and Document 247, 64C, 1S, "Fiscal Relations of the United States to the District of Columbia," Serials 6915 and 6916

Hearings of committees and select joint committees, especially: Subcommittee of the Senate Judiciary Committee, 77C, 1S, Hearings on Senate Joint Resolution 35, "National Representation," and Committee on the District of Columbia, 78C, 1S, Hearings on S1420, "Reorganization of the Government of the District of Columbia"

Index to Hearings in the Senate Library, 2 vols., 1907-1934 and 1935-1958

Index to Laws, Senate Reports, Documents and Committee Prints Relating to the District of Columbia, 1887-1903

Miscellaneous Documents

Reports, especially Report 700, 55C, 1S, "Charities and Reformatory Institutions" and Report 781, 55C, 2S, "Historical Sketches," Serial 3565

Report 711, 56C, 1S, "School Administration," Serial 3889

Report 1230, 85C, 2S, "Growth and Expansion of the District of Columbia and Its Metropolitan Area," 1958

Report 38, 86C, 1S, "Final Report of the Joint Committee on Washington Metropolitan Problems," 1959

Geddes, Anne, *Trends in Relief Expenditures, 1910-1935*, Works Progress Administration Monograph No. 10

Graduate School of the Department of Agriculture, 1961

International Bureau of the American Republics, *Report of the Director to the Fourth Pan American Conference held at Buenos Aires, Argentine Republic, 1910*

Letter from the Secretary of the Treasury transmitting Estimates of Appropriations, 1901-1917

National Capital Park and Planning Commission, *Washington, Past and Future*, 1950

National Gallery of Art, *Bulletin*, I, "General Information," 1941

National Resources Committee, *Research—A National Resource*, I, 1940

Official Register of the United States, 1879-1922

Reports of the President's Homes Commission, 1908

School Bulletin No 9, "Preliminary Report of the Committee on Character Education," 1931

Strayer, George Drayton, *Report of a Survey of the Public Schools of the District of Columbia, conducted under the auspices of the chairmen of the subcommittees on District of Columbia appropriations of the respective appropriations committees of the Senate and House*, Washington, 1949

United States Census, Tenth through Seventeenth, 1880-1950
   Religious Bodies, 1916, 1926, 1936
   Statistics of Cities Having a Population of over 30,000, 1907

United States Commissioner of Education, *Biennial Survey of Education*, 1918-1940

United States Department of Commerce and Labor, *Conditions of Living Among the Poor*, Bureau of Labor Bulletin, 64, 1906
   Forman, Samuel E., *Charity, Relief and Wage Earnings*, 1908

United States Statutes at Large, 1879-1950, cited in notes as *—Stat.—*

War Production Board, *Historical Monograph No. 1*, 1946

RECORDS AND REPORTS OF SOCIAL AGENCIES AND BUSINESS
EDUCATIONAL AND SCIENTIFIC ORGANIZATIONS

American Council on Education, Its History and Activities

American Council of Learned Societies, *Bulletin*, I-X, 1921-1930

American Historical Association, *Annual Report*, 1919, I

Associated Charities of Washington, *Annual Reports*, 1897-1920

Brookings Institution, *A Consideration of the Application of Research in the Social Sciences to the Problems of Modern Civilization*, 1931
——, *Institute for Government Research, An Account of Research Achievements*, 1922

Bulletin of the Philosophical Society of Washington, 1874

Carnegie Institution of Washington, *Annual Reports*, 1910, 1916

Charity Organization Society of the District of Columbia, *Third Annual Report*, 1886

Citizens' Committee on Race Relations, *Second Annual Report*, 1945

Conference for Good City Government, *Proceedings*. 3rd and 16th, 1895 and 1909, Philadelphia.

Consumer's League of Washington, D.C., *Third Annual Report*, 1915

District of Columbia Citizens' Representative Committee of One Hundred, *Proposal to Improve the Present Form of Government of the District of Columbia*, 1888

DuBois, William Edward Burghardt, ed., *Mortality Among Negroes in Cities, together with proceedings of the 1st conference for the study of Negro problems, Atlanta University, 1896*, Atlanta, 1896
——, ed., *Some Efforts of Negroes for Their Own Social Betterment, together with proceedings of the 3rd conference for the study of Negro problems, Atlanta University, 1898*, Atlanta, 1898
——, ed., *The Negro in Business, together with proceedings of the 4th conference for the study of Negro problems, Atlanta University, 1899*, Atlanta, 1899

————, ed., *The College-Bred Negro, together with proceedings of the 5th conference for the study of Negro problems, Atlanta University, 1900*, Atlanta, 1900

Dumbarton Oaks Research Library and Collection, Harvard University, *Bulletin Number One, 1940-1950.*

Forty Years of Achievement: Commemorating the Fortieth Anniversary of the Establishment of the National Commission of Fine Arts, 1910-1950.

Hodson, William, *Preliminary Report of the Commission on Public Welfare Legislation of the District of Columbia*, 1924

McClintock, Miller, *Report on the Parking and Garage Problem of the Central Business District of Washington, D.C.*, 1930

Memorial of the Joint Executive Committee of the Citizens' Associations of the District of Columbia against the Repeal of the Fifty Percent Annual Congressional Appropriation Law, 1894

Monday Evening Club Yearbook, 1930

National Association for the Advancement of Colored People, *Annual Reports*, 1911-

National Committee on Segregation in the Nation's Capital, *Segregation in Washington*, 1948

National Conference on Social Work, 1929

National Society of Fine Arts, *Articles of Incorporation, Constitution and Bylaws*, 1906

New Negro Alliance Yearbook, 1939

Preliminary Report by the Washington Committee of One Hundred on the Federal City to the American Civic Association, 1924

Proceedings of the Sixth Annual Meeting of the Female Union Benevolent Society of Washington City and Report of the Managers, 1844

Proceedings of the Washington Academy of Sciences, 1898-

Report of a Committee from the Geological Society on the History of the Joint Commission of the Scientific Societies of Washington

Washington Board of Trade, *Annual Reports*, 1890-1929, 1936-1938

Washington Federation of Churches, *Year Book*, 1936

AUTOBIOGRAPHIES, REMINISCENCES, LETTERS, AND DIARIES

Allen, George E., *Presidents Who Have Known Me*. New York, 1950.

Anderson, Isabel, *Presidents and Pies; Life in Washington, 1897-1919*. Boston and New York, 1920.

Andrews, Marietta Minnigerode, *My Studio Window*. New York, 1928.

Briggs, Emily Edson, *The Olivia Letters*. Washington, 1906.

Brown, Glenn, *Memories: A Winning Crusade to Revive George Washington's Vision of a Capital City*. Washington, 1931.

Brownlow, Louis, *A Passion for Politics*. Chicago, 1955.

————, *A Passion for Anonymity*. Chicago, 1958.

Butt, Archibald Willingham, *Taft and Roosevelt, The Intimate Letters of Archie Butt*. New York, 1930.

Columbia Historical Society, *Records*, 1894-.

Davidson, Eugene, *Black Boy on a Raft*. Washington, 1958.

DeKoven, Mrs. Reginald, *A Musician and His Wife*. New York and London, 1926.

Donnan, Elizabeth and Leo F. Stock, eds., *An Historian's World: Selections from the Correspondence of John Franklin Jameson*. Philadelphia, 1956.

DuBois, William Edward Burghardt, *Dusk of Dawn: An Essay Toward an Autobiography of a Race Concept*. New York, 1940.

Fairchild, David G., *The World Was My Garden*. New York, 1938.

Foraker, Mrs. Joseph, *I Would Live It Again: Memories of a Vivid Life*. New York and London, 1932.

Gouverneur, Marian, *As I Remember: Recollections of American Society During the Nineteenth Century*. New York, 1911.

Hegermann-Lindencrone, Lillie, *The Sunny Side of Diplomatic Life, 1875-1912*. New York and London, 1914.

Hole, The Very Reverend S. Reynolds, *A Little Tour in America*. London and New York, 1895.

Hoover, Herbert, *Memoirs*, ii, *The Cabinet and the Presidency, 1920-1933*. New York, 1951.

Keyes, Francis Parkinson, *Letters From a Senator's Wife*. New York and London, 1924.

Logan, Mary Simmerson, ed., *Thirty Years in Washington*. Hartford, 1901.

Longworth, Alice Roosevelt, *Crowded Hours*. New York and London, 1933.

Millikan, Robert Andrews, *Autobiography of Robert A. Millikan*, New York, 1950.

Newcomb, Simon, *The Reminiscences of an Astronomer*. New York, 1903.

Sousa, John Philip, *Marching Along: Recollections of Men, Women, and Music*. Boston, 1928.

Starling, E. W., *Starling of the White House*. New York, 1946.

Stokes, Thomas L., *Chip Off My Shoulder*. Princeton, 1940.

Summers, Festus P., ed., *The Cabinet Diary of William L. Wilson, 1896-1897*. Chapel Hill, 1957.

Taft, Mrs. William Howard, *Recollections of Full Years*. New York, 1914.

Terrell, Mary Church, *A Colored Woman in a White World*. Washington, 1940.

Washington, Booker T., *Up From Slavery*. New York, 1909.

White, Walter Francis, *A Man Called White, the Autobiography of Walter White*. New York, 1948.

OTHER PUBLISHED PRIMARY SOURCES

American Biographical Directories: District of Columbia, 1908-09.

An Appeal to the Enlightened Sentiment of the People of the United States for the Safeguarding of the Future Development of the Nation, 1916.

Biographical Directory of the American Congress, 1774-1961.

Dahlgren, Madeline Vinton, *Etiquette of Social Life in Washington*. 5th ed., Philadelphia, 1881.

Elite List of Washington, 1888-1918.

Handbook for District Suffrage, 1938.

Oyster, James, *Annual Address to the Washington Chamber of Commerce, 1913*.

Paynter, John H., *A Souvenir of the Anniversary and Banquet of Oldest Inhabitants Association (Colored) of the District of Columbia, April 14, 1914*.

Programs and announcements of musical events in Washington file, Library of Congress, Music Division.

Sherman's Directory and Ready Reference of the Colored Population of the District of Columbia, 1913.

Social List of Washington, D.C., 1923-

Washington City Directory, 1879-

Washington Social Register, 1900-

Who's Who in the National Capital, 1921-1929, National Cyclopaedia of American Biography

III SECONDARY SOURCES

Abell, George, and Evelyn Gordon, *Let Them Eat Caviar*, New York, 1936.

Allen, Frederick Lewis, *Only Yesterday*. New York, 1957.

American Institute of Architects, *Of Plans and People*. Washington, 1949.

———, A Committee of the Washington Metropolitan Chapter, *Washington Architecture, 1791-1957*. Washington, 1957.

Anderson, Oscar Edward, *The Health of a Nation*. Chicago, 1959.

Anonymous, *The Mirrors of Washington*. New York and London, 1921.

Anonymous, [Robert S. Allen and Drew Pearson], *Washington Merry-go-Round*. New York, 1931.

Baker, Ray Stannard, *Following the Color Line*. New York, 1908.

Bernstein, Irving, *The Lean Years, A History of the American Worker, 1920-1933*. Boston, 1960.

Bicknell, Grace Vawter, *The Inhabited Alleys of Washington, D.C.* Washington, 1912.

Browne, Henry Janvris, *Assessment and Taxation in the District of Columbia and the Fiscal Relation to the Federal Government*. Washington, 1915.

Bruno, Frank John, *Trends in Social Work, 1874-1956; A History Based on the Proceedings of the National Conference of Social Work*. 2nd ed., New York, 1957.

Bulkley, Barry, *Washington, Old and New*. Washington, 1914.

Chapin, Elizabeth M., *American Court Gossip, or Life at the Nation's Capital*. Marshalltown, Ia., 1887.

Church of God, A Pictorial Review. Washington, 1944.

Clephane, Walter C., *Public and Private Hospitals in the District of Columbia*. (Report of Washington Board of Trade) Washington, 1912.

Crane, Katherine Elizabeth, *Mr. Carr of State*. New York, 1960.

Crew, H. W., *Centennial History of the City of Washington*. Washington, 1901.

Cronon, Edmund David, *Black Moses, The Story of Marcus Garvey and the Universal Negro Improvement Association*. Madison, Wis., 1955.

Crowell, Benedict, and Robert Forrest Wilson, *The Armies of Industry, Our Nation's Manufacture of Munitions for a World in Arms, 1917-18*. New Haven, 1921.

Curti, Merle, *The Social Ideas of American Educators*. Paterson, N.J., 1935.

Daly, Victor, *Not Only War, A Story of Two Great Conflicts*. Boston, 1932.

Darrah, William Culp, *Powell of the Colorado*. Princeton, 1951.

Davis, Allison, Burleigh B. Gardner, and Mary B. Gardner, directed by W. Lloyd Warner, *Deep South, A Social and Anthropological Study of Class and Caste*. Chicago, 1941.

D.C. Village, *Fifty Years at Blue Plains, 1906-1956*. Washington, 1957.

District of Columbia Engineer's Office, *Washington Bridges*, 1945.

Dollard, John, *Caste and Class in a Southern Town*. 2nd ed., New York, 1949.

Douglas, Paul H., *Real Wages in the United States, 1890-1926*. Boston and New York, 1930.

Dulles, Foster Rhea, *The American Red Cross, A History*. New York, 1950.

Dupree, A. Hunter, *Science in the Federal Government, A History of Policies and Activities to 1940*. Cambridge, 1957.

Editors of *Fortune*, ed., *Exploding Metropolis*. New York, 1954.

Fairman, Charles E., *Art and Artists of the Capitol of the United States of America*. Washington, 1927.

Federal Writer's Project, *Washington: City and Capital*. Washington, 1937.

Fleming, Walter Lynwood, *The Freedman's Savings Bank: A Chapter in the Economic History of the Negro Race*. Chapel Hill, 1937.

Gabriel, Ralph Henry, *The Course of American Democratic Thought*. New York, 1940.

Gray, Edgar M., *The Washington Race Riot, Its Cause and Effect*. New York, 1919 (Arthur M. Schomburg Negro Collection, New York Public Library).

Grier, Eunice, *Understanding Washington's Population*. Washington Center for Metropolitan Studies, 1961.

Hagedorn, Herman, *Robert Brookings: A Biography*. New York, 1936.

Harmon, John H., Jr., Arnett G. Lindsay, and Carter G. Woodson, *The Negro as a Businessman*. Washington, 1929.

Hart, Hastings Hornell, *Child Welfare in the District of Columbia.* New York, 1924.

Hayes, Laurence J. W., *The Negro Federal Government Worker: A Study of His Classification Status in the District of Columbia, 1883-1938.* Washington, 1941.

Heaton, Herbert, *A Scholar in Action, Edwin F. Gay.* Cambridge, 1952.

History of the League of Women Voters of the District of Columbia, 1960.

Hughes, Langston, *Fine Clothes for the Jew.* New York, 1927.

Hurd, Charles, *Washington Cavalcade.* New York, 1948.

Ingle, Edward, *The Negro in the District of Columbia,* in *The Johns Hopkins University Studies in History and Political Science,* 11th Series, Nos. iii and iv.

James, Henry, "Pandora" in *Stories Revived.* London, 1895.

Johnson, Col. Campbell, *Fifty Years of Progress of the Armed Forces,* reprint from the *Pittsburgh Courier,* 1950.

Jones, William Henry, *Recreation and Amusement Among Negroes in Washington, D.C.: A Sociological Analysis of the Negro in An Urban Environment.* Washington, 1927.

———, *The Housing of Negroes in Washington, D.C.: A Study in Human Ecology.* Washington, 1929.

Joslin, Theodore G., *Hoover Off The Record.* Garden City, N.Y., 1934.

Keim, De Benneville Randolph, *Society in Washington, Its Noted Men, Accomplished Women, Established Customs, and Notable Events.* Harrisburg, Pa., 1887.

Kennedy, Louise Venable, *The Negro Peasant Turns Cityward.* New York, 1930.

Keppel, Frederick P. and R. L. Duffus, *The Arts in American Life.* New York and London, 1933.

Kober, George Martin, *The History and Development of the Housing Movement in the City of Washington, D.C.* 1st ed., Washington, 1907.

Leuchtenburg, William E., *The Perils of Prosperity, 1914-1932.* Chicago, 1958.

Link, Arthur S., *The New Freedom.* Princeton, 1947.

Lowry, Edward G., *Washington Close-Ups: Intimate Views of Some Public Figures.* Boston and New York, 1921.

Lundberg, Emma O. and Mary E. Milburn, *What Child Dependency Means in the District of Columbia And How It Can Be Prevented.* Washington, 1924.

Macfarland, Henry B. F., *The Development of the District of Columbia.* Washington, 1900.

McCormick, Anne O'Hare, *The World at Home.* New York, 1956.

McKenzie, Roderick Duncan, *The Metropolitan Community.* New York and London, 1933.

527

McMurry, Donald LeCrone, *Coxey's Army, A Study of the Industrial Army Movement of 1894.* Boston, 1929.

Matthiessen, F. O., *American Renaissance, Art and Expression in the Age of Emerson and Whitman.* New York and London, 1941.

————, and Kenneth B. Murdock, ed., *The Notebooks of Henry James.* New York, 1947.

Mechlin, Leila, *Works of Art in Washington.* Washington, 1914.

Moore, Joseph West, *Picturesque Washington.* 1st ed., Providence, 1884.

Murray, Pauli, *Proud Shoes, The Story of an American Family.* 1st ed., New York, 1956.

Murray, Robert K., *Red Scare: A Study in National Hysteria, 1919-20.* Minneapolis, Minn., 1955.

Nelson, Bernard H., *The Fourteenth Amendment and the Negro Since 1920.* Washington, 1946.

Nicolay, Helen, *Our Capital on the Potomac.* New York and London, 1924.

————, *Sixty Years of the Literary Society.* Washington, 1934 (Private printing).

Nowlin, William F., *The Negro in American National Politics.* Boston, 1931.

Oehser, Paul H., *Sons of Science, The Story of the Smithsonian Institution and Its Leaders.* New York, 1949.

Ogg, Frederick Austin, *Research in the Humanistic and Social Sciences: Report of a Survey Conducted for the American Council of Learned Societies.* New York and London, 1928.

Quillin, Frank U., *The Color Line in Ohio: A History of Race Prejudice in a Typical Northern State.* Ann Arbor, Mich., 1913.

Reitzes, Dietrich C., *Negroes and Medicine.* Cambridge, 1958.

Republican Campaign Textbook, 1912.

Rose, Arnold M., *The Negro's Morale: Group Identification and Protest.* Minneapolis, Minn., 1949.

Schlesinger, Arthur M., Jr., *The Crisis of the Old Order.* Cambridge, 1957.

————, *The Coming of the New Deal.* Cambridge, 1959.

————, *The Politics of Upheaval.* Cambridge, 1960.

Schmeckebier, Laurence, *The District of Columbia, Its Government and Administration.* Baltimore, 1928.

Sherwood, Robert E., *Roosevelt and Hopkins, An Intimate History.* New York, 1948.

Slauson, Allan B., ed., *A History of the City of Washington,* by the *Washington Post.* Washington, 1903.

Spaulding, Thomas M., *The Literary Society in Peace and War.* Washington, 1947.

Steevens, George Warrington, *The Land of the Dollar.* 2nd ed., Edinburgh and London, 1897.

Sullivan, Mark, *Over Here, 1914-18.* Vol. v of *Our Times.* 6 vol.: New York, 1926-35.

Toomer, Jean, *Cane*. New York, 1923.

Van Rensselaer, Mrs. John King, in collaboration with Frederic Van de Water, *The Social Ladder*. New York, 1924.

Villard, Oswald Garrison, *Some Newspapers and Newspapermen*. New York, 1926.

Washington League of Women Voters, *Washington, D.C.; A Tale of Two Cities*. Washington, 1962.

Waters, Walter T., as told to William C. White, *B.E.F.: The Whole Story of the Bonus Army*. New York, 1933.

Wecter, Dixon, *The Saga of American Society; A Record of Social Aspiration, 1607-1937*. New York, 1937.

Weitzman, Louis G., *One Hundred Years of Catholic Charities in the District of Columbia*. Washington, 1931.

White, William Allen, *A Puritan in Babylon, the Story of Calvin Coolidge*. New York, 1938.

Woodson, Carter G., *The History of the Negro Church*. Washington, 1945.

Woodward, C. Vann, *The Strange Career of Jim Crow*. New York, 1955.

Work, Monroe N., ed., *Negro Year Book, An Annual Encyclopedia of the Negro*. Tuskegee, Ala., 1912.

Wright, Carroll Davidson, *The Economic Development of the District of Columbia* in *Proceedings of the Washington Academy of Sciences*, I, Washington, 1899.

Yerkes, Robert M., ed., *The New World of Science; Its Development During the War*. New York, 1920.

Zueblin, Charles, *A Decade of Civic Development*. Chicago, 1905.

———, *American Municipal Progress*. New York, 1916.